Communications in Computer and Information Science 1006

Commenced Publication in 2007
Founding and Former Series Editors:
Phoebe Chen, Alfredo Cuzzocrea, Xiaoyong Du, Orhun Kara, Ting Liu,
Krishna M. Sivalingam, Dominik Ślęzak, Takashi Washio, and Xiaokang Yang

More information about this series at http://www.springer.com/series/7899

Fuchun Sun · Huaping Liu ·
Dewen Hu (Eds.)

Cognitive Systems and Signal Processing

4th International Conference, ICCSIP 2018
Beijing, China, November 29 – December 1, 2018
Revised Selected Papers, Part II

 Springer

Editors
Fuchun Sun
Department of Computer Science
and Technology
Tsinghua University
Beijing, China

Huaping Liu 🆔
Department of Computer Science
and Technology
Tsinghua University
Beijing, China

Dewen Hu
College of Mechatronics and Automation
National University of Defense Technology
Changsha, China

ISSN 1865-0929   ISSN 1865-0937 (electronic)
Communications in Computer and Information Science
ISBN 978-981-13-7985-7   ISBN 978-981-13-7986-4   (eBook)
https://doi.org/10.1007/978-981-13-7986-4

This Springer imprint is published by the registered company Springer Nature Singapore Pte Ltd.
The registered company address is: 152 Beach Road, #21-01/04 Gateway East, Singapore 189721, Singapore

Preface

Welcome to the proceedings of the International Conference on Cognitive Systems and Information Processing (ICCSIP 2018), which was held in Beijing, the capital of China, from November 29 to December 1, 2018. ICCSIP is the prestigious biennial conference on cognitive systems and information processing with past events held in Beijing (2012, 2014, 2016). Over the past few years, ICCSIP has matured into a well-established series of international conferences on cognitive information processing and related fields over the world. Similar to the previous event, ICCSIP 2018 provided an academic forum for the participants to share their new research findings and discuss emerging areas of research. It also established a stimulating environment for the participants to exchange ideas on future trends and opportunities of cognitive information processing research.

Currently, cognitive systems and information processing are applied in an increasing number of research domains such as cognitive sciences and technology, visual cognition and computation, big data and intelligent information processing, bioinformatics and applications. We believe that cognitive systems and information processing will certainly exhibit greater-than-ever advances in the near future. With the aim of promoting the research and technical innovation in relevant fields domestically and internationally, the fundamental objective of ICCSIP is defined as providing a premier forum for researchers and practitioners from academia, industry, and government to share their ideas, research results, and experiences.

This year, ICCSIP received 169 submissions, all of which are written in English. After a thorough reviewing process, 96 papers were selected for presentation as full papers, resulting in an approximate acceptance rate of 56%. The accepted papers not only address challenging issues in various aspects of cognitive systems and information processing but also showcase contributions from related disciplines that illuminate the state of the art. In addition to the contributed papers, the ICCSIP 2018 technical program included three plenary speeches by Prof. Qionghai Dai, Prof. Feiyue Wang, and Prof. Jianwei Zhang. We would also like to thank the members of the Advisory Committee for their guidance, the members of the international Program Committee and additional reviewers for reviewing the papers, and the members of the Publications Committee for checking the accepted papers in a short period of time. Last but not the least, we would like to thank all the speakers and authors as well as the participants for their great contributions that made ICCSIP2018 successful and all the hard work worthwhile.

December 2018

Fuchun Sun
Huaping Liu
Dewen Hu

Organization

ICCSIP 2018 was organized by the Cognitive Systems and Information Processing Society of Chinese Association for Artificial Intelligence, Cognitive Computing and Systems Society of Chinese Association of Automation, Tsinghua University, Science in China Press, Institute of Software Chinese Academy of Sciences.

Organization

Honorary Chairs

Bo Zhang	Tsinghua University, China
Deyi Li	Chinese Academy of Engineering, China

Advisory Committee Chairs

Nanning Zheng	Xi'an Jiaotong University, China
Wei Li	Beihang University, China
Lin Chen	Chinese Academy of Sciences, China
Ning Xi	Michigan State University, USA
Fuji Ren	Tokushima University, Japan
Donald C. Wunsch	Missouri University of Science and Technology, USA
Cesare Alippi	Politecnico di Milano, Italy
Yinxu Wang	University of Calgary, Canada
Philip Chen	University of Macau, SAR China

General Chairs

Fuchun Sun	Tsinghua University, China
Jennie Si	Arizona State University, USA
Jianwei Zhang	Universität Hamburg, Germany

Program Committee Chairs

Dewen Hu	National University of Defense Technology, China
Angelo Cangelosi	University of Manchester, UK
Michael Y. Wang	Hong Kong University of Science and Technology, SAR China
Chenglin Wen	Hangzhou Dianzi University, China
Changwen Zheng	Institute of Software, Chinese Academy of Sciences, China

Organizing Committee Chairs

Huaping Liu   Tsinghua University, China
Hong Cheng   University of Electronic Science and Technology,
                              China
Guangbin Huang   Nanyang Technological University, Singapore

Plenary Sessions Chairs

Zengguang Hou   Institute of Automation, Chinese Academy of Sciences,
                              China
Chenglin Wen   Hangzhou Dianzi University, China

Special Sessions Chairs

Fei Song   Science China Press, China
Yixu Song   Tsinghua University, China

Publications Chairs

Wei Li   California State University, USA
Quanbo Ge   Hangzhou Dianzi University, China

Publicity Chairs

Jianmin Li   Tsinghua University, China
Bin Fang   Tsinghua University, China

Finance Chair

Chunfang Liu   Tsinghua University, China

Registration Chair

Jianqin Yin   Beijing University of Posts and Telecommunications,
                              China

Local Arrangements Chair

Zhongyi Chu   Beihang University, China

Electronic Review Chair

Xiaolin Hu   Tsinghua University, China

Program Committee

Fuchun Sun	Tsinghua University, China
Dewen Hu	National University of Defense Technology, China
Guojun Dai	Hangzhou Dianzi University, China
Zhiguang Qin	University of Electronic Science and Technology, China
Jingmin Xin	Xi'an Jiaotong University, China
Huaping Liu	Tsinghua University, China
Wanzeng Kong	Hangzhou Dianzi University, China
Yuanlong Yu	Fuzhou University, China
Chenglin Wen	Hangzhou Dianzi University, China
Zhiquan Feng	University of Jinan, China
Yi Ning	Henan University of Technology, China
Rui Nian	Ocean University of China, China
Fang Liu	Shenyang Ligong University, China
Meiqin Liu	Zhejiang University, China
Bin Xu	Northwestern Polytechnical University, China
Weihua Su	Academy of Military Medical Sciences, China
Yujian Li	Beijing University of Technology, China Science China Press, China
Ke Li	Beihang University, China
Yongming Li	Shaanxi Normal University, China
Shunli Li	Harbin Institute of Technology, China
Hongbo Li	Tsinghua University, China
Li Li	Tianjin Normal University, China
Tieshan Li	Dalian Maritime University, China
Zhijun Li	South China University of Technology, China
Xia Li	Shenzhen University, China
Dongfang Yang	Rocket Force University of Engineering, China
Ming Yang	Shanghai Jiao Tong University, China
Jian Yang	Nanjing University of Science and Technology, China
Fengge Wu	Chinese Academy of Sciences, China
Licheng Wu	Minzu University of China, China
Jian He	Beijing University of Technology, China
Haibo Min	Rocket Force University of Engineering, China
Hongqiao Wang	Rocket Force University of Engineering, China
Liejun Wang	Xinjiang University, China
Hui Shen	National University of Defense Technology, China
Pengfei Zhang	China North Vehicle Research Institute, China
Jianhai Zhang	Hangzhou Dianzi University, China
Chun Zhang	Tsinghua University, China
Jinxiang Chen	China Iron and Steel Research Institute Group, China
Liang Chen	Shenzhen University, China
Minnan Luo	Xi'an Jiaotong University, China
Xiong Luo	University of Science and Technology Beijing, China

Fan Zhou	Shenyang Ligong University, China
Erqiang Zhou	University of Electronic Science and Technology, China
Yucai Zhou	Changsha University of Science and Technology, China
Dongbin Zhao	Chinese Academy of Sciences, China
Yuntao Zhao	Shenyang Ligong University, China
Qingjie Zhao	Beijing Institute of Technology, China
Huijing Zhao	Peking University, China
Shiqiang Hu	Shanghai Jiao Tong University, China
Laihong Hu	Rocket Force University of Engineering, China
Ying Hu	Chinese Academy of Sciences, China
Zhansheng Duan	Xi'an Jiaotong University, China
Peijiang Yuan	Beihang University, China
Chen Guo	Dalian Maritime University, China
Deshuang Huang	Tongji University, China
Panfeng Huang	Northwestern Polytechnical University, China
Yongzhi Cao	Peking University, China
Rongxin Cui	Northwestern Polytechnical University, China
Quanbo Ge	Hangzhou Dianzi University, China
Hong Cheng	University of Electronic Science and Technology, China

Organizers

Cognitive Systems and Information Processing Society of Chinese Association for Artificial Intelligence
Cognitive Computing and Systems Society of Chinese Association of Automation
Tsinghua University
Science in China Press
Institute of Software Chinese Academy of Sciences

Technical Co-sponsors

IEEE Computational Intelligence Society
Science in China Series F: Information Sciences
National Natural Science Foundation Committee of China

Co-organizer

Beijing University of Posts and Telecommunications

Contents – Part II

Human-Computer Interaction

Deep Learning

Information Processing and Automatic Driving

Contents – Part I

Algorithms

Robotics

Human-Computer Interaction

How to Understand: Three Types of Bilingual Information Processing?

Mieradilijiang Maimaiti[1], Shunpeng Zou[2], Xiaoqun Wang[3],
and Xiaohui Zou[2,3,4(✉)]

[1] Department of Computer Science and Technology,
Tsinghua University, Beijing, China
meadljmm15@mails.tsinghua.edu.cn
[2] China University of Geosciences (Beijing),
29 Xueyuan Road, Beijing 100083, China
zoushunpeng@xdf.cn, geneculture@icloud.com
[3] Audio-Visual Building, Room 415, Peking University,
Beijing 100871, China
xqwang@pku.edu.cn
[4] Sino-American Searle Research Center, UC Berkeley,
Berkeley 94720-3840, USA

Abstract. Bilingual information processing has been being used widely in many tasks such as Natural Language Understanding (NLU), Cross-Domain, Machine Translation (MT) and Bilingual Cognition. There still remain some problematic phenomena for understanding bilingual information processing. In this work, we aim to fully understand both the principles and methods of bilingual information processing by taking advantage of appropriate comparisons. The major idea of our proposed approach is both human and the machine can cooperate or interact with each other according to their characteristics. Concretely, it is composed of the following three steps: First, find issues from the Chinese-English bilingual translation at phrase sentence level alignment. The challenge in Chinese-English translation lies in an inconsistency of the meanings between the Chinese characters and the English words. Then, analyze the problems from the view of interdisciplinary, cross-domain and cross-industry. Finally, address leveraging human-machine to divide the task and coordinate with each other. As a result, not only we discover both parallel dual formalized approach of big and small strings, but also find and validate both the superiority and followed scientific principles of generalized bilingual information processing method.

Keywords: Bilingual Cognition · Knowledge representation ·
Cross-Domain · Machine Translation ·
Natural Language Understanding

S. Zou—Equal contributor.

F. Sun et al. (Eds.): ICCSIP 2018, CCIS 1006, pp. 3–16, 2019.
https://doi.org/10.1007/978-981-13-7986-4_1

1 Introduction

In a recent couple of years, there have been numerously being increased both in the quality and quantity of explorations [1,2,17,25] in bilingual cognition and language processing development. In some research which is related to assessing the degree of bilingualism in a diverse population by taking advantages of language and social background questionnaires [2], also maintain that there are no any criteria for the definition of bilingualism. Likewise, we also regard that there is a lack of a certain mechanism for evaluating the degree of bilingualism in individual participants. Another interesting research has been being focused on transferring structural patterns into the developing mixed language [6]. Besides, some studies [19] whose effects of bilingual cognition have gained better results by examining the bilingual advantage in attention, working memory and novel-word learning. As their analysis of individual differences showed that bilingual novel-word learning is related to their verbal working memory and ability.

Additionally, the bilingual advantage hypothesis contends that the management of two languages in the brain is carried out through the domain-general mechanism. Some works [18] report the preliminary results of the research of cross-linguistic influence. Moreover, some meaningful work [19] has made an investigation of the effects of that bilingualism and age on executive function. The findings of this work are the different levels of bilingualism and ages, result in varying degrees of executive function. Interestingly, many attractive works [1,13,21] has explored the cross-linguistic evidence and significant challenges in second language learning, respectively. Generally, the main investigation of dialect-switching task relies on cognitive control mechanisms of which, the reminiscent of findings for balanced and unbalanced bilinguals. Furthermore, artificial intelligence technologies made remarkable progress, while many terrific ideas, various mechanisms, and marvelous applications are designed and emerged both in our daily life and study life. Meanwhile, cognitive computation [14,16] filed has also obtained outstanding achievements in the Natural Language Understanding (NLU) situation. Likewise, many fantastic works [3,4,10,22] about bilingualism have been investigated at word embedding level and some works explored bilingual cognition at lexical level [5,24,30,33]. Meanwhile, some of researchers also proposed terrific ideas [9,12,27,28,31] about bilingual cognition take cross-lingual information into account. Likewise, bilingual cognition also plays a vital role during the MT (statistical phrase-based machine translation "SMT" or neural machine translation "NMT"), and the majority of researchers are trying to make bilingual information processing easier, to avoid the significant impediment to process the bilingual information and to clarify the principles of it.

Generally, the information theory is the perspective [26] about information which is used to eliminate the uncertainty, the information philosophy is the standpoint [11] about open issues without clear standards. The major distinction between them is that they stand for two extreme typical point views for formal information and semantic information, respectively. The father of general linguistics discovers that the objects of linguistic research not still as clear as natural sciences [20]. The formal grammarian Chomsky established the basic paradigm of formalization techniques for computing small strings, meanwhile formalized grammar symbolic formulas for that a sentence is equal to noun phrases and verb phrase [8]. However in terms of formal semantics encountered a series of challenges, so far no one could find the unified formal grammar and formal semantics. It demonstrates that there is also still exist problems on formal pragmatics. Mathematicians [29] and empirical philosopher [7] propose object language and meta-language (interpreted language), formally distinguished the language symbol object and formal semantics which produced by the combination of transformation.

In this work, we have proposed the three types of bilingual information processing approaches. More precisely, not only the finding of two major categories formal strategies for different types of work for large string, specifically Chinese characters, and small string particularly ASCII symbols but also the building of the dual formalization method and its generalized bilingual information processing manner. Its performance greatly promotes the research both in these fields and related fields, discovers the logic of order and location among them. We aim to focus on explaining how to further understand the bilingual information processing method and its principle. In here, the three types of bilingual information includes narrow bilingual, such as Chinese and English; alternative bilingual, such as terminologies and popular sayings; generalized bilingual, such as the mathematical language of arithmetic numbers and natural language of Chinese characters. Currently, it mainly involves formal representation of natural language information in a relevant context. To the best of our knowledge, the key idea is a combination of a work with natural sciences [20] on Chinese implicit formal description by taking the differences between the Yan ("言") in language and the Yu ("语") in speech into account.

2   Bilingual Information Processing Method

The proposed method about bilingual information processing in this paper consists of a series of bilingual conversion steps among interpersonal, human-machine and inter-machine. Among them, the rational division of labor and high-level cooperation between the three types of bilingual is the key to information processing. Both human and machine can cooperate or respond to each other according to their respective characteristics, thus forming a three-class bilingual information processing "dividing and combining" synergy linkage mechanism.

2.1   Find Issues from Bilingual (Chinese-English) Translation

In this paper, we are trying better to understand the narrow bilingual such as Chinese-English between human communications Thereby, the general translation task into the problem of "interpret first, then translate" in bilingual information processing that has been given its name as butterfly model as follows:

As illustrated in Fig. 1, it is easy to know the uniqueness from the Character type as a basic symbol object of written Chinese at the right side, each of its

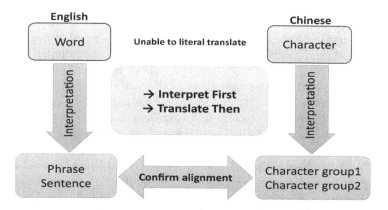

Fig. 1. The sketching graph for narrow bilingual information processing model.

instances is enumerable and it is one of the most significant Characteristics of written Chinese. Therefore, in here we name all the monosyllabic characters as Yan ("言") in language, as well as take it as the indirectly formalized written Chinese object language. The interpretation of indirect formalized written Chinese is meta-language, namely two-syllable and multi-syllable character group (no matter at which level character group1 or character group2) as Yu ("语") in speech. It can be measured by in the collection of large strings of Chinese characters in terms of the number of syllables. The interpretation of the meta-language (formal information) database is carried out step by step. Hereby, all character group equivalent to words, phrases, and sentences taken from the library of written Chinese without any exception. It should be taken attention to the following parts:

First, the consequences of character or character group, formally, the divergence or convergence, division or combination can be used to generate or exclude the corresponding formal ambiguity, involving the determination of formal semantics. Second, because the uniqueness of Chinese is not limited to the number of Chinese characters, but that can be enumerated. Moreover, it is also that the relationship between its large strings and monosyllabic is not a functional relationship. Therefore, not only the various forms of the ambiguity of phonetic symbols' form are asymmetrical, but also the process of giving mean to the meaning of the people is asymmetry, uncertainty, and even ambiguity. It has both the simplicity and convenience of a computer that is easy to enumerate. In order to disambiguate the complexity and the people are also required to participate. Third, combined with historical, geographical and interpersonal complex factors, this has increased the number of ambiguities between its overlapping content and form. This is an intractable and complicated problem. Only the vision of macroscopic philosophical rational reflection and the vision of microscopic scientific experience prediction are combined with each other, and from the practical operation of combining technology and art, under such a multi-pronged system engineering, then can form a series of those bilingual collaborative processing intelligence between interpersonal, human-machine, inter-machine and machine-human. Then it is possible to gradually resolve the series of ambiguities that are inevitably encountered.

Algorithm 1. Bilingual Information Processing.

Input: Given bilingual corpus L, $L = \{\langle \mathbf{x}^{(n)}, \mathbf{y}^{(n)} \rangle\}_{n=1}^{N}$
Output: translation result y
1: **for** $t = 1, 2, 3, 4, 5, ..., N$ **do**
2:     Generate "Phrase Set" and modify sentence structures
3:     Select some words and modify its position among sentence S
4:     Remove the original input from the testset
5:     Feed the revised sentence S' to the testset
6:     Translate final input
7: **end for**

As shown in Fig. 1, the word at the left end has the characteristics of the basic symbol object of written English. It can be seen that since the examples of words can include: monosyllabic, two-syllable and multi-syllables, the syllable attribute of the word as a whole determines that the specific words are not enumerable. If written Chinese word disregards the uniqueness of the enumeration of its own words, rather than directly copying or borrowing the mixed-sentence attribute that cannot be enumerated by foreign words. Furthermore, it is necessary to continue to use the formalization of small strings based on English to continue to use the formalization of small strings to process Chinese character information based on large string sets. Then, it is inevitable that the word segmentation and labeling are inexhaustible. The strategy of "interpret first then translate" actually gives the result of translation, machine translation (MT) and translation memory directly presenting narrow bilingualism. The first is two object languages and interpretation of the internal explanation of the meta-language system, and then further is the conversion, substitution or translation between Chinese and English. Using the unique steps shown in Fig. 1, anyone who can find that NLU could eliminate the bottleneck problem of ambiguity, that is, Chinese words and English words, due to their uniqueness. Therefore, they are not translatable with each other as a whole. Partial interpretation and translation also require precise analysis of specific issues.

Algorithm 1 also shows how our approach generates the revised sentences slightly or heavily if we need. We take L as the bilingual corpus, as well as $L = \{\langle \mathbf{x}^{(n)}, \mathbf{y}^{(n)} \rangle\}_{n=1}^{N}$ and y is translation result which provided by engine (MT model with various architectures in SMT or NMT). Precisely, we need to generate the phrase set before feeding the input into the translation model, as well as modify the input sentence structure slightly in accordance with some context information such as cross-domain, multidisciplinary and specific domain. Select some words and change their position in the original sentence S. Remove the original string (sentence) from the input then feed the revised sentence S' to the test. Finally, translate the revised sentences with moderate modification. In this way, we not only can relieve the burden of translation engine but also mitigate the error rate to some extent.

For instance, physical, physiological, psychological the three words in the context of Chinese and English, it is quite problematic detachable situations. Matter ("物") + reason ("理") = physics ("物理"), health ("生") + reason ("理") = physiology ("生理"), heart ("心") + reason ("理") = psychology ("心里"), the separation mechanism of such a large string can clearly reveal the written Chinese characteristics contained in. However, if we want to translate this form and its Chinese characteristics or rules into English, we need to leverage the proposed approach "interpret first translate then" it may become more reasonable. For example the mechanism of natural or artificial things = physics, the regularity of living things = physiology, the principle of mental activity = psychology. Otherwise, it is very awkward and does not make sense. Besides, the word "meaning" in the Chinese context, the case of division and union is: meaning ("意") + righteousness/meaning ("义") = meaning ("意义"). But in the English context, it cannot be split. If you intent to separate them, you can only "interpret first, then translate", such as: the fundamental rule of sense with a certain choice = meaning. It can be seen that it is essential that there are two sequences between the classical translation (terminology) and the popular interpretation or explanation (popular words or proverbs). Take another example Yufa ("语法") or Wenfa ("文法") in the Chinese, the case of division and union is: language/speech/Yu ("语") + Fa/law ("法") = grammar ("语法"), Wen/literature/letter ("文") + Fa/law ("法") = grammar ("文法"), has actually become the form of two characters. However, in English it is a word, and it cannot be split. If it is hard-released or need to be split, then it can only be "interpret first then translate", such as: the law of Yu in language in the form of formality = syntactic or grammar. The law (rule) or rule (law) of the combination of language ("语") and writing in form = grammar ("语法") or grammar ("文法").

2.2   Analyze Issues from Various Perspectives: Interdisciplinary, Cross-Domain and Cross-Industry

Integration Strategy of Micro, Medium and Macro. This paper regards the expert terminologies and popular sayings bilingual inter-personal as alternative bilingual. Thereby, this can also decompose the surface language problem into language form ("语言形式") formal information ("形式信息") and the problem of language content ("语言内容") content information ("内容信息"), Then it has been further transformed into two sequences namely language form information and knowledge content information. First, a basic qualitative analysis is made from the most qualitative analysis model of Semantic Triangulation ("语义三棱"). Further qualitative analysis for the qualitative analysis model of the Three-Span Division ("三跨划分") is further refined.

As depicted in Fig. 2 that the conceptual framework or architecture of the macroscopic ontology presentation is the analysis model of the Semantic Triangulation (the largest knowledge ontology of the seven Chinese characters refined

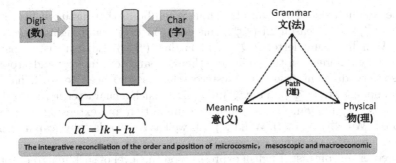

Fig. 2. The architecture for qualitative analysis model.

expression). "Information Identity" links microscopic system of numbers and characters with digital information (Id) and known information (Ik), particularly knowledge and unknown information (Iu), namely semantic information, as a basic division of the three classes. Adopt a dual formal approach to collaboratively address the three-span term of cross-disciplinary, cross-domain, and cross-industry.

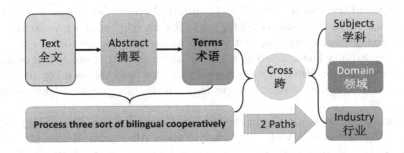

Fig. 3. The sketching graph for bilingual ontology model.

Adopting a Dual Formal Approach to Collaboratively Address the "three-Span" Term of "interdisciplinary, Cross-Domain, and Cross-Industry". We can see from the combination of Figs. 2 and 3 that the meaning and operation of the two qualitative analysis models of Semantic Triangulation and Three-Span Division are characteristic. For example, physics, meaning theory, and grammar are all studies that China has imported from the West. The basic meaning of these scholarships is relatively certain, their connotations and extensions are developed, and in their own context, they are determined by the specific disciplines, fields and the characteristics of the industries they actually apply. Not only can it not be meaningful in its native language, but it must not be just a matter of Chinese translation. Because of culture, technology, philosophy and other thinking behind different contexts the personality side has not just the common side. For example, Chinese can be further distinguished: matter/Wu ("物") and reason/Li ("理"), meaning/Yi ("意") and righteousness/Yi ("义"), Wen/literature/letter ("文") and Fa/law ("法"); English distinguishing mode is very different. In turn, Chinese thoughts and terminology and proverbs are also very different from the Western scholars who need to work hard to understand. e.g., Li ("理") , Yi ("意"), Fa ("法"), such a character not a word, its meaning is very fundamental because its connotation and extension far exceed the words "Wu (物), Yi (义'), Wen (文)", as well as the words "physical, meaning, grammar" are the meanings expressed.

Moreover, in contrast, English expression on the level of such macro-ontology is another pattern. For example, the isomorphism of the world, though, and language as described by Wittgenstein [32]. Another example is the pre-subjectivity, subjectivity, and inter-subjectivity of Husserl and Heidegger [23]. Meanwhile, another example is Plato and Aristotle and the ontology of the medieval philosophers, the epistemology of Descartes and Kant [15]. It is not too hard to find that due to the characteristics of Western languages, description of their "Three-Point" view almost no precision (at best, it can only be equivalent"Wu (物), Yi (义), Wen (文)" division of such phenomena or "physical, meaning, grammar" the expression of this phenomenon mixed with the essence. Likewise, they often overlap each other therefore, it is necessary to analyze the rational reflection of philosophy and the provable prophecy of empirical science, as well as the formal skill operation. On the contrary"Li (理), Yi (意), Fa (法)" such a precise expression of Chinese characters, but just staying at the macroscopic beauty and its micro-changeability lacks coherent scientific arguments. It is not yet developed into a simple and precise unity of macro and micro (and this is a key territory for this study to achieve breakthroughs through the integration of Chinese and Western).

Likewise, the Semantic Triangulation (see Fig. 2) and the Three-Span Division (see Fig. 3) combine with each other to show Alternative Bilingual (terms and proverbs) and its cognitive characteristics. As given in Fig. 1 Butterfly Model the process of "interpret first then translate", two qualitative models combined with Figs. 2 and 3. The process of teaching and managing, learning and using, In essence, it can be said that it is a certain result achieved in the process of interpersonal communication. Alternative Bilingual, a new strategy of consent juxtaposition with expert terminology in different languages, is the cultural background of both sides. Generally, the respect of common sense (referred to as proverbs), interdisciplinary, cross-disciplinary and cross-industry knowledge or the humility of the term is accepted or respected. This process is more than just a process of language translation. At the same time, it is a process of common sense communication or colloquial exchange, knowledge learning and skill training, and terminology mastery. It can be summarized as two telecommuting systems engineering, which is: "Socialized System Engineering for Education, Management, Learning and Application" versus "Formal System Engineering of language, knowledge, software, and hardware". The problem of translation is not limited to text translation of humanities or science and technology. In essence, it is a complex process of interaction. It is the process of learning research and communication between peoples and involves precise understanding and expression of terms and proverbs.

2.3 Address Issues from View of Human-Machine Division and Cooperation

In this work, we look upon bilingual between interpersonal, human-machine, inter-machine and machine-human as a generalized bilingual. In this way, the series of tasks of language form information and knowledge content information between the first two steps can be further promoted to the development environment of human-computer interaction or the shared platform to realize the synergy of three types of bilingual information processing mechanism. The first step of "interpret first then translate" with the second step of "fine term colloquialism", it became "super cloud concrete cloud" of the third step (The human-computer interaction record generated between the various users and the system in the first two steps of storage). If the first two steps are designed to overcome the limitations of Chinese, (Chinese is in a non-mainstream position) It is necessary to launch a group whose native language is Chinese.

In this work, we look upon bilingual between interpersonal, human-machine, inter-machine and machine-human as a generalized bilingual. In this way, the series of tasks of language form information and knowledge content information between the first two steps can be further promoted to the development environment of human-computer interaction or the shared platform to realize the synergy of three types of bilingual information processing mechanism. The first step of "interpret first then translate" with the second step of "fine term colloquialism", it became "super cloud concrete cloud" of the third step (The human-computer interaction record generated between the various users and the system in the first two steps of storage). If the first two steps are designed to overcome the limitations of Chinese, (Chinese is in a non-mainstream position) It is necessary to launch a group whose native language is Chinese.

As we can see from Fig. 4 and the matching double-chessboard can be seen in general bilingualism which is a decimal number (mathematical language) with written Chinese (Natural Language: Collaboration with English-Chinese Bilingual Syllabus). The three types of bilingual collaborative processing mechanisms are implied. Such information processing has the following characteristics: First of all, through the narrow bilingual and alternative bilingual, that can be realized a reasonable division of labor between each other; highly collaborative and optimized interaction. The advantage of this is that it can overcome the limitations of Chinese, and the "cloud platform" can better accomplish the "precise learning ("精准学习")" task. The specific method is to organize the specific disciplines and fields of the distributed subject knowledge center with the teaching classes of each university as the operating unit. The basic knowledge ware-house of specific industries and the targeted derivation knowledge base, namely: form a "super cloud ("超级云") specific cloud ("具体云")". Furthermore, since generalized bilingual information processing has the synergy of human-machine,

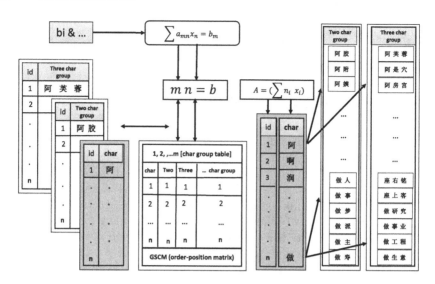

Fig. 4. The mechanism for bilingual function model.

therefore, it is completely possible to be based on the uniqueness of written Chinese. Combining the convenience of converting different arithmetic numbers into each other, realize the synergy of human-machine, in Chinese formal information as well as the three types of bilingual collaborative processing process language, knowledge, and software are targeted for reprocessing especially. Finally, once based on generalized bilingual information processing with three types of bilingual collaborative processing formal system engineering of language, knowledge, software and its hardware to achieve the best point in time, which can form a more reasonable division of labor and complementary advantages with social system engineering of education, management, learning, and application; that is highly collaborative and optimizes interaction. In a nutshell, its characteristics are concentrated in the mechanism of the three types of bilingual collaborative processing that can be driven by general bilingual. A typical example of generalized bilingualism is arithmetic (Mathematical language following mathematical logic) and Chinese (natural language following formal logic) synchronously call its order and location in logic. In this work, This is the key to the new strategy. Therefore, the method part of this paper mainly explains generalized bilingual and alignment in the logic of order-position. How to combine the dual advantages of direct and indirect formalization?

As depicted from Fig. 5, the arithmetic matrix (number matrix) composed of numbers and the Chinese matrix (array matrix) composed of characters or words respectively constitute two symmetric matrices; In the middle is a virtual balance that can be occupied by the order spaces in the twin matrices. In conjunction with Fig. 4, the direct formalized features of the matrix and the indirect formalized features of the Chinese matrix can be found and verified. Based on the abstract model, a dual-constrained dual formalization tool that can conform

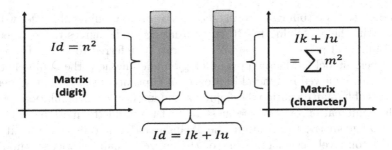

Fig. 5. The sketching graph of symmetrical matrix model.

to the order logic and satisfy the linkage function can be obtained. It has the dual advantages of direct formalization and indirect formalization. It is the most accurate measurement tool for written Chinese. The most basic function of the measurable twin matrix is to realize the quantitative analysis of language and knowledge by sequencing from the Chinese characters. Corresponding to Fig. 5 the abstract model is generalized bilingual information processing. The Super Cloud computing systems work with series Concrete Cloud computing service subsystems from which to access. The actual use case corresponding to this is the relational database of language (Yan ("言") namely character ("字")) and speech (Yu ("语") namely character group ("字组")) described in the double-character chessboard. This shows that by the relationship between character and character group, not only led to narrow bilingual and broad bilingual but also led to alternative bilingual. In particular, three types of bilingual information collaborative processing, this kind of human-computer dual-brain combination cognitive system and information processing method can not only be compatible with both human-machine but also unique. Thus, there will be a series of breakthroughs as follows: First, the key path between linguistics and linguistic philosophy is opened through formal technical methods. Further, through the expansion of the dual formal approach, it also opened up the key path of information science and information philosophy, and also clarified the relationship between language and information. Thus, the relationship between language science and information science has also been rationalized.

3 The Relationship Between Information Processing and Information Basic Rule

Generally, the Model is the Butterfly Model is based on the father of machine translation Weaver with the landmark research results of B. Vauquois the founder of the computational linguistics machine translation pyramid model, it has been further developed. Statistical and rule-based machine translations have envisioned "intermediary", however, you also can re-find that there is actually opposite. If you have to say yes, then you can say that any of a series of bilingual pairs can be used as an "intermediary" for another bilingual pair. Likewise, the key is how to do a series of bilingual construction, the narrow bilingual model works. In particular, the explaining first then translating model agrees to juxtapose a series of bilingual processing strategies that can be referred to as the Bilingual Model. Then, model 2: Macroscopic ontology model, namely, the double knowledge model is reviewed in general improved and optimized several milestones in the process of human cognition development and knowledge accumulation. Moreover, the combination of only the most refined text and the most basic three-dimensional geometric tetrahedron, the Triangular Pyramid, is achieved. It can depict the top-level design blueprint of the entire human knowledge building. The most basic conceptual framework and the method of architecture are concise. Based on the Intellectual Triangle terminology, that can be interdisciplinary, cross-domain, and cross-industry. That is to say, the knowledge learning subdivision system sets up a well-defined knowledge of the basic system. At last, The model 3: three types of bilingual information processing systems, the Double-Melting Model, among them, the generalized bilingual micro-operational model, and its practical relational (char ""字"") and language (char group ""字组"") relational database (Fig. 4) combined its abstract model (Fig. 5), Combined with the father of linguistics, Saussure once thought of Language System as Chess System. As well as the Language Game imagined by Wittgenstein as a master of language philosophy. Simultaneously, combined with models 1 and 2, can form a Super Chess based on three types of bilingual (This is equivalent to the "super cloud" described in Session 2.3 of this article) with Large-Span"language game" (this is equivalent to the "concrete cloud" described in Session 2.3 of this article). A wide variety of ambiguities can be found in the course of the "language game". Follow the three basic laws of information to gradually resolve.

4   Conclusion and Future Work

In this work, we introduce three types of bilingual information processing method and its principles. Meanwhile, we also aim to better understand both the principles and methods by taking advantage of proper comparisons. The major idea of our proposed approach is that both human and machine can cooperate or interact with each other according to their own characteristics. The key idea is shown as follows, finding issues from the bilingual character and word relationship. The main challenge is the meanings between characters only in Chinese and words both in English and Chinese. Then, analyze the problems from the various perspectives such as interdisciplinary, cross-domain and cross-industry Finally, addressed on using human-machine characteristics doing the task and being coordinate with each other. Our main contributions are, we have proposed to let much more people to understand the three types of bilingual information processing methods; besides, provide the understanding bilingual approach of human-machine cooperated architecture. In the future work, we plan to further validate our understanding method incorporate into NLP other tasks. As the unsupervised approach, it can also be used in Low-resource Languages machine translation, dialogue generation and speech recognition, etc tasks. Likewise, we try to exploit the proposed method to morphologically rich, inflectional and derivative languages.

Acknowledgments. Professor Zou and senior engineer Wang had been supported by Peking University Science and Technology Office and National Natural Science Foundation of China under Application No.: 6187022555.

The authors would like to thank those anonymous reviewers for providing valuable comments.

References

1. Álvarez, A.I.: Semantic differences as a function of type of bilingual and cognitive development (2018)
2. Anderson, J.A.E., Mak, L., Chahi, A.K., Bialystok, E.: The language and social background questionnaire: assessing degree of bilingualism in a diverse population. Behav. Res. Methods **50**(1), 250–263 (2018)
3. Artetxe, M., Labaka, G., Agirre, E.: Learning principled bilingual mappings of word embeddings while preserving monolingual invariance. In: EMNLP (2016)
4. Artetxe, M., Labaka, G., Agirre, E.: Learning bilingual word embeddings with (almost) no bilingual data. In: ACL (2017)
5. Artetxe, M., Labaka, G., Agirre, E.: A robust self-learning method for fully unsupervised cross-lingual mappings of word embeddings. In: ACL (2018)
6. Bilingualism, P.M.: Language contact outcomes as the result of bilingual optimization strategies (2018)
7. Carnap, R.: Introduction to Semantics and Formalization of Logic (1959)
8. Chomsky, N.: On certain formal properties of grammars. Inf. Control **2**, 137–167 (1959)
9. Coulmance, J., Marty, J.M., Wenzek, G., Benhalloum, A.: Trans-gram, fast cross-lingual word-embeddings. In: EMNLP (2015)
10. Duong, L.V., Kanayama, H., Ma, T., Bird, S., Cohn, T.: Learning crosslingual word embeddings without bilingual corpora. In: EMNLP (2016)
11. Floridi, L.: Philosophical conceptions of information. In: Sommaruga, G. (ed.) Formal Theories of Information. LNCS, vol. 5363, pp. 13–53. Springer, Heidelberg (2009). https://doi.org/10.1007/978-3-642-00659-3_2
12. Gao, D., Wei, F., Li, W., Liu, X., Zhou, M.: Cross-lingual sentiment lexicon learning with bilingual word graph label propagation. Comput. Linguist. **41**, 21–40 (2015)
13. George, N., Kanero, J.: Bilingualism and second language learning (2018)
14. Pounder, G.A.J., Ellis, R.L.A., Fernandez-Lopez, G.: Cognitive function synthesis: preliminary results. Kybernetes **46**(2), 272–290 (2017)
15. Gillespie, A.: Intersubjectivity: towards a dialogical analysis. J. Theory Soc. Behav. **40**(1), 19–46 (2010)
16. Finch, G., Goehring, B., Marshall, A.: The enticing promise of cognitive computing: high-value functional efficiencies and innovative enterprise capabilities. Strategy Leadersh. **45**(6), 26–33 (2017)
17. Grundy, J.G., Anderson, J.A.E., Bialystok, E.: Neural correlates of cognitive processing in monolinguals and bilinguals. Ann. N. Y. Acad. Sci. **1396**(1), 183–201 (2017)
18. Hervé, C., Serratrice, L.: The development of determiners in the context of French-English bilingualism: a study of cross-linguistic influence. J. Child Lang. **45**(3), 767–787 (2018)

19. Incera, S., McLennan, C.T.: Bilingualism and age are continuous variables that influence executive function. Neuropsychol. Dev. Cogn. Sect. B Aging Neuropsychol. Cogn. **25**(3), 443–463 (2018)
20. Joseph, J.E., Holdcroft, D.: Saussure: Signs, System, and Arbitrariness. Cambridge University Press (1991)
21. Kirk, N., Kempe, V., Scott-Brown, K.C., Philipp, A.M., Declerck, M.: Can monolinguals be like bilinguals? Evidence from dialect switching. Cognition **170**, 164–178 (2018)
22. Maimaiti, M., Zou, X.: Discussion on bilingual cognition in international exchange activities. In: Shi, Z., Pennartz, C., Huang, T. (eds.) ICIS 2018. IAICT, vol. 539, pp. 167–177. Springer, Cham (2018). https://doi.org/10.1007/978-3-030-01313-4_17
23. McGuinness, B.F., et al.: Prototractatus: an early version of Tractatus logico-philosophicus. Anal. Philos. **13**(1), 36–38 (2010)
24. Mogadala, A., Rettinger, A.: Bilingual word embeddings from parallel and non-parallel corpora for cross-language text classification. In: HLT-NAACL (2016)
25. Samuel, S., Roehr-Brackin, K., Pak, H., Kim, H.: Cultural effects rather than a bilingual advantage in cognition: a review and an empirical study. Cogn. Sci. **42**(7), 2313–2341 (2018)
26. Shannon, C.E.: A mathematical theory of communication. Mob. Comput. Commun. Rev. **5**, 3–55 (2001)
27. Shi, T., Liu, Z., Liu, Y., Sun, M.: Learning cross-lingual word embeddings via matrix co-factorization. In: ACL (2015)
28. Täckström, O., McDonald, R.T., Uszkoreit, J.: Cross-lingual word clusters for direct transfer of linguistic structure. In: HLT-NAACL (2012)
29. Tarski, A.: Sur les ensembles définissables de nombres réels. Fundam. Math. **39**, 210 (1939)
30. Upadhyay, S., Faruqui, M., Dyer, C., Roth, D.: Cross-lingual models of word embeddings: an empirical comparison. CoRR abs/1604.00425 (2016)
31. Vulic, I., Moens, M.F.: Monolingual and cross-lingual information retrieval models based on (bilingual) word embeddings. In: SIGIR (2015)
32. Wittgenstein, L.: Goffman unbound!: A new paradigm for social science (the sociological imagination) (1992)
33. Zhang, M., Liu, Y., Luan, H., Sun, M.: Adversarial training for unsupervised bilingual lexicon induction. In: ACL (2017)

Utilizing Chinese Dictionary Information in Named Entity Recognition

Yun Hu[1,2]($\boxtimes$), Mingxue Liao[2], Pin Lv[2], and Changwen Zheng[2]

[1] University of Chinese Academy of Sciences, Beijing, China
[2] Institute of Software, Chinese Academy of Sciences, Beijing, China
{huyun2016,mingxue,lvpin,changwen}@iscas.ac.cn

Abstract. Supervised methods are widely used in Chinese named entity recognition (NER). To achieve state-of-the-art performance, NER systems often use additional resources like gazetteer which is a large dictionary containing well known named entities. However, previous works do not consider the situation that the corpus coverage rate of gazetteer is low and the gazetteer contains noise. In this situation, the effect of the gazetteer is limited. In this paper, we extend the gazetteer with a dictionary which contains common words and part-of-speech (POS) information of the words. We first obtain the Chinese word segmentation (CWS) and part-of-speech information using the dictionary. Then, a feature is developed to contain the CWS and POS information together. Finally, the feature is added to the LSTM-CRF model. Experimental results show that our method yields a 4.71% improvement over the gazetteer feature method.

Keywords: Chinese named entity recognition · Dictionary · Gazetteer

1 Introduction

Name entity recognition is a fundamental Natural Language Process and Intelligent Information Processing task that labels each word in sentences with predefined types, such as Person (PER), Location (LOC), Organization (ORG) and so on. NER system is often realized by supervised methods, such as CRF and neural network methods. When supervised methods are used to realize NER system, a big challenge is out of vocabulary (OOV) problem. Because most of the supervised methods are based on statistical information, these methods are hard to handle unfamiliar words.

The OOV problem can be relieved by gazetteer to some extent. Gazetteer is a dictionary containing well known named entities which may not appear in training dataset. Gazetteer feature is a prevalent feature which is used in both

The work is supported by both National scientific and Technological Innovation Zero (No. 17-H863-01-ZT-005-005-01) and State's Key Project of Research and Development Plan (No. 2016QY03D0505).

F. Sun et al. (Eds.): ICCSIP 2018, CCIS 1006, pp. 17–26, 2019.
https://doi.org/10.1007/978-981-13-7986-4_2

Chinese and English NER systems [2, 4, 12]. A word will have a strong tendency to be an entity when the word appears in gazetteer.

However, previous works do not consider a usual situation that the corpus coverage rate of gazetteer is low and the gazetteer contains noise. The performance of the gazetteer is harmed in this situation. Two reasons lead to this situation. First, the domain of the corpus and gazetteer may be different. In some domain, the gazetteer is hard to obtain and a universal gazetteer is used as an alternative approach. Second, the gazetteer is obtained automatically, which causes noise unavoidably.

In this paper, we explore using dictionary which contains common words and POS information of the words to replace gazetteer. We obtain the Chinese word segmentation information and POS information using the dictionary, and this information is helpful in LSTM-CRF model. Experimental results show that the dictionary feature works better than gazetteer feature in Chinese NER.

2   Related Work

Chinese named entity recognition task is similar to English named entity recognition which can be seen as a sequence labeling task. Lafferty et al. used CRF method to solve sequence labeling task in English [9]. Chen et al. used the CRF method to solve named entity recognition in Chinese [1]. However, CRF method requires hand-engineered features which are difficult and time-consuming to obtain. Recently, the neural network methods can extract the features automatically and achieve state-of-the-art performance in English [2, 10]. Dong et al. explored LSTM-CRF model combining with radical-level features and achieved state-of-the-art performance in Chinese NER [3]. In this paper, we choose LSTM-CRF model as our baseline model.

Gazetteer feature is a widely used feature in previous works. Florian et al. combined various machine-learning classifiers and used a large gazetteer to achieve strong performance in English [4]. Collobert et al. used an additional gazetteer in neural network model and obtained preferable results in English [2]. In Chinese, gazetteer features are also widely used [12]. In this paper, we use the dictionary to extend the usage of gazetteer.

We use the dictionary to extract the word segmentation and POS information which are shown helpful in Chinese named entity recognition task. He and Wang utilized the word segmentation and POS information as the feature when CRF method was used to process the NER [6]. Peng and Dredze introduced a model to jointly train the word segmentation and NER and the model yielded significant improvements in Chinese NER [15]. However, previous works focus on using the off-the-shelf tools or the models trained on large corpus to obtain the CWS or POS information. The tools or models are harder to obtain than dictionary and the performance is affected by the domain adaptation.

3 Method

We consider our method as a pipeline work. We first extract the CWS and POS information using the dictionary. Then, a new feature is created. Finally, the feature is added to the LSTM-CRF model.

3.1 Feature

The dictionary[1] is from jieba project which is a prevalent CWS project. The structure of this dictionary is "word frequency POS". For example, "史铁生   2   nr" means the POS of the word "史铁生" is "nr" ("nr" means "person name" and we do not use the frequency information). We use the dictionary to obtain CWS and POS information, and the two types of information is connected as a new feature. The details of the feature are shown in Table 1.

We first obtain the CWS information. We use the Forward and Backward Maximum Matching (FBMM) algorithm which is based on lexicon [16]. Compared with methods based on large corpus, FBMM is simpler and widely used when only the lexicon is obtained. The FBMM algorithm combines the forward maximum matching (FMM) algorithm and backward maximum algorithm (BMM). The FMM finds the longest matching word from the beginning of the sentence to the end of the sentence. The only difference of BMM is starting from the end of the sentence. We remain the results of least word method when conflict segmentation happens in FMM and BMM.

Table 1. An example of dictionary feature. "B", "M", "E" means begin, middle and end of a word in CWS. In POS, "nr" means person names, "v" means verb, and "n" means noun. In dictionary feature, we connect the CWS and POS. In NER, "B-XXX", "I-XXX" means begin and inside of "XXX" type of entity. "XXX" can be "PER", "LOC", "ORG" and so on. "O" means outside of an entity.

	Si	TieShen		Come to		DiTan		Park	
	史	铁	生	来	到	地	坛	公	园
CWS	B	M	E	B	E	B	M	M	E
POS	nr	nr	nr	v	v	n	n	n	n
Dictionary	B@nr	M@nr	E@nr	B@v	B@v	B@n	M@n	M@n	E@n
NER	B-PER	I-PER	I-PER	O	O	B-LOC	I-LOC	I-LOC	I-LOC

We then obtain the POS information. The POS information of the word can be directly obtained by the dictionary. When the system is realized, two details are emphasized. The first is the POS tag of punctuations, English letters and numbers. These symbols not appear in the dictionary. We set the POS tag of

---

[1] https://github.com/fxsjy/jieba/tree/master/extra_dict.

punctuation as "punc", English letters as "alph" and number as "numb". The second is that we set the POS tag of OOV word as "oov".

3.2 Model

Our model is similar to Dong et al. [3] which achieves state-of-the-art performance in Chinese named entity recognition. Compared with Dong et al. [3], our model does not use the radical-level features and uses an additional dictionary features. The architecture of the model is shown in Fig. 1.

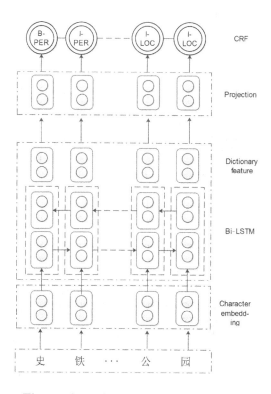

Fig. 1. The architecture of the NER model

First, each character is projected to a vector through character embedding. We use pretrained character embedding to initialize our lookup table. Previous experiments show that using pretrained character embedding can improve the performance significantly [2].

$$e_{x_i} = \text{Character\_Lookup}(W_1, x_i) \qquad (1)$$

where W_1 is the embedding of character, x_i is the character in position i. We use bi-LSTM [5] to process the input sequences. Long Short Term Memory (LSTM) networks can handle gradient vanishing/exploding problems [7]. A LSTM unit is composed of a cell, an input gate, an output gate and a forget gate. The implementations are as follows:

$$i_t = \sigma(W_i h_{t-1} + U_i e_{x_t} + b_i) \tag{2}$$

$$f_t = \sigma(W_f h_{t-1} + U_f e_{x_t} + b_f) \tag{3}$$

$$\tilde{c}_t = tanh(W_c h_{t-1} + U_c e_{x_t} + b_c) \tag{4}$$

$$c_t = f_t \odot c_{t-1} + i_t \odot \tilde{c}_t \tag{5}$$

$$o_t = \sigma(W_o h_{t-1} + U_o e_{x_t} + b_o) \tag{6}$$

$$h_t = o_t \odot tanh(c_t) \tag{7}$$

where e_{x_t} is an input vector at time t, the output vector is h_t, σ is an element-wise sigmoid function, and $\odot$ is an element-wise product function. The bi-LSTM can capture the right and left context information of a character. We simplify the formula as follow:

$$h_{x_i} = \text{bi-LSTM}(W_2, e_{x_i}) \tag{8}$$

where W_2 is the variable in bi-LSTM. We concatenate the bi-LSTM layer output of NER part and the dictionary feature. The dictionary feature can be seen as a feature embedding which is initialized randomly. The different dictionary feature value will project to different vector. We do not use the one hot vector, because different dictionary feature value has similarity. For example, "B@nr" has relation with "M@nr".

$$h_i = [h_{x_i}; f_{dictionary}] \tag{9}$$

We use CRF instead of softmax as the output layer, because CRF can consider neighborhood information. The source of the sentence can be:

$$s(X, y) = \sum_{i=0}^{n} A_{y_i, y_{i+1}} + \sum_{i=1}^{n} P_{h_i, y_i} \tag{10}$$

where X is the sequence list, y is the corresponding NER tag list, $A_{y_i, y_{i+1}}$ is the cost from tag y_i transferring to y_{i+1}. P is the probability from h_i predicting the tag y_i, this can be seen as a projection layer. The probability of all possible tag sequences can be represented as:

$$P(y|X) = \frac{e^{s(X,y)}}{\sum_{\tilde{y} \in Y_{all}} e^{s(X,\tilde{y})}} \tag{11}$$

where Y_{all} is all the possible NER tag. When the model is trained, we maximize the log-probability of the correct tag sequence:

$$logP(y|X) = s(X, y) - log(\sum_{\tilde{y}} e^{s(X,\tilde{y})}) \tag{12}$$

When the model is tested, we obtain the best NER tag sequence by:

$$y^* = \underset{\tilde{y} \in Y_{all}}{\text{argmax}} \, score(X, \tilde{y}) \tag{13}$$

4   Experiments

4.1   Data Sets

The NER dataset is collected by Peng and Dredze from Sina Weibo [14]. The NER dataset contains 1.35K training sentences, 270 developing sentences and 270 testing sentences. The details of name entities in the datasets are shown in Table 3. Four types of entities are labeled: GPE (Geographical/Social/Political Entity), LOC (Location), ORG (Organization), PER (Person)[2].

The dictionary (see footnote 1) is from the jieba which is a prevalent CWS project. The dictionary is widely used as an external resource in CWS [17]. The details of the dictionary are shown in Table 2. The dictionary has 55 types of POS. For example, "nr" means "person name", "ns" means "location name" and "gpe name", and "nt" means "organization name". We obtain the gazetteer by reserved the words labeled "nr", "ns" and "nt" tags. The number of corpus entities that appearing in dictionary and gazetteer is 312 and the coverage rate is 0.2.

Table 2. The details of the dictionary.

Type	Total words	Total entities	nr	ns	nt
Quantity	584429	161567	122962	29743	8862

Table 3. The details of the NER corpus.

Entity type	GPE	LOC	ORG	PER
Quantity	243	88	224	721

4.2   Parameters Setting

The character embedding in the model is initialized using the pre-trained character embedding. The character embedding of the model is pretrained on Chinese social media data using word2vec [13], which is the same as Peng and Dredze [14]. The LSTM dimension is 100. The dimension of the dictionary feature is 50. The projection layer dimension is the same as the number of NER tags (in this paper, the dimension is 9). The optimization method we used is adam [8].

---

[2] GPE is the names of countries, cities, states, provinces, municipalities. LOC is the names of geographical lcations other than GPEs.

4.3   Results

The overview results of our model are shown in Table 4. The baseline uses the model from Dong et al. [3][3]. The gazetteer feature is added to the baseline model, which is similar to our model described in Sect. 3.2. The difference is that the gazetteer feature uses one hot vector. The reason is that different gazetteer features have slight similarity and high dimension may lead to sparse problem. The results show that both gazetteer and dictionary can improve the performance of baseline. We observe that gazetteer obtains a slightly improvement over the baseline. Dictionary gives a 4.83 improvement over the baseline in F1 score. The dictionary obtains better results showing that the performance of the NER system is improved by the common words that are not entities.

Table 4. The overview results of the model.

	P	R	F1
Baseline	56.07	44.5	49.62
Baseline + gazetteer	56.63	44.34	49.74
Baseline + dictionary	59.12	50.47	54.45

In Table 5, we present the results of different entity types. The results show that the dictionary improves the performance in types of ORG and PER significantly. However, the dictionary information may slightly harm the performance in types of GPE and LOC.

Table 5. The results in different types of named entities.

	Gazetteer			Dictionary		
	P	R	F1	P	R	F1
GPE	70.45	65.96	68.13	68.89	65.96	67.39
LOC	33.33	10.53	16.00	22.22	10.53	14.29
ORG	18.52	13.51	15.62	22.58	18.92	20.59
PER	62.92	51.38	56.57	69.79	61.47	65.37

We explore the strategies to achieve the best results and the results are shown in Table 6. First, the different feature positions are tested. We consider the situation that the dictionary feature is concatenated with character embedding and then as the input of LSTM. The results show that our model achieves better results. The reasons may be that the dictionary feature is a high-level feature and has lower similarity to the word features. The second condition, we consider

---

[3] We do not use radical-level features.

Table 6. The strategies used in model.

	P	R	F1
Our model	59.12	50.47	54.45
Feature position	57.84	50.47	53.90
Feature dimension	55.79	50.00	52.74
CWS information	55.32	46.71	50.65

using different feature dimensions. We set the dimension of dictionary feature to 100 and the results become worse. We suppose that the high dimension lead to the sparse problem. Finally, we consider only using the CWS information. The results show that the POS information is helpful.

We simulate two situations that the different corpora coverage rates and different noise levels in dictionary and gazetteer are used. We speculate that we know which words are named entities, and then the dictionary and gazetteer feature are obtained. First, the results of different coverage rates are given in Fig. 2. The figure shows that the performance declines when coverage rate in dictionary declines. The dictionary outperforms the gazetteer in all rates and the declining speed of the dictionary is also lower. Second, the results of different noise level in gazetteer are shown in Table 7. We observe that our model can achieve similar results to the model containing no noise in gazetteer.

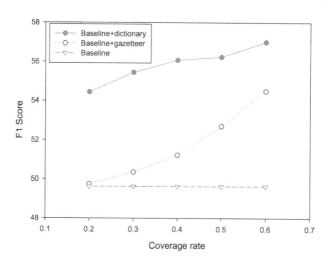

Fig. 2. The results of different corpus coverage rates.

We also test our model in two other corpus. The results are shown in Table 8. The first is news domain corpus which are from Levow [11]. The results show that dictionary information is useful in news domain and achieve better results

Table 7. The results of different noise levels in gazetteer.

	P	R	F1
Baseline + gazetteer (no noise)	59.14	50.46	54.46
Baseline + gazetteer (50% noise remove)	55.32	50.28	52.68
Baseline + dictionary	59.12	50.47	54.45

Table 8. The results in news domain and nominal mentions recognition.

	News domain			Nominal mentions		
	P	R	F1	P	R	F1
Baseline	90.23	88.51	89.36	57.11	51.91	54.39
Baseline + gazetteer	89.88	89.54	89.71	57.99	51.20	54.38
Baseline + dictionary	89.96	89.83	89.90	62.68	52.63	57.22

than gazetteer information. The second is nominal mentions recognition corpus which are from Peng and Dredze [14]. We observe that dictionary model obtains 2.83 improvement compared with the baseline and 2.84 improvement compared with the gazetteer model in F1 score. The domain of nominal mentions recognition is social media domain. We also observe that the dictionary information is more helpful in social media domain than news domain. The results in social media domain obtain 2.84 improvements over the baseline compared with 0.54 improvements in news domain.

5   Conclusion

In this paper, we explore using the dictionary to replace the gazetteer. We first use the dictionary to obtain CWS and POS information. Then, this information is concatenated to construct a dictionary feature. Finally, the dictionary feature is added to the LSTM-CRF model. Experiments show that our model achieves better results than only using the gazetteer. In the future, more complex model can be explored to combine the dictionary information.

References

1. Chen, W., Zhang, Y., Isahara, H.: Chinese named entity recognition with conditional random fields. In: Proceedings of the Fifth SIGHAN Workshop on Chinese Language Processing, pp. 118–121. Association for Computational Linguistics (2006). http://www.aclweb.org/anthology/W06-0116
2. Collobert, R., Weston, J., Bottou, L., Karlen, M., Kavukcuoglu, K., Kuksa, P.: Natural language processing (almost) from scratch. J. Mach. Learn. Res. **12**(Aug), 2493–2537 (2011)

3. Dong, C., Zhang, J., Zong, C., Hattori, M., Di, H.: Character-based LSTM-CRF with radical-level features for Chinese named entity recognition. In: Lin, C.-Y., Xue, N., Zhao, D., Huang, X., Feng, Y. (eds.) ICCPOL/NLPCC -2016. LNCS (LNAI), vol. 10102, pp. 239–250. Springer, Cham (2016). https://doi.org/10.1007/978-3-319-50496-4_20

4. Florian, R., Ittycheriah, A., Jing, H., Zhang, T.: Named entity recognition through classifier combination. In: Conference on Natural Language Learning at HLT-NAACL, pp. 168–171 (2003)

5. Graves, A., Schmidhuber, J.: Framewise phoneme classification with bidirectional LSTM networks. In: IEEE International Joint Conference on Neural Networks, IJCNN 2005, Proceedings, vol. 4, pp. 2047–2052 (2005)

6. He, J., Wang, H.: Chinese named entity recognition and word segmentation based on character. In: Proceedings of the Sixth SIGHAN Workshop on Chinese Language Processing (2008). http://www.aclweb.org/anthology/I08-4022

7. Hochreiter, S., Schmidhuber, J.: Long short-term memory. Neural Comput. 9(8), 1735–1780 (1997)

8. Kingma, D.P., Ba, J.: Adam: a method for stochastic optimization. Computer Science (2014)

9. Lafferty, J.D., Mccallum, A., Pereira, F.C.N.: Conditional random fields: probabilistic models for segmenting and labeling sequence data. In: Eighteenth International Conference on Machine Learning, pp. 282–289 (2001)

10. Lample, G., Ballesteros, M., Subramanian, S., Kawakami, K., Dyer, C.: Neural architectures for named entity recognition. In: Proceedings of the 2016 Conference of the North American Chapter of the Association for Computational Linguistics: Human Language Technologies, pp. 260–270. Association for Computational Linguistics (2016). https://doi.org/10.18653/v1/N16-1030. http://www.aclweb.org/anthology/N16-1030

11. Levow, G.A.: The third international Chinese language processing bakeoff: word segmentation and named entity recognition. In: Proceedings of the Fifth SIGHAN Workshop on Chinese Language Processing, pp. 108–117. Association for Computational Linguistics (2006). http://www.aclweb.org/anthology/W06-0115

12. Mao, X., Dong, Y., He, S., Bao, S., Wang, H.: Chinese word segmentation and named entity recognition based on conditional random fields. In: Proceedings of the Sixth SIGHAN Workshop on Chinese Language Processing (2008). http://www.aclweb.org/anthology/I08-4013

13. Mikolov, T., Sutskever, I., Chen, K., Corrado, G.S., Dean, J.: Distributed representations of words and phrases and their compositionality. In: Advances in Neural Information Processing Systems, pp. 3111–3119 (2013)

14. Peng, N., Dredze, M.: Named entity recognition for Chinese social media with jointly trained embeddings. In: Proceedings of the 2015 Conference on Empirical Methods in Natural Language Processing, pp. 548–554. Association for Computational Linguistics (2015). https://doi.org/10.18653/v1/D15-1064. http://www.aclweb.org/anthology/D15-1064

15. Peng, N., Dredze, M.: Improving named entity recognition for Chinese social media with word segmentation representation learning. In: Proceedings of the 54th Annual Meeting of the Association for Computational Linguistics (vol. 2: Short Papers), pp. 149–155. Association for Computational Linguistics (2016). https://doi.org/10.18653/v1/P16-2025. http://www.aclweb.org/anthology/P16-2025

16. Wong, P.K., Chan, C.: Chinese word segmentation based on maximum matching and word binding force, pp. 200–203 (1996)

17. Zhang, Q., Liu, X., Fu, J.: Neural networks incorporating dictionaries for Chinese word segmentation (2018)

A Computer Vision System to Assist the Early Screening of Autism Spectrum Disorder

Jingjing Liu, Keshi He, Zhiyong Wang, and Honghai Liu(✉)

State Key Laboratory of Mechanical System and Vibration,
Shanghai Jiao Tong University, Shanghai, China
{lily121,lovejessie,yzwang_sjtu,honghai.liu}@sjtu.edu.cn

Abstract. Early identification of autism allows for earlier interventions, which may lead to more positive outcomes in terms of cognitive improvement and a decrease of symptom severity for some autistic children. Based on the evidence that reduced levels of response to languages can be represented as an early marker of Autism Spectrum Disorder (ASD), this paper proposes a computer vision system to assist the early screening of autism from an engineering perspective. Firstly, an experimental paradigm of giving instructions when subjects are playing with toys is well-designed. Then the response of subjects to instructions is measured by vision-based techniques including hand tracking and object recognition. Finally, the feasibility of the proposed system is verified by pre-experiment of ten normal subjects.

Keywords: Autism · Response · Object recognition · Hand tracking

1 Introduction

ASD refers to a group of pervasive developmental disorders which involve many aspects such as social relations, language, behavior and cognition [1]. The core features of ASD are persistent difficulties in social interaction and communication, the presence of stereotypic behaviors, resistance to change and restricted interests. It is estimated that 1/59 children suffer from autism in America in 2018, while the number of autistic patients reaches 67 million in the world [2]. The biggest burden resulted from autistic children is the expensive special education and loss of parental productivity [3]. Although the exact cause of autism is unclear and there is no method to cure, studies [4–6] have shown that proper treatment can improve the symptoms of autism. In particular, in early childhood, early diagnosis and intervention of autism play a very good role in improving the symptoms [7]. The importance of early identification of children with autism has been highlighted in recent practice guidelines issued by the American Academy

Supported by the National Natural Science Foundation of China (No. 61733011, 51575338).

F. Sun et al. (Eds.): ICCSIP 2018, CCIS 1006, pp. 27–38, 2019.
https://doi.org/10.1007/978-981-13-7986-4_3

of Pediatrics [6]. It is noted that identification of autism at young ages would allow broader participation [8] in these specialized early intervention services, which could potentially lead to improved outcomes for more children.

Many researches have been focusing on assisting the early identification technically based on the signs which can be the early indicators for autism. Ozonoff et al. [9] suggest that atypical object play behaviors involving unusual or prolonged visual exploration, spinning, or rotating have potential to be an early indicator for autism. Smart toys embedded with wireless sensors are used to automatically characterize the way in which a child is playing [10]. Thus, objective and quantitative measures of object play interactions are provided for the potential early identification of children with autism. In [11], computer vision tools are provided to measure and identify ASD behavioral markers based on components of the Autism Observation Scale for Infants (AOSI), helping clinicians and general practitioners accomplish this early detection/measurement task automatically. In particular, algorithms are developed to assess visual attention and analyze asymmetrical patterns in unsupported gait. More recently, a parrot-like robot is presented as a screening tool [12] to diagnose autistic children from different aspects such as social interaction, communication, and stereotyped and repetitive behaviors.

There is evidence that reduced levels of social attention and social communication, as well as increased repetitive behavior with objects, are early markers of ASD between 12 and 24 months of age [13]. The reduced levels of response is also essential for the early identification of autism while it is far less common in related researches. Related paradigm and analytic techniques using visual sensors are absent in the domain of autism diagnosis. Therefore, we focus on detecting the response to instructions when the children are interacting with toys.

Collaborating with the professional pediatricians, we propose a system about the response to instructions as an auxiliary function in the process of early identification of autism. Instructions are given when the children are playing with toys freely. The detection of response of children is realized by analyzing the motion of the participants' hands and related objects. With a RGB sensor and a depth sensor at specific locations, the positions of hands and objects are located using real time SSD-based hand tracking and object recognition followed by coordinate transformation. The assessment of response are automatically annotated to reduce costly labor.

The remainder of this paper is organized as follows: Sect. 2 describes the system in detail, including experiment site and equipment in Sub-sect. 2.1, the experimental paradigm in Sub-sect. 2.2, and the evaluation standards in Sub-sect. 2.3. In Sect. 3, corresponding algorithms are introduced. Section 4 gives experiments and results. Finally, the brief conclusion is given in Sect. 5.

2 Experimental System Design

2.1 Experimental Site and Equipment

One table $(length * width * height : 0.6\,\text{m} * 0.6\,\text{m} * 0.6\,\text{m})$ and two chairs$(length * width * height : 0.25\,\text{m} * 0.25\,\text{m} * 0.5\,\text{m})$ facing each other are placed in an indoor field sized $4\,\text{m} * 2.5\,\text{m}$. There are a ball of $5\,\text{cm}$ in diameter and a stuffed toy on the table. A set of cost-effective multiple vision sensors are explored as a platform for recording the interactive activities. As shown in Fig. 1, one RGB sensor(Logitech BRIO) and one depth sensor (Kinect v1) which are fixed at specific locations are used to capture the whole process of the experiment. The camera is distributed on the left front of the child, taking an angle of depression of $15°$. In addition, the Kinect is right above the table, taking an overlook of the whole scene. The behaviors of both the child and the clinician can be recorded as well as the locations of the toys.

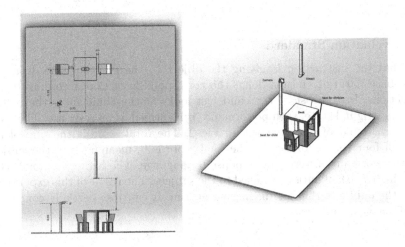

Fig. 1. A diagram of the field.

2.2 Experiment Paradigm

The aim of this work is to explore whether the child responds to the instructions considering his movements. When the child sits on the chair and plays with toys, the clinician sits opposite to the child and gives instructions in a normal and clear tone. The specific experimental process is as follows: first of all, the clinician takes out the ball, gives it to the child and asks the child to play with the ball freely. After 2 to 3 min, the clinician says to the child "give the ball to me" which may be repeated twice within 1 min. If the child has a response to the language, there is no need to take the second round of test. Otherwise, the second round of test which is the same as the first round of the test has to be taken. Whether or not the child has a response, there is a need for the third round of test. Similar to the first round of test, the clinician takes out the stuffed toy, gives it to the child and asks the child to play with the toy freely. After 2 to 3 min, the clinician says to the child, "give the toy to me" which may be repeated twice within 1 min. If the child has a response to the language, there is no need to take the fourth round of test. If the child doesn't respond to the instructions, the fourth round of test which is the same as the third round of the test has to be taken. The interval between each round of test is at least 3 min.

There are several considerations: it should be noted that in the first round of test, the clinician can not reach out for the stuff when giving instructions. The clinician is asked to put his hands on the table. Only when the toy is delivered to the clinician can he stretch out his hand to reach it. The reason is that the action of reaching out may give additional hint to the children. However, in the second round of test, the clinician should reach out as a cue when giving instructions. Similar operations are applied to the third and fourth test. Moreover, the clinician should give instructions when children focus on playing and controlling toys.

2.3   Evaluation Standards

Now that the instruction is giving the object to the clinician, the definition of response naturally means doing the corresponding action according to the instructions. In contrast, if the child just looks at the clinician or the ball or keeps the original state, such performance is identified as no response. The score after each round of test is shown in Fig. 2. The total score is the sum of the scores of four rounds of test. If the final score is 0, meaning that the subject performs normally in terms of response to language. The higher the final score is, the higher risk of autism is linked to the subject. The result of this experiment is not the only criterion for diagnosing autism. It can just partially contribute to the diagnose of autism.

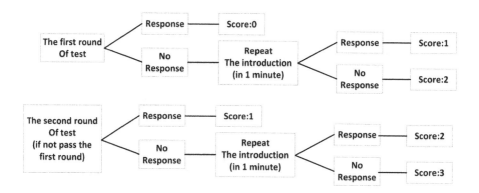

Fig. 2. Schematic diagram of experimental process.

3   Method

Since the definition of response is delivering the object to the clinician, the judgment of response is that whether the distance between the toy and the hands of clinician can be less than a threshold s in 3 s after the instruction is given. Thus the locations of both the hands and the objects have to be obtained. The video stream of the Logitech camera is used for hand tracking while the video stream of the Kinect is used for object recognition. By calibrating the two visual sensors, the 2D coordinates of tracked hands are transferred to the coordinate system of Kinect which is taken as the world coordinate system.

3.1   Object Tracking and Recognition

By tracking and recognizing the ball and the stuffed toy using the Kinect, the locations of the toys can be recorded. This process is divided into two parts: object tracking and object recognition.

Object Tracking. To effectively detect objects in real time, a blob based Otsu [14] object detection method is employed to detect the objects. The area where the table is located is selected as the region of interest. Since the background keeps to be changeless, background subtraction method is used to remove the background and obtain the difference image of current frame. Then Otsu algorithm is employed to find a suitable threshold for image binaryzation. The open operation and closed operation are applied to the binary image successively. With the processed images, blob analysis is utilized to analyze the connected domain of the same pixel which is called blob in the image. Given some requirements such as size and shape, count up the number of blobs satisfying the requirements. Then extract the information of blobs, including minimum circumscribed rectangles, area, circumference and centroid location of the connected domain. For each blob, its boundary is circled by a rectangular box which represents an object. An efficient Gaussian Mixture Probability Hypothesis Density Filter (GM-PHD) tracker [15] is utilized for object tracking due to its good performance in multi-object tracking. An entropy distribution based method is used to estimate the birth intensity of the new objects.

Object Recognition. Object recognition is realized based on Histogram of Oriented Gradient (HOG) [16] and multiple class Support Vector Machine (SVM) [17]. HOG feature is formed by computing the histogram of gradient directions of the local image area. Then a pre-trained multiple class SVM is employed to recognize the image category. The pipeline is shown in Fig. 3.

The ball or the stuffed toy is encircled by a rectangle as shown in Fig. 4. And the center of the rectangle is taken as the position of the detected object. After registering the depth images and color images from the Kinect, the 3D coordinates of object center can be acquired as x_i, y_i, z_i, where $i = 1$ represents the stuffed toy and $i = 2$ represents the ball.

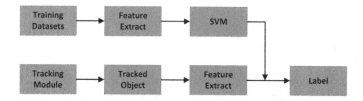

Fig. 3. Object recognition pipeline.

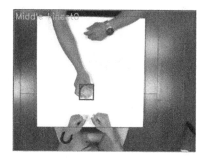

Fig. 4. The position of the detected object. The location of the center of the green rectangle is taken as the position of the object. The red rectangle encircling the desk represents the region of interest (ROI). (Color figure online)

3.2   Hand Tracking

Ideally, finding hands is simply an instantiation of one particular object detection task, for which we could apply any general object detection algorithm. But in practice, detecting hands requires some special considerations. Hands are highly flexible objects whose appearance and position can vary dramatically, but nonetheless we need models that are strong enough to discriminate the hands even if under interactive or occlusion circumstance.

Convolution Neural Networks (CNNs) [18] offer very good performance for classification tasks. Neural networks provide opportunity to train models that perform well and address challenges of existing object tracking/detection algorithms - varied/poor lighting, noisy environments, diverse viewpoints and even occlusion. It is noted that Single Shot MultiBox Detector (SSD) [19] stands out in the domain of image object detection. It reaches a significant improvement in speed but still with high-accuracy detection. Thus, SSD is taken as the preliminary model for real time hand tracking.

Training the Hand Detection Model. The scene of our hand detection is slightly different from the egocentric videos. So The Egohands Dataset [20] can not be directly used for training. To train a model specific to our scene, a pre-trained model followed by transfer learning is used to learn a new hand type. The benefit of transfer learning is that training can be much quicker, and the required data is much less. In practice, the ssd_mobilenet_v1_coco model is taken as our start point since it is currently one of the fastest models.

As shown in Fig. 5, the architecture of SSD is based on VGG16, which is pre-trained on the ILSVRC CLS-LOC dataset. fc6 and fc7 are converted to convolutional layers, and parameters are subsampled from fc6 and fc7. pool5 is changed from $2 * 2 - s2$ to $3 * 3 - s1$, and the atrous algorithm is used to fill the "holes". All the dropout layers and the fc8 layer are removed. The resulting model is fine-tuned using SGD with initial learning rate 10^{-3}, momentum 0.9, weight decay 0.0005, and batch size 32. The network SSD combines predictions from multiple feature mapping with different resolutions to naturally handle objects of various sizes. Compared with other single stage methods, SSD has much better accuracy, even with a smaller input image size. Therefore, it is suitable for real time processing and low requirement for the hardware.

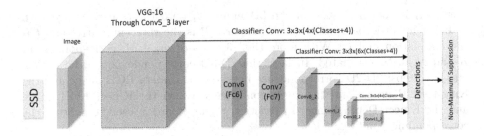

Fig. 5. The architecture of SSD.

Using the Detector to Track Hands. The framework is realized using Tensorflow. The hands of both the child and the clinician are enclosed using bounding boxes as shown in Fig. 6. The center of the boxes are taken as the locations of hands. The 2D coordinates of hand center under the image coordinate system can be acquired as (u, v). This detector can still work even within a small image size. Further more, keeping the input image small can increase fps without any significant accuracy drop.

3.3   Coordinate Transformation

To effectively fuse the data from the camera and Kinect, a coordinate transformation module is proposed to transfer data to a global world coordinate system. The center of the world coordinate system is located at the base of the Kinect.

2D-3D Correspondence. Given intrinsic parameters of the camera and a set of correspondences between 3D points and their 2D projections, the pose of the camera related to the Kinect can be determined using Eq. 1.

$$m_i \approx K(R, t)M_i \tag{1}$$

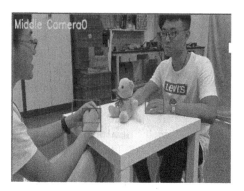

Fig. 6. Hands tracking.

where m_i is the projection of the 3D point M_i onto the camera image with K being intrinsic parameters of the camera. R is the rotation matrix and t is the translation matrix. With more than 3 pairs of $m_i - M_i$ correspondences, R and t can be estimated. In fact, the 2D-3D correspondence can be broken into two steps: 2D-2D correspondence between the camera RGB image and the Kinect RGB image and the correspondence between the Kinect RGB image and the Kinect Depth image. In practice, a chessboard is used to capture the corresponding points.

Camera Pose Estimation. Camera Pose Estimation is mainly based on an iterative process. In each iteration, a Perspective-n-Points (PnP) algorithm [21] is applied along with the 2D-3D correspondence calculated by the previous process.

Local to Global 3D Coordinate Transformation. With the previously obtained results of the camera pose, the coordinates of the 3D points can be easily transformed from the camera coordinate system (local 3D coordinate) to the Kinect coordinate system (global 3D coordinate) using Eq. 2.

$$P = RP' + t \tag{2}$$

where P' is a 3D point in the camera coordinate system and P is the corresponding 3D point in the global coordinate system. R and t are the rotation and translation matrix of the camera, which is also known as the pose of the camera.

With the coordinate transformation module, the 3D coordinates of tracked hand under the global coordinate system can be obtained as x_i, y_i, z_i, where i can be taken as $1l, 1r, 2l, 2r$ which represents the left hand of the clinician, the right hand of the clinician, the left hand of the child and the right hand of the child respectively.

Given the 3D coordinates of tracked objects and hands, the distance between the object and the hand using Eq. 3. Within three seconds after the instruction is issued, the subject is considered as having response once $d_{ij} < s$.

$$d_{ij}^2 = (x_i - x_j)^2 + (y_i - y_j)^2 + (z_i - z_j)^2 \tag{3}$$

where i can be taken as 1 or 2, depending on the related object. j is taken as $1l$ and $1r$.

4   Experiments and Results

4.1   Preparation and Triggering

Preparation includes calibrating both the camera and Kinect. Thus the 3D coordinates of related objects and hands in the scene can be acquired. The judgment of response is triggered by detection of the sentence "give the ball to me" using Kinect. The standard of having a response is that the distance between the toy and the hands of the clinician can be less than a threshold within 3 s after the trigger. Following circumstance may appear: the child may throw or roll the toy toward the clinician instead of handing. This kind of situation is also recognized as having a response according to the professional clinician.

Exceptional case can arise: the child may not want to give the toy to clinician. He may stretch hands out but withdraw later. This results from his consciousness of belongings. The child may not give the toy to others because he likes it very much. But he will do the movement of stretching out the hand at the moment he hear the words "give the ball to me". Although the toy is not delivered to the clinician, such action is also defined as having a response. So even if the distance between the toy and the hands of the clinician is not less than the threshold within 3 s, the moving forward of the hands of child can also be recognized as having response.

4.2   Experiments and Results

In order to verify the feasibility of the proposed paradigm and method, we do the pre-experiments taking ten normal adults as subjects. The behavior of the subjects is judged by our method. The whole process is recorded and annotated by a professional clinician to make a comparison. According to the judgement of clinician, every subject's score is 0. The results given by the proposed method are shown in Table 1. The threshold s is set to 5 cm since the size of the table is 0.6 m ∗ 0.6 m.

Results show that the assessment using proposed method might occasionally go wrong. This is mainly because that the object tracking fails sometimes.

Table 1. Results of the proposed method

Subject	Score				
	Round 1	Round 2	Round 3	Round 4	Sum
Subject 1	1	None	0	None	1
Subject 2	0	None	0	None	0
Subject 3	0	None	0	None	0
Subject 4	0	None	0	None	0
Subject 5	0	None	0	None	0
Subject 6	0	None	0	None	0
Subject 7	0	None	2	1	3
Subject 8	0	None	0	None	0
Subject 9	0	None	0	None	0
Subject 10	0	None	0	None	0

5   Conclusion

Not like most autistic research [22–26] focusing on imitation, turn taking and joint attention, here we have presented the first visual-based system of response to language in the domain of ASD. The detection of response is realized by measuring the movement of hands and objects. In addition, the feasibility of proposed system is validated by a series of preliminary experiments.

Contribution of the article mainly includes the following three parts: (1) the concern of response to language in autistic patients which is rare in recent studies; (2) the authority and standardization of the stated paradigm since the paradigm has got the doctor's approval; (3) the unconstraint of subjects without wearing sensors but in a free mood.

Our future work will focus on taking more complex and possible situations into consideration. More realistic experiments should be done, taking autistics as subjects. In addition, other possible indexes of response will be explored, such as the relationship between the trajectory of the subject and the clinician.

References

1. Rogers, S.J., Pennington, B.F.: A theoretical approach to the deficits in infantile autism. Dev. Psychopathol. **3**(2), 137–162 (1991)
2. Baio, J., Wiggins, L., Christensen, D.L., et al.: Prevalence of Autism Spectrum Disorder Among Children Aged 8 Years Autism and Developmental Disabilities Monitoring Network, 11 Sites, United States, 2014. MMWR Surveill Summ 2018; 67 (No. SS6): 1C23. https://doi.org/10.15585/mmwr.ss6706a1
3. Matthews, R.A., et al.: A qualitative examination of the work-family interface: parents of children with autism spectrum disorder. J. Vocat. Behav. **79**(3), 625–639 (2011)

4. Magiati, I., Charman, T., Howlin, P.: A two-year prospective follow-up study of community-based early intensive behavioural intervention and specialist nursery provision for children with autism spectrum disorders. J. Child Psychol. Psychiatry **48**(8), 803–812 (2010)
5. Ming, S., et al.: Training class inclusion responding in typically-developing children and individuals with autism. J. Appl. Behav. Anal. **51**(1), 53–60 (2017)
6. Whalen, C., Schreibman, L., Ingersoll, B.: The collateral effects of joint attention training on social initiations, positive affect, imitation, and spontaneous speech for young children with autism. J. Autism Dev. Disord. **36**(5), 655 (2006)
7. Liu, X., et al.: Technology-facilitated diagnosis and treatment of individuals with autism spectrum disorder: an engineering perspective. Appl. Sci. **7**(10), 1051 (2017)
8. Nelson, A.C.: Emerging technologies in autism diagnosis, therapy, treatment, and teaching. Educ. Technol. **54**, 32–37 (2014)
9. Ozonoff, S., et al.: A prospective study of the emergence of early behavioral signs of autism. J. Am. Acad. Child Adolesc. Psychiatry **49**(3), 256–266.e2 (2010)
10. Westeyn, T.L., et al.: Monitoring children's developmental progress using augmented toys and activity recognition. Pers. Ubiquit. Comput. **16**(2), 169–191 (2012)
11. Hashemi, J., et al.: Computer vision tools for the non-invasive assessment of autism-related behavioral markers. Computer Science (2012)
12. Dehkordi, P.S., et al.: The design, development, and deployment of roboparrot for screening autistic children. Int. J. Soc. Robot. **7**(4), 1–10 (2015)
13. Zwaigenbaum, L., et al.: Early identification of autism spectrum disorder: recommendations for practice and research. Pediatrics **136**(Suppl. 1), S10 (2015)
14. Otsu, N.: A threshold selection method from gray-level histograms. IEEE Trans. Sys. Man Cybern. **9**(1), 62–66 (2007)
15. Vo, B.N., Ma, W.K.: The Gaussian mixture probability hypothesis density filter. IEEE Trans. Sig. Process. **54**(11), 4091–4104 (2006)
16. Dalal, N., Triggs, B.: Histograms of oriented gradients for human detection. In: Proceedings of International Conference on Computer Vision and Pattern Recognition, vol. 1, no. 12, pp. 886–893 (2005)
17. Chang, C.C., Lin, C.J.: LIBSVM: a library for support vector machines. ACM (2011)
18. Krizhevsky, A., Sutskever, I., Hinton, G.E.: ImageNet classification with deep convolutional neural networks. In: International Conference on Neural Information Processing Systems, pp. 1097–1105. Curran Associates Inc. (2012)
19. Liu, W., et al.: SSD: single shot MultiBox detector. In: Leibe, B., Matas, J., Sebe, N., Welling, M. (eds.) ECCV 2016. LNCS, vol. 9905, pp. 21–37. Springer, Cham (2016). https://doi.org/10.1007/978-3-319-46448-0_2
20. Bambach, S., et al.: Lending a hand: detecting hands and recognizing activities in complex egocentric interactions. In: IEEE International Conference on Computer Vision, pp. 1949–1957. IEEE (2016)
21. Gao, X.S., et al.: Complete solution classification for the perspective-three-point problem. IEEE Trans. Pattern Anal. Mach. Intell. **25**(8), 930–943 (2003)
22. Greczek, J., et al.: Graded cueing feedback in robot-mediated imitation practice for children with autism spectrum disorders. In: IEEE International Symposium on Robot and Human Interactive Communication, pp. 561–566. IEEE (2014)
23. Anzalone, S.M., et al.: How children with autism spectrum disorder behave and explore the 4-dimensional (spatial 3D+ time) environment during a joint attention induction task with a robot. Res. Autism Spectr. Disord. **8**(7), 814–826 (2014)

24. Wainer, J., et al.: A pilot study with a novel setup for collaborative play of the humanoid robot KASPAR with children with autism. Int. J. Soc. Robot. **6**(1), 45–65 (2014)
25. Tapus, A., et al.: Children with autism social engagement in interaction with Nao, an imitative robot: a series of single case experiments. Interact. Stud. **13**(3), 315–347 (2012)
26. David, D.O., et al.: Developing joint attention for children with autism in robot-enhanced therapy. Int. J. Soc. Robot. **8**, 1–11 (2018)

How to Understand the Fundamental Laws
of Information

Shunpeng Zou[1] , Xiaohui Zou[1,2,3(✉)] , and Xiaoqun Wang[3]

[1] China University of Geosciences (Beijing),
29 Xueyuan Road, Beijing 100083, China
407167479@qq.com, 949309225@qq.com
[2] Sino-American Searle Research Center, UC Berkeley,
Berkeley 94720-3840, USA
[3] Room 415, Audio-Visual Building, Peking University, Beijing 100871, China
xqwang@pku.edu.cn

Abstract. The purpose of this paper is to prove the fundamental laws used in the three types of information processing through knowledge content and language form. Thus, the ability showing human-computer as twin smart system of information co-processing is analyzed, and its core intelligence is targeted to produce ambiguity or to reduce ambiguity. The method includes three steps: first, to explore logical rules of thinking process followed by human brain, second, to find out mathematical principles of information processing followed by computer, third, to accumulate a series of translation rules of bilingual information processing followed by human-machine collaboration. The result is that the fundamental laws of information processing are proved by both mental program contents and language expression symbols, including logical rules for content information processing, mathematical rules for formal information processing, generalized translation rules for all kinds of bilingual information processing. Its significance is that it not only clarifies the three rules of human-machine as the generalized bilingual information co-processing, but also finds sequencing and positioning in logic as smart system of language, knowledge, software, hardware, and as super-development environment for big production of knowledge, and all supporting with the generalized text gene information processing within smart system as the common focus collaborated with education, management, learning, using or application.

Keywords: Linguistic cognition · Mind philosophy ·
Brain-machine integration · Fundamental laws

1 Introduction

This article aims to explore the three types of information co-processing through knowledge content and language form that can prove the fundamental laws by using that showing human-computer as twin smart system of information co-processing and its core intelligence which is targeted to produce ambiguity or to reduce ambiguity. The main application is: the actual needs of specific users, or encryption (manufacturing ambiguity), or decryption (disambiguation), or general communication (avoid misunderstanding).

© Springer Nature Singapore Pte Ltd. 2019
F. Sun et al. (Eds.): ICCSIP 2018, CCIS 1006, pp. 39–51, 2019.
https://doi.org/10.1007/978-981-13-7986-4_4

That connects: Aristotle formal logic [1], Frege mathematical logic [2], Turing strong artificial intelligence view [3], Searle weak artificial intelligence view [4], the basis of common sense [5] and expert knowledge [6] ontologically with interdisciplinary, cross-field and cross-industry, Saussure general linguistic view [7] and Chomsky formal linguistic view [8], the reference of English and Chinese and its alternative bilingual [9] to generalized translation on generalized bilingual processing [10]. The Turing test [11–13] and Searle's Chinese room [14–16] thesis have been discussed academically for a long time, which provided the basis for further research. The core of human intelligence is natural language understanding. Artificial intelligence uses human-computer interaction in a programming language development environment, and implants batch programs (appropriate data structures and good algorithms and operational steps or search paths) to give people a feeling that although they also do some natural language understanding. It is not, but only a batch and formal understanding of natural language (only essentially a series of symbolic transformations, data queries, information gathering and repetitive use of expert knowledge) [17–20]. Therefore, in the process of human-computer interaction, two kinds of formal strategies based on Z-ASCII (covering ASCII and Z) can complement each other [21]. The theoretical basis is the formal distinction between language (Yan) and speech (Yu) and the new classification of set under the guidance of reductionism and the basic laws covered [22].

2 Method

In order to focus on the essence of the problem, our argument process in three steps,namely the use of logical, mathematical and linguistic specific steps.

First, to explore logical rules of thinking process followed by human brain, second, to find out mathematical principles of information processing followed by computer, third, to accumulate a series of translation rules of bilingual information processing followed by human-machine collaboration as smart system.

2.1 Using Logical Sequences and Positions to Prove the Existence of the Basic Law of Information

The study found that based on textual genes, it is possible to establish the rules of the sequence and position of the logic that the text combination must follow. It can be called a generalized bilingual logic. In this way, it distinguishes itself from the narrow form of monolingual expressions, such as formal logic described by Aristotle and mathematical logic described by Frege. Different forms of logical expression also have different ways and effects to resolve ambiguities.

Further research has found that the combination of the two language forms in human-computer interaction, represented by natural language as human intelligence and represented by mathematics as artificial intelligence, can be used to improve the intelligence capabilities for both of them (whether there should be a bilingual form of collaborative logical expression? That is a question we raised).

A logical form of bilingual co-expression, obviously, can neither be simply expressed by numbers, nor can it be simply expressed in words. As a result, there is a dual expression that is highly abstract and very specific. One of its typical examples is a digital-textual double chessboard or double bit-list. Its characteristics are:

First, the (narrow and broad sense) text is implemented by using the sequence and position of the logic and its transformation. Has the power of Global Language Positioning System as search engine in the bit-list.

Second, it contains three basic laws, of which the first is the logic rule based on sequence and position and their transformation (the second is mathematics rule, and the third is generalized linguistics or translation rule).

Third, the necessary reminder that there is only one as deductive logic, whether it uses natural language or arithmetic language, or even a narrow or generalized bilingual as its specific expression.

Of course, bilingual expression, (narrow or broad) translation and machine translation make it easier to control the process of ambiguity. In order to facilitate the reader's understanding, the following describes and demonstrates with specific examples: the necessity of its existence, and the scientific nature of its construction or reconstruction. From a practical point of view, it lies in effectiveness as the global positioning system of the language text field it has.

Digital table with alphabet

Digital	1	2	3	4	5	6	7	8
9	10	11	12	13	14	15	16	17
18	19	20	21	22	23	24	25	26

Alphabet	A	B	C	D	E	F	G	H
I	J	K	L	M	N	O	P	Q
R	S	T	U	V	W	X	Y	Z

Fig. 1. The small character set is a complete reference frame

The English alphabet as the small character set is a complete reference frame (thereby composing all the letter combinations - morphemes, words, phrases or phrases, sentences). The digital table is limited by the alphabet, which is limited by the basic stroke table and the Chinese character table in Chinese.

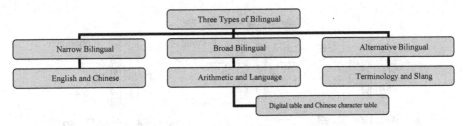

Fig. 2. The large character set is a relatively complete datum reference system in the three types of bilingual system

The Chinese character table as the large character set is a relatively complete datum reference system (all Chinese character combinations can be formed—as morphemes, words, phrases, sentences).

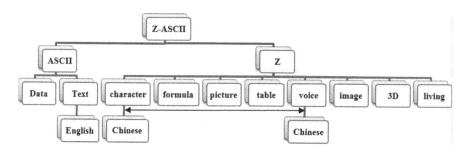

Fig. 3. Two kinds of formal strategies based on Z-ASCII

Therefore, in the process of human-computer interaction, two kinds of formal strategies based on Z-ASCII (covering ASCII and Z) can complement each other. The theoretical basis is the formal distinction between language (Yan) and speech (Yu) and the new classification of set under the guidance of reductionism and the fundamental laws covered. As we know, English is a direct formal text based on the alphabet (small character set) and can realize human-computer interaction according to ASCII; Chinese is a Chinese character table (large character set) based on stroke table and syllable table. The formalization strategy of the class is optional (where the human-computer interaction according to Z can only be indirect formalization). There are several groups of papers that have been introduced in specific details, so they are not covered in this article.

What is really needed to be mentioned here that is the formal understanding mode by using the three types of twin Turing machines. In the minds of the model's constructors, the formal understanding of human-machine generalization is based on mathematics and logic. To the three types of twin Turing machines, it is necessary to distinguish between the three basic situations of complete understanding, that is, equal to ($\cong$), approximate understanding, that is equal to ($\approx$), and roughly understood, that is similar to ($\backsim$). We believe that such a description is clear. Not to mention computers, that is, people, to be able to achieve such three levels of understanding, are very worthy of recognition.

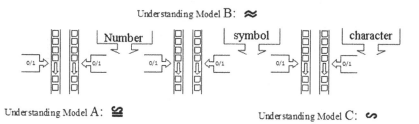

Fig. 4. Three kinds of twin Turing machines

Three kinds of twin Turing machines reveal the bit-list logic and linkage function of generalized bilingual mathematics. Among them, ABC three types of formal understanding models well reveal the three basic information laws understood in this paper, that is, the unique conservation of the bit-list structure (three types of models are observed); the linkage function is synonymous (the bit-list logical structure consistent transformation between various symbologies) corresponding transformations (mutual substitution under constraints); objects or concepts can be substituted (substitute, interpreted or translated) without affecting understanding as long as they agree to juxtapose (provided that the context is specific, the convention is as follows). It is particularly noteworthy that due to differences in history, culture and society between English and Chinese, it is difficult to translate literally between English words and Chinese characters in general. In addition, the theoretical hypothetical intermediaries do not actually exist (or as long as the two parties negotiated and can be almost any object or symbol). Therefore, the following narrowly defined bilingual "first internal interpretation, and then agreed to translate" between the two levels of phrases and sentences, based on object or concept-based symbol substitution, conversion or translation, is also logical.

Fig. 5. First internal interpreting and then agreed to translate as the new model for narrow bilingual by using the butterfly model

The Chinese characters, English words, phrases, and sentences are juxtaposed under the prescriptive conditions. The Chinese characters and the characters group 1 as Zizu 1 as phrases and group 2 as Zizu 2 as sentences (prominent bilingual pairs) are arranged separately.

Figure 4 digital and textual tables namely double bit-list (number and character) as twins giving out (different only in their particular order with the formal system).

As can be seen from Figs. 3, 4 and 5, the formal characteristics of Chinese and English respectively, we can see the logical, mathematical and linguistic or translational integration rules. This study is based on this, can explain, demonstrate and prove the existence mechanism of information on these three levels systematically and simply and explicitly. Among them, the laws of mathematics and linguistics or translation are illustrated and proved in the following two parts.

Figure 1 Description: The relationship between the number table and the alphabet, the dominant alphabet (which determines the sequence and position of the letter combinations and their calculations, statistics, and comparisons - and serves as the basis for analysis). The utility of Figs. 1, 2, 3, 4 and 5: The specific performance of GLPS is using by user for value-taken and confidence-building. Explanation of Fig. 5: Targeted analysis of butterfly model is characterized by first explained each kind of language both in bilingual model internally, and then translated from each other.

Among them, Figs. 3, 4 and 5 has a soul effect. Because, only the Chinese language at all levels of the structure in the world is a combination of finite Chinese characters. Thus, the biggest set of Chinese characters and monosyllables as super big chessboard, this super large collection, once it is indirectly digitized, formalized, and structured, is transformed into a super table (it's like a Chinese character chessboard within many Chinese menus), all process of speaking or writing in Chinese is just making a series of choices in it (this is equivalent to choosing menus). In this way, the original complex Chinese information processing and natural language understanding as well as expert knowledge acquisition and its formal expression and targeted repeated uses and other issues, have also been significantly simplified. The disagreement between the various forms of ambiguity and content selections, once placed in the super double lists (Fig. 4C), can be as accurate as any motorized vehicle in a GPS system. Determine its location (latitude and longitude). Of course, the positioning of carriers is far more extensive than the sequencing of information. Because the most basic information, we must also distinguish the essence (principle or law) and phenomenon (content and form) of information.

2.2   Using Mathematical Functions and Equations to Prove

Continue to use the typical example of the double bit-list for further explanation and argumentation.

That can be seen from Figs. 1 and 4: There is a one-to-one correspondence between the digital table and the textual table. Invisible (but conceivable) is the functional relationship between different id numbers and the functional relationship between different linguistic symbols (in fact, it is not difficult to understand that they exist there). This article seems to be very simple and easy. In fact, it is necessary to thoroughly understand the implied series of joint or link function relationships, and to find concrete linkage functions and equations. It is really necessary to combine specific practical use cases and complete them step by step. The basic training of "understanding, doing, skilled, smart, repeated using" five levels (otherwise the ideas are difficult to penetrate). In a word, it seems simple here, in fact, contains countless flaws. Just think:

On the one hand, it is based on the functions and equations between the arithmetic's digital symbol system and a series of different digital systems. On the other hand, it is based on the language's symbol system and their series of (indirect) functions and equations. This lays a foundation for the double formalization of discovering new (combined) functions and equations under specific constraints in both of them.

For example, take the two tables in Figs. 1 and 4 as an example. Although the two empty tables are identical, once they are filled with text and numbers, in particular, the sequence of the text and the basic position records are clearly defined. When true information has the role of metrics, the relationship between the two will be clear. In this example, the matrix calculations of pure mathematics are separated from the tabular calculations of pure text. Because of this, the function of the sequencing and positioning system possessed by this twin matrix or dual-list can be highlighted. From this it can be seen that it is worth further discussing: the calculation, statistics, comparison or analysis of knowledge menus that include three kinds of points(namely: language point, knowledge point, original point) in the double-list or double chessboard (do not expand here).

In this paper, we only want to emphasize that linkage functions such as Twin Matrix or Double List (Double Chessboard) are operational, valid, and verifiable. The remaining issues are discussed separately.

The above two steps illustrate and demonstrate the "bilingual logic" and "linkage function" based on the "sequencing and position system rules" followed by the two levels of logic and mathematics. "Human-computer bilingual linkage rule" is not only present but also useful. For example, the text in a twin matrix or a double-list can be quickly queried and accurately recalled. Language texts can be fully automated, structured, formalized, and digitized. This provides the basic necessary conditions for big production of knowledge.

2.3   Using Bilingual Form and Content to Prove

If the features of text information processing in the narrow bilingual plain visible language shown in Fig. 5 and its basic rules must be followed, then the alternative bilingual language in Fig. 6 below is: Popular Sayings (Frequently Asked Questions FAQ) and Experts terms (Help File) shows the characteristics of expert knowledge acquisition and formal representation in order to be recalled by human and machine.

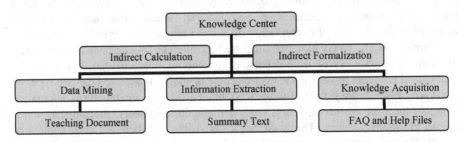

Fig. 6. The knowledge centers from the three types of big data centers can be built

Based on two major categories of formal strategies, three types of big data centers (data collection, information extraction, and knowledge acquisition) can be built. Double chessboard as Global Positioning System for language text and its application for expert knowledge acquisition all are just as easy as selecting menus in Global Language Positioning System GLPS and Global Knowledge Positioning System GKPS.

From Fig. 6, you can see the spot on any of a leopard see expert knowledge acquisition and its formal representation and natural language processing and its formal understanding. This is because, in this process, the ambiguity of content information and form information and essential information has always been very difficult to find and eliminate, just like the negotiating a la carte at a restaurant, or learning to play chess based on a chess score, have a convenient, simple and easy-to-use method. The negotiation between people (experts, teachers, students, experts, and the public) and the interaction between man-machines (systems) are rule-based. Not only can the verbal process of language be documented at any time and any place, but also the process of knowledge accumulation can be documented at any time and any place. Here, almost all of the recording process can be automated and echoed with the machine's automatic learning, forming a super development environment for human-machine mutual assistance.

Thus, the three types of phenomena information (objects, ideas, and texts), and the three types of essential information (mechanism, principle, and rules), and even the total chaotic (Tao) information, can all be in the ordinal logic (sequencing positioning rule). Under the guidance of linkage functions (formal information rules) and conventional conventions (content information rules), three types of global sequencing positioning systems (language, knowledge, and software) are gradually constructed (at the same time).

Later, we will talk about the fundamental information, phenomenon information, essential information and the whole information. It is the basis for our correct understanding of the fundamental laws of information. It can also be seen that the information conceptual framework and the fundamental laws of information described in this paper are strictly limited to the context of logical and mathematical and human-computer combined information processing (especially various types of bilingual information processing). Affirmation and material science (the law of material immortality and the law of conservation of energy) are not one level (Fig. 7).

If we say that narrowly bilingual links are two different languages and cultures, and the brains of two types of natural persons (psycho-intelligence) that they train, the generalized bilingual linkage is the man-machine operation modes and the two types of intelligent systems they train. (two-brains) brain inference model, then, alternative bilingual links are interdisciplinary, cross-domain, cross-industry, multimedia, multilingual knowledge centers. The word "logic" is visible and there are three context of ancient Greece, modern and contemporary with strong and weak artificial intelligence.

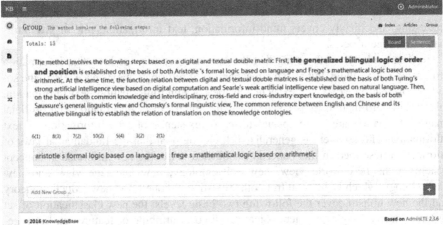

Fig. 7. Double chessboard as global positioning system for language text just as easy as selecting menus

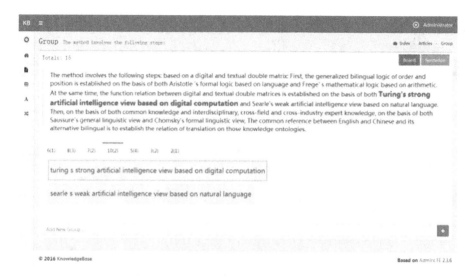

Fig. 7. (*continued*)

3 Result

The result is that the fundamental laws of information processing are proved by both mental program contents and language expression symbols, including the logical rules for content information processing, the mathematical rules for formal information processing, the generalized translation rules for all kinds of bilingual information processing, specifically covers mind information, text information, rule or law information in three aspects.

It is particularly worth noting that the laws are not only the laws that information processing must follow, but also the mechanism of information existence. Here, the so-called information exists: the existence of idea or mind information, text information, rule or law information. It is suggested that natural object information and artificial image information are some special forms of existence of idea information or text information. The text here is generalized. It can be seen that the fundamental laws of information described in this paper is established under the new information concept system in the new world view, new epistemology, new language view and new methodology, which is different from other existing old ones. The new reduction theory and the new holism cover the following two basic levels: the new classification of set system, namely: single set, hierarchical set, logo or attribute or feature set, heterogeneous set; the new reference system, namely: In the reference frame, each of them will respond to the reference frame by using each of the reference systems this way, benchmark or deterministic; each person's seat and order clear; each can do whatever it takes; random or flexible. The new view of information can be expressed formally, that is: physical world or F (W), thought in mind or M (T), grammar language or G (L) and Tao unified or Tao (F, M, G) or D (F, M, G). They can be created by the human brain and also can be recreated and simulated by computers (Figs. 8 and 9).

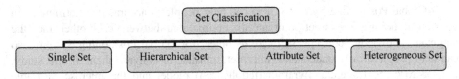

Fig. 8. The new classification of set system

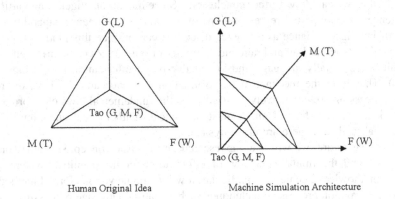

Human Original Idea   Machine Simulation Architecture

Fig. 9. A new world-epistemology-language view or methodology is a new information concept system

We understand that a good and concise formal architecture system can not only be equivalent to other complex formal architecture systems, but also can refine very complex ideas into a clear cognitive system framework and build software module to achieve computer simulation. Therefore, the inscrutable physiological and psychological cognitive system can realize the knowledge processing of human-computer dual-brain collaboration through computer-aided information processing. This provides basic support for the examples of the knowledge center we are working on for ideas and methods. This is the end result of this study.

4   Conclusion

Its significance is that it not only clarifies the three rules of human-machine as the generalized bilingual information co-processing, but also finds sequencing and positioning in logic as smart system of language, knowledge, software, hardware, and as super-development environment for big production of knowledge, and all supporting with the generalized text gene information processing within smart system as the common focus collaborated with education, management, learning, using or application.

Among them, the super development environment for big production of knowledge is based on the three Fundamental Laws of Information described in this article. You can say that:

If Global Positioning System (GPS) can help people to accurately determine from the starting point to the target point and the optimal path between each other, then the language, knowledge concept, software as object for Global Positioning System also can help people clearly understand (interpret, translate or convert) them. In this study, the macroscopic triangular pyramid (tetrahedron) model and the microscopic table model are combined to the formal Global (Language, Knowledge, Software) Positioning System, and the target (language, knowledge, software) positioning effect.

From this, we can draw further conclusions: Since human intelligence and artificial intelligence are only partial representations of the brain's intelligence capabilities, the object of intelligent science as a science discipline can only be this kind of transcendental vehicle (such as human brain and computer or other types of brain) intelligence capabilities (essentially language and knowledge-based information processing capabilities). Therefore, the mechanism of information existence and the laws of information processing are collectively referred to as the fundamental laws of information. The evidence is that, first of all, it must be logical, mathematical and linguistic or translational, and then there are also physical.

In the near future, we will use our research on the basic conceptual framework of information and the fundamental law of information for the cognitive system optimization in knowledge centers. In particular, it will combine various formal methods to improve information processing techniques such as natural language processing and its formal understanding and expert knowledge acquisition and its formal expression.

On the other hand, we will continue to improve our understanding of the fundamental conceptual framework of information and the fundamental laws of information based on the teaching and research practices. In particular, combine with the practice of the construction of knowledge centers to further illustrate the development of our cognitive systems and the improvement of our information processing technology.

Acknowledgement. Thanks to the recent academic exchanges on ICIS2018 in Peking University, we have made clear the formal relationship between human and machine in language cognition! I would like to thank the anonymous reviewers of ICCSIP in Tsinghua University for giving us some pertinent suggestions!

References

1. Beziau, J.-Y.: What is "formal logic"? In: Proceedings of the XXII World Congress of Philosophy, vol. 13, pp. 9–22 (2008)
2. Chiswell, I.: Mathematical Logic. Oxford University Press, Oxford (2007)
3. Turing, A.M.: Computing machinery and intelligence. Mind **49**, 433–460 (1950)
4. Searle, J.: Minds, brains and programs. Behav. Brain Sci. **3**, 417–457 (1980)
5. Taylor, J.M., Raskin, V., Hempelmann, C.F.: From disambiguation failures to common-sense knowledge acquisition: a day in the life of an ontological semantic system. In: Web Intelligence (2011)
6. Ludwig, D.S.: Overlapping ontologies and indigenous knowledge from integration to ontological self-determination. Stud. Hist. Philos. Sci. **59**, 36–45 (2016)
7. Saussure, F.: Selections from the course in general linguistics. In: Kearney, R., Rainwater, M. (eds.) The Continental Philosophy Reader. Routledge, Abingdon (1996)

8. Chomsky, N.: Syntactic Structures. De Gruyter Mouton (1957), 2nd edition 19 November 2002
9. Zou, X.: Collaborative Intelligent Computing System: Theoretical Model with Its Application. AAAS (2012)
10. Zou, X.: Basic law of information: the fundamental theory of generalized bilingual processing. In: ISIS Summit Vienna (2015)
11. Pinar Saygin, A., Cicekli, I., Akman, V.: Turing test: 50 years later. Mind. Mach. **10**, 463 (2000)
12. Charlesworth, A.: The comprehensibility theorem and the foundations of artificial intelligence. Mind. Mach. **24**, 439 (2014)
13. Gonzalez, W.J.: From intelligence to rationality of minds and machines in contemporary society: the sciences of design and the role of information. Mind. Mach. **27**, 397 (2017)
14. Damper, R.I.: The logic of Searle's Chinese room argument. Mind. Mach. **16**, 163 (2006)
15. Rodríguez, D., Hermosillo, J., Lara, B.: Meaning in artificial agents: the symbol grounding problem revisited. Mind. Mach. **22**, 25 (2012)
16. Bozşahin, C.: Computers aren't syntax all the way down or content all the way up. Mind. Mach. **28**, 543 (2018)
17. Zou, S., Zou, X.: Understanding: how to resolve ambiguity. In: Shi, Z., Goertzel, B., Feng, J. (eds.) ICIS 2017. IAICT, vol. 510, pp. 333–343. Springer, Cham (2017). https://doi.org/10.1007/978-3-319-68121-4_36
18. Zou, S., Zou, X., Wang, X.: How to do knowledge module finishing. In: Shi, Z., Pennartz, C., Huang, T. (eds.) ICIS 2018. IAICT, vol. 539, pp. 134–145. Springer, Cham (2018). https://doi.org/10.1007/978-3-030-01313-4_14
19. Wehmeier, K.F.: The proper treatment of variables in predicate logic. Linguist. Philos. **41**, 209 (2018)
20. Kohlhase, M., Koprucki, T., Müller, D., Tabelow, K.: Mathematical models as research data via flexiformal theory graphs. In: Geuvers, H., England, M., Hasan, O., Rabe, F., Teschke, O. (eds.) CICM 2017. LNCS (LNAI), vol. 10383, pp. 224–238. Springer, Cham (2017). https://doi.org/10.1007/978-3-319-62075-6_16
21. Zou, S., Zou, X.: Ecological characteristics of information and its scientific research. In: Multidisciplinary Digital Publishing Institute Proceedings, vol. 1, p. 59 (2017)
22. Zou, X., Zou, S., Ke, L.: Fundamental law of information: proved by both numbers and characters in conjugate matrices. In: Multidisciplinary Digital Publishing Institute Proceedings, vol. 1, p. 60 (2017)

Hand Gesture Recognition Using in Intelligent Transportation

Chao Yang and Jianqin Yin[✉]

Automation School, Beijing University of Posts and Telecommunications,
Beijing, China
{buptyangchao,jqyin}@bupt.edu.cn

Abstract. Hand gesture recognition is important for intelligent transportation. In this paper, C3D neural networks and transfer learning related technologies are used to recognize the traffic police's gestures recognition. Firstly, C3D algorithm is used to model the spatial and temporal information of the gesture. Then, external data set was used for training and the resulted model was saved. Finally, the model is fine-tuned with the idea of transfer learning, so that a good recognition rate can be achieved by training with a small amount of traffic police gesture video. The experimental results show efficacy of our method.

Keywords: Transfer learning · Convolutional neural network · C3D ·
Action recognition

1 Introduction

In recent years, the rapid development of artificial intelligence has pushed forward the development of many researches. One of its most promising technologies, autonomous driving, has been gradually used in practical life. The traffic police's gesture recognition for automatic driving is an extremely important problem. However, in the application of intelligent traffic, intelligent cars will have two modes, motion and static. Therefore, the gesture recognition method oriented to the application of intelligent cars must be able to adapt to these two modes, which increases the difficulty of this problem. In order to solve this problem, this paper proposes a gesture recognition method based on C3D and transfer learning. Since there is no corresponding dataset, this paper first constructs a small simulation gesture dataset for different motion patterns; and proposes a gesture recognition method based on C3D and transfer learning framework.

2 Related Work

In recent years, gestures are recognized based on data gloves and visions, and great progress has been acquired. There are two mainstreams as follows.

© Springer Nature Singapore Pte Ltd. 2019
F. Sun et al. (Eds.): ICCSIP 2018, CCIS 1006, pp. 52–64, 2019.
https://doi.org/10.1007/978-981-13-7986-4_5

(1) Data gloves based gesture recognition.

In the original various gesture recognition technologies, the user was first asked to wear data gloves and then started to make corresponding gestures. Then, sensor devices were used to collect bending Angle or capture the speed of action. The position of hand space was obtained through the position tracking system installed on the gloves. The sensor then feeds back the information to the computer, which processes the information by setting corresponding algorithms, so as to identify and classify the information. Takahashi et al. [1] used VPL data gloves for the study of American standard sign language recognition. Xu et al. [2] used cyber gloves in the robotics research of gesture control. The cyber gloves were used in the Chinese sign language recognition system based on neural network and hidden Markov developed by Wu and Wen [3,4]. Until the 21st century, there are still many techniques for gesture recognition research that still experiment on these data gloves [5].

(2) Vision-based gesture recognition.

Schmid [6] uses a moving camera to correct dense trajectories and extract SURF (accelerated robust features). In order to obtain more robust feature descriptors, the RANSAC (random sampling consistency) algorithm is used to correct the image and remove the moving track of the camera. Based on the data set of RGB video. Song [7] studied the expression of hierarchical characteristics at different time granularity, and then proposed the hierarchical order summary (HSS) model for modeling. Vemulapalli [8] uses three methods of translation and rotation to model the three-dimensional geometric relationship of different body parts in three-dimensional space, using dynamic time warping (DTW) algorithm, Fourier time pyramid expression and linear SVM (support vector Machine) algorithm for action recognition. In order to obtain the spatiotemporal information of the action, the commonly used method is obtained by extracting the spatiotemporal feature points of the action. Therefore, research based on spatiotemporal feature points (STIP) has become a hot research field in the field of action recognition [9–11]. An adaptive method is proposed to integrate RGB and depth information [12], and is optimized by using limited graph-based genetic programming, which effectively improves the accuracy of action recognition system. The recognition based on the traditional human action has made some breakthroughs, but there are also many limitations. Nowadays, human motion recognition based on deep learning is an end-to-end mode, which is more convenient than the traditional human motion recognition method, eliminating the need to process the video, and manually extracting features and other column operations, and the recognition rate is also higher. Convolutional neural networks [13] (CNN) are often used, and the execution speed is fast but the spatio-temporal feature information cannot be extracted. The least squares support vector machine [14] (LS-SVM), three-dimensional convolutional neural network [15] (C3D) can be implemented fast and can extract the time-space feature information, with a high recognition rate.

Residual Network [16] has many layers, and the execution speed is slow, but the recognition rate is high.

In summary, in recent years, many related researches have been done on the gesture recognition problem. The use of deep learning to deal with human motion recognition is an end-to-end mode, which greatly reduces the complexity of video processing, while maintaining a high recognition rate. Therefore, the three-dimensional convolutional neural network is used for traffic police gesture recognition in this paper.

3   Data Collection and Preprocessing

Since there is no public traffic police gesture dataset, so we construct a dataset. For the intelligent car, except waiting the traffic signal, it is moving in most times. That is to say, the intelligent car has 2 motion patterns. In order to simulate the 2 motion pattern, we collect 2 kinds dataset. The first dataset is captured by a static camera, and the 2nd dataset is constructed with a moving camera. For simplicity, we name them as static data and dynamic data respectively. In the first dataset, a total of 24 videos and 4 people in the video screen with traffic gestures, a total of 5 types of traffic police gestures, they are: stop signal, straight line signal, left turn signal, right turn signal, lane change signal. For the 2nd dataset,15 video were captured dynamically through using a moving camera. A total of 3 people appeared in the picture, including 5 types of traffic police gestures, which were: stop signal, straight signal, left turn signal, right turn signal and lane change signal (Table 1).

Two types of traffic police gesture data sets are processed by frame separately, and some frame processing results are shown in Fig. 1.

Table 1. Information of our data sets

Dataset	Category	Number of videos	Number of people appearing on the screen
Static data	5 class	24	4
Dynamic data	5 class	15	3

4   C3D Based Transfer for Gesture Recognition

The algorithms currently used to process video and have a high recognition rate include two-stream convolutional network, residual neural network, C3D, etc. Since the residual neural network and the two-stream convolutional network have more layers and longer processing time, this paper uses the C3D algorithm to perform traffic alert gesture recognition.

Tran [17] proposed C3D network model, which can better acquire temporal feature information by using 3D convolution and 3D pooling operations. At the

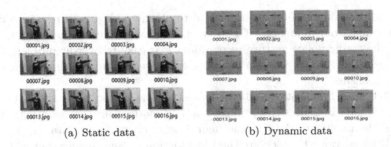

(a) Static data   (b) Dynamic data

Fig. 1. Illustration of our dataset

same time, another purpose of 3D pooling operation is to reduce the number of parameters, reducing the dimensions of the output features and improving the efficiency of the operation. Therefore, after the 3D pooling operation, the output feature map is reduced according to the operation rules defined by us, which can greatly improve the efficiency of our training model. The C3D network model used is the same as [14], which is as shown in Fig. 2.

Fig. 2. C3D network structure

This network model structure consists of 8 convolutional layers, 5 maximum pooling layers, and two fully connected layers. Finally, a softmax layer is connected for classification. All convolutional layers in the network structure are 3D convolution operations. In five of the pooling layers, pool1 is $1 \times 2 \times 2$, and pool2 to pool5 are both $2 \times 2 \times 2$. The first convolution kernel size is $1 \times 2 \times 2$ because we don't need to merge the timing information at the beginning, we need to keep the input dimensions.

After building the network model, the UCF101 data set is used for training, and then the weight is fine-tuned by the traffic police gesture data set. Because the different motion pattern, we use 3 fine-tuning schemes. Firstly, the weight data parameter model trained by UCF101 data set is used to fine-tune the Static data and Dynamic data in parallel. Finally, the weight data parameter model trained by Static data is used to fine-tune the Dynamic data.

The quality of the neural network structure model has the greatest impact on the accuracy of motion recognition, and the second is the choice of parameters in the neural network structure. We use dropout and different batchsize to overcome these problems.

(1) over-fitting: Neural network contains a number of hidden layer, thus it can effectively extract the information of the video and it also appears a series of bad problems, such as the increase in network layer leads to the need of large

data for training. Due to the lack of the traffic police gestures video data, we trained our model on UCF101 first, then when migrat these parameters to the traffic police gesture recognition, it is easy to over-fit problem. This paper discusses the problem of how to solve over-fitting by using the dropout mechanisms.

(2) batch size: Stochastic gradient descent is one of the methods that using for weights and bias to optimize training method in deep learning. When a little amount of data in the neural network model, a data can be as a calculated value to calculate the loss function of convergence, but when the amount of data is very large, we usually select a batch of data to be used for calculating the convergence of a loss function, so the batch size is also one of important parameters to adjust. Choosing a suitable batch size is mainly based on the following two reasons: first, when the video of our training and testing is particularly more, it is impossible to import all of the images or video into our memory, second, in the gradient descent the length of every step also have a great impact on final training testing accuracy. When the batch of we choose is too small, it will make SGD algorithm change so much that it can not converge or to be in a local minimum, at the same time it also makes the length of SGD step is too long, which leads to a very slow convergence speed [18]; When the batch size is too large, it will lead to the loss function of convergence error is too large, thus reduce the accuracy, so it is very important to choose a moderate batch size accuracy of identification.

5   Experimental Results and Analysis

5.1   C3D-Based UCF101 Data Set Gesture Recognition

The UCF101 data set has a total of 13320 videos in which the number of action categories is 101. One video randomly takes in 16 pictures, one batch inputs ten videos, and then predicts the actions of 101 categories. All video is adjusted to a fixed size of 112×112 after being framed. The input video dimension can be described as $3 \times 16 \times 112 \times 112$. All convolutional layers are padded with size of 1, and the stride step is 1. We print out the change in accuracy and loss in the UCF101 training process, as shown in Fig. 3. As the number of training iterations continues to increase, the accuracy and error eventually converge to a certain fixed value. After we achieve a satisfactory accuracy through the UCF101 training test, we save the weight parameter model at this time for the migration test of traffic police gesture. From Fig. 3, we can see that the accuracy of UCF101 has been increasing rapidly from the beginning to about four thousand iterations, but the convergence speed is slower. After that, the accuracy increased relatively slowly during the iteration from 4k to 10k, and finally kept around 0.8. The value of the loss function was also large at first, but it quickly fell after a while, and finally remained relatively flat until 5000 iterations, eventually staying around 3.00. Figure 4 shows the partial confusion matrix of the UCF101 training process. The horizontal axis represents the real label and the vertical axis represents the prediction label. When the prediction label is equal to the real label, the

accuracy

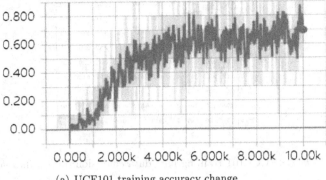

(a) UCF101 training accuracy change

total_loss

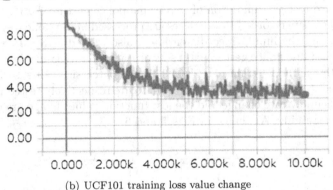

(b) UCF101 training loss value change

Fig. 3. UCF101 training result diagram

prediction is accurate. For example, the value of [1, 1] in the confusion matrix is 0.67, indicating the probability of predicting this action as the second kind is 0.67. Since this figure only shows part of the action, the sum of the vertical axis probabilities is not 1, and the probability of misjudged it as the seventh type of action in the first type of action is 0.11, which may be that their action similarity is large. Some motion recognition probabilities differ greatly from real values. The possible reason is that the neural network does not extract the characteristics of this kind of action well, it may also be because the training method uses random training, that is, the data set of this category is not well fed into the neural network for training, resulting in a low recognition rate of such actions.

5.2 Traffic Police Gesture Migration Test Based on C3D

In the last section, we trained UCF101 data set by using the C3D network model constructed, and adjusted the parameters to achieve a satisfactory recognition

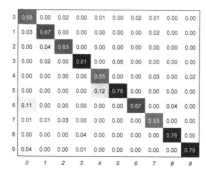

Fig. 4. UCF101 training part data confusion matrix diagram

rate, and then saved the weight parameter model of training. In this section we will use it to test the migration of two traffic police gesture data sets.

Two data sets recorded by ourselves are processed in the same way as UCF101 data sets, and the input video dimension is also resized as $3 \times 16 \times 112 \times 112$. Firstly, the traffic police gesture data sets of static and dynamic data are all fine-tuned with the model trained by UCF101, the batch size value is also taken as 10, and the static data and the dynamic data are respectively tested for training, and the accuracy rate change and the loss function value change are also printed during the training. As shown in Figs. 5 and 6.

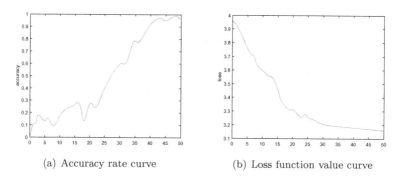

(a) Accuracy rate curve   (b) Loss function value curve

Fig. 5. Accuracy and loss of UCF101 training model migration to static data training

At the same time, the model of the static data of traffic police gesture training was also adopted for preservation. Then, the 5 types of traffic police gesture models of static data were used to test the 5 types of traffic police gestures of dynamic data with the idea of transfer learning. The accuracy change and loss function change were also printed out during the training. As shown in Fig. 7, Table 2 is a table of accuracy rates for UCF101 and two types of traffic police gesture data sets. Since the number of datagrams of the static shooting traffic alert gesture is more than the dataset captured by the mobile camera, we use the

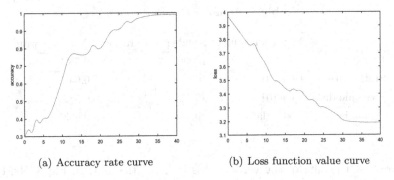

(a) Accuracy rate curve   (b) Loss function value curve

Fig. 6. Accuracy and loss of UCF101 training model migration to dynamic data training

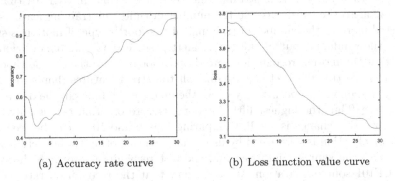

(a) Accuracy rate curve   (b) Loss function value curve

Fig. 7. Accuracy and loss of training in the training model of static data to dynamic data traffic gestures

UCF101 as the source to migrate 50 times and 40 times respectively, and iterate 30 times when the static shooting traffic gesture is used as the source. It can be seen from the table that the accuracy rate of the static shooting traffic alert gesture data set when UCF101 is the source is significantly higher than that of the dynamic shooting data set, indicating that the accuracy of identifying traffic police gestures is lower when the vehicle has speed. At the same time, when the training model of the stationary shooting traffic police gesture data set was used as the source for migration, the accuracy rate of the mobile shooting traffic police gesture data set has increased significantly but still lower than the static shooting with UCF101 as the migration source.

Figure 8 is a confusion matrix diagram of the UCF101 training model as a source to the static shooting traffic police gesture test. Figure 9 is a confusion matrix diagram of the UCF101 training model as the source to the mobile shooting traffic police gesture. Figure 10 Confusion matrix diagram of the training model of still shooting to the mobile shooting traffic police gesture test. As in Fig. 4, the horizontal axis is the real label and the vertical axis is the prediction label. Because the amount of data is small, the accuracy of all data is

Table 2. Accuracy of each data set

Dataset	Migration source	Number of iterations	Accuracy rate
UCF101	-	10000	0.7820
Static data	UCF101	50	0.6425
Dynamic data	UCF101	40	0.5827
Dynamic data	Static data	30	0.6337

displayed, so the sum of the vertical axis probabilities is 1. In Fig. 8, the third type of action recognition rate is the highest, and the fourth type of recognition rate is the lowest. It can be seen that the third type of action feature information is better extracted. It is possible that there are actions in UCF101 that are very similar to the third class, so the number of times the training features are extracted more or the number of trainings of the fourth type of motion is small due to the random input of the traffic alert gesture data set. It is obvious in Fig. 9 that the motion recognition rate drops a lot because the mobile shooting traffic alert gesture data set is more difficult to extract features than still shooting, and the moving shooting may cause the image to be blurred, the distance is too far, etc. Thus the highest fifth class of action recognition rate is only 65%, but the relative change is small. Comparing Figs. 9 and 10, it can be seen that each type of action is performed by using the static shooting traffic alert gesture data set as the source migration, and the test recognition rate is higher than the UCF101 source migration. We can know that the recognition rate will be higher after increasing the number of trainings within a certain range, but it is necessary to prevent over-fitting. Because the probability of misclassification of several types of actions recorded by the user is a bit large, it may be that the traffic alert gestures recorded by the user are not standard, the data noise is large, the data volume is small, or the training feature extraction is insufficient, resulting in a large probability of partial misjudgment.

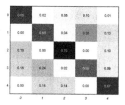

Fig. 8. Confusion matrix of UCF101 training model migration to still shooting traffic police gesture test

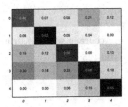

Fig. 9. Confusion matrix of UCF101 training model migration to still shooting traffic police gesture test

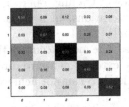

Fig. 10. Confusion matrix of UCF101 training model migration to still shooting traffic police gesture test

5.3 Parameter Tuning

5.3.1 The Optimization of Over-Fitting

Dropout mechanism is that setting up a coefficient of between 0 and 1 in the process of neural network training, then random make dormant part of neurons, the dormant neurons in the training process is equivalent to a weight of zero, which is equivalent to in not connection state, so the Dropout mechanism can effectively prevent the over-fitting problem, at the same time its unique mechanism not only can make the training a neural network to other neural networks are trained at the same time, also can greatly improve the speed of training, reduce the load of hardware resources.

It is selected at random that In choosing a part of the neural network nodes are in a state of body sleeps, In every time, the process of training is randomly selected node. Assumptions in the activation of probabilistic neural network node for f, through the present study showing that f is set to 0.5 or by controlling variable method to verify the value will get better effect, based on the control variable method experiment setting f value is 0.6.

As shown in Table 3. Using Dropout applied to optimize the neural network layer for each model, the result of the identification accuracy improved, but the changes of overall result is not as big as we imagine.

5.3.2 The Optimization of Batch Size

In a reasonable scope, selecting a relatively large batch size has the following benefits:

Table 3. Comparison of accuracy with dropout and no dropout

Dataset	Migration source	Accuracy without dropout	Accuracy with dropout
Static data	UCF101	0.6425	0.6613
Dynamic data	UCF101	0.5827	0.6025
Dynamic data	Static data	0.6337	0.6472

(1) more data can read from the memory at a time, improve memory to use efficiency and the efficiency of training operations;
(2) reducing the number of iterations, in a training, but also improving the training speed of the model;
(3) the more the batch size has, the more accurate the use of stochastic gradient descent algorithm to some extent downward direction will be, it won't make training repeated shocks lead to can not achieve convergence.

Through we collect the batch size 10, 15, 20 were taken to run the program again to get the average accuracy as shown in Table 4. By the table that the batch size parameter has a little influence on accuracy, but not obvious, generally improve accuracy at about 0.02, so long as we get larger, let the memory read more data at a time to reduce the program running time.

Table 4. Accuracy rate of different batch sizes

Dataset	Migration source	batch size 10	batch size 15	batch size 20
Static data	UCF101	0.6613	0.6732	0.6685
Dynamic data	UCF101	0.6025	0.6174	0.6117
Dynamic data	Static data	0.6472	0.6542	0.6586

6   Conclusions

Based on deep learning, this paper uses the open source dataset UCF101 to save the weight parameter model after human body motion recognition training, and then uses the transfer learning idea to identify five types of traffic police gestures. The experimental results show that when UCF101 is used as the source for migration, the recognition rate of static shooting traffic police's gesture is higher than that of mobile shooting; However, when the static shooting traffic police's gesture is used as the source for migration, the traffic police's gesture recognition rate of the mobile shooting is obviously increased, but it is still slightly lower than the static shooting traffic police's gesture recognition rate when the UCF101 is used as the source. At the same time, it is concluded that the two parameters of dropout and batch size have no significant influence on the recognition rate of traffic police's gestures, but dropout is very important to adjust the over-fitting problem.

Future research is to further optimize the method or use other deep learning algorithms to make the traffic police's gesture recognition rate higher and more accurate. At the same time, the smart car can be dynamically captured in the case of speed or the background is more complicated, and finally successfully applied to the automatic driving technology.

Acknowledgement. This work was supported partly by the National Natural Science Foundation of China (Grant No. 61673192), the Fund for Outstanding Youth of Shandong Provincial High School (ZR2016JL023), and the Basic Scientific Research Project of Beijing University of Posts and Telecommunications (2018RC31).

References

1. Takahashi, T., Kishino, F.: Hand gesture coding based on experiments using a hand gesture interfacedevice. ACM SIGCHI Bull. **23**(2), 67–74 (1991)
2. Lee, C., Xu, Y.: Online, interactive learning of gestures for human robot interfaces. In: 1996 IEEE International Conference on Robotics and Automation, Minneapolis, vol. 4, pp. 2982–2987. IEEE (1996)
3. Wen, G.: Enhanced user interface by hand gesture recognition. Chin. J. Adv. Softw. Res. **3**(1), 30–42 (1996)
4. Wu, J., Gao, W., Chen, X.: Recognition of Chinese finger letters based on data glove input. Pattern Recognit. Artif. Intell. **3**(1), 74–78 (1999)
5. Triesch, J., Von Der Malsburg, C.: Robust classification of hand postures against complex backgrounds. In: 2013 10th IEEE International Conference and Workshops on Automatic Face and Gesture Recognition (FG), Shanghai, p. 170. IEEE Computer Society (1996)
6. Wang, H., Schmid, C.: Action recognition with improved trajectones. In: IEEE International Conference on Computer Vision, pp. 3551–3558. IEEE, Piscataway (2013)
7. Song, Y., Morency, L.P., Davis, R.W.: Action recognition by hierarchical sequence summarization. In: IEEE Conference on Computer Vision and Pattern Recognition, pp. 3562–3569. IEEE, Piscataway (2013)
8. Vemulapalli, R., Arrate, F., Chellappa, R.: Human action recognition by representing 3D skeletons as points in a Lie group. In: IEEE Conference on Computer Vision and Pattern Recognition, pp. 588–595. IEEE, Piscataway (2014)
9. Wang, J., Liu, Z.C., Wu, Y., et al.: Mining actionlet ensemble for action recognition with depth cameras. In: IEEE Conference on Computer Vision and Pattern Recognition, pp. 1290–1297. IEEE, Piscataway (2012)
10. Everts, I., van Gemert, J.C., Gevers, T.: Evaluation of color STIPs for human action recognition. In: IEEE Conference on Computer Vision and Pattern Recognition, pp. 2850–2857. IEEE, Piscataway (2013)
11. Everts, I., van Gemert, J.C., Gevers, T.: Evaluation of color spatiotemporal interest points for human action recognition. IEEE Trans. Image Process. **23**(4), 1569–1580 (2014)
12. Liu, L., Shao, L.: Learning discriminative representations from RGB-D video data. In: 23rd International Joint Conference on Artificial Intelligence, pp. 1493–1500. Morgan Kaufmann, Burlington (2013)
13. Ijjina, E.P., Krishna, M.C.: Hybrid deep neural network model for human action recognition. Appl. Soft Comput. **46**, 936–952 (2016)

14. Hoai, M., Zisserman, A.: Improving human action recognition using score distribution and ranking. In: Cremers, D., Reid, I., Saito, H., Yang, M.-H. (eds.) ACCV 2014. LNCS, vol. 9007, pp. 3–20. Springer, Cham (2015). https://doi.org/10.1007/978-3-319-16814-2_1

15. Ji, S.W., Xu, W., Yang, M., et al.: 3D convolutional neural networks for human action recognition. IEEE Trans. Pattern Anal. Mach. Intell. **35**(1), 221–231 (2013)

16. McAllister, P., Zheng, H., et al.: Combining deep residual neural network features with supervised machine learning algorithms to classify diverse food image datasets. Comput. Biol. Med. **95**, 217–233 (2018)

17. Tran, D., Bourdev, L., Fergus, R., et al.: Learning spatiotemporal features with 3D convolutional networks. In: Proceedings of the IEEE International Conference on Computer Vision, pp. 4489–4497 (2015)

18. Byrd, R.H., Chin, G.M., Nocedal, J., Wu, Y.: Sample size selection in optimization methods for machine learning mathematical programming. J. Mach. Learn. Res. **134**(1), 127–155 (2012)

Localization of Human 3D Joints Based on Binocular Vision

Zheng Xu[1], Jinping Li[2], Jianqin Yin[3]([✉]), and Yanchun Wu[1,2,3]

[1] Shandong Provincial Key Laboratory of Network Based Intelligent Computing,
School of Information Science and Engineering, University of Jinan,
Jinan 250022, China
xuzhengqnyh@163.com
[2] Shandong College and University Key Laboratory of Information Processing
and Cognitive Computing in 13th Five-Year University of Jinan,
Jinan 250022, China
[3] School of Automation, Beijing University of Posts and Telecommunications,
Beijing 100876, China
jqyin@bupt.edu.cn

Abstract. With the development of image/video based 3D pose estimation techniques, service robots, human-computer interaction, and 3D somatosensory games have been developed rapidly. However, 3D pose estimation is still one of the most challenging tasks in computer vision. On the one hand, diversity of poses, occlusion and self-occlusion, change in illumination, and complex background increase the complexity of human pose estimation. On the other hand, many application scenarios require high real-time performance for 3D pose estimation. Therefore, we present a 3D pose estimation method based on binocular vision in this paper. For each frame of the binocular videos, the human body is detected firstly; Then Stacked-Hourglass network is used to detect the human joints, and the pixel coordinates of the key joints of all the human bodies in the binocular images are obtained. Finally, with the calibrated camera internal parameters and external parameters, the 3D coordinates of the major joints in the world coordinate system are estimated. This method does not rely on 3D data sets for training. It only requires binocular cameras to perform 3D pose estimation. The experimental results show that the method can locate key joints precisely and the real-time performance is achieved in complex background.

Keywords: Pose estimation · 3D joints localization · Binocular vision

1 Introduction

Human joints motion capture is widely used in medicine, biomechanics, movies, games and other fields. For example, Microsoft's RGB-D camera, Kinect [1], can control the role of the 3D game by capturing the human movement in real time, and realize the interaction between the human and the computer. The depth data provided by the camera greatly simplifies the cumbersome process of the

© Springer Nature Singapore Pte Ltd. 2019
F. Sun et al. (Eds.): ICCSIP 2018, CCIS 1006, pp. 65–75, 2019.
https://doi.org/10.1007/978-981-13-7986-4_6

3D reconstruction of the single camera. However, the disadvantage of Kinect is that it is easy to fail in the outdoors (light interference) or far distance and is expensive and cumbersome compared with other cameras. In recent years, the use of monocular RGB cameras to estimate the 2D pose of human has been widely studied, especially the method based on depth learning, which has achieved good results, for example, OpenPose [2], Stacked-Hourglass [3] and other methods have been able to meet the real-time requirements. However, human 3D pose estimation using monocular RGB images based on depth learning is a difficult task [4,5], and there are few methods at present, and they are usually offline.

Based on the good performance of RGB image in 2D pose estimation and the extensive use of binocular camera in 3D reconstruction, it is becoming more and more important to combine the two to estimate the 3D pose of human. First, the Stacked-Hourglass method is used to detect the human body, and the pixel coordinates of human joints in the left and right images of the binocular camera are obtained. Then, the binocular camera is calibrated accurately and the internal and external parameters of the camera are obtained. Finally, according to the calibrated parameters, the 3D coordinates of each joint are estimated, and 3D modeling of human joints is realized.

2   Related Work

The method of recovering 3D pose is ambiguous and they handle this ambiguity in different ways. These include improving the optimization methods and using rich image features or prior knowledge. We will introduce from the following three aspects:

3D Pose from 2D Joints: Most of the research methods of human 3D pose estimation focused on using 2D joints coordinates to estimate 3D pose. The early method is to recover the 3D pose [6–9] from a single image by using the anatomical knowledge of the human skeleton or joint angle limits. Representing human 3D pose as a linear combination of a sparse set of 3D bases, pretrained using 3D mocap data, has also proved a good approach for articulated human motion.

Structure from motion based methods have gained much popularity. Tomasi et al. [10] proposed a factorization method to estimate the 3D pose of a rigid body from a set of images. Then, a non-rigid structure from motion method (NRSfM) [11–13] is proposed to recover the motion state of the joints given known 2D correspondences for the joints in each frame of the video. As an unsupervised method, the advantage is that they do not need 3D training data, instead they can learn 3D pose directly from the 2D data. However, the main drawback is that they need for significant camera movement throughout the sequence to ensure the accuracy of 3D reconstruction.

3D Pose from Images: Existing work made on estimating 3D body shape from single image. This work often assumes good silhouettes are available. Sigal et al. [14] propose a method for automatically recovering a detailed parametric model of non-rigid body shape and pose from monocular imagery. Specifically, they represent the body using a parameterized triangulated mesh model that is learned from a database of human range scans. Hasler et al. [15] fit a parametric body model to silhouettes. Typically, they require a known segmentation and a few manually provided correspondences. In cases with simple backgrounds, they use four clicked points on the hands and feet to establish a rough fit and then use GrabCut to segment the person. Chen et al. [16] fit a parametric model of body shape and pose to manually extracted silhouettes.

3D Pose Estimation from a Single Image in a Multiple Camera View Scenario: For the 3D pose estimation of a single frame in a multi-camera view scene, it is easy to solve the problem in 3D space if the depth information, such as Kinect, is obtained from the sensor. However, Kinect cannot be used for outdoor applications. As a result, IMUs will often use [17, 18] without these restrictions. Then, these solutions are very expensive.

The proposed method does not require the use of 3D pose data sets, nor does it require significant camera movement. The 3D joint points can be located by a binocular camera only and it performs well.

3   Method

In this section, we mainly introduce how to estimate the 3D joints coordinates of human body in real time by binocular camera. The Sect. 3.1 describes the overall architecture of binocular 3D pose estimation. Section 3.2 will introduce the method of human body positioning. Section 3.3 describe the advantages of the Stacked-Hourglass method in 2D pose estimation, and how to get the pixel coordinates of 2D joints from RGB images. Section 3.4 introduce the specific details of binocular stereo vision for locating 3D joints.

3.1   Overview

As shown in Fig. 1, first of all, we need to detect the human body of the binocular image, and then send the region of the human body into the Stacked-Hourglass network to get the pixel coordinates of the main joints of all the human body. Finally, using the data obtained from camera calibration, the 3D coordinates of the main joints of human body are calculated by using the least-square method.

3.2   Object Detection

We chose Faster-RCNN [19] to detect and locate the human body. Faster-RCNN is one of the most popular detection frameworks. It is an improvement to the Fast-RCNN [20] method. The regional proposal is incorporated into the whole neural network framework, and an end to end target detection model is implemented. Faster-RCNN consists of two parts. The first part is the Fast-RCNN detector, and the other is the regional proposal networks (RPN). Faster-RCNN

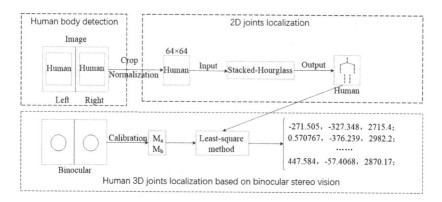

Fig. 1. Overview of the proposed 3D joints localization approach

is faster because it uses RPN to replace traditional regional proposal methods. RPN and Fast-RCNN share the convolution neural network, and the RPN itself is fast. The two sub networks are trained together to improve the ability to extract features of the whole CNN and improve the speed and precision of the detection.

We use Faster-RCNN to detect human body in each frame of the left and right videos. The training code is optimized, and the opened data sets are used to train individually for the human body, so as to improve the accuracy of the detection.

3.3 2D Pose Estimation

For the 2D joints of a single human body, we use the method of Stacked-Hourglass, given RGB images, to determine the exact pixel position of the main joints of the human body, and the entire pose estimation network is composed of multiple stacked Hourglass modules.

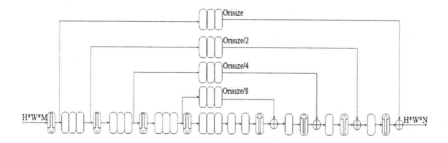

Fig. 2. An illustration of a single 'Hourglass' module

The motivation of Stacked-Hourglass network design is to capture information at every scale. As shown in Figure 2, before each downsampling of a single

Hourglass network, the network retains the original scale information, and the feature map continues the convolution and pooling after the next down-sample. Until the minimum resolution is reached, the network begins to upsample, and after each upsampling, it is added to the data of the previous scale to fuse different scales information. At the same time, between the two downsamplings, three residual modules are used to extract the features. The residual module is shown in Fig. 3. Between the two additions, a residual module is used to extract the features.

Through such a processing, compared with other networks, the Hourglass network structure can get more contextual information by increasing the receptive field. The multi-scale feature is used to capture the spatial position information of human joints. After reaching the output resolution of the network, two consecutive 1×1 convolutions are used to generate the final network prediction. The output of the network is a heat map, where the network predicts the probability of joints at each pixel.

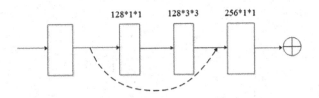

Fig. 3. Residual module

The overall idea of network design is influenced by the ResNet [21] network, and it is hoped that the feature of each scale will be considered to allow the network to learn pose. Repeatedly capture information contained in images at different scales. Pose estimation requires an understanding of the entire human body, the orientation of the human body, the arrangement of the limbs, and the relationship between the adjacent joints. The Stacked-Hourglass network looks for this information at different scales.

3.4   Binocular Stereo Visual Localization of 3D Joints

The brain have a deep understanding of human vision. This kind of cognition is called the stereoscopic effect. The binocular stereo vision imitates the principle by using a pair of RGB image cameras to observe the same object from different angles. At the same time, two images of the observation target are obtained, and the three-dimensional information is restored by the relative parallax of the target in the imaging, thus the stereoscopic positioning is realized.

As shown in Fig. 4, for arbitrary joint J, the two cameras C_1 and C_2 are used to observe the J at the same time. The core of the two cameras is O_1 and O_2 respectively. The J_1 and J_2 points are the pixel coordinates of the joint J at the C_1 and C_2 cameras respectively. The point J can be intersected by a straight line

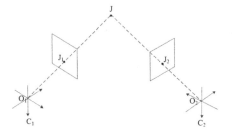

Fig. 4. The principle of binocular stereo vision

O_1J_1 and a straight line O_2J_2, so the joint J is unique, and its three-dimensional spatial position is determined.

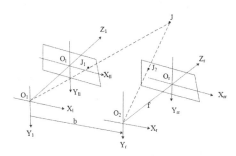

Fig. 5. The principle of joints localization

The ideal binocular stereovision positioning joint model is shown in Fig. 5. At this time, we can use the least-square method to solve the three-dimensional coordinates of the joint J, according to the projective transformation matrices obtained by the calibration. In the world coordinate system, point $J_1(u_l, v_l)$ and $J_2(u_r, v_r)$ are the pixel coordinates of joint J on the left and right images of the cameras. According to the camera pinhole imaging model, we get (1) (2):

$$
Z_l \begin{bmatrix} u_l \\ v_l \\ 1 \end{bmatrix} = M_l \begin{bmatrix} x \\ y \\ z \\ 1 \end{bmatrix} = \begin{bmatrix} m_{l11} & m_{l12} & m_{l13} & m_{l14} \\ m_{l21} & m_{l22} & m_{l23} & m_{l24} \\ m_{l31} & m_{l32} & m_{l33} & m_{l34} \end{bmatrix} \begin{bmatrix} x \\ y \\ z \\ 1 \end{bmatrix} \tag{1}
$$

$$
Z_r \begin{bmatrix} u_r \\ v_r \\ 1 \end{bmatrix} = M_r \begin{bmatrix} x \\ y \\ z \\ 1 \end{bmatrix} = \begin{bmatrix} m_{r11} & m_{r12} & m_{r13} & m_{r14} \\ m_{r21} & m_{r22} & m_{r23} & m_{r24} \\ m_{r31} & m_{r32} & m_{r33} & m_{r34} \end{bmatrix} \begin{bmatrix} x \\ y \\ z \\ 1 \end{bmatrix} \tag{2}
$$

M_l and M_r are the projection matrices of the two cameras. The projection matrix $M = M_a \times M_b$ of a single camera is a matrix of 3×4. M_a is called the internal parameter of the camera, which is determined by the internal structure of the camera (such as the focal length), and the M_b is determined by the camera relative to the azimuth of the world coordinate system (such as the placement position and the shooting angle). It can be described with the rotation matrix R and the translation vector T, known as the external parameters of the camera. The calculation is (3):

$$AJ = b \tag{3}$$

In addition:

$$b = \begin{bmatrix} m_{l14} - m_{l34}u_l \\ m_{l24} - m_{l34}u_l \\ m_{r14} - m_{r34}u_r \\ m_{r24} - m_{r34}u_r \end{bmatrix} \tag{4}$$

$$A = \begin{bmatrix} m_{l31}u_1 - m_{l11} & m_{l31}u_1 - m_{l11} & m_{l31}u_1 - m_{l11} \\ m_{l31}u_1 - m_{l11} & m_{l31}u_1 - m_{l11} & m_{l31}u_1 - m_{l11} \\ m_{l31}u_1 - m_{l11} & m_{l31}u_1 - m_{l11} & m_{l31}u_1 - m_{l11} \\ m_{l31}u_1 - m_{l11} & m_{l31}u_1 - m_{l11} & m_{l31}u_1 - m_{l11} \end{bmatrix} \tag{5}$$

$$J = \begin{bmatrix} x & y & z \end{bmatrix}^T \tag{6}$$

Based on the least-square method, three dimensional coordinates of spatial joints J are obtained:

$$J = (A^T A)^{-1} A^T b \tag{7}$$

4   Experiment

In this section, we use the method proposed in this paper to estimate the 3D coordinates of the key joints of the human body and test the effectiveness of our method in complex background.

4.1   Camera Calibration and Training Model

A fixed camera is used to calibrate using Zhang method [22], and the internal and external parameters of the camera are obtained. We divide the types of detection into two categories, the human body and the background, in order to detect the human body as the sole purpose. We use the AI-Challenger [23] data sets to retrain the Faster-RCNN network to improve the accuracy of the human body detection. After training, mAP increased from 78.14% to 91.62% on the AI-Challenger testing data set.

We also use the AI-Challenger data sets to retrain the Stacked-Hourglass network, the number of data sets, the diversity, and the high complexity (the complex background, a large number of occlusion) greatly improves the robustness and accuracy of the network. On the AI-Challenger testing data sets, the final target mAP increased from 32.93% to 45.11%.

4.2 3D Pose Estimation

Open the calibrated camera, each frame of the video is sent into the Faster-RCNN network. The network can locate the human body position in real time and send the area of the human body into the Stacked-Hourglass network to get the main joint pixel coordinates of the human body in the left and right images. Then, according to the camera's internal and external parameters, the least-square method is used to estimate the 3D coordinates of each joint.

In addition, in order to prevent the individual joint detection errors from causing larger errors in the 3D joint location, we have carried out the identification and optimization. If the depth difference between the left shoulder and the left elbow is greater than 0.5 m, we will judge whether the mistake appears on the left shoulder or the left elbow according to the depth of the neck and left wrist. If it appears on the left shoulder, we will estimate the depth distance according to the average value of the neck and left elbow. If it appears on the left elbow, we will estimate the depth distance based on the average value of the left wrist and the left shoulder.

The experimental results are 3 and 5 m away from the camera, as shown below (Fig. 6).

In addition, in order to estimate the influence of camera calibration error and 2D joints detection error on 3D joints location. We tested the size of the 3D joints positioning error at different detection distances, in which the human body was not covered with a large area (small occlusion), and the experimental results were shown in Table 1.

Table 1. 3D joints localization error at different distances

Detection distance	Maximum error	Average error	Experiment times
1 m	5.4 cm	2.2 cm	50
2 m	9.8 cm	4.5 cm	50
3 m	19.2 cm	10.2 cm	80
4 m	36 cm	17.8 cm	100
5 m	57 cm	26.2 cm	200

4.3 Analysis

Under the complex background (illumination change, etc.), even with partial occlusion, the binocular 3D joints detection also has good results. Under 1980 × 720 resolution, an average of 27.5 frames per second can be processed, and the results can be achieved in real time. As shown in Table 1, with the increase of detection distance, the accuracy of 3D joints location will be lower and lower. This is because there are errors in the binocular calibration and the error is direct proportional to the distance; in addition, there are also errors in the detection of

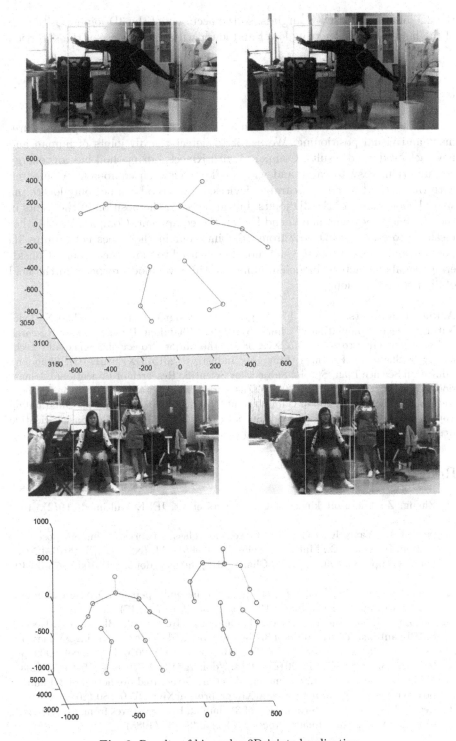

Fig. 6. Results of binocular 3D joints localization

the 2D joints in Stacked-Hourglass, so the accuracy of the 3D joints positioning of the human body is getting lower and lower with the increase of the detection distance.

5   Conclusion

At present, binocular is widely used in 3D reconstruction, stereoscopic measurement and visual positioning. We use it to detect the 3D joints of human and have achieved good results. Compared with Kinect, our method has low energy consumption, easy to carry and wide angle of view on equipment. Compared with the method based on wearable devices, our method can not only locate the spatial coordinates of the 3D joints, but also record the position of the joints in the 2D image by frame and spend less on the equipment. Compared with other methods to estimate 3D pose from 2D joints, our method does not require 3D pose estimation data sets to train, nor does it need to move the camera. Considering the above factors, binocular cameras still have good prospects in the field of 3D pose estimation.

Acknowledgments. I would like to give acknowledgment present to The National Natural Science Foundation of China (61701192), Shandong Provincial Key Research and Development Project (2017CXGC0810), the Major Project of Science and Technology in Shandong Province (Emerging Industry) (2015ZDXX0801A03), Shandong Education Science Plan 'Special Subject for Scientific Research of Educational Admission Examination' (ZK1337212B008). This work was supported partly by the National Natural Science Foundation of China (Grant No. 61673192), the Fund for Outstanding Youth of Shandong Provincial High School (ZR2016JL023), and the Basic Scientific Research Project of Beijing University of Posts and Telecommunications (2018RC31).

References

1. Zhang, Z.: Microsoft kinect sensor and its effect. IEEE Multimed. **19**(2), 4–10 (2012)
2. Newell, A., Yang, K., Deng, J.: Stacked hourglass networks for human pose estimation. In: Leibe, B., Matas, J., Sebe, N., Welling, M. (eds.) ECCV 2016. LNCS, vol. 9912, pp. 483–499. Springer, Cham (2016). https://doi.org/10.1007/978-3-319-46484-8_29
3. Cao, Z., Simon, T., Wei, S.E., et al.: Realtime multi-person 2D pose estimation using part affinity fields. In: CVPR, vol. 1, no. 2, p. 7 (2017)
4. Bogo, F., Kanazawa, A., Lassner, C., Gehler, P., Romero, J., Black, M.J.: Keep it SMPL: automatic estimation of 3D human pose and shape from a single image. In: Leibe, B., Matas, J., Sebe, N., Welling, M. (eds.) ECCV 2016. LNCS, vol. 9909, pp. 561–578. Springer, Cham (2016). https://doi.org/10.1007/978-3-319-46454-1_34
5. Tekin, B., Katircioglu, I., Salzmann, M., et al.: Structured prediction of 3D human pose with deep neural networks. arXiv preprint arXiv:1605.05180 (2016)
6. Lee, H.J., Chen, Z.: Determination of 3D human body postures from a single view. Comput. Vis. Graph. Image Process. **30**(2), 148–168 (1985)

7. Taylor, C.J.: Reconstruction of articulated objects from point correspondences in a single uncalibrated image. Comput. Vis. Image Underst. **80**(3), 349–363 (2000)

8. Parameswaran, V., Chellappa, R.: View independent human body pose estimation from a single perspective image. In: 2004 Proceedings of the 2004 IEEE Computer Society Conference on Computer Vision and Pattern Recognition, CVPR 2004, vol. 2, p. II. IEEE (2004)

9. Barrón, C., Kakadiaris, I.A.: Estimating anthropometry and pose from a single uncalibrated image. Comput. Vis. Image Underst. **81**(3), 269–284 (2001)

10. Tomasi, C., Kanade, T.: Shape and motion from image streams under orthography: a factorization method. Int. J. Comput. Vis. **9**(2), 137–154 (1992)

11. Akhter, I., Sheikh, Y., Khan, S., et al.: Trajectory space: a dual representation for nonrigid structure from motion. IEEE Trans. Pattern Anal. Mach. Intell. **33**(7), 1442–1456 (2011)

12. Gotardo, P.F.U., Martinez, A.M.: Computing smooth time trajectories for camera and deformable shape in structure from motion with occlusion. IEEE Trans. Pattern Anal. Mach. Intell. **33**(10), 2051–2065 (2011)

13. Lee, M., Cho, J., Choi, C.H., et al.: Procrustean normal distribution for non-rigid structure from motion. In: IEEE Conference on Computer Vision and Pattern Recognition (CVPR), pp. 1280–1287. IEEE (2013)

14. Sigal, L., Balan, A., Black, M.: Combined discriminative and generative articulated pose and non-rigid shape estimation. In: NIPS, pp. 1337–1344 (2008)

15. Hasler, N., et al.: Multilinear pose and body shape estimation of dressed subjects from image sets. In: IEEE, vol. 238, no. 6, pp. 1823–1830 (2010)

16. Chen, Y., Kim, T.-K., Cipolla, R.: Inferring 3D shapes and deformations from single views. In: Daniilidis, K., Maragos, P., Paragios, N. (eds.) ECCV 2010. LNCS, vol. 6313, pp. 300–313. Springer, Heidelberg (2010). https://doi.org/10.1007/978-3-642-15558-1_22

17. Pons-Moll, G., Baak, A., Helten, T., et al.: Multisensor-fusion for 3D full-body human motion capture. In: 2010 IEEE Conference on Computer Vision and Pattern Recognition (CVPR), pp. 663–670. IEEE (2010)

18. von Marcard, T., Pons-Moll, G., Rosenhahn, B.: Human pose estimation from video and IMUs. IEEE Trans. Pattern Anal. Mach. Intell. **38**(8), 1533–1547 (2016)

19. Ren, S., He, K., Girshick, R., et al.: Faster R-CNN: towards real-time object detection with region proposal networks. In: Advances in Neural Information Processing Systems, pp. 91–99 (2015)

20. Girshick, R.: Scale-aware fast R-CNN for pedestrian detection. Comput. Sci. (2015)

21. He, K., Zhang, X., Ren, S., et al.: Deep residual learning for image recognition. In: Proceedings of the IEEE Conference on Computer Vision and Pattern Recognition, pp. 770–778 (2016)

22. Zhang, Z.: A flexible new technique for camera calibration. IEEE Trans. Pattern Anal. Mach. Intell. **22**(11), 1330–1334 (2000)

23. Wu, J., Zheng, H., Zhao, B., et al.: AI challenger: a large-scale dataset for going deeper in image understanding. arXiv preprint arXiv:1711.06475 (2017)

Development of Multi-person Pose Estimation Method Based on PAFs

Menghan Guo[1], Ye Gao[1], Bin Wang[2,3(✉)], and Fuchun Sun[2]

[1] College of Computer Science and Technology,
Xi'an University of Science and Technology, Xi'an, China
[2] State Key Laboratory of Intelligent Technology and Systems,
Tsinghua University, Beijing 100084, China
wangbinth@tsinghua.edu.cn
[3] Beijing Little Wheel Co., Beijing 100084, China

Abstract. Human keypoints are effective human pose descriptions. Human behavior can be recognized by the motion of keypoints of human bodies. In this paper, we propose a method, which is based on a PAFs approach, for human keypoints detection. The proposed method makes improvements in two aspects: (1) It perfects the joint points matching algorithm by re-matching. (2) It uses multi-branch PAFs to correct the keypoint connections, thus improving the wrong connection problem of upper and lower limbs for multi-person keypoint detection. The improved PAFs method, whose mAP reaches 53.6% on HKD dataset, improved the score of the original method by 2%.

Keywords: Human pose estimation · Keypoints detection · Part affinity fields

1 Introduction

The keypoints of human skeleton are essential for describing human posture and predicting human behavior. The action of human body can be described as the movement of some major joint points. A skeleton with only 10–16 keypoints can characterize many behaviors. The characteristics of skeleton information are clear and straightforward, which is not easily affected by appearance factors. Consequently, the detection of human keypoints is particularly important.

At present, human pose estimation has attracted more and more attention, and many researchers have done related works. However, when it comes to real applications, there are some challenging problems need to be solved. Firstly, in practical applications, real-time is a problem which we must consider. Moreover, skeleton errors also need to be solved. For example, the interaction of multi person often causes the human body parts occlusion, especially the upper and lower limbs (arms and legs), which is easy to cause the disordered skeleton and joint point loss (Fig. 1) in detection process.

F. Sun et al. (Eds.): ICCSIP 2018, CCIS 1006, pp. 76–84, 2019.
https://doi.org/10.1007/978-981-13-7986-4_7

Fig. 1. Top: When the person in the scene are not overlapped, the recognition result is more accurate. Bottom: As shown in the red shaded area, if limbs are crossed, the skeletons are prone to disorder and loss. (Color figure online)

In this work, we improved the method of Cao et al. [1]. Firstly, we discuss the weaknesses of their method. Secondly, to solve these existing problems, we propose to enhance the limb joints matching algorithm by re-matching. Moreover, the PAFs are extended by increasing the limb connection on upper and lower limbs, which are less dependent on the anterior joint points, so as to correct the connection of the subsequent joint points. Finally, we validate our method on the HKD dataset [2]. The results show that the mAP of proposed method is 2–2.5% higher than the original PAFs method.

2   Related Work

Previously, the detection of human skeleton keypoints was mainly conducted with Kinect [3], which is a kind of 3D somatosensory camera. One of its functions is to extract 3D skeleton information, including the coordinators of keypoints in x, y, and z directions. But Kinect has many limitations in some application scenarios and is far less convenient than ordinary camera. Furthermore, it is more expensive and not suitable for wide application.

How to get the human keypoints in the 2D RGB images with the ordinary camera has become a hot spot of the human pose estimation research [17]. Normally, the location of the human body and the number of people in the scene are unknown, which requires us to perform multi-person pose estimation, not only to detect the keypoints of all people in the image, but also to connect the points of the same person to form a skeleton. There are two popular methods for these problems: (1) top-down approaches. (2) bottom-up approaches.

The first top-down method based on deep learning was proposed by Toshev et al. [4]. In their work, the human pose estimation is regarded as a keypoint regression problem. The first step of the top-down approach is to detect person from a given image and then perform single person keypoints detection in each of the detected bounding boxes [5, 6, 9]. This approach takes advantage of the single-person estimation method, which is simple and accurate. But it relies heavily on the reliability of the human body detector, and when the number of people in the image increases, the computational complexity will increase linearly. Mask R-CNN [8] predicts the human bounding box and keypoints simultaneously, which make the process faster by sharing the features for each branch.

In contrast to the top-down approach, the bottom-up approach first detects all the body keypoints in an image [16], and then associates all the points to human instances [11, 12, 14, 15]. The inference of this method is faster because there is no need to detect each person's posture separately. But how to connect the keypoints from the same person is a problem that needs to be considered. Pishchulin et al. [10] proposed the first deep learning based bottom-up method, which models part candidates as vertices and relation between part candidates as edges. Cao et al. [1] proposed a new feature, part affinity fields (PAFs), which is constructed by the keypoints position, and then a greedy algorithm is exploited to generate human skeleton.

A novel network structure, Stacked hourglass, is designed by Newell et al. [7]. This structure is proved to be important for improving human pose detection performance by repeating bottom-up, top-down processing with intermediate supervision.

HKD (Human Keypoint Detection) dataset is a sub-dataset of AIC (AI Challenger). The HKD dataset [3] is the largest human pose image set at present. It has a total of 300K images, which are labeled with 14 human keypoints. The images are crawled from the Internet using web crawlers. The scenes are more richer, complex, and challenging.

3   Part Affinity Fields

For the affiliation of each keypoint belongs to which person in the image, Cao et al. [1] used two adjacent joint points to construct a new limb feature called PAFs (Part Affinity Fields), which is a 2D vector field that records the position and direction of the limbs. As shown in Fig. 2. First, input an image, and extract the feature maps by a convolution network (here is VGG19). Then, split the feature maps into two branches that using the CNN to output the part confidence maps and PAFs respectively. After that, with these two kinds of information, the keypoints of the same person can be connected to form a human skeleton. The PAFs represent the connection information between joints. The main function of which is to combine keypoints belonging to the same person when there are more than one person in the image.

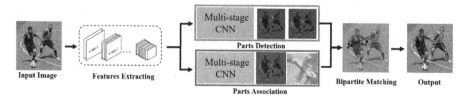

Fig. 2. Overall pipeline

Fig. 3. Left: There is a limb overlap at point **p**, so its vector is shown by the blue arrow, which is the sum of the vectors v_1 and v_2. Right: Matching the bipartite graph of keypoints. Red dots and blue dots, blue dots and green dots are matched respectively. (Color figure online)

For Example, there are two adjacent joint points, $x_{j1,k}$ and $x_{j2,k}$, belonging to the same person k, so these two points can form a c limb part, expressed as $limb_{c,k}$. There is a unit vector between them

$$v_{c,k} = \frac{x_{j2,k} - x_{j1,k}}{\left\| x_{j2,k} - x_{j1,k} \right\|^2} \tag{1}$$

At a point **p** in the image, if **p** is a point on $limb_{c,k}$, then $L_c(p)$ is equal to $v_{c,k}$. If there are multiple people's limbs overlapping at **p**, calculate the value of **p** on each limb separately, and then sum them up (shown in Fig. 3 Left),

$$L_c(p) = \frac{\sum_k L_{c,k}(p)}{n} \tag{2}$$

where n is the number of overlapping limbs.

When evaluating the reliability of the association between the join points j_1 and j_2, connect the two points and calculate the linear integral,

$$S = \int_0^1 L_c(p(u))du \tag{3}$$

where u is the point on the line connecting j_1 and j_2. Then calculating the projection length L of S in the direction of $\overrightarrow{J_1J_2}$, shown in Eq. (4). If S and $\overrightarrow{J_1J_2}$ are in the same direction, the value of L will be large relatively, and the reliability that the connection of these two points is limb c will be more higher. So L can be used as a weight to evaluate the connection quality.

$$L = S \cdot \frac{(j_2 - j_1)}{\left\| j_2 - j_1 \right\|^2} \tag{4}$$

They decomposed the matching problem into a set of bipartite graph matching sub-problems, determined the matching of adjacent nodes independently, and then used the Hungarian method for the optimal match, as shown in Fig. 3 Right. But the problem with PAFs was that it consider the connection of adjacent keypoints only, which using n-1 lines to connect n points. That was, in order to get a complete human skeleton, all keypoints prediction and connection prediction must be completely correct. At the same time, these joint points were connected one by one in a tree structure. Once the parent connection is broken, the subsequent child connection and joint points will be discarded, even if the children are correct. For instance, consider three joint points together in sequence, e.g., shoulder, elbow and wrist. And if the connection between the shoulder and the elbow was missing, the wrist joint would not be able to connect to the human body. That makes the mechanics less robust.

4   Improve Part Affinity Fields

For the problems mentioned in the previous section, first we increased the number of connecting line between the joint keypoints, for example, the shoulder and the wrist connected directly, so that there are two connections from the shoulder to the wrist (Fig. 4 Left). When one of the connection is wrong, it can be corrected by another connection to improve the robustness.

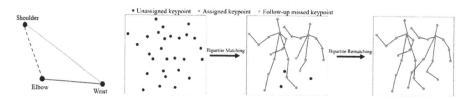

Fig. 4. Left: When the connection between shoulder and elbow is broke (blue dotted line), the wrist joint can be find through another connecting line (red line). Right: The bipartite graph re-matching process. (Color figure online)

For the upper and lower extremities, add the connecting lines from shoulder to wrist and hip to ankle. There has

$$J^* = \{LSho, LElb, LWri, LHip, LKne, LAnk, RSho, RElb, RWri, RHip, RKne, RAnk\}$$

We define a variable p_j, which represents the position of the keypoint j, with $j \in J^*$. E is the final weight score of the limbs,

$$O = \{E_{j_x j_y} : for\ j \in J^*, x, y \in \{1...N_{J^*}\}\} \tag{5}$$

For the joint points j_1, j_2, j_3 on arm or leg, there are two connection routes, $j_1 \rightarrow j_2 \rightarrow j_3$ and $j_1 \rightarrow j_3$. Then we perform weighted calculations on the two connections (Eq. (6)). When the connection of $j_1 \rightarrow j_2$ or $j_2 \rightarrow j_3$ is lost, we can retrieve the joint point j_3 through the connection of $j_1 \rightarrow j_3$.

$$\varphi = (1 - \mu)E_{j_1 j_2} + \mu E_{j_2 j_3} \tag{6}$$

If $E_{j_1 j_3} > \varphi$, the points of j_1, j_2, j_3 are sequentially connected.

These are not enough to improve the effect of connection. In our testing, we observed that some keypoints have been predicted, but they are not matched in the end. We use the re-matching method to improve the problem.

Firstly, we traverse the well-matched skeletons to find the missing keypoints from the human body. The existing anterior joint points which connected to these keypoints are Q, where $Q = \{q_{j_x} : for j_x \in J\}$. The remaining predicted keypoints which not matched are P, where $P = \{p_{j_y} : for j_y \in J\}$. The Hungarian method will be used again to perform bipartite graph re-matching between Q and P. The process is shown in Fig. 4. Right. After the first matching, some keypoints are not connected. The keypoints which missed the subsequent node (red dots) and the unassigned keypoints (black dots) are re-matched by the method of bipartite matching. It can eliminate the impact of the other points.

5 Experiments and Results

We have experimented on the HKD dataset. The experimental results show that the improved PAFs and re-matching method can solve the problems of disordered skeleton and missing keypoints, which caused by human occlusion, to a certain extent. As shown in Fig. 5.

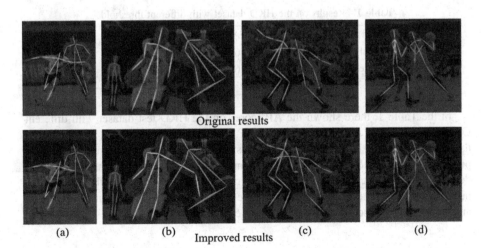

Fig. 5. Some result cases: (a) The left wrist is wrongly connected to another person. (b) The crossed arms cause the disordered skeleton. (c) The keypoints on left arm are missing. (d) Because the knee point is not detected, the ankle point is lost.

We trained on the training set (a total of 210K images without adding external data) and tested on the validation set (a total of 30K images). The evaluation metric is the mAP (mean Average Precision), and using the OKS (Object Keypoint Similarity) [13] to measure the predicted result. The s, threshold of OKS, is set to (0.50:0.05:0.95). The OKS is defined as follows [3]:

$$OKS_p = \frac{\sum_i \exp\{-d_{pi}^2/2s_p^2\sigma_i^2\}\sigma(v_{pi} = 1)}{\sum_i \delta(v_{pi} = 1)} \tag{7}$$

where p is the human index; i is the index of human skeleton keypoint; δ_i is the normalization factor of keypoint, which is calculated by the standard deviation of the annotation; v_{pi} is the state (visible, invisible) of the keypoint i of the person p; d_{pi} is the Euclidean distance of the predicted keypoint position and the groundtruth; s_p is the scale factor of human p, which is defined as the square root of the human body bounding box; $\delta(\cdot)$ is the Kroneck function, which means that only the keypoints of human marked as visible ($v = 1$) are considered in the evaluation.

The AP (Average Precision) formula under different s is as follows:

$$AP@s = \frac{\sum_p \delta(OKS_p > s)}{\sum_p 1} \tag{8}$$

We initialized the VGG-19 model from the pre-trained model of ImageNet. Our model was trained with 16 batch_size for 180000 iterations using four Quadro P5000 GPU, where lr = 4e−5, gamma = 0.333, step_size = 100000. The final experimental results are as follow tables:

Table 1. Results on the HKD dataset with different threshold

Method	$AP^{0.50}$	$AP^{0.60}$	$AP^{0.70}$	$AP^{0.80}$	$AP^{0.90}$	mAP
Original PAFs	80.4	73.4	62.3	44.1	16.3	51.5
Improved PAFs	81.8	75.6	65.2	48.0	18.7	53.6

In the Table 1, there shown the AP scores on the HKD test dataset with different OKS threshold. The mAP is the average AP with 10 thresholds. Cao [1] pointed out that the performance of top-down approaches rely heavily on the person detector. The performance difference will exceed more than 10% with different methods of human detection. In contrast, the bottom-up method of PAFs is not affected by the accuracy of human detection. The original method achieves 51.5% mAP. With our optimization and improving, the score increased 2.1% to 53.6%.

Table 2. The mAP scores of each keypoint on extremity. Calculate the OKS of each part individually which including the left and right limbs.

Method	Shoulder	Elbow	Wrist	Hip	Knee	Ankle	mAP
Original PAFs	52.3	54.5	45.3	55.6	48.7	31.4	51.5
Improved PAFs	52.4	**55.4**	**47.8**	55.6	49.2	**33.5**	**53.6**

As can be seen from Table 2, the accuracy of the wrist and ankle are improved about 2–2.5% significantly. The reason is that the limbs of human body are most prone to cross-occlusion, which can easily cause the skeleton points to be disordered and lost on 2D image. With the method of this paper, the keypoints reduce the dependence on the previous nodes, and the bipartite re-matching can compensate for the lost keypoints to a certain extent. So the accuracy of these two positions are increased significantly.

6 Conclusions

In this paper, we have studied the skeletal disorder and loss of limbs in multi-human pose estimation, and used re-matching method and extended PAFs to solve these problems. Experiments proved that our research and exploration are effective, but at the same time, these difficulties can not be solved completely. How to further improve the accuracy of keypoints detection in multi-human pose estimation requires us to study in-depth.

Acknowledgment. Research supported by NVIDIA Corporation with the donation of the Quadro P5000 GPU, National High-Tech Research and Development Plan under Grant 2015AA042306 and Beijing Little Wheel research project.

This work was supported partly by the Innovation Leading Action of Suzhou-Tsinghua (No. 016SZ0219).

References

1. Cao, Z., Simon, T., et al.: Realtime multi-person 2D pose estimation using part affinity fields. In: IEEE Conference on Computer Vision and Pattern Recognition (CVPR), pp. 1302–1310 (2017)
2. Han, J., Shao, L., Xu, D., et al.: Enhanced computer vision with microsoft kinect sensor: a review. IEEE Trans. Cybern. **43**(5), 1318–1334 (2013)
3. Wu, J., Zheng, H., Zhao, B., Li, Y., et al.: AI Challenger: A Large-scale Dataset for Going Deeper in Image Understanding. arXiv:1711.06475 (2017)
4. Toshev, A., Szegedy, C.: DeepPose: human pose estimation via deep neural networks. In: IEEE Conference on Computer Vision and Pattern Recognition (CVPR), pp. 1653–1660 (2014)
5. Sapp, B., Taskar, B.: MODEC: multimodal decomposable models for human pose estimation. In: IEEE Conference on Computer Vision and Pattern Recognition (CVPR), pp. 3674–3681 (2013)

6. Fang, H.S., Xie, S., Tai, Y.W., et al.: RMPE: Regional Multi-person Pose Estimation. arXiv: 1612.00137 (2016)
7. Newell, A., Yang, K., Deng, J.: Stacked hourglass networks for human pose estimation. In: Leibe, B., Matas, J., Sebe, N., Welling, M. (eds.) ECCV 2016. LNCS, vol. 9912, pp. 483–499. Springer, Cham (2016). https://doi.org/10.1007/978-3-319-46484-8_29
8. He, K., Gkioxari, G., Dollar, P., Girshick, R.: Mask R-CNN. IEEE Trans. Pattern Anal. Mach. Intell. (2017)
9. Iqbal, U., Gall, J.: Multi-person pose estimation with local joint-to-person associations. In: Hua, G., Jégou, H. (eds.) ECCV 2016. LNCS, vol. 9914, pp. 627–642. Springer, Cham (2016). https://doi.org/10.1007/978-3-319-48881-3_44
10. Pishchulin, L., Insafutdinov, E., Tang, S., et al.: DeepCut: joint subset partition and labeling for multi person pose estimation. In: IEEE Conference on Computer Vision and Pattern Recognition (CVPR), pp. 4929–4937 (2016)
11. Newell, A., Huang, Z., Deng, J.: Associative embedding: end-to-end learning for joint detection and grouping. In: Advances in Neural Information Processing Systems, pp. 2274–2284 (2017)
12. Wei, S.E., Ramakrishna, V., Kanade, T., Sheikh, Y.: Convolutional pose machines. In: IEEE Conference on Computer Vision and Pattern Recognition (CVPR), pp. 4724–4732 (2016)
13. Lin, T.-Y., et al.: Microsoft COCO: common objects in context. In: Fleet, D., Pajdla, T., Schiele, B., Tuytelaars, T. (eds.) ECCV 2014. LNCS, vol. 8693, pp. 740–755. Springer, Cham (2014). https://doi.org/10.1007/978-3-319-10602-1_48
14. Insafutdinov, E., Pishchulin, L., Andres, B., Andriluka, M., Schiele, B.: DeeperCut: a deeper, stronger, and faster multi-person pose estimation model. In: Leibe, B., Matas, J., Sebe, N., Welling, M. (eds.) ECCV 2016. LNCS, vol. 9910, pp. 34–50. Springer, Cham (2016). https://doi.org/10.1007/978-3-319-46466-4_3
15. Insafutdinov, E., Andriluka, M., Pishchulin, L., et al.: Arttrack: articulated multi-person tracking in the wild. In: IEEE Conference on Computer Vision and Pattern Recognition (CVPR), vol. 4327 (2017)
16. Papandreou, G., Zhu, T., Kanazawa, N., Toshev, A., et al.: Towards accurate multiperson pose estimation in the wild. arXiv:1701.01779, 8 (2017)
17. Wang, B., et al.: Development of operation estimation method based on tracking records captured by kinect. In: Sun, F., Liu, H., Hu, D. (eds.) ICCSIP 2016. CCIS, vol. 710, pp. 136–143. Springer, Singapore (2017). https://doi.org/10.1007/978-981-10-5230-9_15

Background of Semantic Intelligence Research and the Principle of Technical Framework

Wang Ye[1], Bolin Chen[2], Shuming Chen[1], and Xiaohui Zou[3](✉) 🆔

[1] Sino Cosmocreating Group, Room 1001-2, Building 7, Yard 30,
Shijingshan District, Beijing 100041, China
warren.ye@foxmail.com, digitalgod@263.net
[2] Chongqing Institute of Geology and Mineral Resources,
Chongqing Engineering Research Center of Automatic Monitoring
for Geological Hazards, No. 111. Lanxin Road, Yubei District,
Chongqing 401120, China
261761985@qq.com
[3] Sino-American Searle Research Center, Beijing, China
949309225@qq.com

Abstract. Through semantic analysis of the words "sweet" and "good", this thesis aims to understand the cognitive methods and limitations of human beings, trying to reveal the research background, technical framework and resonance principle of semantic intelligence. The method is as follows: Firstly, based on the application perspective, the artificial intelligence technology is divided into three categories: motion, perception and semantics. Furthermore, from the perspective of technical framework, it is based on semantic concepts and cosmic energy material system, human self-perception and functional system, computer artificial intelligence system, energy material logic function system, human language grammar system, computer artificial intelligence function logic software programming system, etc. the internal logic of the five aspects advances the principles of semantic intelligence systems, engineering implementation techniques, and systematic research of product systems. The result is: from its research background, it highlights the logic relationship between Chinese classical religion, philosophy and culture, people and people, consciousness and the nature of the universe, and assists with the modern scientific and technological methods to propose a new framework of semantic intelligence technology content and ideas. The significance is that it can construct a system intelligence theory and principle that integrates the universe's natural, material world, philosophy, science, graphic and symbolic systems, human consciousness and semantic virtual world, and realizes the breakthrough of semantic intelligence research.

Keywords: Sensation · Sensory organs · Semantic intelligence research · Graphic and symbolic systems · Human cognitive methods

© Springer Nature Singapore Pte Ltd. 2019
F. Sun et al. (Eds.): ICCSIP 2018, CCIS 1006, pp. 85–92, 2019.
https://doi.org/10.1007/978-981-13-7986-4_8

1 Introduction

The purpose of this paper is to show how to understand the cognitive methods and limitations of human beings, trying to reveal the research background, technical framework and resonance principle of semantic intelligence.

1.1 Re-understanding of artificial intelligence technology

1.2. Analysis of the background of artificial intelligence research in the modern science and technology system

1.3. Principle of semantic intelligence technology framework

2 Method

The method is as follows: Firstly, based on the application perspective, the artificial intelligence technology is divided into three categories: motion, perception and semantics. Furthermore, from the perspective of technical framework, it is based on semantic concepts and cosmic energy material system, human self-perception and functional system, computer artificial intelligence system, energy material logic function system, human language grammar system, computer artificial intelligence function logic software programming system, etc. the internal logic of the five aspects advances the principles of semantic intelligence systems, engineering implementation techniques, and systematic research of product systems.

2.1 Theoretical Discussion: Re-understanding of AI Technology

Artificial intelligence technology is the inevitable result of the comprehensive development of mathematics, automation control, electronic computer and other related theories and technologies [1]. Based on the application perspective, artificial intelligence technology can be roughly divided into three categories: sports intelligence, perceived intelligence and semantic intelligence (decision intelligence or thinking intelligence) [2]:

1.1.1 Sports intelligence is an intelligent technology system that aims to simulate human flexible controllability and motion balance. It involves cutting-edge technologies such as automation control and robotics. This field of research is suitable for applying reductionism thinking. In fact, it has made great progress [3].

1.1.2 Perceptual intelligence is a related technical system that simulates the sensing, acquisition, feature extraction, feature recognition, structural modeling, and cognition of human vision, sound, taste, and smell. Among them, the fields of induction (acquisition), feature extraction and feature recognition are still suitable for the application of reductionism thinking. Therefore, the direction of artificial intelligence technology such as deep learning [4, 5] is in full swing; in the fields of structural modeling and cognition, It is not only a representation of spatial features, but also a relational model between spatial features, such as topographical, geomorphological, geological and other structural fine-grained artificial intelligence modeling problems. The research progress of related technologies is extremely limited.

1.1.3 Semantic intelligence (decision intelligence or thinking intelligence, etc.) is an artificial intelligence technology system that simulates human consciousness, thinking, emotion, mind, understanding, learning, innovation, etc. This part should be the crown of artificial intelligence technology [6] as the key part of human intelligence stems from its inexpressible experience, it is obvious that reductionism and empirical logic in the modern science and technology system cannot provide effective technical means for it.

2.2 Theoretical Analysis of the Background of AI

Modern science and technology systems, especially in the past sixty years, have made great progress in the fields of astrophysics, quantum, materials, information, aerospace, biology, energy, etc., although the current artificial intelligence technologies such as AlphaGo and deep learning are in full swing [7] It still cannot conceal the most core of the modern science and technology system - the fact that the actual progress of artificial intelligence is still stagnant [8].

The modern science and technology system, the inevitable product of industrial science and technology civilization, its fundamental methodology is reductionism and empirical logic. Its essence is to study the relationship and law between nature and matter [9–11]. Human beings are the spirit of the natural world of the universe. Artificial intelligence is the intelligence of simulating human beings. Its core content has gone far beyond the logical category of nature and matter. Therefore, the development of modern western science and technology system based on reductionism and empirical logic, going to the bottleneck is also an inevitable result [12].

Chinese classical religion, philosophy and culture have been deeply rooted in the study of the relationship and logic between people, between consciousness and the nature of the universe based on the profound experience and sentiments of the sages. The essence of this is the Confucianism, Buddhism, and Chinese, Chinese medicine, etc. Including the achievements of "Heaven and Man, Liding, Buddha, Yinyang and Five Elements, hieroglyphics", the essence of the methodology is holistic thinking; that is to say, among the historical treasures of Chinese classical religion, philosophy and culture, the Chinese nation is included. The millennium continues to perceive the insights of experiential insights, and in it can profoundly reveal the laws and logics of human wisdom deduction, and if it is assisted by modern scientific and technological methods, it can make the development of strong artificial intelligence technology possible [13–16].

2.3 Principle of Semantic Intelligence Technology Framework

The basic research logic of the semantic intelligence technology framework is:

3.1 To study the state, mode, characteristics, and rules of self-consciousness, thinking, emotion, mind, understanding, learning, innovation, and trust.

3.2 Supported by the theoretical system and knowledge of modern science and technology (natural science and social science).

3.3 In-depth thinking, re-creation and application of mathematical methods and theoretical systems.

3.4 profoundly explore the relationship and logic between human beings, consciousness and cosmic nature from Chinese classical religion, philosophy, language and culture, fully understand and integrate the essence of Western philosophy system [17–22].

3.5 From the universe as a whole, profoundly analyze the fundamental differences and internal logic relations between different systems of computers and human beings.

The essence of the semantic intelligence technology framework is to construct a system intelligence theory and principle that integrates the universe's natural, material world, philosophy, science, and graphic symbolic systems, human consciousness and semantic virtual world [23–26].

3 Research Contents and Approach of Technical Framework of Semantic Intelligence

The result is: from its research background, it highlights the logic relationship between Chinese classical religion, philosophy and culture, people and people, consciousness and the nature of the universe, and assists with the modern scientific and technological methods to propose a new framework of semantic intelligence technology content and ideas.

Semantic intelligence technology has four main aspects, which are text semantic intelligence, image semantic intelligence, voice semantic intelligence and integrated semantic intelligence, among which text semantic intelligence is the core, image semantic intelligence and sound semantic intelligence are the key, and integrated semantic intelligence is the main body. Systematic research of semantic intelligence, including principle, engineering implementation technologies and products, is currently conducted in five aspects.

3.1 Research on the Inherent Logic and Relationship Based on Semantic Concepts and Cosmic Energy Material System

Research on the inherent logic and relationship between semantic concept and the energy and material system in real world.

Based on the discovered natural laws from the modern science and technology, and the energy and material basis of human beings, the essence of the conceptual models in the language system and the mapping logic between the conceptual models and the energy and material system in real world should be analyzed, so as to propose the principle and approach to construct the essential and unified conceptual models which can be resonantly comprehended by both humans and AI systems.

Taking the logic of conceptual model of taste perception as an example, "sweet" is a concept formed through experience of human's taste perception, of which the essence is a resonant response of the human body's perception system, i.e. taste buds, to the various concentrations of sweet molecules in saliva. Therefore, based on the logic mentioned above, a conceptual model of "sweet" based on energy and material of computer, which is similar to human's comprehension, can be established.

3.2 Research on the Inherent Logic and Relationship Based on Human Self-perception and Functional System

Research on the internal logic and relationship of human's ego-perception and function system: The inherent logic rules of human's ego perception, consciousness, thought, emotion, mind, comprehension, learning, innovation, trust, etc., should be systematically studied, so as to construct various corresponding logical function models [27]. Taking the logical function model of "favor", which is one of human's affections, as an example, it is found that the evolvement of "favor" model in the process of getting along with others follows the following three principles:

(1) Law of Incremental Benefit to Maintain Favor: The "favor" between humans is maintained by incremental benefits. For instance, A feels B is good for A when B gives A 10 dollars the first time. However, the good feel gradually fades when A gets used to the favor of 10 dollars which offered by B everyday until B start to give 20 dollars to A, which brings an increment of 10 dollars.

(2) Law of Harm Once to Reverse Favor to Antipathy: Once B does harm to A, the good feeling of A for B will be cleared to zero regardless of the whole history of B's goodness for A, further more, a will even become disgusted with B.

(3) Law of Persistence of Negative Effect on Affection: Once B does harm to A, the negative effect might last forever and the former affection could never be fixed no matter how good B will be for A, because A tends to remember the harm everlastingly.

It can be seen that the key to the solution of ambiguity lies in distinguishing between human intelligence and artificial intelligence [28].

It is easy for misunderstandings of a large number of causes on the complexity not only in mental information but also in social ecology [29, 30].

3.3 Research on Energy and Material System of Computer AI System

The logic background and logic law of energy and material of computer artificial intelligence system should be analyzed, based on which the support system of energy and material function system for AI will be constructed, which conforms to the inherent requirements of the overall objective law of the universe and nature, and can resonate with human beings. Taking the spatial intelligent function system of computer AI as an example, it is to explore the technical implementation to enable the capability to understand and cognize space by computer itself. Traditional Geographic Information

System and CAD Graphic Model are essentially to assist people in understanding the space, rather than to cognize the space by computer itself. For instance, a large number of annotated information in CAD drawings is not to describe the graph itself, but to assist people in understanding, which will become superfluous if it is provided for AI to comprehend it.

3.4   Research on the Inherent Logic of Human Language and Grammar System

The inherent logic of the grammatical system of human language and characters involves many new technical fields, such as (1) the evolution of human language and characters in the evolution of human history, as well as its absolute position and role in human wisdom; (2) the inherent logic law and the deductive logic law of various words and sentences, parts of speech and grammar in human language and characters; (3) the commonness and difference between different languages of Chinese and English; (4) the inherent logic relationship between grammar and concepts etc.

Take the logic of evolution of human language and characters in the evolution of human history as an example: (1) the evolution of bipedalism brought the liberation of hands; (2) the liberation of hands brought convenience for symbolic marking, which led to the development of language and characters; (3) the development of language and characters has boosted the progress of human brain, vision, hearing and verbal capability, which universally promote the humans' intelligence, thus bringing about the memory and inheritance of individuals' experience and knowledge, and promoting the all-round development of human wisdom and human society.

3.5   Research on Intelligent Programming Based on Computer AI

Research on The inherent law and relationship between the functional logic system of computer artificial intelligence and computer programming language are to be ana- lyzed, and the organic interaction and the inherent logical relationship among data (files), programming language, variables (concepts), functions and system (agents) and their roles in AI should be studies, so as to explore the essence of intelligent pro- gramming and a comprehensive and effective approach to implement it. For example, how to construct the intelligent programming system with data, functions, variables and functional modules? (1) data is the content of variables; (2) variables are the structural carriers of data; (3) functions are the structural carriers of variables; (4) data, functions and variables constitute the main part of functional modules; (5) the changes of data in variables trigger the call of functions to release specific functional modules of software; (6) the execution of functional modules changes the contents of variables to form new data models; (7) the iterating loops mentioned above form an autonomous cognition and self-deduction system of the function and content based on computer.

4 Conclusion: Our Progress of Study on Semantic Intelligence

The significance is that it can construct a system intelligence theory and principle that integrates the universe's natural, material world, philosophy, science, graphic and symbolic systems, human consciousness and semantic virtual world, and realizes the breakthrough of semantic intelligence research.

Some substantial progress in semantic intelligence and related fields has been made so far.

(1) The theoretical system of geometric and graphical topological space which can be comprehended by computer itself based on its material logic has been basically constructed.

(2) Intelligent geospatial modeling technology covering micro-topography, micro-geomorphology and micro-geology in the global geographic framework has been basically realized by artificial intelligence, and some technical products have reached the level of practicality, and have begun to be applied in the market, which lays a foundation for the realization of semantic intelligence in the field of computer-based autonomous spatial intelligent analysis.

(3) Semantic intelligence study, which integrates human consciousness, thought, emotion, mind, comprehension, learning, innovation and trust, etc., has made breakthroughs. The relevant basic principles and frameworks have been preliminarily formed. The prototype system of semantic intelligence, which has man-like consciousness, thought, emotion, mind, comprehension, learning and innovation, and its substantial progress of industrialization trial expected to be realized in the next 2–5 years.

References

1. Cai, Z., Wang, Y.: Principles, Algorithms and Applications of Intelligent Systems, pp. 2–11. Mechanical Industry Press, Beijing (2014)
2. Cai, Z., Xu, G.: Artificial Intelligence and Its Application, pp. 6–15. Tsinghua University Press, Beijing (1996)
3. Eppe, M., et al.: A computational framework for conceptual blending. Artif. Intell. **256**, 105–129 (2018)
4. Ian, G., et al.: Deep Learning. People's Posts and Telecommunications Press, Beijing (2017)
5. Han, L.: Artificial Neural Network Theory and Application. Mechanical Industry Press, Beijing (2016)
6. Jurafsky, D., Martin, J.H.: Speech and Language Processing: An Introduction to Natural Language Processing, Computational Linguistics, and Speech Recognition. Stanford University, Stanford (2018)
7. Liu, W., Ni, S.: Review of artificial intelligence research and development in 2017. Sci. Technol. Rev. **36**(1), 98–103 (2018)
8. Carters, W.A., Kinnucan, E., Elliot, J.: A National Machine Intelligence Strategy for the United States, pp. 8–9. Center for Strategic & International Studies, US (2018)

9. Zhong, Y.: Mechanismal artificial intelligence theory—a general theory of artificial intelligence. J. Intell. Syst. **13**(1), 2–18 (2018)

10. Wang, P.: Factor space theory—the mathematical foundation of mechanismal artificial intelligence theory. J. Intell. Syst. **13**(1), 37–54 (2018)

11. He, H.: The theory of universal logic—the logical basis of mechanismal artificial intelligence theory. J. Intell. Syst. **13**(1), 19–36 (2018)

12. Huang, C.: A description of earthquake risk perception in intelligent mathematics. J. Risk Anal. Crisis Response **8**(3), 163–176 (2018)

13. Brenner, J.E.: Intelligence Science and Intelligence Philosophy: Another Convergence? CDUT (2016)

14. Zhang, G., Gao, L., Zhang, Y.: Science Education and Similarity Theory. Jiangsu Science and Technology Press, Jiangsu (2000)

15. Zhao, C.: Frontier of Intelligent Science Research. Science Press, Beijing (2013)

16. Martel, F.: Intelligence – The Cultural Frontier of the Internet Age. The Commercial Press, Beijing (2015)

17. Laozi: Tao Te Ching. Beijing United Press, Beijing (2015)

18. The Analects: Beijing Publishing House, Beijing (2005)

19. Yi, J.: Peking University Press, Beijing (1996)

20. Huang Di Nei Jing: Zhonghua Book Company, Beijing (2010)

21. The Bible: Chinese Christian Association, Nanjing (1996)

22. The Qur'an Interpretation: Ningxia People's Publishing House, Ningxia (2005)

23. Putnam: Reason, Truth, and History. Shanghai Translation Publishing House, Shanghai (1997)

24. Martinique: Language Philosophy. The Commercial Press, Beijing (1998)

25. Cai, Y.: Speech Acts and Pragmatic Logic. China Social Sciences Press, Beijing (1998)

26. Ma, Y.: Research on thinking science and geographical thinking. Acta Geographica Sinica **56**(2), 29–34 (2001)

27. Wu, C.: From Representation to Action: The Naturalistic Approach of Intentionality. China Social Sciences Press, Beijing (2010)

28. Zou, S., Zou, X.: Understanding: how to resolve ambiguity. In: Shi, Z., Goertzel, B., Feng, J. (eds.) ICIS 2017. IAICT, vol. 510, pp. 333–343. Springer, Cham (2017). https://doi.org/10.1007/978-3-319-68121-4_36

29. Zou, S., Zou, X., Wang, X.: How to do knowledge module finishing. In: Shi, Z., Pennartz, C., Huang, T. (eds.) ICIS 2018. IAICT, vol. 539, pp. 134–145. Springer, Cham (2018). https://doi.org/10.1007/978-3-030-01313-4_14

30. Zou, S., Zou, X.: Ecological characteristics of information and its scientific research. In: Multidisciplinary Digital Publishing Institute Proceedings, vol. 1, p. 59 (2017)

Leavs: A Learning-Enabled Autonomous Vehicle Simulation Platform

Weizheng Wu, Yizhi Wei, Cuiying Gao, and Zichen Xu[⊠]

Nanchang University, Nanchang, China
{wuweizheng,yizhiwei,arry}@email.ncu.edu.cn, xuz@ncu.edu.cn

Abstract. Self-driving vehicle simulation exhibits human-computer interaction. There already exist many commercial autonomous vehicle simulation tools, however, they all require human inputs, which is limited. In this paper, we present our early work as building learning enabled autonomous vehicle simulations, or LEAVS. We started from forking an open-sourced tool AirSim, and legoed it up with our smart sensors, data collection tools, and algorithm platform, to test learning-based algorithm, such as object detection. We report our current platform now can successfully enable many state-of-the-art object recognition algorithm, combined with smart vehicles control to drive independently in thousands of simulations. LEAVS is the platform to perform learning-based simulations for unmanned autonomous vehicles.

1 Introduction

Human computer interaction plays an important role that bridges cyber-physical systems. Unmanned driven vehicles exhibit a perfect example for such interaction as it provides the feedback loop from environmental sensing, to intelligent decision from cyber-space, and reaches fault-free decisions. However, it is very expensive to carry out a large quantities of such tests in a cyber-physical world, usually, we use simulations. Typical simulation tools are commercial from large manufacture companies, such as Honda, Toyota, Buick, etc. There exist a few other free tools, such as AirSim [1], CARLA [2], and Apollo [3].

The current simulation tools usually support human inputs, but not all of them can perform reasoning and understanding on human decisions as well as driving interaction with the ever-changing environment. To have a real "autonomous" driving vehicle test, the simulation platform shall behave the ability of learning. However, learning is not an easy task in simulations. Though it is easy to access a large amount of data in simulation platform, it is hard to deal with those data, and turns those data into effective commands read by the vehicles, such as automatic road guide, environmental sensing, traffic collision detection and recovery, etc. These problems shall be analyzable and emulated in a simulation environment.

Another important problem with the current tool sets is scalability and adaptivity. Commercial tools are close-developed thus new sensors or detection tools

© Springer Nature Singapore Pte Ltd. 2019
F. Sun et al. (Eds.): ICCSIP 2018, CCIS 1006, pp. 93–103, 2019.
https://doi.org/10.1007/978-981-13-7986-4_9

are hard to be modeled in. Open-sourced platforms have limited access to up-to-date learning algorithms. We need a tool to bridge the gap between the two and improve the scope of simulation for autonomous driving.

In this paper, we propose an open-sourced simulation platform with the ability to deploy new sensors, perform data analysis, and adopt novel learning algorithms, called LEAVS. LEAVS provides smart sensing services by programming new sensors, such as scene graph sensor, depth sensor, etc. in different position of a target vehicle or many vehicles. With these new sensors, LEAVS provides data analysis on many runtime collected data traces. At last, LEAVS adopts many state-of-the-art algorithms for performance evaluation and algorithm analysis. At last, LEAVS provides a rich set of functions, as a novel autonomous driving simulation platform.

We prototyped LEAVS based on an open-source platform AirSim, made by Microsoft. We extend the current API of AirSim to enable many more sensors onto the target vehicles with user-defined functions. All these sensors output information, such as position in a global map, etc., or features, for later stage behavior learning and object detection. Our prototype runs in a GPU-CPU machine box for weeks and we have collected many pieces of performance analysis on state-of-the-art learning algorithms.

The main contribution of this paper are:

- We identify the limitation of today's autonomous driving simulation platform and provide our own solution–LEAVS. We deploy many new types of smart sensors on LEAVS and it can collect large amount of data on running vehicles.
- We provide an accessible approach to analyze the data derived from sensors and make further research in autonomous vehicles.
- We have prototyped LEAVS and evaluate many vision learning algorithms.

The remainder of this paper is organized as follows: we first compare our work with other projects in Sect. 2. We then provide the design of our experiments on AirSim in Sect. 3. We describe the technical details of our experiments in Sect. 4, analyze those data derived form the experiments, and discuss their limitations in Sect. 5. Finally, we conclude the paper in Sect. 6.

2   Related Work

While a variety of autonomous vehicles simulators are developed, the research is concentrated in three areas: smart sensors, data collection tools, and algorithm platform.

Smart Sensors. Sensors in autonomous vehicles have been an active field of research for many years. Croke and Hrabar [4] work on a sensor network deployment method, which is suitable for tasks such as large-scale environmental monitoring or for command and control in emergency situations. Several other teams [5,6] also provide some generation dynamic vision systems to guide the autonomous vehicles. However, their methods are far more complex and not flexible enough to obtain needed data than LEAVS. LEAVS can provide various kinds of sensors and place them into different positions so as to collect plenty of data in a more straightforward approach.

Data Collection Tools. Data processing is another focus with a great deal of research. Gregor and Lutzeler [7] turn path-planning and dynamic steering data into a computationally feasible scheme for real-time feedback control of autonomous vehicles, and use this method to compute critical points along a globally desirable path using a priori information and sensor data. Moreover, other researchers [8,9] intrinsically segment the scene in autonomous into its constituting dynamic components and set fixed transmission instants in each receiver in order to transfer and analyze data on autonomous vehicles. Developing on all such work, LEAVS provides a simple and convenient way to access and export data, and information can be directly derived from running vehicles.

Algorithm Platform. Another notable research area is algorithm implement. Michalon [10] develops and tests algorithms for autonomous vehicles in order to developed further in deep learning and machine intelligence. Pereira [11] models an integration architecture of autonomous vehicles which enables autonomous vehicles to be deployed in a rather realistic traffic flow as an agent entity, at the same time it simulates all its sensors and actuators. Moreover, Bojarskiz [12] trains a convolutional neural network (CNN) to map raw pixels from a single front-facing camera directly to steering commands. Similarly, Al-Shihabi and Mourant [13] address the problem of modeling realistic and humanlike behaviors, such as the aggressive driving model, the alcoholic driving model, the elderly driving model and the generic normal model on stimulated systems by capturing the details of human driving at the microscopic level on stimulated highway. All these algorithms are of great importance. However, they have many limitations to implement. On LEAVS, various kinds of algorithms can be implemented and tested without multifarious prerequisites.

3   Design

LEAVS enables more sensors, and thus more complex data analysis and learning algorithms onto the original self-driving simulation. In this section, we present our LEAVS design and detailed parameters.

3.1   Sensor Objects

From Fig. 1, we can know the architecture of LEAVS. LEAVS is based on an open-sourced tool AirSim, which is composed of our smart sensors, data collection tools, and algorithm platform, to test learning-based algorithm, such as object detection. LEAVS can collect raw data from the sensors and extract features by using data analysis tool. From getting the features, LEAVS can learn the algorithm and can feedback on itself for better decision. The basic function of LEAVS is a feedback loop of AirSim, Sensor Objects, Data Analysis and Learning Algorithm. The feedback loop can continuously enhance the ability of

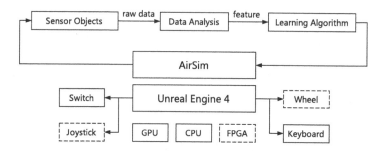

Fig. 1. The architecture of LEAVS

learning and making decisions on LEAVS. LEAVS needs Unreal Engine to load the scene map. Loading maps requires a lot of computation and graphical rendering. In order to have faster loading speed and better rendering effect, we deploy LEAVS in a server with GPUs. In the future, we will use FGPA to accelerate further. With the help of Unreal Engine, we can control the vehicle by Nintendo Switch, joystick, wheel and the keyboard on LEAVS. The support of multiple control tools enriches LEAVS's human-computer interactive ability.

We provide more user-defined sensors to emulate new techniques and tools in today's self-driving. Originally, there are two kinds of sensors on the vehicle, as vehicle information sensors and environment information sensors. Vehicle information sensors collect the driving information of the vehicle, including position, speed, gear, steer, RPM, brake and so on. Environment information sensors collect environment information around the vehicle. Environment information sensors have five types, scene graph sensor, depth map sensor, grayscale sensor, infrared sensor sensor and object segmentation sensor. There are five positions on the vehicle for users to place those sensors. They are respectively front_center, front_right, front_left, FPV (FPV is driver's head position in the car) and back_center. To meet the research needs, we can place those five sensors on these five positions on the vehicle. Furthermore, we can write a program to set stabilization for pitching, rolling or yawing for any sensors to collect omni-directional data. LEAVS also offers sensor models for accelerometer, gyroscope, barometer, magnetometer and GPS. All our sensor models are implemented

Fig. 2. Depth map example

Fig. 3. Scene graph example

Fig. 4. Grayscale image example

through C++ header-only library and can be independently used outside Air-Sim. Like other components, sensor models are expressed as abstract interfaces so it is easy to replace or add new sensors.

Figures 2, 3 and 4 are the examples captured by the environment information sensors. Figure 2 is captured by the depth map sensor. Figure 3 is from the scene graph sensor. Figure 4 is captured by the grayscale sensor. Each pixel of the grayscale image captured by the gray sensor corresponds to a luminance test. We can extract gray values on the grayscale image and use OSTU algorithm (An efficient algorithm for two valued images) [14] to do two valued operations. We also can use the grayscale image to detect objects. The pixel value of gray image is influenced by many factors, such as ambient light intensity, surface reflection and texture features. Depth image directly reflects the depth of the object rather than other factors. Therefore, the depth image has been widely used in three-dimensional object recognition based on the geometric information of the object.

3.2   Data Analysis

Data collection is for analysis. Using the data collected by vehicle information sensors, we can analyze the relationship between gear and speed, influence of throttle on vehicle speed and the effect of parameter brake on braking time. Table 1 is an example of our collected vehicle information. It shows that we can take the name of the corresponding image while we are collecting data. From analysis of the corresponding images, we should be able to determine how to steer the car only by focusing on the red part of the image shown in Fig. 6. In order to reduce the training time and the quantity of the data, we have sufficient grounds to extract the part of red frame while training autonomous vehicle models. The red frame part can also prevent the model from getting confused by focusing on irrelevant features in the environment (e.g. mountains, trees, etc.) (Fig. 5).

From Fig. 9, we analyze the change of steer angle in the two different driving strategies, normal and swerve. By observing a obvious difference between the two driving strategies, we can draw some conclusions. The blue points show that when driving the car normally, the steering angle is almost zero, which makes our car nearly go straight on the road. There is a heavy imbalance and if this portion of the data is not downsampled, the model will always predict zero, and the car will not be able to turn. When driving the car with the swerve strategy, we can

Table 1. Part of collected vehicle information

Index	Timestamp	Speed(km/h)	Throttle	Steering	Brake	Gear	ImageName
0	94044195	0	0.031373	0.0	0.0	N	img_0.png
1	94044195	0	0.031373	0.0	0.0	N	img_1.png
2	94044247	0	0.047059	0.0	0.0	N	img_2.png
3	94044299	0	0.082353	0.0	0.0	N	img_3.png
4	94044347	0	0.082353	0.0	0.0	N	img_4.png

Fig. 5. Sample image

Fig. 6. The red part of the sample image (Color figure online)

get examples of sharp turns that do not appear in normal strategy dataset. This validates our reasoning based on those data above. These conclusions are vital in training end-to-end deep learning models. Since we are not doing any feature engineering, our model mostly relies on the dataset which can provide all the necessary information to it.

Figure 7 shows that when the throttle is less than 0.8, the speed will increase first and then remain unchanged. However, when the throttle is greater than 0.8, the speed will continue to increase to maximum. It is like the real-world when the clutch of the car is released a bit, the car will accelerate first and then at a stable pace. When the clutch is released a lot, the car will accelerate continuously to maximum speed. The throttle design of the vehicle power system in AirSim is very close to the actual power system of the vehicle. As for the brake, from Fig. 8, we can see that the value of the brake has nothing to do with deceleration. When the brake is greater than zero, the car will slow down at the same speed. I think the brake plays an significant role in handbrake.

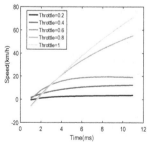

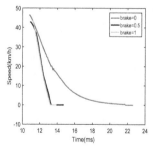

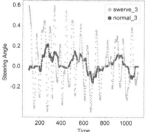

Fig. 7. Influence of throttle value on vehicle speed

Fig. 8. Influence of brake value on brake

Fig. 9. The comparison of steer angle of two driving strategies (Color figure online)

3.3 Algorithm Platform

Object Recognition. As a platform for AI researchers to experiment with deep learning, computer vision and reinforcement learning algorithms for autonomous vehicles, AirSim also exposes APIs to retrieve data and control vehicles without assistance from platform. We choose a deep learning model. This model takes a convolution neural network (CNN) [15] as the main learning object of image processing, and uses SSD [16] to detect image features. CNN can construct a multilayer neural network more easier through image convolution and pooling steps. SSD obtains the final result by multi-layer convolution (Fig. 10).

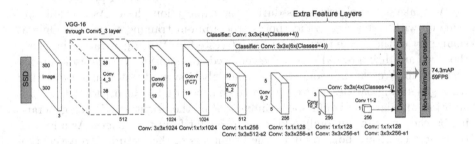

Fig. 10. SSD algorithm structure [16]

Autonomous Vehicle. We choose an autonomous driving model using end-to-end deep learning named DQN. End-to-end deep learning is a modeling strategy that is a response to the success of deep neural networks [17]. Unlike traditional methods, this strategy is not built on feature engineering. Instead, it leverages the power of deep neural networks, along with recent hardware advances (GPUs, FPGAs etc.) to harness the incredible potential of large amounts of data. It is closer to a human-like learning approach than traditional ML, as end-to-end deep learning lets a neural network map raw input to direct output. With real-world simulators like AirSim, we collect a large amount of data to train our autonomous vehicle models without having to use an actual car. We train a model to learn how to steer a car through a portion of the Landscape map in AirSim using only one of the front facing webcams on the car as visual input.

4 Experiment

4.1 Object Recognition

First, we choose a tensorflow detection model, whose model speed is fast and detector performance is not bad. Fast and accurate object recognition is critical to the driving vehicle. Next, we use a handle to control the vehicle driving on the city scene, while we write a script to record image data captured by vehicle sensors. Next, we use the model to recognize the images. Besides, we also use Python, OpenCV, and threading to make the model recognize objects dynamic while driving.

4.2   Autonomous Vehicle Using End-to-End Deep Learning

In this section, we train the model. We also discuss some of the transformations on the data in response to observations that we have made in the result section. For image data, it is too expensive to load the entire dataset into memory. Fortunately, Keras has the concept of DataGenerators. A DataGenerator is nothing more than an iterator that can read data from disk in chunks. This allows researchers to keep both CPU and GPU busy, increasing productivity.

We make a few observations during the exploration phase. As a result, we come up with a strategy to incorporate them in our training algorithm. Only a small part of the image is what we are interested in. When generating batches, those we are disinterested should be removed. In addition, the dataset can be vertical flip. We can flip some images and labels around the Y axis randomly when generating batches, so we can get some new data for the model to learn. In addition, the dataset should not be influenced by the brightness. When generating batches, we can randomly add or remove light from the images. As a result, the model can learn how to ignore the brightness of the picture. Moreover, the dataset has a huge number of zero-valued images. When analyzing the dataset, we can give up some data points randomly where the steering angle is zero, so the model can see a balanced dataset when training. We need to exemplify how the model swerve hastily from the swerving strategy in our dataset. Here, we will initialize the generator with the following parameters:

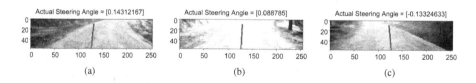

Fig. 11. Image data before training (Color figure online)

- **Zero_Drop_Percentage**: 0.80 - That is, we randomly drop 80% of the data points with label = 0, but not 90%, because the amount of zero steering angle images also influence the result.
- **Brighten_Range**: 0.3 - That is, the brightness of each image can be modified by up to 30%. To compute "brightness", we transform the image from RGB to HSV space, scale the 'V' coordinate up or down, and transform back to RGB space.
- **ROI**: [76, 140, 0, 255] - This is the x1, x2, y1, y2 rectangle that represents the area of interest for the images.

To avoid overwhelming parameterization, we adapt a few data augmentation strategies, in order to improve model stability and convergence. By adding or removing hidden layers, as well as changing layer width, LEAVS can improve the network structure to meet the training efficiency goal. Keras is able to declare callbacks, so these functions will be executed while each epoch is training. We can look at a sample batch. The steering angle is represented by the red line in the Fig. 11.

We train our model using the Tensorflow platform. The whole training process takes about 45 mins. It can repeat itself when the regression loss is above our pre-defined thresholds (i.e., p = 0.5). At last, we have a workable mode in LEAVS.

5   Result

5.1   Object Recognition

From Fig. 12, we can see a good result from our training. Our model is able to recognize the vehicles and pedestrians on the road. This will provide timely warning information for vehicles to avoid other vehicles and pedestrians, which will reduce the occurrence of traffic accidents.

(a)   (b)

Fig. 12. Object recognition results

5.2   Autonomous Vehicle

In Fig. 13, the blue line and the red line are very close. We get a good result. We load the model and connect it with AirSim in the Landscape environment. We keep the speed of the car at 5 ms to 10 ms. Moreover, the model controls the steer. Though there exists some collisions, the model is still a huge ingress to make autonomous vehicle come true.

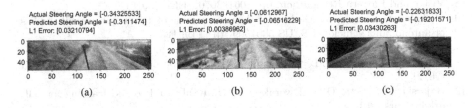

(a)   (b)   (c)

Fig. 13. Image data after training (Color figure online)

6   Conclusion

This paper presents a learning enabled autonomous vehicles simulations, LEAVS. Based on an open-sourced platform AirSim, we build it up with our smart sensors, data collection tools and algorithm platform. Through our current platform, some algorithms such as object recognition, autonomous vehicles can be implemented. With plenty of simulations, the test result shows that LEAVS can perform learning-based simulations for unmanned autonomous vehicles. Further discussions and research on evaluation and implementation of the accuracy of object recognition and autonomous vehicles are also presented for future improvement.

Acknowledgement. This research was supported by the grant from the Tencent Rhino Grant award (11002675), by the grant from the National Science Foundation China (NSFC) (617022501006873), and by the grant from Jiangxi Province Science Foundation for Youths (708237400050).

References

1. Shah, S., Dey, D., Lovett, C., et al.: AirSim: high-fidelity visual and physical simulation for autonomous vehicles (2017)
2. Dosovitskiy, A., Ros, G., Codevilla, F., et al.: CARLA: an open urban driving simulator (2017)
3. Fan, H., Zhu, F., Liu, C., et al.: Baidu Apollo EM Motion Planner (2018)
4. Corke, P., Hrabar, S., Peterson, R., et al.: Autonomous deployment and repair of a sensor network using an unmanned aerial vehicle. In: 2004 Proceedings of the IEEE International Conference on Robotics and Automation, ICRA, vol. 4, pp. 3602–3608. IEEE (2004)
5. Cao, X.R., Shen, H.X., Milito, R., Wirth, P.: Internet pricing with a game theoretical approach: concepts and examples. IEEE/ACM Trans. Netw. **10**(2), 208–216 (2002)
6. Pagac, D., Nebot, E.M., Durrant-Whyte, H.: An evidential approach to mapbuilding for autonomous vehicles. IEEE Trans. Robot. Autom. **14**(4), 623–629 (2002)
7. Gregor, R., Lutzeler, M., Pellkofer, M., et al.: EMS-Vision: a perceptual system for autonomous vehicles. IEEE Trans. Intell. Transp. Syst. **3**(1), 48–59 (2002)
8. Xu, Z., Stewart, C., Deng, N., et al.: Blending on-demand and spot instances to lower costs for in-memory storage. In: International Conference on Computer Communications, pp. 1–9 (2016)
9. Menze, M., Geiger, A.: Object scene flow for autonomous vehicles. In: Computer Vision and Pattern Recognition, pp. 3061–3070. IEEE (2015)
10. Michalon, G., Auger, G.: Method for the transmission of data among mobile bodies or autonomous vehicles. US, US 5307509 A[P] (1994)
11. Pereira, J.L.F., Rossetti, R.J.F.: An integrated architecture for autonomous vehicles simulation. In: ACM Symposium on Applied Computing, pp. 286–292. ACM (2012)
12. Bojarski, M., Testa, D.D., Dworakowski, D., et al.: End to end learning for selfdriving cars (2016)

13. Al-Shihabi, T., Mourant, R.R.: Toward more realistic driving behavior models for autonomous vehicles in driving simulators. Transp. Res. Rec. J. Transp. Res. Board **1843**(1), 1150–1154 (2003)
14. Jiang, H.Y., Si, Y.P., Luo, X.G.: Medical image segmentation based on improved Ostu algorithm and regional growth algorithm. J. Northeast. Univ. **27**(4), 398–401 (2006)
15. Chua, L.O., Roska, T.: CNN paradigm. IEEE Trans. Circuits Syst. I: Fundam. Theory Appl. **40**(3), 147–156 (1993)
16. Liu, W., et al.: SSD: single shot multibox detector. In: Leibe, B., Matas, J., Sebe, N., Welling, M. (eds.) ECCV 2016. LNCS, vol. 9905, pp. 21–37. Springer, Cham (2016). https://doi.org/10.1007/978-3-319-46448-0_2
17. Xiao, T., Li, S., Wang, B., et al.: End-to-end deep learning for person search (2016)

Research on Dynamic and Static Fusion Polymorphic Gesture Recognition Algorithm for Interactive Teaching Interface

Zhiquan Feng[1,2(✉)], Tao Xu[1,2], Xiaohui Yang[1,2], Jinglan Tian[1,2],
Jiangyan Yi[3], and Ke Zhao[4]

[1] School of Information Science and Engineering,
University of Jinan, Jinan 250022, China
ise_fengzq@ujn.edu.cn
[2] Shandong Provincial Key Laboratory of Network Based Intelligent
Computing, Jinan 250022, China
[3] Institute of Computing Technology Chinese Academy of Sciences,
Beijing 100190, China
[4] Institute of Psychology Chinese Academy of Sciences, Beijing 100101, China

Abstract. In order to solve the problem of teachers' excessive energy dissipation due to interaction with teaching equipment in traditional classrooms, an interactive and intelligent teaching interface is proposed to enable teachers to use the gestures to give students a geometry lesson. The traditional algorithm of gesture recognition mainly consists of feature extraction and classifier, which requires human-designed features. The recognition is mainly based on static gesture or dynamic gesture singular state recognition algorithm. The recognition accuracy is not robust enough and different people Identification results do not have the universality and ease of operation. In order to solve this problem, we propose a multi-state gesture recognition algorithm based on the deep learning network, which combines the large database of hand gestures and the deep learning algorithms. The innovation of this algorithm is as follows: Aiming at the static gesture images, a sequence reduction algorithm is proposed. According to the sequence of dynamic gestures, the first and last frame fixed and intermediate frame traversal combination algorithm are proposed to get the dynamic and static fusion gesture training datasets, and then the dynamic and static fusion datasets are input to the deep learning network GoogLeNet for training. After repeated training, we found the optimal rule of deep learning network training. According to the optimization law, we got GoogLeNet_model which can recognize 23 kinds of dynamic and static fusion gestures, the recognition rate is 97.09%. We use this model in interactive teaching interface, and achieved good application effect.

Keywords: Interactive teaching interface · Gesture database · Deep learning · Dynamic · Static fusion gesture recognition

© Springer Nature Singapore Pte Ltd. 2019
F. Sun et al. (Eds.): ICCSIP 2018, CCIS 1006, pp. 104–115, 2019.
https://doi.org/10.1007/978-981-13-7986-4_10

1 Introduction

With the development of electronic technology and the emergence of electronic audio and video equipment, the form of classrooms has gone through traditional classrooms, electronic classrooms, multimedia classrooms, and today's intelligent classrooms. The application of more and more electronic devices in the classroom makes it necessary for teachers to constantly improve the control skills of these multimedia devices in the teaching process. Even the most widely used electronic whiteboard [1] requires teachers to engage in contact interactions for control purposes. This makes the teacher pay too much attention to the interaction itself, and limited energy can not be fully used for teaching. Therefore, we propose an intelligent teaching interface based on inter-active teaching application, which allows the teacher to use the natural gestures during the lecture to teach the students, without having to focus on the method of interaction. The core of the intelligent teaching system based on interactive gestures is the gesture recognition algorithm [2, 4]. The purpose of this paper is to use a better recognition algorithm for 6 dynamic gestures in interactive teaching interface, to improve the recognition rate and robustness, and to make the whole interactive teaching interface better serve the intelligent teaching system.

At present, the commonly used gesture recognition algorithms need artificial feature extraction and classifier, the robustness and generalization of the recognition results and the recognition rate of multiple types of gestures is difficult to meet the requirements of the intelligent gesture teaching interface. For example, Dardas et al. [5] extracted the scale invariance feature and vectorization feature of the image, and then use the feature packet and the multi class support vector machine [6] to identify the gestures. This method can get better effect of gesture recognition. However, because of the high computational complexity of the SIFT algorithm [7], the recognition speed is slow and the real-time performance is poor. A gesture recognition method based on dynamic programming (DP) is proposed by Kuremoto et al. [8]. First, the skin color region is segmented with hsv-rgb filter, and then a simple motion estimation is made with the retina-v1 model in the 8 neighborhood. Finally, the gesture recognition is carried out by the DP algorithm. Haithamet et al. [9] proposed a method of gesture recognition using neural network. This method extracts geometric moment features and contour features of samples by edge detection, and then uses neural network to identify gestures. This method effectively recognize dynamic gestures and can improve the dynamic gesture recognition accuracy. Li et al. [10] proposed a gesture recognition method using hier-archical elastic graph matching (HEGM). The Boosting algorithm is used to determine the hierarchy of a given graph, and the gradient direction histogram (HOG) is used to extract the visual features. Priyal et al. [11] proposed a static gesture recognition algorithm based on geometric normalization and Krawtchouk moment features. According to the gesture measurement method, the handle is extracted from the hand and forearm regions, and the gesture profile is normalized by the Krawtchouk moment feature and the minimum distance classifier, which can identify small training sample sets very well. Miao et al. [12] proposed a multi-modal gesture recognition method, which first eliminates the mechanism independent of gestures, and then proposed a key frame injection mechanism to find the most representative frames, extract features through Res3d network, and finally mixed them with the canonical correlation analysis. Devineau et al. [13] proposed a new convolutional neural network which uses only the human skeleton sequence to classify and identify. This method is faster than the traditional method of using image sequences. These gesture recognition algorithms have obvious drawbacks: insufficient learning ability, low efficiency, and the correct rate of gesture recognition has certain limitations and does not have universality.

2   The Design and Creation of Interactive Teaching Interface

The interactive intelligent teaching interface proposed in this paper is mainly for the purpose of "letting the teacher can give the students a three-dimensional geometry less hand". Therefore, we designed a geometry class that "proves that the volume of the vertebral body is one-third of the volume of the cylinder." Let the teacher use gestures to control the objects in the OPENGL scene, instead of the traditional PPT lectures, only switch slides, and can not manipulate the geometric objects in the ppt according to the actual impromptu of the lecture. Gestures used in the interface are teachers' customary and subconscious gestures. For example, the left or right hand waving can be used to switch the scene, three finger grasping or placing, the two finger grasping or placing or five fingers grasping or amplifying the geometry in the scene (simulating the object on the touch screen). In this way, teachers do not have to distract too much energy on how to operate various teaching equipment.

On the basis of interactive teaching interface, we fuse the gesture recognition model GoogLeNet_model of dynamic and static fusion, and the application process is shown in Fig. 1.

Input: the dynamic image sequence captured by Kinect.
Output: the teaching interface executes the command.
Step1. After entering the intelligent teaching interface, Kinect continues to capture user gestures.
Step2. The gesture sequence is input into the system, and the input samples are synthesized by preprocessing such as segmentation, normalized size, dynamic and static gesture synthesis algorithm.
Step3. The synthesized pictures are input into the trained deep learning model GoogLeNet_model for identification.
Step4. The interactive interface responds according to the recognized gesture commands.

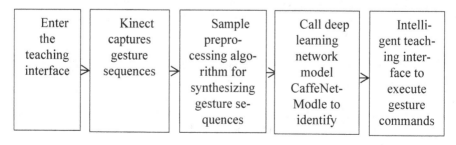

Fig. 1. Operation flow chart of interactive teaching interface

3   The Large Database and Gesture Preprocessing Algorithm

3.1   Database Acquisition and Segmentation Preprocessing Based on Two Thousand People

For the purpose of the interactive teaching interface, we surveyed 50 teachers and students, and counted the natural gestures commonly used by teachers during class, a total of 23 kinds, including 17 static gestures, 6 non-track dynamic gestures. Then, organized 1000 people collected the gesture database, mainly from the freshman to the senior, and also the teacher in the school. The ratio of male to female is even. When the gesture library is collected, we use the Kinect2.0 device to collect, dynamic and static gestures. The pictures are collected separately. In order to avoid the influence of lighting skin color on the gesture picture, and also to avoid the complicated preprocessing work for color RGB images, we select the depth image to establish the large database. It can avoid the influence of complex background and avoid the influence of illumination on the human hand.

For static gestures, the volunteers are about 1.5 m away from Kinect. They naturally extend their hands to face Kinect, make gestures that need to be collected, and then freely rotate the gestures, so that Kinect can capture gestures at different angles, ensuring the gesture library. Diversity. Collect 50 images for each volunteer to build our large database of static gestures.

Dynamic gestures are gestures in which the shape and position of the hand change over time. The expansion of the dynamic gesture by the time axis is a combination of static gesture sequence frames of one frame. Therefore, we use Kinect to collect sequence frames that make up dynamic gestures. For the recognition training of dynamic gestures. we use Kinect 2.0 to collect gestures. Volunteers are about 1.5 m away from Kinect, and naturally extend their hands to face Kinect, making dynamic gestures that need to be collected, Kinect Capture and save sequence frames from start to finish, and then freely transform an angle to make gestures, so Kinect can capture gesture sequence frames at different angles, ensuring the diversity of gesture libraries. Group dynamic gesture sequence, 5 groups are facing Kinect, 5 groups are side to Kinect, in order to build our dynamic gesture large database design of restoration sequence processing algorithm for static gestures

Dynamic and static gestures can be seen as a process on a time series. The difference is that dynamic gestures change in time series, while static gestures are static in time series. For this law, we propose a static gesture set restoration sequence. Processing the algorithm, the specific process is as follows:

Input. The depth map captured by Kinect.
Output. Synthesized static gesture sequence training samples.
Step 1: Kinect captures the depth information and generates a depth map based on the depth information.
Step 2: Kinect obtains the human skeleton information and locks the coordinates of the centroid point of the human hand to determine the position of the human hand.
Step 3: According to the depth information and the position of the centroid point of the human hand, we think that the distance of 3 cm before and after the centroid

point is the human hand area. If it is larger than this threshold, it is not the human hand area. According to this standard, the human hand is cut out from the depth image to generate the human hand.

Step 4: Split the static gesture map according to the bounding box of the human hand in the figure, cut the human hand from the picture, normalize it to the size of 60 * 60, and then perform self-splicing processing, that is, copy the gesture for 3 copies to restore the sequence combination.

3.2 Synthetic Sequence Processing of Dynamic Sequence Gestures

After the dynamic gesture sequence frame is segmented from the depth map of the whole body, it is a set of dynamic gesture sequences. It cannot be directly input into the Caffe platform to train the model we need, and the proportion of the human hand in each picture is too small. It is beneficial for the deep network to extract effective learning features. Therefore, we divide the segmented image into a bounding box to obtain a sequence of images. However, the dynamic image sequence we obtained cannot be directly input into the CNN network for training, so we propose a kind The first and last frames are fixed, and the intermediate frame is traversed in combination (Eq. 1) to preprocess the dynamic gesture sequence frame.

$$F(X,M) = \begin{cases} m = 0, & No\ Done \\ 0 < m < M, & F(X,M) = (x_1, x_m, x_M) \\ m = M, & No\ Done \end{cases} \tag{1}$$

M is the length of each group of picture sequence frames. The specific process of the algorithm is as follows:

Input: the depth map captured by Kinect.

Output: synthetic dynamic gesture sequence training samples.

Step1. Kinect captures depth information and human bone information, and generates a depth map of the human hand based on the depth information and the centroid point coordinates of the human hand.

Step2. Kinect captures the gesture sequence frame and divides the depth image of each frame of the gesture sequence. According to the depth information and the position of the centroid point of the human hand, we think that the distance of 3 cm before and after the centroid point is the human hand area. If it is greater than this threshold, it is not Human hand area. According to this standard, the human hand is cut out from the depth image to generate a depth map of the human hand.

Step3. After obtaining the split gesture, find the bounding box of the gesture picture, divide each picture according to the bounding box, and then zoom to 60 * 60 ps.

Step4. Split the good picture sequence X, obtain the sequence length M of each group of picture sequences, and synthesize the training samples according to the method of formula 1.

3.3 Dynamic and Static Pictures Are Unified and Normalized

After the processing of Sects. 3.2 and 3.3, we can get the dynamic and static gesture normalization sequence (Fig. 2), and the training samples can be trained and recognized uniformly. However, due to the size requirements of the network selected in this paper, need to perform a unified normalization of the image.

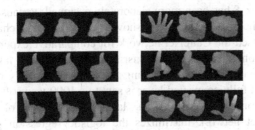

Fig. 2. Dynamic and static fusion training sequence sample display

The processed gesture size is 60 * 180 ps, unified input into MATLAB and normalized size to 200 * 200 ps (Fig. 3), a total of 23 gesture sequences, the number of training for each gesture sequence set, where the training set does not contain a test set.

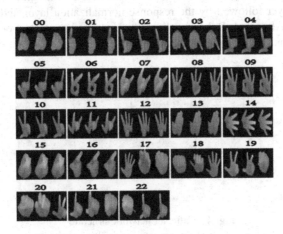

Fig. 3. Example of normalized image sample

3.4 GoogLeNet and CaffeNet

After the introduction of the third chapter, we have unified processing of the static and dynamic images in the gesture database, and restore the static images to dynamic sequences, so that dynamic and static gesture images can be uniformly trained. Training based on the GoogLeNet Inception V3 network for gesture recognition models. GoogLeNet Incepetion v3 is a deep network with more than 130 layers. One of the most important improvements on the basis of V1 and V2 is Factorization, which will be 7 × 7 volumes. The integral is solved into two one-dimensional convolutions (1 × 7, 7 × 1), and the convolution of 3 × 3 is the same (1 × 3, 3 × 1). This has the advantage of speeding up the calculation (excessive computing power can be used to deepen the network), and Splitting 1 conv into 2 convs further increases the network depth and increases the nonlinearity of the network. It is also worth noting that the input of the network has changed from 224 × 224 to 299 × 299, and the module of 35 × 35/17 × 17/8 × 8 has been more elaborately designed. Because the GoogLeNet network is more complex, its structure is shown in the form of a chart.

In addition, we used the CaffeNet network for comparative experiments. CaffeNet was modified based on AlexNet, which consists of eight weighted layers, the first five layers are convolution Layer, and remaining three layers are fully connected layers. The output of the last fully connected layer is sent to a 1000-way softmax layer, which produces a distribution covering 1000 class labels. The 23 types of tags used in this article. The CaffeNet network maximizes the logistic regression goal of multiple classifications, which is equivalent to maximizing the logarithmic probability mean of the correct labels in the training samples under the predicted distribution. The cores of the second, fourth and fifth convolutional layers are only connected to the front. A convolutional layer is also located on those core maps in the same GPU (see Fig. 4). The core of the third convolutional layer is connected to all the core maps in the second convolutional layer. The element is connected to all neurons in the previous layer. The response normalization layer follows the first and second convolutional layers. The largest pooling layer followed by the response normalization layer and the fifth convolutional layer. After that, ReLU nonlinearity is applied to the export of each convolutional layer and fully connected layer.

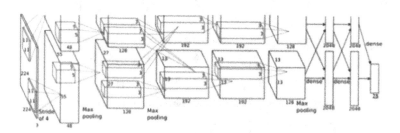

Fig. 4. CaffeNet network structure

3.5   Optimization of Training Parameters for GoogLeNet Network Solver

In Caffe, solver updates the parameters by coordinating Net's Forward Inference and Backward Gradients to reduce the loss. The learning of the Caffe model is divided into two parts: Optimized by Solver, updated parameters, and loss and gradient calculated by Net. We have learned through extensive and iterative training, the value of the training parameters in the solver file during the deep network training model, and the training of the deep learning network model. The result is huge.

We did a lot of experiments on the value of the base learning rate base_lr in solver. In the range of 0.0001–0.9 of the valid value range of base_lr, the CaffeNet and GoogLeNet networks were tested by means of interval sampling, and found along with base_lr. The value of the change, the recognition rate of the highest recognition rate model trained by the two networks shows a regular change, base_lr is used to set the basic learning rate, and in the process of iteration, the basic learning rate can be adjusted to improve the recognition effect of overall network model. Therefore, we follow this rule to find the optimal parameter configuration in the solver file, so as to achieve the purpose of optimizing the deep learning network model.

In addition to the value of base_lr taking samples, the other parameters of our training for gesture recognition pictures are set as follows:

Lr_policy: "poly", gamma: 0.96, power: 1.0, these parameters are set for the learning rate. lr_policy is the adjustment strategy, "poly" is the learning rate for polynomial error, return base_lr (1 - iter/max_iter) ^ (power); momentum: 0.9 refers to the weight of the last gradient update; display: 50 is 50 times per training, displayed once on the screen, if set to 0, it is not displayed; max_iter: 300000 this is the maximum number of iterations. This parameter is set too small, it will lead to no convergence, the accuracy is very low. Setting too large will cause shock and waste time. After repeated experiments, we find that 300 k is the most suitable. weight_decay: 0.0002 is the weight attenuation term, preventing over-fitting one parameter. In the initial data input of the network, in addition to adding the shuffle function when converting the data format, the original data is scrambled, which ensures that the input picture is as diverse as possible, and the efficiency of the model training is improved. In addition to setting the mirror to false in the network, the reason is that the sequence order of each picture represents different gesture types.

4   Experiment and Analysis

The hardware environment is 2xXeon E5-2620 V3 CPU, dual K40 M GPU, 64G memory. The experimental software environment is Win10 64-bit Caffe for Windows + CUDA8.0 + CUDNN7.5 + VS2013. The image (Fig. 3) is captured by the Kinect 2.0. The experimental gesture library is 23 gesture image libraries arranged in this paper. The models used in the experiment include the network model GoogLe_-model before optimization of GoogLeNet network, the optimized model GoogLeNet_model, and the CaffeNet_model after optimization of CaffeNet network.

4.1   Comparison of Recognition Rate Before and After Model Optimization

We've collected 23 gestures from 20 people (Including undergraduate and postgraduate students, proportional to gender balance) each with 100 sets of data (There are two kinds of color RPG and depth graphs, color maps are used for 5.2 contrast test) as explained in Sect. 3. The method collects and processes the pictures, each of which is 100 sheets. The 100 sample maps are not included in the test set and training set used in the training model. The recognition effect before and after the test model optimization (identifying the correct number of pictures/the total sample size, test results are shown in Table 1. According to statistics, before the model optimization, the average recognition rate of 23 non-trajectory gestures was 92.48%. After optimization, the average recognition rate of 23 gestures reached 97.07%, and the recognition rate increased by 4.59%. After testing, the recognition time is 18.98 ms, the rate is very fast, the human eye is almost imperceptible, and used in the interactive intelligent teaching interface, almost no delay, basically realize real-time recognition.

Table 1. Comparison experiment of recognition rate before and after GoogLenet_model optimization.

Gesture number	00	01	02	03	04	05	06	07	08	09	10	11
Recognition rate before model optimized (%)	94	92	91	94	91	93	94	90	91	94	92	95
Recognition rate after model optimized (%)	**100**	**99**	**98**	**97**	**97**	**99**	**96**	**94**	**96**	**97**	**96**	**99**
Gesture Number	12	13	14	15	16	17	18	19	20	21	22	
Recognition rate before model optimized (%)	95	92	93	94	92	90	91	93	94	89	93	
Recognition rate after model optimized (%)	**97**	**95**	**98**	**97**	**96**	**98**	**99**	**95**	**97**	**95**	**96**	

4.2   Comparison with Traditional Methods HCDF and CaffeNet_Model

On this basis, we compare the model recognition rate with that based on the spatial gesture coordinate point distribution feature (HCDF) and the class-Hausdorff distance (hereinafter referred to as HCDF-H) algorithm. The collected 20 students' gesture recognition images were used, CaffeNet_model and GoogLeNet_model used the depth pictures of the 20 students, and the HCDF algorithm used RGB color images. Each algorithm tested 100 pictures for each gesture. Test results as shown in Table 2.

Table 2. Comparison of GoogLeNet_model and CaffeNet_model recognition rate test.

Gesture number	00	01	02	03	04	05	06	07	08	09	10	11
CaffeNet_model(%)	90	81	88	87	88	85	86	86	82	84	85	82
HCDF(%)	95	91	93	88	89	93	92	92	89	91	91	93
Googe-Net_model(%)	**100**	**99**	**98**	**97**	**97**	**99**	**96**	**94**	**96**	**97**	**96**	**99**
Gesture Number	12	13	14	15	16	17	18	19	20	21	22	
CaffeNet_model(%)	81	86	88	87	82	84	88	80	86	81	83	
HCDF(%)	95	93	91	92	89	89	92	94	92	93	91	
GoogLeNet_model(%)	**97**	**95**	**98**	**97**	**96**	**98**	**99**	**95**	**97**	**95**	**96**	

From the comparison of the recognition rates of 23 gestures in Table 2, we calculated that the average recognition rate of CaffeNet_model is 84.78%, and the average recognition rate of HCDF algorithm is 91.65%, while the optimized GoogLeNet_model recognition rate is 97.07% for similar gestures. The recognition rate and robustness are significantly better than CaffeNet-model and the traditional HCDF algorithm. We summarize the two sets of comparison experiments in Fig. 5, which proves the success and usability of the optimization model again. We use GoogLeNet_model for the intelligent teaching of this paper. In the interface, it has achieved good results.

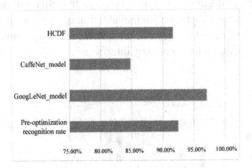

Fig. 5. The average recognition rate of the two groups of comparative experiments.

4.3 User Experience Statistics

We set the four evaluation indicators of fatigue level, effort level, pleasure level and feasibility to evaluate the game. The degree of fatigue is the user's hard work during the user operation; the effort level is the user needs to pay during the operation. How much effort the user needs to pay, the degree of pleasure is the degree of pleasure that the user feels during the operation; the feasibility is the feasibility of the entire interactive interface design for the user. The lower the degree of fatigue and effort, the better the user experience, feasible higher the score of sex and pleasure, the better the user experience. We have designed a three-dimensional geometry class with a triangular pyramid volume of three prisms in two forms. Please experience 50 experience for each of the 50 experience participants.

Fig. 6. Application of gesture recognition algorithm in smart classrooms.

Figure 6 (intelligent teaching system based on interactive teaching interface): using an interactive intelligent teaching interface give the students a geometry lesson. After the experiment is completed, ask the experimenter to follow the above four evaluation indicators for the two versions of the classroom operation. Total is divided into 100 points.

From the results of Fig. 7, the interactive teaching interface based on the interactive evaluation of the four indicators, the degree of fatigue decreased by 46%, the effort reduced by 18.6%, the degree of pleasure increased by 51.8%, and the feasibility analysis, the experience is common It is believed that the interactive teaching interface is completely feasible, and almost everyone believes that this will be a trend in future teaching. This user experience gives a high evaluation of our research. The naturalness and simplicity of the operation Interesting has provided a good development prospect for the research of the interactive teaching interface.

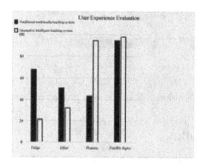

Fig. 7. User experience evaluation statistics.

5   Conclusion

The main innovations of this paper are as follows: (1) Propose an interactive intelligent teaching interface to solve the problem of teachers distracting too much energy in the traditional classroom because of interaction with teaching equipment. (2) This thesis is oriented to interactive teaching. Based on the large database of gestures, this thesis proposes a static gesture segmentation algorithm for static gestures and dynamic gestures. It provides the basis and guarantee for deep learning for gesture recognition research. (3) Based on the large database of gestures and the deep learning network GoogLeNet Inception V3 network, the sequence restoration algorithm for static images in the gesture library is proposed. The first and last frames of the dynamic sequence picture are fixed, and the synthetic sequence algorithm of the intermediate frame traversal combination is proposed. Based on this, a dynamic recognition model based on the deep learning network is proposed. The optimized deep learning model can uniformly identify the dynamic and static gestures. And the recognition rate is as high as 97.09%, and it has been successfully applied in the interactive intelligent teaching interface. Through the intelligent teaching interface, the teacher can use the gesture to operate the interactive interface, and the student can use the above-mentioned three-dimensional geometry class, the teacher can use the gestures to directly manipulate the OPENGL scene and the objects in the scene to give the students a demonstration, giving the students direct visual impact, and also allowing the teacher to focus on the teaching content itself rather than the interaction itself.

Acknowledgement. This paper is supported by the National Key R&D Program of China (No. 2018YFB1004901) and the National Natural Science Foundation of China (No. 61472163, 61603151).

References

1. Kong, J., Zhao, J., Liu, J.: Interactive whiteboard supports the process of inquiry learning activities. Audio-Visual Educ. Res. (12), 86–92 (2014)
2. Qian, H.: Augmented Reality Education Aid System Using Kinect and Gesture Recognition. Shanghai Jiaotong University (2011)
3. Wang, X.: Research on Intelligent Classroom Gesture Recognition Algorithm and Interactive Prototype System Design. Xidian University (2009)
4. Zabulis, X., Baltzakis, H., Argyros, A.A.: Vision-based hand gesture recognition for human computer interaction. In: The Universal Access Handbook, chap. 34, pp. 1–30 (2009)
5. Dardas, N.H., Georganas, N.D.: Real-time hand gesture detection and recognition using bag-of-features and support vector machine techniques. IEEE Trans. Instrum. Meas. **60**, 3592–3607 (2011)
6. Weston, J., Watkins, C.: Support vector machines for multi-class pattern recognition. In: Proceedings of the seventh European symposium on artificial neural networks, Bruges, pp. 219–224 (1999)
7. Lowe, D.G.: Distinctive image features from scale-invariant keypoints. Int. J. Comput. Vis. **60**, 91–110 (2004)
8. Kuremoto, T., Kinoshita, Y., Feng, L., et al.: A gesture recognition system with retina-V1 model and one-pass dynamic programming. Neurocomputing **116**, 291–300 (2013)
9. Haitham, H., Abdul-Kareem, S.: Static hand gesture recognition using neural networks. Artif. Intell. Rev. **41**, 1–35 (2012)
10. Li, Y.T., Wachs, J.P.: HEGM: a hierarchical elastic graph matching for hand gesture recognition. Pattern Recogn. **47**, 80–88 (2014)
11. Priyal, S.P., Bora, P.K.: A robust static hand gesture recognition system using geometry based normalizations and Krawtchouk moments. Pattern Recogn. **46**, 2202–2219 (2013)
12. Miao, Q., et al.: Multimodal gesture recognition based on the ResC3D network. In: 2017 IEEE International Conference on Computer Vision Workshops (ICCVW), Venice, pp. 3047–3055 (2017)
13. Devineau, G., Moutarde, F., Xi, W., Yang, J.: Deep learning for hand gesture recognition on skeletal data. In: 2018 13th IEEE International Conference on Automatic Face & Gesture Recognition (FG 2018), pp. 106–113 (2018)

RBF Network Imitation Posture Judgment Algorithm Based on Improved PSO

Shuhuan Wen[1(✉)], Xiaohan Lv[1], Fuchun Sun[2], and Leibo Zheng[1]

[1] Department of Key Lab of Industrial Computer Control Engineering of Hebei Province, Yanshan University, Qinhuangdao 066004, China
swen@ysu.edu.cn, 635987378@qq.com, zlb_ysu@163.com
[2] Department of Computer Science and Technology,
State Key Lab of Intelligent Technology and Systems, Tsinghua University,
Beijing 100084, People's Republic of China
fcsun@tsinghua.edu.cn

Abstract. In this paper, because the robot is easy to fall during the imitation process, a novel Radical Basis Function (RBF) neural network algorithm based on heuristic simulated annealing adaptive particle swarm optimization Particle Swarm Optimization (PSO) algorithm is proposed to judge the mimic posture of the robot. In order to solve the problem of poor convergence speed and low accuracy of traditional RBF neural network, the PSO algorithm is used to optimize it. At the same time, in order to solve the problem that the classical PSO algorithm is easy to fall into the local optimal value, heuristic simulated annealing adaptive PSO algorithm is proposed. Experiment shows that the proposed algorithm has higher convergence speed and accuracy than BP neural network, Support Vector Machines (SVM) and traditional RBF neural network.

Keywords: Humanoid robot · Imitation · RBF neural network

1 Introduction

Today, in the rapid development of the humanoid robot industry, how to make robots better integrated into the human social environment has become a key issue facing the development of robots [1,2]. A friendly interaction will make the robot better to get along with humans. Traditional human-computer interaction achieves robotic control by a professional researcher, using a specific programming language and a large amount of time [3]. Therefore, robots exist only in scientific research institutions and laboratories, and cannot be applied to various fields of society.

In recent years, computer peripheral devices have developed at a high speed, and various types of visual and voice sensors have become more and more mature.

© Springer Nature Singapore Pte Ltd. 2019
F. Sun et al. (Eds.): ICCSIP 2018, CCIS 1006, pp. 116–126, 2019.
https://doi.org/10.1007/978-981-13-7986-4_11

Then the way of human-computer interaction has gradually diversified. Human-computer interaction technologies relying on visual and voice gradually emerged, such as face recognition, gesture recognition, speech recognition, etc. These technologies make the communication between humans and robots more and more humanized and convenient [4]. Among them, imitation learning is one of the simplest and the most friendly human-computer interaction mode.

Compared with the traditional human-computer interaction mode, imitation learning enables the robot to acquire the ability of self-learning. The control of the robot no longer requires a lot of time for the professional to achieve, which is very helpful for the application of the robot in various fields [5]. At present, there have been many outstanding achievements in the study of robotic imitation learning.

Kulic et al. used the method of body marking to study robotic imitation [6]. Since the marker points are highly susceptible to occlusion, it is difficult to deal with this problem solely by means of image processing. Moreover, it is necessary to mark the key positions of the human body before each imitation, and the operation steps are relatively complicated. Therefore, the convenience and reliability of the method need to be improved. Koenemann et al. used a wearable device to study robotic imitation [7]. However, since the apparatus used in this method is too expensive and the action after wearing is not convenient, the practicality of the method needs to be improved. Li et al. used the method of human body part detection and image segmentation to realize the imitation of the robot [8]. Zhu et al. studied the spatiotemporal consistency of robot imitation [9], and improved the spatiotemporal consistency and motion smoothness of robot imitation. Yu et al. used the method of centroid compensation to ensure the balance in the robot imitation process [10], which achieves the balance of robotic imitation. Stadie et al. proposed an unsupervised the third-person imitation learning method that solved the simple third-person imitation task [11].

Throughout the development history and research status of humanoid robot imitation learning, people mainly studied from two aspects. One is the spatiotemporal consistency of robot imitation. People use different hardware and different algorithms to conduct a lot of research on the spatiotemporal consistency of robot imitation learning, and also put forward many effective methods. The other is the performance optimization of imitation learning. The purpose of robot imitation is to learn, its security needs to be concerned. People have studied from the perspective of robot safety and self-collision.

At present, most of the research on robot safety is kinematics modeling. However, the quality and centroid position of each link of the robot is difficult to obtain. Each link of the robot is regarded as a cylinder of uniform quality. However, this method greatly reduces the accuracy of the model, the experimental results are often not ideal [12]. So this paper intends to determine whether the robot falls by using a machine learning method.

Due to the structural difference between the robot and the human body, in the process of robot imitation, it is easy to cause the center of gravity unstable and falling, so that the imitation task cannot continue or even damage the robot.

The robot falls or not refers to whether the current posture of the robot can stand stably. It is divided into two states: falling and not falling, which is a binary classification problem. Based on the imitation action, this paper adds online judgment of machine learning. Before the computer transmits the motion command to the robot, the motion sequence is predicted to ensure the stability of the robot, thereby avoiding the falling of the robot and ensuring the safety of the robot.

Neural network is a mathematical model that simulates the structure of biological neural networks. Because of its advantages of self-adaptation and self-learning, neural network is widely used in the fields of automatic control, pattern recognition, advertising recommendation, searching optimization and so on. There are currently dozens of shallow neural network models, including BP neural network, RBF neural network, self-organizing neural network [13], Hopfield network [14] and so on. Among them, BP neural network and RBF neural network are popular among scientific researchers because of their stability and feasibility.

Statistical Learning Theory (SLT) is established by Vapnik [15]. The theory is based on the statistical methods and explores the machine learning principles under the condition of limited sample space capacity. Support vector machine (SVM) is a machine learning method based on SLT, and has been widely studied and applied due to its fast training speed and high accuracy.

In this paper, RBF neural network is used to determine whether imitation action of the robot will cause the falling. Aiming at the problem of poor convergence speed and low accuracy of RBF neural network, PSO algorithm is used to optimize it. At the same time, an improved PSO algorithm is proposed to solve the problem of the local optimum for classical PSO algorithm, which can improve the convergence speed and accuracy of the improved RBF neural network, and compare with the BP neural network and the SVM.

2   RBF Neural Network Algorithm Based on Improved Particle Swarm Optimization

Because traditional RBF neural network has insufficient accuracy, slow convergence rate and easy overfitting, this section uses Particle Swarm Optimization (PSO) algorithm to optimize the RBF neural network. At the same time, because the classical PSO algorithm is easy to fall into the local optimum, PSO algorithm based on heuristic simulated annealing is proposed. And combined with RBF neural network, the convergence speed and accuracy of the model are improved, and the overfitting phenomenon is avoided.

2.1   Adaptive PSO Algorithm Based on Heuristic Simulated Annealing Algorithm

Because classical PSO algorithm is easy to fall into the local optimum, this paper proposes an adaptive particle swarm optimization algorithm based on heuristic simulated annealing algorithm. In the early stage of the algorithm, w is given a larger value, which can improve the convergence speed of the algorithm and be easy to jump out of the local optimum. As the iteration number of the algorithm increases, w is gradually attenuated, which can allow the algorithm to improve the search accuracy in the later stage, and finally obtain a more accurate algorithm model. Specific steps are as follows:

(1) Within the search space, randomly initialize the position $X_i = (x_1, x_2, \cdots, x_N)$ and velocity $V_i = (v_1, v_2, \cdots, v_N)$ of each particle.
(2) Calculate the fitness of each particle based on the fitness function.
(3) If the ith particle position is better than all previous positions, then the current position is the historical best position $\widehat{p_i}$ of the particle. If the current position of a particle is better than the historical best position of all particles, then it is noted that the particle is the best position of the particle group history as $\widehat{g}$.
(4) The inertia weight w is updated according to the heuristic simulated annealing formula $w = w/(1 + kd)$.
(5) Update the movement speed of each particle according to the formula $v_i = wv_i + c_1 r_1(\widehat{p_i} - x_i) + c_2 r_2(\widehat{g} - x_i)$.
(6) Update the position of each particle according to the formula $x_i = x_{i-1} + v_i$.
(7) Iterate the steps (2)–(6) until the end condition is met.

where k is the number of iterations; d is the attenuation coefficient, indicating the decay rate of the weight, which is generally 10^{-3}.

Figure 2 shows the global optimization process of the improved PSO algorithm in two dimensions, and the blue four-pointed star is the two optimized particles of the improved PSO algorithm. It can be seen that the particle velocity is greatly affected by its own historical speed in the initial iteration of the improved PSO algorithm, and has the characteristics of high convergence speed and is easy to jump out of local optimum. With the iteration, the weight gradually decreases. The proportion of particle velocity updating influenced by self-recognition and social experience increases and a more accurate location updating is obtained. It causes the particles to gradually stabilize at the global optimal solution shown in the purple four-pointed star.

The fitness curve comparison of the traditional classical PSO algorithm with the improved PSO algorithm is shown in Fig. 3. Compared with the classical PSO algorithm, the improved PSO algorithm has faster convergence speed in the early stage and higher accuracy in the later stage.

2.2 RBF Neural Network Algorithm Based on Heuristic Simulated Annealing Adaptive PSO

In order to improve the convergence speed and accuracy of RBF neural network, in this paper, the RBF neural network is optimized by the PSO algorithm based on heuristic simulated annealing algorithm. The specific implementation steps are as follows:

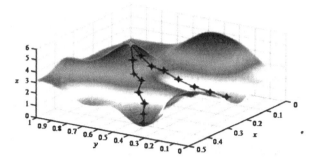

Fig. 1. Local optimal solution of PSO algorithm

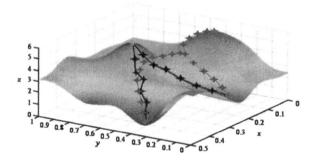

Fig. 2. Global optimization process of improved PSO algorithm (Color figure online)

(1) Load training samples and sample tags.

14 degrees of freedom which effects the falling of the robot greatly is regarded as a model input, and the falling judgment of the robot is regarded as the output of the model.

(2) Data normalization.

In order to improve the training speed and generalization ability of the network model, the normalization of data is required before training. The sample data is normalized to the (0, 1) interval, and the lower and upper values are 0 and 1 respectively. Then normalization is performed by

$$F(x) = \sum_{i=1}^{N} w_i R_i(x) \tag{1}$$

(3) Pre-training of the RBF neural networks.

In order to obtain the solution space of PSO algorithm, K-means algorithm is used to train the RBF neural network, and the initial model of RBF neural network is obtained.

(4) Optimization of RBF neural networks.

The steps of optimizing RBF neural network model by adaptive PSO are as follows:

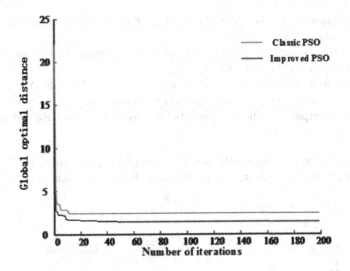

Fig. 3. Convergence process of classical PSO algorithm and improved PSO algorithm

(1) Establish the mapping relationship between the output weight of RBF neural network and the PSO particle dimension. Set the parameters according to the classical PSO algorithm parameter set, that is $c_1 = 2.8$, $c_2 = 1.3$ and $N = 30$. Since the PSO typically achieves better results within 500 iterations, the maximum number of iterations is set to 500. The initial position $X_i = (x_1, x_2, \cdots, x_N)$ and the initial velocity $V_i = (v_1, v_2, \cdots, v_N)$ are randomly assigned to 30 particles.

(2) The fitness function is used to calculate the fitness of each particle. The fitness function formula is

$$f_i = \frac{1}{1 + D(x_{i1}, x_{i2}, \cdots, x_{iM})} \tag{2}$$

where, $M = h(N + 1)$, h is the number of hidden layer nodes, and N is the number of particles.

$$D = \frac{1}{p} \sum_{j=1}^{p} \sum_{i=1}^{m} (y_{ji} - \widehat{y}_{ji})^2 \tag{3}$$

is the mean square error between the actual output and the desired output of RBF neural network. p is the total number of samples, and m is the number of output layer nodes.

(3) Compare the current fitness with the historical best fitness of each particle. If the current fitness is better, update the historical best position $\widehat{p}_i$ to the current position.

(4) Compare the current fitness of each particle with the historical best fitness of the particle swarm. If the current fitness is better, update the particle swarm historical optimal position $\widehat{g}$ to the current position.

(5) The inertia weight w is updated according to the heuristic simulated annealing formula $w = w/(1 + kd)$.
(6) Update the movement speed of each particle according to the formula $v_i = wv_i + c_1r_1(\widehat{p_i} - x_i) + c_2r_2(\widehat{g} - x_i)$.
(7) Update the position of each particle according to the formula $x_i = x_{i-1} + v_i$.
(8) Iterate the steps (2)–(6) until the end condition is met.
(9) The test sample and the sample label are loaded to evaluate the accuracy of the optimized model.

The error curves of PSO-RBF neural network and the improved PSO-RBF neural network on the training set under the different iteration times are shown in Fig. 4.

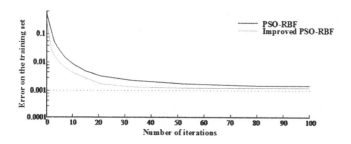

Fig. 4. Error comparison of improved PSO-RBF and PSO-RBF error under the different iterations on training set

It can be seen from the figure that the improved PSO-RBF neural network has faster convergence speed and higher nonlinear learning ability than the traditional PSO-RBF neural network.

The error comparison between the 200 randomly selected samples on the test set in the improved PSO-RBF neural network and the traditional neural network is shown in Fig. 5. It can be seen that compared with the traditional PSO-RBF neural network, the improved PSO-RBF neural network has a significant improvement in accuracy.

3   Experimental Research

In order to illustrate the effectiveness of the proposed algorithm, BP neural network, SVM, and the traditional RBF neural network methods are compared with the PSO-RBF neural network based on heuristic simulated annealing proposed in this paper.

According to the research task of this paper, a three-layer BP neural network is designed. The input is 14 degrees of freedom that have a greater impact on robot falling. The output is the falling judgement of the robot, and is encoded with one-hot. The model input of imitation attitude based on the SVM also is 14

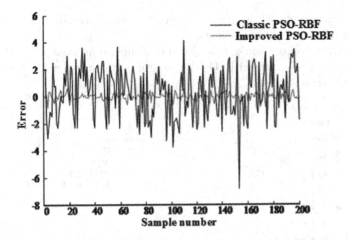

Fig. 5. Error comparison between the improved PSO-RBF and the PSO-FBF

degrees of freedom influencing robot falling. The output is whether the current posture will cause the robot to fall, and is encoded with one-hot. At the same time, in order to improve the speed and accuracy of the model training, the sample data is normalized. The data is scaled to the $[-1, 1]$ interval, so the lower and the upper are -1 and 1 respectively.

3.1   Imitative Posture Judgment of the RBF Neural Network Based on Heuristic Adaptive PSO

The error curve of the PSO-RBF neural network and the improved PSO-RBF neural network in the test set under the different iteration times is shown in Fig. 6.

In Fig. 6, the improved PSO-RBF neural network has higher accuracy and better generalization ability. As the number of iterations increases, the improved

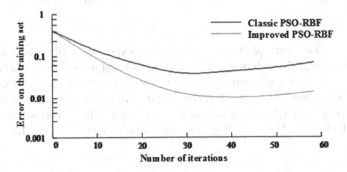

Fig. 6. Error comparison of classical PSO-RBF and improved PSO-RBF under the different iterations in the test set

RBF-PSO neural network gradually approaches the optimal value due to the attenuation of the weight coefficients.

The accuracy comparison of traditional RBF neural network, PSO-RBF neural network and the improved PSO-RBF neural network under different hidden layer nodes is shown in Fig. 7.

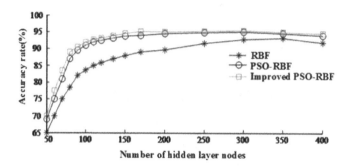

Fig. 7. Comparison of accuracy between RBF, PSO-RBF and improved PSO-RBF

In Fig. 7, the improved PSO-RBF neural network has higher accuracy than the traditional RBF neural network and the PSO-RBF neural network, and it can be up to 95.4%.

As shown in Table 1, all kinds of machine learning models are adjusted to the best parameters. Compared with BP neural network, SVM, RBF neural network, PSO-RBF and other machine learning models, the improved PSO-RBF neural network has higher accuracy and ensures the safety of robot mimicking tasks. However, the accuracy rate still needs to be further improved.

Table 1. Accuracy comparison of various machine learning models

Algorithm model	BP neural network	SVM	RBF neural network	PSO-RBF	Improved PSO-RBF
Accuracy rate (%)	91.8	92.6	93.2	95.0	95.4

Figure 8 is the photo of the robot imitation experiment process using RBF neural network algorithm based on heuristic simulated annealing adaptive PSO. The values of 14 joint angle corresponding to the action of the robot is input, and the falling judgment of the robot is the output. After the judgment is made by the improved PSO-RBF neural network, the robot predicts whether the action will be performed stably, so falling is avoided due to instability of the center of gravity.

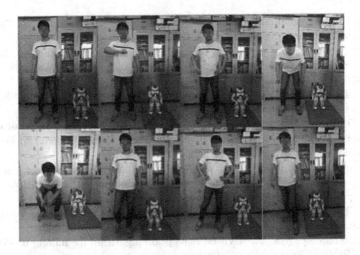

Fig. 8. Robot imitation experiment of the RBF neural network determination method based on heuristic simulated annealing PSO

4   Conclusion

Aiming at the problem that the humanoid robot is easy to fall during the imitation process, RBF neural network algorithm based on simulated annealing adaptive PSO is proposed and used to judge the stable state of mimicking action of the robot. Because of the problems of slow convergence and low accuracy of traditional BP neural network, SVM and RBF neural networks, PSO algorithm is used to optimize RBF neural network. At the same time, the classical PSO algorithm is easy to fall into the local optimal solution, so the PSO algorithm based on heuristic simulated annealing is proposed to improve the convergence speed and accuracy of the RBF neural network. Experiments show that the RBF neural network algorithm based on improved PSO has higher convergence speed and model accuracy than traditional BP neural network, SVM and RBF neural networks.

Acknowledgements. This work was partly supported by the National Natural Science Foundation of China (Project No. 61773333, 61473248), and the major project of Science and technology in Hebei Provincial Education Department (Project No. ZD2016150).

References

1. Huang, D.W., Katz, G., Langsfeld, J., et al.: A virtual demonstrator environment for robot imitation learning. In: 2015 IEEE International Conference on Technologies for Practical Robot Applications, Wobum, USA, pp. 1–6 (2015)
2. Liu, H.Y., Wang, W.J., Wang, R.J., et al.: Image recognition and force measurement application in the humanoid robot imitation. IEEE Trans. Instrum. Meas. **61**(1), 149–161 (2012)

3. Shihai, D.: Progress and challenge of human-computer interaction. J. Comput.-Aided Des. Comput. Graph. **16**(1), 1–13 (2004)
4. Finn, C., Levine, S.: Deep visual foresight for planning robot motion. In: 2017 IEEE International Conference on Robotics and Automation, Wobum, USA, pp. 2786–2793 (2017)
5. Hu, X., Li, B., Zhao, Y., et al.: Humanoid robot using Kinect sensor, Electronic Measurement Technology (2017)
6. Kulic, D., Lee, D., et al.: Incremental learning of full body motion primitives for humanoid robots. In: Humanoids 2008-8th IEEE-RAS International Conference on Humanoid Robots, pp. 326–332 (2008)
7. Koenemann, J., Bennewitz, M.: Whole-body imitation of human motions with a Nao humanoid. In: ACM/IEEE International Conference on Human-Robot Interaction, pp. 425–425. IEEE (2012)
8. Li, S., Zhao, Y., Zhao, Q., et al.: Algorithm of human posture action recognition and imitation for robots. Comput. Eng. **39**(8), 181–186 (2013)
9. Zhu, T., Zhao, Q., Xia, Y.: A visual perception algorithm for human motion by a Kinect. ROBOT **36**(6), 647–653 (2014)
10. Yu, J., Zhang, Y., Zuo, G., et al.: Humanoid robot imitation learning based on COM correction and compensation. J. Beijing Univ. Technol. **44**(2), 193–199 (2018)
11. Stadie, B.C., Abbeel, P., Sutskever, I.: Third-person imitation learning. Comput. Sci. **23**(6), 1–16 (2017)
12. Yang, P.C., Sasaki, K., Suzuki, K., et al.: Repeatable folding task by humanoid robot worker using deep learning. IEEE Robot. Autom. Lett. **15**(99), 1 (2017)
13. Kohonen, T.: Self-organized formation of topologically correct feature maps. Biol. Cybern. **43**(1), 59–69 (1982)
14. Hopfield, J.J.: Neural networks and physical systems with emergent collective computational abilities. Proc. Natl. Acad. Sci. U. S. A. **79**(8), 2554–2558 (1982)
15. Vapnik, V.N.: The nature of statistical learning theory. IEEE Trans. Neural Netw. **8**(6), 1564–1564 (2002)

Path Planning of Maritime Autonomous Surface Ships in Unknown Environment with Reinforcement Learning

Chengbo Wang[1], Xinyu Zhang[1]([⊠]), Ruijie Li[1], and Peifang Dong[2]

[1] Key Laboratory of Marine Simulation and Control for Ministry of Communications, Dalian Maritime University, Dalian, China
wangcb@dlmu.edu.cn, zhang.xinyu@sohu.com
[2] School of Mechanical Engineering,
Nanjing University of Science and Technology, Nanjing, China

Abstract. Recently, artificial intelligence algorithms represented by reinforcement learning and deep learning have promoted the development of autonomous driving technology. For the shipping industry, research and development of maritime autonomous surface ships (MASS) has academic value and practical significance. In an unknown environment, MASS interacts with the environment to conduct behavioral decisions-making, intelligent collision avoidance, and path planning. Reinforcement learning balances exploration and exploitation to improve its own behavior by interacting with the environment to obtain rewarded data. Thus, to achieve intelligent collision avoidance and path planning for MASS in unknown environments, a path planning algorithm of MASS based on reinforcement learning is established. Firstly, the research status of unmanned ships and reinforcement learning is reviewed. The four basic elements of reinforcement learning are analyzed: environment model, incentive function, value function and strategy. Secondly, the port environment model, sensor model, MASS behavioral space, reward function, and action selection strategy were designed separately. Besides, the reward function consists of avoiding obstacles and approaching the target point. Finally, based on the python and pygame platform, a simulation experiment was carried out with Rizhao Harbor District as a case study to verify that this method has better self-adaptability. The model successfully avoids obstacles through online trial and error self-learning and plans adaptive paths in unknown environments.

Keywords: Reinforcement learning · Collision avoidance · Path planning · Maritime autonomous surface ships

1 Introduction

With the rapid development of artificial intelligence, unmanned technologies can better serve various fields, including environmental monitoring, object tracking, industrial manufacturing, and hazardous environment exploration. From mobile robots to drones and unmanned boats, the path planning technology has been continuously improved and matured. However, for marine autonomous systems, path planning and obstacle avoidance are new research subjects and hot topics for scholars and experts.

© Springer Nature Singapore Pte Ltd. 2019
F. Sun et al. (Eds.): ICCSIP 2018, CCIS 1006, pp. 127–137, 2019.
https://doi.org/10.1007/978-981-13-7986-4_12

Path planning is one of the key technologies of the Marine Autonomous System (MAS). Its essence is to avoid obstacles and reach the target point with the optimal path. According to the degree of knowledge of the environmental information, the path planning is divided into a global path planning based on prior knowledge of the environment or an expert system, and a local path planning based on perception information. The disadvantage of the global path planning based on expert system is that it is difficult to obtain information on the marine environment. It is difficult to form a complete and accurate knowledge base and expert system, and it cannot meet online learning. Local path planning requires sensors to acquire environmental information in real time, real-time positioning of unmanned ships, determining the distribution of local obstacles, and calculating an optimal path online. At present, in the field of mobile robots, drones and unmanned boats, effective path planning methods include artificial potential field method, neural network method, fuzzy logic and genetic algorithm. Among them, Chen, Qi, Zhang [1] and others proposed that the improved artificial potential field method avoids the problem of the local minimum point of the unmanned boat and realizes the path planning of the unmanned boat. The effectiveness of the method is verified by simulation. Guo and Wang [2] and others proposed an improved quantum particle swarm optimization algorithm based on modified particle update location, which improved the global optimization ability and convergence performance of UAV path planning algorithms. Yan, Huang, Zhu et al. [3] proposed an underwater robot path planning method based on biological neural dynamics, and Yan simulated and implemented tasks such as autonomous planning of observation paths, return routes, and obstacle avoidance in unknown dynamic underwater environments. The multi-objective genetic algorithm for the local path planning of surface water unmanned boats was designed by Chen [4], taking the shortest local route and the minimum heading variation as the optimization objectives, and the ship's close encounter distance model and the "International Convention on the rules of collision avoidance by sea in 1972" are the constraints.

However, these methods usually need to assume complete environmental information. However, MAS in unknown environments rarely have prior knowledge of the environment. In large number of practical applications, the system needs a strong ability to adapt to uncertain environments. Reinforcement Learning has the advantage of interacting with the environment. Reinforcement learning completes online learning through trial and error algorithms, meeting adaptive learning without prior knowledge of the environment. Duan, Zhang, and Zhang [5] proposed a fuzzy control rule that can realize real-time motion planning of underwater robots based on reinforcement learning self-learning and self-adjusting planning algorithms. Liang [6] proposed an autonomous learning method based on Q-learning algorithm to solve the problem of adaptive path planning for mobile robots in unknown environments, and they completed adaptive path planning through simulation experiments. Zhao, Zheng, Zhang, Liu [7] and others used adaptive and random detection methods (ARE) to complete the mission of UAV navigation and obstacle avoidance, and the UAV path planning is realized with reinforcement learning. Konar, Chakraborty, Singh [8] and others used Q-learning four derived features to propose a new deterministic Q-learning algorithm for path planning of mobile robots, and simulations validated the modified algorithm applicability in path planning. A model-based reinforcement learning algorithm - Dyna-Q algorithm was proposed by Hwang, Jiang, Chen [9] et al. KS Hwang extracts status information between virtual neighbors for indirect learning and combines depth-first search methods to solve the problem of path planning and labyrinth of mountain bikes. Cruz and Yu [10] and others proposed a modified multi-agent reinforcement learning algorithm to perform greedy search by estimating unknown environmental information combined with neural networks and kernel smoothing techniques to implement multi-agent path planning.

The above domestic and foreign route planning methods have achieved good results in the fields of mobile robots, unmanned aerial vehicles and unmanned boats, but they are still at a preliminary stage of research in the intelligent navigation and route planning of MAS. In response to these challenges, this paper will innovate the application of reinforcement learning to the path planning of MAS of unmanned cargo ships. This article uses reinforcement learning selection strategies to complete obstacle avoidance for unmanned cargo ships, realizing the adaptive path planning of Rizhao Port area under the unknown prior knowledge.

2 Reinforcement Learning and Basic Elements

2.1 Reinforcement Learning Principle

Reinforcement learning is also known as enhanced learning and further learning [11]. Unmanned ships learn online by interacting with the environment in a reinforcement learning system. Figure 1 shows the reinforcement learning schematic. In reinforcement learning, MASS selects an action A_t based on the current state S_t and has an impact on the environment. MASS receive environmental feedback R_t (award or punishment). The MASS selects the next action based on the current feedback signal and the environment. The principle of choice is to maximize the probability of positive feedback from the environment. In simple terms, the purpose of reinforcement learning is to choose an optimal strategy that maximizes the total return of unmanned ships in interaction with the environment.

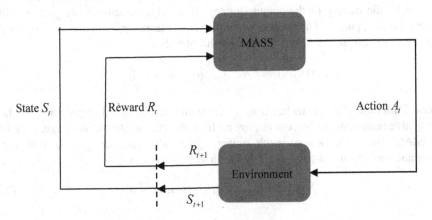

Fig. 1. The reinforcement learning schematic.

Reinforcement learning in discrete time can essentially be regarded as Markov Decision Process (MDP). A Markov decision process for MAS is defined by the following five-tuple: (S, A, P_a, R_a, γ). S represents the limited state space of the unmanned ship; A represents the action space of the unmanned ship, that is, the collection of all the behavior spaces of the unmanned ship in any state, such as left rudder, right rudder, acceleration, deceleration, follow-up, and ship stopping. $P_a(s, s') = P(s'|s, a)$ is a conditional probability that represents the probability that the unmanned ship will reach the next state s' under state s and action a. $R_a(s, s')$ is reward function that represents the incentive obtained from the state s to the state s' of an unmanned ship under action a. $\gamma \in (0, 1)$ is the attenuation factor of the reward, and the reward at the next moment is attenuated according to this factor [12, 13].

Currently used reinforcement learning algorithms include Q-Learning, SARSA-Learning, TD-Learning, and adaptive dynamic programming [14]. This article uses Q-Learning online learning algorithm. Q-Learning is considered as an incremental dynamic programming. By optimizing the action function to find the optimal strategy, the expectation of cumulative returns is maximized. The Q-Learning algorithm not only satisfies the adaptability of the system in the environment, but also ensures that the algorithm converges in the learning process [15].

2.2   Basic Elements of Reinforcement Learning Model

In the reinforcement learning of MAS, in addition to the unmanned ship and the environment, there are four major elements [15]: environment model, reward function R, value function $Q(s)$ and strategy π.

Environment Model. MASS environment models include unmanned ships, obstacles, starting points, target points, and sensors. In the environment model, the MASS acquires information on obstacles and target points through the sensors. After executing the search strategy, the model will make feedback to judge the rewards and punishments of the action strategies.

Reward Function. The reward function is the enhanced signal fed back by the environment after the MASS's action strategy interacts with the environment. It is used to evaluate the quality of the action strategy. If it helps to achieve the goal, it will reward. Instead, punish. The purpose of reinforcement learning is to choose the optimal strategy to maximize the ultimate return of the MASS.

$$r(s_t, a_t) = \mathbb{E}_{P(s_{t+1}|s_t, a_t)}[r(s_t, a_t, s_{t+1})] \tag{1}$$

Value Function. The value function refers to the mathematical expectation of the cumulative returns in the process of moving from the current state to the target state of the MASS under the action search strategy. The value function $Q^\pi(s, a) \in \mathbb{R}$ will determine the action search strategy of the driverless system.

$$Q^\pi(s, a) = \mathbb{E}_{P^\pi(t)}[G(t)|s_1 = s, a_1 = a] \tag{2}$$

Strategy. The problem to be solved in the path planning of MASS is to find an optimal "strategy", to make the greatest return. Essentially, the strategy is a mapping of the state S of MASS to the action A, denoted as $\pi : S \rightarrow A$.

$$\pi^* = \arg \max_{\pi} \mathbb{E}_{P^{\pi}(t)}[G(t)] \tag{3}$$

3 Design of MASS Track Decision Model

3.1 Environmental Model Establishment

This research builds a two-dimensional simulation environment based on python and pygame. In the two-dimensional coordinate system, each coordinate point corresponds to a state of MASS. Each state can be mapped to each element of the set of environmental states S. In the simulation environment model, there are two state values for each coordinate point, which are 1 and 0, respectively, where 1 represents the navigable area, which is displayed as a white area in the environmental model; 0 represents the area of the obstacle and is shown as a black area in the environmental model. Figure 2 shows the simulation environment model, which simulates the two-dimensional map of the environment state size 656×808. In the environmental model, obstacles such as static ships, breakwaters, and basin foundations were simulated, which positional information is unknown to MASS.

Fig. 2. The simulation environment.

3.2 Expression of Action Space

After setting the initial point and target point of the MASS, it is considered as a mass point during the simulation. The autonomous navigation of MASS is a continuous state during the actual navigation. Thus, research needs to generalize the observational behavior of MASS O into discrete actions $\hat{A} = Generalization(A', O)$. Generally, the search movement of MASS is four discrete actions: up, down, left, and right. When the environment appears corners, the searching behavior in the diagonal direction is increased.

Focusing on the unmanned ship's particle quality, the study defines the actual operational space model of MASS as eight discrete actions: up, down, left, right, $up_{-45°}$, $up_{+45°}$, $down_{+45°}$, $down_{-45°}$. That is the matrix of formula (4):

$$A = [-1,1 \quad 0,1 \quad 1,1 \quad -1,0 \quad 1,0 \quad -1,-1 \quad 0,-1 \quad 1,-1] \qquad (4)$$

3.3   Design of Reward Function

The reward function plays an important role in the reinforcement learning system of MASS. Function can be used to evaluate the effectiveness of decision-making of MASS and the safety of obstacle avoidance. It is search-oriented. For MASS, the reward function consists of safety, comfort, and arrival targets. In designing the reward function, the following elements should be considered as much as possible [16]:

Approaching Target Point. Searching behavior of MASS with reinforcement learning in unknown environmental conditions should bring MASS closer to the target point. Closer to the incentive function will choose rewards, otherwise it will punish:

$$R_{distance} = -\lambda_{distance} \sqrt{(x - x_{goal})^2 + (y - y_{goal})^2} \qquad (5)$$

Safety. In the Q-Learning algorithm model, the unknown environment where the MASS is located is divided into state spaces, which are divided into safety state areas and obstacle areas. The MASS should select the action search strategy that satisfies the safety of the ship in the local area of obstacles, and avoid the obstacles "early, clear, and large". Thus, in the reward function, the penalty value will be added to the behavior near the obstacle, and vice versa. This paper generalizes the excitation function as a nonlinear piecewise function:

$$R = \begin{cases} 10, & d_g(t) = 0 \\ 2, & s = 1 \text{ and } (d_g(t) - d_g(t-1)) < 0 \\ -1, & s = 0 \\ -1, & s = 1 \text{ and } (d_o(t) - d_o(t-1)) < 0 \\ 0, & \text{else} \end{cases} \qquad (6)$$

Where: $s = 0$ represents collision between unmanned ship and obstacle; $s = 1$ represents MASS sailing in a safe area. $d_g(t)$ represents the distance between the target point and the MASS at time t; $d_g(t-1)$ represents the distance between the target point and the MASS at time $t-1$; $d_o(t)$ represents the distance between the obstacle and the MASS at time t; $d_o(t-1)$ represents the distance between the obstacle and the MASS at time $t-1$.

3.4   Action Selection Strategy

In the reinforcement learning system, on the one hand, the MASS needs online trial and error to find the optimal search strategy, namely exploration; On the other hand, it is necessary to consider the entire route planning. The expectation of the entire MASS to obtain rewards is maximum, namely, utilization. This study uses $\varepsilon - greedy$ strategy, which balances exploration and utilization. Its meaning is that when the search behavior maximizes the action value function, the probability of selecting the action is $1 - \varepsilon + \frac{\varepsilon}{|A(s)|}$, and the probability of selecting other actions is $\frac{\varepsilon}{|A(s)|}$:

$$\pi(a|s) \leftarrow \begin{cases} 1 - \varepsilon + \frac{\varepsilon}{|A(s)|} & \text{if} \quad a = \text{argmax}_a Q(s, a) \\ \frac{\varepsilon}{|A(s)|} & \text{else} \end{cases} \tag{7}$$

4   Experiments

Based on the model in Sect. 3, a design simulation experiment was established to verify the effectiveness of Q-Learning-based obstacle avoidance and path planning for MASS. The model validation platform uses python and pygame. The path planning framework of the unmanned ship consists of two parts: approaching the target point and avoiding obstacles. When there are no obstacles in the environment or the obstacles are not within the safe encounter distance, the unmanned ship will randomly select the action near the target point with probability $\varepsilon/|A(s)|$; When an obstacle appears within a safe encounter distance, an unmanned ship navigates obstacles by interacting with the environment through the reward function. Some of the model parameters in the experiment were set to: gamma $gamma = 0.005$, $\gamma = 0.9$, $\omega = 0.02$, $v_0 = 8kn$.

This study sets the initial position (529, 364) and target point (164, 279) of MASS. In the early stage of experimental iteration shown in Fig. 3(a), the MASS collides with obstacles at different time steps. After the collision, the MASS will return to the previous step and reselect the action strategy. In the initial iteration, the MASS cannot judge the temptation area in the simulation environment and it is trapped in the "trap" sea area in the simulation port pool; After 100 iterations, the system gradually plans effective paths, but collision obstacles occur many times in the process and the planning path fluctuates greatly. From 200 iterations to 500 iterations in Fig. 3(b), the collision phenomenon gradually decreases and the planned path fluctuates. As is shown in Fig. 3(c) in the 1000 iterations, all obstacles are effectively avoided and the planned path is weak and gradually stable; Until the 1500th iteration, shown in Fig. 3(d), the probability of random search is the smallest, and the reinforcement learning system plans the final fixed path to reach the target point. The simulation experiment results are shown in Fig. 3.

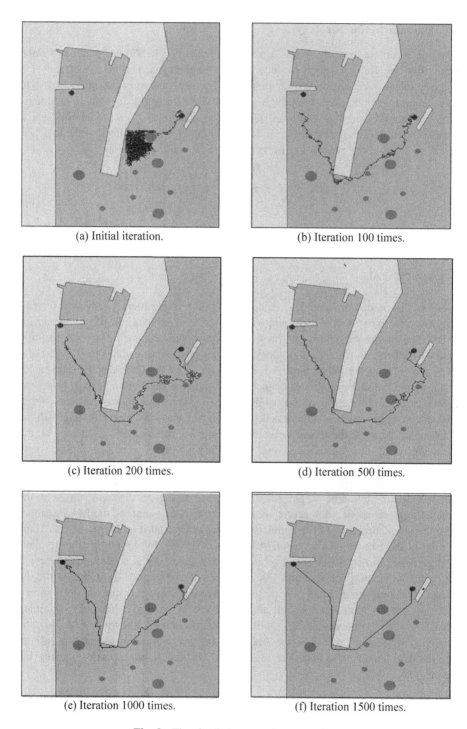

(a) Initial iteration.

(b) Iteration 100 times.

(c) Iteration 200 times.

(d) Iteration 500 times.

(e) Iteration 1000 times.

(f) Iteration 1500 times.

Fig. 3. The simulation experiment results.

The number of epochs of the model is taken as the abscissa, and the number of steps required to move from the starting to the end of each iteration is plotted as the ordinate to visually observe the training speed and training effect of this method. The iterative convergence trend is shown in Fig. 4. The MASS has too little information about the state of the environment in the early stage of interacting with the environment, and collisions and path planning are fluctuating. As the number of iterations increases, the MASS accumulates learning experience and completes the adaptation to the environment, ultimately successfully planning the path and reaching the target point.

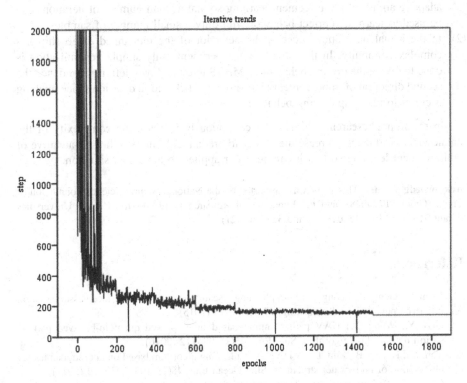

Fig. 4. Iterative trends.

5   Conclusion

This research proposes a path planning method for MASS based on the Q-Learning algorithm. Based on the four basic elements of Q-Learning, an unmanned ship path planning model was established. Simulation experiments verify that this method has better self-adaptive ability. Through the online trial-and-error self-learning, MASS can avoid the obstacles and plan the adaptive path in the unknown environment, which verified the effectiveness of the method.

In the early stage of interacting with the environment, the MASS has too little information about the state of the environment, and there are collisions and large fluctuations in route planning. As the number of iterations increases, the unmanned ship system accumulates learning experience and completes adaptation to the environment, ultimately successfully planning the path and reaching the target point. However, reinforcement learning algorithms still require many improvements, if reinforcement learning is required to be applied in an unmanned scenario.

(1) The Q-Learning algorithm based on Markov decision process can obtain the optimal path through trial and error algorithm, but its convergence speed is slower and the number of iterations is more. The first improvement is to improve the adaptive ability of reinforcement learning so that a small number of iterations can be used to learn the correct behavior with only a small number of samples.

(2) In the actual navigation process, the behavior of the unmanned cargo ship has complex continuity. In this simulation experiment, only simple generalization is done to divide the driving behavior of MASS into up, down, left, right and etc., the second direction of improvement is to enrich the behavioral decision space, making it closer to real ship driving behavior.

In the future research, we also can continuously increase the complexity of the unknown environment, increase the ability to predict and improve the self-adaptive of reinforcement learning so that it can be better applied to the actual situation.

Acknowledgements. This work was supported by the National Natural Science Foundation of China (Grant 51779028), and the Fundamental Research Funds for the Central Universities (Grant 3132018146, 3132016315 and 3132016321).

References

1. Chen, C., Geng, P., Zhang, X.: Path planning research on unmanned surface vessel based on improved potential field. Ship Eng. **37**(9), 72–75 (2015)
2. Guo, Y., Wang, X.: UAV path planning based on improved quantum-behaved particle swarm optimization algorithm. Ship Eng. **45**(1), 99–112 (2016)
3. Yan, M., Huang, B., Zhu, D.: A novel path planning algorithm based on neurodynamics for observation of underwater structures. Ship Ocean Eng. **46**(2), 103–107, 112 (2017)
4. Chen, H.: Preliminary research on local path planning for unmanned surface vehicle. Doctoral dissertation of Dalian Maritime University (2016)
5. Duan, Q., Zhang, M., Zhang, J.: Underwater robot local path planning method based on fuzzy neural network. Ship Eng. **1**, 54–58 (2001)
6. Liang, Q.: Reinforcement learning based mobile robot path planning in unknown environment. Mech. Electr. Eng. Mag. **29**(4), 477–481 (2012)
7. Zhao, Y., Zheng, Z., Zhang, X., et al.: Q learning algorithm-based UAV path learning and obstacle avoidance approach. In: 36th Chinese Control Conference (CCC), Dalian, pp. 3397–3402. IEEE CPP (2017)
8. Konar, A., Chakraborty, I.G., Singh, S.J., et al.: A deterministic improved Q-learning for path planning of a mobile robot. IEEE Trans. Syst. Man Cybern. Syst. **43**(5), 1141–1153 (2013)

9. Hwang, K.S., Jiang, W.C., Chen, Y.J.: Pheromone-based planning strategies in Dyna-Q learning. IEEE Trans. Industr. Inf. **13**(2), 424–435 (2017)
10. Cruz, D.L., Yu, W.: Path planning of multi-agent systems in unknown environment with neural kernel smoothing and reinforcement learning. Neurocomputing **233**, 34–42 (2017)
11. Dong, W.: Research on mobile robot piath planning based on Q-learning. Doctoral dissertation of Shandong University of Science and Technology (2013)
12. Liu, Q., Zhai, J., Zhang, Z., et al.: A survey on deep reinforcement learning. Chin. J. Comput. **41**(1), 1–27 (2018)
13. Zhao, D., Shao, K., Zhu, Y., et al.: Review of deep reinforcement learning and discussions on the development of computer Go. Control Theory Appl. **33**(6), 701–717 (2016)
14. Huang, B., Cao, G., Wang, Z.: Reinforcement learning theory, algorithms and application. J. Hebei Univ. Technol. **35**(6), 34–38 (2006)
15. Szepesvari, C.: Algorithms for reinforcement learning. In: International Conference on Computing, pp. 103–127. Morgan & Claypool, San Rafael (2010)
16. Cheng, Y., Zhang, W.: Concise deep reinforcement learning obstacle avoidance for underactuated unmanned marine vessels. Neurocomputing **272**, 63–73 (2017)

Evaluation of sEMG-Based Feature Extraction and Effective Classification Method for Gait Phase Detection

Fang Peng[1,2], Wei Peng[3], and Cheng Zhang[2,4(✉)]

[1] School of Automation Science and Engineering,
South China University of Technology, Guangzhou, China
fion_peng@163.com
[2] Zhongshan Institute, University of Electronic Science and Technology,
Zhongshan, China
[3] University of Electronic Science and Technology, Chendu, China
646141118@qq.com
[4] Department of Computer Science and Communications Engineering,
Waseda University, Tokyo, Japan
cheng.zhang@akane.waseda.jp

Abstract. Gait phase detection is an essential procedure for amputated person with an artificial leg to walk naturally. However, a high-performance gait phase detection system is challenging due to (1) the complexity of surface electromyography (sEMG) and redundancy among the numerous features; (2) a robust recognition algorithm which can satisfy the real-time and high accuracy requirement of the system. This paper presents a gait phase detection method based on feature selection and ensemble learning. Four kinds of features extraction methods of sEMG, including time, frequency, time/frequency domain and entropy, are quantitatively analyzed by statistical analysis and calculation complexity to select the best features set. Furthermore, a multiclass classifier using Light Gradient Boosting Machine (LightGBM) is first introduced in gait recognition for discriminating six different gait phases with an average accuracy (94.1%) in a reasonable calculation time (85 ms), and the average accuracy is 5%, which is better than the traditional multiple classifiers decision fusion model. The proposed robust algorithm can effectively reduce the effect of speed on the result, which make it a perfect choice for gait phase detection.

Keywords: sEMG · Features extraction · Gait phase detection · Classifier · LightGBM

1 Introduction

Surface electromyography (sEMG) signals are the electrical potential generated by muscle cells when neurologically activated or muscle cells are electrical. In

This work was partially supported by Guangdong Science and Technology Plan Project under Grant 2016A020220003.

F. Sun et al. (Eds.): ICCSIP 2018, CCIS 1006, pp. 138–149, 2019.
https://doi.org/10.1007/978-981-13-7986-4_13

recent years, sEMG signal has been widely used in the fields of bionic legs, assisted gait robots [1]. Movement state of the lower limb is complicated, and the stage detection is significant in the application of lower limb robot.

In previous studies of gait detection, researchers usually classified the gait phase by using physical sensors [2,3]. However gait phase detection using physical sensors has shortcomings in that it causes unnatural gait behavior and does not sufficiently recognize subject's intentions. To solve this problem, the researchers introduced the sEMG signal for the recognition. sEMG is a complex signal, and it is necessary to deeply study the signal characteristics.

Feature extraction is a significant method to extract the useful information which is hidden in sEMG signal. Feature extraction of sEMG is generally divided into the time domain, frequency domain, time-frequency domain, and entropy spectrum. Among these, the time domain analysis is the most common method because it is synthesized based on the signals' amplitude [4]. For the frequency domain, two modified mean and median frequencies are presented for robust feature extraction [5]. Time-frequency domain can characterize varying frequency information at different time locations, provide plenty of non-stationary information about the analyzed signals [6]. One of the methods is wavelet transform (WT), which has been a research hotspot in recent decades and is more suitable for short pulse string or long time slow signal which can characterize high-frequency signal [7]. The sEMG data produced by human motion is proved to be not static, and the results show that the characteristics of these data can be represented by the combination of time-frequency domain features [8]. There are many different types of entropy methods have been used in many different applications in the biomedical field [9]. However, in this multitude of characteristic categories, there are a lot of redundancy features. The traditional solution is to descend the dimension, but this method lacks the qualitative analysis of sEMG signal during gait phase, and it is hard to achieve optimal recognition efficiency [10,11].

In recognition methods, the traditional research method is to use linear discriminant analysis (LDA) and other linear models to classify human physiological data to infer intention [12]. LDA has been proved to be highly efficient and unsusceptible to overfitting [13]. Furthermore, using multiple classifiers and using classifier fusion methods to combine them together has shown a better combination accuracy than any single classifier [14]. However, the fusion decision of multiple classifiers based on LDA is not particularly ideal for gait recognition with sEMG signals.

Based on the above discussion, the traditional gait phase detection researches lack the quantitative analysis of surface EMG signals, resulting in the waste of computational resources. Moreover, further research on the algorithm of gait phase detection is required. The contribution of this paper is to select the most suitable feature combination for gait detection and to establish an ideal gait phase detection and recognition model.

2   EMG Data Acquisitions

2.1   Experimental Design

A cycle of human gait is usually divided into 6 different phases: pre-stance, mid-stance, terminal-stance, pre-swing, mid-swing, terminal-swing. In this study, sEMG signals were collected from healthy males, and related works show that there is no difference in the sEMG signal between the disabled and the healthy people. The sEMG electrodes were attached to the experimenter's designated position as shown in Fig. 1, the experimental data were collected from the three participants, and the physical characteristics of the participants are shown in Table 1. The gait data were collected with a speed of 2 km/h, 3 km/h, 4 km/h on the treadmill. The training and test data were collected as each subject performed 500 steps level walk.

Table 1. Physical characteristics of study participants.

Subject	Age	Height	Weight
A01	23 years	178 cm	62 kg
A02	24 years	174 cm	64 kg
A03	26 years	172 cm	65 kg

The sEMG signals were collected with Myomove EMG Instrument, which provided a 16-bit resolution, a 50-m wireless WiFi transmission, and a sEMG signal sampling frequency of 1024 Hz. The sEMG electrodes were placed at the right limb of the femoral rectus muscle, the lateral femoral muscle, the medial femoral muscle, and the femoral two head muscles, which have been identified in the study as key muscles in the lower limbs of the gait process [15].

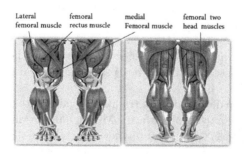

Fig. 1. The reflective position were used to get sEMG data.

2.2   Pre-processing

The surface EMG signals are generated by electrical activity of muscle nerve fibers, which is a weak electrical signal. The research shows that amplitude of sEMG is in the 0–10 mv range and the frequency of useful sEMG is in 10 Hz–500 Hz range.

As a weak signal, the sEMG signal is susceptible to noise during the acquisition, so the effective noise removal is an important step in the whole process. In this paper, the preprocessing method of sEMG signal was firstly comb filtered to reduce the superposition effect of useful signal and noise, and then filtered by IIR (Forward-backward band-pass filtering) bandpass filter between 10 Hz–500 Hz to subtract exception offset from the normalizing signals.

3   Algorithm Description

3.1   Feature Extraction

For the purpose of comparison, 20 sEMG feature types are considered, there are some simple statistical features such as mean, standard deviation, upper-quantile are not shown below. In the following formula, where N and x_i denote the number of samples and the ith sEMG sample, respectively, $sgn(x)$ is sign function and $u(x)$ is a unit-step function.

(1) Mean absolute value (MAV)

For discrete signals, MAV feature is an average of absolute value of the sEMG signal amplitude in a segment [11], which is defined as $MAV = \frac{1}{N}\sum_{i=1}^{N}|x|$.

(2) Variance and Logarithm of variance (Var and Logvar)

In the stochastic process, the variance is used to measure the discrete degree of the random variable [11], which is defined as $Var = \frac{1}{N-1}\sum_{i=1}^{N}x_i^2$ and naturally Logvar is defined as the natural logarithm of Var.

(3) Willison amplitude ($Wamp$)

Wilson's amplitude refers to the number of times the difference exceeds a certain threshold for two consecutive points [16], which is defined as $Wamp = \sum_{i=1}^{N}sgn(|x_{i+1} - x_i| - T)$. In this study, the threshold T is 50 mv, which is the indicator of muscle contraction level.

(4) Zero crossing (ZC)

Zero crossing refers to a number of times that amplitude values of the sEMG signal cross zero amplitude level [16], which is defined as $ZC = \sum_{i=1}^{N-1}sgn(-x_ix_{i+1})$.

(5) Root mean square (RMS)

RMS is the characteristic of the signal amplitude [16], which is defined as $RMS = \sqrt{\frac{\sum_{i=1}^{N}x_i^2}{N}}$.

(6) Slope sign change (SSC)

The SSC represents the frequency information of EMG signals [10], it counts the changes of the positive and negative slopes of EMG signals:

$$SSC = \sum_{i=2}^{N-1} f((x_i - x_{i+1}) * (x_i - x_{i-1})) \tag{1}$$

where $f(x) = \begin{cases} 0, if & x \geq T \\ 1, otherwize \end{cases}$. Through experiments and comparison, we set the threshold T as 50 mv in this paper.

(7) Waveform length (WL)

Waveform length is a kind of characteristic of measuring the complexity of surface EMG signals [18], which is defined as $WL = \sum_{i=1}^{N-1} |x_{i+1} - x_i|$.

(8) Auto-regressive coefficients (AR)

Autoregressive model is a predictive model, which describes the relationship between the samples of EMG signals by a linear combination [10]. It is defined as $x_i = \sum_{p=1}^{P} a_p x_{i-p} + w_i$. P represents the order of AR regression model, and the experimental and theoretical studies show that the model order $P = 4$ is suitable for the application of EMG signal [19].

(9) Mean Frequency (MF)

The mean frequency is the change of the distribution center point of the surface EMG Signal Band [19], which is defined as $MF = \frac{\sum_{i=1}^{N} f_i p_i}{\sum_{i=1}^{N} p_i}$, where f_i represents the frequency of the ith Sample Point, p_i represents the power spectral density of the ith Sample Point, and M represents the length of the band.

(10) Median Frequency (MDF)

The median frequency is to divide the signal spectrum into two equal regions [19], and the formula is expressed as $\sum_{i=1}^{MDF} p_i = \sum_{i=MDF}^{M} p_i = \frac{1}{2} \sum_{i=1}^{M} p_i$, where p_i represents the power spectral density of the ith Sample Point, and M represents the length of the band.

(11) Sample Entropy (SampEn)

Sample entropy is usually used to evaluate the complexity of physiological time series signals [20]. For the given vector, m is the dimension, r is the distance threshold, and N is the number of point, now using $SampEn(m, r, N)$ to represent the sample entropy, defining a vector template of length m, which is written as the $X_m(i) = (x_i, x_{i+1}, x_{i+3}, x_{i+m-1})$. The distance function is: $d[x_m(i), x_m(j)] = \sqrt{\sum_{i,j=1}^{m}(x_i - x_j)^2}$, A is the number of the vector with a length of $m + i$ that satisfied $d[X_m(i), X_m(j)] < r$, B is the number of the vector with a length of m that satisfied $d[X_m(i), X_m(j)] < r$, the expression of sample entropy is $SampEn(m, r, N) = -\log \frac{A}{B}$. In this paper, we set $m = 3$, r is set to 0.2 times of the sample variance.

(12) Fuzzy Approximate Entropy (FuzzyEn)

Fuzzy approximate entropy [21] is to take the exponential function as the fuzzy function instead of the two value judgment function. Now the distance function is defined as d_{ij}^m which represents the maximum value of the absolute value of the difference between the vector corresponding elements, the fuzzy function $\mu(d_{ij}^m, n, r) = \exp(-(\frac{d_{ij}}{r})^n)$, now defining

$$\phi^m(n, r) = \frac{1}{N-m} \sum_{i=1}^{N-m} (\frac{1}{N-m-1} \sum_{j=1, j\neq i}^{N-m} \mu(d_{ij}^m, n, r)) \qquad (2)$$

and finally the fuzzy approximate entropy can be expressed as $FuzzyEn(m, n, r, N) = -\log \frac{\phi^m}{\phi^{m+1}}$. Compared with the sample entropy, the fuzzy approximate entropy has an extra n parameter, which represents weight, FuzzyEn will lost a lot of information when n takes a large number, this article takes $n = 3$.

(13) Wavelet Transform

Wavelet transform is widely used in time-frequency domain feature extraction. The mathematical expression of the feature extraction of the data by continuous wavelet transform is as $C = \frac{1}{\sqrt{a}} \int_{-\infty}^{\infty} x(t)\varphi^*(\frac{t-b}{a})dt$, where the φ^* is the wavelet base, b is the translation parameter, a is the transformation scale, commonly uses the scale a as: $a = 2^k, k = [1, 2, 3...7]$, C denotes coefficients generated by wavelet transform. For the selection of wavelet bases, the application of db1, db4, db7 wavelet in lower limb gait is studied in this paper [14,22], and the medium-low frequency band after the signal decomposition is studied.

3.2 Evaluation Criteria

The Davidson Index and Scattering criterion method described below are two kinds of classical clustering algorithms, which are used to evaluate the performance of surface EMG signals in gait detection [10]. The Davidson index is to evaluate the overlap severity between clusters by calculating the distance between clusters and cluster, and the mapping evaluation method is to evaluate the spatial distribution quality of the whole cluster.

Davies Bouldin (DB) index is an evaluation metric for clustering, which is calculated as $DBI = \frac{1}{k} \sum_{i=1}^{k} \max(\frac{s_i+s_j}{D_{i,j}})$, where k is number of classes, S_i and S_j are the dispersions of the ith and jth clusters,respectively, and $D_{i,j}$ is the distance between their mean values.

The Scattering criterion method is an overall evaluation of all the clusters in the sample space. By calculating the covariance matrix between the clusters and the traces of the covariance matrix, the overall condition of the sample space is represented. It is expressed as $SCAT = \frac{trace(S_W)}{trace(S_B)}$, where S_W is the covariance matrix of all classes and S_B is the covariance matrix of between-classes.

3.3 Classification

In this paper, four representative ensemble learning methods were considered:

(1) Simple majority voting fusion based on LDA (SV-LDA)

The Linear Discriminant Analysis (LDA) is the most commonly used method of EMG signal recognition. LDA is a classification method for finding the maximal interval through projection. The research shows that the accuracy of fused classifiers based on LDA is better than any single classifier, and in this study, we used a simple majority voting fusing based on LDA to implement a combination of classifiers [14].

(2) Weighted majority voting fusion based on LDA (WT-LDA)

If different characteristics have different recognition effects on different gait stages, then it is reasonable to weight the classifiers in a manner, the more accurate classifiers can have more decision-making power in the final result [14].

(3) Extreme Gradient Boosting (XGboost)

XGboost [23] is a king of Gradient Boosting Decision Tree algorithm which is a highly effective and widely used ensemble learning method. XGboost can get higher accuracy by iterative operation of weak-learning methods, meanwhile, XGboost is an efficient algorithm which can process data smoothly by utilizing more available resources.

(4) Light Gradient Boosting Machine (LightGBM)

LightGBM [24] is an efficient parallel algorithm for decision tree which is an open source Gradient Boosting Decision Tree algorithm by Microsoft. Its operation is extremely efficient because it uses the histogram algorithm to speed up an arithmetic process and combines communication optimization to improve parallel learning, it is worth mentioning that LightGBM uses the strategy of leaf growth (leaf-wise tree Growth) with largest splitter gain which greatly improves recognition performance.

4   Results and Discussion

4.1   Evaluation of EMG Features

In order to effectively determine the current gait phase from sEMG signals, we need to find out the difference in signals at different gait stages.

Figure 2 illustrates class separability of 20 EMG features. Lower values of the score imply higher degree of cluster separability. We compared the mean absolute value (MAV) calculated by the coefficients of 50 Hz–100 Hz and 100 Hz–150 Hz which is decomposed by db1, db4, db7. Results show that SSC feature is the most separable feature at gait phases, and secondly, waveform length (WL), Willison amplitude (Wamp), logarithm of variance (logvar) and absolute mean value based on db7 wavelet decomposition coefficients within 50 Hz–100 Hz (DB7-MAV) and fuzzy approximate entropy (FuzzyEn) also have good performance in gait phase detection. Computational complexity is an important criterion in the real-time application, in the current study, the calculation uses the I5-3230M, 2.6 GHz CPU and 4G RAM, Spyder IDE. Figure 3 illustrates the calculation time of features:

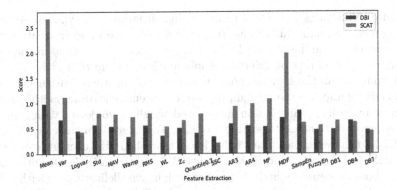

Fig. 2. The separability values of features.

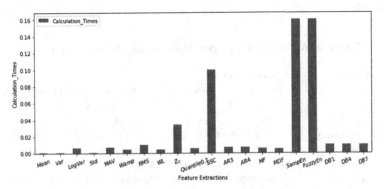

Fig. 3. The calculation time of features.

Reviewing the Figs. 2 and 3, it can be observed that the overall separable properties of these six features, different features differ in different gait stages, such as the SSC feature can perfect distinct the mid-stance stage and other stages and the other stages are a little blurry, and the logvar feature has a better separation in the blurry area. In terms of computational time, the FuzzyEn feature and SSC feature have a large computational complexity that is not conducive to the real-time requirements of the system, considering the good separation of SSC feature, we select only SSC and other four features as model input.

4.2 Activities Recognition Results

The feature dataset of gait phases is input into four types of ensemble learning methods, the models are evaluated with the accuracy rate and calculation complexity.

Figure 4 illustrates the actual identification situation four types of ensemble learning methods, and Table 2 illustrates the detailed data and calculation time of four models. It can be observed that the speed has a slight effect on the result and the recognition rate of different people in 3 km/h is up to 97.3%.

We compare all the four methods, result shows that weak learner can actually effectively improve the recognition rate by ensemble learning methods, such as simple majority voting fusion model and weighted majority voting model, but compared to Gradient Boosting Decision Tree algorithm such as XGboost, LightGBM, the average accuracy is 5% lower than them, the average accuracy of LightGBM is 94.3%. Obviously, the LightGBM algorithm is significantly faster than XGboost because LightGBM is a lightweight parallelization algorithm benefits from histogram algorithm and strategy of leaf growth. Although LightGBM has a slightly longer computational time than the voting method, it is still an ideal model.

Table 2. Accuracy of four ensemble learning for each subject

Subject	Label	Classifier km/h											
		SV-LDA			WV-LDA			XGboost			LightGBM		
		2	3	4	2	3	4	2	3	4	2	3	4
A01	Overall	0.868			0.885			0.938			0.942		
	Pre-swing	0.81	0.85	0.83	0.86	0.88	0.87	0.92	0.93	0.92	0.93	0.94	0.93
	Mid-swing	0.84	0.87	0.84	0.87	0.91	0.89	0.93	0.94	0.92	0.94	0.95	0.95
	Terminal-swing	0.87	0.89	0.88	0.91	0.93	0.9	0.96	0.95	0.92	0.95	0.96	0.94
	Pre-stance	0.91	0.95	0.93	0.93	0.95	0.91	0.94	0.96	0.93	0.95	0.96	0.94
	Mid-stance	0.84	0.86	0.88	0.89	0.93	0.90	0.94	0.96	0.92	0.94	0.95	0.93
	Terminal-stance	0.81	0.83	0.82	0.85	0.93	0.91	0.93	0.95	0.92	0.93	0.94	0.92
A02	Overall	0.846			0.905			0.936			0.951		
	Pre-swing	0.80	0.83	0.79	0.87	0.89	0.86	0.92	0.93	0.91	0.92	0.95	0.92
	Mid-swing	0.82	0.83	0.82	0.88	0.90	0.89	0.93	0.95	0.92	0.95	0.97	0.96
	Terminal-swing	0.86	0.87	0.84	0.90	0.93	0.94	0.95	0.95	0.94	0.95	0.98	0.95
	Pre-stance	0.90	0.94	0.92	0.92	0.94	0.91	0.93	0.94	0.92	0.95	0.97	0.94
	Mid-stance	0.80	0.84	0.81	0.88	0.89	0.84	0.89	0.93	0. 90	0.93	0.97	0.92
	Terminal-stance	0.81	0.86	0.83	0.84	0.91	0.90	0.92	0.93	0.91	0.92	0.95	0.94
A03	Overall	0.838			0.894			0.928			0.936		
	Pre-swing	0.79	0.82	0.79	0.88	0.88	0.87	0.91	0.92	0.91	0.91	0.94	0.93
	Mid-swing	0.80	0.81	0.79	0.88	0.87	0.90	0.93	0.94	0.92	0.94	0.95	0.92
	Terminal-swing	0.83	0.84	0.80	0.87	0.89	0.86	0.94	0.95	0.92	0.95	0.96	0.94
	Pre-stance	0.91	0.93	0.91	0.92	0.94	0.92	0.93	0.94	0.93	0.94	0.95	0.94
	Mid-stance	0.81	0.86	0.84	0.87	0.90	0.88	0.95	0.95	0.92	0.93	0.94	0.92
	Terminal-stance	0.83	0.86	0.85	0.87	0.92	0.90	0.92	0.95	0.92	0.92	0.94	0.93
Calculation time		65 ms			83 ms			190 ms			85 ms		

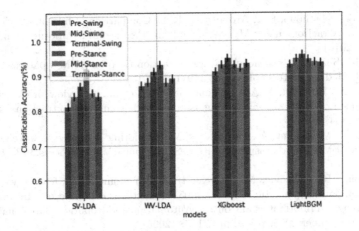

Fig. 4. Classification result of four models.

5   Conclusions

In order to recognize the gait phase effectively, we have evaluated sEMG-based feature extraction and have proposed to use LightGBM algorithm for gait phase detection in this paper. After the quantitative analysis of four types of features extraction methods, the SSC is the most separable features and a reasonable computational complexity, and the final selection of the Slope sign change (SSC), Waveform length (WL), Willison amplitude (Wamp), Logarithm of variance (Logvar) and absolute mean value of DB7 wavelet decomposition coefficients (DB7-MAV) as the optimal feature set.

Furthermore, after considering the accuracy rate and the calculation time synthetically, LightGBM is found to be superior to traditional fusion decision making algorithm in gait phase recognition, with the computing time of 85 ms and the average accuracy rate of 94.3%. This research can be applied on the application of sEMG signals, such as walking assist devices, and robotics or prosthetic devices. It can effectively improve the recognition rate of motion intention and meet the real-time requirements.

References

1. Chen, B., Zheng, E., Fan, X., et al.: Locomotion mode classification using a wearable capacitive sensing system. IEEE Trans. Neural Syst. Rehabil. Eng. **21**, 744–755 (2013)
2. Hargrove, L.J., Simon, A.M., Young, A.J., et al.: Robotic leg control with EMG decoding in an amputee with nerve transfers. N. Engl. J. Med. **369**, 1237–1242 (2013)
3. Ivanenko, Y.P., Cappellini, G., Solopova, I.A., et al.: Plasticity and modular control of locomotor patterns in neurological disorders with motor deficits. Front. Comput. Neurosci. **7**, 123 (2013)

4. Arief, Z., Sulistijono, I.A., Ardiansyah, R.A.: Comparison of five time series EMG features extractions using Myo Armband. In: Electronics Symposium, pp. 11–14. IEEE (2016)
5. Veer, K., Sharma, T.: A novel feature extraction for robust EMG pattern recognition. J. Med. Eng. Technol. 40(4), 149–154 (2016)
6. Nazmi, N., Rahman, M.A.A., Yamamoto, S.I., et al.: A review of classification techniques of EMG signals during isotonic and isometric contractions. Sensors 16(8), 1304 (2016)
7. Kakoty, N.M., Saikia, A., Hazarika, S.M.: Exploring a family of wavelet transforms for EMG-based grasp recognition. Signal Image Video Process. 9(3), 553–559 (2015)
8. Carreoñ, I.R., Vuskovic, M.: Wavelet transform moments for feature extraction from temporal signals. In: ICINCO 2005, Proceedings of the Second International Conference on Informatics in Control, Automation and Robotics, Barcelona, Spain, 14–17 September 2005, vol. 4, pp. 71–78 (2005)
9. Marta, B.: Entropy-based algorithms in the analysis of biomedical signals. Stud. Log. Gramm. Rhetor. 43(1), 21–32 (2015)
10. Boostani, R., Moradi, M.H.: Evaluation of the forearm EMG signal features for the control of a prosthetic hand. Physiol. Meas. 24(2), 309–319 (2003)
11. Phinyomark, A., Phukpattaranont, P., Limsakul, C.: Feature reduction and selection for EMG signal classification. Expert Syst. Appl. 39(8), 7420–7431 (2012)
12. Ha, K.H., Varol, H.A., Goldfarb, M.: Volitional control of a prosthetic knee using surface electromyography. IEEE Trans. Biomed. Eng. 58(1), 144–151 (2010)
13. Abumostafa, Y.S., Magdonismail, M., Lin, H.T.: Learning from Data: A Short Course. AMLBook, New York (2012)
14. Kadrolkar, A., Sup IV, F.C.: Intent recognition of torso motion using wavelet transform feature extraction and linear discriminant analysis ensemble classification. Biomed. Signal Process. Control 38, 250–264 (2017)
15. Wentink, E.C., Beijen, S.I., Hermens, H.J., et al.: Intention detection of gait initiation using EMG and kinematic data. Gait Posture 37(2), 223–228 (2013)
16. Chang, G.C., Kang, W.J., Luh, J.J., et al.: Real-time implementation of electromyogram pattern recognition as a control command of man-machine interface. Med. Eng. Phys. 18(7), 529–537 (1996)
17. Kang, S.K., Choi, H.H., Chang, S.M., et al.: Comparison of k-nearest neighbor, quadratic discriminant and linear discriminant analysis in classification of electromyogram signals based on the wrist-motion directions. Curr. Appl. Phys. 11(3), 740–745 (2011)
18. Hargrove, L.J.: Non-weight-bearing neural control of a powered transfemoral prosthesis. J. Neuroeng. Rehabil. 10(1), 1–11 (2013)
19. Aishwarya, R., Prabhu, M., Sumithra, G., et al.: Feature extraction for EMG based prostheses control. ICTACT J. Soft Comput. 3(2), 472–477 (2013)
20. Yentes, J.M., Hunt, N., Schmid, K.K., et al.: The appropriate use of approximate entropy and sample entropy with short data sets. Ann. Biomed. Eng. 41(2), 349–365 (2013)
21. Navaneethakrishna, M., Karthick, P.A., Ramakrishnan, S.: Analysis of biceps brachii sEMG signal using multiscale fuzzy approximate entropy. In: Engineering in Medicine and Biology Society, p. 7881. IEEE (2015)

22. Bastiaensen, Y., Schaeps, T., Baeyens, J.P.: Analyzing an sEMG signal using wavelets. In: Vander Sloten, J., Verdonck, P., Nyssen, M., Haueisen, J. (eds.) 4th European Conference of the International Federation for Medical and Biological Engineering. IFMBE, vol. 22, pp. 156–159. Springer, Heidelberg (2009). https://doi.org/10.1007/978-3-540-89208-3_39
23. Chen, T., Guestrin, C.: XGBoost: a scalable tree boosting system. In: ACM SIGKDD International Conference on Knowledge Discovery and Data Mining, pp. 785–794. ACM (2016)
24. Meng, Q., Ke, G., Wang, T., et al.: A communication-efficient parallel algorithm for decision tree (2016)

Computer-Based Attention Training Improves Brain Cognitive Control Function: Evidences from Event-Related Potentials

Lei Zheng[1,2], Dong-ni Pan[1,2], Yi Wang[1,2], and Xuebing Li[1,2(✉)]

[1] Key Laboratory of Mental Health, Institute of Psychology,
Chinese Academy of Sciences, No. 16 Lincui Road, Chaoyang District,
Beijing 100101, China
zhenglei309@sohu.com, psydrina@163.com,
w.wy.y@163.com, lixb@psych.ac.cn
[2] Department of Psychology, University of Chinese Academy,
Beijing 100101, China

Abstract. The present study explored the mechanism of attention bias modification (ABM) on Social Anxiety Disorder (SAD). The participants were assigned into training group (attention modification program, AMP) or attention bias holding group (attention control condition, ACC) randomly. To examine the underlying neural mechanism of ABM training, we used the event-related potentials (ERPs) technology and combined with a Stroop task reflecting the function of cognitive control. The behavioral results showed that after attention training, anxiety symptoms were relieved in both groups. The ERP results showed that, in Stroop task, both AMP and ACC group had an increasing N450 and an increasing SP after training, showing an improvement of cognitive control through this long-term repeated training. We also found the reduced P2 amplitudes after AMP training, but not after ACC training, which suggested that ABM training can reduce the early attention resource allocation of the individual to the relevant stimulus. Therefore, computer-based attention training could generally improve the cognitive control function in anxiety individuals, while manipulative training contingency in ABM mainly modulated the early stage of attention processing.

Keywords: Cognitive control · Stroop task ·
Attention bias modification training · ERP

1 Introduction

Anxiety disorder is the most common mental disorder. An international epidemiological study showed that the lifetime prevalence of anxiety disorders was up to 14.6% [1]. Therefore, anxiety disorders, as a major public health problem, require effective, feasible and acceptable treatment.

This research was supported by National Nature Science Foundation of China [NSFC 31671136; 31530031].

© Springer Nature Singapore Pte Ltd. 2019
F. Sun et al. (Eds.): ICCSIP 2018, CCIS 1006, pp. 150–161, 2019.
https://doi.org/10.1007/978-981-13-7986-4_14

In the last decade, researchers have found that Attentional Bias Modification (ABM), a systematic training program to alter or correct ones exaggerated negative attention bias, has a potential relieving effect on anxiety disorders, such as reduced anxiety arousal when facing speech challenge and overall decrease of distress [2, 3]. The dot-probe paradigm is widely used during ABM training. In the task, a probe certainly appeared in the location of neutral stimuli instead of negative stimuli. The negative stimuli were social threatening words or disgust faces, which were especially threatening to anxiety people. This attention bias modification (known as ABM) training can direct a person's attention bias away from threatening stimuli. A lot of researchers demonstrated that this ABM program can effectively alter attention bias, relieve anxiety symptoms, and make people do better in the subsequent stressor events [4–6]. But other researchers found ABM can't change attention bias, nor can it relieve anxiety symptoms compared with ACC group (attention control condition, in which the probe replace the neutral or negative stimuli with 50% probability for each) [7, 8].

However, it is unclear that the underlying mechanism of the ABM training up to now. Researchers have shown that the anxiety-reducing effects of attention training may be due to increase in general attention control [9–11]. That is to say, attention training may increase attention control via enhancement of top-down cognitive function which may in turn inhibit threat processing [12]. Cognitive control refers to processes that support the ability of individuals to regulate, coordinate, and sequence thoughts and actions according to internally maintained behavioral goals [13].

Several behavioral tasks have been developed to examine the cognitive control function. For example, the Stroop task reflecting the interference effect between word-reading and color-naming for a color word. A number of ERP (event-related potentials) studies demonstrated that there were mainly two important ERP components N450 and SP (slow potential) induced by the Stroop task. N450 is a negative component occurring about 400–500 ms after the stimulus onset, and is more pronounced for incongruent trials than congruent (or neutral) ones [14]. N450 is usually located fronto-centrally, and recent ERP source localization studies have revealed that most variance in the topography of the N450 can be explained by dipoles found in the ACC [15–17]. SP starts with about 500 ms after the stimulus onset, and sustains until the response is made [14]. SP is more positive for incongruent than congruent trials [18]. It is interpreted as an index of conflict resolution (not conflict detection) that leads to response selection [19, 20]. Another ERP component is P2, a frontally distributed P2 which has been related to attention and feature-based stimulus evaluation [21] or the recall of task rules [22–24]. The time window of P2 is usually 150–300 ms.

The goal of the present study was to investigate the neural mechanisms of cognitive control improved by attention training in social anxious individuals. In the study, 44 anxiety students were asked to complete attention training. They were randomly divided into two groups, training group (attention modification program, AMP) or attention bias holding group (attention control condition, ACC). We recorded electroencephalogram (EEG) activity during pre-test and post-test, and we assumed that the symptoms of social anxiety would be alleviated during training, and for ERP results we hypothesized that attention training would modulate the change of P2, N450 and SP in the Stroop task.

2 Methods

2.1 Participants

Forty-four college students with social anxiety were included in our study. They were recruited from a sample pool of 679 South China Normal University students. All participants met all of the following criteria: (a) scoring above 32 on the Liebowitz Social Anxiety Scale self-report version (LSAS-SR; Baker, Heinrichs, Kim, Hofmann 2002); (b) scoring above the top 20% on the Social Interact Anxiety Scale (SIAS; Mattick 1998); (c) not undergoing any other psychological treatments when training; (d) not taking any drugs for anxiety or depression; (e) not having the other serious mental disorders which could influence the outcome of our study. All the participants were right handed, had normal or corrected to normal eyesight. They signed the informed consent before the experiment and were paid after the experiment. The study was approved by the local ethics committee.

2.2 Procedure

Participants were randomly assigned to the AMP (n = 22) or the ACC (n = 22) group. The average age of the AMP group is 20.05 ± 1.0 (M ± SD), and the average age of the ACC group is 19.94 ± 1.03 (M ± SD). Since 3 participants in AMP group and 6 participants in ACC group rejected the collection of EEG, the data used for ERP analysis were 19 in AMP and 16 in ACC at last.

At the pre-training assessments, participants in both AMP and ACC groups completed the self-report scales. After that, all participants finished the spatial cuing task to assess their attention bias to threat, the Stroop task combining with EEG recording to assess their ability of cognitive control. One or two days after the pre-training assessments, participants came to our lab to accomplish their training task twice a week. The training procedures lasted 4 weeks. The AMP group accomplished the attention bias modification program and the ACC group accomplished the attention bias holding program. A single training session lasted about 21 min.

After training, all participants came back to our lab to finish the same post-training assessments as they did in pre-training assessments. The whole pre-training and the post-training assessment lasted about 40 min respectively.

Self-report Measures. Self-report scales included the Social Phobia Scale (SPS; Mattick et al. 1998), the Spielberger State-Trait Anxiety Inventory (STAI; Spielberger et al. 1983), and the Liebowitz Social Anxiety Scale self-report version (LSAS-SR).

Attention Bias Assessment. We used a modified version of spatial cuing task to assess attention bias, as reported by Amir [4]. The formal task involved 192 computerized trials. There were totally 16 words [eight socially threatening words (e.g., stupid, embarrassed, shamed) and eight neutral words (e.g., smooth, easy, busy)] cuing on the left or the right of the screen. At the beginning of the task, a fixation cross on the center of the screen presented 500 ms. Then the word cue appeared 600 ms and then disappeared, followed by a probe (*) appeared on either the cue location or the opposite location of the cue word for 1500 ms. Participants were instructed to press "F" or "J" to indicate the location of the probe. Of the 192 trials, 128 were valid [16(word) * 2 (location: left/right) * 4(repetition)], which means the probe appeared in the same location as the cue; 32 were invalid [16(word) * 2(location: left/right)], which means the probe appeared in the opposite location of the cue; 32 were uncued, which means the probe appeared with the same word in both side of the cross. Additionally, there were 24 practice trials before the experiment.

Cognitive Control Assessment. A traditional Stroop task was used to assess the ability of cognitive control. In the Stroop task, four color words (green, yellow, red, blue) were printed in their corresponding color ink or in one of the non-matching colors (e.g., the word "red" was printed in yellow.) In the trial, a fixation cross was presented for 500 ms, and then a centralized color word was presented for 300 ms, followed by a fixation cross 1000 ms for participants response. Participants were asked to indicate the word color by pressing the buttons as soon as possible when the stimulus was presented, the letter "D" represents red, the letter "F" represents yellow, the letter "J" represents green, the letter "K" represents blue. After the initial practice 20 trials, two blocks with each consisting of 72 trials (50% congruence probability) were completed. During this task, both EEG and behavior data were recorded (Fig. 1).

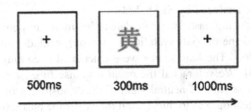

Fig. 1. The procedure of the Stroop Task. (Color figure online)

Attention Bias Modification. There were totally eight sessions for the ABM procedure. A single training session was just the same version of the dot probe task as Amir' study [4]. A fixation cross was presented on the center of the screen for 500 ms. Then a pair of faces was presented on the top and the bottom of the screen 800 ms. After the presentation of faces, a probe (either the letter "E" or "F") appeared in the location of one of the two faces. Participants were instructed to judge the probe was the letter "E" or "F". Each session contained 160 trials repeating three times, consisting of all combinations of probe type (E/F), probe position (top/bottom), face type (neutral/disgust), and person (four male faces and four female faces). Participants were allowed to have a rest every 40 trials.

In the AMP condition, on trials with disgust-neural face pairs, the probe always replaced the neutral faces. Of every 160 trials in each session, 32 included only neutral face pairs: 2 (probe type) * 2 (probe position) * 8 (person). The remaining 128 trials were disgust-neutral face pairs: 2 (disgust face position) * 2 (probe type) * 8 (person) * 4 (repetition).

The ACC condition was same like the AMP condition except that on trials with disgust-neutral face pairs, the probe presented in the position of disgust and neutral face with equal frequency. Thus of every 160 trials in each session, 32 included only neutral face pairs: 2 (probe type) * 2 (probe position) * 8 (person). The remaining 128 trials were disgust-neutral face pairs: 2 (disgust face position) * 2 (probe type) * 2 (probe position) * 8 (person) * 2 (repetition).

2.3   EEG Recording

We recorded the EEG data for the Stroop task for both pre-training assessment and post-training assessment. The EEG was recorded from 32 Ag-AgCl electrodes placed on the scalp according to the extended International 10/20 system (Waveguard 64 cap, Cephalon A/S). Vertical electro-oculograms (VEOG) were recorded above and below the left eye. Horizontal electro-oculograms (HEOG) was recorded as the left and right orbital rim. The EEG activity was recorded using a right mastoid reference electrode and re-referenced off-line to the mean of bilateral mastoid electrodes. All electrode impedances were maintained below 5 KΩ. EEG and EOG activity was amplified with a AC 0.05–100 Hz band-pass and continuously sampled at the rate of 500 Hz.

2.4   Data Analysis

Behavioral data were analyzed by SPSS 17.0.

For the spatial cueing task, we calculated the mean response time to probes respectively on each type of trials (validity * emotion), exclude the trails that exceed two standard deviation. The bias scores were calculated according to the criteria in MacLeod' study [25]. We subtracted the mean response time of negative-valid-trials from the mean response time of neutral-valid-trials. A positive score revealed that the participant had an attention bias to threat. And the larger the bias score was, the greater the bias to threat was.

For Stroop task, we calculated the mean response time (RT) for consistent and inconsistent conditions as assistant index. What's more, we subtracted response time of consistent case from inconsistent case, that is an index for the effect amount of Stroop task.

Continuously EEG data were subsequently submitted to Scan 4.5 environment for off-line analysis. The data were first visually screened for any noisy part. Eye blinks and eye movement artifacts were removed using Scan 4.5 software. EEG was filtered off-line with a low bandpass of 30 Hz (24 dB/oct, zero phase shift). The target ERP epoch lasted from −200 ms to 800 ms. Trials with amplitude exceeding ±100 μV in any scalp channels were rejected. The time-domain averaging procedure was completed for each participant and each condition. Time windows of P2, N450, SP components of Stroop task were established based on the averaged potentials of each task condition. Finally, the interval of P2 component was 150–300 ms, the interval of N450 component was 400–550 ms, the interval of SP component was 600–800 ms. The following two electrode sites Cz, FCz were further selected for statistical analysis for P2 and N450 components, the electrode site Pz was selected for statistical analysis for SP components.

3 Results

3.1 Questionnaires

For LSAS-SR, STAI-T, STAI-S we submitted the data to a 2 (Group: AMP/ACC) * 2 (Time: pre-training/post-training) mixed model ANOVA with repeated measurement on the second factor.

For the LSAS-SR, the main effect of time $[F(1, 42) = 28.392, p < 0.0001, \eta_p^2 = 0.403]$, was significant, the score of post-training decreased significantly compared with pre-training. The main effect of group was not significant $[F(1, 42) = 0.733, p = 0.397, \eta_p^2 = 0.017]$, and the interaction of group and time was significant. Further simple effect analysis, the post-test score of the experimental group was significantly lower than that of the pre-test $[t(21) = 6.119, p < 0.0001]$. There was no significant difference between pre-test and post-test scores in the control group $[t(21) = 2.002, p = 0.058]$.

For the STAI-T, the main effect of time $[F(1, 42) = 28.392, p < 0.0001, \eta_p^2 = 0.403]$, was significant, the score of post-training decreased significantly compared with pre-training. The main effect of group and the interaction of group and time were not significant.

For the STAT-S, the main effect of time, the main effect of group and the interaction of group and time were not significant.

3.2 Behavioral Data

The Spatial Cueing Task. For attention bias scores, we ran a 2 (Group: AMP/ACC) * 2 (Time: pre-training/post-training) mixed model ANOVA with repeated measurement on the second factor. The result of the repeated ANOVA didn't find a significant effect of time $[F(1, 42) = 1.847, p = 0.181, \eta_p^2 = 0.042]$, nor the effect of group $[F(1, 42) = 1.82, p = 0.185, \eta_p^2 = 0.042]$. Also the interaction of group and time were not significant $[F(1, 42) = 0.344, p = 0.561, \eta_p^2 = 0.008]$. This meant that there was no significant change in the attentional bias score of the two groups after training.

The Stroop Task. We ran a 2 (Group: AMP/ACC) * 2 (Time: pre-training/post-training) * (Condition: consistent/conflict) mixed model ANOVA for RT. We found that effect of time was significant $[F(1, 42) = 10.578, p = 0.002, \eta_p^2 = 0.201]$, RT before training is longer than the time after training. There was also a significant main effect of condition on RT $[F(1, 42) = 94.669, p < 0.0001, \eta_p^2 = 0.693]$, with longer RT in the conflict condition than in the consistent condition. The main effect of group and the interaction of group and time were not significant. This meant both groups had Stroop effects, and both had shortened responses.

We ran a 2 (Group: AMP/ACC) * 2 (Time: pre-training/post-training) mixed model ANOVA for Stroop effects. The analysis revealed no significant main effects or interaction between the group and the time.

3.3 ERP Data

P2. We ran a [2 (Group: AMP/ACC) * 2 (Time: pre-training/post-training) * 2 (Condition: consistent/conflict) * 2 (Electrode sites: Cz/FCz)] mixed model ANOVA on the averaged amplitudes of P2 components. We found that the main effect of time was significant [$F(1,33) = 21.015, p < 0.0001, \eta_p^2 = 0.389$], averaged amplitude before training is larger than the amplitude after training. The interaction of group and time were significant [$F(1,33) = 4.137, p = 0.05, \eta_p^2 = 0.111$]. Further analysis showed that the amplitude before training is larger than the amplitude after training in the AMP group [$F(1,18) = 23.953, p < 0.0001, \eta_p^2 = 0.421$]. There was no significant difference in the control group. The main effect of condition and other main effect or interaction were not significant (Fig. 2).

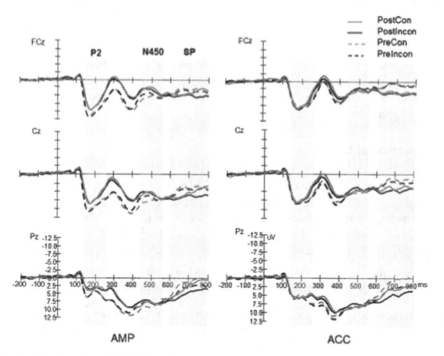

Fig. 2. Grand-averaged ERPs from three electrodes (Cz/Pz/FCz) to Stroop targets in AMP and ACC group before and after training.

N450. We ran a [2 (Group: AMP/ACC) * 2 (Time: pre-training/post-training) * 2 (Condition: consistent/conflict) * 2 (Electrode sites: Cz/FCz)] mixed model ANOVA on the averaged amplitudes of N450 components. We found significant main effect of time [$F(1,33) = 5.577, p = 0.024, \eta_p^2 = 0.145$], which showed increased N450 after training. The main effect of condition was significant [$F(1,33) = 4.612, p = 0.039, \eta_p^2 = 0.123$], indicating that the conflict condition induced larger N450 than the consistent condition. The main effect of electrodes was also significant, which showed N450 of FCz was larger than that of Cz [$F(1, 33) = 101.926, p < 0.0001, \eta_p^2 = 0.755$]. No significant interaction effects were found.

SP. We ran a [2 (Group: AMP/ACC) * 2 (Time: pre-training/post-training) * 2 (Condition: consistent/conflict) mixed model ANOVA on the averaged amplitudes of SP components. We found that main effect of time was significant [$F(1, 33) = 8.086$, $p = 0.008, \eta_p^2 = 0.197$], averaged amplitude before training is lower than the amplitude after training. The main effect of condition was significant, with larger averaged amplitude in the conflict condition than in the consistent condition [$F(1, 33) = 26.48, p < 0.0001, \eta_p^2 = 0.45$]. The analysis revealed no significant main effects or interaction except these.

4 Discussion

The current study aimed to investigate the neural mechanism of ABM training with ERP technique, especially to investigate whether Computer-based attention training improves brain cognitive control function. According to the self-report scores of anxiety symptoms, both the AMP and the ACC group were able to reduce the anxious level of the participants, but the AMP group was more effective. This is consistent with many previous studies [26, 27]. For example, Schmidt et al. found that ABM training relieved social anxiety, and the effect maintained and enhanced over 2–4 months [26].

We did not find any changes of attention bias in both AMP group and ACC group. This was different from the Amir's study [3]. This result might be due to the different attention bias score before training, only 13 participants in AMP group showed attention bias to threat. Many researchers have confirmed that only when the participants showed attention bias to threat before training, ABM training can have an impact on attention bias score [28–31]. In the present study, most of the participants did not have attention bias before training in AMP group, which probably lead to no changes in the attention bias score after training. Some researchers suggested that the attention bias to threat was caused by the decline of attention control ability [32], and declared that the attention training can modulated the general ability of attention control [33]. Hereby, the ABM training maybe have an effect through increasing attention control, rather than a change in attention bias.

The response time reduced in the Stroop task in both groups, which suggested that both AMP and ACC trainings improve cognition control functions of participants. The current training programmers required participants to repeatedly response to the stimuli position by pressing buttons on keyboard in both AMP and ACC group. Wealthy studies have found that repetition of the same stimuli would benefit for behavioral performance, such as a short reaction time [34, 35]. The ERP data showed the consistent results with Behavioral Data. In neural level, we found that both group showed an increased N450 and an increased SP after training, no group difference was found. According to the previous studies, the increased N450 and SP reflected the improvement of cognition control function. N450 represents the monitoring of conflict [16, 36], and the SP reflects the conflict resolution [16, 37]. Gajewski et al. found that enhanced performance in the Stroop task may be driven by a larger N2 and N450 ERP components [38]. Suárez-Pellicioni et al. found a negative correlation between the interference in hit rates and the amplitude of the N450 when preceded by congruence [39]. Hereby, the present ERP results implied that the relieved anxiety symptoms after attention training could come out from improving of the cognitive control function. These results also gave some support to the DMC (dual mechanisms of control) account [40], suggesting that high anxious individuals are characterized by a tendency to exert attentional control in a reactive way, that is, only when conflict is encountered in processing. On the other hand, low anxious individuals are considered to exert attentional control in a proactive way, by maintaining task goals over time. The greater amplitude of N450 and SP components after training maybe mean the participants can exert attentional control in a more proactive way.

More interesting ERP result was found on the P2 component. Although, we did not observe a main effect of condition on P2, but we found the decreased P2 amplitude after training only in AMP group. P2was used to be related to attentive and feature-based stimulus evaluation [21, 41] or reflected the recall processing of task rules. It reflected early attention distribution and was not a major component of cognitive control. The decreased amplitude of P2 in AMP group after training meant that ABM training can reduce the early attention resource allocation of the individual to the stimulus. That might imply that ABM training mainly affects the early processing stage of attention (for example, the attention engagement). Corbetta and Shulman proposed that there are two kinds of attention systems in our brain, one is a top-down goal-directed system influenced by an individual's current goals, expectations, and knowledge [42]. Another is a bottom-up stimulus-driven system affected by prominent stimuli in the current environment. These two systems interact with each other. And ACT theory suggested that anxiety affects the balance of the two attention systems, and damages the goal-directed system and enhances the stimulus-driven system, thus affects individual attention control. In this way, before training anxious individuals would be more influenced by the distractor dimension of the stimuli as compared with the task-relevant dimension, which would explain why they needed more time to respond to incongruent trials. In AMP condition, as the detection stimulus was always fixed in the position of neutral face, individuals were prompted to obtain a preference for neutral stimuli and implicitly modulate early hyperactive processing of emotional stimuli. Therefore, based on our ERP results, we suggested that the ABM training allow the paper to more focus on goal-oriented systems rather than stimuli not relevant to the task, which reflected by decreased P2 showing reduced attention resource inputs and improved efficiency.

Some limitations in our study are worth mentioning. Firstly, the participants we selected were subclinical social anxiety, and clinical social anxiety disorder should be involved in future studies. Secondly, it is suggested that the attention bias score of participants at the pre-training baseline stage should be taken into account in the future research. Thirdly, ERP data only show the time-course processing in cognitive control. Thus, further studies could employ fMRI technique to investigate the functional activation of brain areas and their functional connectivity.

In conclusion, the aim of this study was to explore the underlying mechanism of attention training. The ERP results suggested that the computer-based attention training no matter attention bias modification or not could improve the general cognitive control ability in anxious individuals. However, the attention bias modification training could change the early attention resource allocation as comparing with the attention bias holding training.

References

1. Regier, D.A., Rae, D.S., Narrow, W.E., Kaelber, C.T., Schatzberg, A.F.: Prevalence of anxiety disorders and their comorbidity with mood and addictive disorders. Br. J. Psychiatry **173**(34), 24–28 (1998)
2. Beard, C., Sawyer, A.T., Hofmann, S.G.: Efficacy of attention bias modification using threat and appetitive stimuli: a meta-analytic review. Behav. Ther. **43**(4), 724–740 (2012)
3. Amir, N., Beard, C., Burns, M., Bomyea, J.: Attention modification program in individuals with generalized anxiety disorder. J. Abnorm. Psychol. **118**(1), 28–33 (2009)
4. Amir, N., Weber, G., Beard, C., Bomyea, J., Taylor, C.: The effect of a single-session attention modification program on response to a public-speaking challenge in socially anxious individuals. J. Abnorm. Psychol. **117**(4), 860–868 (2008)
5. Amir, N., Taylor, C.T., Donohue, M.C.: Predictors of response to an attention modification program in generalized social phobia. J. Consult. Clin. Psychol. **81**(1), 112 (2013)
6. Brosan, L., Hoppitt, L., Shelfer, L., Sillence, A., Mackintosh, B.: Cognitive bias modification for attention and interpretation reduces trait and state anxiety in anxious patients referred to an out-patient service: results from a pilot study. J. Behav. Ther. Exp. Psychiatry **42**(3), 258–264 (2011)
7. Boettcher, J., Hasselrot, J., Sund, E., Andersson, G., Carlbring, P.: Combining attention training with internet-based cognitive-behavioural self-help for social anxiety: a randomised controlled trial. Cogn. Behav. Ther. **4**(1), 1–8 (2014)
8. Carlbring, P., et al.: Internet-delivered attention bias modification training in individuals with social anxiety disorder - a double blind randomized controlled trial. BMC Psychiatry **12**(1), 66 (2012)
9. Heeren, A., Mogoaşe, C., Philippot, P., McNally, R.J.: Attention bias modification for social anxiety: a systematic review and meta-analysis. Clin. Psychol. Rev. **40**(40), 76–90 (2015)
10. Neubauer, K., von Auer, M., Murray, E., Petermann, F., Helbig-Lang, S., Gerlach, A.L.: Internet-delivered attention modification training as a treatment for social phobia: a randomized controlled trial. Behav. Res. Ther. **51**(2), 87–97 (2013)
11. Bardeer, J.R., Daniel, T.A., Hinnant, J.B., Orcutt, H.K.: Emotion dysregulation and threat-related attention bias variability. Motiv. Emot. **41**(3), 1–8 (2017)
12. Pessoa, L.: How do emotion and motivation direct executive control? Trends Cogn. Sci. **13**(4), 160–166 (2009)
13. Braver, T.S.: The variable nature of cognitive control: a dual-mechanisms framework. Trends Cogn. Sci. **16**(2), 106–113 (2012)
14. West, R., Alain, C.: Effects of task context and fluctuations of attention on neural activity supporting performance of the Stroop task. Brain Res. **873**(1), 102–111 (2000)
15. Hanslmayr, S., Pastötter, B., Bäuml, K.H., Gruber, S., Wimber, M., Klimesch, W.: The electrophysiological dynamics of interference during the Stroop task. J. Cogn. Neurosci. **20**(2), 215–225 (2008)
16. Liotti, M., Woldorff, M.G., Perez, R., Mayberg, H.S.: An ERP study of the temporal course of the Stroop color-word interference effect. Neuropsychologia **38**(5), 701–711 (2000)

17. Szűcs, D., Soltész, F., White, S.: Motor conflict in Stroop tasks: direct evidence from single-trial electro-myography and electro-encephalography. Neuroimage **47**(4), 1960–1973 (2009)
18. Chuderski, A., Senderecka, M., Kałamała, P., Kroczek, B., Ociepka, M.: ERP correlates of the conflict level in the multi-response Stroop task. Brain Res. **1650**, 93–102 (2016)
19. Larson, M.J., Clayson, P.E., Clawson, A.: Making sense of all the conflict: a theoretical review and critique of conflict-related ERPs. Int. J. Psychophysiol. **93**(3), 283–297 (2014)
20. Pires, L., Leitao, J., Guerrini, C., Simoes, M.R.: Event-related brain potentials in the study of inhibition: cognitive control, source localization, and age-related modulations. Neuropsychol. Rev. **24**(4), 461–490 (2014)
21. O'Donnell, B.F., Swearer, J.M., Smith, L.T., Hokama, H., McCarley, R.W.: A topographic study of ERPs elicited by visual feature discrimination. Brain Topogr. **10**(2), 133–143 (1997)
22. Finke, M., Barceló, F., Garolera, M., Cortinas, M., Garrido, G., Pajares, M.: Impaired preparatory re-mapping of stimulus-response associations and rule-implementation in schizophrenic patients–the role for differences in early processing. Biol. Psychol. **87**(3), 358–365 (2011)
23. Schapkin, S.A., Gajewski, P.D., Freude, G.: Age differences in memory-based task switching with and without cues: an ERP study. J. Psychophysiol. **28**(3), 187–201 (2014)
24. Van, E.M., Crajé, C., Beeren, M.E., Steenbergen, B., Schie, H.T., Bekkering, H.: Neural evidence for impaired action selection in right hemiparetic cerebral palsy. Brain Res. **1349**(18), 56–67 (2010)
25. William, J.M., Mathews, A., Macleod, C.: The emotional Stroop task and psychopathology. Psychol. Bull. **120**(1), 3–24 (1996)
26. Ollendick, T., Allen, B., Benoit, K., Cowart, M.: The tripartite model of fear in children with specific phobias: assessing concordance and discordance using the behavioral approach test. Behav. Res. Ther. **49**(8), 459–465 (2011)
27. Schmidt, N.B., Richey, J.A., Buckner, J.D., Timpano, K.R.: Attention training for generalized social anxiety disorder. J. Abnorm. Psychol. **118**(1), 5–14 (2011)
28. Amir, N., Taylor, C.T.: Combining computerized home-based treatments for generalized anxiety disorder: an attention modification program and cognitive behavioral therapy. Behav. Ther. **43**(3), 546–559 (2012)
29. Boettcher, J., et al.: Internet-based attention bias modification for social anxiety: a randomised controlled comparison of training towards negative and training towards positive cues. PLoS ONE **8**(9), e71760 (2013)
30. Kuckertz, J.M., Gildebrant, E., Liliequist, B., Karlström, P., Väppling, C., Bodlund, O., et al.: Moderation and mediation of the effect of attention training in social anxiety disorder. Behav. Res. Ther. **53**(1), 30–40 (2014)
31. O'Toole, L., Dennis, T.A.: Attention training and the threat bias: an ERP study. Brain Cogn. **78**(1), 70–73 (2012)
32. Heeren, A., Raedt, R.D., Koster, E.H.W., Philippot, P.: The (neuro)cognitive mechanisms behind attention bias modification in anxiety: proposals based on theoretical accounts of attentional bias. Front. Hum. Neurosci. **110**(3), 119–204 (2013)
33. Kim, S.H., Hamann, S.: Neural correlates of positive and negative emotion regulation. J. Cogn. Neurosci. **19**(5), 776–798 (2007)
34. Bertelson, P.: Serial choice reaction-time as a function of response versus signal-and-response repetition. Nature **206**(4980), 217–218 (1965)
35. Henson, R.N., Rugg, M.D.: Neural response suppression, haemodynamic repetition effects, and behavioural priming. Neuropsychologia **41**(3), 263–270 (2003)

36. Milham, M.P., Banich, M.T., Webb, A., Barad, V., Cohen, N.J., Wszalek, T., et al.: The relative involvement of anterior cingulate and prefrontal cortex in attentional control depends on nature of conflict. Cogn. Brain. Res. **12**(3), 467–473 (2001)
37. Donohue, S.E., Liotti, M., Perez, R., Woldorff, M.G.: Is conflict monitoring supramodal? Spatiotemporal dynamics of cognitive control processes in an auditory Stroop task. Cogn. Affect. Behav. Neurosci. **12**(1), 1–15 (2011)
38. Gajewski, P.D., Falkenstein, M.: Long-term habitual physical activity is associated with lower distractibility in a Stroop interference task in aging: behavioral and ERP evidence. Brain Cogn. **98**, 87–101 (2015)
39. Suárez-Pellicioni, M., Núñez-Peña, M.I., Colomé, À.: Reactive recruitment of attentional control in math anxiety: an ERP study of numeric conflict monitoring and adaptation. PLoS ONE **9**(6), 1476–1491 (2014)
40. Braver, T.S., Gray, G.R., Burgess, G.C.: Explaining the many varieties of working memory variation: dual mechanisms of cognitive control. In: Variation in Working Memory, pp. 76–106. Oxford University Press, Oxford (2007)
41. Wild-Wall, N., Falkenstein, M., Gajewski, P.D.: Neural correlates of changes in a visual search task due to cognitive training. Neural Plast. **2012**(3), 216–225 (2012)
42. Corbetta, M., Kincade, J.M., Shulman, G.L.: Neural systems for visual orienting and their relationships to spatial working memory. J. Cogn. Neurosci. **14**(3), 508–523 (2002)

Comparison of Facial Emotion Recognition Based on Image Visual Features and EEG Features

Yanfang Long[1], Wanzeng Kong[1(✉)], Wenfen Ling[1], Can Yang[2], and Jieyong Zhu[1]

[1] Hangzhou Dianzi University, Hangzhou 310018, Zhejiang, China
yanfang_longsun@163.com, kongwanzeng@hdu.edu.cn, wenfen_ling@163.com, zjsczjy04@gmail.com
[2] Hong Kong University of Science and Technology, Hong Kong, China
macyang@ust.hk

Abstract. Automatic facial emotion recognition plays an important role in human-computer interaction. Although humans can recognize emotions with little or no effort, reliable emotion recognition by machines is always a challenge. To explore the doubt that whether machines can discriminate better than humans or not, we proposed two different ideas about facial emotion recognition. One is based on image visual features, the other is based on EEG signals which were recorded when the subject is watching facial emotion pictures. Correspondingly, the Deep Convolutional Neural Network (DCNN) model is adopted to enable the machine to learn visual features from facial emotion pictures automatically. The Gated Recurrent Unit (GRU) model is used to extract specific emotional EEG features from EEG signals. These two methods were verified on the Chinese Facial Affective Picture System (CFAPS) and our developed Emotion EEG data (EMOT), and the recognition performance based on EEG features was found to be significantly better than the image visual.

Keywords: Deep learning · EEG · Facial emotion recognition

1 Introduction

Automatic facial emotion recognition is an important part of human-computer interaction, which can be used in psychology/behavior analysis, clinical practice and other fields. Although humans can recognize emotions with little or no effort, reliable emotion recognition by machines is always a challenge. It is worth mentioning that researchers have made considerable progress in developing automatic emotion classifiers over the past decade [1–4]. Most of them were based on the Face Action Coding System (FACS) Action Unit (AU) by tracking changes in facial features including lips, eyes, eyebrows, cheeks and related wrinkles to recognize facial expressions. However, feature parameters of such methods were

© Springer Nature Singapore Pte Ltd. 2019
F. Sun et al. (Eds.): ICCSIP 2018, CCIS 1006, pp. 162–172, 2019.
https://doi.org/10.1007/978-981-13-7986-4_15

primarily calculated by manually defined thresholds and rules. To some extend, it is not really automatic emotion recognition through machines.

In recent years, deep learning technology has been widely applied in object classification, speech recognition, machine translation and other fields due to its powerful autonomous learning ability. Up to now, researchers have also used the deep learning method to facial emotion recognition research. Shima et al. [5] used combination of raw pixels and histogram gradient (HOG) features to train a CNN model on the data set provided by Kaggle [6] to identify seven emotions: anger, neutrality, sadness, happiness, surprise, fear, and disgust. They designed a model consisting of four convolutional layers and two full-connected layers as the best network for this data set. Accuracies on the validation set and test are 65% and 64% respectively. Ng et al. [7] proposed using transfer learning approach in deep learning to challenge the emotion recognition on small data sets. Their team participated in the 2015 Field Emotion Recognition Competition with the best overall accuracy of 48.5% in the validation set and 55.6% in test after twice fine-tune. Giannopoulos et al. [8] examined the performance of two well-known deep learning models (GoogLeNet [9] and AlexNet [10]) on the FER-2013 data set [6]. They divided this data set into two parts, the neutral and emotional. Accuracy of this binary classification problem was 85%. And accuracy of the seven emotions, including anger, neutrality, sadness, happiness, surprise, fear and disgust, is about 60%.

Nevertheless, compared to humans, recognition of facial emotion by the machine is often limited due to contours, angles, and light of faces. In order to explore whether machines can be able to discriminate better than humans or not, we proposed two different ideas about facial emotion recognition: one is based on image visual features; the other is based on EEG signals which were recorded when the subject is watching facial emotion pictures. EEG-based emotion recognition is considered to be a common and reliable method. Because potential differences of EEG signals correspond to different emotions perceived by humans brain, and people cannot hide or control them deliberately [11].

In this paper, we utilized Deep Convolutional Neural Networks (DCNN) and Gated Recurrent Units (GRU) models to compare the recognition of facial emotion based on image visual features and EEG features. We conducted experiments on the Chinese Facial Affective Picture System (CFAPS) and our developed Emotion EEG data (EMOT) with these two methods.

The structure of this paper is as follows: the Sect. 2 introduces materials and methods, the Sect. 3 presents experimental results, and some conclusions are drawn in the Sect. 4.

2   Material and Method

In this study, images we used were from the Chinese Facial Affective Picture System (CFAPS) [12]. This system collected a total of 870 emotional faces, including 74 anger, 47 disgust, 64 fear, 95 sadness, 150 surprise, 222 neutrality, 248 happiness. One hundred college students (1:1 male and female, average age

22.6 years old.) were invited to judge the category and intensity of these pictures. Recognition index of each picture is greater than 60%. Therefore, these images can be used as emotional stimuli materials for our experiments.

2.1 Data Acquisition and Participant

The experimental paradigm designed for the EEG-based emotion recognition experiment as shown in Fig. 1. At the beginning of this experiment, a '+' character displays on the screen for 0.8 s to remind the subject to concentrate. When the "open your eyes" message appears on the screen, the subject is required to keep eyes open and avoid blinking as much as possible. This process lasts for 60 s. After another '+' character, when the screen emerges "close your eyes", the subject is required to keep eyes closed for 60 s, during which the subject's eyes cannot move frequently. Then, the subject starts to watch different facial emotion pictures. Each emotional face appears 0.5 s, and is presented in order of emotional type. In addition, there is a black image showing 10 s between different classes emotion as a buffer. The total duration of this experiment lasted around 13 min. EEG signals were recorded by the Neuroscan 68 channel brain cap which includes 62 scalp electrodes, 4 EOG electrodes and 2 reference electrodes. These electrodes' impedances were kept below 5 kΩ, the signal sampling frequency was 1000 Hz, and a notch filter 50 Hz was set up.

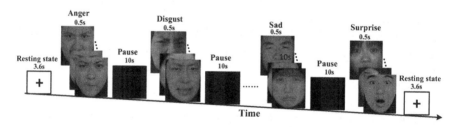

Fig. 1. The experimental paradigm designed for the EEG-based emotion recognition experiment.

Subjects sat comfortably in a bass and dimly lit room and adjusted the height of the chair to keep his/her eyes fixed in the middle of the computer screen. Six volunteers (3 female), aged 23–25 years old with normal or corrected vision participated in this experiment.

2.2 GRU-Based EEG for Emotion Recognition

The EEG-based emotion recognition framework is shown in Fig. 2. Before extracting EEG features, we need to execute some pre-processing operations. Firstly, eye's artifacts were eliminated by manually. Secondly, a band pass filter is applied to obtain EEG signals of four frequency bands: theta band (4–8 Hz), alpha band (8–13 Hz), beta band (13–30 Hz) and gamma band (30–40 Hz) as they convey information about the cognitive processes involved in the visual perception [13].

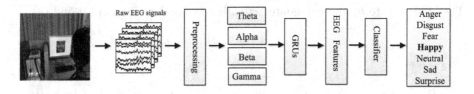

Fig. 2. The EEG-based emotion recognition framework.

In order to obtain more important emotional features from EEG signals, we proposed to use the Gated Recurrent Unit (GRU) [14] to extract EEG features. GRU is a popular variation of the Long Short-term Memory Unit (LSTM) [15], both of which have ability to remember time-domain dependent information dynamically. Therefore, GRU is suitable for analyzing the correlation property between EEG channels in the time domain. At the same time, the GRU has only two gates compared to the LSTM, with fewer parameters and easier convergence. Figure 3 shows the basic structure of the GRU unit.

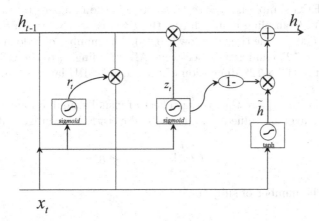

Fig. 3. The basic structure of the GRU unit.

Two gates of the GRU are updated gate z_t and reset gate r_t. The gate z_t selects whether the hidden state is to be updated with a new hidden state in the form:

$$z_t = \sigma(W_{xz}x_t + U_{hz}h_{t-1} + b_z) \tag{1}$$

The second gate r_t decides whether the previous hidden state is ignored, this decision made as follows:

$$r_t = \sigma(W_{xr}x_t + U_{hr}h_{t-1} + b_r) \tag{2}$$

The hidden state h_t and candidate activation $\widetilde{h}_t$ are described in (3) and (4):

$$\widetilde{h}_t = tanh(W_{xh}x_t + U_{rh}r_t + b_h) \tag{3}$$

$$h_t = z_t h_{t-1} + (1 - z_t)\widetilde{h}_t \tag{4}$$

where σ is the logistic sigmoid function, x_t is the input vector, W_{xz}, W_{xr}, W_{xh}, U_{hz}, U_{hr}, U_{rh} are the weight matrices, and b_z, b_r, b_h are bias vectors.

The GRUs model designed in the experiment consists of two common GRU layers. The architecture and parameters are shown in Table 1.

Table 1. Our GRUs model architecture and parameters

Type	Neurons	Output	Parameters
gru_1	256	62×256	581376
gru_2	128	1×128	147840

A single EEG sample is $x_i = (c, t)$, where c is the number of channels and t is the number of sampling points during the given time window. In this study, c is 62 and t is 500 (ie, the time window is 0.5 s). The number of hidden neurons of GRUs model are 256 and 128 respectively. After feeding x_i to the GRUs model, a output vector of 1×128 dimension of the second GRU layer is defined as the EEG feature e_i.

In addition, to explore the average effect of visual stimuli on all subjects, we calculated the average value $\bar{e}_i$ of all subjects' e_i as EEG-average features.

$$\bar{e}_i = \frac{\sum_{s=1}^{M} e_i}{s}, 1 \leq s \leq 6 \tag{5}$$

where M is the number of subjects.

2.3   DCNN-Based for Emotion Recognition

In this study, emotion recognition based on image visual features mainly uses deep convolutional neural network (DCNN), and the flow chart is shown in Fig. 4.

Since the image data set is not large in scale, our convolutional network applies LeNet [16] and AlexNet [10] with fewer layers than VGG [17] or GoogleNet [9] to prevent overfitting. LeNet is a classic convolutional neural network that has achieved well results on the ImageNet [18]. It consists of two

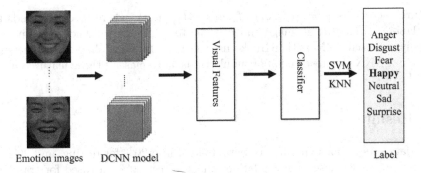

Fig. 4. The emotion recognition framework based on image visual.

layers of convolution, two layers of max-pooling and two layers of full connectivity. Geoffrey Hinton and his students Krizhevsky et al. [10] proposed the AlexNet model to refresh the result on the ImageNet in 2012. This new model is composed of five convolutional layers, three max-pooling layers, and three full connected layers. Compared to LeNet, AlextNet uses convolutional layers of different kernel sizes, similar to the receptive field of the retina. These two DCNN models can learn the visual-level features from emotional pictures. Figure 5 shows the visualization of several visual-level features of the first layer of the DCNN model.

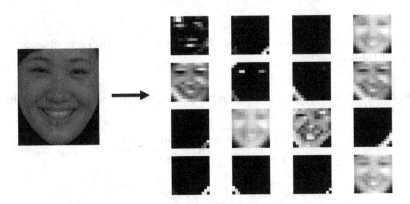

Fig. 5. The visualization of several visual-level features of the first layer of the DCNN model.

The input of the DCNN model is a normalized pixel image. In order to compare with EEG features, a dense layer with neuron number of 128 is added before the softmax layer. And a 1×128 dimensional output vector of the added layer is defined as the image visual feature f_i.

We constructed EEG feature vectors as $E = \{(e_1, y_1), (e_2, y_2), ..., (e_n, y_n)\}$, EEG-average feature vectors as $\bar{E} = \{(\bar{e}_1, y_1), (\bar{e}_2, y_2), ..., (\bar{e}_n, y_n)\}$ and image feature vectors as $F = \{(f_1, y_1), (f_2, y_2), ..., (f_n, y_n)\}$, where y_i corresponds to the label of a emotional image and n is the total number of emotional images. Finally, we used SVM with RBF kernel (decision_function_shape is one-versus-rest) and KNN (nearest neighbor number k is 4) to classify those features E, $\bar{E}$ and F.

3   Result

The data sets in our experiments were divided into 20% for testing, and 20% of the remaining was used for validation, and the rest 60% was used for training. To evaluate the performance of DCNN and GRUs models, 5-fold cross-validation was used for the verification of above mentioned methods. Hyper-parameters of GRUs, LeNet and AlexNet models are shown in Table 2. Keras [19] library with TensorFlow backend is used to implement GRUs and DCNN models.

Table 2. Hyper-parameters of GRUs, LeNet and AlexNet models.

Model	Learning_rate	Batch_size	Optimizer	Activation	Epochs
GRUs	0.001	32	RMSprop	tanh	50
LeNet	0.01	16	SGD	relu	80
AlexNet	0.01	16	SGD	relu	60

Accuracies of recognition based on DCNN models and different classifiers are shown in Table 3.

Table 3. Classification accuracies (in percent) using different classifiers and different DCNN models

DCNN	Classifiers	Accuracy(%)
Lenet	SVM	**67.83**
	KNN	64.71
Alexnet	SVM	**74.60**
	KNN	74.48

From Table 3, we can see the best accuracy of LeNet is 67.83%, and AlexNet is 74.60%. This is because deeper convolutional neural networks and convolutional layers with different kernel sizes can extract more representative features.

Classification results for each subject on different classifiers and different frequency bands are shown in Table 4. Although the difference of recognition performance of different classifiers is no significant, there are obvious distinctions between different frequency bands. Obviously, the alpha and gamma bands are

Table 4. Classification accuracies (in percent) using different classifiers and different frequency bands for each subject.

Subject	Classifier	Total(%)	Theta(%)	Alpha(%)	Beta(%)	Gamma(%)
#1	SVM	68.86	73.18	70.23	62.10	**86.36**
	KNN	70.51	73.35	70.74	63.30	**86.53**
#2	SVM	70.85	81.02	80.17	54.55	**87.27**
	KNN	67.27	81.42	80.51	54.32	**86.65**
#3	SVM	60.06	**76.02**	74.09	63.30	72.67
	KNN	60.40	**76.36**	74.15	62.33	72.61
#4	SVM	62.84	71.25	75.63	60.74	**79.94**
	KNN	63.47	70.63	75.80	60.51	**80.00**
#5	SVM	67.61	47.90	71.31	57.90	**78.18**
	KNN	67.05	46.70	72.27	58.24	**76.99**
#6	SVM	68.18	73.18	69.20	70.63	**83.64**
	KNN	67.27	72.50	69.60	69.60	**83.86**
Mean	SVM	66.40	70.43	73.44	61.53	**_81.34_**
	KNN	65.99	70.16	73.84	61.38	**_81.11_**

much better than others. And we found that the best result was in the gamma high band, which is consistent with the findings of Zheng and Lu et al. [20].

Recognition results based on the average of all the subjects' EEG features $\bar{E}$ using different frequency bands and different classifiers are shown in Table 5.

Table 5. Classification accuracies using different classifiers, different frequency bands and EEG-average features.

Classifier	Total(%)	Theta(%)	Alpha(%)	Beta(%)	Gamma(%)
SVM	80.11	76.14	85.80	79.55	**97.16**
KNN	82.95	76.14	84.66	78.98	**97.73**

Note that the accuracy values of the EEG-average are significantly better than EEG, and the accuracy of the gamma band can achieve more than 97%. This is in line with the literature on cognitive neuroscience, for which changes in EEG signals elicited by visual object stimuli are typically observed when averaging data from multiple trials and subjects [21]. Confusion matrices of $\bar{E}$ on the test set of gamma band using different classifiers are shown in Fig. 6.

Only the sadness and surprise in the prediction results have some minor errors, and other emotions can be identified correctly. Here we assume that the brain's cognitive sensitivity to different emotions may have subtle differences, but it needs to be confirmed.

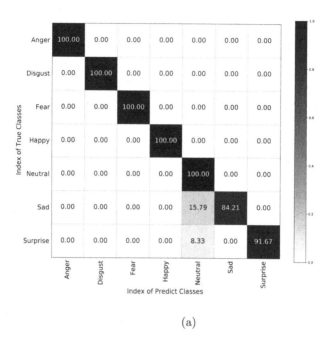

(a)

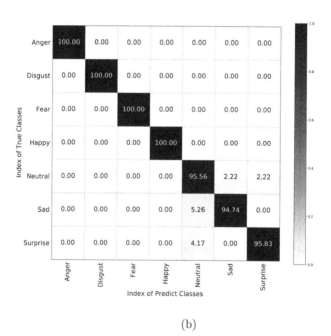

(b)

Fig. 6. (a) Confusion matrix on the test set of gamma band and SVM classifier with an accuracy of 97.16%. (b) Confusion matrix on the test set of gamma band and KNN classifier with an accuracy of 97.73%.

4   Conclusion

This paper presents two emotion recognition methods based on image visual features and EEG features. Correspondingly, we utilized DCNN (AlexNet and LeNet) and GRUs models to extract visual features from pixel images and extracted emotional features from EEG signals. Among the two proposed methods, the recognition performance based on EEG features was found to be significantly better than the image visual. It is potentially possible that the EEG contains a perceptual emotional process from which high-level features can be extracted. At the same time, it can improve the recognition accuracy when averaging EEG features from multiple subjects. In the future work, we intend to explore the potential cognitive implications for different emotional stimuli, as well as the method of emotional recognition that integrates the image visual and EEG signal.

Acknowledgements. This work was supported by National Key R&D Program of China for Intergovernmental International Science and Technology Innovation Cooperation Project (2017YFE0116800), National Natural Science Foundation of China (61671193), Science and Technology Program of Zhejiang Province (2018C04012).

References

1. Tian, Y.L., Kanade, T., Cohn, J.F.: Recognizing action units for facial expression analysis. IEEE Trans. Pattern Anal. Mach. Intell. **23**(2), 97–115 (2001)
2. Cohen, I., Sebe, N., Sun, Y., Lew, M.S., Huang, T.S.: Evaluation of expression recognition techniques. In: Bakker, E.M., Lew, M.S., Huang, T.S., Sebe, N., Zhou, X.S. (eds.) CIVR 2003. LNCS, vol. 2728, pp. 184–195. Springer, Heidelberg (2003). https://doi.org/10.1007/3-540-45113-7_19
3. Bartlett, M.S., Littlewort, G., Frank, M., Lainscsek, C., Fasel, I., Movellan, J.: Fully automatic facial action recognition in spontaneous behavior. In: International Conference on Automatic Face and Gesture Recognition, pp. 223–230 (2006)
4. Pantic, M., Rothkrantz, L.J.: Facial action recognition for facial expression analysis from static face images. IEEE Trans. Syst. Man Cybern. Part B Cybern. **34**(3), 1449–1461 (2004)
5. Alizadeh, S., Fazel, A.: Convolutional neural networks for facial expression recognition. arXiv preprint arXiv:1704.06756 (2017)
6. https://www.kaggle.com/c/challenges-in-representation-learning-facial-expression-recognition-challenge/data. Accessed 2013
7. Ng, H.W., Nguyen, V.D., Vonikakis, V., Winkler, S.: Deep learning for emotion recognition on small datasets using transfer learning. In: ACM on International Conference on Multimodal Interaction, pp. 443–449 (2015)
8. Giannopoulos, P., Perikos, I., Hatzilygeroudis, I.: Deep learning approaches for facial emotion recognition: a case study on FER-2013. In: Hatzilygeroudis, I., Palade, V. (eds.) Advances in Hybridization of Intelligent Methods. SIST, vol. 85, pp. 1–16. Springer, Cham (2018). https://doi.org/10.1007/978-3-319-66790-4_1
9. Szegedy, C., et al.: Going deeper with convolutions. In: Proceedings of the IEEE Conference on Computer Vision and Pattern Recognition, pp. 1–9 (2015)

10. Krizhevsky, A., Sutskever, I., Hinton, G.E.: ImageNet classification with deep convolutional neural networks. In: Advances in Neural Information Processing Systems, pp. 1097–1105 (2012)

11. Bajaj, V., Pachori, R.B.: Detection of human emotions using features based on the multiwavelet transform of EEG signals. In: Hassanien, A.E., Azar, A.T. (eds.) Brain-Computer Interfaces. ISRL, vol. 74, pp. 215–240. Springer, Cham (2015). https://doi.org/10.1007/978-3-319-10978-7_8

12. Li, X., Li, X., et al.: Effects of emotion on cognitive processing: series of event-related potentials study. Adv. Psychol. Sci. **14**(04), 505–510 (2006)

13. Niedermeyer, E., da Silva, F.L.: Electroencephalography: Basic Principles, Clinical Applications, and Related Fields. Lippincott Williams & Wilkins (2005)

14. Cho, K., Van Merriënboer, B., Bahdanau, D., Bengio, Y.: On the properties of neural machine translation: encoder-decoder approaches. arXiv preprint arXiv:1409.1259 (2014)

15. Hochreiter, S., Schmidhuber, J.: Long short-term memory. Neural Comput. **9**(8), 1735–1780 (1997)

16. LeCun, Y., Bottou, L., Bengio, Y., Haffner, P.: Gradient-based learning applied to document recognition. Proc. IEEE **86**(11), 2278–2324 (1998)

17. Simonyan, K., Zisserman, A.: Very deep convolutional networks for large-scale image recognition. arXiv preprint arXiv:1409.1556 (2014)

18. Deng, J.: A large-scale hierarchical image database. In: 2009 Proceedings of IEEE Computer Vision and Pattern Recognition (2009)

19. https://github.com/keras-team/keras. Accessed 2015

20. Zheng, W.L., Lu, B.L.: Investigating critical frequency bands and channels for EEG-based emotion recognition with deep neural networks. IEEE Trans. Auton. Ment. Dev. **7**(3), 162–175 (2017)

21. Stewart, A.X., Nuthmann, A., Sanguinetti, G.: Single-trial classification of EEG in a visual object task using ICA and machine learning. J. Neurosci. Methods **228**, 1–14 (2014)

A Measure of the Consciousness Revealed by the Cerebral Cortex Spontaneous Activity

Fuquan Li, Chong Jiao, Ming Li, and Dewen Hu[(✉)]

College of Artificial Intelligence,
National University of Defense and Technology,
Changsha 410073, Hunan, People's Republic of China
{lifuquan16, dwhu}@nudt.edu.cn

Abstract. Building a real artificial intelligence system is a big dream for human for many years. One of the main problems is that we do not have a good indicator to measure the conscious level both for biological system and human-made system. To solve this problem, we combined the method of human-made communication system (Radio system) and the major idea about the biological origin of consciousness, namely, the corporation of a huge number of neurons. And we proposed an approximate indicator: the frequencies of the spontaneous activity - very low frequency oscillation (vLFO ∼0.03 Hz) and low frequency oscillation (LFO ∼0.18 Hz). The results showed that the vLFO became faster and the LFO stayed consistent when the brain changed into a lower conscious level. Thus, we may probably try to build a bionic brain by combining this phenomena and other conclusion.

Keywords: Biological conscious system ·
Human-made communication system · Conscious level · Spontaneous activity

1 Introduction

In recent years, the artificial intelligence (AI) is popular again with the great advancement in Deep learning [1]. It solved many difficult problems, such as Medical Image Analysis [2], playing video games [3]. However, we still could not build a real artificial intelligence system. Somebody thought that if we build a bigger neuro network, we would get a real artificial intelligent system. But others did not agree with that. They thought this idea may be too naïve, because the critical problem about what is consciousness was still unclear. This problem, what is the biological basis of consciousness, confused us for centuries [4].

Recently, Dehaene et al. [5] discussed this fundamental problem. He divided consciousness into two types of information-processing computations: choosing information for global broadcasting and self-monitoring. This described a potential approach to achieve a real intelligence system. But, there is still a problem remained. The mainstream view is that biological consciousness comes from the incorporation of

© Springer Nature Singapore Pte Ltd. 2019
F. Sun et al. (Eds.): ICCSIP 2018, CCIS 1006, pp. 173–181, 2019.
https://doi.org/10.1007/978-981-13-7986-4_16

a huge amount of neurons [6, 7]. This leads to another important problem with respect to what is the communication mechanism of neurons. Is the communication system like the human-made communication system? The human-made communication system used the low frequency wave to carry high frequency information, for example, frequency modulation radio. In radio system, the frequencies of the low-frequency wave ware steady. So, we could use the information to modulated it. The receiver could obtain the information by demodulation. Is the communication method consistent or various during different conscious level? As far as we knew, there were not any public report about this problem.

Here, we used different anesthetic concentration of Isoflurane (ISO) as the tool to change the conscious level and explore the relationship between conscious level and properties of spontaneous activity (vLFO and LFO). When the anesthetic concentration was in a specific range, the frequencies of LFOs tended to be consistent and the rhythms of vLFOs tended to be accelerated with increased concentrate-on. These results are different from the human-made communication system. We supposed that the special communication mechanisms had a unique contribution to the biological consciousness. Understanding what is the rule behind may help us understand more biological consciousness and design a human-like cognitive system.

2 Materials and Methods

2.1 Animal Preparation

All experiment protocols were implemented in compliance with the guidelines of Xiangya Medical College at Central South University for research involving animals. Ten male adult KM mouse (40 ± 3 g) were anaesthetized before surgery with Isoflurane (1%) by a Rodent Anesthesia Machine (RWD 510; RWD Inc., Shenzhen, Guangdong China).

The mice were positioned in a standard stereotaxic frame after anesthesia. The skull on the cerebral cortex was polished with a saline-cooled dental drill to visualize the cerebral cortex. Then, a chamber was constructed by dental cement and filled with silicon oil that increased the translucency of the thinned skull. Body temperature was monitored and maintained at 37.0 ± 0.5 °C with a feedback-controlled heating pad. The heart-beat and respiration were monitored using a physiological recording system (Mouseox Plus; STARR Life Science Corp Inc., Oakmont, Pennsylvania, USA). The eyes of each mouse were covered with Vaseline to prevent drying.

2.2 Data Acquisition and Experiment Setup

The image sequence of the somatosensory cortex was captured under green (546 ± 10 nm) illumination using an Intrinsic Optical Imaging system (Imager 3001; Optical Imaging Inc., Germantown, New York, USA) equipped with two front-to-front camera lenses connected to a CCD (12-bit, 1024 × 1024 pixels, 60 dB) [8]. Since the artery and vein are visible under green light, we chose artery and vein in the somatosensory cortex as the research object. The anesthetic would make animal become unconscious. The higher the concentration of anesthetics, the lower the consciousness of animals. So, we supposed that the concentration of the anesthetics had a relationship with the conscious level.

This enabled us to use the anesthetic concentration as an indicator. Different concentration of anesthesia (0.8%, 1%, 1.2%, 1.5%, 2.0%) were presented in random order during separate recordings within the same mouse. Two identical data were recorded for each parameter, and the recording interval was nearly the same (∼ 30 min). When the two recordings for a single parameter were completed, the mouse was put back to cages. After one or two days, we would continue the experiment with a second parameter.

One of the two trials for each parameter was randomly chosen for use in the statistical analysis, because the results of different trials for the same parameter were quite similar. After data acquisition, the mice were euthanized with high anesthetic concentration.

2.3 Data Analysis

To explore the frequency change of vLFO and LFO signals, the mean timeseries of the chosen region of interest (ROI) was defined as the change in the average grey level within the ROI, namely, $(R_j - R_0)/R_0$, where R_j is the mean intensity of the ROI for the jth image and R_0 is the baseline, defined as the average of the recorded timeseries. After that we used detrend function to remove the obvious trend under the timeseries.

Spectral properties of the processed time series was obtained using the traditional FFT method, in which the choice of FFT point, NFFT, was typically 1024.

We utilized a feature to depict the signal-Peak Frequency (PF) [9], which means the highest amplitude of the chosen spectral section. difference of vLFO and LFO signals with different anesthetic concentration, were examined using t-test, and the differences were considered significant at the 95% level (P < 0.05).

3 Results

3.1 The Very Low-Frequency Oscillation on Artery Is Accelerated with the Increasing Anesthetic Concentration

The rhythms of vLFO were visible under the 1.5% anesthetic concentration, as shown in Fig. 1. The specific anesthetic concentration induced a significant vLFO on artery (0.05 Hz) (the green region in Fig. 1a).

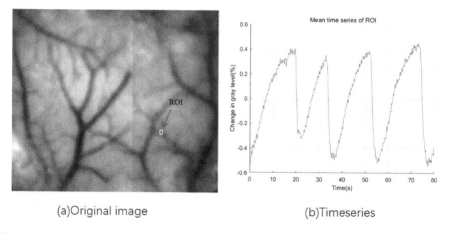

(a)Original image   (b)Timeseries

Fig. 1. The very low-frequency oscillation on artery was significant after the increased anesthetic concentration. (a) An image recorded after a 1.5% ISO. The green region was the artery. (b) The mean time series of the region of interest (ROI) shown in (a). Note that the very low-frequency oscillation (0.05 Hz) on artery was visible. (Color figure online)

The grey image was collected after the mouse's breath became steady with the physiological recording system. Figure 1b shows the mean time series of the ROI marked in Fig. 1a. The peak frequency of vLFO increased from 0.0213 to 0.0500 Hz with 1%–1.5 anesthetic concentration. While, the peak frequency of vLFO was accelerated from 0.0238 to 0.0500 Hz with 1.2%–1.5 anesthetic concentration.

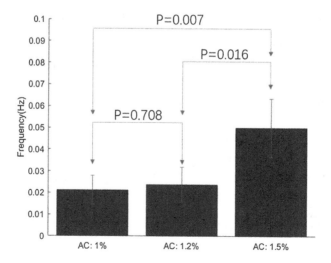

Fig. 2. The statistical results for the vLFO on artery

Statistical results for all animals are shown in Fig. 2. The average vLFO PF increased from 0.0213 ± 0.0066 to 0.0500 ± 0.0135 Hz (mean $\pm$ SE) (n = 20, P = 0.0073, t-test) after increased Anesthetic concentration from 1% to 1.5%. Anesthetic concentration at 1.2%–1.5% changed the mean vLFO PF from 0.0238 ± 0.0080 to 0.0500 ± 0.0135 Hz (n = 20, P = 0.0166). However, the anesthetic concentration stayed nearly steady (0.0213 ± 0.0066 to 0.0238 ± 0.0080 Hz, n = 20, p = 0.7088).

3.2 The Low-Frequency Oscillation on Artery Stayed Consistent with Different Anesthetic Concentration

The PF of LFO retained nearly consistent from 0.1913 to 0.1850 Hz with 1%–1.5 anesthetic concentration.

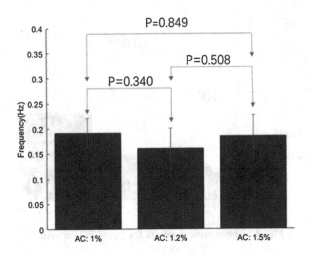

Fig. 3. The statistical results for the LFO on artery

And the PF of LFO kept nearly steady from 0.1600 to 0.1850 Hz with 1.2%–1.5 anesthetic concentration.

Statistical results for all animals are shown in Fig. 3. The average vLFO rhythm kept consistent from 0.1913 ± 0.0296 to 0.1850 ± 0.0419 Hz (n = 20, P = 0.8493, t-test) after increased Anesthetic concentration at 1%–1.5%.

Anesthetic concentration at 1%–1.2% altered the mean LFO rhythm from 0.1913 ± 0.0296 to 0.1850 ± 0.0419 Hz (n = 20, P = 0.3409). And anesthetic concentration at 1.2%–1.5% changed the mean LFO rhythm from 0.1600 ± 0.0409 to 0.1850 ± 0.0419 Hz (n = 20, P = 0.5080). They were not significant.

3.3 The Very Low-Frequency Oscillation on Vein Is Accelerated with the Increasing Anesthetic Concentration

The peak frequency of vLFO on vein increased from 0.0163 Hz to 0.0415 Hz with 1%–1.5 anesthetic concentration. And the PF of vLFO was accelerated from 0.0213 Hz to 0.0415 Hz with 1.2%–1.5 anesthetic concentration.

Statistical results for all animals are shown in Fig. 4. The average vLFO PF was accelerated from 0.0163 ± 0.0054 Hz to 0.0415 ± 0.0175 Hz (n = 20, P = 0.0006, t-test) after increased Anesthetic concentration from 1% to 1.5%.

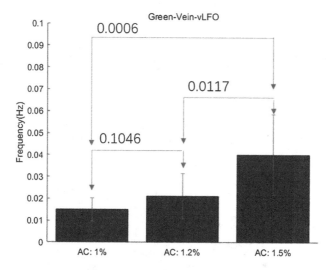

Fig. 4. The statistical results for the vLFO on vein

Anesthetic concentration at 1%–1.2% altered the mean LFO rhythm from 0.0163 ± 0.0054 Hz to 0.0215 ± 0.0105 Hz (n = 20, P = 0.1046), which was not significant. And anesthetic concentration from 1.2% to 1.5% changed the mean vLFO PF from 0.0215 ± 0.0105 Hz to 0.0415 ± 0.0175 Hz (n = 20, P = 0.0117), which was not significant.

3.4 The Low-Frequency Oscillation on Artery Retained Consistent with Different Anesthetic Concentration

The PF of LFO on vein stayed nearly consistent from 0.1515 to 0.1615 Hz with 1%–1.5 anesthetic concentration. And the PF of LFO kept nearly steady from 0.1714 to 0.1615 Hz with 1.2%–1.5 anesthetic concentration.

Statistical results for all animals are shown in Fig. 5. The average LFO rhythm kept consistent from 0.1515 ± 0.0505 to 0.1615 ± 0.0815 Hz (n = 20, P = 0.7970, t-test) after increased Anesthetic concentration from 1% to 1.5%.

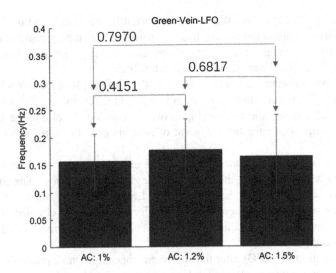

Fig. 5. The statistical results for the LFO on vein

Anesthetic concentration from 1% to 1.2% altered the mean LFO PF from 0.1515 ± 0.0505 to 0.1715 ± 0.0535 Hz ($n = 20$, $P = 0.4151$). And anesthetic concentration at 1.2%–1.5% changed the mean LFO PF from 0.1715 ± 0.0535 to 0.1615 ± 0.0815 Hz ($n = 20$, $P = 0.5080$). They were not significant.

4 Discussion

Researchers have generally changed the physiological state to study the conscious level [10]. The methods that the neurons used to cooperate in the whole brain is difficult to research. Because a suitable experiment mode is hard to find. The anesthetic concentration may be a good approach to solve this problem. Others used different anesthetic to explore the spontaneous activity (vLFO and LFO) and found some interesting result [11, 12]. We used different anesthetic concentration to investigate the relationship between conscious level and spontaneous activity (vLFO, LFO) and used a relatively broad concentration to research it.

The acceleration and consistent phenomena induced by various anesthetic concentration implied that the biological communication system, i.e., spontaneous activity, has a unique operational mechanism.

Our results were against our assumptions, which thought that the biological communication system was like human-made communication system. In human-made communication system, the high-frequency wave is the information and the low-frequency wave keeps steady to be a carrier. However, our results were not all the same. The LFO keeps consistent, which agreed with the suppose. The basic communication system is responsible for monitoring the basic physiological state. It may belong to the lowest conscious level-unconscious state. But the vLFO accelerated significantly when the anesthetic concentration changed to 1.5%. The mechanism behind this is worth exploring. We would explore it in the future, and try to find the behind cognitive computation system that controls it. Thus, it may provide an insight for building the communication system in artificial intelligence system that has consciousness, which would help us to have a better life.

It would be important to confirm whether the similar phenomena could be discovered in neural activities through calcium imaging [13]. Therefore, it would be more essentially to understand the relationship between conscious level and the communication mechanism, which the huge amount of neurons used to cooperate and transfer information.

Using various anesthetic concentration in the experiment may serve as a potential approach with which to explore the origin of biological consciousness. The consistence or acceleration of spontaneous activity (vLFO, LFO) elicited by the anesthetic concentration was an interesting phenomenon, which remained to be clarified. This result is similar to previous studies, which proposed that the response time, played a crucial role in the conscious level [14].

The acceleration of vLFOs after the anesthetic concentration increasing may reflect some internal mechanisms. Behavioral experiments involving neural activity are required to verify this hypothesis and may reveal some important mechanism about the brain [15].

Moreover, the observed stationary LFO phenomena was consistent with our previous study, which observed Significant Granger causal relationships from local field potentials to cerebral blood flow [16]. They both implied the spontaneous activity is tight to neuro activity. And the observed accelerated vLFO phenomena was similar to our previous research, which found the high frequency light would accelerate the frequency of LFO in the rat visual cortex [17]. They both told us the spontaneous activity played a important role in the brain [18]. We may build a more precise cognitive computation model by understanding it.

Our research may also provide a solution to the difficult problem that whether the vegetative people have consciousness? The properties (frequency and amplitude) of the spontaneous activity may be a good indicator.

Acknowledgements. This work was supported by the National Science Foundation of China (61420106001).

References

1. LeCun, Y., Bengio, Y., Hinton, G.: Deep learning. Nature **521**, 436–444 (2015)
2. Litjens, G., et al.: A survey on deep learning in medical image analysis. Med. Image Anal. **42**, 60–88 (2017)
3. Mnih, V., et al.: Human-level control through deep reinforcement learning. Nature **518**, 529 (2015)
4. Miller, G., et al.: What is the biological basis of consciousness? Science **309**, 79–102 (2005)
5. Dehaene, S., Lau, H., Kouider, S.: What is consciousness, and could machines have it? Science **358**, 486 (2017)

6. Heit, E.: Brain imaging, forward inference, and theories of reasoning. Front. Hum. Neurosci. **8**, 1056 (2014)
7. Dehaene, S.: The eternal silence of neuronal spaces. Science **336**, 1507 (2012)
8. Li, M., Liu, Y.D.: Spatio-temporal analysis of stimuli-modulated spontaneous low frequency oscillations. Chin. Sci. Bull. **52**, 1475–1483 (2007)
9. Hirschberg, H., et al.: Hemodynamic low-frequency oscillation reflects resting-state neuronal activity in rodent brain, vol. 9305, p. 930517 (2015)
10. Horikawa, T., Tamaki, M., Miyawaki, Y., Kamitani, Y.: Neural decoding of visual imagery during sleep. Science **340**, 639–642 (2013)
11. Astashev, M.E., Serov, D.A., Tankanag, A.V.: Anesthesia effects on the low frequency blood flow oscillations in mouse skin. Ski. Res. Technol. **25**, 40–46 (2018)
12. Mitra, A., et al.: Spontaneous infra-slow brain activity has unique spatiotemporal dynamics and laminar structure. Neuron **98**, 297–305 (2018)
13. Shih, A.Y., Driscoll, J.D., Drew, P.J., Nishimura, N., Schaffer, C.B., Kleinfeld, D.: Two-photon microscopy as a tool to study blood flow and neurovascular coupling in the rodent brain. J. Cereb. Blood Flow Metab. **32**, 1277–1309 (2012)
14. Kouider, S., et al.: A neural marker of perceptual consciousness in infants. Science **340**, 376–380 (2013)
15. Winder, A.T., Echagarruga, C., Zhang, Q., Drew, P.J.: Weak correlations between hemodynamic signals and ongoing neural activity during the resting state. Nat. Neurosci. **20**, 1761–1769 (2017)
16. Huang, L., Liu, Y., Li, M., Hu, D.: Hemodynamic and electrophysiological spontaneous low-frequency oscillations in the cortex: directional influences revealed by Granger causality. Neuroimage **85**, 810–822 (2014)
17. Huang, L., Liu, Y., Gui, J., Li, M., Hu, D.: Stimulus-dependent modulation of spontaneous low-frequency oscillations in the rat visual cortex. NeuroReport **25**, 823–828 (2014)
18. Fox, M.D., Raichle, M.E.: Spontaneous fluctuations in brain activity observed with functional magnetic resonance imaging. Nat. Rev. Neurosci. **8**, 700–711 (2007)

Deep Learning

Multi-scale Neural Style Transfer Based on Deep Semantic Matching

Jiachen Yu[1], Li Jin[1], Jiayi Chen[2], Zhiqiang Tian[1(✉)],
and Xuguang Lan[2]

[1] School of Software Engineering, Xi'an Jiaotong University,
Xi'an 710049, Shaanxi, China
zhiqiangtian@xjtu.edu.cn
[2] Institute of Artificial Intelligence and Robotics, Xi'an Jiaotong University,
Xi'an 710049, Shaanxi, China

Abstract. Existing Neural Style Transfer (NST) algorithms do not migrate styles well to a reasonable location where the output image can render the correct spatial structure of the object being painted. We propose a deep semantic matching-based multi-scale (DSM-MS) neural style transfer method, which can achieve the reasonable transfer of styles guided by the prior spatial segmentation and illumination information of input images. First, according to real drawing process, before an artist decides how to paint a stroke, he/she needs to observe and then understand subjects, segmenting space into different regions, objects and structures and analyzing the illumination conditions on each object. To simulate the two visual cognition processes, we define a deep semantic space (DSS) and propose a method for calculating DSSs using manual image segmentation, automatic illumination estimation and convolutional neural network (CNN). Second, we define a loss function, named deep semantic loss, which uses DSS to guide reasonable style transfer. Third, we propose a multi-scale optimization strategy for improving the efficiency of our method. Finally, we achieve an interdisciplinary application of our method for the first time–painterly rendering 3D scenes by neural style transfer. The experimental results show that our method can synthesize images in better original structures, with more reasonable placement of each styles and visual aesthetic feeling.

Keywords: Neural style transfer · Image segmentation ·
Illumination estimation · Patch matching

1 Introduction

In recent years, the development of computer vision, deep learning theory and computer graphics processor (GPU) has provided new ideas for style transfer. Gatys et al. first utilized the strong feature extraction capability of convolutional neural network (CNN) to realize the extraction and use of complex art styles [6], and initiated the NST genre. Since the algorithm does not limit the type of the style image, it breaks the style constraint of the previous method. The pioneering work of Gatys and others has attracted wide attention in the industry.

© Springer Nature Singapore Pte Ltd. 2019
F. Sun et al. (Eds.): ICCSIP 2018, CCIS 1006, pp. 185–196, 2019.
https://doi.org/10.1007/978-981-13-7986-4_17

On the basis of Gatys et al., the scientific researchers respectively promoted NST from three aspects: speed, flexibility and image generation quality. Risser et al. considered that advanced art styles can also be measured by the mean value and variance of feature layers [8]. In addition to the loss function of Gayts method, a "deep histogram loss" was added to improve the synthesis effect. Liu et al. added an image depth estimation module and depth loss function based neural network to limit the placement of artistic styles in the target image [10]. Gatys et al. tried to improve their previous strategies by mixing multiple works of a painter to construct the style loss function. Before the algorithm is executed, the artistic style of the style image with the largest stroke scale (or with the desired size scale) is migrated to other style images. All style images are changed to have the same stroke scale [9]. Johnson et al. added an image generation network before Gayts loss model [2]. Training a generation network for each style image before compositing the target greatly improves the efficiency of the algorithm. Some style transfer apps (eg. Prisma) on websites and mobile phones use this approach [4, 5]. Based on this idea, Ulyanov et al. changed the location of the image generation network to a multi-scale generation network [3]. However, these methods take about 3.5 h to train a style network, and you can't pick your own style.

Li et al. provided a theoretical explanation for the accidental discovery of Gram matrix in the method proposed by Gatys et al., and proved that the nature of the style loss function based on the Gram method is the maximum average difference (MAD) between the data of two feature layers [7]. Currently, most deep style transfer methods use Gram matrix statistics to represent complex art styles. Li et al. proposed an algorithm based on Markov Random Field, which directly used the depth feature block of the style image to replace Gram matrix as the high-level art style [11]. Similarly, Liao et al. put forward a kind of similar frame of depth image [15]. The disadvantage of this algorithm is that it can only aim at the style transfer between the same objects, and it will cause the output image to be slightly distorted.

To sum up, whether Gram statistics or deep style feature blocks are used in NST, the following problems exist: the process of extracting and using complex textured styles has no connection with the structures of actual object space; some methods keep internal continuity, but deform the whole of the original structure. Some methods are proposed to solve the above problems. But these methods cannot be applied to style transfer between different objects.

To solve this problem, we propose a deep semantic matching-based multi-scale neural style transfer method, which uses the prior space segmentation and illumination information of the input image. It guides rational style transformation, and makes various art styles of style image placed in a more appropriate location. Therefore, the visual aesthetic feeling is improved.

The main work of this paper is presented as follows: (1) the guiding role of spatial segmentation and illumination analysis in the process of real painting is analyzed. A Deep Semantic Space (DSS) is defined to simulate two kinds of visual understanding mechanism. Then, a deep semantic matching-based multi-scale neural style transfer algorithm is proposed, which enables the art style to be effectively guided by space segmentation and illumination information in the process of transfer. At the same time, the performance is improved by using the DSM algorithm. A multi-scale iterative strategy for the target image is proposed, which greatly reduces the total computing time of the algorithm. (2) A method is proposed to apply the DSM-MS algorithm for rendering the 3D scenes in artistic sense.

2 Methods

2.1 Overview of the Proposed Method

The proposed method consists of three parts that include the calculation of DSS, the deep semantic loss function obtained by DSS, the multi-scale iteration strategy. In this algorithm, we defined a Deep Semantic Space (DSS) containing spatial segmentation and contextual illumination information. Based on the spatial segmentation and illumination information contained in the above deep semantic space, we defined the deep semantic loss function and realized the reasonable transfer of the style of DSS guided brushwork. Furthermore, we introduced the deformation of style features, which greatly improved the computational efficiency. We integrated content loss function [6] proposed by Gatys et al. and style loss function based on Gram statistics, and added DSS loss term. Compared with the method proposed by Gatys et al., the result of work synthesis is better. After solving the spatial rationality of the synthesis effect, the proposed multi-scale iteration strategy greatly improves the algorithm speed when synthesizing high-resolution images.

2.2 Deep Semantic Space

Deep Semantic Space (DSS) contains spatial segmentation and contextual illumination information. The semantic exists in the form of convolution neural network characteristic graph. There are three steps to calculate DSS.

Spatial Segmentation
Our approach is to treat this spatial segmentation as a precondition. We use manual space segmentation in this article. For the input images of each group, the first step is to obtain the spatial segmentation image S_c of the source image I_c, and the spatial segmentation image S_s of the style image I_s.

Integrate Illumination Information into Space Segmentation
The existing methods of NST do not take into account the importance of illumination for artistic stylization. Our algorithm integrates light information into space segmentation image to calculate. The way to obtain a comprehensive semantic map containing spatial segmentation and illumination information is as follows (Fig. 1):

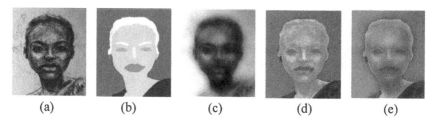

(a)   (b)   (c)   (d)   (e)

Fig. 1. Process of integrate illumination information into space segmentation estimated illumination L_s and L_c. (a) is I_s, (b) is S_s, (c) is L_s, (d) is untextured-filtering I_{ss}. (e) is textured-filtering I_{ss}

- Estimated illumination L_s and L_c

Firstly, converting RGB image into YCrCb color space, we do not use Y channel as illumination directly, but use Guided Filter [14] to do fuzzy filtering on the brightness channel of the style image, that is, $L_s = F_\sigma * Y_s$ and F_σ is the boot filter of 5% size of the style image. And the illumination estimation of the source image does not require fuzzy processing, that is $L_c = Y_c$.

- Integrated light estimation into the spatial segmentation image

We use the linear fusion method in (1) to realize the combination of illumination and space segmentation. In algorithm, we set $\lambda = 1/2$.

$$\begin{cases} I_{sc} = \lambda S_c + (1 - \lambda) L_c \\ I_{ss} = \lambda S_s + (1 - \lambda) L_s \end{cases} \tag{1}$$

Calculate Deep Semantic Space
We use the response of I_{ss} and I_{sc} in CNN's deep feature to calculate the deep semantic space. We define the Deep Semantic space of the source image and style image as the Vector space containing M_{cl} and M_{sl} deep semantic vectors (DSV):

$$\begin{cases} D_c^l = \left[d_c^l(1), d_c^l(2) \ldots d_c^l(M_{cl}) \right] \\ D_s^l = \left[d_s^l(1), d_s^l(2) \ldots d_s^l(M_{sl}) \right] \end{cases} \tag{2}$$

in (2), the value of each DSV consists of the response value of F_{sc}^l (or F_{ss}^l) at the same coordinate in all channels:

$$\begin{cases} d_c^l(p) \left[\left(F_{sc}^l \right)_{p,1}, \left(F_{sc}^l \right)_{p,2}, \ldots \left(F_{sc}^l \right)_{p,N_l} \right]^T, \forall p \leq M_{cl} \\ d_s^l(p) \left[\left(F_{ss}^l \right)_{p,1}, \left(F_{ss}^l \right)_{p,2}, \ldots \left(F_{ss}^l \right)_{p,N_l} \right]^T, \forall p \leq M_{sl} \end{cases} \tag{3}$$

$\left(F^l\right)_{p,n}$ – characteristic response at layer l, feature channel n and pixel position p (Fig. 2).

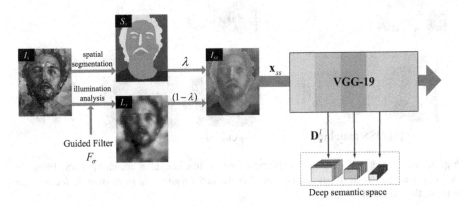

Fig. 2. The complete DSS calculation process of an oil painting image. Only relu2_1, relu3_1 and relu4_1 of VGG-19 [16] are used to calculate the deep semantic space.

2.3 DSS - Guided Deep Semantic Loss Function

Deep Semantic Mapping Function

We aim to find a certain stylized target for each object and light in the source image. For each feature response $\left(F_x^l\right)_{p,n}$ of the target image, if the source image has semantic $d_c^l(p)$ here, then we hope that the value of $\left(F_x^l\right)_{p,n}$ can be as close as possible to the feature response value $\left(F_s^l\right)_{\delta(p),n}$ with the most similar semantic $d_s^l(\delta(p))$. Hereinto, $\delta(p)$ is the semantic mapping function, which means each $d_c^l(p)$ of the source image, finds the $d_s^l(\delta(p))$ that matches it best in the style image:

$$\delta(p) = q \leftarrow \underset{q}{\arg \min}\left\{similarity\left(d_c^l(p), d_s^l(q)\right)\right\} \tag{4}$$

$similarity(z_1, z_2)$ – similarity function, using the Euclidean distance between two feature blocks of size $3 \times 3 \times N_l$ centered on feature vectors z_1, z_2.

$d_c^l(p)$ and $d_s^l(\delta(p))$ in (4) are known information, thus $\delta(p)$ can complete the calculation before optimizing the image. In practice, we use PatchMatch algorithm [1] to calculate semantic mapping function, namely:

$$\delta(p) = NNF_{D_c^l, D_s^l}(p) \tag{5}$$

where: $NNF_{D_c^l, D_s^l}$ – the nearest neighbor space obtained by similarity matching between two deep semantic Spaces $\left\{D_c^l, D_s^l\right\}$ (Fig. 3).

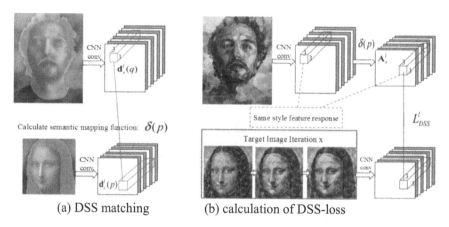

(a) DSS matching   (b) calculation of DSS-loss

Fig. 3. The process of obtaining semantic mapping function after matching DSS. From the optimization process in (b), it can be seen that the deformation treatment of style features can achieve the expected effect.

Deformation of Style Features

When the algorithm iterates, it will take unnecessary computation time to find the target value $\left(F_s^l\right)_{\delta(p),n}$ for each $\left(F_x^l\right)_{p,n}$. In order to eliminate this step, after calculating $\delta(p)$, we firstly deform the style feature space F_s^l [13] and obtain the new style feature space A_s^l, namely: $A_s^l = align\left(F_s^l\right)$

$$\left(A_s^l\right)_{p,n} = \left(F_s^l\right)_{\delta(p),n}, \forall n \leq N_l \tag{6}$$

Loss Function of the Algorithm

The deformed style feature space A_s^l has three properties. First of all, the style feature space A_s^l after deformation retains the brushstroke style of these three levels. Secondly, feature graphs of A_s^l, F_c^l and F_x^l are of the same size. Finally, A_s^l and F_c^l [12] have the same object labeling and contextual illumination at the same spatial location.

The total loss function we need to optimize is

$$L_{total} = \alpha \sum_l L_{content}^l + \beta \sum_l L_{style}^l + \gamma \sum_l L_{DSS}^l \tag{7}$$

where α – weight of content loss; β – weight of style loss; γ – weight for DSS. In experiments, the fixed values of the parameters in the loss function are shown in Table 1. Among them, $L_{content}^l$ is the content loss function in algorithm [6] of Gayts et al., L_{style}^l is the style loss function based on Gram statistics, and the last item is our proposed deep semantic loss function L_{DSS}^l:

$$L_{DSS}^l = \left\| F_x^l - A_s^l \right\|^2 \tag{8}$$

Table 1. Loss function parameter experience value of DSM-MS

α/β	α/γ	$L_{content}^l$	L_{style}^l	L_{DSS}^l
5×10^{-4}	2×10^{-2}	{relu4_1, relu5_1}	{relu1_1, relu2_1, relu3_1, relu4_1, relu5_1}	{relu2_1, relu3_1, relu4_1}

Since A_s^l is known quantity before the iteration, the derivative of L_{DSS}^l with respect to each characteristic response is

$$\frac{L_{DSS}^l}{\delta(F_x^l)_{i,j}} = \begin{cases} (F_x^l - A_s^l)_{j,i} & if\,(F_x^l)_{i,j} > 0 \\ 0 & if\,(F_x^l)_{i,j} \leq 0 \end{cases} \qquad (9)$$

2.4 Multi-scale Iteration Strategy

The multi-scale iteration strategy can be summarized as:

a. Downsample the input image to get $\{X_c^k\}_{k=1,2,3}$, $\{X_s^k\}_{k=1,2,3}$, and $\{X_{sc}^k\}_{k=1,2,3}$, and the downsampling coefficient is $\alpha = 1/2$.
b. When k = 1, the target image is initialized to $X^{1(0)} = random\left(\frac{W}{4}, \frac{H}{4}\right)$ or $X^{1(0)} = X_c^1$; When k > 1, the target image is initialized to $X^{k(0)} = upsampling\left(X^{k-1(T)}\right)$, and the upsampling coefficient is $1/\alpha = 2$.
c. The objective function of each scale is set as (7), and feature space is replaced by the input image of the corresponding scale:

$$X^k \leftarrow \arg\min L_{total}\left(X^k | X_c^k, X_s^k, X_{cs}^k, X_{ss}^k\right), k = 1, 2, 3 \qquad (10)$$

d. The iterative update process of the target is: $X^{k(0)} \rightarrow X^{k(1)} \rightarrow X^{k(2)} \ldots \rightarrow X^{k(T)}$. Generally speaking, each scale can get good results after T = 10 iterations. At this point, the loss function starts to slow down with L_{DSS}^l converged.
e. The composite image is $X = X^{3(T)}$.

3 Experimental Result

3.1 Implementation Details

The experimental environment in this paper is shown in Table 2. The programming language environment of DSM-MS algorithm is Python, and the computing language environment of light estimation and comprehensive semantic graph is Matlab. In all the experiments below, we fix the number of iterations of Gatys et al. [6] to 1000 times. The weight of style loss function is 1000 times of the weight of content loss. Other algorithms directly extract the results of their papers. As shown in Table 1, we fixed the parameters of loss function of the proposed DSM-MS algorithm, and made the optimization of objective x be divided into 3 scales, and each scale was iterated for 7 times.

Table 2. Experimental environment

Language	DeepLearning-Lib	GPU	OS
Python/Matlab	Theano	NVIDIA Tesla K4	CentOS 7

3.2   Data and Pre-treatment

The data sets of experimental input images come from Internet and other algorithms. In this paper, these input images are divided into two categories: face image and natural landscape image. Each image is pre-calibrated to simulate space segment. We used the Wand tool of Photoshop to label the images, which took an average of 4 min to complete the task. In the following experiments, the images of natural landscapes were uniformly divided into foreground (green) and background (red). In addition, we divided face image into background, skin, clothes, hair and other areas (for example, as shown in S_c and S_s in Fig. 4(a) and (b)). The latter method of face segmentation refers to NeuralDoodle algorithm [17].

3.3   Result and Analysis

Verify the Guiding Effect of Illumination Information on Style Transfer

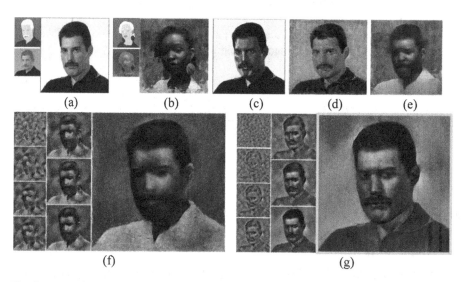

Fig. 4. Comparison of the output of the traditional style migration algorithm and the algorithm in this paper. (a) and (b) are the source image and style image, respectively. (c) is the result of matching the light information I_{sc} and I_{ss} at the pixel level. Secondly, (d) shows the output of the algorithm of Gatys et al. [6], which presents wrong illumination information compared with the source image (a). (e) shows the output of the algorithm of Neural Doodle [17]. (f) and (g) initialized to white noise show two groups of contrast experiments, aiming to verify the validity of illumination information in deep semantic space (DSS). Where (g) contains illumination information and (f) does not. (Color figure online)

Discussion on the Effect of Style Transfer Between Objects of Different Categories

In the following experiments, we will divide validation of our algorithm into three cases:

- the stylization of facial images using portrait (Fig. 5)

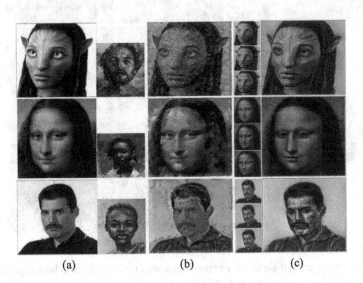

(a)   (b)   (c)

Fig. 5. Three groups of stylistic transfer experiments from portraiture to face images, proving that our DSM-MS algorithm is also applicable to other art styles. (a) includes the source image and the style image, (b) shows the output of the algorithm of Gatys et al. [6], (c) shows the output of the algorithm of DSM-MS

- the stylization of natural scenes by using portraits (Fig. 6)

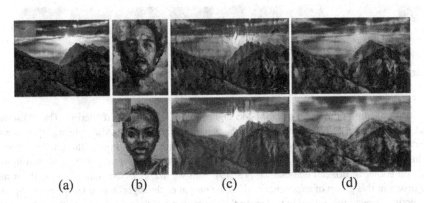

(a)   (b)   (c)   (d)

Fig. 6. Two experiments using portraits to stylize images of natural landscapes. (a) and (b) are the source image and style image, respectively. (c) shows the output of the algorithm of Gatys et al. [6], (d) shows the output of our algorithm of DSM-MS

- the stylization of natural scenes with landscape paintings (Fig. 7)

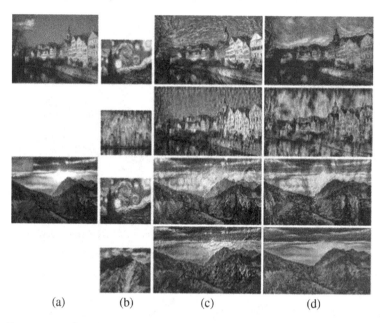

(a)   (b)   (c)   (d)

Fig. 7. Four groups of stylistic transfer experiments from natural scenes to landscape paintings. (a) and (b) are the source image and style image, respectively. (c) shows the output of the algorithm of Gatys et al. [6], (d) shows the output of our algorithm of DSM-MS. Compared with the third image in (c), the third and fourth images in (d) achieve more delicate texture migration.

Application of DSM-MS 3D Scene Art Rendering
See Fig. 8.

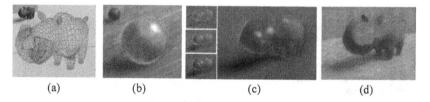

(a)   (b)   (c)   (d)

Fig. 8. Application of a group of DSM-MS algorithm in 3D scene art rendering. The 3D scene in (a) includes two objects, buffalo and a rectangular background. After placing the virtual camera, mapping of color materials, rendering of LPEs illumination to three illumination effects, and linear superposition of four illumination effects, the target semantic graph I_{sc} shown in the upper left corner of (a), can be obtained [18, 19]. And we use I_{sc} as the source image. (b) is the style image in this group of experiment. (d) is the output of the algorithm of Gatys et al. [6] and incorrectly migrated the red stripe texture in the background of the style image to the red buffalo. In our DSM-MS algorithm (c), the DSS of target scene and style image control the placement of texture. (Color figure online)

Algorithm Efficiency Analysis

In the experiment in this paper, it takes 700–1000 iterations for Gayts' original framework to achieve a better synthesis effect. Our DSM-MS algorithm adopts a multi-scale iterative strategy, and the deformed style feature space enables the target to converge faster, only about 20 iterations can achieve a better synthesis effect.

4 Conclusion

We define DSS to simulate the spatial and illumination visual guidance information, and give the algorithm of using DSS to guide the style transfer process. Also, we use a multi-scale iteration method to optimize the target, which improve the total computing efficiency and save computing resources, and have a significant effect on the HD image synthesis rate. In addition, the DSM-MS algorithm can also be used for 3D scene rendering.

This work is a semi-automated approach that requires user intervention to initialize the source image and the style image. The automatic segmentation method can simplify the process. Therefore, it is important to develop a completely automatic segmentation method which can get a high degree of acceptability at the same time. Our future work will focus on developing robust, accurate, and fully automatic methods

Acknowledgement. This work was supported in part by the National Key Research and Development Program of China (No. 2017YFB1302200) and key project of Shaanxi province (No. 2018ZDCXL-GY-06-07).

References

1. Barnes, C., Shechtman, E., Finkelstein, A., et al.: PatchMatch: a randomized correspondence algorithm for structural image editing. ACM Trans. Graph.-TOG **28**(3), 24 (2009)
2. Johnson, J., Alahi, A., Fei-Fei, L.: Perceptual losses for real-time style transfer and super-resolution. In: Leibe, B., Matas, J., Sebe, N., Welling, M. (eds.) ECCV 2016. LNCS, vol. 9906, pp. 694–711. Springer, Cham (2016). https://doi.org/10.1007/978-3-319-46475-6_43
3. Ulyanov, D., Lebedev, V., Lempitsky, V.: Texture networks: feed-forward synthesis of textures and stylized images. In: International Conference on Machine Learning, pp. 1349–1357 (2016)
4. Prisma Labs: Prisma: turn memories into art using artificial intelligence (2018). https://prisma-ai.com
5. Champandard, A.J.: Deep forger: paint photos in the style of famous artists (2018). https://deepforger.com/
6. Gatys, L.A., Ecker, A.S., Bethge, M.: Image style transfer using convolutional neural networks. In: 2016 IEEE Conference on Computer Vision and Pattern Recognition (CVPR), pp. 2414–2423. IEEE (2016)
7. Li, Y., Wang, N., Liu, J., et al.: Demystifying neural style transfer. In: Proceedings of the 26th International Joint Conference on Artificial Intelligence, pp. 2230–2236. AAAI Press (2017)
8. Wilmot, P., Risser, E., Barnes, C.: Stable and controllable neural texture synthesis and style transfer using histogram losses. arXiv preprint arXiv:1701.08893 (2017)

9. Gatys, L.A., Ecker, A.S., Bethge, M., et al.: Controlling perceptual factors in neural style transfer. In: Proceedings of the IEEE Conference on Computer Vision and Pattern Recognition (CVPR), pp. 3985–3993 (2017)
10. Liu, X.C., Cheng, M.M., Lai, Y.K., et al.: Depth-aware neural style transfer. In: Proceedings of the Symposium on Non-Photorealistic Animation and Rendering, p. 4. ACM (2017)
11. Li, C., Wand, M.: Combining Markov random fields and convolutional neural networks for image synthesis. In: Proceedings of the IEEE Conference on Computer Vision and Pattern Recognition (CVPR), pp. 2479–2486 (2016)
12. Yosinski, J., Clune, J., Fuchs, T., et al.: Understanding neural networks through deep visualization. In: ICML Workshop on Deep Learning (2015)
13. Gatys, L., Ecker, A.S., Bethge, M.: Texture synthesis using convolutional neural networks. In: Advances in Neural Information Processing Systems, pp. 262–270 (2015)
14. He, K., Sun, J., Tang, X.: Guided image filtering. In: Daniilidis, K., Maragos, P., Paragios, N. (eds.) ECCV 2010. LNCS, vol. 6311, pp. 1–14. Springer, Heidelberg (2010). https://doi.org/10.1007/978-3-642-15549-9_1
15. Liao, J., Yao, Y., Yuan, L., et al.: Visual attribute transfer through deep image analogy. ACM Trans. Graph. (TOG) 36(4), 120 (2017)
16. Simonyan, K., Zisserman, A.: Very deep convolutional networks for large-scale image recognition. arXiv preprint arXiv:1409.1556 (2014)
17. Champandard, A.J.: Semantic style transfer and turning two-bit doodles into fine artworks. arXiv preprint arXiv:1603.01768 (2016)
18. Fišer, J., Jamriška, O., Lukáč, M., et al.: StyLit: illumination-guided example-based stylization of 3D renderings. ACM Trans. Graph. (TOG) 35(4), 92 (2016)
19. Heckbert, P.S.: Adaptive radiosity textures for bidirectional ray tracing. ACM SIGGRAPH Comput. Graph. 24(4), 145–154 (1990)

A Method of Attitude Control Based on Deep Deterministic Policy Gradient

Jian Zhang[✉], Fengge Wu, Junsuo Zhao, and Fanjiang Xu

Beijing, China
eholy.zh@gmail.com, {fengge,junsuo,fanjiang}@iscas.ac.cn

Abstract. The traditional methods of attitude control of satellite are represented by PID control, adaptive control, optimal control and intelligent control, etc. With these methods, lots of work of parameter adjustment and simulation needs to do on the earth. We proposed a method based on Deep Deterministic Policy Gradient (DDPG) to learn attitude control strategy in orbit in order to reduce the work and establish the ability of adapting to space environment. Through constructing training environment by using the attitude control system of satellite platform (ACSoSP), we trained an attitude control model and used the model to generate the strategy of attitude control. Validate the method by experiments in simulation environment.

Keywords: Attitude control · Micro/nano-satellite · Deep reinforcement learning · DDPG

1 Introduction

The satellite attitude control algorithm is the core of the attitude control system, and its performance determines whether the task can be successfully executed. In general, the verification of the attitude control system relies on the method of simulation. By establishing a mathematical model, numerical simulation is used to apply the control algorithm to the model for verification. Because the attitude control has strong dependence on the environment, and the attitude sensor and actuator also have various measurement and execution deviations, the simulation results of the control algorithm on the earth are often quite different from the results running on the actual space environment. Especially for micro/nano-satellite with short development cycle, low cost and simple structure (YU (2004)), it is not realistic to use a backup attitude control system or an attitude control system which is designed excellently. Therefore, we need a method that can adapt to the actual environment and be trained to learn the attitude control strategy in orbit.

From another point of view, we can collectively call this type of method designed and verified on the earth "Offline" method. This type of control method is generally based on knowledge, starting from the establishment of mathematical models, and verified by simulation experiments. Though these methods can

© Springer Nature Singapore Pte Ltd. 2019
F. Sun et al. (Eds.): ICCSIP 2018, CCIS 1006, pp. 197–207, 2019.
https://doi.org/10.1007/978-981-13-7986-4_18

adapt to the disturbance in orbit to a certain extent, the overall structure is determined on the earth, and the adjustment range is limited. They are generally represented by PID control, robust control, adaptive control, optimal control and intelligent control, etc. This type of method requires a lot of parameter adjustment, which is often unacceptable for micro/nano-satellite of which cost is constrained.

The method proposed in this paper is based on the deep reinforcement learning framework, defines the tuples required by the reinforcement learning method, and trains an agent to learn the attitude control strategy by using the actual payload on the satellite to achieve the expected control effect. The traditional "Offline" method differs in that the training of the agent is done in orbit, so we call it "Online" method.

The article consists of four parts: 1. Background introduction, including the satellite kinematics and attitude dynamics model required by this paper, and the reinforcement learning method. 2. A METHOD of ATTITUDE CONTROL BASED ON DEEP DETERMINISTIC POLICY GRADIENT (DDPG) (Lillicrap (2016)). 3. Simulation and model training. 4. Conclusion.

2   Background

2.1   Deep Reinforcement Learning

Reinforcement learning strategy can effectively adapt to the environment. Through interacting with the environment in trial-and-error mechanism, it learns optimal strategies by maximizing cumulative reward. The classical reinforcement learning methods (SUTTON (1998)) include Monte Carlo method, TD (temporal difference), Sarsa (RUMMERY (1994)), Q learning (Watkins (1989)), REINFORCE (Williams (1992)), etc. These methods rely on the selection of artificial features to achieve success in classical control problems, but the quality of learning is greatly related to the selected features. Deep learning method based on neural network can effectively reduce the dependence on feature selection quality for specific applications, and it makes it possible to extract high-level features directly from the original data under the condition of reducing feature engineering work through its strong representational ability. Deep learning has strong perception ability, but lacks decision-making ability. Reinforcement learning has decision-making ability, but cannot solve representation problem. Therefore, the combination of the deep learning and reinforcement learning will provide one possible solution to complex perceptual and decision-making problem such as attitude control.

2.2   The Kinematic and Dynamic Module of Attitude in Satellite

We choose three reference coordinate systems: geocentric inertial coordinate system, orbital coordinate system and satellite body coordinate system (Lu (2007)).

1. Geocentric inertial coordinate system $O_I X_I Y_I Z_I$

We define the geocentric inertial coordinate system as follows. The origin is the center of the earth, and the $O_I Z_I$ axis points to the North Pole, that is, the earth's rotation axis. The $O_I X_I$ axis points to the vernal equinox along the intersection of the Earth's equator plane and the ecliptic plane. The $O_I Y_I$ axis forms a right-hand rotation coordinate system with the $O_I X_I$ axis and the $O_I Z_I$ axis. The geocentric inertial coordinate system is a coordinate system that is stationary relative to the inertial space.

2. Orbital coordinate system $O X_O Y_O Z_O$

We define the orbital coordinate system as follow. The origin is the satellite centroid. The $O Z_O$ axis points to the center of the earth, and the $O Y_O$ axis points to the opposite direction of the normal direction of orbital plane. The $O X_O$ axis forms a right-handed coordinate system with the $O Y_O$ axis and the $O Z_O$ axis in the orbital plane. The $O X_O$ axis is the satellite velocity direction.

3. Satellite body coordinate system $O X_B Y_B Z_B$

We define the satellite body coordinate system as follow. The origin is the satellite's center of mass, and the $O X_B$ axis, $O Y_B$ axis and $O Z_B$ axis are fixed on the satellite. The $O X_B$ axis, $O Y_B$ axis and $O Z_B$ axis is parallel to the inertial reference coordinate axis that is fixed on the satellite respectively (Fig. 1).

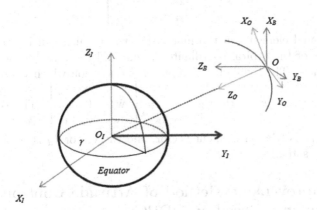

Fig. 1. Reference coordinate systems

The rotation angular velocity of the satellite body coordinate system with respect to the geocentric inertial and orbital coordinate systems is represented by three component vectors w, w_{bo} respectively.

$$w = [w_x, w_y, w_z]^T, \quad w_{bo} = [w_{box}, w_{boy}, w_{boz}]^T.$$

With the orbital coordinate system as the reference coordinate system, the attitude quaternion of the satellite body coordinate system relative to the orbital coordinate system is q_bo. The attitude kinematics equation described by quaternion is

$$\begin{bmatrix} \dot{q}_{bo1} \\ \dot{q}_{bo2} \\ \dot{q}_{bo3} \\ \dot{q}_{bo4} \end{bmatrix} = \frac{1}{2} \begin{bmatrix} 0 & w_{box} & -w_{boy} & w_{boz} \\ -w_{boz} & 0 & w_{box} & w_{boy} \\ w_{boy} & -w_{box} & 0 & w_{box} \\ -w_{box} & -w_{boy} & -w_{box} & 0 \end{bmatrix} \begin{bmatrix} q_{bo1} \\ q_{bo2} \\ q_{bo3} \\ q_{bo4} \end{bmatrix} \tag{1}$$

Equation 1 can be abbreviated as

$$\dot{q}_{bo} = \frac{1}{2} \Omega \left(w_{bo} \right) q_{bo} \tag{2}$$

The attitude dynamics equation of the satellite is

$$I\dot{w} + w^{\times} Iw = T_c + T_d \tag{3}$$

I is the moment of inertia matrix, can be written in matrix form as

$$I = \begin{bmatrix} I_x & -I_{xy} & I_{xz} \\ -I_{xy} & I_y & -I_{yz} \\ -I_{xz} & -I_{yz} & I_z \end{bmatrix} \tag{4}$$

The diagonal elements in the matrix are the moments of inertia of the x, y, and z axes of the orbital coordinate system and the other elements are the inertia products. The Symbol "$\times$" represents operation which is taken on any vector $w = [w_x, w_y, w_z]^T$, then get $w^{\times} = \begin{bmatrix} 0 & -w_z & w_y \\ w_z & 0 & w_x \\ -w_y & w_x & 0 \end{bmatrix}$. The vector $T_c = [T_{cx}, T_{cy}, T_{cz}]^T$ is triaxial moment vector, and the vector T_d is the disturbance torque on the satellite.

3   An Improvement Method of Attitude Controls Performance Based on DDPG

In the attitude control of satellite, the goal of reinforcement learning is to obtain the attitude control strategy through learning. Reinforcement learning requires interaction with the environment to learn, so we need to construct the training environment when the ACSoSP works normally. Tuples of reinforcement learning are defined as follows.

The satellite's attitude relative to geocentric inertial coordinate system is described by the quaternion q as [q1, q2, q3, q4]^T. The target attitude is represented by q'.

The state space in the reinforcement learning structure is defined as

$$S = [q, q', dist, keep\_count] \in R^{10}$$

where q is current attitude quaternion and q' is target attitude quaternion. The Euclidean distance between current attitude quaternion and target attitude quaternion is represented by dist.

$$dist = D(q, q') = \sqrt{\sum_1^4 (q_i - q_i')^2}$$

The number of current attitude quaternion kept within a radius centered on the target attitude is represented as keep_count. The state space is a real number space of ten dimensions. The action space in the reinforcement learning structure is defined as $A = [a1, a2, a3] \in R^3$ where components are three-axis torque scalar and the directions are coaxial with satellite body coordinate system. The accuracy function is defined as

$$H(h, q, q') = \begin{cases} 1 \ when \ D(q, q') \leq h \\ 0 \ otherwise \end{cases}$$

where h is the accuracy radius. The function describes whether the Euclidean distance between the current attitude quaternion and the target attitude quaternion is less than the accuracy radius h.

The reward function is defined as

$$R(s, s', a) = \begin{cases} - \| a \| \ if \ H(h, s'.q, \ s'.q') = 0 \\ - \| a \| + \alpha^{s.keep\_count+1} \ if \ H(h, s'.q, \ s'.q') = 1 \end{cases}$$

where s is the current state and s' is the next state to which is transferred after taking action a. The reward function will give high reward to the strategy in which the distance is kept in the accuracy radius continuously. The hyperparameter is set to bigger than 1. The overall structure of the proposed method is shown in Fig. 2. It is divided into three phases: pre-learning phase, adjustment phase and execution phase. We define the pre-learning phase in which phase the control accuracy of ACSoSP is not degraded. In this phase, the training environment is constructed through adjusting the satellite's attitude to a 4-dimensional sphere of which center is target attitude and radius is H1. In this situation, the accuracy radius is H1. According to the accuracy radius, we can know whether the training environment is constructed. Figure 3(a) is the schematic diagram. We define the adjustment phase in which the control accuracy of ACSoSP is degraded. The ACSoSP can only control the attitude to a 4-dimensional sphere of which center is target attitude and the radius is H2. In this phase, the model pre-trained in pre-learning phase will be used to interact with environment directly. Model's parameters will be updated to adapt to the new environment. We define the execution phase when the model is updated and the neural network's parameters are fixed. In this phase, the model and ACSoSP will complete the attitude control task together. There is no difference between the adjustment stage and the execution stage in the structure. The work schematic diagram is given in Fig. 3(b).

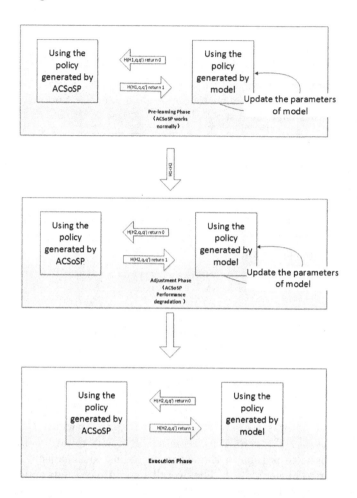

Fig. 2. The overall structure of the proposed method

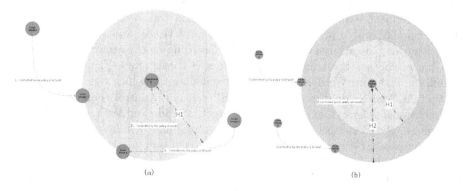

Fig. 3. (a) Schematic diagram in pre-learning phase, (b) Schematic diagram in adjustment phase and execution phase

In this paper, the model trained to learn control strategy is based on DDPG. Silver et al. proved that updating the parameters of the policy network along the direction of the policy gradient can improve the performance of the strategy (Silver (2014)). In general, the usage of optimization algorithm is based on assumption that samples are subjected to independent and identical distribution. However, in the reinforcement learning problem, the data obtained by executing any strategy is correlated. In Deep Q-Learning Network, experience replay is used to solve the problem that the data sampled with specific strategy is correlated. Usually, experience replay uses data buffer R of which capacity is limited. When the policy interacts with the environment, one experience represented by a tuple (s_t, a_t, r_t, s_{t+1}) is stored into the buffer R. When the buffer is full, the earliest records will be eliminated. Experience replay makes historical data to be used more effectively, but it requires the method is Off-Policy. As a class of Off-Policy Actor-Critic algorithm, DDPG can use experience replay to improve learning efficiency. In real world, Q-Learning may be divergent if neural networks are used as approximations. To solve this problem, DDPG establishes two target networks for the policy network and the value network, and uses "soft update" to reduce the update speed of the target network. The update rule of the policy network is given by formula as

$$\begin{cases} \theta_{t+1}^{\mu} = \theta_t^{\mu} + \alpha_t * \nabla_{\theta^{\mu}} J \\ \nabla_{\theta^{\mu}} J \approx \frac{1}{N} \sum_{i=1}^{N} \nabla_{\theta^{\mu}} Q\left(s_i, a|\theta^Q\right) \left(\text{Where } a = \mu\left(s_i|\theta^{\mu}\right)\right) = \frac{1}{N} \sum_{i=1}^{N} \nabla_a Q\left(s_i, a|\theta^Q\right) \nabla_{\theta^{\mu}} \mu\left(s_i\right) \end{cases} \tag{5}$$

where θ_t^{μ} represents the parameters of the policy network μ at time step t and the policy network μ is a function which maps the state space to the action space. The goal of updating the value network is to fit the target value network. For any one experience (st, at, rt, st + 1), the target Q value is

$$y_t = r_t + \gamma Q'\left(s_{t+1}, \mu'\left(s_{t+1}\right)\right),$$

and the Q value estimated by the value network is

$$y_t' = Q(s_t, a_t),$$

The rule of updating the value network is to make the MSE (mean squared error) of an estimator of a parameter y_t in batch samples minimized. The MSE is

$$L = \frac{1}{N} \sum_{i=1}^{N} (y_i - y_i')^2$$

The update rule of the value network is given by formula as

$$\begin{cases} \theta_{t+1}^Q = \theta_t^Q + \alpha_t * \nabla_{\theta^Q} L \\ \nabla_{\theta^Q} L = \frac{1}{N} \sum_{i=1}^{N} (y_i - y_i') * \nabla_{\theta^Q} Q(s_i, a_i) \end{cases} \tag{6}$$

where θ_t^Q represents the parameters of the value network Q at time step t and the value network Q is a function which maps the pair of state and action to the Q value. Soft update is taken to update the target policy network and the value network. The update rule is given by formula as

$$\begin{cases} \theta_{t+1}^{Q'} = \tau * \theta_{t+1}^{Q} + (1 - \tau) * \theta_t^{Q'} \\ \theta_{t+1}^{\mu'} = \tau * \theta_{t+1}^{\mu} + (1 - \tau) * \theta_t^{\mu'} \end{cases} \tag{7}$$

Algorithm 1. Learning algorithm based on DDPG

1: Initialize the value network Q(s,a) and the policy network $\mu(s)$ where the parameters of two network are θ^Q, θ^μ respectively.
2: Initialize the target value network $Q'(s, a)$ and the target policy network $\mu'(s)$ where the parameters of two networks are $\theta^{Q'}, \theta^{\mu'}$ respectively.
3: Initialize the experience replay buffer R, and the maximum capacity is denoted as C.
4: **for** $epoch\_num = 0$ to max_epoch **do**
5:     Initialize a random process N which will be mixed with the action outputted by the policy network in order to realize the exploration of action space.
6:     Initialize the state s_1 and the accuracy radius H_1.
7:     **for** $step = 0$ to max_steps **do**
8:         **if then**
9:             Execute the action $a = \mu(s, \theta^\mu) + N$ generated by the policy network with the random process.
10:        **else**
11:            Execute the action generated by the ACSoSP until the current attitude is in a 4-dimensional sphere of which center is the target attitude and the radius is H_1.
12:        **end if**
13:        Observe the reward r and the new state s'.
14:        Store the experience (s, a, r, s') into the replay buffer R.
15:        Randomly sample a batch of N samples from R, represented as $S_1, \ldots, S_N$.
16:        According to the formula 6, update the parameters θ^Q of the value network.
17:        According to the formula 5, update the parameters θ^μ of the value network.
18:        According to the formula 7, update the parameters $\theta^{Q'}, \theta^{\mu'}$ of the target networks.
19:        $step = step + 1$
20:    **end for**
21:    $epoch\_num = epoch\_num + 1$
22: **end for**

---

4   Simulation Environment and Model Training

To validate the method described in this paper, we develop the simulation environment based the attitude dynamics equation and the attitude kinematics equation described in sect. 2. The multilayer neural networks are used as the structure of DDPG policy network and value network. The policy network consists of 2 hidden layers, each with 300 neurons, and the input layer's dimension is the same as the state space. The activation function is Relu, and the output layer's dimension is 3 equivalents to the action space's dimension. The detail is shown in Fig. 4(a). The value network is used to describe function Q(S, A). The network's structure consists of 2 parts. The first part consists of the first 4 layers. Input layer is combined with action input after encoded by a fully-connected hidden layer. The second part consists of the last 4 layers. These layers are fully connected. The output layer of which dimension is 1 is viewed as a scalar to represent Q value. The detail structure is shown in Fig. 4(b).

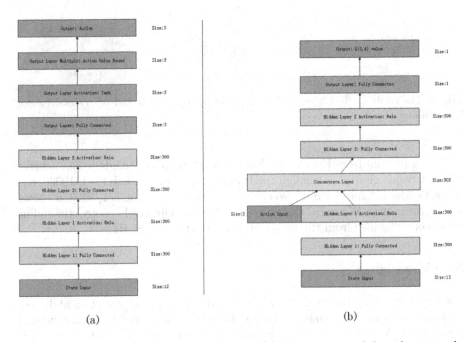

(a)   (b)

Fig. 4. (a) The structure of the policy network, (b) The structure of the value network

In pre-learning phase, the maximum steps in each epoch are 500 and the ACSoSP uses PID as default attitude control strategy. We set H1 as 0.0001. When the current attitude is in range of which center is target attitude and radius is H1, PID stops and model's training starts. When the current attitude is out of the range, PID works and model's training is suspended. Loop the process described above until the training model learned the strategy. Our work is built on environment which is Python3.5 + Tensorflow1.8 + Nvidia-GeForce-GTX-TITAN-X. After trained in 20000 epochs, the pre-learning phase is end, and we found the model has learned the control strategy. Different H2 value means different capacity of default attitude control strategy. The bigger the value of H2, the harder the control strategy learned is to achieve. We want to find in which situation the control strategy learned still work. H2 = 0.000125 (1/8000), 0.00016667 (1/6000) and 0.0002 (1/5000) were used as test values respectively. Each H2 value was taken and the model obtained in the pre-learning phase was used to run 100 epochs (500 steps per epoch). The results of the experiment are counted, and the data is obtained as shown in Fig. 5(a-c). The X axis represents the steps in epoch and the Y axis represents current attitude distance from the target attitude. The red dot line shows the average distance in which step the x axis tells.

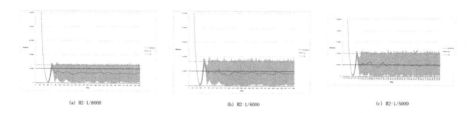

(a) H2=1/8000   (b) H2=1/6000   (c) H2=1/5000

Fig. 5. The control effect when H2 is (a) 1/8000, (b) 1/6000 and (c) 1/5000 (Color figure online)

It can be seen from Fig. 5(a-c) that the learned control strategy can achieve stable attitude control. Although the training environment is H1 = 1/10000, the control under H2 condition is also effective. When H2's value is 1/8000, it shows high performance. When H2's value is 1/5000, it can effectively control the radius of attitude distance from the target attitude to the level of H1.

5   Conclusion

Aiming at reducing the work of parameter adjustment and providing ability to adapting to space environment, a DDPG-based attitude control learning method is proposed. An online learning environment to train control strategy model is constructed by using ACSoSP. The trained control strategy model can be used to realize the attitude control effectively. At the same time, we believe that by choosing several groups of H1 values to train several models, the model used in execution phase will have better robustness and better control performance. These need to be in the next step of the work.

References

Lillicrap, T.P.: Continuous control with deep reinforcement learning. In: ICLR (2016)

Lu, J.: Study on attitude control algorithm of three-axis stabilization satellite. Ph.D. thesis, Harbin Institute of Technology (2007)

RUMMERY: On-Line Q-Learning Using Connectionist Systems. University of Cambridge, Cambridge (1994)

Silver, D.: Deterministic policy gradient algorithms. In: ICML (2014)

Sutton, R.S.: Reinforcement Learning: An Introduction. The MIT Press, Cambridge (1998)

Watkins, C.J.: Learning from delayed rewards. Ph.D. thesis. University of Cambridge, Cambridge (1989)

Williams, R.J.: Simple statistical gradient-following algorithms forconnectionist reinforcement learning. Mach. Learn. **8**(2), 229–256 (1992)

Yu, J.: Modern Micro-Sat Technology and Application. Shanghai Popular Technology Press, Shanghai (2004)

The Semaphore Identification and Fault Troubleshooting Modus for Spacecraft Originating from Deep Learning and RF Method

Wei Lan[1], Chun He[2], Mingju Wang[3], Ke Li[3(✉)], and Zhijian Zhao[4]

[1] School of Economics and Management, Beihang University, Beijing, China
lanwei@buaa.edu.cn
[2] Beijing Institute of Control and Electronic Technology, Beijing, China
he302@sohu.com
[3] School of Aeronautics Science and Engineering,
Beihang University, Beijing, China
{dtm,like}@buaa.edu.cn
[4] Naval Aeronautical and Astronautical University, Yantai, China
hyz0504@163.com

Abstract. The spacecraft environment and reliability test brings the huge type of data, traditional algorithm has many shortcomings when handling big data especially huge storage space and massive compute time. According to the deep learning network, the writer design a algorithm with the ability that gain the initial parameters of the multi-layer neutral network. After initialize the parameters with gradient descent method, we will select the parameters to help to classifying information more easily. By researching generated data, there is expert information which could help to build a platform to manage the health of spacecraft. Experimental data show that the deep neural network algorithm could be proved to achieve a desired accuracy through classification with multi-kind of spacecraft data environment and reliability experiment.

Keywords: Prognostic and health management · Deep learning · Data compression · Signal identification · Random-forest · Deep belief network

1 Introduction

Satellite have a longer and longer life span, so the Prognostics and Health Management of the satellite are very essential in the launch and operation, which could help to make the spacecraft safer and more reliable [1, 2]. It is necessary for the health risk appraisal of satellite to use unified the signal identification algorithm with expert system infor-

© Springer Nature Singapore Pte Ltd. 2019
F. Sun et al. (Eds.): ICCSIP 2018, CCIS 1006, pp. 208–219, 2019.
https://doi.org/10.1007/978-981-13-7986-4_19

mation and current data to recognize the false signal and predict possible order [2, 3]. As the Pivotal key of the expert system, knowledge acquisition, which is mainly generate from the raw signal through deep learning algorithm [4]. Compare to the original data, the learning characteristics obtained depict more essentially by using deep learning method. Furthermore, the deep learning also surmounts the problem called gradient diffusion when it uses layer-by-layer to initialize when train gradient descent [5–8]. And the characteristics of multithreading calculating is kept learning more kernel from complicated information. Recently, this method has been successfully applicated in many places in natural language processing [9]. Because of these advantages, the deep learning method is introduced to be used to aerospace data analysis generating the chief features of the raw spacecraft signals and utilizing the traditional algorithm (such as support vector machine (SVM), K nearest neighbor (KNN), logic regression (LR), simple Bias, etc.) to classify, proposes a multi-features separate algorithm on basis of random forest and further research for the health risk appraisal of satellite [10–14].

2 Structure and Algorithm

The practical spacecraft detected measurement system could create a 50-channel data in all and each channel collects higher than 30 MB/S rate signals. The information that different channels acquire is very large, however, we might only need a few information for satellite fault diagnosis, while most other data afford little information. We list a flow chart of learning approach that conflated with the neural networks characteristics. It is shown in the Fig. 1.

The chart has three parts: signal acquirement, electrical type recognition and network training. The original information is generated from the recorded ground station offline database in, obtained from other channels as well as cut into the Individual events. The writer could build simultaneous training network or support the prepared network that already set for fault diagnosis in the total procedure. Features of the original data that play an important role in satellite situation estimate are abstracted from the network that has been trained and apply traditional classification algorithms to classifying. The following discussion is about building basic network framework, initializing network and fine-tuning training parameters.

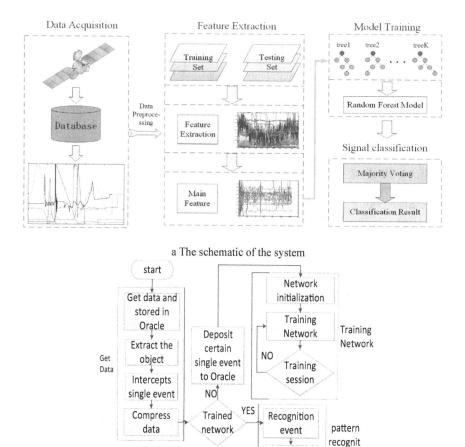

a The schematic of the system

b The Flowchart of whole processing

Fig. 1. The total system flow chart

2.1 Network Parameters Initialization

Network Structrue

There is more hidden layers in deep learning neural network in form of shallow layer. But the network could process the complicate nonlinear problem with any precision as well as could exploit more characteristics from the data. Every hidden layer net parameter will be given a initial value by auto-encoder, then, use the sample label and gradient descent method to fine tune the weights of the network. The depth learning network of this paper is shown in Fig. 2.

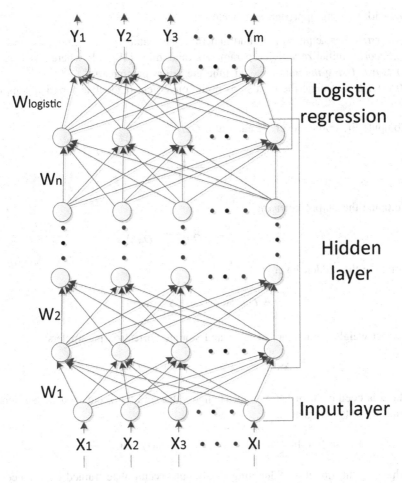

Fig. 2. Structrue of deep learning network.

The network contains an input layer, the hidden layer and an output layer. Input channel numbers in the input layer is obtained by the features of the sample data. Hidden layer nodes could be determined from empirical formula and we will use experimental methods to obtain them. The output layer neuron number is three. Hidden layer activation function selection sigmoid are exhibited as follows:

$$f(x) = \frac{1}{1 + e^{-x}} \tag{1}$$

Network training approach is as follows:

(a) First: Filter acquired data and generate one feature;
(b) Second: Initialize weights parameters randomly, $\{\mathbf{W_i}, \mathbf{b_i}\}$, where $i = 1, \ldots, n$;
(c) Third: Using the auto-encoder tune the initial parameters;
(d) Fourth: Circulate the next steps until convergent (Calculate for each sample in turn):

Compute the output result of each unit Out_j

$$Out_j = \frac{1}{1 - e^{-\sum_i W_{ij}x_i}} \tag{2}$$

Compute the output layer σ_j:

$$\sigma_j = (y - Out_j)Out_j(1 - Out_j) \tag{3}$$

Compute the hidden layer σ_j:

$$\sigma_j = Out_j(y - Out_j) \sum_k w_{jk}\sigma_k \tag{4}$$

Correct weight parameters of layer and storage correction parameters:

$$\Delta w_{ij}(t) = \alpha \Delta w_{ij}(t - 1) + \eta \sigma_j Out_j \tag{5}$$

The α is coefficient of last weight change value and the η determines step length; Tune weights parameters:

$$w_{ij}(t + 1) = w_{ij}(t) + \Delta w_{ij}(t) + \rho[w_{ij}(t) - w_{ij}(t - 1)] \tag{6}$$

Where ρ (the impulse of learning rate) could accumulate trained experience and help the network come to convergence faster.

2.2 Stack Auto-Encoder [5, 17]

If writer use iterative algorithm to train deep neural network, as the depth of the network increases, the magnitude of the gradient of back propagation (from the output layer to the initial layers of the network) decreases dramatically, which is called vanishing gradient problem. To resolve this problem, in each layer the writer extract features with unsupervised method from unlabeled data and uses these features to build auto ceding network and train network. The processes is shown in Fig. 3.

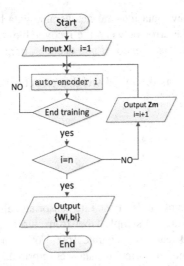

Fig. 3. The stack auto-encoder diagram.

The most important effect that auto-encoder method takes is to improve the network weight value, using the raw data to initialize the network weight which is core information extracted from the data. The Automatic Encoding Basic approach: First, by the transforming high-dimension signal to low-dimension code. Second, the decoder compiles the code into original signal. Finally, according to the deviation of reconstructed data and the original signal, correct the parameters of modified encoder and decoder. Inspired by this method, the writer proposes auto-encoder for this paper.

The equations of third step are revealed as follows:

$$\mathbf{O}_m = \mathbf{W}_{mn} * \mathbf{X}_n + \mathbf{B} \tag{7}$$

$$\mathbf{Y}_n = \mathbf{W}1_{nm} * \mathbf{O}_m + \mathbf{B}1 \tag{8}$$

Where n is the training samples dimension; m is the hidden layer neurons number.

The penalty function is selected from the training sample error and the reconstructed signals:

$$error = \sum_{i=1}^{n} |X_i - Y_i| \tag{9}$$

The algorithm main steps:

(e) *First:* Input samples that are used for training;
(f) *Second:* Use the encoder to reduce dimension of samples for training, maintain the dimension of reconstructed data has the same number as neurons number of the hidden layer;

(g) Third: Transform new data into the recoverable data by decoder;

(h) Fourth: Compute the error between the recoverable data and original signal;

(i) Fifth: Correct parameters of encoder and decoder, minimizing the reconstruction error;

(j) Sixth: Consider $\mathbf{W}_{mn}$ as the initial weights of network input layer and hidden layer.

3 Experiment

3.1 Data Acquisition

There are 19 selected different kinds of satellite sensor signals and the 13th mode of a spacecraft flying data with added sample label from. writer acquire 22400 parts that every parts including 1000 features; Separate 16000 original signals for training and other 6400 used for testing. The original data were normalized before input the network. The physical signification of the part of the data as shown in Fig. 4.

3.2 Relationship Between Classification Accuracy and the Sample Size

The classification accuracy will float as the number of cycles and classes change. As shown in Fig. 5. After initialization, the deep learning network could validly simplify the sample data and extract major characteristics of sample data. But deep learning network cannot directly be used to classifying, so use the labeled sample to fine tune the initial weights and offsets is very essential. It could guarantee the network to convergent, also will make the training time increase rapidly and reduce the algorithm efficiency when the number of cycles or the amount of fine-tuning sample has large amount. To figure out the best fit fine-tuning sample for the data set has been used, writer design experiments to prove that the accuracy rate of the classification is varied with the number of samples. The results obtained are shown in Fig. 5.

All kinds of algorithms could get ideally classification accuracy when classes are few. Such as the two kinds classification accuracy of deep learning network could be nearly 100% if the class is less than 8. When the number of classes increase, the classification accuracy of the different algorithms could cut down. The results reveal that the classification accuracy of algorithm including KNN, SVM and NBM is significantly lower. Meanwhile, the abatement of classification accuracy using deep learning becomes obviously lower than other algorithms, deep learning could improve the result of classification through ameliorating the cycles number to offset the reduction.

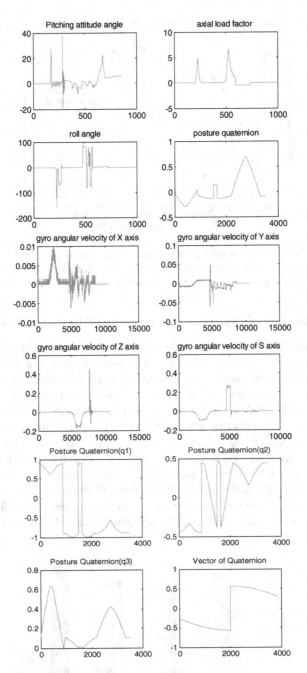

Fig. 4. Partial data and its physical meaning.

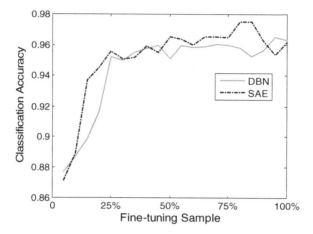

Fig. 5. Curve of classification accuracy varying with the fine-tuning part. *(Every curve consists of 20 points; Each point is the average of the experiment 6 times in the case of the same parameters; Horizontal coordinates percentage of fine-tuning sample compare to the total sample.)*

3.3   The Coalescent of Deep Neural Network and Other Algorithms

The accuracy of classifying shall be reduced because the characteristic the sample has too large dimension, which is called the dimension disaster. The reduction of the sample dimension could improve the calculating speed and reduce memory account, besides, it could also enhance the accuracy of classifying. In engineering, there has been a lot application of dimension reduction method utilizing the kernel function, such as linear method like principal component analysis and nonlinear method. Linear method has poor performance when it is used to classify nonlinear separable samples. Meanwhile, nonlinear method has the advantage of aggrandizing the numerical difficulty when separate data by projecting to the high dimensional space. By unsupervised initializing the parameters, the separability of data will enhance and avert the problem of high dimension, which will make generating the characteristics that fitting primary data well The classification results of different algorithms are shown in Fig. 6, memory

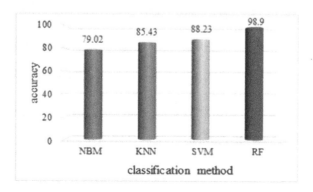

Fig. 6. The results of different algorithms classifying

usage and running time are given in Table 1 gives the classification accuracy of different classification algorithms.

Table 1. Classification accuracy and training time variation chart for dimension reduction data

Method	Raw data	Compressed data	
		DEN	SEA
KNN	79.67%	97.48%	97.46%
NBM	80.26%	81.27%	85.55%
SVM	82.97%	99.12%	90.98%

From Table 1, writer could see that it could save the memory footprint and the entire time of the calculation that extracts 50 features from the 1000 features by DBN and SEA. Table 1 shows that the effect of classifying the original data is obviously worse than classifying same data that has been reduced dimension. The KNN classification accuracy increased significantly for the k nearest neighbor is based on linear separable theory. From the simulation, it could improve accuracy of classifying and the separability of data, as also it could save computing time that use deep learning to extract the major characteristics of the original data.

4 Conclusion

The writer presents the main progress of spacecraft fault diagnosis which is on basis of deep learning network. Experimental information reveals that: the deep learning algorithm in the case of huge samples and a quantity of labels could still have ideally effect by targeted training to classifying. The new structure is improved in stability, speed of convergence and accuracy rate of classification. Besides it also could be used for the satellite fault diagnosis directly for it uses the raw spacecraft signal to train. Finally, new algorithm is convenient in designs, moreover, is greatly flexible and adaptable on the data when detailed rules are ambiguous. It could elevate accuracy rate and real-time of the satellite fault diagnosis, which also help writer do further research with other algorithms based on deep learning method. There is a great space for improvement considering deep belief network in this paper is simple designed.

Acknowledgment. The authors are supported by the Chinese National Natural Science Foundation (No. 61773039), The Aeronautical Science Foundation of China (No. 2017ZD51043), 'Fanzhou' Youth Scientific Funds (No. 20100504), and Fundamental Research Funds for the Central Universities (No. YWF-14-HKXY-017, YWF-13-HKXY-033).

References

1. Luo, R., Sun, B., Zhang, L., et al.: Analysis of PHM technology for spacecraft. Spacecr. Eng. **22**(4), 95–102 (2012)
2. Long, B., et al.: A study of integrated vehicle and ground health management technology for spacecrafts. Aerosp. Control **21**(2), 56–61 (2003)
3. Gang-De, L.V., Yang, Z.C.: Study on prognostics and health management system modeling technology. Meas. Control Technol. (2011)
4. Xin, M.A.: Knowledge acquisition methods for expert systems based on machine learning. J. Beijing Univ. Chem. Technol. **35**(5), 89–93 (2008)
5. Hinton, G.E., Osindero, S.: A fast learning algorithm for deep belief nets. Neural Comput. **18**(7), 1527–1554 (2006)
6. Bengio, Y.: Learning deep architectures for AI. Found. Trends® Mach. Learn. **2**, 1–127 (2009)
7. Rodrigues, L.R., Gomes, J.P.P., Ferri, F.A.S., et al.: Use of PHM information and system architecture for optimized aircraft maintenance planning. IEEE Syst. J. **9**(4), 1–11 (2014)
8. Xu, J., Wang, Y., Xu, L.: PHM-oriented integrated fusion prognostics for aircraft engines based on sensor data. IEEE Sens. J. **14**(4), 1124–1132 (2014)
9. Batzel, T.D., Swanson, D.C.: Prognostic health management of aircraft power generators. IEEE Trans. Aerosp. Electron. Syst. **45**(2), 473–482 (2009)
10. Anand, I.M.: Reverse multiple-choice based clustering for machine learning and knowledge acquisition. In: 2014 International Conference on Computational Science and Computational Intelligence (CSCI), pp. 431–436. IEEE Computer Society (2014)
11. Liu, Y., Li, K., Huang, Y., et al.: Spacecraft electrical characteristics identification study based on offline FCM clustering and online SVM classifier. In: 2014 International Conference on Multisensor Fusion and Information Integration for Intelligent Systems (MFI), pp. 1–4. IEEE (2014)
12. Li, K., Liu, Y., Wang, Q., et al.: A spacecraft electrical characteristics multi-label classification method based on off-line FCM clustering and on-line WPSVM. PloS One **10**(11) (2015)
13. Liu, Y., Li, K., Song, S., et al.: The research of spacecraft electrical characteristics identification and diagnosis using PCA feature extraction. In: 2014 12th International Conference on Signal Processing (ICSP), pp. 1413–1417. IEEE (2014)
14. Li, K., Liu, W., Wang, J., et al.: Multi-parameter decoupling and slope tracking control strategy of a large-scale high altitude environment simulation test cabin. Chin. J. Aeronaut. **27**(6), 1390–1400 (2014)
15. Li, K., Liu, W., Wang, J., et al.: An intelligent control method for a large multi-parameter environmental simulation cabin. Chin. J. Aeronaut. **26**(6), 1360–1369 (2013)
16. Martínez, A.M., Kak, A.C.: PCA versus LDA. IEEE Trans. Pattern Anal. Mach. Intell. **23**(3–4), 228–233 (2001)
17. Carmona, P.L., Sánchez, J.S., Fred, A.L.N.: Editorial: advances in pattern recognition applications and methods. Neurocomputing **123**, 1–2 (2014)
18. Thomas, S., Seltzer, M.L., Church, K., et al.: Deep neural network features and semi-supervised training for low resource speech recognition. In: Acoustics, Speech, and Signal Processing, pp. 6704–6708 (2013)
19. Luus, F.P.S., Salmon, B.P., van den Bergh, F., et al.: Multiview deep learning for land-use classification. IEEE Geosci. Remote Sens. Lett. **12**(12), 2448–2452 (2015)
20. Wersing, H., Körner, E.: Learning optimized features for hierarchical models of invariant object recognition. Neural Comput. **15**(7), 1559–1588 (2003)

21. Zabalza, J., Clemente, C., Caterina, G.D., et al.: Robust PCA micro-doppler classification using SVM on embedded systems. IEEE Trans. Aerosp. Electron. Syst. **50**(3), 2304–2310 (2014)
22. Keerthi, S.S., Shevade, S.K., Bhattacharyya, C., et al.: Improvements to Platt's SMO algorithm for SVM classifier design. Neural Comput. **13**(3), 637–649 (1999)
23. Chen, H., Chang, K.C.: K-nearest neighbor particle filters for dynamic hybrid bayesian networks. IEEE Trans. Aerosp. Electron. Syst. **44**(3), 1091–1101 (2008)
24. Yu, C., Ooi, B.C., Tan, K.L., et al.: Indexing the distance: an efficient method to KNN processing. In: VLDB (2001)
25. Zhou, X.Y., Tian, X.W., Lim, J.S.: Fuzzy Naive Bayesian for constructing regulated network with weights. Bio-Med. Mater. Eng. **26**(s1), S1757–S1762 (2015)
26. Zhang, X., Hao, S., Xu, C., et al.: Image classification based on low-rank matrix recovery and Naive Bayes collaborative representation. Neurocomputing **169**, 110–118 (2015)
27. Friedman, J., Hastie, T., Tibshirani, R.: Additive logistic regression: a statistical view of boosting. Ann. Stat. **28**(1), 337–407 (2000)
28. Pregibon, D.: Logistic regression diagnostics. Ann. Stat. **9**(4), 705–724 (1981)
29. Zhao, L., Jia, Y.: Neural network-based distributed adaptive attitude synchronization control of spacecraft formation under modified fast terminal sliding mode. Neurocomputing **171**(C), 230–241 (2015)
30. Hinton, G.E.: Reducing the dimensionality of data with neural networks. Science **313**(5786), 504–507 (2006)

Network Improved by Auxiliary Part Features for Person Re-identification

Zhongji Liu$^{(\boxtimes)}$, Hui Zhang$^{(\boxtimes)}$, Rui Wang$^{(\boxtimes)}$, Haichang Li$^{(\boxtimes)}$, and Xiaohui Hu$^{(\boxtimes)}$

Institute of Software Chinese Academy of Sciences,
No. 4 Zhongguancun South Road, Haidian District, Beijing, China
{zhongji2016,wangrui,haichang,hxh}@iscas.ac.cn, zhzaozao@126.com

Abstract. Person re-identification (ReID) is an important issue in computer vision area. It focuses on identifying people under different scenarios. In this paper, we test the contributions of local part features in ReID system. With the auxiliary of local part features, our model achieves significantly improvements, which achieves rank-1 accuracy of 91.7% on market1501 dataset and 82.6% on MARS dataset. We also test the feasibility of using densenet as backbone model in ReID system. With densenet as our backbone model, our method achieves state-of-art performance and simultaneously reduces the model size enormously.

Keyword: Re-Identification densenet part-feature

1 Introduction

Person re-identification is an important task in computer vision. Technically speaking, a practical person re-ID system is consist of three modules, i.e., person detection, person tracking and person retrieval. The first two modules are thought to be independent computer vision tasks, so most re-ID works focus on person retrieval. The key purpose of this issue is to identifying a person from a gallery that have been taken using different cameras, or at different time with a single camera. This is a challenging problem, like other visual recognition problems, because of large significant appearance variations, usually caused by variations in pose, viewpoints, illumination and occlusion.

The key challenges for person re-identification lie in two fundamental problems: feature description and distance metrics. For the first problem, traditional methods focus on low-level features such as colors, shapes and local features [5,7]. With the development of deep learning, the convolutional neural network becomes the principal method. Generally speaking, two types of CNN models, identification model and verification model, have been used to solve the problem. The first type is the classification model as used in image classification and

---

This work is supported in part by the Youth Innovation Foundation of the 4th China High Resolution Earth Observation Conference under Grant GFZX04061502.

F. Sun et al. (Eds.): ICCSIP 2018, CCIS 1006, pp. 220–230, 2019.
https://doi.org/10.1007/978-981-13-7986-4_20

object detection. The second type is using image pairs or triplets as input and output a similarity score between the images.

Another problem of re-identification system is how to learn a similarity function to match the input images. Many metric learning algorithms have been proposed to measure similarity between images. Deep metric learning methods transform raw images into embedding features and then compute the feature distances as their similarities. The commonly used learning losses include softmax loss, contrastive loss [18], center loss [28], triplet loss [14] and triplet hard loss [10] (Fig. 1).

Fig. 1. Person re-id: matching with manually cropped pedestrians.

In this paper, beside extracting a global feature as descriptor of input image, our model also adds a local feature branch to predict the identity using local part features. With the combination of global feature and local part features, we achieve better performance than only using the global features. With the auxiliary of local part features, our model can focus on body rather than the background. We also test the feasibility of using densenet as backbone model in ReID system, rather than the most common used Resnet model. Resnet has become the domain model to extract feature map but we found out that densenet model has its advantages for this task. Densenet model has much fewer parameters and include the low-level features naturally. In our experiments, with densenet as backbone model rather than using resnet, we achieve better accuracy performance and save much memory utilization.

2   Related Work

CNN-Based Re-ID Work. CNN-based methods have become the principal method in re-identification problem and can be classified into two categories: verification model and identification model [29]. Verification model can achieve good results in small datasets. In verification model, image pairs or triplets are fed into the network and output whether the input images are the same or different person. For triplets, a triplet loss is proposed to get the relative distance between images [14]. Verification model focuses on the similarities of the input images and many articles apply the idea of part matching, which divide the images into serval parts and synthesis the similarities between parts. These methods include horizontal stripe [11,12], square neighborhood [31], body parts [4,22] and attention matching [14,16,30].

Identification model has gained increasing popularity because it achieves superior accuracy coupled with the efficiency, such as [13,14,34,35]. Xiao et al. [34] train the classification model with multiple datasets and proposes a new dropout function. Geng et al. [6] collect some commonly used trick and achieve pretty good performance. Lin et al. [13] combine attribute recognition and ReID issues and achieves good performance. Zheng et al. [33] use GAN model to perform data augmentation. Xiao et al. [14] use a approach similar to faster-RCNN to train the classification model to automatically predict the position of pedestrians in the image, thereby reducing the detection error of the dataset itself.

Metric Learning. Deep metric learning methods measure the similarities of images by computing the distances between the extracted features. Usually, two images of the same person are defined as a positive pair, whereas two images of different persons are a negative pair. Classification loss combining verification loss is efficient but they both have disadvantages [3]. However, triplet loss is end-to-end and the features are highly embedded. Triplet loss is hard to train and we choose triplet hard loss, which choose hard positive and negative samples mining as triplets [10].

Local Part Features. Many methods just take a global feature extracted from cnn model as feature representation, which lose the important local details. Without the help of local features, pose changes or body deformations will make the metric learning difficult. What's more, the accuracy with be impacted greatly if the appearances of two people are similar. Recently, many articles have applied the idea of part matching. Liao et al. [12] divide images into horizontal stripes and compute the similarities between parts. BPM [11] proposed a model to conduct a 'soft' and adaptive partition to refine the original 'hard' and uniform partition. GLAD [23] detects key pose points and extracts local features from corresponding regions. SpindleNet [36] uses a region proposed network (RPN) to generate several body regions, gradually combining the response maps from adjacent body regions at different stages. Our method combines global and local features and uses local part features to improve the performance of global features.

3 Our Architecture

In this section, we present our cnn model improved by auxiliary part features, as shown in Fig. 2. We will describe the architecture and introduce the loss function we use below.

3.1 Network Structure

In our architecture, we have one global branch to extract a global feature as the final output of the input image and one local branch using local parts features to predict the IDs. The similarities of two images is the summation of their global distance and local distances. The global distance is simply the L2 distance of the global features. Local features will be fed into softmax and during training the loss will be supervised by cross entropy loss. The final loss function is the summation of cross entropy loss and triplet loss.

We use a Densenet121 [9] model pretrained on ImageNet to extract feature map F for each input image. The structure before the original global average pooling layer is maintained exactly the same as the backbone model. On all datasets, before entering the first dense block, all images are resized to 256×128. The data augmentation includes random horizontal flipping and cropping. The global feature is extracted by directly applying global average pooling on the feature map. To represent the local features, we replace the original global pooling layer with a conventional pooling layer, to spatially down-sample F into p pieces of column vectors g. A following 1×1 kernel-sized convolutional layer reduces the dimension of g. Finally, each dimension-reduced column vector h is input into a classifier respectively. Each classifier is implemented with a fully-connected layer and a Softmax layer to predict the identity.

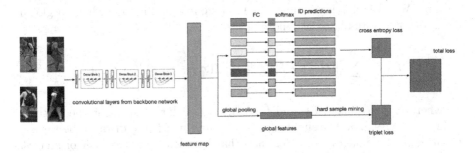

Fig. 2. Block diagram of the proposed method. Both the global feature and local feature are computed based on the feature map extraction model. The global feature branch and local part feature branch are joint learned during training.

During the learning stage, we take triplet hard loss [10] as the metric learning loss for global features. According to global feature, the most dissimilar one with the same identity and the most similar one with a different is chosen to form a triplet for each sample. We don't apply local features to find hard triplet due to its computation cost. During inferencing, we only use the global features to compute the similarity between images. The local features are not used in inference stage, which does not influence the result much. But with local features jointly learned is better than learning the global feature alone. The local features help the global feature pay more attention to the body rather than the background.

3.2   Loss Computation

In our experiments, we take cross entropy loss [11] in part features branch and triplet hard loss [10] in global features branch to supervised the learning stage.

We test the performance of each branch and our method achieve best performance with the combination of both branches.

Cross Entropy Loss. During training stage, to classify all the columns vectors f, we put each column vector into a classifier which is implemented with a linear layer followed by a softmax layer. During training, the loss is optimized by minimizing the sum of cross entropy loss over all ID predictions as follows:

$$L_{xent} = -log \frac{exp(W_i^T f)}{\sum_{j=1}^{p}(W_j^T(f))}. \tag{1}$$

$$L_{total} = \alpha_{xent} L_x + \alpha_t L_{trp}. \tag{2}$$

where W is the trainable weight matrix of classifier.

Triplet Loss. The triplet loss is normally trained on a series of triplets $\{x_i, x_j, x_k\}$, where x_i and x_j are images from same person, and x_k is from a different person. We select triplet samples by hard sample mining according to global distances. It is formulated as following:

$$L_{trp} = \sum_{i,j,k}^{N}[||f(x_i) - f(x_j)||_2^2 - ||f(x_i) - f(x_k)||_2^2 + \alpha_{trp}]_+. \tag{3}$$

where $[z]_+ = \max(z, 0)$, and $f(x_i)$, $f(x_j)$ and $f(x_k)$ represent the features of input images. The threshold α_{trp} is a margin which the distance between a negative pair of images is greater than that between a positive pair of images. The triplet loss adopts the Euclidean distance to measure the similarity between features.

4   Experiments

In this section, we present our results and compare with several other deep learning method on two widely used ReID datasets: Market1501 [1] and MARS [19]. For performance measure, we use the cumulative matching characteristic (CMC) and mean Average Precision (mAP) metrics.

4.1   Implementation Details

We use Densenet121 as the base model. We choose the novel Densenet model as backbone network, which requires much less memory comparing with the common used Resnet in ReID system. We adopt a ResNet-50 [8] model as the base network for comparison. Given the base model, we extract a 2048-dim feature map from the pool5 layer. For each query, we calculate the Euclidean distance between the query and gallery features, before a ranking step.

The training images are augmented with horizontal flip and normalization. We set batch size to 32 and train the model for 60 epochs with base learning rate initialized at 0.0003 and decayed by 0.1 every 10 epochs. The margins of triplet hard loss is set to 0.3 empirically.

4.2 Performance Evaluation

Part Features Contributions. We present the experiments results in Table 1, in which densenet121 and resnet50 represents the base feature extraction model respectively. We tested how much local part features contribute to our architecture. For the convenience of description, global model represents the architecture only using global features, part model represents the model we remove the global feature branch and concentrate the local parts features as the output feature instead. Joint model represents the architecture we combine these both branches. With the help of local part features, joint model goes ahead than global model in rank-1 accuracy by 3.2%, which implies the importance of local detailed informations in person re-identification. Local part features can help the model focus on body rather than the background. But the final representation in global model is easy to compute, while part model require larger computation cost. So in our method, with the help of local part features during training stage, the rank-1 accuracy obtains a very big enhancement and the time cost in inference stage is lower simultaneously.

Table 1. Joint model achieves better rank-1 and mAP performance than the part model or the global model.

Branch	Backbone model	Param size (M)	Rank-1(%)	mAP(%)
Part model	densenet121	7.7	87.7	69.6
	resnet50	25.1	88.24	70.5
Global model	densenet121	7.7	88.5	73.7
	resnet50	25.1	88.7	74.1
Joint model	densenet121	7.7	91.7	77.2
	resnet50	25.1	91.4	77.6

Backbone Model Differences. Besides the accuracy performance, with the advantage of densenet model comparing with resnet50, our model size shrinks enormously from 25.1M to 7.7M and gets the equal performance simultaneously. Usually, resent model converges faster than densenet and we verify that in Fig. 3. With resnet as backbone, the train losses of global part and local part converged faster. But we find that the train loss of joint model converged faster with densenet121 model. With NVIDIA TITAN XP GPUs and Pytorch as the platform, training our joint model on Market1501, with densenet and resnet as the backbone network, consumed about 24 and 26 min respectively. What's more, with densenet121 as backbone model, our model has fewer parameters and is lighter and suitable for more scenes. During training, densenet is harder to train but we can bear this small defect.

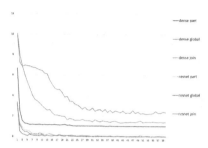

Fig. 3. The train loss comparison. With densenet as backbone model, our joint model converged faster.

Evaluation on Market1501. Market1501 dataset contains 32,668 images of 1,501 labeled persons of six camera views. There are 751 identities in the training set and 750 identities in the testing set. In the original study on this proposed dataset, the author also uses mAP as the evaluation criterial to test the algorithms.

We evaluated our model against the state-of-art methods on Market1501 dataset summarized by the author of Market1501 dataset in Table 2. We will report both mAP and ran-1,5,10 accuracies. On market1501, GLAD [23] achieves an 89.9% rank-1 accuracy and obtains 81.1% for mAP with the help of re-ranking. Our model achieves a 91.7% rank-1 accuracy and a 77.2% for mAP without the use of re-ranking. Our method achieves the state-of-art level performance on Market-1501. Comparing with the GLAD [23], which is the best method recorded, our method outperforms by 1.8%.

Evaluation on MARS. MARS (Motion Analysis and Re-identification Set) dataset is an extended version of the Market1501 dataset. Because all bounding boxes and tracklets are generated automatically, it contains distractors, and each identity may have more than one tracklet. There were five 1080×1920 HD cameras and one 640×480 SD camera during collection. MARS consists of 1,261 different pedestrians whom are captured by at least 2 cameras. Given a query tracklet, MARS aims to retrieve tracklets that contain the same ID.

We also evaluated our model against the state-of-art methods in Table 3. For each tracklet, its feature is calculated by averaging features of all its bounding boxes. Our method achieves 82.6% rank-1 accuracy which is better than all other state-of-art methods.

Table 2. Comparison on Market-1501 in single query mode

Method	Market1501			
	rank-1	rank-5	rank-10	mAP
Scalable [1]	44.42	63.90	72.18	20.76
Multiregion [42]	66.36	85.01	90.17	41.17
Multi-scale [44]	45.1	70.1	78.4	-
Synthetic [2]	73.87	88.03	92.22	47.89
Pose [22]	79.33	90.76	94.41	55.95
Re-ranking [21]	77.11	-	-	63.63
Discriminatively [28]	79.51	90.91	94.09	59.87
Divide [37]	82.3	-	-	72.42
Improving [13]	84.29	93.20	95.19	64.67
Pedestrian [43]	85.78	93.38	-	76.56
In defense [10]	84.92	94.21	-	69.14
Multi-loss [40]	88.8	-	-	72.9
GLAD [23]	89.9	-	-	73.9
Our method	**91.7**	**96.1**	**97.6**	**77.2**

Table 3. Comparison on MARS in single query mode

Method	MARS			
	rank-1	rank-5	rank-10	mAP
MARS [19]	65.0	81.1	88.9	49.3
Compact [24]	55.5	70.2	80.2	-
Multi-target [25]	68.22	-	-	-
Re-ranking [21]	73.94	-	-	68.45
Context-aware [41]	71.77	86.57	93.08	56.05
See [27]	70.6	90.0	97.6	50.7
Quality [26]	73.74	84.90	91.62	51.70
In defense [10]	81.21	90.76	-	77.43
Our method	**82.6**	**93.2**	**95.4**	**74.6**

5   Conclusion

In this paper, we tested the contributions of local part features in ReID system. With the help of local parts features, the accuracy of our method obtains a very big enhancement. We also tested the feasibility of using densenet as backbone model in ReID system. With densenet as backbone feature extraction model, our model achieves state-of-art performance and simultaneously reduces the model size enormously. Our model still has a lot of room to improve, we will try to extract more deep local features or take alignment idea into consideration in the future work.

References

1. Bai, S., Bai, X., Tian, Q.: Scalable person re-identification on supervised smoothed manifold. arXiv preprint arXiv:1703.08359 (2017)
2. Barbosa, I.B., Cristani, M., Caputo, B., Rognhaugen, A., Theoharis, T.: Looking beyond appearances: synthetic training data for deep CNNs in re-identification. arXiv preprint arXiv:1701.03153 (2017)
3. Chen, W., Chen, X., Zhang, J., Huang, K.: Beyond triplet loss: a deep quadruplet network for person re-identification. arXiv preprint arXiv:1704.01719 (2017)
4. Cheng, D., Gong, Y., Zhou, S., Wang, J., Zheng, N.: Person re-identification by multi-channel parts-based CNN with improved triplet loss function. In: Proceedings of the IEEE Conference on Computer Vision and Pattern Recognition, pp. 1335–1344 (2016)
5. Farenzena, M., Bazzani, L., Perina, A., Murino, V., Cristani, M.: Person re-identification by symmetry-driven accumulation of local features. In: 2010 IEEE Conference on Computer Vision and Pattern Recognition (CVPR), pp. 2360–2367. IEEE (2010)
6. Geng, M., Wang, Y., Xiang, T., Tian, Y.: Deep transfer learning for person re-identification. arXiv preprint arXiv:1611.05244 (2016)
7. Hamdoun, O., Moutarde, F., Stanciulescu, B., Steux, B.: Person re-identification in multi-camera system by signature based on interest point descriptors collected on short video sequences. In: 2008 Second ACM/IEEE International Conference on Distributed Smart Cameras, ICDSC 2008, p. 16. IEEE (2008)
8. He, K., Zhang, X., Ren, S., Sun, J.: Deep residual learning for image recognition. In: Proceedings of the IEEE Conference on Computer Vision and Pattern Recognition, pp. 770–778 (2016)
9. Huang, G., Liu, Z., Maaten, L.V.D., et al.: Densely connected convolutional networks (2016)
10. Hermans, A., Beyer, L., Leibe, B.: In defense of the triplet loss for person re-identification. arXiv preprint arXiv:1703.07737 (2017)
11. Sun, Y., Zheng, L., Yang, Y., et al.: Beyond part models: person retrieval with refined part pooling (and a strong convolutional baseline) (2017)
12. Liao, S., Hu, Y., Zhu, X., Li, S.Z.: Person re-identification by local maximal occurrence representation and metric learning. In: Proceedings of the IEEE Conference on Computer Vision and Pattern Recognition, pp. 2197–2206 (2015)
13. Lin, Y., Zheng, L., Zheng, Z., Wu, Y., Yang, Y.: Improving person re-identification by attribute and identity learning. arXiv preprint arXiv:1703.07220 (2017)
14. Liu, H., Feng, J., Qi, M., Jiang, J., Yan, S.: End-to-end comparative attention networks for person re-identification. IEEE Trans. Image Process. **26**, 3492–3506 (2017)
15. Liu, H., et al.: Video-based person re-identification with accumulative motion context. arXiv preprint arXiv:1701.00193 (2017)
16. Liu, X., et al.: Hydraplus-net: attentive deep features for pedestrian analysis (2017)
17. Martinel, N., Das, A., Micheloni, C., Roy-Chowdhury, A.K.: Temporal model adaptation for person re-identification. In: Leibe, B., Matas, J., Sebe, N., Welling, M. (eds.) ECCV 2016. LNCS, vol. 9908, pp. 858–877. Springer, Cham (2016). https://doi.org/10.1007/978-3-319-46493-0_52

18. Matsukawa, T., Suzuki, E.: Person re-identification using CNN features learned from combination of attributes. In: 2016 23rd International Conference on Pattern Recognition (ICPR), pp. 2428–2433. IEEE (2016)
19. Zheng, L., et al.: MARS: a video benchmark for large-scale person re-identification (2016)
20. Zhang, L., Xiang, T., Gong, S.: Learning a discriminative null space for person re-identification. In: Proceedings of the IEEE Conference on Computer Vision and Pattern Recognition, pp. 1239–1248 (2016)
21. Zhong, Z., Zheng, L., Cao, D., Li, S.: Re-ranking person re-identification with k-reciprocal encoding. arXiv preprint arXiv:1701.08398 (2017)
22. Zheng, L., Huang, Y., Lu, H., Yang, Y.: Pose invariant embedding for deep person re-identification. arXiv preprint arXiv:1701.07732 (2017)
23. Wei, L., Zhang, S., Yao, H., Gao, W., Tian, Q: GLAD: global-local-alignment descriptor for pedestrian retrieval. arXiv preprint arXiv:1709.04329 (2017)
24. Zhang, W., Hu, S., Liu, K.: Learning compact appearance representation for video-based person re-identification. arXiv preprint arXiv:1702.06294 (2017)
25. Tesfaye, Y.T., Zemene, E., Prati, A., Pelillo, M., Shah, M.: Multi-target tracking in multiple non-overlapping cameras using constrained dominant sets. arXiv preprint arXiv:1706.06196 (2017)
26. Liu, Y., Yan, J., Ouyang, W.: Quality aware network for set to set recognition. arXiv preprint arXiv:1704.03373 (2017)
27. Zhou, Z., Huang, Y., Wang, W., Wang, L., Tan, T.: See the forest for the trees: joint spatial and temporal recurrent neural networks for video-based person re-identification (2017)
28. Zheng, Z., Zheng, L., Yang, Y.: A discriminatively learned CNN embedding for person re-identification. arXiv preprint arXiv:1611.05666 (2016)
29. Zheng, L., Yang, Y., Hauptmann, A.G.: Person re-identification: past, present and future. arXiv preprint arXiv:1610.02984 (2016)
30. Varior, R.R., Haloi, M., Wang, G.: Gated siamese convolutional neural network architecture for human re-identification. In: Leibe, B., Matas, J., Sebe, N., Welling, M. (eds.) ECCV 2016. LNCS, vol. 9912, pp. 791–808. Springer, Cham (2016). https://doi.org/10.1007/978-3-319-46484-8_48
31. Ahmed, E., Jones, M., Marks, T.K.: An improved deep learning architecture for person re-identification (2015)
32. Liu, W., et al.: SSD: single shot multibox detector. In: Leibe, B., Matas, J., Sebe, N., Welling, M. (eds.) ECCV 2016. LNCS, vol. 9905, pp. 21–37. Springer, Cham (2016). https://doi.org/10.1007/978-3-319-46448-0_2
33. Zheng, Z., Zheng, L., Yang, Y.: Unlabeled samples generated by GAN improve the person re-identification baseline in vitro. arXiv:1701.07717 (2017)
34. Xiao, T., Li, H., Ouyang, W., Wang, X.: Learning deep feature representations with domain guided dropout for person re-identification (2016)
35. Su, C., Zhang, S., Xing, J., Gao, W., Tian, Q.: Deep attributes driven multi-camera person re-identification. In: Leibe, B., Matas, J., Sebe, N., Welling, M. (eds.) ECCV 2016. LNCS, vol. 9906, pp. 475–491. Springer, Cham (2016). https://doi.org/10.1007/978-3-319-46475-6_30
36. Zhao, H., et al.: Spindle Net: person re-identification with human body region guided feature decomposition and fusion. In: CVPR (2017)
37. Yu, R., Zhou, Z., Bai, S., et al.: Divide and fuse: a re-ranking approach for person re-identification (2017)
38. Zhao, L., Li, X., Wang, J., Zhuang, Y.: Deeply-learned part-aligned representations for person re-identification. In: ICCV (2017)

39. Dai, J., Li, Y., He, K., Sun, J.: R-FCN: object detection via region-based fully convolutional networks. In: NIPS (2016)
40. Li, W., Zhu, X., Gong, S.: Person re-identification by deep joint learning of multi-loss classification, pp. 2194-2200 (2017)
41. Li, D., et al.: Learning deep context-aware features over body and latent parts for person re-identification. In: IEEE Conference on Computer Vision and Pattern Recognition. IEEE (2017)
42. Ustinova, E., Ganin, Y., Lempitsky, V.: Multiregion bilinear convolutional neural networks for person re-identification **48**(10), 2993–3003 (2015)
43. Zheng, Z., Zheng, L., Yang, Y.: Pedestrian alignment network for large-scale person re-identification (2017)
44. Liu, J., Zha, Z.J., Tian, Q.I., et al.: Multi-scale triplet CNN for person re-identification. In: ACM on Multimedia Conference. ACM, pp. 192-196 (2016)
45. Ustinova, E., Lempitsky, V.: Learning deep embeddings with histogram loss. In: NIPS (2016)

A Unified Framework of Deep Neural Networks by Capsules

Yujian Li[✉] and Chuanhui Shan

Faculty of Information Technology, Beijing University of Technology,
Beijing 100124, China
liyujian@bjut.edu.cn, chuanhuishan@emails.bjut.edu.cn

Abstract. Deep learning has made a great deal of success in processing images, audios, and natural languages. With the growth of deep learning, how to describe deep neural networks unifiedly is becoming an important issue. We first formalize neural networks mathematically with their directed graph representations, and prove a generation theorem about the induced networks of connected directed acyclic graphs. Then, we set up a unified framework for deep learning with capsule networks. This capsule framework could simplify the description of existing deep neural networks, and provide a theoretical basis of graphic designing and programming techniques for deep learning models, thus would be of great significance to the advancement of deep learning.

Keywords: Formalization · Induced network · Generation theorem ·
Capsule network · Capsule framework

1 Introduction

Deep learning has made a great deal of success in processing images, audios, and natural languages [1–3], influencing academia and industry dramatically. It is essentially a collection of various methods for effectively training neural networks with deep structures. A neural network is usually regarded as a hierarchical system composed of many nonlinear computing units (or neurons, nodes). The most popular neural network was once multilayer perceptron (MLP) [4]. A MLP consists of an input layer, a number of hidden layers and an output layer, as shown in Fig. 1. The depth of it is the number of layers excluding the input layer. If the depth is greater than 2, a neural network is now called "deep". For training MLPs, backpropagation (BP) is certainly the most well-known algorithm in common use [4], but it seemed to work only for shallow networks. In 1991, Hochreiter indicated that typical deep neural networks (DNNs) suffer from the problem of vanishing or exploding gradients [5]. To overcome training difficulties in DNNs, Hinton et al. started the new field of deep learning in 2006 [6,7].

© Springer Nature Singapore Pte Ltd. 2019
F. Sun et al. (Eds.): ICCSIP 2018, CCIS 1006, pp. 231–242, 2019.
https://doi.org/10.1007/978-981-13-7986-4_21

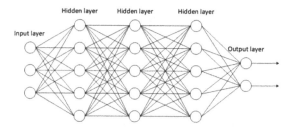

Fig. 1. The structure of a MLP.

Besides deep MLPs, DNNs also include convolutional neural networks (CNNs) and recurrent neural networks (RNNs). Here, we omit RNNs for saving space. Theoretically, a CNN can be regarded as a special MLP or feedforward neural network. It generally consists of an input layer, alternating convolutional and pooling layers, a fully connected layer, and an output layer, as shown in Fig. 2. Note that "convolutional layers" are also called "detection layers", and "pooling layers" are also called "downsampling layers". There have been a large number of CNN variants, for example, LeNet [8], AlexNet [1], VGGNet [9], GoogLeNet [10], ResNet [11], Faster R-CNN [12], DenseNet [13], Mask R-CNN [14], YOLO [15], SSD [16], and so on. They not only take the lead in competitions of image classification and recognition as well as object localization and detection [9–12], but also in other applications such as deep Q-networks [17], AlphaGo [18], speech recognition [2], and machine translation [3]. To cope with the disadvantages of CNNs, in 2017 Hinton et al. further proposed a capsule network [19], which is more convincing from the neurobiological point of view. So many deep models are dazzling with different structures. Some of them have added shortcut connections, parallel connections, and even nested structures to traditional layered structures. How to establish a unified framework for DNNs is becoming a progressively important issue in theory. We are motivated to address it.

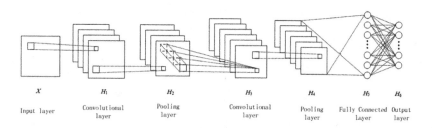

Fig. 2. The structure of a CNN.

This paper is organized as follows. In Sect. 2, we propose a mathematical definition to formalize neural networks, give their directed graph representations, and prove a generation theorem about the induced networks of connected directed acyclic graphs. In Sect. 3, we use the concept of capsule to extend neural networks, define an induced model for capsule networks, and establish a unified framework for deep learning with a universal backpropagation algorithm. Finally, in Sect. 4 we make a few conclusions to summarize the significance of the capsule framework to advance deep learning in theory and application.

2   Formalization of Neural Networks

2.1   Mathematical Definition

A neural network is a computational model composed of nodes and connections. Nodes are divided into input nodes and neuron nodes. Input nodes can be represented by real variables, e.g. $x_1, x_2, \cdots, x_n$. The set of input nodes is denoted as $X = \{x_1, x_2, \cdots, x_n\}$. A neuron node can receive signals through connections both from input nodes and the outputs of other neuron nodes, and perform a weighted sum of these signals for a nonlinear transformation. Note that the weight measures the strength of a connection, and the nonlinear transformation is the effect of an activation function. Let F be a set of activation functions, such as sigmoid, tanh, ReLU, and so on.

On X and F, a neural network can be formally defined as a 4-tuple $net = (S, H, W, Y)$, where S is a set of input nodes, H is a set of neuron nodes, W is a set of weighting connections, and Y is a set of outputs. The neural network is recursively generated by four basic rules as follows:

(1) **Rule of variable.** For any $z \in X$, let $y_z = z$. If $S = \{z\}$, $H = \emptyset$, $W = \emptyset$, $Y = \{y_z\}$, then the 4-tuple $net = (S, H, W, Y)$ is a neural network.

(2) **Rule of neuron.** For any nonempty subset $S \subseteq X$, $\forall f \in F$, $\forall b \in \mathbb{R}$, construct a node $h \notin X$ that depends on (f, b) and select a set of weighting connections $w_{x_i \to h}(x_i \in S)$. Let $y_h = f(\sum_{x_i \in S} w_{x_i \to h} x_i + b)$ be the output of node h. If $H = \{h\}$, $W = \{w_{x_i \to h} | x_i \in S\}$, and $Y = \{y_h\}$, then $net = (S, H, W, Y)$ is a neural network.

(3) **Rule of growth.** Suppose $net = (S, H, W, Y)$ is a neural network. For any nonempty subset $N \subseteq S \cup H$, $\forall f \in F$, $\forall b \in \mathbb{R}$, construct a node $h \notin S \cup H$ that depends on (f, b) and select a set of weighting connections $w_{z_j \to h}(z_j \in N)$. Let $y_h = f(\sum_{z_j \in N} w_{z_j \to h} y_{z_j} + b)$ be the output of node h. If $S' = S$, $H' = H \cup \{h\}$, $W' = W \cup \{w_{z_j \to h} | z_j \in N\}$, and $Y' = Y \cup \{y_h\}$, then $net' = (S', H', W', Y')$ is also a neural network.

(4) **Rule of convergence.** Suppose $net_k = (S_k, H_k, W_k, Y_k)(1 \leq k \leq K)$ are K neural networks, satisfying that $\forall 1 \leq i \neq j \leq K$, $(S_i \cup H_i) \cap (S_j \cup H_j) = \emptyset$. For any nonempty subsets $A_k \subseteq S_k \cup H_k (1 \leq k \leq K)$, $N = \bigcup_{k=1}^{K} A_k$, $\forall f \in F$, $\forall b \in \mathbb{R}$, construct a node $h \notin \bigcup_{k=1}^{K}(S_k \cup H_k)$ that depends on (f, b), select a set of weighting connections $w_{z \to h}(z \in N)$. Let $y_h = f(\sum_{z \in N} w_{z \to h} y_z + b)$ be the output of the node h. If $S = \bigcup_{k=1}^{K} S_k$, $H = (\bigcup_{k=1}^{K} H_k) \cup \{h\}$, $W = (\bigcup_{k=1}^{K} W_k) \cup \{w_{z \to h} | z \in N\}$, and $Y = (\bigcup_{k=1}^{K} Y_k) \cup \{y_h\}$, then $net = (S, H, W, Y)$ is also a neural network.

Among the four generation rules, it should be noted that the rule of neuron is not independent. This rule can be derived from the rule of variable and the rule of convergence. Moreover, the weighting connection $w_{z \to h}$ should be taken as a combination of the weight and the connection, rather than just the weight. Additionally, if a node h depends on (f, b), f is called the activation function of h, and b is called the bias of h.

2.2   Directed Graph Representation

Let X be a set of real variables and F be a set of activation functions. For any neural network $net = (S, H, W, Y)$ on X and F, a directed acyclic graph $G_{net} = (V, E)$ can be constructed with the vertex set $V = S \cup H$ and the directed edge set $E = \{z \to h | w_{z \to h} \in W\}$. $G_{net} = (V, E)$ is called the directed graph representation of $net = (S, H, W, Y)$. Two cases of the representation generation are discussed in the following.

(1) **The case of $X = \{x_1\}$**

Using the rule of variable, for $x_1 \in X$, let $y_{x_1} = x_1$. If $S = \{x_1\}$, $H = \emptyset$, $W = \emptyset$, and $Y = \{y_{x_1}\}$, then $net = (S, H, W, Y)$ is a neural network. Since this network has only one input node without any function for nonlinear transformation, it is also called a trivial network, as shown in Fig. 3(a). Using the rule of neuron, for a nonempty subset $S = \{x_1\} \subseteq X$, $\forall f \in F$, $\forall b \in \mathbb{R}$, construct a node $h_1 \notin S$ that depends on (f, b), select a weighting connection $w_{x_1 \to h_1}$, and let $y_{h_1} = f(w_{x_1 \to h_1} x_1 + b)$. If $H = \{h_1\}$, $W = \{w_{x_1 \to h_1}\}$, and $Y = \{y_{h_1}\}$, then $net = (S, H, W, Y)$ is a neural network, which has one input and one neuron. It is also called a 1-input-1-neuron network, as shown in Fig. 3(b). Using the rule of growth on the network, three new neural networks with different structures can be generated, as shown in Fig. 4(a-c). Likewise, they are called 1-input-2-neuron networks. Using the rule of growth on the three networks, twenty-one new neural networks with different structures can be totally generated further. Seven out of them for Fig. 4(a) are displayed in Fig. 5(a-g). They are called 1-input-3-neuron networks.

(2) **The case of $X = \{x_1, x_2\}$**

Using the rule of variable, for $x_1, x_2 \in X$, let $y_{x_1} = x_1$ and $y_{x_2} = x_2$. If $S_1 = \{x_1\}$, $S_2 = \{x_2\}$, $H_1 = H_2 = \emptyset$, $W_1 = W_2 = \emptyset$, $Y_1 = \{y_{x_1}\}$, and $Y_2 = \{y_{x_2}\}$, then $net_1 = (\{x_1\}, \emptyset, \emptyset, \{y_{x_1}\})$ and $net_2 = (\{x_2\}, \emptyset, \emptyset, \{y_{x_2}\})$ are neural networks. Obviously, both of them are trivial networks. Using the rule of neuron, for a nonempty subset $S \subseteq X$, if $S = \{x_1\}$ or $S = \{x_2\}$, the neural network can be similarly constructed with the case of $X = \{x_1\}$.

If $S = \{x_1, x_2\}$, $\forall f \in F$, $\forall b \in \mathbb{R}$, construct a node $h_1 \notin S$ that depends on (f, b), select a set of weighting connections $w_{x_i \to h_1}(x_i \in S)$ and let $y_{h_1} = f(\sum_{x_i \in S} w_{x_i \to h_1} x_i + b)$. If $H = \{h_1\}$, $W = \{w_{x_1 \to h_1}, w_{x_2 \to h_1}\}$, and $Y = \{y_{h_1}\}$, then $net = (S, H, W, Y)$ is a neural network. This is a 2-input-1-neuron network, as depicted in Fig. 6. Using the rule of growth on this network, seven 2-input-2-neuron networks with different structures can be generated, as shown in Fig. 7(a-g).

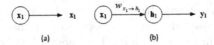

Fig. 3. (a) A trivial network; (b) A 1-input-1-neuron network.

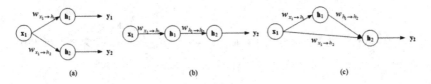

Fig. 4. Three 1-input-2-neuron networks.

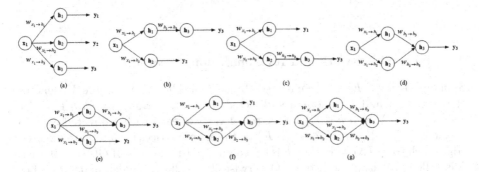

Fig. 5. Seven 1-input-3-neuron networks.

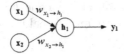

Fig. 6. A 2-input-1-neuron network.

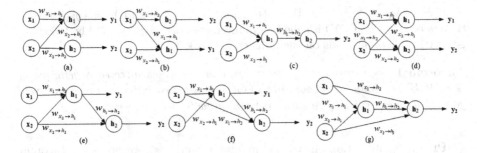

Fig. 7. Seven 2-input-2-neuron networks.

Finally, the rule of convergence is necessary. In fact, it cannot generate all neural networks only using the three rules of variable, neuron and growth. For example, the network in Fig. 8(c) cannot be generated without using the rule of convergence on the two in Fig. 8(a-b).

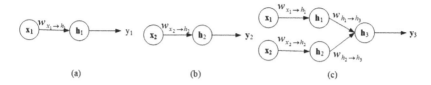

(a)   (b)   (c)

Fig. 8. A necessary explanation for the rule of convergence.

2.3   Induced Network and Its Generation Theorem

Suppose $G = (V, E)$ is a connected directed acyclic graph, where V denotes the vertex set and E denotes the directed edge set. For any vertex $h \in V$, let $IN_h = \{z | z \in V, z \to h \in E\}$ be the set of vertices each with a directed edge to h, and $OUT_h = \{z | z \in V, h \to z \in E\}$ be the set of vertices for h to have directed edges each to. If $IN_h = \emptyset$, then h is called an input node of G. If $OUT_h = \emptyset$, then h is called an output node of G. Otherwise, h is called a hidden node of G. Let X stand for the set of all input nodes, O for the set of all output nodes, and M for the set of all hidden nodes. Obviously, $V = X \cup M \cup O$, and $M = V - X \cup O$.

Furthermore, let y_h be the output of node h, and $w_{z \to h}$ be the weighting connection from z to h. Then, a computational model of graph G can be defined as follows:

(1) $\forall z \in X, y_z = z$.
(2) $\forall h \in M \cup O$, select $f \in F$ and $b \in \mathbb{R}$ to compute $y_h = f(\sum_{z \in IN_h} w_{z \to h} y_z + b)$.

If $S = X$, $H = M \cup O$, $W = \{w_{z \to h} | z \to h \in E\}$, and $Y = \{y_h | h \in V\}$, then $net_G = (S, H, W, Y)$ is called an induced network of graph G. The following generation theorem holds on the induced network.

Theorem 1 *(Generation Theorem): For any connected directed acyclic graph $G = (V, E)$, its induced network net_G is a neural network that can be recursively generated by the rules of variable, neuron, growth, and convergence.*

Proof: By induction on $|V|$ (i.e. number of vertices), we prove the theorem as follows.

(1) When $|V| = 1$, we have $|X| = 1$ and $|O| = 0$, so the induced network net_G is a neural network that can be generated directly by the rule of variable.

(2) When $|V| = 2$, we have $|X| = 1$ and $|O| = 1$, so the induced network net_G is a neural network that can be generated directly by the rule of growth.

(3) Assume that the theorem holds for $|V| \leq n$. When $|V| = n + 1 \geq 3$, the induced network net_G has at least one output node $h \in O$. Let $E_h = \{z \to h \in E\}$ denote the set of edges heading to the node h. Moreover, let $V' = V - \{h\}$ and $E' = E - E_h$. Based on the connectedness of $G' = (V', E')$, we have two cases to discuss in the following:

(i) If $G' = (V', E')$ is connected, then applying the induction assumption for $|V'| \leq n$, the induced network $net_{G'} = (S', H', W', Y')$ can be recursively generated by the rules of variable, neuron, growth, and convergence. Let $N = IN_h$. In $net_G = (S, H, W, Y)$, we use $f \in F$ and $b \in \mathbb{R}$ to stand for the activation function and bias of node h, and $w_{z \to h}(z \in N)$ for the weighting connection from node z to the node h. Then, net_G can be obtained by using the rule of growth on $net_{G'}$, to generate the node h and its output $y_h = f(\sum_{z \in N} w_{z \to h} y_z + b)$.

(ii) Otherwise, G' comprises a number of disjoint connected components $G_k = (V_k, E_k)$ $(1 \leq k \leq K)$. Using the induction assumption for $|V_k| \leq n (1 \leq k \leq K)$, the induced network $net_{G_k} = (S_k, H_k, W_k, Y_k)$ can be recursively generated by the rules of variable, neuron, growth, and convergence. Let $A_k = (S_k \cup H_k) \cap IN_h$, and $N = \bigcup_{k=1}^{K} A_k$. In $net_G = (S, H, W, Y)$, we use $f \in F$ and $b \in \mathbb{R}$ to stand for the activation function and bias of the node h, and $w_{z \to h}(z \in N)$ for the weighting connection from node z to node h. Then, net_G can be obtained by using the rule of convergence on $net_{G_k}(1 \leq k \leq K)$, to generate the node h and its output $y_h = f(\sum_{z \in N} w_{z \to h} y_z + b)$.

As a result, the theorem always holds.

3   Capsule Framework of Deep Learning

3.1   Mathematical Definition of Capsules

In 2017, Hinton et al. pioneered the idea of capsules and considered a nonlinear "squashing" capsule [19]. From the viewpoint of mathematical models, a capsule is essentially an extension of the traditional activation function. It is primarily defined as an activation function with a vector input and a vector output. More generally, a capsule can be an activation function with a tensor input and a tensor output.

As shown in Fig. 9, a general capsule may have n input tensors $X_1, X_2, \cdots, X_n$, n weight tensors $W_1, W_2, \cdots, W_n$, and a capsule bias B, and n weighting operations $\otimes_1, \otimes_2, \cdots, \otimes_n$. Note that a weighting operation may be taken as an identity transfer, a scalar multiplication, a vector dot product, a matrix multiplication, a convolution operation, and so on. Meantime, $W_i \otimes_i X_i (1 \leq i \leq n)$ and B must be tensors with the same dimension. The total

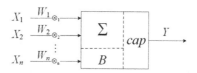

Fig. 9. The mathematical model of a general capsule.

input of the capsule is $U = \sum_i W_i \otimes_i X_i + B$, and the output Y is a tensor computed by a nonlinear capsule function cap, namely,

$$Y = cap(U) = cap(\sum_i W_i \otimes_i X_i + B). \tag{1}$$

For convenience, we use $\mathcal{F}$ to stand for a nonempty set of capsule functions, and $\mathbb{T}$ for the set of all tensors.

3.2 Capsule Networks

Suppose $\mathcal{G} = (\mathcal{V}, \mathcal{E})$ is a connected directed acyclic graph, where $\mathcal{V}$ denotes the vertex set and $\mathcal{E}$ denotes the directed edge set. For any vertex $H \in \mathcal{V}$, let IN_H be the set of vertices each with a directed edge to H, and OUT_H be the set of vertices for H to have a directed edge each to. If $IN_H = \emptyset$, then H is called an input node of $\mathcal{G}$. If $OUT_H = \emptyset$, then H is called an output node of $\mathcal{G}$. Otherwise, H is called a hidden node of $\mathcal{G}$. Let $\mathcal{X}$ stand for the set of all input nodes, $\mathcal{O}$ for the set of all output nodes, and $\mathcal{M}$ for the set of all hidden nodes. Obviously, $\mathcal{V} = \mathcal{X} \cup \mathcal{M} \cup \mathcal{O}$, and $\mathcal{M} = \mathcal{V} - \mathcal{X} \cup \mathcal{O}$.

Furthermore, let Y_H be the output of node H, and $(W_{Z \to H}, \otimes_{Z \to H})$ be the tensor-weighting connection from Z to H. If $\forall H \in \mathcal{M} \cup \mathcal{O}, \forall Z \in IN_H$, $W_{Z \to H} \otimes_{Z \to H} Y_Z$ and B are tensors with the same dimension, then a tensor-computational model of graph $\mathcal{G}$ can be defined as follows:

(1) $\forall Z \in \mathcal{X}, Y_Z = Z$.
(2) $\forall H \in \mathcal{M} \cup \mathcal{O}$, select $cap \in \mathcal{F}$ and $B \in \mathbb{T}$ to compute $Y_H = cap(\sum_{Z \in IN_H} W_{Z \to H} \otimes_{Z \to H} Y_Z + B)$.

If $\mathcal{S} = \mathcal{X}$, $\mathcal{H} = \mathcal{M} \cup \mathcal{O}$, $\mathcal{W} = \{(W_{Z \to H}, \otimes_{Z \to H}) | Z \to H \in \mathcal{E}\}$, and $\mathcal{Y} = \{Y_H | H \in \mathcal{V}\}$, then $net_\mathcal{G} = (\mathcal{S}, \mathcal{H}, \mathcal{W}, \mathcal{Y})$ is called a tensor-induced network of graph $\mathcal{G}$. This network is also called a capsule network.

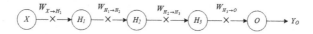

Fig. 10. The capsule structure of a MLP.

Using a capsule network, a MLP can be simplified as a directed acyclic path of capsules. For example, the MLP in Fig. 1 has five layers: an input layer, three hidden layers, and an output layer. On the whole, each layer could be thought of as a capsule. Let $X = (x_1, x_2, \cdots, x_5)^T$ stand for the input capsule node, $H_i = (cap_i, B_i)(i = 1, 2, 3)$ for the hidden capsule nodes, and $O = (cap_4, B_4)$ for the output capsule node. Note that capsule function cap_i and capsule bias B_i are defined by the elementwise activation function and the bias vector respectively of the corresponding layer in the MLP. If the weighting operations $\otimes_{X \to H_1}$, $\otimes_{H_1 \to H_2}$, $\otimes_{H_2 \to H_3}$, and $\otimes_{H_3 \to O}$ are all taken as matrix multiplication "$\times$", then we have $(W_{X \to H_1}, \otimes_{X \to H_1}) = ((w_{m,n}^{X \to H_1})_{7 \times 5}, \times)$, $(W_{H_1 \to H_2}, \otimes_{H_1 \to H_2}) = ((w_{m,n}^{H_1 \to H_2})_{7 \times 7}, \times)$, $(W_{H_2 \to H_3}, \otimes_{H_2 \to H_3}) = ((w_{m,n}^{H_2 \to H_3})_{7 \times 7}, \times)$ and $(W_{H_3 \to O} \otimes_{H_3 \to O}) = ((w_{m,n}^{H_3 \to O})_{4 \times 7}, \times)$, which are the tensor-weighting connections from X to H_1, H_1 to H_2, H_2 to H_3 and H_3 to O. Finally, let $Y_{H_i}(i = 1, 2, 3)$ stand for the output vector of H_i, and Y_O for the output vector of O. Setting $Y_{H_O} = X$ and $Y_{H_4} = Y_O$, we obtain $Y_{H_i} = cap_i(W_{H_{i-1} \to H_i} \times Y_{H_{i-1}} + B_i)$. Therefore, the capsule structure of the MLP is a directed acyclic path, as displayed in Fig. 10.

Besides MLPs, capsule networks can also be used to simplify the structures of other DNNs. Let us consider the CNN in Fig. 2. This CNN has 7 layers: one input layer, two convolutional layers, two downsampling (pooling) layers, one fully connected layer, and one output layer. On the whole, each of the layers could be thought of as a capsule. Let X stand for the input capsule node, $H_i = (cap_i, B_i)(i = 1, \cdots, 5)$ for the hidden capsule nodes, and $O = (cap_6, B_6)$ for the output capsule node. Note that cap_1 and cap_3 are capsule functions defined by elementwise ReLUs. cap_2 and cap_4 are capsule functions defined by downsampling "$\downarrow$". cap_5 is an identity function. cap_6 is a capsule function defined by softmax. In addition, $B_i(i = 1, \cdots, 6)$ are capsule biases each defined by the bias tensor of the corresponding layer in the CNN. Let both $\otimes_{X \to H_1}$ and $\otimes_{H_2 \to H_3}$ be the convolution operation "$*$", both $\otimes_{H_1 \to H_2}$ and $\otimes_{H_3 \to H_4}$ be the identity transfer "$\to$", $\otimes_{H_4 \to H_5}$ be the tensor-reshaping operation "$\triangleleft$", and $\otimes_{H_5 \to O}$ be the matrix multiplication "$\times$". Then, $(W_{X \to H_1}, \otimes_{X \to H_1}) = (W_{X \to H_1}, *)$, $(W_{H_1 \to H_2}, \otimes_{H_1 \to H_2}) = ("", \to)$, $(W_{H_2 \to H_3}, \otimes_{H_2 \to H_3}) = (W_{H_2 \to H_3}, *)$, $(W_{H_3 \to H_4}, \otimes_{H_3 \to H_4}) = ("", \to)$, $(W_{H_4 \to H_5}, \otimes_{H_4 \to H_5}) = ("", \triangleleft)$, and $(W_{H_5 \to O}, \otimes_{H_5 \to O}) = (W_{H_5 \to O}, \times)$, which are the tensor-weighting connections from X to H_1, H_1 to H_2, H_2 to H_3, H_3 to H_4, H_4 to H_5, and H_5 to O. Finally, let $Y_{H_i}(i = 1, 2, 3, 4, 5)$ stand for the output tensor of H_i, and Y_O for the output tensor of O. This leads to the following computations:

$$\begin{cases} Y_{H_1} = cap_1(W_{X \to H_1} * X + B_1) = \mathrm{ReLU}(W_{X \to H_1} * X + B_1), \\ Y_{H_2} = cap_2(W_{H_1 \to H_2} \otimes_{H_1 \to H_2} Y_{H_1} + B_2) = cap_2(\to Y_{H_1} + B_2) = \downarrow Y_{H_1} + B_2, \\ Y_{H_3} = cap_3(W_{H_2 \to H_3} * X + B_3) = \mathrm{ReLU}(W_{H_2 \to H_3} * Y_{H_2} + B_3), \\ Y_{H_4} = cap_4(W_{H_3 \to H_4} \otimes_{H_3 \to H_4} Y_{H_3} + B_4) = cap_4(\to Y_{H_3} + B_4) = \downarrow Y_{H_3} + B_4, \\ Y_{H_5} = cap_5(\triangleleft Y_{H_4} + B_5) = \triangleleft Y_{H_4}, \\ Y_O = cap_6(W_{H_5 \to O} \times Y_{H_5} + B_6) = softmax(W_{H_5 \to O} \times Y_{H_5} + B_6). \end{cases}$$

$$(2)$$

Therefore, the capsule structure of the CNN is also a directed acyclic path, as depicted in Fig. 11.

Fig. 11. The Capsule structure of a CNN, with "∗" standing for convolution, "→" for identity transfer, "◁" for tensor reshaping, and "×" for matrix multiplication.

Besides simplifying the description of existing DNNs, the capsule networks can also be used to graphically design a variety of new structures for complex DNNs, such as displayed in Fig. 12.

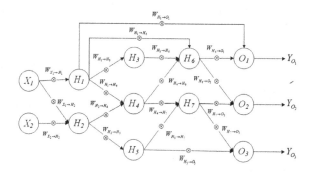

Fig. 12. Structure of a general capsule network.

3.3   Universal Backpropagation of Capsule Networks

Suppose $\mathcal{G} = (\mathcal{V}, \mathcal{E})$ is a connected directed acyclic graph. Let $\mathcal{X} = \{X_1, X_2, \cdots, X_n\}$ stand for the set of all input nodes, $\mathcal{O} = \{O_1, O_2, \cdots, O_m\}$ for the set of all output nodes, and $\mathcal{M} = \mathcal{V} - \mathcal{X} \cup \mathcal{O} = \{H_1, H_2, \cdots, H_l\}$ for the set of all hidden nodes. $net_{\mathcal{G}} = (\mathcal{S}, \mathcal{H}, \mathcal{W}, \mathcal{Y})$ is an tensor-induced network of graph $\mathcal{G}$. This is also a capsule network. If the number of nodes $|\mathcal{S} \cup \mathcal{H}| \geq 2$, then for $\forall H \in \mathcal{H}$,

$$\begin{cases} U_H = \sum_{Z \in IN_H} W_{Z \to H} \otimes_{Z \to H} Y_Z + B_H, \\ Y_H = cap_H(U_H) = cap_H(\sum_{Z \in IN_H} W_{Z \to H} \otimes_{Z \to H} Y_Z + B_H). \end{cases} \quad (3)$$

For any output node $H \in \mathcal{O}$, let Y_H and T_H be its actual output and expected output for input $\mathcal{X}$, respectively. The loss function between them is defined as $L_H = Loss(Y_H, T_H)$. Accordingly, we have the total loss function $L = \sum_{H \in \mathcal{O}} L_H$. Let $\delta_H = \frac{\partial L}{\partial U_H}$ denote the backpropagated error signal (or sensitivity) for capsule node H. By the chain rule, we further obtain:

$$\forall H \in \mathcal{O}, \begin{cases} \delta_H & = \frac{\partial L}{\partial U_H} = \frac{\partial Loss(Y_H, T_H)}{\partial Y_H} \cdot \frac{\partial cap_H}{\partial U_H}, \\ \frac{\partial L}{\partial B_H} & = \frac{\partial L}{\partial U_H} \cdot \frac{\partial U_H}{\partial B_H} = \delta_H, \\ \frac{\partial L}{\partial W_{Z \to H}} & = \frac{\partial L}{\partial U_H} \cdot \frac{\partial U_H}{\partial W_{Z \to H}} = \delta_H \cdot \frac{\partial U_H}{\partial W_{Z \to H}}. \end{cases} \quad (4)$$

$$\forall H \in \mathcal{M}, \begin{cases} \delta_H & = \frac{\partial L}{\partial U_H} = \sum_{P \in OUT_H} \frac{\partial L}{\partial U_P} \cdot \frac{\partial U_P}{\partial Y_H} \cdot \frac{\partial Y_H}{\partial U_H} \\ & = \sum_{P \in OUT_H} \delta_P \cdot \frac{\partial U_P}{\partial Y_H} \cdot \frac{\partial cap_H}{\partial U_H}, \\ \frac{\partial L}{\partial B_H} & = \frac{\partial L}{\partial U_H} \cdot \frac{\partial U_H}{\partial B_H} = \delta_H, \\ \frac{\partial L}{\partial W_{Z \to H}} & = \frac{\partial L}{\partial U_H} \cdot \frac{\partial U_H}{\partial W_{Z \to H}} = \delta_H \cdot \frac{\partial U_H}{\partial W_{Z \to H}}. \end{cases} \quad (5)$$

Note that in formulae (4)–(5), $\frac{\partial cap_H}{\partial U_H}$ depends on the specific form of capsule function cap_H. For example, when cap_H is an elementwise sigmoid function, the result is $\frac{\partial cap_H}{\partial U_H} = sigmoid(U_H)(1 - sigmoid(U_H))$. Meanwhile, $\frac{\partial U_H}{\partial W_{Z \to H}}$ and $\frac{\partial U_P}{\partial Y_H}$ also depend on the specific choice of the weighting operation $\otimes_{Z \to H}$.

Based on formulae (4)–(5), a universal backpropagation algorithm can be designed theoretically for capsule networks, with one iteration detailed in Algorithm 1. In practice, this algorithm should be changed to one of many variants with training data [20].

Algorithm 1: One iteration of the universal backpropagation algorithm.

1) Select a learning rate $\eta > 0$,
2) $\forall H \in \mathcal{M} \cup \mathcal{O}$, $\forall Z \in IN_H$, initialize $W_{Z \to H}$ and B_H,
3) $\forall H \in \mathcal{O}$, compute $\delta_H = \frac{\partial Loss(Y_H, T_H)}{\partial Y_H} \cdot \frac{\partial cap_H}{\partial U_H}$,
4) $\forall H \in \mathcal{M}$, compute $\delta_H = \sum_{P \in OUT_H} \delta_P \cdot \frac{\partial U_P}{\partial Y_H} \cdot \frac{\partial cap_H}{\partial U_H}$,
5) Compute $\Delta W_{Z \to H} = \delta_H \cdot \frac{\partial U_H}{\partial W_{Z \to H}}$ and $\Delta B_H = \delta_H$,
6) Update $W_{Z \to H} \leftarrow W_{Z \to H} - \eta \cdot \Delta W_{Z \to H}, B_H \leftarrow B_H - \eta \cdot \Delta B_H$.

---

4 Conclusions

Based on the formalization of neural networks, we have developed capsule networks to establish a unified framework for deep learning. This capsule framework could not only simplify the description of existing DNNs, but also provide a theoretical basis of graphical designing and programming for new deep learning models. As future work, we will try to define an industrial standard and implement a graphic platform for the advancement of deep learning with capsule networks, and even with a similar extension to recurrent neural networks.

Acknowledgement. This research is supported by the National Natural Science Foundation of China (No.61876010).

References

1. Krizhevsky, A., Sutskever, I., Hinton, G.E.: ImageNet classification with deep convolutional neural networks. In: Pereira, F., Burges, C.J.C., Bottou, L., Weinberger, K.Q. (eds.) Advances in Neural Information Processing Systems, vol. 25, pp. 1097–1105. MIT Press, Cambridge (2012)

2. Amodei, D., Ananthanarayanan, S., Anubhai, R., et al.: Deep speech 2: end-to-end speech recognition in English and Mandarin. In: International Conference on Machine Learning, pp. 173–182 (2016)
3. Wu, Y., Schuster, M., Chen, Z., et al.: Google's neural machine translation system: bridging the gap between human and machine translation. arXiv preprint arXiv:1609.08144 (2016)
4. Rumellhart, D.E.: Learning internal representations by error propagation. In: Parallel Distributed Processing: Explorations in the Microstructure of Cognition, vol. 1, pp. 319–362 (1986)
5. Schmidhuber, J.: Deep learning in neural networks: an overview. Neural Netw. **61**, 85–117 (2015)
6. Hinton, G.E., Salakhutdinov, R.R.: Reducing the dimensionality of data with neural networks. Science **313**(5786), 504–507 (2006)
7. Hinton, G.E., Osindero, S., Teh, Y.W.: A fast learning algorithm for deep belief nets. Neural Comput. **18**(7), 1527–1554 (2006)
8. LeCun, Y., Bottou, L., Bengio, Y., et al.: Gradient-based learning applied to document recognition. Proc. IEEE **86**(11), 2278–2324 (1998)
9. Simonyan, K., Zisserman, A.: Very deep convolutional networks for large-scale image recognition. Comput. Sci. (2014)
10. Szegedy, C., Liu, W., Jia, Y., et al.: Going deeper with convolutions. In: IEEE Conference on Computer Vision and Pattern Recognition. IEEE Press, New York (2015)
11. He, K., Zhang, X., Ren, S., et al.: Deep residual learning for image recognition. In: Proceedings of the IEEE Conference on Computer Vision and Pattern Recognition, pp. 770–778. IEEE Press, New York (2016)
12. Ren, S., He, K., Girshick, R., et al.: Faster R-CNN: towards real-time object detection with region proposal networks. In: Advances in Neural Information Processing Systems, pp. 91–99 (2015)
13. Huang, G., Liu, Z., Weinberger, K.Q., et al.: Densely connected convolutional networks. In: Proceedings of the IEEE Conference on Computer Vision and Pattern Recognition, vol. 1, no. 2, p. 3. IEEE Press, New York (2017)
14. He, K., Gkioxari, G., Dollr, P., et al.: Mask R-CNN. In: 2017 IEEE International Conference on Computer Vision (ICCV). IEEE, pp. 2980–2988. IEEE Press, New York (2017)
15. Redmon, J., Divvala, S., Girshick, R., et al.: You only look once: unified, real-time object detection. In: Proceedings of the IEEE Conference on Computer Vision and Pattern Recognition, pp. 779–788. IEEE Press, New York (2016)
16. Liu, W., et al.: SSD: single shot multibox detector. In: Leibe, B., Matas, J., Sebe, N., Welling, M. (eds.) ECCV 2016. LNCS, vol. 9905, pp. 21–37. Springer, Cham (2016). https://doi.org/10.1007/978-3-319-46448-0_2
17. Mnih, V., Kavukcuoglu, K., Silver, D., et al.: Human-level control through deep reinforcement learning. Nature **518**(7540), 529 (2015)
18. Silver, D., Schrittwieser, J., Simonyan, K., et al.: Mastering the game of go without human knowledge. Nature **550**(7676), 354–359 (2017)
19. Sabour, S., Frosst, N., Hinton, G.E.: Dynamic routing between capsules. In: Guyon, I., et al. (eds.) Advances in Neural Information Processing Systems, vol. 30, pp. 3859–3869. MIT Press, Cambridge (2017)
20. Ruder, S.: An overview of gradient descent optimization algorithms. arXiv preprint arXiv:1609.04747 (2016)

Reformative Vehicle License Plate Recognition Algorithm Based on Deep Learning

Xinggan Peng[1], Long Wen[2], Diqiu Bai[2], and Bei Peng[2(✉)]

[1] The Ohio State University,
Columbus, OH, USA
peng.647@osu.edu
[2] University of Electronic Science and Technology of China,
Chengdu, China
huxi1000@gmail.com, baidq@tamu.edu, beipeng@uestc.edu.cn

Abstract. As the surge of the number of vehicles in modern cities, it has become more and more difficult to recognize vehicle plates in high accuracy from different shooting situations. Traditional image processing methods like edge or color detection [12, 18] become incapable of detecting plates shooting from side view or with distorted resolution input. Additionally, optical character recognition methods based on graphic features sometimes have high error rate, even when the plate is detected from the front view. Therefore, we present a reformative vehicle license plate recognition algorithm combined with two networks: MobileNet-Single Shot MultiBox Detector (SSD) and Convolutional Neural Network (CNN). We use the SSD to locate the region of interest (ROI) and the CNN to identify the characters on the plate. In the experiments, we show that the SSD and CNN are small and easy to train. What's more, the results prove that our algorithm performs much higher accuracy than traditional methods in the side view and distorted problems.

Keywords: MobileNet-SSD · CNN · Vehicle license plate recognition

1 Introduction

As the development of the modern cities, the demand of purchasing private vehicles is becoming more and more eager for citizens. At the meantime, as citizens enjoy the huge profits and great convenience that auto industry brought to them, people are also exposed to problems like traffic jams [17], accidents and air pollution. Nowadays, traffic condition has become worse and worse in cities, and has already impeded the development of major cities [5] in a large number of countries. Governments spend a large share of their budget on dealing with traffic issues. Plate Recognition plays a critical role in dealing with traffic issues, such as vehicle violation, vehicle parking and so on. Traditional image processing method

© Springer Nature Singapore Pte Ltd. 2019
F. Sun et al. (Eds.): ICCSIP 2018, CCIS 1006, pp. 243–255, 2019.
https://doi.org/10.1007/978-981-13-7986-4_22

like edge detection is frequently applied to vehicle license plate detection. However it is incapable of recognizing plates shooting from oblique shooting angle or with distorted resolution input. Alternately, the traditional character recognition method based on graphic features also have high error rate, even when, the plate is direct towards the camera. Additionally, end to end (E2E) networks based on deep learning methods can make them more adaptive to different types of input images. However these models always need tens of thousands of training set and they are hard to converge during the training. Also some are still in low accuracy in recognizing oblique image. Therefore, we present a reformative vehicle license plate recognition model with two networks: MobileNet -Single Shot MultiBox Detector (SSD) [8,13] and Convolutional Neural Network (CNN). We use the SSD to locate the region of interest (ROI) and the CNN to identify the characters on plate. In the experiments, on the one hand, two small networks are easier to train. On the other hand, during the side view and distorted input tests, our algorithm performs much higher accuracy than traditional methods.

1.1 Technical Background

Single Shot MultiBox Detector (SSD) discretizes the output space of a number of bounding boxes into a series number of default boxes for every small pix location of the feature map in different aspect ratios and scales. During the detection time, the detector network produces scores for the presence of each object category in each default box and produces offset to each box to get better location matching. Compared with other former detection network such as Faster R-CNN [15] or YOLO [14], SSD have significantly improved the detection speed and kept the high accuracy at the meantime. Instead of using bounding box proposals and the subsequent pixel or feature resampling stage, SSD combines all computation in a single network and this design change results in fundamental detection speed improvement [13]. The detection process of SSD can be concluded in Fig. 1 below. In Fig. 1(a) during the training, the input image of SSD only needs ground truth boxes for each target object. In a convolutional process, the network first evaluates a small set (e.g. 4) of default boxes in different aspect ratios at each location in several feature maps with different scales (e.g. 8×8 and 4×4 in (b) and (c)). For every default box, network produces scores in both the location offsets and confidences for all target categories ((c1; c2; ... ; cp)) [13]. During the training, numbers of positives and negatives default boxes are roughly set to be 3:1. The sum of the model loss is calculated by localization loss (e.g. Smooth L1) and confidence loss (e.g. Softmax) [11]. Additionally, MobileNets which uses depthwise separable convolutions as their core architecture are one new type of light weight deep neural networks that can be applied for embedded applications and mobile devices. MobileNets have advantages in size, financial cost and speed in a number of popular tasks such as object detection and classification.

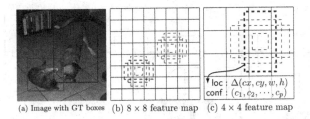

(a) Image with GT boxes   (b) 8 × 8 feature map   (c) 4 × 4 feature map

Fig. 1. Detection process of SSD

1.2 Algorithm Objective

The objective of this plate recognizer can be concluded as:

1. Detect the plate from different shooting angles with high confidence;
2. Compared with other traditional recognizer, this plate recognizer improves the recognizing performance with low resolution input, distorted input and side view input;
3. This plate recognizer finishes the recognizing process in an acceptable time period with high accuracy during the field test;

2 Algorithm Model

Figure 2 represents the algorithm design scheme of the plate recognizer. The Plate Recognizer is contained five crucial operation parts: plate detection, fine mapping, fast rectify, plate segmentation and plate recognition. The input of the algorithm is an image which contain the plate (can be taken from a side angle or in low resolution quality) and the output of the algorithm contains the location, province character, letter and number information of the target plate. In the first part, the rough region of the plate will be detected and then sent to the next part. The region will be further accurately mapped and rectified in the second and the third part. In the fourth part, the plate will be divided into 7 subpart and each subpart will be sent to be recognized in the last part to get the output result. In addition, each part of the algorithm can work separately with appropriate input, which makes this algorithm easier to be further optimized by changing advanced subparts.

2.1 Plate Detection

The plate detection part applies MobileNet -SSD technology to get the rough location region of the target plate, which includes tasks of determine the existence and location of the plate. The architecture of MobileNet-SSD is shown in Fig. 3. The network consist of 47 convolution layers [11] whose size is gradually decreased to generate different size of feature maps. The change of size is determined by the size of the kernel and stride in that layer. If the size of the layer

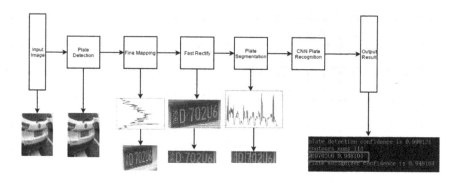

Fig. 2. Algorithm design scheme

is m × n × q, the size kernel is set to be 3 × 3 × q and some layers will generate scores of confidence for labels in the category (background or plate) and the relative offset relative to the default boxes. Therefore, the offset of the bounding box is measured by different default boxes with different feature maps which makes it more accurate in location prediction.

In this model, default boxes are separately added in layers of conv11, conv13, conv14_2, conv15_2, conv16_2 and conv17_2. There are 6 kind of sizes of default boxes will be generated for each layer and the rule of the size in each layer is given by the expression

$$\begin{cases} W_k = S_k \sqrt{a_r} \\ h_k = \frac{S_k}{\sqrt{a_r}} \end{cases} \tag{1}$$

where w_k and h_k are width and height of the default boxes respectively and S_k is the scale factor for each layer and k is the sequence for these 7 layers (k=1 to 7 and k=1 for conv11). The expression of S_k is given by

$$\begin{cases} S_k = S_{min} + (k+1)\frac{S_{max}-S_{min}}{\sqrt{5}}. & a_r \neq 0 \\ S_k = \sqrt{S_k S_k + 1}. & a_r = 0 \end{cases} \tag{2}$$

where $S_{min} = 0.2$, $S_{max} = 0.95$ and a_r is the aspect ratio of the default boxes whose value can take from $[0, 1, 2, 3, \frac{1}{2}, \frac{1}{3}]$.

After collecting data form layers, scores for labels produced by these 6 layers are collected in Concat 1 layer to generate the general confidence of the prediction and similarly location offsets information is collected in Concat 2 layer to generate location prediction of the plate. After the training, the SSD network will generate the x and y coordinates of the left top point, height and width of the region of interest (ROI). Then ROI will be extended and one crop operation will be processed according to data of ROI, which makes only the ROI of the original image will be sent to the Fine mapping part.

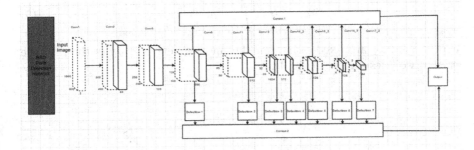

Fig. 3. MobileNet-SSD model

2.2 Fine Mapping

After being processed by plate detection operation, the partial ROI will be processed to have more accurate plate region. The input image will be separately processed by vertical operations and horizontal operations. As for horizontal operations, at first, Sobel operator [10] method is applied to detect the vertical edges of the ROI. The second step is to calculate the vertical sum according to the X axis of the output. The third step is to put theses sum into one histogram and find the valid horizontal domain of the plate according to their X axis values. In addition, the first step of Fine mapping vertical operations is getting structure elements by MORPH_ELLIPSE [2] and then proceed binary adaptive operation with the adaptive threshold parameter k from -50 to 0 in the second step. The next step is finding the contour box that satisfy the default area and aspect ratio requirements for each character. The last step is marking the left-top and right-bottom points of each character and then using RANSAC fitting [4] method to generate the top and bottom edge of the plate. After being processed horizontally and vertically, the four more accurate edges of the plate are generated and ready to be sent to the next operation part.

2.3 Fast Rectify

If the input image is distorted or oblique, the character segmentation and the recognition can be interfered which may leads to fake results. Therefore the ROI which has been proceed by fine mapping process should be rectified before being sent to the next step.

In geometry in order to verify two line segment are parallel, one method is to set one line segment to be reference and vertically move another line until it intersect the reference one, which will generate an angle θ and a "gap" area S. Therefore, by calculating whether the area of S is 0 or not, we can determine whether two lines are parallel or not. As shown in Fig. 5, the area of the "gap" S can be calculated by integration as:

$$S = \int_{x_1}^{x_2} dy \tag{3}$$

where x_1 and x_2 are fixed points on the line segment and dy is the distance between two lines segment (Fig. 4).

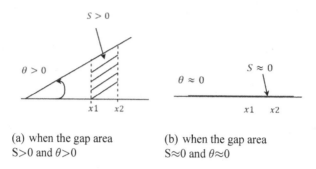

(a) when the gap area
S>0 and θ>0

(b) when the gap area
S≈0 and θ≈0

Fig. 4. The angles values between two line segment with different geometric region area

Under this geometric property, we can ensure the lower boundary of the plate is horizontal by minimizing the "gap" area S. Figure 5 shows the coordinates transformation of the points of the boundary of the plate which is about to be rectified. (The imaged has already been under binary adaptive operation and background information is set to be 0 and valid information is set to be 1) And for every points the rectified expression is given by

$$\begin{cases} x_1 = x_0 cos\theta + y_0 sin\theta \\ y_1 = y_0 sin\theta - x_0 sin\theta \end{cases} \tag{4}$$

where (x_0, y_0) and (x_1, y_1) are the original and the rectified coordinates of the points of plate, respectively. We change the angle θ from 0 to 0.9 rad by 0.001 rad each time. In addition, the area of the S can be equivalently represented by the expression as:

$$S = \sum_{x_1}^{x_2} y_i \tag{5}$$

where the y_i is the y coordinate of the ith first "one value" point of the among the x-axis after the rectification and x_1 and x_2 are the upper and lower domain of the "one value" points. Therefore, after 900 times of calculations the minimal value of S can be collected and the corresponding rectified angle θ' can be found.

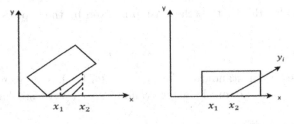

(a) Coordinates before rectify   (b) Coordinates after rectify

Fig. 5. Coordinates transformation of the plate

2.4 Plate Segmentation and Recognition

After rectification, the direction towards plate picture is found. We add the matrix at every column as shown in the Fig. 7. Then, the every local maximum is corresponding to one character, and we can set a threshold value to get the character section on the picture (Fig. 6).

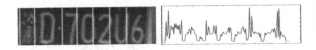

Fig. 6. Add up columns of matrix

During this process, one Convolutional Neural Network (CNN) [11] is applied to determine the rough space between each characters. Then Gaussian filter is used to suppress the noise. In order to find the proper segmentation points, the default template slide from left to right with different length of stride (each time stride plus 1). Additionally, during every stride of the slide, the loss function is calculated. After the stride equal to the columns of the input image, choosing the segmentation points whose loss is lowest. Finally, the segmented plate is sent to the trained CNN [11] to be recognized and eventually to get the output plate information.

As Shown in Fig. 7, the CNN network consists of 5 weighted layers: three convolution layers [11] (Conv1, Conv2 and Conv3) and two inner product layers (Inner Product 1 and Inner Product 2). And there are 3 unweighted layers: two max pooling layers and one flatten layer [9].

Also each layer is connected to one Rectified Linear Units (ReLU) layer [11] to increase the training speed of the network. This improvement of the training speed comes from the property that standard relationship between one neuron's output and input (x) is given by the expression

$$f(x) = tanh(x) \quad or \quad f(x) = \frac{1}{(1+e^{-x})} \tag{6}$$

However, as for ReLUs the relationship is given by the expression

$$f(x) = max(0, x) \tag{7}$$

So compared with standard relationship, ReLUs has non-saturating non-linearity which leads to much faster training speed with stochastic gradient descent [1].

The input image is with size of $30 \times 14 \times 3$ and in the first convolution layer, there are 32 kernels of size $3 \times 3 \times 3$ with a stride of 4 pixels to filter the input image. The second convolution layer filters the normalized and max pooled results from the first convolution layer with 64 kernels of size $3 \times 3 \times 16$. Similarly, the third convolutional layer takes the normalized and max pooled results from the second convolution layer and then filters it using 128 kernels of size $2 \times 2 \times 32$. The kernels of convolution layers are connected to all kernel maps in the previous layer. The neurons in the second inner product layer are connected to all neurons in the first inner product layer. In addition, two max pooling layers are set after the first and the second convolution layer respectively to summarize the maximum output of adjacent set of neurons in the same kernel map and gradually decrease the size of the convolution layers by the following expression

$$outputwidth : w_0 = \frac{w_i + 2 \times number\ of\ padding}{length\ of\ stride} + 1 \tag{8}$$

$$outputheight : h_0 = \frac{h_i + 2 \times number\ of\ padding}{length\ of\ stride} + 1 \tag{9}$$

After being convoluted to extract features in these three convolution layers, the output of the third convolution layer is sent to the flatten layer and the two inner product layers and final output is a single vector (with the blob's height and width set to 1). Then the output processes a 65-way Softmax regression [11] to produce a distribution over the 65 class labels (31 Chinese Characters, 10 numbers and 24 letters).

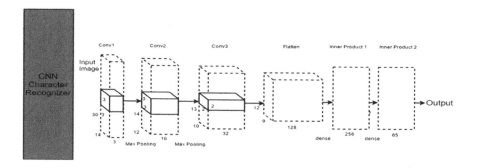

Fig. 7. Architecture of the CNN recognition network

2.5 Training

In order to prevent overfitting during the training, two strategies are used: Local Response Normalization and Dropout [7]. As for Local Response Normalization, this strategy is applied after the ReLU and the relationship between the response normalized output $y(m,n)^i$ for i^{th} kernel at position (m,n) and input $x(m,n)^i$ is given by the expression

$$y_{m,n}^i = \frac{x_{m,n}^i}{(\partial + p\sum_{min(N,i+0.5k)}^{j=max(0,i-0.5k)} x_{m,n}^j)^q} \tag{10}$$

where k is the number of the adjacent kernel maps at the positon (m, n), N is the number of the kernels in the same layer and ∂, p, q are training parameters which can be determined during the training to keep it valid. After comparing the results, Local Response Normalization reduce the error by 3%.

Another strategy named Dropout [7] is also applied in the two inner product layers. Every neuron is set to be zero with probability of 0.5, which means if the neuron is set to be zero, it will not participate in the forward not the backward propagation. Therefore, the network would have different paths for each training but the weights are shared. Under this random circumstances, the number of iterations is doubled which leads to more robust features that the network should be equipped.

In the training process, stochastic gradient descent [1] algorism is used and the size of the batch is 128 examples. The initial momentum is set to be 0.8 and initial weights of every weighted layer collected from a zero-mean Gaussian distribution with a standard deviation of 0.01 and the decay of weight is 0.0005. The iterations rule of the weight the weight w and momentum parameter v is given by the expressions:

$$w_{i+1} = w_i + v_{i+1} \tag{11}$$

$$v_{i+1} = 0.8v_{i+1} - 0.0005 \cdot a \cdot w_i - a \cdot \overline{\frac{\partial y}{\partial w}|_{w_i}} \tag{12}$$

where α is learning rate which is initially set to be 0.005 for all layers and $\frac{\partial y}{\partial w}|_{w_i}$ is the average of the derivate of the objective with respective to the current weight evaluated at w_i over the ith batch. The total time consumed in training is about 12 h for the training set of 4000 image for around 100 cycles with $4 \times$ Titan X.

In addition, besides using Softmax [11] to calculate confidence, the SSD network also require calculating location loss [13] by Smooth L1 [6]. And the expression of the default bounding boxes location offsets [3,16] are given by

$$\begin{cases} x_i = \frac{g_i^x - p_i^x}{p_i^w} \\ y_1 = \frac{g_i^y - p_i^y}{p_i^h} \\ w_i = log(\frac{g_i^w}{p_i^w}) \\ h_i = log(\frac{g_i^h}{p_i^h}) \end{cases} \tag{13}$$

where p, g are parameters for prediction results, ground truth boxes respectively. And i is the points in the range of default boxes, (x, y),w, h are coordinates and width and height of the boxes.

3   Experiment Result

The main task of license plate detection is to find the location of the license plate in the image of the automobile, and accurately separate the license plate from the region for character segmentation. Therefore, the accuracy of license area is one of the most important factors affecting the algorithm performance. The position of license plate directly affects the accuracy of character segmentation and character recognition. At present, there are many methods for license plate position, but generally they can be divided into the following four categories : (1) color-based segmentation method, which mainly uses the information of color space to realize license plate segmentation, including color edge algorithm, color distance and similarity algorithm, etc. (2) texture based segmentation method, which mainly uses the horizontal texture features of license plate area for segmentation, including small ripple, horizontal gradient difference texture and so on; (3) segmentation method based on edge detection; (4) segmentation method based on mathematical morphology. Our side view input tests will compare performances of these traditional methods with our SSD+DNN method.

3.1   Side View Input

Due to the fact that camera can not always taking pictures in the front of the plate in practice, a number of input images will be side viewed. We use the deep learning algorithm to detect the licence plate instead of traditional methods said above. In addition, we also use neural network to recognize the character rather than thinning the character and then extracting the features to compare with ground truth and recognize the character. Therefore the license plate can also be recognized when the camera is tilted in the direction of the camera by our algorithm.

The cyan line means our algorithm that uses SSD and neural network. The green dash line represents the traditional method detection and CNN recognition. The blue dash line is SSD detection and traditional method recognition. Finally, the red dash line means the accuracy of using traditional method to detect the car plate and recognize the character (Fig. 8).

Apparently, the highest accuracy can be obtained by using deep learning methods to both detect the location of the plate and to identify the character. Therefore, compared with the green and red dash line, it can be found that using our algorithm to identify characters can improve the accuracy significantly in 60° or 120°. When the angle comes to below 30 or above 150°, the accuracy of four algorithms are all very low, because the angle between camera and plate is small, which leads to some strokes may overlap in picture and make it hard to be divided.

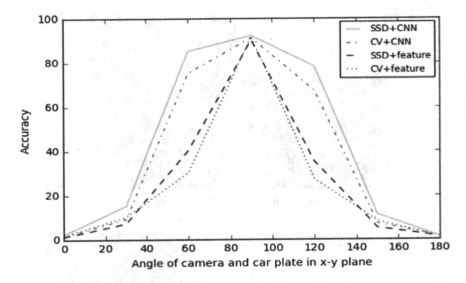

Fig. 8. Car plate recognition accuracy in difference algorithms (Color figure online)

Additionally, the result shows that the accuracies of four algorithms are higher at 30 and 60° than 120 and 150°. It is because the Chinese character is on the right side and the Chinese character is the most complex character on the licence plate. When the camera is at 30 and 60°, the overlapped strokes of Chinese character are less than at 120 and 150°.

3.2   Distorted Input Test Results

Images may be compressed during transmission, which leads to the distorted input picture. Most traditional plate recognition method use edge detection or color edge to detect and identify the plate, but it is very limited in dealing with distorted input image.

However, our algorithm can avoid this problem, because we use SSD algorithm to detect the car plate and CNN to recognize the characters. No matter how the picture distorted, before the image sent to the SSD network, it need to be resized to 1000×800 resolution, and segmented characters also need to be resized to 30×14 resolution. Therefore, in fact we even have no need to do transfer training specially for every case of input images with different sizes. In additional, during the training of CNN network, we combine images of characters with different sizes and even some incomplete pictures to improve the character recognition capability and reduce the error caused by character segmentation deviation. Moreover, we also add some rotated samples in training dataset to make our model can detect the position of plate even when the picture is rotated, as shown in Fig. 9(d). Though the area of detected plate is slant, we can also use fast rectify algorithm to set right the plate and then recognize the characters on it.

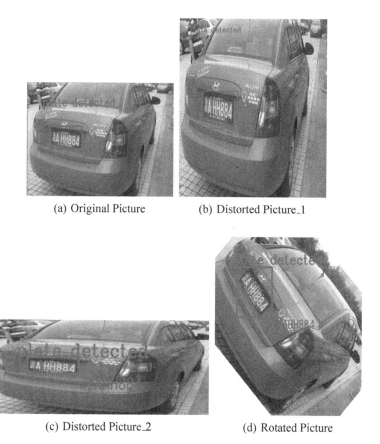

(a) Original Picture   (b) Distorted Picture_1

(c) Distorted Picture_2   (d) Rotated Picture

Fig. 9. Compare of recognition result

4   Conclusion and Further Work

After few adjustments of parameters of the recognizer, the MobileNet-SSD technology compared with other traditional recognizer shows competitive advantages in processing side view input and distorted input images. The test result (the total dataset is 5000) show that the overall accuracy of the standard input is 92% and for the side view (60 or 120°) input the accuracy can keep in a very high level (85%). In addition, compared with most traditional recognizers which are not qualified to recognize distorted input, our algorithm can reach the accuracy of 90% in distorted input tests. Therefore, the overall performance of the detection and recognition of plate is acceptable. Further work can be focused on finding the effect of the angles to the recognition results and improve the system robustness for shooting angle.

References

1. Bottou, L.: Large-scale machine learning with stochastic gradient descent. In: Lechevallier, Y., Saporta, G. (eds.) Proceedings of COMPSTAT 2010, pp. 177–186. Springer, Heidelberg (2010). https://doi.org/10.1007/978-3-7908-2604-3_16
2. Bradski, G., Kaehler, A.: Learning OpenCV: Computer Vision with the OpenCV Library. O'Reilly Media, Inc., Sebastopol (2008)
3. Erhan, D., Szegedy, C., Toshev, A., Anguelov, D.: Scalable object detection using deep neural networks. In: Proceedings of the IEEE Conference on Computer Vision and Pattern Recognition, pp. 2147–2154 (2014)
4. Fischler, M.A., Bolles, R.C.: Random sample consensus: a paradigm for model fitting with applications to image analysis and automated cartography. Commun. ACM **24**(6), 381–395 (1981)
5. Guo, J.F., Liu, Y., Yu, L.: Traffic congestion in large metropolitan area in china. Urban Transp. China **2**(006) (2011)
6. He, K., Gkioxari, G., Dollár, P., Girshick, R.: Mask R-CNN. IEEE Trans. Pattern Anal. Mach. Intell. (2018)
7. Hinton, G.E., Srivastava, N., Krizhevsky, A., Sutskever, I., Salakhutdinov, R.R.: Improving neural networks by preventing co-adaptation of feature detectors. arXiv preprint arXiv:1207.0580 (2012)
8. Howard, A.G., et al.: MobileNets: efficient convolutional neural networks for mobile vision applications. arXiv preprint arXiv:1704.04861 (2017)
9. Jia, Y., et al.: Caffe: convolutional architecture for fast feature embedding. In: Proceedings of the 22nd ACM International Conference on Multimedia, pp. 675–678. ACM (2014)
10. Kanopoulos, N., Vasanthavada, N., Baker, R.L.: Design of an image edge detection filter using the sobel operator. IEEE J. Solid-State Circuits **23**(2), 358–367 (1988)
11. Krizhevsky, A., Sutskever, I., Hinton, G.E.: ImageNet classification with deep convolutional neural networks. In: Advances in Neural Information Processing Systems, pp. 1097–1105 (2012)
12. Lee, E.R., Kim, P.K., Kim, H.J.: Automatic recognition of a car license plate using color image processing. In: 1994 IEEE International Conference Proceedings Image Processing ICIP-1994, vol. 2, pp. 301–305. IEEE (1994)
13. Liu, W., et al.: SSD: single shot multibox detector. In: Leibe, B., Matas, J., Sebe, N., Welling, M. (eds.) ECCV 2016. LNCS, vol. 9905, pp. 21–37. Springer, Cham (2016). https://doi.org/10.1007/978-3-319-46448-0_2
14. Redmon, J., Divvala, S., Girshick, R., Farhadi, A.: You only look once: unified, real-time object detection. In: Proceedings of the IEEE Conference on Computer Vision and Pattern Recognition, pp. 779–788 (2016)
15. Ren, S., He, K., Girshick, R., Sun, J.: Faster R-CNN: towards real-time object detection with region proposal networks. In: Advances in Neural Information Processing Systems, pp. 91–99 (2015)
16. Szegedy, C., Reed, S., Erhan, D., Anguelov, D., Ioffe, S.: Scalable, high-quality object detection. arXiv preprint arXiv:1412.1441 (2014)
17. Wen, H., Sun, J., Zhang, X.: Study on traffic congestion patterns of large city in China taking Beijing as an example. Proc. Soc. Behav. Sci. **138**, 482–491 (2014)
18. Yu, M., Kim, Y.D.: An approach to Korean license plate recognition based on vertical edge matching. In: 2000 IEEE International Conference on Systems, Man, and Cybernetics, vol. 4, pp. 2975–2980. IEEE (2000)

Performance Comparison Between Genetic Fuzzy Tree and Reinforcement Learning in Gaming Environment

Wenda Wu[1,2(✉)], Mingxue Liao[2], Pin Lv[2], Xueyu Duan[1,2], and Xinwei Zhao[1,2]

[1] University of Chinese Academy of Sciences,
Beijing, People's Republic of China
wenda2016@iscas.ac.cn
[2] Institute of Software, Chinese Academy of Sciences,
Beijing, People's Republic of China
{mingxue,lvpin,xueyu2016,xinwei2016}@iscas.ac.cn

Abstract. Wargame systems are artificial combat simulation platforms which would be practical in game research. The widely used methods in wargame systems mostly rely on refined experience of human experts. We suppose to apply artificial intelligence methods rather than expert-experience-based methods to complicated game environments. Reinforcement learning methods provide a human-like normative way which guides agents upgrade their behaviors in game environments without expert experience. This paper reveals the performances of both experience-based models and reinforcement-learning-based models in game environments. This environment presented in this paper is a type of zero-sum game which means there only be one winner. Our experiments show that reinforcement-learning-based models is more robust and powerful than expert-experience-based methods but cost more time.

Keywords: Wargame · Reinforcement learning · Genetic Fuzzy Tree · Deep learning

1 Introduction

Intelligence decision systems [12] engage to fulfill a task in specific environments. It works efficiently on both gaming environments and cooperating environments. Chess games and video games are widely-used domains of intelligence decision systems.

Traditional method to construct intelligence decision systems rely on supervised learning [1] which is based on rules and human experience, Deep Blue [4]

The work is supported by both National scientific and Technological Innovation Zero (No. 17-H863-01-ZT-005-005-01) and State's Key Project of Research and Development Plan (No. 2016QY03D0505). The contributions of authors of this paper are as follows: Wu proposed this problem, built computational models and do experiments; Liao, Lv, Duan and Zhao provided various supports for this work.

© Springer Nature Singapore Pte Ltd. 2019
F. Sun et al. (Eds.): ICCSIP 2018, CCIS 1006, pp. 256–267, 2019.
https://doi.org/10.1007/978-981-13-7986-4_23

and Genetic Fuzzy Tree [6] for instance. There is a defect that supervised learning results are totally determined by artificial labels. Its performance would be poor when the data we got could not fully present the problem we want to solve.

In contrast, reinforcement learning [20] does not rely on data with artificial labels. Decision strategy is improved by interaction between agents and environment. Agents choose actions according to present state via some algorithms and execute them in the environment. After that, agents receive instant rewards and new state of the environment. In other words, reinforcement learning methods search for the best policy through trails.

Reinforcement learning methods can also be used in game environments. There are two forces in the environment and only one winner left at last. Both experience-based model and reinforcement-learning-based model worked efficiently and we want to compare the performances of two different types of models in gaming environment.

2   Related Work

In 2016, the artificial intelligence [18] named Alpha AI defeated the experienced US Air Force Colonel Keen Lee in the air combat simulator according to the information released from official website of the University of Cincinnati. Alpha AI extracts high-level features from basic features using genetic fuzzy tree method and outputs the proper actions of agents. It divides input features into several fuzzy levels [17]. Different fuzzy features are combined to form high-level features through fuzzy inference system [10]. Finally, outputs of different fuzzy inference systems form a cascaded fuzzy inference system. Agents get their actions from the cascaded fuzzy inference system. The whole model is evaluated by genetic algorithm [7].

DeepMind presented "Playing Atari with Deep Reinforcement Learning" [16] trying to teach computer playing video games in 2013. In this paper, they trained computer playing Atari 2600 video games [14] via Deep Q-Network (DQN). Atari 2600 is a compilation including a bunch of classical games designed for human and each game has its own goal to reach. DQN model performed better than human in 3 games. After that, they upgraded DQN and presented another paper [15] which was on the cover of Nature in 2015. They applied their model to 49 different games. The model performed better than human in more than half of games this time. DQN combined convolution neural network (CNN) [2,11] and reinforcement learning method together. They took the screen shot of the game as input and fed the output of model to controller. Every screen shot produced a command for controller which guides the action of agent in environment. After agents executing actions, model received instant rewards and the new screen shot.

Apart from video games, DeepMind also works in chess domain. There were already AI models playing Go against amateur human players in 2014 [13] but the capacity of AI models are still far behind from top professional players. Two years later, DeepMind presented AlphaGo and caused a hit. Its a mixture model of convolution neural network, supervised learning, reinforcement learning and Monte Carlo tree search methods [3,5,8].

One year later, DeepMind presented AlphaGo Zero [19] in Nature. AlphaGo Zero fully abandoned human experience and learned Go from tabula rasa to superhuman master. It took residual network [9] instead of convolution neural network and combined policy network and value network together. AlphaGo Zero thrashed AlphaGo with 100:0.

3   Method

3.1   Gaming Environment Construction

Basic Layout. We set two forces in limited grid playground. Each force controls the same numbers of agents. These agents can move freely in playground. Each agent has 6 hit-points (HP) and infinite ammunition. Agents have the same field of fire and would fire to enemy who is exposed in their field of fire. Once all agents of one force are destroyed, battle round ends.

Rules. Gaming process is pushed by timesteps. Every agent gets an action in a single timestep. Agent would stay in-place if it wants to move out of playground or its destination of this step is obtained by another agent. One movement takes a single timestep and an attack does not take any time. If two opposing agents are exposed in the field of fire of the other, they are encountering and attack automatically in a single timestep. If one agent encounters with two or more opposing agents, on the one hand, it could be attacked by all the enemies. On the other hand, the single agent would attack one of its enemies randomly. Each attack causes one damage and each agent has 6 HP which means that an agent can suffer 6 attacks.

If one agent arrives 0 HP, it is destroyed and takes no position. Other agents can take this position again. Damages are computed at the end of a single timestep so that two opposing agents could be destroyed simultaneously. A single game round ends when agents of one force are all destroyed and the other force wins this round.

Playground Initialization. As a primary exploration for experience-based models and reinforcement-learning-based models, we set two agents for each force in playground. Two forces are named as red force and blue force. Our models control red force and try to win in every round. We locate two blue-force agents in the center and two red-force agents in the corner. Blue-force agents can support each other because they could fire to the same enemy which are trapped into the common area of blue-force agents. Two red-force agents are far away from each other so they must learn to band together for winning.

Reward Setting. There are two types of reward systems in our game environment. First reward system does not pay attention to game process but the final results. There are seven different rewards that agents can get. If all red-force agents are destroyed and all blue-force agents are alive, models get −3 points; If all red-force agents are destroyed and one blue-force agents is alive, models get −2 points; If one red-force agents is alive and all blue-force agent are alive, models get −1 point; If all red-force agent are alive and one blue-force agents is alive, models get +1 point; If one red-force agents is alive and all blue-force agents are destroyed, models get +2 points. If all red-force agents are alive and all blue-force agents are destroyed, models get +3 points. Models get 0 points.

The other reward system is more complicated. We want to encourage red-force agents to fire to enemies rather than escape from damages. Models get +0.31 points when a blue-force agent lose 1 HP and −0.2 points when red-force agent lose 1 HP. Furthermore, we expect red-force agents pursue and attack moribund opposing agents so we give models +6 points when one blue-force agent is destroyed. We expect red-force agents reserve themselves and give models −4 points when one red-force agent is destroyed. We do not want agents waste timesteps in useless movements, swinging left and right or circling for instance. Models get a small minus reward when there are no rewards feed-backed from environment.

Pay attention to the reward system, old rewards should be saved and new rewards of current time-step minus old rewards are fed to models.

Graphical Interface. Graphical interface can show what strategy models have learned and check what have happened during the whole process. We use a white grid map describes our playground. Red-force agents are presented by red squares and blue-force agents are presented by blue squares. Red-force agents turn to green and blue-force agents turns to black when they are destroyed. Below the white grid map is an information text block. It shows every agent's HP, action and location. Graphical interface updates information between the point that agent gets action and execute action in playground. Graphical interface was shown as Fig. 1.

3.2 Genetic Fuzzy Tree Method

Genetic Fuzzy Tree (GFT) is an experience-based method. We construct Genetic Fuzzy Tree for every agent. Our Genetic Fuzzy Tree has four basic-level-features fuzzy inference systems (FIS) and two high-level-features fuzzy inference systems. These FISs construct a Genetic Fuzzy Tree in cascaded form.

For sake of solving the problem that location coordinates are hard to be described in FIS, we adopt distances between agents instead of coordinates. We give five actions to every agent: moving away from first enemy, moving close to first enemy, moving away from second enemy and moving close to second enemy and stay-in-place.

We need 12 basic features including HP of first enemy agent, ammunition of first enemy agent, distance to first enemy agent, HP of second enemy agent,

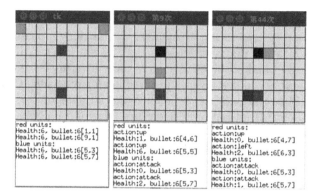

Fig. 1. Graphical interface. Red-force agent is red square and blue agent is blue square. Red-force agent turns to green and blue-force agent turns to black when destroyed. Left image describes the start of one round. Image in the middle shows one blue-force agent was destroyed. Right image shows one red-force agent and one blue-force agent was destroyed. (Color figure online)

ammunition of second enemy agent, distance to second enemy agent, HP of itself, ammunition of itself, HP of friend agent, ammunition of friend agent, distance to friend agent and distances between friend agent and two enemies.

We fuzz every feature to three levels with the help of membership functions. Membership functions are shown in Fig. 2. We put enemy HP, enemy ammunition and distance from enemy together to construct enemy threat; put own HP and own ammunition together to construct own capability; put HP of friend agent and ammunition of friend agent to construct friend capability; put distance to friend agent and distances between friend agent and two enemies to construct friend location feature. Friend capability and friend location are bonded together as friend support. Finally, enemy threat, own capability and friend support decide which action agent would choose. Fig. 3 provides the structure of GFT and Tables 1, 2, 3, 4, 5 and 6 provide details of every FIS.

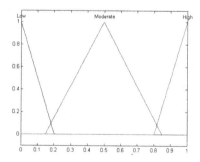

Fig. 2. Membership function

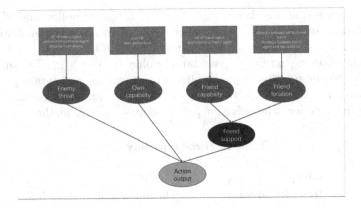

Fig. 3. GFT structure

Table 1. Enemy threat FIS

Input	Output
HP of enemy agent	Enemy threat (0–2)
Ammunition of enemy agent	\
Distance to enemy	\

Table 2. Own capability FIS

Input	Output
Own HP	Own capability (0–2)
Own ammunition	\

We construct a chromosome with two parts to upgrade the rules in GFT. One part consists of all rules in GFT. The other part consists of shifting of key point in membership functions. A chromosome gets a score after every game round ends. The chromosome with higher score takes advantage during genetic algorithm [7] process.

3.3 Traditional Reinforcement Learning Method

Traditional reinforcement learning methods record rewards that every action can get in different states via value table. We establish a Q-value table for game environment.

Q-value table includes HP and location of agents. Every action in different state gets an initial random score which presents the penitential reward agent would get if it executes this action. The value's update equation showed as following.

$$Q(s_t, a_t) = Q(s_t, a_t) + \alpha(R_{t+1} + \gamma Q(s_{t+1}, a'_{t+1}) - Q(s_t, a_t)) \qquad (1)$$

In (1), a means that we choose an action via behavior policy and a' means that we choose an action via target policy. $Q(s_t,a_t)$ means rewards obtained by choosing action a_t via behavior policy in state s_t. $Q(s_{t+1},a'_{t+1})$ means reward obtained by choosing action a'_{t+1} via target policy in state s_{t+1}. The subscripts t and t+1 present the timestep. We allow both behavior and target policies to be improved. In other words, we balance exploitation and exploration with the aid of behavior policy. The behavior policy adopts ϵ-greedy method.

Table 3. Friend capability FIS

Input	Output
HP of friend agent	Friend capability (0–2)
Ammunition of friend agent	\

Table 4. Friend location FIS

Input	Output
Distance to friend agent	Friend location (0–2)
Distances between friend agent and two enemies	\

3.4   Deep Q-Network Method

Traditional reinforcement learning methods store an action-value table for any possible state. The biggest problem we face to is that even in a simple environment, the action-value table could be enormous. Deep Q-network method constructs model without action-value table. There is a restriction that only Q-learning can be used in CNN in terms of convergence.

State Matrix. Original DQN captures video game images as input of neural network [15]. It is inappropriate to capture graphical interface images in our environment as inputs. Finally, we decide to use state matrices instead of images.

State matrices have the same scale with playground. As a single state matrix can't describe complete state, we make three matrices for every state, presenting own state, enemy state and location relationship individually. We put the value of agents according to their real location in our environment. The value of an agent in matrix is equal to HP plus playground basic value. State matrices have two advantages: firstly, model takes raw information from state matrices rather than second-hand information of graphic interface images. Secondly, state matrices have less scale than images and need no extra preprocessing.

Table 5. Friend support FIS

Input	Output
Friend capability (0–2)	Friend support (0–2)
Friend location (0–2)	\

Table 6. Action FIS

Input	Output
Enemy threat (0–2)	Action (0–4)
Own capability (0–2)	\
Friend support (0–2)	\

Convolution Neural Network. Whole network is divided into two parts, action-value network and target action-value network. These two networks have the same structure (see Fig. 4). We use convolution layers, pooling layers and fully connected layers in our network. Our activation function is Relu.

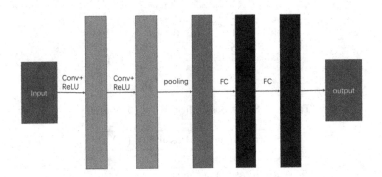

Fig. 4. CNN construct

The final fully connected layer outputs the probability of choosing each action individually. Different from Genetic Fuzzy Tree, our DQN is a centralized system which means that one model controls all agents. The ultra-output action probabilities are encoded for action-combination of all agents.

The training process follows DeepMind's standard process.

4   Experiments

4.1   State Estimation

We start our experiments in a simple basic environment. Every agent gets 6 HP and its field of fire is 3. Red-force agents start in the two top corners of map while blue-force agents are in the middle of the map. Red-force agents can move freely around the map while blue-force agents only stay in their own location. Red-force agents receive commands from our models and try to destroy all blue-force agents.

We estimate which force gets advantages in initial environment setting. We record results of $1 * 10^8$ game rounds. Results are shown in Tables 7 and 8.

We determine red-force is lost when two forces have the same number of agents left or number of red-force agents left are less than Blue's. As we can see from Table 8, blue-force agents dominate.

Table 7. Advantages estimate Table

	Red force	Blue force	Score
Agents left	0	2	−3
	0	1	−2
	1	2	−1
	0	0	0
	1	1	0
	2	2	0
	2	1	1
	1	0	2
	2	0	3

Table 8. Score possibility in $1 * 10^8$ gaming

Score	Rounds	Possibility (%)
−3	302834	0.3
−2	6342454	6.3
−1	0	0
0	57511594	57.5
1	697	0
2	34146705	34.1
3	1695716	1.8

4.2   Experiments for Models

We apply models to our environment and their performances can be seen in Table 9. Since DQN takes more time to get converged and relies on the initial setting of hyper-parameters, we do not take it into account when comparing converge rounds of models.

As we can see, red-force agents can defeat blue-force agents and reserve themselves as many as possible. All methods can find the best way to destroy enemies and save own HP. Comparing to complicated reward system, our reinforcement-learning-based model prefers succinct one. Reinforcement-learning-based model with succinct reward system takes less rounds to get the best policy. We deem that complicated reward system would mislead convergence direction of model in some specific situations. It is worth to take more experiments in future works to prove that.

Furthermore, we choose the best chromosome of Genetic Fuzzy Trees as the strategy of blue-force in next series of experiments. Blue-force agents are located in the two bottom corners as red-force agents do. We also want red-force agents to win. The following experiments are presented as Table 10.

As we can see from experiments, Genetic Fuzzy Tree method is limited by experts knowledge. The defect is more apparent as enemys strategy improving step by step whereas reinforcement-learning-based model can adjust with strategy upgrading of enemies. DQN seems less powerful but still performs better than Genetic Fuzzy Tree.

In other hand, traditional reinforcement-learning-based model takes the shortest time in training and Genetic Fuzzy Tree follows. DQN takes very long time to arrive stable contrast to other methods but gifted for stronger expansion ability. Considering about memory space cost, traditional reinforcement-learning-based model holds huge data even in simple environment because it needs to save Q-value for every possible state. This is the problem reinforcement-learning-based method can not avoid. The data scale is shown in Table 11.

We can't ignore that different reward systems influence model's performance badly. It is a hard way to find the proper reward system to describe the task we want to accomplish.

Table 9. State of red force agents

Model	Gaming rounds	Win	Agents left	Total HP left	Average rounds
GFT	100000	Yes	2	6	290
T.RL (reward1)	100000	Yes	2	6	3331.44
T.RL (reward2)	100000	Yes	2	6	2155.3
DQN (reward1)	100000	Yes	2	6	\
DQN (reward2)	100000	Yes	2	6	\

5   Future Works

Genetic Fuzzy Tree is easy to understand but performs poor.

Reinforcement-learning-based models are powerful but black boxes. We expect to combine advantages of these two types of models together in the future.

Table 10. State of red force agents

Turn 1					
Model	Gaming rounds	Win	Agents left	Total HP left	Average rounds
GFT	100000	Yes	2	5	2256.14
T.RL (reward1)	100000	Yes	2	5	3025.79
T.RL (reward2)	100000	Yes	2	5	778.56
DQN (reward1)	100000	Yes	2	5	\
DQN (reward2)	100000	Yes	2	5	\
Turn 2					
GFT	100000	No	\	\	\
T.RL (reward1)	100000	No	\	\	\
T.RL (reward2)	100000	Yes	2	5	5447.8
DQN (reward1)	100000	No	\	\	\
DQN (reward2)	100000	Yes	2	3	\

Table 11. Space and time occupancy

Model	Space occupancy	Time occupancy
GFT	5.9 KB	Long
T.RL	2 GB	Short
DQN	102.3 KB	Very long

If Genetic Fuzzy Tree can learn feature combination rules from reinforcement-learning-based models, it could be more powerful and helpful to enrich human knowledge base.

Reward system is the most important part in reinforcement learning. We would test model performance in different types of reward systems and find something helpful for reward designing.

It is would be a hard but exciting way.

References

1. Aha, D.W., Kibler, D., Albert, M.K.: Instance-based learning algorithms. Mach. Learn. **6**(1), 37–66 (1991)
2. Bishop, C.M.: Neural networks for pattern recognition. Agric. Eng. Int. CIGR J. Sci. Res. Dev. Manuscript Pm **12**(5), 1235–1242 (1995)
3. Browne, C.B., et al.: A survey of monte carlo tree search methods. IEEE Trans. Comput. Intell. AI Games **4**(1), 1–43 (2012)
4. Campbell, M., Hoane Jr., A.J., Hsu, F.H.: Deep blue. Artif. Intell. **134**(1), 57–83 (2002)
5. Coulom, R.: Efficient selectivity and backup operators in Monte-Carlo tree search. In: van den Herik, H.J., Ciancarini, P., Donkers, H.H.L.M.J. (eds.) CG 2006. LNCS, vol. 4630, pp. 72–83. Springer, Heidelberg (2007). https://doi.org/10.1007/978-3-540-75538-8_7

6. Ernest, N.D.: Genetic fuzzy trees for intelligent control of unmanned combat aerial vehicles. Dissertations & Theses - Gradworks (2015)
7. Goldberg, D.E.: Genetic Algorithm in Search Optimization and Machine Learning, vol. xiii, no. 7, pp. 2104–2116. Addison Wesley, Boston (1989)
8. Guo, X., Singh, S., Lee, H., Lewis, R., Wang, X.: Deep learning for real-time Atari game play using offline Monte-Carlo tree search planning. In: International Conference on Neural Information Processing Systems, pp. 3338–3346 (2014)
9. He, K., Zhang, X., Ren, S., Sun, J.: Deep residual learning for image recognition. In: IEEE Conference on Computer Vision and Pattern Recognition, pp. 770–778 (2016)
10. Jang, J.S.R.: ANFIS: adaptive-network-based fuzzy inference system. IEEE Trans. Syst. Man Cybern. **23**(3), 665–685 (1993)
11. Krizhevsky, A., Sutskever, I., Hinton, G.E.: ImageNet classification with deep convolutional neural networks. In: International Conference on Neural Information Processing Systems, pp. 1097–1105 (2012)
12. Kuhlmann, T., Lamping, R., Massow, C.: Intelligent decision support. J. Mater. Process. Technol. **76**(13), 257–260 (1998)
13. Maddison, C.J., Huang, A., Sutskever, I., Silver, D.: Move evaluation in go using deep convolutional neural networks. Comput. Sci. (2015)
14. Miller, F.P., Vandome, A.F., Mcbrewster, J.: Atari 2600. Alphascript Publishing (2013)
15. Mnih, V., et al.: Human-level control through deep reinforcement learning. Nature **518**(7540), 529 (2015)
16. Mnih, V., et al.: Playing Atari with deep reinforcement learning. Comput. Sci. (2013)
17. Passino, K.M., Yurkovich, S.: Fuzzy Control. Tsinghua University Press, Beijing (2001)
18. Russell, S.J., Norvig, P.: Artificial intelligence: a modern approach. Appl. Mech. Mater. **263**(5), 2829–2833 (2010)
19. Silver, D., et al.: Mastering the game of go without human knowledge. Nature **550**(7676), 354–359 (2017)
20. Sutton, R.S., Barto, A.G.: Reinforcement learning: an introduction, bradford book. IEEE Trans. Neural Netw. **16**(1), 285–286 (2005)

The Third Kind of Bayes' Theorem Links Membership Functions to Likelihood Functions and Sampling Distributions

Chenguang Lu[✉][iD]

College of Intelligence Engineering and Mathematics,
Liaoning Engineering and Technology University,
Fuxin 123000, Liaoning, China
lcguang@foxmail.com

Abstract. For given age population prior distribution $P(x)$ and the posterior distribution $P(x|\text{adult})$, how do we obtain the denotation of a label y = "adult"? With the denotation, e.g., the membership function of class {Adult}, we can make new probability prediction, e.g., likelihood function, for changed $P(x)$. However, existing methods including Likelihood Method and Bayesian Inference cannot resolve this problem. For this purpose, the author proposes and proves the third kind of Bayes' Theorem, which includes two asymmetrical Bayes' formulas. The membership function so obtained is equivalent to that from random set statistics proposed by Peizhuang Wang. When samples are very big so that there are continuous sampling distributions $P(x, y)$, we can directly derive a group of membership functions by a new Bayes formula. If samples are not big enough, we can use the semantic information formula, a generalized Kullback-Leibler formula, to optimize the membership functions by sampling distributions. The semantic information criterion is compatible with maximum likelihood criterion and Regularized Least Squares (RLS) criterion. In comparison with the likelihood function and the Bayesian posterior, the membership function so obtained as the predictive model can be used with new source $P(x)$ to produce new likelihood function for better generalization performance. New Bayes' formulas and the semantic information method can be applied to machine learning. The paper simply introduces their applications to (1) multi-label classifications; (2) maximum mutual information classifications for unseen instances; and (3) mixture models. It is shown that new methods are very simple and reliable. It seems that the membership function so obtained can bridge the gap between logic and probability. With this membership function, we can develop a new mathematical tool: Logical Bayesian Inference.

Keywords: Bayes' theorem · Membership function · Likelihood function · Semantic information · Machine learning · Multi-label classification · Natural language processing · Logical probability

© Springer Nature Singapore Pte Ltd. 2019
F. Sun et al. (Eds.): ICCSIP 2018, CCIS 1006, pp. 268–280, 2019.
https://doi.org/10.1007/978-981-13-7986-4_24

1 Introduction

The main task of machine learning is classification. The membership function proposed by Zadeh [1] indicates the membership relation of different instances to a fuzzy class and hence should be a good tool for machine learning. The relationship between statistical probabilities and membership functions has been discussed for a long time [2–6]. Wang [2] explained the membership function with random set falling shadow. Thomas et al. [3, 4] proposed a Bayes' formula to produce a likelihood function from a membership function and an instance prior distribution (e.g., a source). The author used Wang's random set falling shadow theory to derived the above Bayes' formula and used it to set up a semantic information theory [7–9]. However, existing methods still cannot obtain a membership function, which is compatible with random set statistics, from a likelihood function or a sampling distribution directly.

We use an example to explain this problem. Assume there is age population prior distribution $P(x)$ and the posterior distribution $P(x|\text{adult})$ or $P(x|$ "adult" is true), which are continuous. How do we obtain the denotation of "adult" (see Fig. 1)? With the denotation, e.g., the feature function or the membership function of class {Adult}, we can make new probability prediction or produce new likelihood function after $P(x)$ is changed. Can we obtain the feature function of set {Adult}? If the set {Adult} is fuzzy, can we obtain the membership function of the fuzzy set {Adult}?

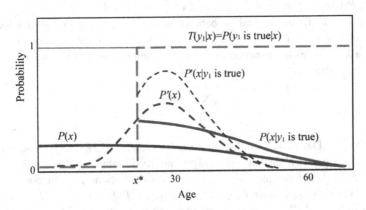

Fig. 1. Solving the denotation of "Adult" and the posterior distribution $P'(x|y_1$ is true).

Further, if we only know a not big enough sample with unsmooth or discontinuous distribution $P(x, y)$, can we construct a smooth membership function with parameters as we do for a likelihood function, and train it with the sampling distribution? This is a label learning issue.

Furthermore, given a group of membership functions and a changed $P(x)$, how do we classify the instance space with maximum likelihood criterion or maximum mutual information criterion? This is a multi-label classification issue.

In this paper, to resolve above problems with membership functions, we first propose the third kind of Bayes' theorem and prove that the membership function obtained from the new Bayes' formula is equivalent to that obtained from the random set statistics. Two resolve the above two issues, we use the semantic information method [11–13].

In next section, we introduce new mathematical methods. In Sect. 3, we simply introduce the applications of the new methods to multi-label classification, maximum mutual information classifications for unseen instances, and mixture models. Section 4 provides discussions. The last section is the summary.

2 Mathematical Methods

2.1 Distinguishing Statistical Probability and Logical Probability

Definition 1. Let U denote an instance set, and X denote a discrete random variable taking a value x from U. That means $X \in U = \{x_1, x_2, \ldots\}$. Let V denote the set of selectable labels, including some atomic and compound labels and let $Y \in V = \{y_1, y_2, \ldots\}$.

Definition 2. A label y_j is also a predicate $y_j(X) = $ "$X \in A_j$". For each y_j, U has a subset of A_j, every instance of which makes y_j true. Let $P(Y = y_j)$ denote the statistical probability of y_j, and $P(X \in A_j)$ denote the Logical Probability (LP) of y_j. For simplicity, let $P(y_j) = P(Y = y_j)$ and $T(y_j) = T(A_j) = P(X \in A_j)$.

We call $P(X \in A_j)$ the logical probability because according to Tarski's theory of truth [14], $P(X \in A_j) = P(``X \in A_j"$ is true$) = P(y_j$ is true$)$. Hence the conditional LP of y_j for given X is the feature function of A_j and the truth function of y_j. We denote it with $T(A_j|X)$. Hence there is

$$T(A_j) = \sum_i P(x_i) T(A_j|x_i) \tag{2.1}$$

According to Davidson's truth-conditional semantics [15], $T(A_j|X)$ ascertains the semantic meaning of y_j. Note that statistical probability distributions, such as $P(Y)$, $P(Y|x_i)$, $P(X)$, and $P(X|y_j)$, are normalized; however, LP distributions are not normalized. In general, $T(A_1) + T(A_2) + \ldots + T(A_n) > 1; T(A_1|x_i) + T(A_2|x_i) + \ldots + T(A_n|x_i) > 1$.

If A_j is fuzzy, $T(A_j|X)$ becomes the membership function, and $T(A_j)$ is also the fuzzy event probability defined by Zadeh [16]. For fuzzy sets, we use θ_j to replace A_j. Then $T(\theta_j|X)$ becomes the membership function of θ_j. There is

$$m_{\theta_j}(X) = T(\theta_j|X) = T(y_j|X) \tag{2.2}$$

We can also treat θ_j as a sub-model of a predictive model θ. In this paper, likelihood function $P(X|\theta_j)$ is equal to $P(X|y_j; \theta)$ in popular likelihood method.

2.2 The Three Kinds of Bayes' Theorems

There are three kinds of Bayes' theorem, which are used by Bayes [17], Shannon [18], and the author respectively.

Bayes' Theorem I (used by Bayes): Assume that sets $A, B \in 2^U, A^c$ is the complementary set of A, $T(A) = P(X \in A)$, and $T(B) = P(X \in B)$. Then

$$T(B|A) = T(A|B)T(B)/T(A), T(A) = T(A|B)T(B) + T(A|B^c)T(B^c) \qquad (2.3)$$

There is also an asymmetrical formula for $T(A|B)$. Note there are only one random variable X and two logical probabilities.

Bayes' Theorem II (used by Shannon):

$$P(x_i|y_j) = P(y_j|x_i)P(x_i)/P(y_j), \ P(y_j) = \sum_i P(x_i)P(y_j|x_i) \qquad (2.4)$$

There is also an asymmetrical formula for $P(y_j|x_i)$. Note there are two random variables and two statistical probabilities.

Bayes' Theorem III: Assume that $P(X) = P(X = \text{any in } U)$ and $T(\theta_j) = P(X \in \theta_j)$. Then

$$P(X|\theta_j) = T(\theta_j|X)P(X)/T(\theta_j), \ T(\theta_j) = \sum_i P(x_i)T(\theta_j|x_i) \qquad (2.5)$$

$$T(\theta_j|X) = P(X|\theta_j)T(\theta_j)/P(X), \ T(\theta_j) = 1/\max(P(X|\theta_j)/P(X)) \qquad (2.6)$$

The two formulas are asymmetrical because there is a statistical probability and a logical probability. $T(\theta_j)$ in (2.5) may be call longitudinally normalizing constant.

The Proof of Bayes' Theorem III: Assume the joint probability $P(X, \theta_j) = P(X = \text{any}, X \in \theta_j)$, then $P(X|\theta_j)T(\theta_j) = P(X = \text{any}, X \in \theta_j) = T(\theta_j|X)P(X)$. Hence there is

$$P(X|\theta_j) = P(X)T(\theta_j|X)/T(\theta_j), T(\theta_j|X) = T(\theta_j)P(X|\theta_j)/P(X)$$

Since $P(X|A_j)$ is horizontally normalized, $T(\theta_j) = \sum_i P(x_i)T(\theta_j|x_i)$. Since $T(\theta_j|X)$ is longitudinally normalized and has the maximum 1, there is

$$1 = \max\left[T(\theta_j)P(X|\theta_j)/P(X)\right] = T(\theta_j)\max\left[P(X|\theta_j)/P(X)\right]$$

Hence $T(\theta_j) = 1/\max[P(X|\theta_j)/P(X)]$. **QED.**

Equation (2.5) can be directly written in

$$T(\theta_j|X) = [P(X|\theta_j)/P(X)]/\max[P(X|\theta_j)/P(X)] \tag{2.7}$$

By this formula, we can obtain the denotation of "Adult" and the posterior distribution $P'(x|y_1 \text{ is true})$ as shown in Fig. 1 where the set is not fuzzy.

2.3   Relationships Between Likelihood Functions, Membership Functions, and Sampling Distributions

In Shannon's information theory [18], $P(X)$ is called the source and $P(Y)$ is called the destination, the transition probability matrix $P(Y|X)$ is called the channel. A Shannon's channel consists of a group of transition probability functions: $P(y_j|X), j = 1, 2, \ldots, n$.

$P(y_j|X)$ has two important properties: (1) It can be used for Bayes' prediction to get $P(X|y_j)$; after $P(X)$ becomes $P'(X)$, $P(y_j|X)$ still works; (2) $P(y_j|X)$ by a constant k can make the same probability prediction because

$$\frac{P'(X)kP(y_j|X)}{\sum_i P'(x_i)kP(y_j|x_i)} = \frac{P'(X)P(y_j|X)}{\sum_i P'(x_i)P(y_j|x_i)} = P'(X|y_j) \tag{2.8}$$

Similarly, a semantic channel consists of a group of membership functions: $T(\theta|X) : T(\theta_j|X), j = 1, 2, \ldots, n$. According to (2.8), if $T(\theta_j|X) \propto P(y_j|X)$, there is $P(X|\theta_j) = P(X|y_j)$. Hence the optimized membership function is

$$T^*(\theta_j|X) = P(y_j|X)/\max(P(y_j|X)) \tag{2.9}$$

The relationships between membership functions, likelihood functions, and several probability distributions are:

$$\begin{aligned}
T^*(\theta_j|X) &= [P^*(X|\theta_j)/P(X|)]/\max[P^*(X|\theta_j)/P(X|)] \\
&= [P(X|y_j)/P(X|)]/\max[P(X|y_j)/P(X|)] = P(y_j|X)/\max(P(y_j|X))
\end{aligned} \tag{2.10}$$

2.4   The Consistency of the Bayes' Theorem III and Random Set Statistics

We can prove that the membership function derived from (2.10) is the same as that from the random set statistics [2].

Assume that a Shannon channel $P(Y|X)$ is obtained from a big sample **D** where whose size is $N \to \infty$; X is equiprobable; there are N/m examples $(x_i; y_j)$ for every x_i with different y_j. We pick out all examples with y_j. Assume x' is the most instance in these examples. We denote it by x_j^*, whose number is N_j^*. Existing multi-instance multi-label learning method [19] reminds us that we can merge these examples with y_j into N_j^* multi-instance examples $S_k = (x_{k1}, x_{k2}, \ldots; y_j)$, $k = 1, 2, \ldots, N_j^*$, every one of which contains x_j^*. Then we can treat S_k as a set-value taken by the random set. Let its feature function be denoted by $F_k(X)$ (Fig. 2).

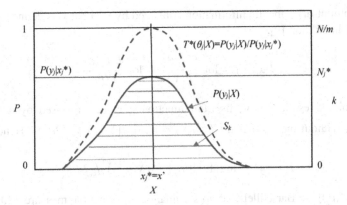

Fig. 2. The Bayes' Theorem III is compatible with the random sets falling shadow theory.

According to Wang's random set falling shadow theory [2], the membership function of θ_j is

$$m_{\theta_j}(X) = \frac{1}{N_j^*} \sum_{k=1}^{N_j^*} F_k(X) \qquad (2.11)$$

According to classical statistics, the transition probability function of y_j is

$$P(y_j|X) = \frac{1}{(N/m)} \sum_{k=1}^{N_j^*} F_k(X) \qquad (2.12)$$

Comparing the above two formulas, we have

$$
\begin{aligned}
m_{\theta_j}(X) &= P(y_j|X)/[N_j^*/(N/m)] \\
&= P(y_j|X)/\max[P(y_j|X)] = T^*(\theta_j|X)
\end{aligned} \qquad (2.13)
$$

If X is not equiprobable, we can randomly remove some examples to get an equiprobable sample. Its $P(Y|X)$ is the same, and hence the conclusion is the same.

2.5 Optimizing Membership Functions with Unsmooth or Discontinuous Sampling Distributions

If sampling distributions are unsmooth or discontinuous, but we wish that membership functions are smooth, then we can use the semantic information method to optimize the membership function.

The (amount of) semantic information conveyed by y_j about x_i is defined with log-normalized-likelihood [9]:

$$I(x_i; \theta_j) = \log \frac{P(x_i|\theta_j)}{P(x_i)} = \log \frac{T(\theta_j|x_i)}{T(\theta_j)} \tag{2.14}$$

For an unbiased estimation y_j, its truth function may be expressed by a Gaussian distribution without the coefficient: $T(\theta_j|X) = \exp\left[-(X - x_j)^2/(2d^2)\right]$. Hence

$$I(x_i; \theta_j) = \log\left[1/T(\theta_j)\right] - (X - x_j)^2/(2d^2) \tag{2.15}$$

The $\log[1/T(\theta_j)]$ is Bar-Hillel-Carnap's semantic information measure [20]. Equation (2.15) tells us that the larger the deviation is, the less information there is; the less the logical probability is, the more information there is; and, a wrong estimation may convey negative information. These conclusions accord with Popper's thought [21].

To average $I(x_i; \theta_j)$, we have

$$I(X; \theta_j) = \sum_i P(x_i|y_j) \log \frac{P(x_i|\theta_j)}{P(x_i)} = \sum_i P(x_i|y_j) \log \frac{T(\theta_j|x_i)}{T(\theta_j)} \tag{2.16}$$

where $P(x_i|y_j)$ $(i = 1, 2, \ldots)$ is the sampling distribution, which may be unsmooth or discontinuous. Hence, the optimized membership function is

$$T^*(\theta_j|X) = \arg \max_{T(\theta_j|X)} I(X; \theta_j) = \arg \max_{T(\theta_j|X)} \sum_i P(x_i|y_j) \log \frac{T(\theta_j|x_i)}{T(\theta_j)} \tag{2.17}$$

It is easy to prove that when $P(X|\theta_j) = P(X|y_j)$ or $T(\theta_j|X) \propto P(y_j|X)$, $I(X; \theta_j)$ reaches its maximum and is equal to the Kullback-Leibler information. When $P(y_j|X)$ is known and $P(X)$ is unknown, we may assume X is equiprobable to have

$$T^*(\theta_j|X) = \arg \max_{T(\theta_j|X)} I(X; \theta_j) = \arg \max_{T(\theta_j|X)} \sum_i \frac{P(y_j|x_i)}{\sum_k P(y_j|x_k)} \log \frac{T(\theta_j|x_i)}{\sum_k T(\theta_j|x_k)} \tag{2.18}$$

To average $I(x_i; \theta_j)$ in (2.15) for different X and Y, we have

$$\begin{aligned} I(X; \theta) &= H(\theta) - H(\theta|X) \\ &= -\sum_j P(y_j) \log T(\theta_j) - \sum_j \sum_i P(x_i, y_j)(x_i - x_j)^2/\left(2d_j^2\right) \end{aligned} \tag{2.19}$$

It is easy to find that the Maximum Semantic Information (MSI) criterion is a special Regularized Least Squares (RLS) criterion. $H(\theta|X)$ is the mean squared error, and $H(\theta)$ is the negative regularization term.

3   Applications to Machine Learning

3.1   Multi-label Learning and Classification

There have been many valuable studies in Multi-label learning and classification [22–24]. In popular methods, the learning and the classification are made by the same agent. However, from the viewpoint of semantic communication, the sender's classification and the receiver's logical classification are different. The receiver learns from a sample to obtain labels' denotations, e.g., membership functions, whereas the sender needs, for a given instance, to select a label with the most information. The sender partitions the instance space whereas the receiver does not.

Section 2.5 has discussed how to obtain optimized membership functions, which makes multi-label learning much easier because the learning is naturally converted into several single label learning. We may improve Binary Relevance method [24] to optimize the membership function of a label with both positive and negative examples by

$$
\begin{aligned}
T^*(\theta_j|X) &= \underset{T(\theta_j|X)}{\arg\ \max}[I(X;\theta_j) + I(X;\theta_j^c)] \\
&= \underset{T(\theta_j|X)}{\arg\ \max} \sum_i [P(x_i|y_j)\log\frac{T(\theta_j|x_i)}{T(\theta_j)} + P(x_i|y_j')\log\frac{1-T(\theta_j|x_i)}{1-T(\theta_j)}]
\end{aligned}
\tag{3.1}
$$

where $T^*(\theta_j|x_i)$ is only affected by $P(y_j|X)$ and $P(y_{j'}|X)$. For a given label, this method divides all instances into three kinds: the positive, the negative, and the unclear. $T^*(\theta_j|x_i)$ is not affected by unclear instances. However, popular One-vs-Rest or Binary Relevance method [24, 25] divides all instances into two kinds: the positive and the negative, for every label, and hence it needs a lot of time to prepare samples.

This binary logical learning allows the second part of Eq. (3.1) to be 0. Any big enough sample with distribution $P(X, Y)$ may be used for the membership function.

Now we discuss multi-label classifications with maximum semantic information criterion. For a visible instance X, the label sender selects y_j by the classifier

$$
y_j^* = h(X) = \underset{y_j}{\arg\max} \log I(\theta_j;x_i) = \underset{y_j}{\arg\max} \log \frac{T(\theta_j|X)}{T(\theta_j)}
\tag{3.2}
$$

This classifier produces a noiseless Shannon channel. Using $T(\theta_j)$ can overcome the class-imbalance problem [22]. If $T(\theta_j|X) \in \{0,1\}$, the above semantic information measure becomes Bar-Hillel and Carnap's information measure [20]; the classifier becomes

$$
y_j^* = h(X) = \underset{y_j \text{ with } T(A_j|X)=1}{\arg\max} \log[1/T(A_j)] = \underset{y_j \text{ with } T(A_j|X)=1}{\arg\min} T(A_j)
\tag{3.3}
$$

It means that we should select a label with the least logical probability and hence with the richest connotation. The above classifier encourages us to select a compound label such as y_1 and y_2 and y_3' (' means negation). Unlike canonical Binary Relevance method

[25], it does not add label "Adult" or "Non-youth" to an example with label "Old person". See [14] for details about the new method for multi-label classifications.

3.2 Maximum Mutual Information Classifications for Unseen Instances

For unseen instance classifications, we assume that observed condition is $Z \in C = \{z_1, z_2, \ldots\}$; the classifier is $Y = f(Z)$; a true class or true label is $X \in U = \{x_1, x_2, \ldots\}$; a sample is $\mathbf{D} = \{(x(t); z(t)) | t = 1, 2, \ldots, N; X(t) \in U; z(t) \in C\}$. From $\mathbf{D}$, we can obtain $P(X, Z)$. If $\mathbf{D}$ is not big enough, we may use the likelihood method to obtain $P(X, Z)$ with parameters. The aim is to solve the optimal partition of C. The problem is that Shannon's channel is not fixed and also needs optimization. Hence, we need semi-supersized learning method. We may use the Channels' Matching (CM) iteration algorithm [12, 13].

Let C_j be a subset of C and $y_j = f(Z|Z \in C_j)$. Hence $S = \{C_1, C_2, \ldots\}$ is a partition of C. Our aim is, for given $P(X, Z)$ from D, to find optimized S, which is

$$S^* = \arg\max_S I(X; \theta|S) = \arg\max_S \sum_j \sum_i P(C_j) P(x_i|C_j) \log \frac{T(\theta_j|x_i)}{T(\theta_j)} \quad (3.4)$$

First, we obtain the Shannon channel for given S:

$$P(y_j|X) = \sum_{z_k \in C_j} P(z_k|X), j = 1, 2, \ldots, n \quad (3.5)$$

From this Shannon's channel, we can obtain the semantic channel $T(\theta|X)$ in numbers or with parameters. For given Z, we have conditional semantic information

$$I(X_i; \theta_j|Z) = \sum_i P(X_i|Z) \log \frac{T(\theta_j|X_i)}{T(\theta_j)} \quad (3.6)$$

Then let the Shannon channel match the semantic channel by

$$y_j = f(Z) = \arg\max_{y_j} I(X; \theta_j|Z), \quad j = 1, 2, \ldots, n \quad (3.7)$$

Repeat (3.5)–(3.7) until S does not change. The convergent S is S^* we seek. Some iterative examples show that the above algorithm is fast and reliable. The convergence can be proved with the help of the $R(G)$ function [12].

3.3 Mixture Models

Assume a sampling distribution $P(X)$ is produced by two or several conditional probability functions $P^*(X|y_j)$ $(j = 1, 2, \ldots, n)$, where $P^*(X|y_j)$ is some kind of function such as Gaussian distribution. We only know n, without knowing $P(Y)$. We need to find $P(Y)$ and model parameters θ so that the predicted distribution, denoted by $P_\theta(X)$, is as close to $P(X)$ as possible, e.g., the relative entropy or Kullback-Leibler divergence $H(P\|P_\theta) = \sum_i P(x_i)\log[P(x_i)/P_\theta(x_i)]$ is close to 0.

The Expectation-Maximization (EM) algorithm and its improved versions [23, 24] are popular for solving mixture models. We can improve the EM algorithm or Maximization-Maximization algorithm [24] by the CM algorithm as follows:

Left-step a: Construct Shannon's channel by

$$P(y_j|X) = P(y_j)P(X|\theta_j)/P_\theta(X)$$
$$P_\theta(X) = \sum_j P(y_j)(X|\theta_j) \qquad ,j = 1, 2, \ldots, n \qquad (3.8)$$

This formula has been used in the E-step of the EM algorithm.

Left-step b: Use the following equation to obtain a new $P(Y)$ repeatedly until the inner iteration converges:

$$P(y_j) \Leftarrow \sum_i P(x_i)P(y_j|x_i)$$
$$= \sum_i P(x_i)\frac{P(x_i|\theta_j)}{\sum_k P(y_k)P(x_i|\theta_k)}P(y_j), j = 1, 2, \ldots, n \qquad (3.9)$$

If $H(P\|P_\theta)$ is less than a small number, such as 0.001 bit, then end the iteration.

Right-step: Optimize the parameters in the likelihood function $P(X|\theta)$ on the right of the following log to maximize the semantic mutual information:

$$I(X;\theta) = \sum_i \sum_j P(x_i)\frac{P(x_i|\theta_j)}{P_\theta(x_i)}P(y_j)\log\frac{P(x_i|\theta_j)}{P(x_i)} \qquad (3.10)$$

Then go to Left-step a.

Fortunately, to prove $H(P\|P_\theta) \to 0$, we derived an important formula [25]

$$\min H(P\|P_\theta) = \min_{P(Y),\theta}(I(X;Y) - I(X;\theta)) = \min_{P(Y),\theta}(R(G) - G)) \qquad (3.11)$$

where G is the semantic information and $R(G)$ is the minimum Shannon's mutual information for given G. In every step, $H(P\|P_\theta)$ is decreasing. In comparison with the EM algorithm, the CM algorithm has faster speed and clearer convergence reason [28].

The package with Excel files and Word files illustrating the CM algorithm for mixture models and maximum mutual information classifications can be obtained from http://survivor99.com/lcg/CM-iteration.zip. These Excel files also contain the data of iterative processes.

4   Discussions

4.1   The Significance to the Unification of Logic and Probability

It has been being an important issue to unify logic and probability [21, 28, 29]. Although logical probability has been discussed for a long time, people defined logical probability only with classical sets and hence truth functions can only be 0 or 1. In this way, it is hard to unify statistical probability and logical probability.

Zadeh proposed fuzzy sets and membership functions and explained a membership function as the truth function of a hypothesis [1]. This theory is an important advance because the truth function is between 0 and 1 and hence is closer to statistical probability. Wang [2] and others also made important advances in setting up relationship between statistics and fuzzy logic. However, there is still a gap between statistical probability and fuzzy logic because we cannot convert a sampling distribution such as $P(y_j|X)$ into a membership function reasonably. And, it is still unclear to derive membership functions from likelihood functions. It seems that the Bayes' Theorem III and the semantic information method can bridge this gap well.

4.2   From Bayesian Inference to Logical Bayesian Inference

In comparison with the likelihood function $P(X|\theta_j)$ and the Bayesian posterior $P(\theta|X)$ [30], the membership function $T(\theta_j|X)$ so obtained seems to be a better tool for machine learning because the main task of machine learning is classification. And, a fuzzy set indicates a fuzzy class and a membership function indicates the denotation of a label. The learning is just for the denotation of a label.

An important advantage of a group of membership functions, or a semantic channel, as a predictive model is that when the source $P(X)$ is changed, this model still works well and hence has good generalization performance [14].

The above methods for membership functions may be called Logical Bayesian Inference [31], an improved version of Bayesian inference.

5   Summary

This paper proposed and proved the third kind of Bayes' theorem including two asymmetrical formulas for transform between likelihood functions and the membership functions. Letting a semantic channel match a Shannon's channel, we can obtain a group of optimized membership functions from a sampling distribution. If the sampling distribution is unsmooth or discontinuous, we can obtain a group of optimized membership functions by the semantic information formula. The paper introduced the applications of new methods to multi-label classification, maximum mutual information classifications, and mixture models. It discussed the significance of the new methods for membership functions to the unification of logic and probability. As a new and general tool, Logical Bayesian Inference was proposed.

References

1. Zadeh, L.A.: Fuzzy sets. Inf. Control **8**, 338–353 (1965)
2. Wang, P.Z.: From the fuzzy statistics to the falling random subsets. In: Wang, P.P. (ed.) Advances in Fuzzy Sets, Possibility Theory and Applications, pp. 81–96. Plenum Press, New York (1983)
3. Dubois, D., Moral, S., Prade, H.: A semantics for possibility theory based on likelihoods. J. Math. Anal. Appl. **205**, 359–380 (1997)
4. Thomas, S.F.: Possibilistic uncertainty and statistical inference. In: ORSA/TIMS Meeting, Houston, Texas (1981)
5. Civanlar, M.R., Trussell, H.J.: Constructing membership functions using statistical data. Fuzzy Sets Syst. **18**, 1–13 (1986)
6. Pota, M., Esposito, M., De Pietro, G.: Transforming probability distributions into membership functions of fuzzy classes: a hypothesis test approach. Fuzzy Sets Syst. **233**, 52–73 (2013)
7. Lu, C.: B-fuzzy quasi-Boolean algebra and a generalize mutual entropy formula. Fuzzy Syst. Math. (in Chin.) **5**, 76–80 (1991)
8. Lu, C.: A Generalized Information Theory (in Chinese). China Science and Technology University Press, Hefei (1993)
9. Lu, C.: Meanings of generalized entropy and generalized mutual information for coding. J. China Inst. Commun. (in Chin.) **15**, 37–44 (1994)
10. Lu, C.: A generalization of Shannon's information theory. Int. J. Gen Syst **28**, 453–490 (1999)
11. Lu, C.: Semantic channel and Shannon channel mutually match and iterate for tests and estimations with maximum mutual information and maximum likelihood. In: 2018 IEEE International Conference on Big Data and Smart Computing, pp. 227–234. IEEE Conference Publishing Services, Piscataway (2018)
12. Lu, C.: Channels' matching algorithm for mixture models. In: Shi, Z., Goertzel, B., Feng, J. (eds.) ICIS 2017. IAICT, vol. 510, pp. 321–332. Springer, Cham (2017). https://doi.org/10.1007/978-3-319-68121-4_35
13. Lu, C.: Semantic channel and Shannon's channel mutually match for multi-label classification. In: Shi, Z., Pennartz, C., Huang, T. (eds.) ICIS 2018. IAICT, vol. 539, pp. 37–48. Springer, Cham (2018). https://doi.org/10.1007/978-3-030-01313-4_5
14. Tarski, A.: The semantic conception of truth: and the foundations of semantics. Philos. Phenomenol. Res. **4**, 341–376 (1944)
15. Davidson, D.: Truth and meaning. Synthese **17**, 304–323 (1967)
16. Zadeh, L.A.: Probability measures of fuzzy events. J. Math. Anal. Appl. **23**, 421–427 (1986)
17. Bayes, T., Price, R.: An essay towards solving a problem in the doctrine of chance. Philos. Trans. R. Soc. Lond. **53**, 370–418 (1736)
18. Shannon, C.E.: A mathematical theory of communication. Bell Syst. Tech. J. **27**, 379–429 and 623–656 (1948)
19. Zhou, Z.H., Zhang, M.L., Huang, S.J., Li, Y.F.: Multi-instance multi-label learning. Artif. Intell. **176**, 2291–2320 (2012)
20. Bar-Hillel, Y., Carnap, R.: An outline of a theory of semantic information. Technical report, No. 247, Research Laboratory of Electronics, MIT (1952)
21. Popper, K.: Conjectures and Refutations. Repr. Routledge, London and New York (1963/2005)
22. Zhou, Z.H.: Machine Learning (in Chinese). Tsinghua University Press, Beijing (2016)

23. Zhang, M.L., Zhou, Z.H.: A review on multi-label learning algorithm. IEEE Trans. Knowl. Data Eng. **26**, 1819–1837 (2014)

24. Zhang, M.L., Li, Y.K., Liu, X.Y., et al.: Binary relevance for multi-label learning: an overview. Front. Comput. Sci. **12**, 191–202 (2018)

25. Dempster, A.P., Laird, N.M., Rubin, D.B.: Maximum likelihood from incomplete data via the EM algorithm. J. R. Stat. Soc. Ser. B **39**, 1–38 (1977)

26. Neal, R., Hinton, G.: A view of the EM algorithm that justifies incremental, sparse, and other variants. In: Jordan, M.I. (ed.) Learning in Graphical Models, pp. 355–368. MIT Press, Cambridge (1999)

27. Lu, C.: Problems with the EM algorithm and the way out (in Chinese). http://survivor99.com/lcg/CM/Recent.html. Accessed 10 Apr 2018

28. Jaynes, E.T.: Probability Theory: The Logic of Science (Ed. by Bretthorst, L.). Cambridge University Press, New York (2003)

29. Russell, S.: Unifying logic and probability. Commun. ACM **58**, 88–97 (2015)

30. Lu, C.: From Bayesian inference to logical Bayesian inference. In: Shi, Z., Pennartz, C., Huang, T. (eds.) ICIS 2018. IAICT, vol. 539, pp. 11–23. Springer, Cham (2018). https://doi.org/10.1007/978-3-030-01313-4_2

Speech Signal Classification Based on Convolutional Neural Networks

Xiaomeng Zhang, Hao Sun$^{(\boxtimes)}$, Shuopeng Wang, and Jing Xu

School of Artificial Intelligence, Hebei University of Technology,
Tianjin 300130, China
ZXMhebut@163.com, sunhao@hebut.edu.cn,
wangsp_hebut@163.com, xjhebut@163.com

Abstract. In the field of intelligent human-computer interaction, speech signal is the hotspot research field, and has been widely used. For the traditional classification algorithm, the computational complexity is high and the classification accuracy is low. This paper proposes a convolutional neural network based on convolutional neural network. The speech signal classification method converts the speech signal into a form of a spectrogram and inputs it into a convolutional neural network to realize classification of the speech signal. Finally, the training and testing of convolutional neural networks are completed by using the framework of tensorflow. Compared with the traditional classification algorithm, the accuracy of the classification algorithm proposed in this paper reaches about 98%. The results show the feasibility and effectiveness of the experimental method.

Keywords: Speech signal classification · Spectrogram ·
Convolutional neural networks

1 Introduction

Language is one of the important sources of communication and access to information for human communication. As a high-tech technology, speech processing technology involves many disciplines, including digital signal processing, linguistics, phonetics, pattern recognition, etc. It has become an important means of developing artificial intelligence and man-machine dialogue, and the basic theory of speech processing. And the research of various processing algorithms mainly includes two aspects: one is to study from the generation of speech and the perception of speech; the other is to process speech as a signal, such as digital filter, FFT, etc., which are closely related to speech signal processing contact [1–3].

At present, some scholars have proposed several classification algorithms to process the input signal. Reference [4] proposed the use of KNN algorithm for speech signal classification. The performance difference of KNN algorithm in different types of signals is analyzed. Reference [5] proposed a SVM-based classification algorithm to reduce the execution time and energy consumption of SVM-based speech/music classifiers by optimizing the support vector access mode. Reference [6] proposed a content-based audio classification and retrieval method, which improved the accuracy

© Springer Nature Singapore Pte Ltd. 2019
F. Sun et al. (Eds.): ICCSIP 2018, CCIS 1006, pp. 281–287, 2019.
https://doi.org/10.1007/978-981-13-7986-4_25

of 9% compared with the nearest neighbor (NN) method. In [7], the classification method based on decision tree is used for speech classification, and the hierarchical oblique decision tree is used to extract multiple short-term features and long-term features. However, these algorithms need to extract many feature parameters in order to improve the correct rate. This greatly increases the complexity of the classification algorithm, and the algorithm training time is too long.

In recent years, in-depth learning has achieved great success and greatly promoted the development of machine learning. The convolutional neural network is a typical deep neural network. The weight sharing network structure makes it more similar to the biological neural network, which reduces the complexity of the network model and reduces the number of weights. Convolutional neural networks have been widely used in image processing [8]. As a visual representation of the time-frequency distribution of speech energy, the spectrogram itself contains speech features such as energy, pitch, and fundamental frequency. Researchers have used the profilogram to combine image processing into speech processing and achieved good results [9].

2   Methods

2.1   Data Processing

The recognition of speech signals mainly comes from the time domain and the frequency domain, but the time domain signal cannot represent the frequency characteristics, and the frequency domain cannot represent the characteristics that change with time. So this paper considers the use of the spectrogram as an input to the convolutional neural network. The spectrogram shows a large amount of information related to the speech characteristics of the speech. It combines the characteristics of the spectrogram and the time domain waveform, and clearly shows the variation of the speech spectrum over time, or a dynamic spectrum [10]. The basic mathematical expression is [11],

$$x'(t) = STFT\{x(t)\} = X(t,f) = \int_{-\infty}^{+\infty} x(\tau)\omega(t-\tau)e^{-j2\pi f\tau}d\tau \tag{1}$$

Where: $x(t)$ indicates the time signal of the voice, t indicating the time; $\omega(t)$ representing the window function. The implementation process of the spectrogram is shown in Fig. 1:

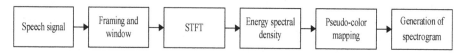

Fig. 1. The realization process of the spectrogram

The spectrogram corresponding to the time domain waveform of the speech signal is shown in Fig. 2:

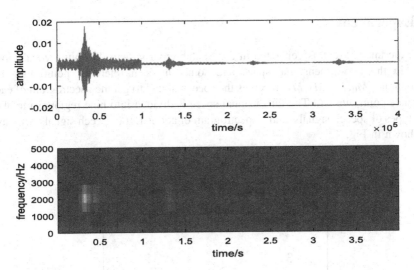

Fig. 2. Time domain waveform and spectrogram of speech signals

2.2 Model Analysis

The convolutional neural network is a feedforward neural network, which mainly includes an input layer, a feature extraction layer composed of one or more sets of convolution layers + pooling layers, a fully connected layer and an output layer. A convolutional layer contains several different volume machines. The pooling layer controls the complexity of the model by pooling the convolutional layer and reducing the number of input nodes in the next layer. The general pooling layer uses the maximum pooling algorithm. Multiple convolutional layers and pooled layers are alternately combined to form a feature extraction phase. Finally, the output values of the pooled layers are combined through a fully connected layer to obtain a final classification. The convolutional neural network model of this experiment consists of four convolutional layers, four pooling layers and three fully connected layers. The specific structure is shown in Fig. 3:

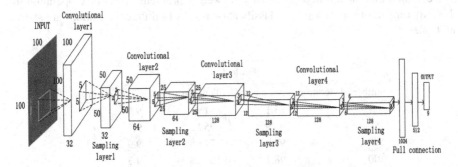

Fig. 3. The network structure of CNN

3 Experiment

The experimental data is generated in the Matlab environment. We put a vocalization point in the two-dimensional space and sound at each reference point, then the microphone (M_0, M_1, M_2, M_3) receives the speech signal to get the spectrogram of each reference point, we will The dimensional space is divided into nine regions, a total of nine types of speech signals, and a spectrogram of about 1,100 speech signals per class. As shown in Fig. 4:

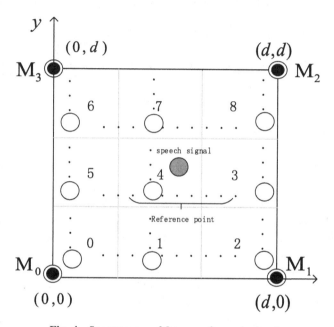

Fig. 4. Spectrogram of 9 types of speech signals

3.1 Experimental Result

The convolutional neural network solves the weight problem by iterative operation. In this experiment, the speech signal classification results of different iterations are shown in Table 1:

Table 1. .

Number of iterations	Accuracy/%	Training time/s	Testing time/s
1	83.1	15.1	9.6
50	93.9	259.3	9.2
100	97.8	774.8	9.9
200	98.1	1549.9	9.3
500	98.1	3984.1	9.0
1000	98.1	7718.3	9.4

Tensorboard is a visual tool embedded in tensorflow. It can display various drawing data during the training process by reading the event log. We visualize the results of one training and test using the tensorboard tool, as shown in Figs. 5 and 6.

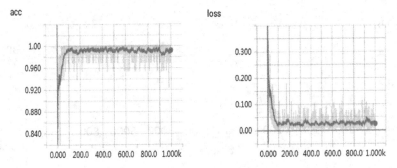

Fig. 5. The accuracy and loss function on the training set

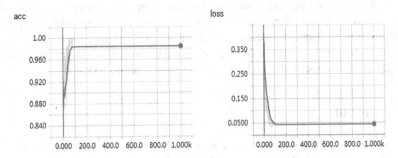

Fig. 6. The accuracy and loss function on the testing set

According to the experimental results, under the condition that the number of iterations is small, the network learning is not sufficient, the training model is not ideal, and the training classification effect is poor. As the number of iterations increases, the network parameters are continuously optimized, and the classification accuracy increases. When the number of iterations reaches 200, the number of iterations tends to be stable. The final classification accuracy rate is around 98%.

3.2 Comparative Experimental

In order to verify the performance of convolutional neural networks in speech signal classification, this paper compares it with KNN (K-Nearest Neighbor), BP (Back Propagation) neural network and SVM (Support Vector Machine). Test and implement these three machine learning methods using sklearn [12]. For KNN, we use KNeighborsClassifier; for SVM, we use SVC; for BP neural network, we use MLPClassifier. The experimental results are shown in Fig. 7.

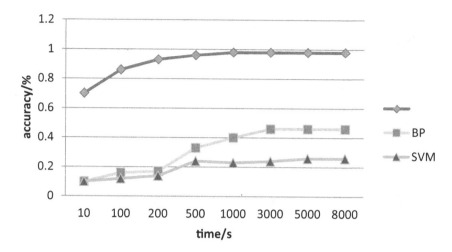

Fig. 7. Classification accuracy of different methods

Since KNN has no parameter training process, it makes direct classification decisions based on the distribution of training data. Therefore, it is impossible to reproduce the relationship between the accuracy of the KNN method and the time in the line graph. According to the test results, we get the classification accuracy rate based on KNN algorithm is about 89%, and the training time is about 553 s.

4   Conclusion

In this paper, a speech signal classification method based on convolutional neural network is designed, which solves the problems of high computational complexity and long training time of existing classification algorithms. The matlab simulation experiment proves that the classification accuracy of speech signal can be improved by transforming the speech signal into the form of the spectrogram and inputting the convolutional neural network. Finally, we demonstrate the effectiveness and feasibility of the proposed method through comparative experiments.

References

1. Mowlaee, P., Saeidi, R., Stylianou, Y.: Advances in phase-aware signal processing in speech communication. Speech Commun. **81**, 1–29 (2016)
2. Huang, C., Gong, W., Fu, W., et al.: A research of speech emotion recognition based on deep belief network and SVM. Math. Probl. Eng. **2014**(5), 1–7 (2014)
3. Tychkov, A.Y., Alimuradov, A.K., Frantsuzov, M.V., et al.: Program implementation of an algorithm for recognition of speech signals in the labview graphics programming environment. Meas. Tech. **58**(9), 965–969 (2015)
4. Llasat, V.: Classification of audible signals by characteristics of the human vocal apparatus. IEEE Lat. Am. Trans. **11**(1), 77–80 (2013)

5. Lim, C., Lee, S.R., Chang, J.H.: Efficient implementation of an SVM-based speech/music classifier by enhancing temporal locality in support vector references. IEEE Trans. Consum. Electron. **58**(3), 898–904 (2012)
6. Li, S.Z.: Content-based audio classification and retrieval using the nearest feature line method. IEEE Trans. Speech Audio Process. **8**(5), 619–625 (2000)
7. Wang, J., Wu, Q., Deng, H., et al.: Real-time speech/music classification with a hierarchical oblique decision tree. In: IEEE International Conference on Acoustics, Speech and Signal Processing. IEEE, pp. 2033–2036 (2008)
8. Badshah, A.M., Ahmad, J., Rahim, N., et al.: Speech emotion recognition from spectrograms with deep convolutional neural network. In: International Conference on Platform Technology and Service. IEEE, pp. 1–5 (2017)
9. Aykanat, M., Kılıç, Ö., Kurt, B., et al.: Classification of lung sounds using convolutional neural networks. Eurasip J. Image Video Process. **2017**(1), 65 (2017)
10. Reynolds, D.A., Quatieri, T.F., Dunn, R.B.: Speaker verification using adapted gaussian mixture models. Digital Signal Process. **10**(1), 19–41 (2000)
11. Lu, W.K., Zhang, Q.: Deconvolutive short-time fourier transform spectrogram. IEEE Signal Process. Lett. **16**(7), 576–579 (2009)
12. Ahmed, I., Witbooi, P., Christoffels, A.: Prediction of human-Bacillus anthracis protein-protein interactions using multi-layer neural network. Bioinformatics **34**, 4159–4164 (2018)

Two-Input Gegenbauer Orthogonal Neural Network with Growing-and-Pruning Weights and Structure Determination

Zhijun Zhang[1(✉)], Jie He[1], and Luxin Tang[2]

[1] School of Automation Science and Engineering,
South China University of Technology, Guangzhou 510640, China
auzjzhang@scut.edu.cn, auhjaystephen@mail.scut.edu.cn
[2] School of Electromechanical Engineering,
Guangdong University of Technology, Guangzhou 510006, China
tangluxin@21cn.com

Abstract. Based on the probability theory and polynomial interpolation and approximation theory, a two-input Gegenbauer orthogonal neural network (TIGONN) is investigated and constructed in this paper. In order to avoid inherent problems of back-propagation (BP) training algorithm, a weights-direct-determination (WDD) is applied to calculate the optimal connecting weights of TIGONN proposed. Then, based on WDD, a growing and pruning weights and structure determination (GPWSD) is developed to determine the optimal connecting weights and optimal number of neurons in hidden layer, by combining growing weights and structure determination (GWSD) and post-pruning scheme. Furthermore, numerical verifications are also conducted to substantiate the superiority and efficacy of TIGONN with GPWSD in terms of approximation and denoising.

Keywords: Gegenbauer orthogonal polynomials ·
Weights direct determination ·
Growing and pruning weights and structure determination

1 Introduction

With its excellent capabilities of data-fitting and generalization, artificial neuronets (ANN) can help to set up a computational model containing system

Supported by the National Key R&D Program of China under Grant 2017YFB1002505, National Natural Science Foundation of China under Grants 61603142 and 61633010, Guangdong Foundation for Distinguished Young Scholars under Grant 2017A030306009, The Guangdong Youth Talent Support Program of Scientific and Technological Innovation under Grant 2017TQ04X475, the Fundamental Research Funds for Central Universities under Grant 2017MS049, National Key Basic Research Program of China (973 Program) under Grant 2015CB351703.

© Springer Nature Singapore Pte Ltd. 2019
F. Sun et al. (Eds.): ICCSIP 2018, CCIS 1006, pp. 288–300, 2019.
https://doi.org/10.1007/978-981-13-7986-4_26

characteristics through training without knowing the exact information of the objective system. Also, due to its outstanding features of parallelism, fault-tolerance and adaptive self-learning [1,2], ANN, especially with back-propagation (BP) proposed by Rumelhart and McClelland [3], has become one of the most widely applied tools in pattern recognition. However, BP-type neural networks, as self-organization neural networks [4,5] have some inherent problems, such as slow convergence, local minima [6] and uncertainties in optimal structure (i.e., optimal number of neurons in a hidden layer) [7].

Although many improved BP-type algorithms have been proposed and widely investigated, the problems above still exist. In this paper, different from many algorithmic improvements, we, inspired by the previous works [5,8], focus on the usage of different activation functions (e.g. orthogonal basis functions) and design special structure determination methods to avoid those inherent weaknesses of BP iterative algorithms, thus to improve the network performance. Therefore, a two-input Gegenbauer orthogonal neural network (TIGONN) is studied and constructed, based on the probability theory [9,10] and polynomial interpolation and approximation theory [11–13]. Then, a weights direct determination (WDD) method based on pseudo-inverse (Moore-Penrose), which has been proved effective and efficient in previous work [8,13], is investigated and adopted in our work. With this algorithm, the optimal weights of TIGONN can be determined in only one step, while avoiding problems of lengthy iteration and local minima.

Moreover, since the performance of network is highly related to the network structure [14,15], in this paper, we elegantly design a growing weights and structure determination (GWSD), to search for the optimal structure, where the approximation error is minimized. In addition, to simplify the network structure and improve effectiveness, a post-pruning scheme is proposed and this finally leads us to the growing and pruning weights and structure determination (GPWSD) by combining GWSD and pruning scheme. Finally, numerical verifications based on different two-variables objective functions substantiate the superiority and efficacy of the TIGONN with GPWSD in terms of approximation and denoising (with training error accuracies less than 10^{-20}).

2   Theoretical Basis

In this section, the theoretical basis for constructing TIGONN is discussed. First, to lay a solid foundation for the later analysis, Proposition 1 is given here [9,10]:

Proposition 1 *(Probability Theory). For the cases of two continuous independent variables u and v, the generalized joint probability density functions (PDFs) f(u, v) can be written as:*

$$f(u, v) = f_U(u)f_V(v) \tag{1}$$

where $f_U(u)$ and $f_V(v)$ denote the generalized marginal PDFs on u and v, respectively.

Note that the joint PDFs and the marginal PDFs in Proposition 1 differ from the PDFs in traditional probability theory [9,10], since they are much more generalized in 3 aspects: 1, those PDFs can be positive, negative or even zero; 2, those PDFs can increase or decrease monotonically, or both; 3, the integral values of those PDFs can be positive, zero, negative or even not definite [14]. Here, Lemma 1 [16] is given as below:

Lemma 1. *The general formula of Gegenbauer polynomials is [16]*

$$G_n(x, \lambda) = \sum_{k=0}^{n} \frac{1}{k!(n-k)!} \frac{(2\lambda)_n(2\lambda+n)_k}{(\lambda+1/2)_k} (\frac{x-1}{2})^k, n = 0, 1, 2, \cdots \quad (2)$$

where $(\theta)_k = \theta(\theta+1)\cdots(\theta+k+1)$, *($\theta$ represents 2λ, $2\lambda+n$ and $\lambda+1/2$ in Eq. 2). Based on this, the recurrent formula of Gegenbauer orthogonal polynomials can be denoted as below [16]:*

$$G_n(x, \lambda) = \frac{2(n+\lambda-1)}{n} x G_{n-1}(x, \lambda) - \frac{n+2\lambda-2}{n} G_{n-2}(x, \lambda), n = 2, 3, \cdots, \quad (3)$$

where $G_0(x) = 1$ *and* $G_1(x) = 2\lambda x$, *Note that λ is fixed to $\frac{2}{3}$ in this paper.*

Before constructing the two-input neural network, we first present a simple theoretical analysis on function approximation $\phi(x)$ with one variable x. Based on polynomial interpolation and approximation theory [11–13], it is evident that the unknown objective function $\phi(x)$ can be approximated by a polynomial $\varphi(x)$. For the approximation ability of $\varphi(x)$, we have the following Proposition 2:

Proposition 2 *(Least-Squares Approximation). Let $\phi(x)$ denote the continuous objective function in a closed interval $[a, b]$ and every polynomial sequence $\varphi_j(x)$ is continuous in $[a, b]$ (i.e., $\phi(x)$, $\varphi_j(x) \in C[a, b]$, $j = 0, 1, 2, \cdots, n-1$). And we define $\{\varphi_j(x)\}_{j=0}^{n-1}$ as a set of linearly-independent (or orthogonal) polynomial sequences in interval $[a, b]$, and polynomial function $\varphi(x)$ can be formed by this set of sequences:*

$$\varphi(x) = \sum_{j=0}^{n-1} w_j \varphi_j(x). \quad (4)$$

According to the analysis in [11–13], there always exists a group of optimal weights $[w_0, w_1, w_2, \cdots, w_{n-1}]$ that minimizes the approximation error, which means to minimize the values of equation below:

$$\int_a^b |\phi(x) - \varphi(x)|^2 dx. \quad (5)$$

For such case, $\varphi(x)$ is considered as the least-squares approximation function (LSAF) of unknown objective function $\phi(x)$. And according to [11, 12], the uniqueness and existence of LSAF is confirmed.

By combining Propositions 1 and 2, and Lemma 1, we introduce the following theorem on approximating objective functions with two variables:

Theorem 1. *For an objective function $\phi(u,v)$ with two continuous independent variables u and v, it can be best estimated by the product of LSAFs of two generalized functions $\phi_U(u)$ and $\phi_V(v)$ simultaneously via Gegenbauer orthogonal polynomial.*

Proof. According to Proposition 1, the objective function $\phi(u,v)$ can be reformed:

$$\phi(u,v) = \phi_U(u)\phi_V(v). \tag{6}$$

Then, on the basis of Proposition 2 and Lemma 1, the generalized PDFs $\phi_U(u)$ and $\phi_V(v)$ can be best approximated by the LSAFs via Gegenbauer orthogonal polynomials with optimal weights, respectively. Thus, the Eq. (6) is modified:

$$
\begin{aligned}
\phi(u,v) &= \phi_U(u)\phi_V(v) \\
&\cong \left(\sum_{i=0}^{N_1-1} \alpha_i G_i(u) \right)\left(\sum_{j=0}^{N_2-1} \beta_j G_2(v) \right) \\
&= \sum_{i=0}^{N_1-1} \sum_{j=0}^{N_2-1} w_{ij} G_i(u) G_j(v),
\end{aligned} \tag{7}
$$

where $w_k = w_{ij} = \alpha_i \beta_j$ ($i = 0,1,2,\cdots,N_1-1$ and $j = 0,1,2,\cdots,N_2-1$) denotes the optimal weights of basis function $\{G_i(u)G_j(v)\}$. Thus, the proof of Theorem 1 is completed.

Based on Theorem 1 and its Proof, a group of Gegenbauer orthogonal basis functions with optimal weights can approximate objective function $\phi(u,v)$ in minimized error. Thus, in this way, we successfully obtain the LSAF of two-variable objective function with the product of two Gegenbauer polynomials. Thus, Eq. can be reformed:

$$\phi(u,v) \cong \varphi(u,v) = \sum_{i=0}^{N_1-1} \sum_{j=0}^{N_2-1} w_{ij} G_i(u) G_j(v) = \sum_{k=1}^{M} w_k q_k(u,v), \tag{8}$$

where $w_k = w_{ij}$ is termed as the weight for the kth basis function $q_k(u,v) = G_i(u)G_j(v)$ with $k = (i+j)(i+j+1)/2+i+1$. and maximum value of k is termed as K ($k = 1,2,\cdots,K$, and $K = N_1 \times N_2 = (d+1)(d+2)/2$), denoting the total number of basis functions used to approximate objective function $\phi(u,v)$. Note that, the basis functions are organized and sorted in graded lexicographer order [17]. To be detailed, we let d denote the total degree of $G_i(u)$ and $G_j(v)$, i.e., $d = i+j$.

3   Network Model and Weights Direct Determination

Based on the theoretical analysis in Sect. 2, in this section, we introduce the network topological model of TIGONN and then the weights direct determination (WDD) [8,13,14] to obtain the optimal connecting weights is discussed.

3.1   TIGONN Model

As is shown in Fig. 1, the topological model of TIGONN based on Eq. (8) is presented. This three-layer forward network model includes input layer, hidden layer and output layer. In this model, the neurons in input layer and output layer are both linearly activated, and the number of neurons in input and output layer is 2 and 1 respectively. Besides, the mth $(m = 1, 2, \cdots, M)$ hidden neuron is activated by the kth basis function $q_k(u, v) = G_i(u)G_j(v)$, (note that k is not equal to m for not every basis function is used in network). All connecting weights between input neurons and hidden neurons are 1, and all the threshold values of neurons are fixed to 0. Such design can help to simplify network structure and make hardware implementations easier, while not affecting the approximation ability. For the network structure above, the input-output relationship can be expressed by Eq. (8).

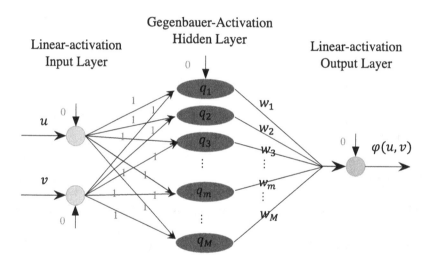

Fig. 1. The network model of TIGONN.

3.2   Weights Direct Determination

For the three-layer TIGONN shown in Fig. 1, the conventional BP-type iterative training algorithms can be exploited to obtain the optimal connection weights w_m, such as stochastic gradient descend [18]. However, the conventional BP-type gradient-based iterative training algorithms have some inevitable weaknesses in obtaining optimal weights, such as local minima, lengthy training time [6]. In order to overcome those weaknesses, in this paper, a weights direct determination (WDD) method based on pseudo-inverse [8,13,14] is adopted. With WDD, the optimal connecting weights from hidden layer to output layer can be calculated in only one step.

Theorem 2. *The optimal connecting weights can be directly determined by:*

$$w = (Q^{\mathrm{T}}Q)^{-1}Q^{\mathrm{T}}\phi = Q^{+}\phi, \tag{9}$$

where superscript ^{T} *denotes the transpose of matrix, and* $(Q^{\mathrm{T}}Q)^{-1}Q^{\mathrm{T}}$ *denotes the pseudo-inverse of matrix* Q, *also termed as* Q^{+}. *In Eq. (9),* w *is the connecting weights vector,* ϕ *is the desired output vector and* Q *denotes the activation matrix.*

$$w := \begin{bmatrix} w_1 \ w_2 \ \cdots \ w_m \ \cdots \ w_M \end{bmatrix}^{\mathrm{T}} \in \mathbb{R}^M,$$

$$Q := \begin{bmatrix} q_1^{(1)} & q_2^{(1)} & \cdots & q_M^{(1)} \\ q_1^{(2)} & q_2^{(2)} & \cdots & q_M^{(2)} \\ \vdots & \vdots & \ddots & \vdots \\ q_1^{(S)} & q_2^{(S)} & \cdots & q_M^{(S)} \end{bmatrix} \in \mathbb{R}^{S \times M},$$

$$\phi := \begin{bmatrix} \phi^1 \ \phi^2 \ \cdots \ \phi^s \ \cdots \ \phi^S \end{bmatrix}^{\mathrm{T}} \in \mathbb{R}^S$$

where $q_m^{(s)}$ *denotes the activation response of the* m^{th} *hidden neuron corresponding to the* s^{th} *training sample, and* M *is termed as the total number of neurons. The number of samples of variable* u *and* v *is* s_u *and* s_v *respectively, thus* $S = s_v \times s_u$. *To be more specific, we defined* $((u^{(s)}, v^{(s)}), \phi^s)$ *as the training sample pairs.*

Proof. Due to space limitations and plenty of proof done by previous work [13–15], we here only give a brief proof of WDD.

Based on BP iterative gradient-based algorithm in [2,3,18], for feed-forward neural network, the weights updating equation in matrix-vector form should be:

$$w(t+1) = w(t) - \eta Q^{\mathrm{T}}(Qw(t) - \phi), \tag{10}$$

where t denotes the tth iteration, η denotes the learning rates.

According to Ref. [8,13,14], in light of learning rate η larger than zero, when training process reaches a steady state (i.e., $t \to \infty$), we will have $w(t+1) = w(t) := w$. Then, based on Eq. (10), we have $Q^{\mathrm{T}}(Qw(t) - \phi) = 0$. Thus, Eq. (9) is finally established. Therefore, the proof of validity of WDD is finished.

4   Growing and Pruning Weights and Structure Determination

According to the analysis in [14,15], the performances of neural network are closely related to the number of neurons in hidden layer. In this section, based on the TIGONN model constructed and WDD in Sect. 3, we elegantly design a growing weights and structure determination (GWSD) algorithm. To be detailed, by adding neurons in a trial-and-evaluate fashion, GWSD can determine the optimal weights and number of neurons in hidden layer, which minimize the approximation error. And WDD, as a part of GWSD, is responsible for calculating the

---

Algorithm 1. Growing WSD

Input: max value of counter, c_{max}; training samples pairs, $\{((u^{(s)}, v^{(s)}), \phi^{(s)})\}_{s=1}^{S}$;
Output: optimal error, $\bar{E}_h$; optimal number of neurons, M;
       optimal weights w_{opt}; optimal activation matrix, Q_{opt};
1: **initialize:** $k \leftarrow 1$; $M \leftarrow 1$; $c \leftarrow 0$; $d \leftarrow 0$; $\bar{E}_h \leftarrow 10$;
2: **while** $(k < (d+1)(d+2)/2)$ **or** $(c < c_{max})$ **do**
3:     Update d based on k, according to graded lexicographer order;
4:     Calculate the kth basis function (i.e, generate the Mth neuron);
5:     Generate corresponding activation matrix Q and then calculate the optimal weights w of it through WDD, when number of hidden neurons is M;
6:     Calculate the corresponding MSE $\bar{E}$;
7:     **if** $\bar{E} < \bar{E}_h$ **then**
8:         Keep the Mth neuron;
9:         $c \leftarrow 0$;
10:        $M \leftarrow M + 1$;
11:        $\bar{E}_h \leftarrow \bar{E}$;
12:        $Q_{opt} \leftarrow Q$;
13:        $w_{opt} \leftarrow w$;
14:     **else**
15:         Delete the Mth neuron;
16:        $c \leftarrow c + 1$;
17:     **end if**
18:     $k \leftarrow k + 1$;
19: **end while**
20: **return:** $\bar{E}_h$, M, w_{opt} and Q_{opt};

---

optimal connecting weights. Further, to simplify the structure, a post-pruning scheme is also introduced to delete those unimportant neurons (i.e, neurons with extremely small weights) in the network. By combining GWSD with post-pruning scheme, the growing and pruning weights and structure determination (GPWSD) algorithm is finally proposed.

Specifically, the discussions and verifications in this work are mainly based on three objective functions as below:

$$\phi(u, v) = \frac{v cos(\sqrt{100u^2 + 100v^2 + 1})}{e^{-2u^2 - 2v^2} + 2} + 20, \tag{11}$$

$$\phi(u, v) = (7 + v)e^{-sin(u^2 v^2)}, \tag{12}$$

$$\phi(u, v) = (1 - u)^3 cos(v)e^{-u^2 - v^2} + 10. \tag{13}$$

4.1 Growing WSD

Before introducing the GWSD, we need to give following specific definitions:

✓ $E := \frac{1}{2} \| Qw - \gamma \|_2^2$ denotes the training error of network;

✓ $\bar{E} := E/S$ denotes the mean square error (MSE) of network;

✓ $\bar{E}_h$ denotes the optimal MSE ever found, which should be initialized largely enough, Q_{opt} denotes the activation matrix corresponding to $\bar{E}_h$;

✓ c denotes the counter in training, with initial value 0 and max value c_{max}.

Based on the previous studies on relationship between number of hidden neurons and approximation error in Ref. [14,15], we present the specific procedure and pseudo-code of the proposed GWSD in Algorithm 1, which determine the optimal number of hidden neurons through adding neurons in a trial-and-evaluation fashion.

4.2   Post-Pruning Scheme

In Subsect. 4.1, we have successfully obtained the optimal structure by GWSD. However, according to the results of magnitude distribution of w_m ($m = 1, 2, \cdots, M$) in Fig. 2, there exists a lot of neurons with tiny weights, which implies that they should have no important influence on the network performance. Note that, for this experiments, the datasets of each of training sample pairs $\{((u^{(s)}, v^{(s)}), \phi^{(s)})\}$ ($s = 1, 2, 3, \cdots, 2116$) are obtained by sampling uniformly over the area $u, v \in [-0.9, 0.9]^2$, with gap-size being 0.04.

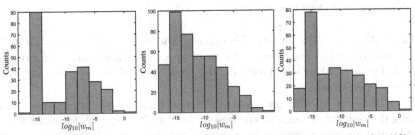

(a) Objective Function (11). (b) Objective Function (12). (c) Objective Function (13).

Fig. 2. The distribution of $log_{10}|w_m|$ before pruning.

To simplify the structure of network, a post-pruning scheme is presented. Before specific post-pruning scheme given, we also need to give the following definition:

✓ $\bar{E}_{del}$ denotes the current mean square error (MSE) in the post-pruning process, Q_{del} and w_{del} denote the corresponding activation matrix and weights vector;

✓ M_{opt} denotes the number of hidden neurons after post-pruning;

✓ g denotes the threshold of pruning.

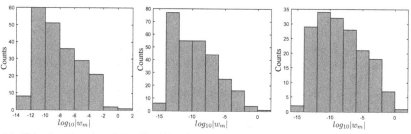

(a) Objective Function (11). (b) Objective Function (12). (c) Objective Function (13).

Fig. 3. The distribution of $log_{10}|w_m|$ after pruning.

The pseudo-code of the proposed post-pruning is presented in Algorithm 2.

By combining GWSD in Algorithm 1 and post-pruning scheme in Algorithm 2, we finally propose the growing and pruning weights and structure determination (GPWSD) algorithm. Here, the magnitude distribution of weights w_m ($m = 1, 2, \cdots, M_{opt}$) after pruning are shown in Fig. 3. By comparing it to Fig. 2, we can see that a lot of neurons with tiny w_m are deleted, and the total number of neurons decreases greatly.

5   Numerical Verifications

In this section, to substantiate the efficacy and superiority of the TIGONN trained by GPWSD algorithm (in terms of approximation, testing and denoising), numerical verifications based on two-variables objective functions (see in Sect. 4) are performed.

Note that, for approximation and denoising verification experiments, the training dataset is the same as the one in Sect. 4. Besides, for denoising experiments, random noises, subject to gaussian distribution, are added to objective functions simulating noises in nature. The mean value of noises is 0 and the range of noises is $[-10\%(\max Y - \min Y), 10\%(\max Y - \min Y)]$. Further, for testing verifications, the sample pairs $\{((u^{(s)}, v^{(s)}), \phi^{(s)})\}_{s=1}^{S=4489}$ are generated by sampling the region $[-1, 1]^2$ which covers the training region and the unlearned region (i.e, $\{[-1, 1]^2 - [-0.9, 0.9]^2\}$) with new gap-size 0.03, to test the approximation and predicting ability of the network.

Table 1. Approximation, testing and denoising results of TIGONN with GPWSD.

Function	M_{opt}	$\bar{E}_{app}$	$\bar{E}_{test}$	$\bar{E}_{dn}$	Training time /s
(11)	138	1.173×10^{-20}	1.116×10^{-9}	6.354×10^{-6}	218.827
(12)	204	1.732×10^{-25}	1.992×10^{-17}	9.734×10^{-6}	242.754
(13)	153	3.840×10^{-26}	1.534×10^{-21}	4.903×10^{-6}	100.017

Algorithm 2. Post-Pruning Scheme

Input: $\bar{E}_h$, w_{opt} and Q_{opt} obtained in the Alg. 1;
Output: final optimal error, $\bar{E}_{opt}$; optimal number of hidden neurons, M_{opt};
     w_{opt}; Q_{opt};

1: **initialize:** $\bar{E}_{del} \leftarrow \bar{E}_h$; $w_{del} \leftarrow w_{opt}$; $Q_{del} \leftarrow Q_{opt}$;
2: $g \leftarrow 2 \times \min |w_{opt}|$;
3: **while** 1 **do**
4:     $\bar{E}_{opt} \leftarrow \bar{E}_{del}$;
5:     $w_{opt} \leftarrow w_{del}$;
6:     $Q_{opt} \leftarrow Q_{del}$;
7:     Delete the elements in w_{del} with absolute values less than g, and the corresponding vectors in Q_{del};
8:     Calculate the corresponding MSE $\bar{E}_{del}$;
9:     **if** $\bar{E}_{del} < 2\bar{E}_h$ **then**
10:         $g \leftarrow 5g$;
11:         continue;
12:     **else**
13:         $M_{opt} \leftarrow \text{length}(w_{opt})$;
14:         break;
15:     **end if**
16: **end while**
17: **return:** $\bar{E}_{opt}$, M_{opt}, Q_{opt}, and w_{opt};

The corresponding numerical verifications results of approximation, denoising and testing are shown in Table 1. According to them, we can see that the mean training errors $\bar{E}_{app}$ (i.e, $\bar{E}_{opt}$ in GPWSD), and testing errors $\bar{E}_{test}$ of TIGONN with GPWSD are tiny enough (i.e., of order $10^{-20} - 10^{-26}$), which substantiates the superiority of TIGONN trained by GPWSD in terms of approximation. Besides, the results of denoising experiments are also recorded in Table 1, and the denoising errors $\bar{E}_{dn}$ (with the denoising outputs compared to the corresponding objective functions) are also quite small too, which proves the denoising ability of the network, even though the objective functions are polluted by large noises.

To show the superiority of TIGONN with GPWSD more intuitively, Fig. 4 illustrates the corresponding numerical results of network working on objective function (12) (with the results on objective function (11) and (13) omitted due to results' similarity and space limitation). For approximation ability, we can see the curves of network approximation output and network testing output are basically identical to the curves of objective functions (12), according to Fig. 4(a), (b) and (g). And the tiny relative error (i.e., $\bar{E}_{rel} := (\varphi - \phi)/\phi$) of approximation and testing also further substantiate the superiority of the network in terms of approximation, as is shown in Fig. 4(c) and (h). As for denoising ability of network, although the objective function is added with multitude of random noises (see in Fig. 4(d)), network with GPWSD can still approximate original objective function (12) with small relative error (shown in Fig. 4(e) and (f)).

In Subsect. 4.2, we have already demonstrated the efficacy of post-pruning scheme (See in Figs. 2 and 3). Here, to further show the effects brought by

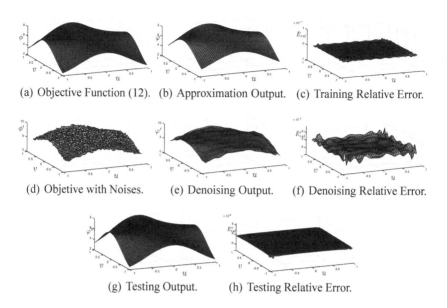

(a) Objective Function (12).   (b) Approximation Output.   (c) Training Relative Error.

(d) Objetive with Noises.   (e) Denoising Output.   (f) Denoising Relative Error.

(g) Testing Output.   (h) Testing Relative Error.

Fig. 4. The numerical verifications on objective function (12).

the post-pruning scheme, experiments on comparisons of GWSD and GPWSD are conducted and the results are recorded in Table 2. Also, we present the learning curves of GPWSD on three objective functions in Fig. 5, which reveals the relationships between the training errors and number of hidden neurons of three objective functions. In Table 2, the optimal number of neurons (i.e, M) of TIGONN where $\bar{E}_h$ is achieved for each target function determined through GWSD, which is marked with an arrow in Fig. 5 and number of neurons after pruning M_{opt} is also marked, respectively.

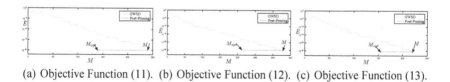

(a) Objective Function (11).   (b) Objective Function (12).   (c) Objective Function (13).

Fig. 5. The Learning Curves of GPWSD.

According to Table 2, a great many neurons in network have been deleted in the post-pruning process (also seen in Figs. 2 and 3), while the orders of magnitude of training approximation errors remain unchanged on three objective functions (by comparing $\bar{E}_h$ to $\bar{E}_{opt}$). In addition, the testing error accuracies $\bar{E}_{test}$ do not decline while the testing time(s) of network have been much shortened, showing the improvements in effectiveness brought by post-pruning.

Table 2. Comparisons on performance of GWSD and GPWSD on three objective functions.

Function	M/M_{opt}	$\bar{E}_h/\bar{E}_{opt}$	$\bar{E}_{test}$	Testing time /s
(11)	241/138	$1.17 \times 10^{-20}/1.79 \times 10^{-20}$	$1.12 \times 10^{-9}/1.11 \times 10^{-9}$	10.52/3.31
(12)	330/204	$1.28 \times 10^{-25}/1.73 \times 10^{-25}$	$1.99 \times 10^{-17}/1.99 \times 10^{-17}$	8.53/2.17
(13)	227/153	$3.95 \times 10^{-26}/3.84 \times 10^{-26}$	$1.53 \times 10^{-21}/1.53 \times 10^{-21}$	3.87/0.92

[1] GWSD results/GPWSD results.

6   Conclusion

In this work, we have investigated and proposed a two-input Gegenbauer orthogonal neural network (TIGONN) based on probability theory and polynomial interpolation and approximation theory. To avoid the weaknesses of traditional BP-type gradient based iterative training method, we have adopted weights direct determination (WDD) to obtain the optimal weights of network proposed. Based on this, we have elegantly designed a growing and pruning weights and structure determination (GPWSD) training method for network by combining growing weights and structure determination (GWSD) proposed before and post-pruning scheme, which can help to determine the optimal structure of network (i.e., optimal number of hidden neurons) and then simplify it automatically. According to numerical verifications on different two-variables objective functions, the TIGONN with GPWSD has shown superiority in terms of approximation, predicting and denoising, with tiny error accuracies. Further, comparison experiments on GPWSD and GWSD have substantiated the efficacy of post-pruning scheme, which indeed simplify the network and improve the effectiveness of network.

References

1. Zhang, G.P.: Neural networks for classification: a survey. IEEE Trans. Syst. Man Cybern. Part C: Appl. Rev. **30**(4), 451–462 (2000)
2. Cenggoro, T.W., Kridalaksana, A.H., Arriyanti, E., Ukkas, M.I.: Recognition of a human behavior pattern in paper rock scissor game using backpropagation artificial neural network method. In: Proceedings of the 2nd International Conference on Information and Communication Technology (ICoICT), pp. 238–243 (2014)
3. Rumelhart, D.E., McClelland, J.L.: Parallel Distributed Processing. The MIT Press, Cambridge (1986)
4. Wan, Y., Wu, C.W.: Fitting and prediction for crack propagation rate based on machine learning optimal algorithm. In: 2009 International Conference on E-Learning, E-Business, Enterprise Information Systems, and E-Government, vol. 1, pp. 96–96 (2009)
5. Zhang, Y., Zhong, T., Li, W., Xiao, X., Yi, C.: Growing algorithm of laguerre orthogonal basis neural network with weights directly determined. In: Huang, D.-S., Wunsch, D.C., Levine, D.S., Jo, K.-H. (eds.) ICIC 2008. LNCS (LNAI), vol. 5227, pp. 60–67. Springer, Heidelberg (2008). https://doi.org/10.1007/978-3-540-85984-0_8

6. Zhang, L., Suganthan, P.N.: A survey of randomized algorithms for training neural networks. Inf. Sci. **364**, 146–155 (2016)
7. Yu, X.H., Chen, G.A.: Euler neural network with its weight-direct-determination and structure-automatic-determination algorithms. In: Ninth International Conference on Hybrid Intelligent Systems, pp. 319–324 (2009)
8. Zhang, N.Y., Y, X.T., Lin, X., Li, W.B., Fan, Z.P.: Weights and structure determination of artificial neuronets. Self-organ. Theor. Methods **5370**, 109–154 (2014)
9. Wang, F., Li, H.: Towards reliability evaluation involving correlated multivariates under incomplete probability information: a reconstructed joint probability distribution for isoprobabilistic transformation. Struct. Saf. **69**(5), 99–110 (2016)
10. Robert, V.H., Joseph, W.M., Allen, T.C.: Introduction to Mathematical Statistics, 6th edn. Pearson, Upper Saddle River (2003)
11. Smith, G.K.: Polynomial Approximation. Encyclopedia of Biostatistics, 2nd edn, Armitage, P., Colton, T. (eds.), vol. 6, pp. 4136–4140. Wiley, London (2004)
12. Lin, C.: Numerical Analysis. Science Press, China (2007)
13. Zhang, Y.N., Li, W., Yi, C., Chen, K.: A weights-directly-determined simple neural network for nonlinear system identification. In: IEEE International Conference on Fuzzy Systems, pp. 455–460 (2008)
14. Zhang, Y.N., Yu, X.T., Guo, D.S., Li, J., Fan, Z.P.: Weights and structure determination of feed-forward two-input neural network activated by Chebyshev polynomials of Class 2. In: Proceedings of the 24th Chinese Control and Decision Conference (CCDC), pp. 1100–1105 (2012)
15. Zhang, Y.N., Chen, J.H., Guo, D.S., Yin, Y.H., Lao, W.C: Growing-type weights and structure determination of 2-input Legendere orthogonal polynomial neuronet. In: Proceedings of IEEE International Symposium on Industrial Electronics, pp. 852–857 (2012)
16. Lin, C.H., Hsu, H.Y.: Blend recurrent Gegenbauer orthogonal polynomials neural network control of a SynRM servo-drive CVT system using amended artificial bee colony optimization. In: IEEE International Conference on Applied System Innovation (ICASI), pp. 1–4 (2016)
17. Charles, D.F., Yuan, X.: Orthogonal Polynomials of Several Variables, pp. 112–115. Cambridge University Press, Cambridge (2009)
18. Bottou, L.: Large-scale machine learning with stochastic gradient descent. In: Lechevallier, Y., Saporta, G. (eds.) Proceedings of COMPSTAT, pp. 177–186. Springer, Heidelberg (2010). https://doi.org/10.1007/978-3-7908-2604-3_16

A Lightweight Convolutional Neural Network for Silkworm Cocoons Fast Classification

Wei Feng, Geng Jia, Wei Wang, Zukui Zhang,
Jing Cui[✉], Zhongyi Chu, and Bo Xu

Beijing University of Technology, Beijing, China
fw422@qq.com, 15810505011@163.com, cuijing@bjut.edu.cn

Abstract. Silk clothing is very popular all over the world, and the annual demand is very large each year. Silkworm cocoons as raw materials for silk will be selected much more to meet market demand. At present, high quality cocoons and defective cocoons are identified mainly by manual selection, the main problem of this situation is that the identification process is inefficient. It is necessary to develop automated visual equipment to assist workers in silkworm cocoons selection. In recent years, deep learning especially the convolutional neural network (CNN) has achieved high success and gradually become the main method in the area of image classification. In order to establish silkworm cocoon classification model, we made a silkworm cocoon data set and designed a convolutional neural network to classify silkworm cocoons. For traditional convolutional neural networks, the fully connection layer often contains most of the parameters of the whole model, which consumes a lot of computing resources and time in the forward propagation. In order to improve this, we use global average pooling (GAP) layer to connect the convolutional layer and classify layer to reduce some fully connection layers. And all improvements were accomplished on the basis of the structure of AlexNet. As a result, the AlexNet (GAP) is obtained. Experimental results demonstrate that the proposed architecture achieves a mean accuracy of 98.22%, which makes it possible to apply cocoons classification in industry very soon.

Keywords: Cocoons classification · Convolutional neural networks · Global average pooling

1 Introduction

Silk is an important clothing material and the annual economic benefit of the silk industry is very high. The export of silk products is huge, and the annual need is increasing. As the raw material of silk, the quality of silkworm cocoons also has a great impact on the quality of silk products. Therefore, selecting high quality silkworm cocoons is essential for producing high-quality silk goods.

© Springer Nature Singapore Pte Ltd. 2019
F. Sun et al. (Eds.): ICCSIP 2018, CCIS 1006, pp. 301–309, 2019.
https://doi.org/10.1007/978-981-13-7986-4_27

At present, selecting cocoons by hand is the usual method in the industry. This method is not only inefficient, but also the evaluation criteria highly relies on the experience of the workers. Besides, the results of the selecting are very easy to be influenced by emotions, which may result in a little difference in the standard of good cocoons and affect the subsequent operation.

In order to increase the efficiency of work, the need for automatic selecting of silkworm cocoons to assist people is increasing. The automated selecting system mainly includes three parts: the conveying device, the visual detection system and the sorting device. Distinguishing the qualified silkworm cocoons and defective silkworm cocoons by machine vision is the key technology for automatic selecting of silkworm cocoons.

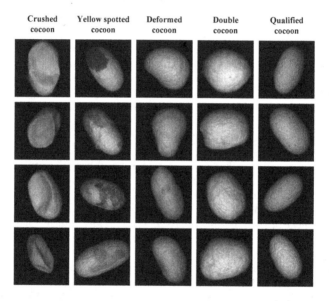

Fig. 1. Images of different kinds of silkworm cocoons (Color figure online)

For the classification of silkworm cocoons, in order to determine the category of each cocoon, the most difficult thing is how to extract the features of all kinds of cocoons as many as possible. Most of the methods for feature extraction of silkworm cocoon is digital image processing algorithm. Song et al. [1] proposed a method through calculating Mathematical Morphology, the area, correlation coefficient and values of RGB of cocoons and then using these values to judge the category of different cocoons including deformity cocoon, doupion double cocoon, rotten cocoon, fungi cocoon and special small cocoon. The problem with this method is that all images of silkworm cocoons are collected under the sunlight. If the environment changes, many parameters may change at the same time. Therefore, the standard for classification is not very robust.

Jin et al. [2] from Zhejiang University use image binarization, contrast adjust, image inverse digital and other image processing technology to process the cocoon images and extract the surface region of silkworm cocoon by calculating a series of parameters of the surface region and using Bayesian Discriminant to classify silkworm cocoons, but this method still has a gap from the application. The reason is that the color of certain locations of some defective cocoons and background are similar. Although enhancing the contrast, the feature area cannot be completely extracted.

In recent years, convolutional neural network (CNN) has higher and higher achievements in computer vision especially in classification tasks, such classical networks as AlexNet [3], VGG [4], GoogLeNet [5], etc. The AlexNet achieved big success and showed the huge potential of the convolutional neural network in the ILSVRC-2012 competition. And the structure of AlexNet has very essential impact on the subsequent convolutional neural network. CNN is an end-to-end method. It can extract so many features automatically from the images and gives the final classification results directly. So compared with traditional digital image processing methods, the CNN can solve the problem of insufficient feature extraction of silkworm cocoons. However, the traditional convolutional neural networks, for example, the AlexNet we used takes a lot of time to determine the category of one input image and can't make real-time judgments. The reason is that the amount of parameters is so large that the forward propagation takes more time. Therefore, we modified the structure of AlexNet to reduce the amount of parameters and proposed the convolutional neural network (AlexNet (GAP)) to classify the different kinds of silkworm cocoons more accurately and quickly. The structure of the network we proposed constitutes eleven layers: five convolution layers, two max-pooling layers, two LRN layers, one global average pooling layer and one fully-connected layer.

The rest of this paper is organized as follows. The methodology for image preprocessing and the network architecture are reviewed in Sect. 2. The experiments are introduced in Sect. 3. Section 4 shows results and discussion from our experiments. Section 5 draws conclusions and prospects.

2   Image Processing Method and Network Structure Design

2.1   Image Acquisition and Processing

In current cocoon factory, cocoons are usually piled up together and workers select the good cocoons out by watching the surface of every cocoon. In order to relieve the pressure of workers, using industrial camera at specific positions to capture the cocoons image is an available way. As the cocoons are oval, so every cocoon is captured in several times to check the global surface of cocoon completely. All the cocoons we obtained have been classified by the experienced workers. We captured the images of five kinds of cocoons includes crushed cocoon, yellow spotted cocoon, deformed cocoon, double cocoon (or called doupion) and qualified cocoon.

As it shows in Fig. 1, each image contains a cocoon. To enhance the contrast, we use black cloth as the background. The most area of the image is the black background which is useless to classify cocoons, so we drew a bounding box to surround the cocoon and extracted the content of the bounding box as the dataset. To let all kinds of cocoons can be surrounded by bounding box, we designed the size of bounding box is 400×400, so the background outside the bounding box can be removed. And finally, we rescale the image resolution from 400×400 to 256×256 as the input data.

2.2   Network Architecture

Our proposed AlexNet (GAP) architecture, the schematic diagram of the entire network design is provided in Fig. 2, contains eleven layers: five convolution layers, two max-pooling layers, two Local Response Normalization (LRN) layers, one global average pooling layer and one fully-connected layer. The input data is RBG image and we cropped the size from 256×256 to 227×227, they are fed to the network after the normalization, subtracting the mean activity over the training set from each pixel [3]. The overall architecture is based on AlexNet and the details of network are designed as follows. The first six layers are stacked by convolutional layer, Local Response Normalization layer and Max-pooling layer alternately and then followed by three convolutional layers. After that, a global Average-pooling layer is applied and finally using a fully-connected layer with softmax operation to output results of the cocoons classification. There are 96 filters in the first convolutional layer, and the size of the filters is 11×11 with a stride of 4 pixels, followed by a ReLU activation function. Then the 3×3 Max-pool operation is used with a stride of 2 pixels. The second convolutional layer

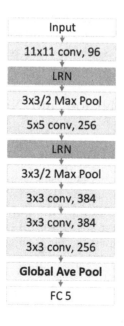

Fig. 2. The AlexNet (GAP) structure

has 256 kernels with stride of 1 pixels, followed by a Max-Pooling layer with the kernel size of 3 × 3. The third, fourth and sixth convolutional layer has 384, 384 and 256 kernels respectively with kernel size of 3 × 3. The details of AlexNet (GAP) structure are showed in Table 1. All the activation method we used is ReLU as the same as the first layer. As the development of CNN structure, the global Average-pooling layer acts as a structural regularizer that prevents overfitting globally [6] and it becomes more and more popular in the design of CNN. Especially it can reduce the number of parameters greatly. So we use the global Average-pooling layer connecting the fifth convolutional layer. To make the final classification, a fully-connected layer which has only 5 neurons with softmax operation is designed at the end of the network.

Table 1. The details of AlexNet (GAP) structure

Layer	Type	Kernel size	Stride	Pad	Output size
1	Input				$227 \times 227 \times 3$
2	Convolution1	11×11	4	0	$55 \times 55 \times 96$
3	LRN1				
4	Max pooling	3×3	2		$27 \times 27 \times 96$
5	Convolution2	5×5	1	2	$27 \times 27 \times 256$
6	LRN2				
7	Max pooling	3×3	2		$13 \times 13 \times 256$
8	Convolution3	3×3	1	1	$13 \times 13 \times 384$
9	Convolution4	3×3	1	1	$13 \times 13 \times 384$
10	Convolution5	3×3	1	1	$13 \times 13 \times 256$
11	Global Ave pooling	13×13			256
12	Fc				5

3 Classification Experiments

We evaluated our architecture for cocoon classification on the cocoon dataset we made. The cocoons we used in this paper is obtained from the cocoon factory. Five types of common cocoons are collected to build the dataset and the method we reprocessed has been described in the Sect. 2. There are 13514 images in total, including 3138 images of qualified cocoon, 2155 images of crushed cocoon, 2405 images of yellow spotted cocoon, 2040 images of deformed cocoon and 3776 images of double cocoon.

To analyze the performance comprehensively, we made five datasets (datasetA, datasetB, ..., datasetE). Each dataset contains all the images we collected, consisting of training set and validation set. The ratio between them is about 9.2:0.8. The five validation set do not overlap. In the experiment, we selected three criterions to evaluate the model, the accuracy, the number of parameters and the test time for one image.

The weights in each layers are initialized from a zero-mean Gaussian distribution with standard deviation 0.01 as the same as AlexNet [3]. The neuron biases in the first, third convolutional layer and the final output layer are initialized with the constant 0. And the neuron biases in other convolutional layer including the second, fourth, and the fifth convolutional layers, are initialized with constant 0.1.

The training course was not very complex. We fixed the learning rate at 0.001 and trained the network for 600 epochs. And the method of optimization was stochastic gradient descent with a batch size of 256 examples, momentum of 0.9, and weight decay of 0.00005. We applied the Caffe framework in the NVIDIA Deep Learning GPU Training System (DIGITS) using two NVIDIA GTX 1080Ti GPU to train our model.

4   Results and Disscussion

In this paper, we compare the result between the AlexNet [3] and AlexNet (G-AP) we proposed. Three evaluation indexes including the accuracy, the amount of parameters and the speed of the two networks are conducted to compare them.

Table 2 shows the mean classification accuracy of different kinds of cocoons on five validation datasets by using AlexNet and our network respectively. Most results are very close, but the classification accuracy of deformed cocoon increased by more than four percentage. Table 3 shows the Top-1 accuracy of the two networks. We achieve an mean accuracy of 98.22%, and our network achieves more than 0.6% better accuracy than the AlexNet. The reason is that we used the global average pooling layer to replace the first two fully-connected layers. This structure has regularization effect [6] and improves the generalization ability of the model.

Table 2. Mean recall for different categories

Network architecture	Crushed cocoon	Qualified cocoon	Yellow spotted cocoon	Deformed cocoon	Double cocoon
AlexNet	100%	97.9%	99.53%	93.22%	97.14%
AlexNet (GAP)	99.88%	97.51%	100%	**97.68%**	97.32%

Table 3. Top-1 accuracy of classification

Network architecture	Mean accuracy
AlexNet	97.58%
AlexNet (GAP)	**98.22%**

In Table 4 we show the best confusion matric. We achieved a mean accuracy of 98.66%, especially in crushed cocoon and yellow spotted cocoon. The recall of both is up to 100%. But nine samples of qualified cocoon were misclassified as deformed cocoon. We looked up the images and found that there were some details which were a little similar to deformed cocoon in the misclassified images and misclassification also occurs in other data sets. Therefore, classifying one cocoon in just one image or one position may make a wrong decision, and it is necessary to make a machine that can take photos of cocoons from multiple positions.

Table 4. Best confusion matrix

		Actual class				
		Crushed cocoon	Qualified cocoon	Yellow spotted cocoon	Deformed cocoon	Double cocoon
Prediction	Crushed cocoon	171	0	0	0	0
	Qualified cocoon	0	238	0	9	0
	Yellow spotted cocoon	0	0	183	0	0
	Deformed cocoon	1	0	0	158	0
	Double cocoon	0	0	1	3	277

Table 5. Comparison of the parameters of the two networks

AlexNet layer name	Parameter amount	AlexNet (GAP) layer name	Parameter amount
Convolution1	34,944	Convolution1	34,944
Convolution2	307,456	Convolution2	307,456
Convolution3	885,120	Convolution3	885,120
Convolution4	663,936	Convolution4	663,936
Convolution5	442,624	Convolution5	442,624
Fc1	**37,752,832**	**Fc**	**1,285**
Fc2	16,781,312	N/A	N/A
Fc3	20,485	N/A	N/A

In addition to the improvement of accuracy, the parameters of our model are much smaller than the AlexNet and the speed has improved a lot. Table 5 shows the parameter of two networks in details and the Table 6 shows the total amount of parameter and time cost of two networks. The amount of parameters of our network is only 4.1% of the AlexNet. The size of the our model file is just 8.9 MB, and the other is 217 MB. For fair comparison, we made the test on the same platform of a PC (CPU is i5-7300HQ, RAM is 8G). Our network only takes 0.57 s to test one image. The speed increased by 53%. This is because the global average pooling layer reduces the connection between the convolutional layer and the output layer, the computation is much reduced. And all the results support that our network has better performance over AlexNet for cocoon classification both in accuracy and speed.

Table 6. Parameters and time cost for different methods

Network architecture	The amount of parameters	Time cost for single image
AlexNet	56,888,709	1.22 s
AlexNet (GAP)	**2,335,365**	**0.57 s**

5   Conclusions

This paper presents an efficient method for cocoon classification based on a well-designed shallow convolution neural network. First, we collect cocoon images and remove the most area of background to highlight every silkworm cocoon. Then we select 5 common types of cocoons to build dataset and the size (resolution) of all the images in the dataset have been rescaled. Finally, we proposed a shallow convolution neural network for the classification of cocoons, to reduce the parameters greatly and speed up the course of forward propagation. We applied the Global Average-pooling (GAP) layer to replace the fully-connected layers except the classification layer. The results show the AlexNet (GAP) we proposed has good performance both in accuracy and test time, and the network makes it possible to classify cocoons in real-time application very soon.

For future work, we would like to combine the sorting machinery with the AlexNet(GAP) together to accomplish the sorting task. The machine can take photos of cocoons from multiple positions to detect the cocoons more comprehensively. Whether the network can achieve high precision is still a problem worth exploring. It may be necessary to use different methods of data augmentation in the training process and we will continue looking for ways to make the model more robust to apply in industry as soon as possible.

Acknowledgements. The authors acknowledge the financial support from the Natural Science Foundation of China (61773028), the Natural Science Foundation of Beijing (4172008).

References

1. Song, Y.J., Xie, S.Y., Ran, R.L.: Applied research on machine vision technology in non-destructive test of cocoon. Mod. Agric. Equipments **9**, 48–51 (2006)
2. Jin, H.F.: Research on nondestructive determination of cocoon quality based on spectroscopy and hyperspectral imaging techniques, Zhejiang University (2015)

3. Krizhevsky, A., Sutskever, I., Hinton, G.E.: ImageNet classification with deep convolutional neural networks. In: International Conference on Neural Information Processing Systems, vol. 60, pp. 1097–1105 (2012)
4. Simonyan, K., Zisserman, A.: Very deep convolutional networks for large-scale image recognition. Comput. Sci. (2014)
5. Szegedy, C., et al.: Going deeper with convolutions. In: Proceedings of the IEEE Conference on Computer Vision and Pattern Recognition, pp. 1–9 (2015)
6. Lin, M., Chen, Q., Yan, S.: Network in network. Comput. Sci. (2013)
7. Ioffe, S., Szegedy, C.: Batch normalization: accelerating deep network training by reducing internal covariate shift, pp. 448–456 (2015)
8. He, K., Zhang, X., Ren, S., Sun, J.: Deep residual learning for image recognition. In: 2016 IEEE Conference on Computer Vision and Pattern Recognition (CVPR), Las Vegas, NV, United States, pp. 770–778 (2016)
9. Huang, G., et al.: Densely connected convolutional networks. In: IEEE Conference on Computer Vision and Pattern Recognition IEEE Computer Society, pp. 2261–2269 (2017)
10. Lin, T.Y., et al.: Feature pyramid networks for object detection. In: IEEE Conference on Computer Vision and Pattern Recognition IEEE Computer Society, pp. 936–944 (2017)
11. Xie, S., Girshick, R., Dollar, P., Tu, Z., He, K.: Aggregated residual transformations for deep neural networks. In: 2017 IEEE Conference on Computer Vision and Pattern Recognition (CVPR), pp. 5987–5995 (2017)
12. Ren, S., et al.: Faster R-CNN: towards real-time object detection with region proposal networks. IEEE Trans. Pattern Anal. Mach. Intell. 39(6), 1137–1149 (2015)
13. Redmon, J., et al.: You only look once: unified, real-time object detection. In: IEEE Conference on Computer Vision and Pattern Recognition IEEE Computer Society, pp. 779–788 (2016)
14. Redmon, J., Farhadi, A.: YOLO9000: better, faster, stronger. In: 2017 IEEE Conference on Computer Vision and Pattern Recognition (CVPR), pp. 6517–6525 (2017)
15. Liang, M., Hu, X.: Recurrent convolutional neural network for object recognition. In: Proceedings of the IEEE Conference on Computer Vision and Pattern Recognition, pp. 3367–3375 (2015)
16. Hamester, D., Barros, P., Wermter, S.: Face expression recognition with a 2-channel convolutional neural network. In: International Joint Conference on Neural Networks IEEE, pp. 1–8 (2015)

A Novel Convolutional Neural Network for Facial Expression Recognition

Jing Li[1], Yang Mi[1], Jiahui Yu[2], and Zhaojie Ju[3,4(✉)]

[1] School of Information Engineering, Nanchang University,
Nanchang 330031, China
jingli@ncu.edu.cn, 997562713@qq.com
[2] School of Information Science and Engineering, Shenyang Ligong University,
Shenyang 110159, China
[3] School of Computing, University of Portsmouth, Portsmouth PO1 3HE, UK
zhaojie.ju@port.ac.uk
[4] The State Key Laboratory of Robotics, Shenyang Institute of Automation,
Chinese Academy of Sciences, Shenyang 110016, China

Abstract. Facial expression recognition is becoming a hot topic due to its wide applications in computer vision research fields. Traditional methods adopt hand-crafted features combined with classifiers to achieve the recognition goal. However, the accuracy of these methods often relies heavily on the extracted features and the classifier's parameters, and thus cannot get good result with unseen data. Recently, deep learning, which simulates the mechanism of human brain to interpret data, has shown remarkable results in visual object recognition. In this paper, we present a novel convolutional neural network which consists of local binary patterns and improved Inception-ResNet layers for automatic facial expression recognition. We apply the proposed method to three expression datasets, i.e., the Extended Cohn-kanade Dataset (CK+), the Japanese Female Expression Database (JAFFE), and the FER2013 Dataset. The experimental results demonstrate the feasibility and effectiveness of our proposed network.

Keywords: Facial expression recognition · Deep learning · LBP · Inception-ResNet layers

1 Introduction

In human daily communications, audio and visual signals are mixed to understand each other. Audio signal is the most direct way to express ourselves and visual signals help us get potential information. As a part of visual signals, facial expressions, which refer to the movements of the mimetic musculature of the face [25], provide rich information about one's real emotions and intentions. A study [23] reported that facial expressions constitute 55% of the effect of a communication message which is higher than language and voice do. Due to the important role in conveying information, automatic facial expression analysis is becoming an interesting and challenging topic in today's computer vision research area, including human-computer interaction, data-driven animation, and so on. Though much progress has made in this study, with the variability,

© Springer Nature Singapore Pte Ltd. 2019
F. Sun et al. (Eds.): ICCSIP 2018, CCIS 1006, pp. 310–320, 2019.
https://doi.org/10.1007/978-981-13-7986-4_28

complexity and subtlety of facial expressions, it is still difficult to achieve a desirable recognition accuracy in practical applications.

Ekman and Friesen [26] provided six basic facial expression forms, i.e., anger, happiness, disgust, sadness, surprise and fear, which are widely accepted, and most of the current articles are aiming at automatically identifying these six prototypic expressions. Early in 1978, Suwa et al. [28] presented a preliminary investigation on automatic facial expression analysis. Picard [24] showed that affective computing could be a useful way to expand human-computing communication. Ekman and Friesen [27] developed the famous Facial Action Coding System (FACS) to detect subtle variations in facial expressions. Since then, extracting facial features and classifying different facial expressions based on computer technologies have attracted more and more attention. However, these works did not significantly progress until the last decade, Hinton et al. [29] proposed that with many hidden layers in deep learning neural network, the ability of learning characteristics could be improved, as well as the model prediction and classification accuracy.

Our aim is to explore and design a system that could perform automated facial expression analysis. Generally, three main steps are involved in tackling the problem: (1) facial detection and preprocessing; (2) facial feature extraction; and (3) facial expression classification. As we can see in Fig. 1. In order to accomplish the classification tasks, traditional approaches such as Support Vector Machine (SVM) perform well on classifying posed facial expressions in a controlled environment and lab settings. However, in a spontaneous uncontrolled circumstance, these methods cannot work effectively. In 1980 s, LeCun et al. [30] proposed the Convolutional Neural Network (CNN), which contains convolutional layers (C layers) and subsampling layers (S layers) as two basic layers, made the classification more robust.

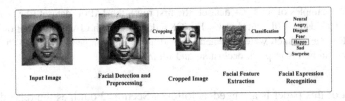

Fig. 1. An example of a facial expression recognition system.

In this paper, we propose a novel deep convolutional neural network for recognizing facial expressions. Inspired by [7], improved Inception-ResNet is used since it would allow Inception to reap the benefits of the residual approach while maintaining its computational efficiency. Furthermore, Local Binary Patterns (LBPs), which contains image texture information, is entered into the network. We conduct our proposed method on three well-known facial expression datasets, which are CK+ [14], JAFFE [16], and FER2013 [33].

The main contributions of this paper are as follows:

(1) We introduce an improved double-input feature extraction block to recognize facial expressions automatically. Except for the raw images, we add LBPs to the two middle-layers of the network, because they contain texture information of the face and can reflect subtle face changes. In this way, the performance can be significantly improved.

(2) Traditional datasets (CK+ and JAFFE) only containing frontal facial images were collected in specific environments. Some expressions are even unnatural and exaggerated which are not suitable for practical good social communications. In order to make the network generalize better for communication in daily life, we use the FER2013 dataset that contains more variations in pose, occlusion, and illumination.

(3) We employ data augmentation and batch normalization to avoid overfitting. For data augmentation, we randomly rotate, flip, and shift the images to expand the size of datasets. Batch normalization can reduce intra-class variation while does not distort the images. Section 3 describes this procedure in detail (Fig. 2).

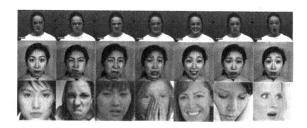

Fig. 2. Some examples of the CK+ dataset (the first row), the JAFFE dataset (the second row), and the FER2013 dataset (the third row). The CK+ dataset and the JAFFE dataset only contain frontal facial images, which were collected in conditional environments. The FER2013 dataset includes more variations in pose, occlusion, and illumination.

The rest of this paper is arranged as follows. Section 2 outlines the related work in the field of facial expression recognition. Section 3 describes the newly proposed network. Section 4 presents the experimental results and Sect. 5 concludes the whole paper.

2 Related Work

Facial expressions represent one's most powerful and immediate means for emotions and intentions communication [15]. Because of its potential applications, facial expression recognition can be used in many fields, such as human-robot interaction [16], surveillance [17], health-care [18], and so on.

The facial action coding system developed by Ekman [27] is the inspiration for many research papers. Luecy et al. [14] created the Extended Cohn-kanade dataset (CK+).

In the classification stage, the dataset was evaluated using Active Appearance Models (AAMs) in combination with SVMs. The architecture achieved the final accuracy over 65% for each expression. In [21], facial expressions were classified into six basic emotions. First, the active patches, which are the most useful parts when people give an expression, were extracted from the facial region. Then, LBP used as the feature descriptor were fed into Support Vector Machines (SVMs) for classification. The system achieved 94.39% and 92.22% for extended Cohn-Kanade (CK+) dataset and JAFFE dataset respectively.

Recently, it has been a popular way to use deep neural network to recognizing facial expression and visual objects. In [19], the earliest convolutional neural network LeNet-5 was presented for handwriting recognition. Then, many variants of this basic design are prevalent in image classification. In 2012, Hinton proposed the AlexNet [20] as the beginning of the larger and deeper convolutional neural networks. It classifies 1.2 million high-resolution images into 1,000 different classes.

Szegedy et al. [9] proposed GoogLeNet, which increases both the width and depth of the network to improve the architecture performance. This is a 22-layer deep network and the main structure is "Inception" layers, which allow the architecture to make a more complex decision. In 2015, He et al. [5] produced the deep residual learning framework called ResNet to address the degradation problem. The residual block uses shortcut connection to add outputs to the outputs of the stacked layers. When the model layer to deepen, the simple operation can solve the degradation problem.

The previous studies [3, 4] had shown remarkable improvement in recognition rates by using Inception, and also ResNet had achieved remarkable results in very deep networks [5, 6]. Inspired by these advantages, the Inception architectures were combined with residual connections in [7], which was called as Inception-ResNet layers. Wherein, it also presented clear empirical evidence that residual connections accelerate the training stage of Inception networks, meanwhile maintain the computation effectiveness.

3 A Double Input Architecture

In this paper, we utilize a double-input Inception-ResNet block (DIB) to address the facial expression recognition problem. In the proposed neural network, we incorporate LBP features during the training step. These features provide texture information and thus reflect slight changes on the face, which helps the network pay attention to the facial feature so as to improve the recognition accuracy. Beyond that, we employ batch normalization to guarantee the stable distribution of the input data at each layer. Last but not the least, we use data augmentation to prevent overfitting. We will explain each module in detail in the following sub-sections.

3.1 A Double Input Inception-ResNet Block

We propose a modified Inception-ResNet architecture, which has double-input feature blocks to automatically recognize seven expressions. As inspired by the Inception-ResNet architecture [7], we choose Inception-v4 layers, which achieve better recognition rates compared with the other models. Figure 3 shows the overall schema for the modified Inception-ResNet network. We feed the input images with the size of 299 * 299 * 1 into the "stem" module and add LBP features into the Inception-ResNet-A module and the Inception-ResNet-B module. The LBP feature maps are resized to their corresponding filter size in the network. Batch normalization layer is added to all of the convolution layers to avoid overfitting and ReLU [10] activation function is added to all of the batch normalization layers to avoid the vanishing gradient problem.

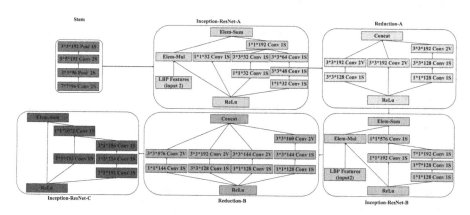

Fig. 3. The overview of the architecture.

3.2   Local Binary Pattern

Robust facial features should minimize within-class variations of expressions while maximize between-class variations. There are two types of facial feature extraction methods: Geometric feature-based methods and appearance-based methods. The geometric feature-based methods aim to use the geometric relationships between facial feature points to extract facial features, but commonly require accurate and reliable facial feature detection and tracking, which is difficult to accommodate in many situations. The appearance-based methods reflect the underlying information in a face image that can help determine the expression attributes accurately. However, this method may ignore overall information of the face to some extent. Although either of these two methods can effectively represent facial expressions, we employ appearance-based methods since it can pay attention to the changes in skin texture that is important for facial expression modelling. As a representative of the appearance-based methods, we extract local binary patterns (LBPs) [11] as the facial features. The LBPs can reflect subtle changes of the face such as wrinkles and furrows, which makes it convenient for a more detail study. The LBP operator is rotation invariant and grey invariant, and thus can solve the problem of imbalanced displacement, rotation and illumination in an image.

There are several types of LBPs. The original LBP operator introduced in [11] was defined in a 3 * 3 neighborhood. It thresholds each pixel with the center value, and then considers the result as a binary number. The LBP feature at this pixel can be expressed as follows:

$$LBP(x_c, y_c) = \sum_{p=0}^{7} s(i_p - i_c)2^p. \tag{1}$$

where p is the number of different pixels, (x_c, y_c) as the center pixel with intensity i_c, and i_p being the intensity of the neighborhood pixel, and s is the sign function defined as:

$$s(x) = \begin{cases} 1 & if \quad x \geq 0 \\ 0 & if \quad x < 0 \end{cases}. \tag{2}$$

In order to make it suitable for different scales of texture features and achieve gray-scale invariance, the operator extends to use different-size neighborhoods [12, 13]. The local neighborhoods are defined as a set of sampling points evenly spaced on a circle, which are centered at the pixel to be labeled. It allows any radius and number of sampling points. Bilinearly interpolating is used when sampling points do not fall in the center of a pixel. Given a pixel at (x_c, y_c), the resulting LBP can be expressed as:

$$LBP_{P,R}(x_c, y_c) = \sum_{P=0}^{P-1} s(i_p - i_c)2^p. \tag{3}$$

where U is the uniformity measure and the superscript "rius2" denotes rotation-invariant uniform pattern (Fig. 4).

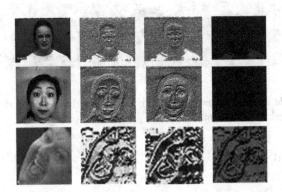

Fig. 4. Each row shows the LBP images of the CK+ dataset, the JAFFE dataset, and FER2013 dataset, respectively. From left to right is the input image, original LBP image, circle LBP image, and uniform LBP image.

3.3 Batch Normalization

In previous tasks, such as face detection [25] and face identification [34], one class only contains one person. While in facial expression recognition, the same expression class may contain numerous individuals, which leads to intra-class variations. In order to solve this problem, traditional methods always apply face alignment. However, it may distort the images. Current deep learning networks always apply batch normalization [1], which makes the network focus on images that are more real by distorting them less. Batch normalization adds standardized processing to the input data of each layer during the training process in deep neural networks. Thus, it ensures that each layer of the input data distribution is stable. Batch normalization also alleviates the covariate shift phenomenon [2] caused by the input distribution changes. It allows the networks to decrease the need for dropout and local response normalization. In our network, we add batch normalization layers after all of the convolutional layers.

3.4 Data Augmentation

It is important to consider overfitting in our deep convolutional neural network. Overfitting makes the model perform too well on the training data, but leads to poor performance in validation data and test data. Data augmentation and dropout are two primary ways to prevent overfitting. For data augmentation, the easiest and most common way is to artificially enlarge the dataset using label-preserving transformation. In this paper, considering the images in the three datasets are grayscale, we do not manipulate the contrast, brightness or color. First, we take a random rotation on the images to capture different-angle invariance. Second, we flip the images horizontally to capture the reflection invariance. Finally, we randomly shift the images to capture the translation invariance (Fig. 5).

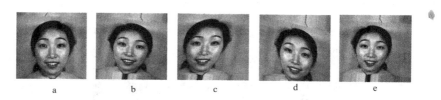

a   b   c   d   e

Fig. 5. An example for data augmentation: (a) is the original facial image, (b), (c), (d), (e) are the images after random data augmentation

4   Experiment Result

4.1 Face Datasets

In this work, we design a double-input Inception-ResNet block to automatic classifying static images. Except for the famous facial expression datasets, such Cohn-Kandade [14] and JAFFE [16], we also evaluate our proposed method on FER2013 [33] that is more challenging with large variations in pose, illumination and occlusion.

CK+: The Extended Cohn-Kanade database [14] contains 593 video sequences recorded from 123 subjects. Participants were from 18 to 50 years old. There are seven basic expressions, which are anger, disgust, fear, happy, sad, and surprise. Each sequence began in a neural face and ended in a peak expression. All the images are 640 * 490 or 640 *480 pixel arrays with 8-bit gray-scale or 24-bit color values. In this paper, we select 5,287 images as the dataset.

JAFFE: The Japanese Female Facial Expression (JAFFE) database [16] contains 213 images of seven facial expressions (neutral, angry, disgust, fear, happy, sad and surprise) from 10 Japanese female models, each of which has 2–4 samples for one expression. Each image is 256 * 256.

FER2013: The Facial Expression Recognition Challenge 2013 (FER2013) [33] is a dataset for spontaneous facial expression. It contains 28,709 training images and 3,589 testing images of seven expressions (six basic facial expressions and neutral), which are 48 * 48. Unlike CK+ and JAFFE, FER2013 contains more variations in pose, illumination and occlusion.

4.2   Results

We evaluate our architecture on three datasets mentioned above, i.e. the CK+ dataset, the JAFFE dataset, and the FER2013 dataset. The model is trained with an initialized learning rate 0.001, and the batch size is around 64–128. We add batch normalization after each convolutional layer. The model obtains the best classification accuracy after 300 epochs. Our network is trained on one GTX1080 TI GPU.

We compare the performance of our proposed method with the state-of-the-art facial expression recognition methods on the three dataset. The methods include Inception-ResNet with Conditional Random Field (Inception-ResNet+CRF) [8], Salient Facial Patches (SFP) [21], VGGNet and Long Short Term Memory (VGGNet +LSTM) [22], Face Parsing and Stacked Autoencoder (FP+SAE) [31], Inception layer and Network in Network theory (Inception+NIN) [3], and Linear Support Vector Machine (LSVM) [32]. In order to demonstrate the merit of incorporating LBP features, we also provide the result of our network without LBP features, which are replaced with a simple shortcut between the input and output of the residual unit in the Inception-ResNet A and Inception-ResNet B modules. We call this Single-Input Inception-ResNet Block (SIB) (Table 1).

Table 1. Recognition rates (%) on the CK+ dataset, the JAFFE dataset and FER2013 dataset.

Methods	Datasets		
	CK+	JAFFE	FER2013
DIB (ours)	**97.34**	**98.92**	**67.71**
SIB (ours)	94.38	97.78	58.21
Inception-ResNet+CRF [8]	93.04	–	–
SFP [21]	94.39	92.22	–
VGGNet+LSTM [22]	97.2	–	–
FP+SAE [31]	–	90.95	–
LSVM [32]	–	–	69.3
Inception+NIN [3]	–	–	66.4

5   Conclusion and Future Work

This paper presents a double-input Inception-ResNet block for facial expression recognition in static images. The network explores the texture information in order to improve the architecture performance. Considering the depth of the network, we first increase the number of images to prevent overfitting, then put the facial images into the network and classify them into either of the six basic expressions or the neutral one. The proposed method is evaluated on three well-known datasets: the CK+ dataset, the JAFFE dataset, and the FER 2013 dataset. Our experimental results show that the proposed method is more superior to many state-of-art methods when performing in FER2013.

Acknowledgments. This work is supported by National Natural Science Foundation of China under Grant 61463032 and 61703198, Natural Science Foundation for Distinguished Young Scholars of Jiangxi Province under Grant 2018ACB21014, Open Fund of State Key Laboratory of Management and Control for Complex Systems, Institute of Automation, Chinese Academy of Sciences under Grant 20180109.

References

1. Ioffe, S., Szegedy, C.: Batch normalization: accelerating deep network training by reducing internal covariate shift. arXiv preprint arXiv:1502.03167 (2015)
2. Shimodaira, H.: Improving predictive inference under covariate shift by weighting the log likelihood function. J. Stat. Plan. Inference **90**(2), 227–244 (2000)
3. Mollahosseini, A., Chan, D., Mahoor, M.H.: Going deeper in facial expression recognition using deep neural networks. In: IEEE Winter Conference on Applications of Computer Vision. IEEE, pp. 1–10 (2016)
4. Szegedy, C., Liu, W., Jia, Y., et al.: Going deeper with convolutions. In: IEEE Conference on Computer Vision and Pattern Recognition. IEEE Computer Society, pp. 1–9 (2015)
5. He, K., Zhang, X., Ren, S., et al.: Deep residual learning for image recognition. In: IEEE Conference on Computer Vision and Pattern Recognition. IEEE Computer Society, pp. 770–778 (2016)

6. He, K., Zhang, X., Ren, S., Sun, J.: Identity mappings in deep residual networks. In: Leibe, B., Matas, J., Sebe, N., Welling, M. (eds.) ECCV 2016. LNCS, vol. 9908, pp. 630–645. Springer, Cham (2016). https://doi.org/10.1007/978-3-319-46493-0_38

7. Szegedy, C., Ioffe, S., Vanhoucke, V., et al.: Inception-v4, Inception-ResNet and the impact of residual connections on learning. arXiv:1602.07261 (2016)

8. Hasani, B., Mahoor, M.H.: Spatio-temporal facial expression recognition using convolutional neural networks and conditional random fields. In: IEEE International Conference on Automatic Face & Gesture Recognition. IEEE, pp. 790–795 (2017)

9. Hasani, B., Mahoor, M.H.: Facial expression recognition using enhanced deep 3D convolutional neural networks. In: Computer Vision and Pattern Recognition Workshops, pp. 2278–2288 (2017)

10. Krizhevsky, A., Sutskever, I., Hinton, G.E.: ImageNet classification with deep convolutional neural networks. In: International Conference on Neural Information Processing Systems. Curran Associates Inc., pp. 1097–1105 (2012)

11. Ojala, T., Harwood, I.: A comparative study of texture measures with classification based on feature distributions. Pattern Recognit. 29(1), 51–59 (1996)

12. Ali, A., Hussain, S., Haroon, F., et al.: Face recognition with local binary patterns. Bahria Univ. J. Inf. Commun. Technol. 5(1), 46–50 (2014)

13. Ojala, T., Pietikinen, M., Menp, T.: Multiresolution grayscale and rotation invariant texture classification with local binary patterns. IEEE PAMI 24(7), 971–987 (2002)

14. Lucey, P., Cohn, J.F., Kanade, Y., Saragih, J., Ambadar, Z., Matthews, I.: The extended Cohn-Kanade dataset (CK+): a complete dataset for action unit and emotion-specified expression. In: 2010 IEEE Computer Society Conference on Computer Vision and Pattern Recognition-Workshops, pp. 94–101 (2010)

15. Tian, Y., Brown, L., Hampapur, A., Pankanti, S., Senior, A., Bolle, R.: Real world real-time automatic recognition of facial expression. In: Proceedings of IEEE Workshop on (2003)

16. Lyons, M., Akamatsu, S., Kamachi, M., et al.: Coding facial expressions with gabor wavelets. In: IEEE International Conference on Automatic Face and Gesture Recognition, pp. 200–205 (1998)

17. Song, Z., Ni, B., Guo, D., Sim, T., Yan, S.: Learning universal multi-view age estimator using video context. In: Proceedings of IEEE International Conference Computer Vision, pp. 241–248 (2011)

18. Lucey, P., Cohn, J., Lucey, S., Matthews, I., Sridharan, S., Prkachin, K.: Automatically detecting pain using facial actions. In: IEEE International Conference on Affective Computing and Intelligent Interaction, pp. 1–8 (2009)

19. Lecun, Y., Bottou, L., Bengio, Y.: Gradient-based learning applied to document recognition. Proc. IEEE 86(11), 2278–2324 (1998)

20. Krizhevsky, A., Sutskever, I., Hinton, G.E.: ImageNet classification with deep convolutional neural networks. Commun. ACM 60(2), 1097–1105 (2012)

21. Happy, S.L., Routray, A.: Automatic facial expression recognition using features of salient facial patches. IEEE Trans. Affect. Comput. 6(1), 1–12 (2015)

22. Rodriguez, P., Cucurull, G., Gonzàlez, J.: Deep pain: exploiting long short-term memory networks for facial expression classification. IEEE Trans. Cybern. 1–11 (2017). https://doi.org/10.1109/TCYB.2017.2662199

23. Mehrabian, A.: Communication without words. Psychol. Today 2(4), 53–56 (1968)

24. Picard, R.W.: Affective computing. MIT Press, vol. 1, no. 1, pp. 71–73 (1997)

25. Viola, P., Jones, M.J.: Robust real-time face detection. Int. J. Comput. Vis. 57(2), 137–154 (2004)

26. Ekman, P., Friesen, W.V.: Constants across cultures in the face and emotion. Pers. Soc. Psychol. 17(2), 124–129 (1971)

27. Ekman, P., Friesen, W.: Facial Action Coding System: A Technique for the Measurement of Facial Movement. Consulting Psychologists Press, Palo Alto (1978)
28. Suwa, M., Sugie, N., Fujimora, K.: A preliminary note on pattern recognition of human emotional expression. In: Proceedings of the Fourth International Joint Conference on Pattern Recognition, Kyoto, Japan, pp. 408–410 (1978)
29. Hinton, G.E., Salakhutdinov, R.R.: Reducing the dimensionality of data with neural networks. Science **313**, 504–507 (2006)
30. Lecun, Y.: Generalization and network design strategies. In: Connectionism in Perspective (1989)
31. Lv, Y., Feng, Z., Xu, C.: Facial expression recognition via deep learning. In: International Conference on Smart Computing. IEEE, pp. 347–355 (2015)
32. Tang, Y.: Deep learning using linear support vector machines. Eprint Arxiv (2013)
33. The FER2013 dataset. https://www.kaggle.com/c/challenges-in-representation-learning-facial-expression-recognition-challenge/data
34. Zheng, L., Shen, L., Tian, L.: Person re-identification meets image search. Comput. Sci. 1 (2015). https://doi.org/10.1109/TPAMI.2015.2505297

Deep CNN-Based Radar Detection for Real Maritime Target Under Different Sea States and Polarizations

Ningyuan Su[1], Xiaolong Chen[1($\boxtimes$)], Jian Guan[1], and Yuzhou Li[2]

[1] Radar Detection Research Section, Naval Aviation University,
Erma Road 188, Yantai, China
cxlcxl1209@163.com
[2] Huazhong University of Science and Technology, Wuhan, China

Abstract. Maritime target detection, because of the difficulties in the extraction and recognition of target and clutter micro-motion characteristics, has always been one of the difficulties in radar target detection. In this paper, convolutional neural networks are used for the detection of maritime target micro-Doppler. Firstly, using the IPIX measured sea clutter and target signal data, the two-dimensional time-frequency signal dataset is built by time-frequency analysis. Two Deep CNN models, LeNet and GoogLeNet are trained and used for the detection of maritime targets, and their performances are compared. Then the method is tested under different sea states and polarization. The results show that the proposed method can achieve high detection probability under different circumstance, which provides a new approach for the detection of maritime targets.

Keywords: Radar target detection · Deep learning ·
Convolutional neural network (CNN) · Sea clutter · Time-frequency analysis

1 Introduction

The detection of maritime targets is widely used in military and civilian applications. Radar is an important means of maritime target detection and surveillance. However, due to the sea clutter generated by complex marine environment and the diversification of maritime target types, reliable and robust maritime target detection is always one of the key technologies to be studied [2]. At present, the difficulty in maritime target detection mainly lies in sea clutter suppression, target high-resolution feature extraction, "low-slow-small" (low glancing angle, slow or stationary, small size) target detection. Traditional detection methods are usually based on statistical theory, which considers sea clutter as a stochastic process. But due to the diversified trend of target

This work was supported in part by the National Natural Science Foundation of China (61871391, U1633122, 61871392, 61531020), Project of Shandong Province Higher Educational Science and Technology Program (J17KB139), Young Elite Scientist Sponsorship Program of CAST.

and clutter models, it is difficult for traditional methods to achieve high performance detection in complex backgrounds [7]. The development of micro-Doppler technology provides an effective way for target detection [1]. The research shows that the maritime target also has micro-motion characteristics, which are mainly represented by changes in target speed and changes in posture such as roll, pitch and yaw caused by the impact of the wave. These changes are expressed as changes in the instantaneous velocity of the target or scattering point [7, 8], which can reflect the motion state of the target and provide more effective information for the detection of the maritime target. However, the micro-motion characteristics of the maritime target do not have the characteristics of regular frequency modulation period. Its time-varying causes difficulties in detection and extraction [9], and it is urgent to develop intelligent methods and means.

The deep learning method, which is rapidly developing in recent years, is an efficient intelligent processing method. Compared with the traditional Support Vector Machine (SVM [3]), it is more suitable for mining higher-dimensional abstract features [4], and has good generalization ability. And it has begun to be applied in the radar field. For example, detection method based on SAR image and deep learning can be used for detection and recognition of ground objects. Human body gesture recognition methods based on deep learning and Doppler radar have been used for gesture command recognition [7], gait recognition, abnormal posture (such as falling, drowning) detection and other fields. In addition, it has a very good application prospect in the recognition of high resolution range images, micro-Doppler spectra and distance Doppler spectra [5]. At present, most widely used deep learning models include Convolutional Neural Network (CNN), Recurrent Neural Network (RNN [10]), and Deep Belief Network (DBN [6]). Among them, CNN is the most commonly used algorithm in computer vision. This method can not only achieve high-precision classification, but also use the original image as input. Besides, no human intervention is required in the feature extraction process [11]. The method of ground armored target recognition, which is mentioned in document [12], can attain an accuracy of 99.13%. Since the micro-motion characteristics are time-varying, the time-frequency image is an effective analysis tool. Therefore, using deep learning for maritime target detection can not only make full use of the target micro-motion information, but also take advantage of the deep learning method in image processing, and realize the intelligent extraction and recognition of the micro-motion characteristics of target and clutter. In this paper, a maritime target detection method based on CNN is proposed. The time-frequency images of radar echo are distinguished by CNN (binary classification) to realize the differentiation of target and clutter. First, time-frequency analysis is performed on the IPIX [13] measured data to obtain time-frequency images. Then the time-frequency images are used to build datasets, which is used for CNN training and testing. Based on the results of testing, we compare the target detection performance of different CNN models, and analyze the influence of sea states and radar polarization on the model performance. Finally the research direction suitable for engineering applications is put forward.

2 Construction of Target Detection Model

In this paper, LeNet and GoogLeNet, which are common in CNN, are selected for the simulation of maritime target detection. A CNN mainly consists of multiple convolution layers, pooling layers and fully connected layers, and finally uses softmax to classify and output.

2.1 CNN Models

LeNet

A LeNet network consists of 7 layers (and an input layer). The structure of LeNet is shown in Fig. 1(a). It consists of two convolution layers, two fully connected layers and one softmax output layer. Each convolution layer is followed by a pooling layer. The input layer normalizes the input image to the size of 32 × 32 and inputs them to the convolution layer 1. The convolution layer 1 has six kinds of convolution kernel, and the size of each convolution kernel is 5 × 5. The output of convolution layer 1 are feature maps, size of 28 × 28, which is input to the pooling layer 1. The pooling layer 1, with a sampling area of 2 × 2 in size, uses max pooling function for down-sampling, which takes the largest feature point in the area. The fully connected layer computes the dot product between the input vector and the weight vector, plus an offset, and the result is output through the sigmoid function.

$$S(x) = \frac{1}{1 + e^{-x}} \tag{1}$$

The size of output feature map is 14 × 14. The input of convolution layer 2 is the combination of several feature maps in the output of the pooling layer 1. It has six kinds of convolution kernel, and the size of each convolution kernel is 5 × 5. The output of convolution layer 2 are feature maps, size of 10 × 10, which is input to the pooling layer 2. In pooling layer 2, the sampling area of the pooling layer 2 is 2 × 2, and the sampling mode is the same as that of the pooling layer 1. The size of output feature map is 5 × 5. The fully connected layer 1 is actually also a convolution layer, which has a convolution kernel size of 5 × 5. Since the convolution kernel is the same as the input in size, 120 convolution results of size 1 × 1 (120-dimensional vector) are formed after convolution operation, making this layer a fully connected layer. The input of the fully connected layer 2 is a 120-dimensional vector, and the dot product between the input vector and the weight vector is calculated, with an offset added. And the result is output through the sigmoid function.

The output layer uses a radial basis function (RBF) as network connection.

$$y_i = \sum_j (x_j - w_{ij})^2 \tag{2}$$

The closer the RBF output value is to 0, the closer the recognition result is to the i-th category.

GoogLeNet

GoogLeNet, as is shown in Fig. 1(b), is a convolutional neural network model built by increasing the depth and width of the network model. Its structure is shown in Fig. 1(c). It consists of 22 layers with more than 100 parameters. It uses RGB tri-color channels and the size of the sensed pixels is 224 × 224. To prevent the gradient from disappearing, it sets two loss functions of different depths to guarantee the return gradient. In order to avoid over-fitting and speed up the convergence, ReLU operations are performed after each convolution operation.

$$f(x) = \max(0, x) \tag{3}$$

It also increases the width of the network by using the inception module.

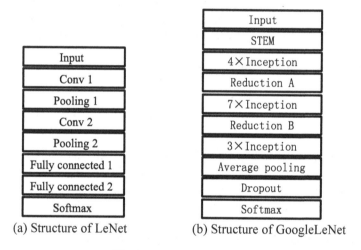

(a) Structure of LeNet   (b) Structure of GoogLeNet

Fig. 1. Structure of models

2.2   Model Training

This article is based on an environment architecture of Python2.7, VS2013, CUDA7.5, cudnn5.1, caffe, and realize the graphical interface processing of images through NVIDIA Digits. And the computer configuration includes a dual E5 processor, NVIDIA Quadro M2000 graphics card and an RAM of 24 GB. According to the convergence of loss value in the training process, the model training parameters are set as follows (Table 1):

Table 1. Parameter settings of model training

Parameter		Value
Iterations		30
Parameter solving algorithm		Stochastic gradient descent (SGD)
Learning rate	Initial learning rate	0.01
	Step size	30%
	Change rate	0.1

During training, the performance of network changes with the number of iterations done, which is shown in Fig. 2(b).

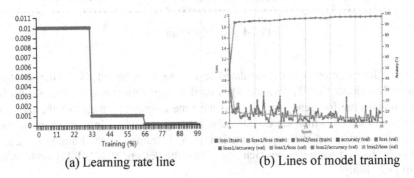

(a) Learning rate line   (b) Lines of model training

Fig. 2. Learning rate line

Digits can realize the visualization of data, weights and hidden layer output, etc. As shown in Fig. 3, (a) and (c) are the convolution kernels of the convolution layer 1 and the convolution layer 2, respectively. Figure 3(b) and (d) are feature maps of the convolution layer 1 and the convolution layer 2, respectively.

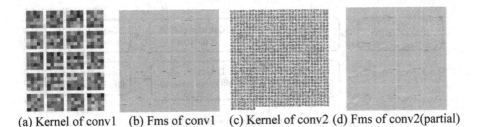

(a) Kernel of conv1   (b) Fms of conv1   (c) Kernel of conv2 (d) Fms of conv2(partial)

Fig. 3. Data characteristics of each convolution layer in Digits (e.g., LeNet).

2.3   Simulation and Algorithm Flow

The algorithm flow mainly includes three parts: (1) data preprocessing (2) dataset construction (3) target detection, and the flow chart is shown in Fig. 4.

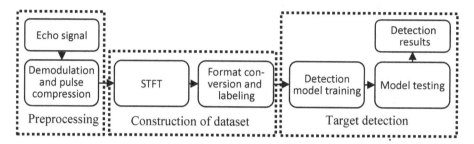

Fig. 4. The algorithm flow

First, the radar echo is demodulated and pulse compressed. Next, the short-time Fourier Transform (STFT, formula 4) is used to transform the echo signal into two-dimensional time-frequency images and the time-frequency images of the target and clutter are obtained, which are used to build training set and testing set. Then, the target detection is performed, the target detection model is trained by the training set, and the testing set is used for testing, which can obtain the detection probability and the false alarm probability.

$$\mathrm{STFT}(t,f) = \int_{-\infty}^{+\infty} [s_p(t)g^*(u-t)]\mathrm{e}^{-\mathrm{j}2\pi fu}\mathrm{d}u \tag{4}$$

In formula 4, $g(t)$ is the function of Hamming window, and $S_P(t)$ is the preprocessed signal.

The process of simulation is shown in Fig. 5.

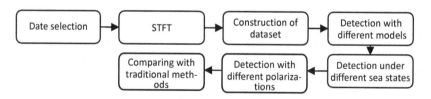

Fig. 5. Flow of process of simulation

First, the processed signal is transformed to time-frequency images through short-time Fourier transform. Then the datasets are built with time-frequency images, after format conversion and labeling. Two different target detection models were trained with the training sets, and the testing sets were used to test and compare the performance of trained models. The model with better performance is selected to classify the target and clutter samples under different sea states, to analyze the influence of sea states on the performance of target detection. Then a new model is trained and tested with clutter and target samples obtained under a certain sea state, and the results are compared with previous ones to analyze the generalization ability of models. Then, new models are trained and tested by the target and clutter samples obtained under four different polarization modes, to compare the performance of different polarization modes in target detection.

3   Simulation and Analysis Based on IPIX Data

3.1   Dataset

This paper uses the standard measured data of sea clutter and targets collected by MacMaster University using IPIX [13] radar in the Dartmouth area of in Canada in 1989. The parameters of IPIX radar are as follows (Table 2):

Table 2. Radar parameters

Parameter	Value	Parameter	Value
Peak power	8 kW	Antenna diameter	2.4 m
Width of beam	0.9° pencil beam	Antenna gain	44 dB
Sidelobes	<−30 dB	Polarization mode	HH; HV; VH; VV
Instantaneous dynamic range	>50 dB	Radar transmitting frequency	9.39 GHz
Pulse repetition frequency	1000 Hz	Distance resolution	30 m

The data we use includes data collected under the level 2, 3, 4 sea states with four different polarization modes: HH, HV, VH and VV. The weather and sea state information are as follows (Table 3):

Table 3. Weather and sea state information

Sea state	Temperature	Wave height	Wave period	Wind speed
Level 2	4.9 °C	1.0 m	5.5 s	4 m/s
Level 3	8.6 °C	1.5 m	5.2 s	6 m/s
Level 4	7.7 °C	2.1 m	8.2 s	9 m/s

The data sampling time is 131 s, with the first 90 s of signal used to build the training set and the last 41 s of signal used to build the testing set. The length of each sample is 1024 points, and the time-frequency image, generated through the short-time Fourier transform (STFT), are the original image to build datasets. During the construction of the dataset, the original image is compressed into a 256×256 color image and labeled according to the category (Table 4).

Table 4. Examples of dataset

	Sea state level 2		Sea state level 3		Sea state level 4	
	Clutter	Target	Clutter	Target	Clutter	Target
HH						
HV						
VH						
VV						

In IPIX data, the target is of low velocity. Under the level 2 sea state, the Doppler shift of clutter is small, and the spectra of clutter is overlap with that of target. Under the level 3 sea state, the clutter has a larger Doppler shift, making its spectra separated with that of target. Under the level 4 sea state, the clutter is close to Gaussian distribution and sea spikes are more dispersed

3.2   Analysis of Performance of Target Detection

Comparison of Target Detection Performance of Different Models
In the simulation experiment of comparison of different detection models' performance, the data's signal polarization mode uses HH polarization, and the training set consists of 9000 samples, including 4500 clutter samples and 4500 target samples. In each category, the samples collected under each sea state consists 1/3 of the dataset. 20% of the samples of training set are separated as validation set. The testing set consists of 3000 samples including 1500 clutter samples and 1500 target samples, and the samples collected under each sea state consists 1/3 of the dataset. Training and testing results are shown in the Table 5.

Table 5. Results of detection of two models

Model	Detection probability	False alarm probability	Time
LeNet	91.06%	5.28%	195 s
GoogLeNet	95.43%	4.37%	242 s

The results show that under the HH polarization mode, compared with LeNet, GoogLeNet has better performance in target detection under various sea conditions, with lower false alarm probability and higher detection probability.

Influence of Sea States on Target Detection Performance

According to the results above, the trained GoogLeNet model is used to test the dataset built by echo signals in different sea conditions. The testing set of each sea state contains 1500 target samples and 1500 clutter samples collected under the corresponding sea state. The results are shown in the Table 6.

Table 6. Results of target detection under different sea states

Sea states	Level 2	Level 3	Level 4
Detection probability	85.98%	100.00%	99.67%
False alarm probability	1.86%	8.04%	5.05%

Under the level 2 sea state, the false alarm probability is the lowest, but the corresponding detection probability is also the lowest. The detection probability under level 3 and level 4 sea states are close to 100%, but the false alarm probability is also much higher.

We then consider using the samples collected under a certain sea state to train the model. The training set consisted of 4,500 clutter samples and 4,500 target samples in the same sea state, from which 20% of the samples were isolated as a validation set. Then we test the model with the same testing set as above simulation. The results are shown in Table 7.

Table 7. Results of target detection of models trained by certain sea state samples

Sea states	Level 2	Level 3	Level 4
Detection probability	88.11%%	100.00%	95.55%
False alarm probability	2.72%	0.27%	1.99%

By comparing the simulation results, it can be found that under high sea conditions, using the signal of a certain sea state as samples for model training can reduce the false alarm probability of target detection, which is maintain within 0.03.

Influence of Polarizations on Target Detection Performance

In the simulation experiment of comparison of different polarization modes, the training set and testing set are built with signals collected with the same polarization, under sea state 2. The training set includes 4500 clutter samples and 4500 target samples (including 10% proof set samples), and the testing set includes 1500 clutter samples and 1500 signal samples. The simulation results are shown in the Table 8.

Table 8. Results of target detection with different polarization modes

Polarization mode	HH	HV	VH	VV
Detection probability	89.57%	87.04%	87.18%	88.70%
False alarm probability	3.26%	3.85%	2.72%	2.92%

The polarization mode has influence on the target detection performance. The detection probability is higher under HH polarization mode, reaching 89.57%, while the false alarm probability is lower under VH polarization mode, which is 0.0272.

The results above shows that: (1) the maritime target can be detected by the method of deep learning and time-frequency analysis. Under the sea states of level 2, 3, 4, the detection probability exceeds 85.98%. (2) Training the models with samples collected under a certain sea state to adapt to certain environment can improve the performance of the model by reducing false alarm probability, especially under higher sea states. (3) Radar polarization mode has influence on detection performance. The detection probability is the highest under HH polarization mode, and the false alarm probability is the lowest under VH polarization mode. (4) Among the two models mentioned in this paper, LeNet is more efficient in radar echo processing, but GoogLeNet has better performance in terms of detecting probability and false alarm probability. (5) The results obtained in this paper are obviously worse than the results based on the simulation data. In addition to the diversity of the measured data itself, the targets' low speed and acceleration in IPIX data may also contribute to this difference. Under this circumstance, the Doppler spectrum of targets overlap with that of sea clutter.

4   Conclusion

This paper proposes a maritime target detection method based on CNN. In this method, the time-frequency images of the radar echo signal is classified using the CNN model. The clutter unit and target unit data in the IPIX radar real measured data are used for CNN training and testing for the detection of maritime targets. The detection results reflect the high-precision and intelligent advantages of CNN in target and clutter feature extraction and recognition of radar signal time-frequency image processing applications. Next, study of judgment criteria, simulation process optimization and use of other measured data will be carried out, based on the problems such as high false alarm probability and weak generalization ability of the model. Further studies will be done to verify and improve the detection performance of the method for different targets in different environments.

References

1. Luo, Y., Zhang, Q., Wang, G., Guan, H., Bai, Y.: Micro-motion signature extraction method for wideband radar based on complex image OMP decomposition. J. Radars **1**(4), 361–369 (2012)
2. Darzikolaei, M.A., Ebrahimzade, A., Gholami, E.: Classification of radar clutters with artificial neural network. In: 2015 2nd International Conference on Knowledge-Based Engineering and Innovation, pp. 577–581 (2015)
3. Wagner, S.A.: SAR ATR by a combination of convolutional neural network and support vector machines. IEEE Trans. Aerosp. Electron. Syst. **52**(6), 2861–2872 (2016)
4. Tian, Z., Zhan, R., Hu, J., Zhang, J.: SAR ATR based on convolutional neural network. J. Radars **5**(3), 320–325 (2016)
5. Wang, J., Zheng, T., Lei, P., Wei, S.: Study on deep learning in radar. J. Radars **7**(4), 395–411 (2018)
6. Wang, X., Zhou, Y., Zhou, D., Chen, Z., Tian, Y.: Research on low probability of intercept radar signal recognition using deep belief network and bispectra diagonal slice. J. Electron. Inf. Technol. **38**(11), 2972–2976 (2016)
7. Chen, X., Guan, J., He, Y.: Applications and prospect of micro-motion theory in the detection of sea surface target. J. Radars **2**(1), 123–134 (2013)
8. Chen, X., Guan, J., Bao, Z., He, Y.: Detection and extraction of target with micro-motion in spiky sea clutter via short-time fractional Fourier transform. IEEE Trans. Geosci. Remote Sens. **52**(2), 1002–1018 (2014)
9. Chen, X., Guan, J., Li, X., He, Y.: Effective coherent integration method for marine target with micromotion via phase differentiation and radon-Lv's distribution. IET Radar Sonar Navig. (Spec. Issue: Micro-Doppler) **9**(9), 1284–1295 (2015)
10. Xu, B., Chen, B., Liu, H., Jin, L.: Attention-based recurrent neural network model for radar high-resolution range profile target recognition. J. Electron. Inf. Technol. **38**(12), 2988–2995 (2016)
11. Xu, Z., Wang, R., Li, N., Zhang, H., Zhang, L.: A novel approach to change detection in SAR images with CNN classification. J. Radars **6**(5), 483–491 (2017)
12. Xu, F., Wang, H., Jin, Y.: Deep learning as applied in SAR target recognition and terrain classification. J. Radars **6**, 1–13 (2017)
13. Yan, L., Sun, P., Yi, L., Han, N., Tang, J.: Modeling of compound-gaussian sea clutter based on an inverse gaussian distribution. J. Radars **2**(4), 461–465 (2013)

Information Processing and Automatic Driving

Rapid Precipitation Shifts in a Black Soil Region

Wenfeng Wang[1], Xi Chen[1(✉)], Xiaoliang Zhang[2], Hongwei Zheng[1],
Ruide Yu[1], and Jianjun Yu[3]

[1] CAS Research Center for Ecology and Environment of Central Asia,
Xinjiang Institute of Ecology and Geography, Chinese Academy of Sciences,
Urumqi 830011, China
chenxi@ms.xjb.ac.cn
[2] Laboratory of Computational Mathematics,
College of Statistics and Management,
Shanghai University of Finance and Economics, Shanghai 200433, China
[3] Environmental Change Institute, University of Oxford, Oxford OX1 3QY, UK

Abstract. Improving remote sensing precipitation products is essential important for a correct understanding of regional climate action and land surface feedbacks although, until now, influence of precipitation distribution and its evolution on retrieval accuracies remains poorly understood, especially in black soil regions, which characterize about 3% of the Earth's total land surface. This study examines precipitation shifts in the Hulan River Basin - a cold watershed located in a black soil region in Northeast China, analyzes influences of such precipitation shifts on performance of the current remote sensing precipitation products within the considered region, and particularly in sub-regions with rapid precipitation shifts, investigates how well can precipitation occurrence, amounts and trends be detected from space. Utilizing local precipitation data and three latest TRMM products (3B42V7, 3B42RT, CHIRPS), rapid precipitation shifts in the region and their evident influences on retrieval accuracies are proved. Nevertheless, there are still considerable uncertainties associated with the mechanisms and drivers of such precipitation shifts and it remains undetermined whether such rapid precipitation shifts are representative in other black soil regions. These two unresolved issues are essentially significant, and therefore, should be future research priorities towards a better performance of remote sensing precipitation products in black soil regions.

Keywords: Retrieval · Climate action · Land surface feedbacks

1 Introduction

Satellite remote sensing has provided major advances in understanding the climate system and its changes, but the short duration of observation series and their uncertainties still pose challenges for capturing the robust long-term trends of many climate variables [1]. Improving remote sensing precipitation products is hence important for a correct understanding of regional and global climate action although, until now, accurate observation of precipitation in different regions of the world is still a great

F. Sun et al. (Eds.): ICCSIP 2018, CCIS 1006, pp. 335–349, 2019.
https://doi.org/10.1007/978-981-13-7986-4_30

challenge, especially in regions with sparse gauge networks and its high spatiotemporal variability [2]. Recent studies confirmed strong feedbacks between the atmosphere and terrestrial biosphere and indicated that variability in terrestrial vegetation growth and phenology can modulate water fluxes from/to the atmosphere [3, 4]. Consequently, there are still considerable uncertainties associated with the mechanisms and controls of precipitation patterns [5–7]. Complexity in estimating the past and future extreme short-duration rainfall demands a better understanding of regional precipitation evolution and its potential effect on local performance of remote sensing products [8].

A substantial amount of frictional dissipation in the atmosphere occurs in the microphysical shear zones surrounding falling precipitation shown that changes in the hydrological cycle could potentially have a direct impact on the amount of kinetic energy generated and dissipated by the atmospheric circulation [9]. Taking it together with strong feedbacks between the atmosphere and terrestrial biosphere, such a direct impact also implies that bias in the precipitation retrieval can be partly attributed to the evolution of precipitation patterns [9–11]. For the convenience of statement, the regional evolution of precipitation patterns is termed as precipitation shifts throughout the paper, which can also be explained as a part of hydrological shifts [12]. Improving remote sensing products by considering effect of precipitation shifts is feasible and exactly, some previous studies described the procedure to correct high resolution satellite rainfall estimation for parallax error and shows how these adjustments can be performed on any satellite rainfall estimation technique [13–16].

Black regions represent the most fecund lands in the world although, they are only no more than 3% of the Earth's total land surface. Because of high sensitivity of the fecund soils to precipitation changes, the land surface feedbacks to precipitation shifts are also more sensitive in black soil regions. Black soil region in Northeast China is one of the three largest black lands in the world - the four provinces/autonomous regions in Northeast China, namely Heilongjiang, Jilin, Liaoning and Inner Mongolia (except for the west part of Liaoning, Chifeng City, the South part of Tongliao City and the west part of Hulunbeir City) belong to the black soil region [17–19]. Furthermore, it has been proved that there was a significant variability in precipitation amounts and distribution within Northeast China over the past decades [20–22]. Detection of precipitation shifts in this region and validation of shifts effect on retrieval accuracies can motivate a better explanation of overall performance of remote sensing precipitation products in black soil regions and meanwhile, can present a new direction to improve the regional and global remote sensing precipitation products [23–25].

The major objectives in this study were to address three questions, as follows:

(1) Do precipitation changes in the considered region indicate a significant shift on annual scale?
(2) If so, are such rapid precipitation shifts significantly influencing performance of the current remote sensing precipitation products within the considered region?
(3) Under the background, particularly in sub-regions with rapid precipitation shifts, how well can precipitation occurrence, amounts and trends be detected from space?

2 Materials and Methods

2.1 Study Area and Datasets

A small watershed, named the Hulan River basin, was selected as the study area, which locates in a black soil region of Heilongjiang Province, China, constituting the region between longitude 125.9°E to 128.8°E and latitudes 46.18°N to 48.13°N. DEM data with a resolution of 90 m generated by GSC (the geospatial data cloud) in Chinese Academy of Sciences and ASTER (the Advanced Space-borne Thermal Emission and Reflection Radiometer) and GDEM (the Global Digital Elevation Model) from the NASA and METI (the Ministry of Economy, Trade, and Industry) in the United States, the elevation range within the basin is of 7–1427 km. The total area of the basin is about 35683 km^2 (Fig. 1).

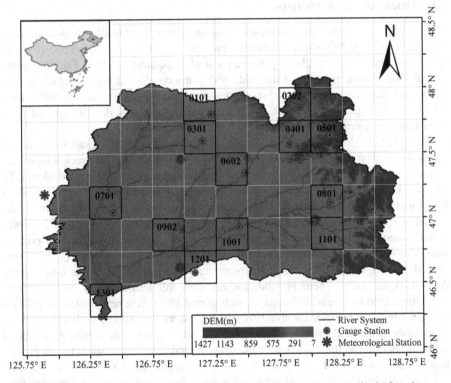

Fig. 1. Location of the study area and distribution of gauge and meteorological stations.

Climate in the Hulan River Basin is cold and semi-humid. There are four meteorological stations, and particularly for observation of precipitation amounts, there are sixteen additional gauge stations. According to the observed data collected from the local meteorological stations over the past decades (1953–2010), the average precipitation amounts within the basin is about 547 mm and annual mean air temperature is about 4.5 °C. Period considered in this study is 2001–2006 (gauge data after 2006 are governmentally secret), for which three remote sensing products (3B42V7, 3B42RT, CHIRPS) and the gauging precipitation data (collected from the meteorological and gauge stations) are available. Both the gauge observations and remote sensing products are sufficiently utilized on explicit temporal scales (daily, monthly and annually) to present a fully understanding of the effect of precipitation shifts on retrieval accuracies. Note that 3B42V7 is available after March 2000 and the available time of 3B42RT, CHIRPS are a little earlier, investigation on 2001–2006 is enough for our major objectives. For a direct cell to cell comparison with the gauge data, retrieval precipitation data were evaluated, originally at grids of 0.25° which were aggregated to a resolution of 0.05°.

2.2   Calculation and Analyses

The 16 gauge observations and remote sensing products were interpolated onto the same grid using IDW, whose robustness has been validated in widespread practical applications and does not rely on particular statistical assumptions [11]. Daily, monthly annual precipitation amounts at the grids within the considered region, which are the major basic data for partition of sub-regions and abstraction of precipitation shifts, were calculated after gap filling of the gauge data and the amounts data interpreted from three remote sensing products.

Precipitation shifts considered in the present study include spatial shifts in the distribution of precipitation, temporal shifts in the amounts of precipitation and majorly, integration of the spatial and temporal shifts (termed as integrated shifts). To abstract the spatial shifts, annual distribution of precipitation within the Hulan River Basin was partitioned as four sub-regions, respectively in each year, according to the annual average precipitation amount based on the data collected from four meteorological stations, denoted by x. Four spatial sub-regions are areas with annual precipitation amounts falling into four intervals, $(-\infty, x - 100)$, $[x - 100, x)$, $[x, x + 100)$, $(x + 100, +\infty)$, respectively, and the sub-regions with spatial shifts in the k-th year are defined as the areas where precipitation amounts fall into different intervals from $k - 1$-th year to k-th year. Sub-regions with spatial shifts were represented by colorful areas, while the sub-regions without spatial shifts were represented by blank areas. In accordance with the definition of spatial shifts, sub-regions with significant temporal shifts are defined as the areas where the absolute value of difference between precipitation amounts of $k - 1$-th year and k-th year are larger than 100 mm. Consequently, sub-regions with significant integrated shifts are defined as the areas with precipitation amounts falling into different intervals from $k - 1$-th year to k-th year and at the same time, with absolute value of annual difference between precipitation amounts larger than 100 mm. Integrated shifts are also defined as the final effective shifts.

Only the final effective shifts were employed to examine the shifts effect on retrieval accuracies, where evaluation of shifts effect was carried out. Utilizing the gauge data and remote sensing data in 13 grids and the corresponding gap filling data, the overall performance of three remote sensing products was examined and the shifts degree (defined as $1 - \sigma$, where σ is slope of the slope-intercept line between the gauging data to the remote sensing data) and shifts distance (defined as the intercept of the slope-intercept line between the gauging data to the remote sensing data) were calculated and preliminarily attributed to shifts effect. Finally, sub-regions with significant integrated shifts and the best remote sensing product chosen from 3B42V7, 3B42RT, CHIRPS by the overall performance, were employed to detect misdiagnosis of precipitation occurrence (validated by the conditional successful index, denoted by CSI)), overestimates and underestimates of precipitation amounts (bias) and scrambled precipitation trends (validated by the time series dependence, denoted by CC) were also presented, which displays the retrieval performance during 2001–2006 in a direct, simple and visual way within the sub-regions with significant integrated shifts.

Definitions of CSI, bias and CC are as follows [16, 26, 27]:

$$CSI = \frac{U}{U + V + W} \tag{1}$$

$$BIAS = \frac{\sum\limits_{i=1}^{n}(R_i - G_i)}{\sum\limits_{i=1}^{n}G_i} \times 100\% \tag{2}$$

$$CC = \frac{\sum\limits_{i=1}^{n}(G_i - \overline{G})(R_i - \overline{R})}{\sqrt{\sum\limits_{i=1}^{n}(G_i - \overline{G})^2}\sqrt{\sum\limits_{i=1}^{n}(R_i - \overline{R})^2}} \tag{3}$$

where U is the frequency of precipitation occurrence in gauge and retrieval data, V is the frequency of precipitation occurrence in gauge data but not in retrieval data, W is the frequency of precipitation occurrence in retrieval data but not in gauge data, G_i, R_i are gauge and retrieval data of precipitation amounts (mm), $\overline{G}$, $\overline{R}$ the average gauge and retrieval data of precipitation amounts (mm), respectively.

3   Results and Discussions

3.1   Rapid Precipitation Shifts

There are evident spatial shifts in precipitation distribution in the Hulan River Basin during 2001–2006. The total area of the sub-regions with spatial shifts in precipitation distribution from 2001 to 2002 is 5422 km^2, which occupies more than 15% area of the basin. The total area of the sub-regions with spatial shifts in precipitation distribution from 2002 to 2003 is 15717 km^2, which occupies more than 44% area of the basin. The total area of the sub-regions with spatial shifts in precipitation distribution from 2003 to 2004 is 8210 km^2, which occupies more than 23% area of this basin. The total area of the sub-regions with spatial shifts in precipitation distribution from 2004 to 2005 is 6256 km^2, which occupies about 18% of the basin area.

The total area of the sub-regions with spatial shifts in precipitation distribution from 2005 to 2006 is 13983 km^2, which occupies more than 39% area of the Hulan River Basin. Consequently, the accumulated area of the sub-regions with spatial shifts in precipitation distribution during 2001–2006 is 20788 km^2, which occupies more than 58% area of the considered region. Spatial shifts in precipitation distribution during 2001–2006 in the Hulan River Basin are rapid, with an average rate of 3465 km^2/year (Fig. 2).

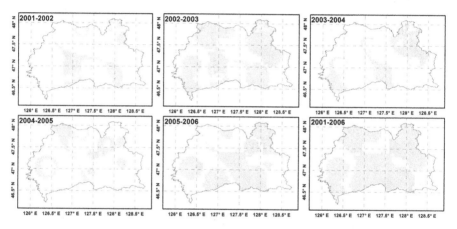

Fig. 2. Sub-regions (colorful) with significant shifts in precipitation distribution during 2001–2006. (Color figure online)

Significant temporal shifts in precipitation amounts (>100 mm) almost covered the whole basin during 2001–2006. The total area of the sub-regions with temporal shifts in precipitation amounts from 2001 to 2002 is 26561 km^2, which occupies more than 74% area of the basin. The total area of the sub-regions with temporal shifts in precipitation amounts from 2002 to 2003 is 28339 km^2, which occupies more than 79% area of the basin. The total area of the sub-regions with temporal shifts in precipitation amounts from 2003 to 2004 is 28558 km^2, which occupies more than 80% area of the basin. The total area of the sub-regions with temporal shifts in precipitation amounts from 2004 to 2005 was significantly reduced, which is 9856 km^2 and occupies more than 28% area of the basin. The total area of the sub-regions with temporal shifts in precipitation amounts from 2005 to 2006 was further reduced, which is 3666 km^2 and occupies only about 10% area of the basin.

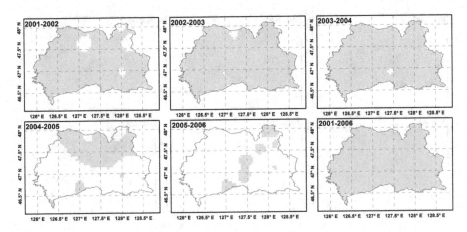

Fig. 3. Sub-regions (colorful) with significant temporal shifts (>100 mm) in precipitation amounts during 2001–2006. (Color figure online)

Consequently, the accumulated area of the sub-regions with temporal shifts in precipitation amounts during 2001–2006 is 28690 km^2. Alternatively, more than 80% area of the considered region have significant temporal shifts in precipitation amounts (>100 mm) during 2001–2006.

Temporal shifts in precipitation distribution during 2001–2006 in the Hulan River Basin are rapid (Fig. 3).

There are unneglectable integrated shifts in precipitation distribution and amounts in the Hulan River Basin during 2001–2006. The total area of the sub-regions with integrated shifts in precipitation from 2001 to 2002 is 4478 km^2, which occupies about 13% area of the basin. The total area of the sub-regions with integrated shifts in precipitation from 2002 to 2003 is 15432 km^2, which occupies more than 43% area of the basin. The total area of the sub-regions with integrated shifts in precipitation was significantly reduced from 2003 to 2004, which is 8078 km^2 and occupies about 23% area of the basin. The total area of the sub-regions with integrated shifts in precipitation from 2004 to 2005 was further reduced, which is 3907 km^2 and occupies about 11% area of the basin. The total area of the sub-regions with integrated shifts in precipitation from 2005 to 2006 is 3644 km^2, which occupies only about 10% area of the basin. Consequently, the accumulated area of the sub-regions with integrated shifts in precipitation during 2001–2006 is more than 57% area of the Hulan River Basin, implying a rapid integrated shift with an average rate almost equal to that of spatial shifts (Fig. 4).

Therefore, precipitation changes in the considered region indicated a significant shift in the local precipitation distribution and amounts on annual scale. It is certainly worthy to investigate whether such rapid precipitation shifts can significantly influence performance of the current remote sensing precipitation products within the considered black soil region.

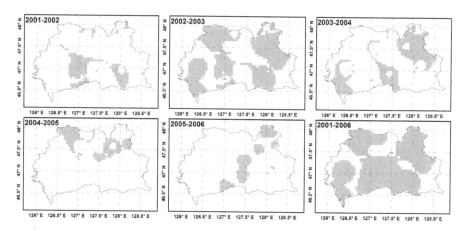

Fig. 4. Sub-regions (colorful) with significant integrated shifts in local precipitation during 2001–2006. (Color figure online)

3.2   Evident Shifts Effect

Improving remote sensing precipitation products is important for a correct understanding of regional climate action and land surface feedbacks although, until now, there are still considerable uncertainties associated with the reasons for difference between the performance of different retrieval products. Hypothesizing that shifts degree and shifts distance of three remote sensing products within the Hulan River Basin in the precipitation retrieval performance can be partly attributed to the rapid precipitation shifts, then effect of the rapid precipitation shifts on retrieval accuracies of precipitation distribution and amounts, which was evaluated utilizing the gauge and remote sensing data in 13 grids within the Hulan River station, is much more evident in the overall performance of 3B42RT than that in the overall performance 3B42V7 and CHIRPS. The shifts effect is universally evident on daily, monthly and seasonal scales. The shifts degree of 3B42RT on daily, monthly and seasonal scales are 1.007, 1.099, 1.182, respectively, and the shifts distance of 3B42RT on daily, monthly and seasonal scales are 2.082, 67.541, 213.935, respectively, implying significant bias in retrieval performance. Shifts degree of 3B42V7 on daily, monthly and seasonal scales are 0.336, 0.007, 0.047, respectively, and the shifts distance of 3B42V7 on daily, monthly and seasonal scales are 0.619, 3.252, 4.340, respectively. Shifts degree of CHIRPS on daily, monthly and seasonal scales are 0.471, 0.055, 0.027, respectively, and the shifts distance of CHIRPS on daily, monthly and seasonal scales are 0.768, 4.411, 2.084, respectively. The overall performance of 3B42V7 is much better than the performance of 3B42RT and is a little better than CHIRPS performance (Fig. 5), which was further validated by performance of remote sensing precipitation products, particularly in the overestimates and underestimates of precipitation amounts and the diagnosis of precipitation occurrence within the considered region (Fig. 6).

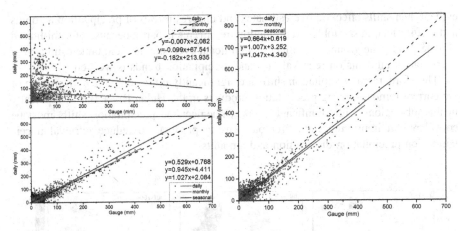

Fig. 5. Temporal performance of remote sensing precipitation products within the considered region.

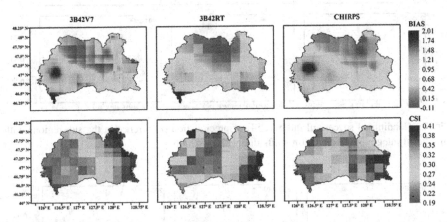

Fig. 6. Performance of remote sensing precipitation products, particularly in estimates of precipitation amounts (validated by bias) and diagnosis of precipitation occurrence (validated by conditional successful index (CSI) in the basin.

Further investigation on the retrieval performance of the best remote sensing product - 3B42V7, particularly in sub-regions with rapid precipitation shifts, implies that the current remote sensing products are suffering from reduced accuracies in these sub-regions, which resulted in misdiagnosis of precipitation occurrence (Fig. 7; the average probability of correct judgement is less than 0.34 during 2001–2006), overestimates and underestimates of precipitation amounts (Fig. 8; there is an average overestimate of 9.6% during 2001–2006, where the largest overestimates amounted to 27% in 2002 and only in 2005, the overall performance indicated an average underestimate) and scrambled precipitation trends (Fig. 9; the average of time series correlation efficient is 58.5%, implying an undistinguished performance on characterizing the precipitation trends). Over in all, shifts effect on diagnosis of precipitation occurrence is much more evident than shifts effect on overestimates and underestimates of precipitation amounts and shifts effect on scrambled precipitation trend. This is partly because of semi-humid climate. Under the ground, the effect of significant overestimates and underestimates of precipitation amounts on retrieval bias and precipitation trends is weaken.

Therefore, rapid precipitation shifts are significantly influencing the performance of the current remote sensing precipitation products in the Hulan River Basin, especially in the sub-regions with significant shifts. Unneglectable precipitation shifts must be considered in improving future remote sensing products to reduce retrieval uncertainties on precipitation distribution and amounts.

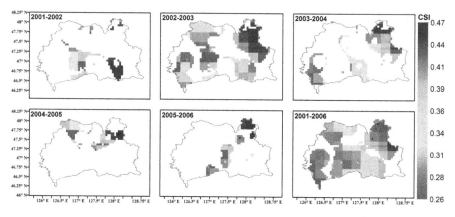

Fig. 7. Conditional successful index (CSI) of precipitation occurrence in the sub-regions with significant integrated precipitation shifts during 2001–2006.

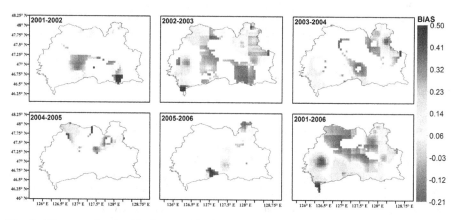

Fig. 8. Bias associated with the precipitation overestimates and underestimates in the sub-regions with significant integrated precipitation shifts during 2001–2006.

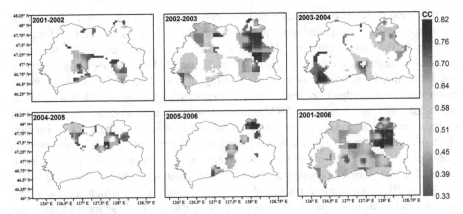

Fig. 9. Time series dependence (CC) associated with precipitation trends in the sub-regions with significant integrated precipitation shifts during 2001–2006.

It has been widely recognized that distribution of precipitation and its evolution play a vital role in regulating regional climate, atmospheric environments and land vegetation coverage, but response of precipitation shifts to the local vegetation changes and land surface feedbacks are still poorly understood [30–34]. Despite of these studies, a key problem is still unresolved - how well can these precipitation shifts be detected from space, alternatively, can such shifts been properly interpreted by the current remote sensing products of precipitation [35–39]? This research presents a solution to the issue and cautions that rapid precipitation shifts in black soil regions have not been properly interpreted by the current remote sensing products of precipitation. Precipitation changes in the considered region indicate a significant shift on annual scale and such rapid precipitation shifts have significantly influenced retrieval performance of the current remote sensing precipitation products within the considered region. Under the background, the current remote sensing products are suffering from a series of problems, such as misdiagnosis of precipitation occurrence, overestimates and underestimates of precipitation amounts and scrambled precipitation trends, which are evident especially in sub-regions with rapid precipitation shifts.

It is worthy to note that analyses in the present study was carried out under the hypothesis that shifts degree and shifts distance of three remote sensing products within the Hulan River Basin in the precipitation retrieval performance can be partly attributed to the rapid precipitation shifts. Such a hypothesis is exactly necessary and reasonable - improving remote sensing precipitation products is important for a correct understanding of regional climate action and land surface feedbacks although, until now, there are still considerable uncertainties associated with the explanations of the difference between the performance of different retrieval products [40]. One essential reason is the uncertainties in spectral properties have significant implications to remote sensing of precipitation and assimilation of the retrieval data [41]. Because of these intractable uncertainties, any attempts to explain the difference between the performance of different retrieval products should be encouraged. Results in the present study suggest difference in the spectral responses to precipitation shifts as a possible explanation although, further evidences are still necessary.

Black soil region in Northeast China is one of the three major black lands in the world - except the west part of Liaoning Province, Chifeng City, the South part of Tongliao City and the west part of Hulunbeir City, all other areas in the four provinces/autonomous regions in Northeast China, namely Heilongjiang, Jilin, Liaoning and Inner Mongolia, belong to the black soil region [29]. This study detected precipitation shifts in the hulan river basin - a cold watershed located in a black soil region in Northeast China, and three latest TRMM products are utilized to examine the shifts effect on local retrieval accuracy. Therefore, rapid precipitation shifts in the black soil region are highlighted and the shifts effect on precipitation retrieval accuracies are proved. Consequently, the results about the rapid precipitation shifts and their effect on accuracies of remote sensing products are also representative in Northeast China [42–44].

About 3% of the Earth's total land surface are black lands, which represents the most fecund lands in the world. Because of high sensitivity of these most fecund soils to precipitation changes, the land surface feedbacks to rapid precipitation shifts are also most sensitive in black soil regions. Consequently, the response of the precipitation shifts to the vegetation changes and land surface feedbacks are also unneglectable in the subsequent studies [45]. For a better understanding of the regional climate action and land surface changes, it is also emergent to characterize precipitation shifts in black soil regions and examine the effect of such shifts on local retrieval accuracies within the other black soil regions around the world [40, 46–51]. Especially, there are still considerable uncertainties associated with the overall magnitude of precipitation shifts in black soil regions and the mechanisms and drivers of such rapid shifts. Considering the vital role of black soil in protect the local agricultural production and its significant contributions to improve the local environments, these unresolved issues are essentially significant, and therefore, should be future research priorities towards a better performance of remote sensing precipitation products in black soil regions.

4   Concluding Remarks

Precipitation in the Hulan River basin has significant shifts on annual scale. Such rapid shifts are significantly influencing the retrieval performance on local precipitation. Alternatively, the current remote sensing products are suffering from a series of problems, such as misdiagnosis of precipitation occurrence, overestimates and underestimates of precipitation amounts and scrambled precipitation trends, which are evident especially in sub-regions with rapid precipitation shifts. To improve remote sensing precipitation products in black soil regions, understanding of the mechanisms and drivers of rapid precipitation shifts and determining whether such shifts are representative in other black soil regions should be future research priorities.

Acknowledgments. This research was financially supported by the National Natural Science Foundation of China (41571299) and the "Thousand Talents" plan (Y474161).

Competing Interests
None declared.

References

1. Yang, J., Gong, P., Fu, R., et al.: The role of satellite remote sensing in climate change studies. Nat. Clim. Chang. **3**(10), 875–883 (2013)
2. Sapiano, M.R.P., Arkin, P.A.: An intercomparison and validation of high-resolution satellite precipitation estimates with 3-hourly gauge data. J. Hydrometeorol. **10**(1), 149–166 (2009)
3. Green, J.K., Konings, A.G., Alemohammad, S.H., et al.: Regionally strong feedbacks between the atmosphere and terrestrial biosphere. Nat. Geosci. (2017). https://doi.org/10.1038/ngeo2957
4. Wicaksono, S.A., Russell, J.M., Holbourn, A., et al.: Hydrological and vegetation shifts in the Wallacean region of central Indonesia since the Last Glacial Maximum. Quat. Sci. Rev. **157**, 152–163 (2017)
5. Wang, G., Wang, D., Trenberth, K.E., et al.: The peak structure and future changes of the relationships between extreme precipitation and temperature. Nat. Clim. Chang. **3**(7), 268–274 (2017)
6. Wilhelm, B., Arnaud, F., Sabatier, P., et al.: 1400 years of extreme precipitation patterns over the Mediterranean French Alps and possible forcing mechanisms. Quat. Res. **78**(1), 1–12 (2012)
7. Nosetto, M.D., Jobbágy, E.G., Tóth, T., et al.: Regional patterns and controls of ecosystem salinization with grassland afforestation along a rainfall gradient. Glob. Biogeochem. Cycles **22**(2), 65 (2008)
8. Zhang, X., Zwiers, F.W., Li, G., et al.: Complexity in estimating past and future extreme short-duration rainfall. Nat. Geosci. **3**(7), 423–427 (2017)
9. Pauluis, O., Dias, J.: Satellite estimates of precipitation-induced dissipation in the atmosphere. Science **335**(6071), 953–956 (2012)
10. Treacy, M.M., Borisenko, K.B.: The local structure of amorphous silicon. Science **335**(6071), 950–953 (2012)
11. Ye, T., Zheng, D., Disse, M., et al.: Evaluation of precipitation input for SWAT modeling in Alpine catchment: a case study in the Adige river basin (Italy). Sci. Total Environ. **573**, 66–82 (2016)
12. Zörner, J., de Vries, M.P., Beirle, S., et al.: Multi-satellite sensor study on precipitation-induced emission pulses of NOx from soils in semi-arid ecosystems. Atmos. Chem. Phys. **18**(14), 1–39 (2016)
13. Buishand, T.A.: Tests for detecting a shift in the mean of hydrological time series. J. Hydrol. **73**(1–2), 51–69 (1984)
14. Vicente, G.A., Davenport, J.C., Scofield, R.A.: The role of orographic and parallax corrections on real time high resolution satellite rainfall rate distribution. Int. J. Remote Sens. **23**(2), 221–230 (2002)
15. Kuligowski, R.J.: A self-calibrating real-time GOES rainfall algorithm for short-term rainfall estimates. J. Hydrometeorol. **3**(2), 112–130 (2002)
16. Andermann, C., Bonnet, S., Gloaguen, R.: Evaluation of precipitation data sets along the Himalayan front. Geochem. Geophys. Geosyst. **12**(7), 785–814 (2011)
17. Schroeder, W., Csiszar, I., Morisette, J.: Quantifying the impact of cloud obscuration on remote sensing of active fires in the Brazilian Amazon. Remote Sens. Environ. **112**(2), 456–470 (2008)
18. Liang, A.Z., Zhang, X.P., Yang, X.M., et al.: Estimation of total erosion in cultivated Black soils in northeast China from vertical profiles of soil organic carbon. Eur. J. Soil Sci. **60**(2), 223–229 (2009)

19. Zhang, Y., Wang, P., Wang, L., et al.: The influence of facility agriculture production on phthalate esters distribution in black soils of Northeast China. Sci. Total Environ. **506–507**, 118–125 (2015)

20. Liu, J., Wang, G., Zheng, C., et al.: Specific assemblages of major capsid genes (g23) of T4-type bacteriophages isolated from upland black soils in Northeast China. Soil Biol. Biochem. **43**(9), 1980–1984 (2011)

21. Liang, L., Li, L., Qiang, L.: Precipitation variability in Northeast China from 1961 to 2008. J. Hydrol. **404**(1–2), 67–76 (2011)

22. Alessio, S., Taricco, C., Rubinetti, S., et al.: Temperature and precipitation in Northeast China during the last 150 years: relationship to large-scale climatic variability. Ann. Geophys. **32**(7), 749–760 (2014)

23. Wang, B., Zhang, M., Wei, J., et al.: Changes in extreme precipitation over Northeast China, 1960–2011. Quat. Int. **298**(298), 177–186 (2013)

24. Crow, W.: Improving long-term, retrospective precipitation datasets using satellite-based surface soil moisture retrievals and the soil moisture analysis rainfall tool. J. Appl. Remote Sens. **6**(1), 063604 (2012)

25. Stenz, R., Dong, X., Xi, B., et al.: Improving satellite quantitative precipitation estimation using GOES-retrieved cloud optical depth. J. Hydrometeorol. **17**(2), 557–570 (2016)

26. Kühnlein, M., Appelhans, T., Thies, B., et al.: Improving the accuracy of rainfall rates from optical satellite sensors with machine learning—a random forests-based approach applied to MSG SEVIRI. Remote Sens. Environ. **141**(141), 129–143 (2014)

27. Nastos, P.T., Kapsomenakis, J., Philandras, K.M.: Evaluation of the TRMM 3B43 gridded precipitation estimates over Greece. Atmos. Res. **169**, 497–514 (2016)

28. Chronis, T.G., Anagnostou, E.N., Dinku, T.: High-frequency estimation of rainfall from thunderstorms via satellite infrared and a long-range lightning network in Europe. Q. J. R. Meteorol. Soc. **130**(599), 1555–1574 (2004)

29. Xu, X.Z., Xu, Y., Chen, S.C., et al.: Soil loss and conservation in the black soil region of Northeast China: a retrospective study. Environ. Sci. Policy **13**(8), 793–800 (2010)

30. Meroni, M., Rembold, F., Fasbender, D., et al.: Evaluation of the Standardized Precipitation Index as an early predictor of seasonal vegetation production anomalies in the Sahel. Remote Sens. Lett. **8**(4), 301–310 (2017)

31. Domingo, F., Villagarcía, L., Boer, M.M., et al.: Evaluating the long-term water balance of arid zone stream bed vegetation using evapotranspiration modelling and hillslope runoff measurements. J. Hydrol. **243**(1), 17–30 (2017)

32. Millán, H., Rodríguez, J., Ghanbarian-Alavijeh, B., et al.: Temporal complexity of daily precipitation records from different atmospheric environments: Chaotic and Lévy stable parameters. Atmos. Res. **101**(4), 879–892 (2011)

33. Kulshrestha, U.C., Engardt, L.G., Rodhe, H.: Review of precipitation monitoring studies in India—a search for regional patterns. Atmos. Environ. **39**(38), 7403–7419 (2005)

34. Buda, A.R., Dewalle, D.R.: Using atmospheric chemistry and storm track information to explain the variation of nitrate stable isotopes in precipitation at a site in central Pennsylvania, USA. Atmos. Environ. **43**(29), 4453–4464 (2009)

35. Ciabatta, L., Marra, A.C., Panegrossi, G., et al.: Daily precipitation estimation through different microwave sensors: verification study over Italy. J. Hydrol. **545**, 436–450 (2017)

36. Palerme, C., Genthon, C., Claud, C., et al.: Evaluation of current and projected Antarctic precipitation in CMIP5 models. Clim. Dyn. **48**(1–2), 1–15 (2017)

37. Meng, X., Li, R., Luan, L., et al.: Detecting hydrological consistency between soil moisture and precipitation and changes of soil moisture in summer over the Tibetan Plateau. Clim. Dyn. **51**, 1–12 (2017)

38. Siuki, S.K., Saghafian, B., Moazami, S.: Comprehensive evaluation of 3-hourly TRMM and half-hourly GPM-IMERG satellite precipitation products. Int. J. Remote Sens. **38**(2), 558–571 (2017)
39. Kolassa, J., Gentine, P., Prigent, C., et al.: Soil moisture retrieval from AMSR-E and ASCAT microwave observation synergy. Part 2: product evaluation. Remote Sens. Environ. **195**, 202–217 (2017)
40. Kulie, M.S., Bennartz, R., Greenwald, T.J., et al.: Uncertainties in microwave properties of frozen precipitation: implications for remote sensing and data assimilation. J. Atmos. Sci. **67** (11), 3471–3487 (2010)
41. Aghakouchak, A., Bárdossy, A., Habib, E.: Copula-based uncertainty modelling: application to multisensor precipitation estimates. Hydrol. Process. **24**(15), 2111–2124 (2010)
42. Liu, D., Wang, Z., Zhang, B., et al.: Spatial distribution of soil organic carbon and analysis of related factors in croplands of the black soil region, Northeast China. Agric. Ecosyst. Environ. **113**(1), 73–81 (2006)
43. Wu, Y., Zheng, Q., Zhang, Y., et al.: Development of gullies and sediment production in the black soil region of northeastern China. Geomorphology **101**(4), 683–691 (2008)
44. Liang, W., Qi, L.I., Jiang, Y., et al.: Effect of cultivation on spatial distribution of nematode trophic groups in black soil. Pedosphere **13**(2), 97–102 (2003)
45. Wen, L.L., Zheng, F.L., Yang, Q.S., et al.: Effects of rainfall patterns on hillslope farmland erosion in black soil region of Northeast China. J. Hydraul. Eng. **43**(9), 1084–1091 (2012)
46. Stephens, G.L.: The remote sensing of clouds and precipitation from space: a review. J. Atmos. Sci. **64**(11), 3742–3765 (2007)
47. Michaelides, S., Levizzani, V., Anagnostou, E., et al.: Precipitation: measurement, remote sensing, climatology and modeling. Atmos. Res. **94**(4), 512–533 (2009)
48. Brunsell, N.A.: Characterization of land-surface precipitation feedback regimes with remote sensing. Remote Sens. Environ. **100**(2), 200–211 (2006)
49. Alexakis, D.D., Hadjimitsis, D.G., Agapiou, A.: Integrated use of remote sensing, GIS and precipitation data for the assessment of soil erosion rate in the catchment area of "Yialias" in Cyprus. Atmos. Res. **131**(2), 108–124 (2013)
50. Velmourougane, K., Venugopalan, M.V., Bhattacharyya, T., et al.: Soil dehydrogenase activity in agro-ecological sub regions of black soil regions in India. Geoderma **197–198**(3), 186–192 (2013)
51. Dwivedi, R.S., Sreenivas, K., Ramana, K.V.: Detecting soil information in a predominantly black soil region using Indian remote sensing satellite (IRS-1B) linear imaging self-scanning sensor (LISS-II) data. Int. J. Remote Sens. **21**(17), 3293–3302 (2000)

Temperature Dependence of Soil Respiration in Arid Region Is Reconciled

Wenfeng Wang[1], Xi Chen[1(✉)], Xiaoliang Li[2], Jing Qian[3],
and Jianjun Yu[4]

[1] State Key Laboratory of Desert and Oasis Ecology,
Xinjiang Institute of Ecology and Geography, Chinese Academy of Sciences,
Urumqi 830011, China
chenxi@ms.xjb.ac.cn
[2] College of Statistics and Management,
Shanghai University of Finance and Economics, Shanghai 200433, China
[3] Center for Geo-Spatial Information, Shenzhen Institutes of Advanced
Technology, Chinese Academy of Sciences, Shenzhen 518055, China
[4] Environmental Change Institute, University of Oxford, Oxford OX1 3QY, UK

Abstract. This article suggests that temperature dependence of soil respiration in arid region is reconciled by highlighting a gap in our knowledge by examining the hypothesis that diel temperature sensitivities (i.e. Q_{10}) of soil respiration flux (R_s) are in essence the same, ignoring the negative R_s data in arid regions that characterize more than 30% of the earth's land area. Analyses on data collected from previous studies revealed diel turbulence in Q_{10} values even if excluding negative R_s data. Such turbulence was inherently controlled by temperature and soil water content. On the basis of utilizing the soil data collected from the Xinjiang and Central Asia Scientific Data Sharing Platform, four coupling models indicated that soil water content and temperature were equally significant in determining Q_{10}. Therefore, taking into account negative R_s data in arid regions is strongly needed to reduce uncertainties in the current global/regional carbon balance and in predictions of future feedback in the coupled carbon-climate system.

Keywords: Temperature sensitivity · Soil respiration · Carbon-climate system

1 Introduction

Over the long-term period, rapid carbon release from soil respiration fluxes (R_s) provided the second largest CO_2 efflux between terrestrial ecosystems and the atmosphere [1, 2]. R_s were conventionally thought to be comprised of two biological components, controlled by two distinct processes: the plant root respiration (autotrophic respiration) and the soil organic carbon (SOC) decomposition by soil fauna and soil microbes (heterotrophic respiration) [3–5]. CO_2 released from both two biological processes are highly sensitive to temperature change, and with the onset of global warming, significant implications to the global carbon balance are likely to occur. Supposing, for instance, that warming would lead to a 1% increase of global R_s per year, this extra

© Springer Nature Singapore Pte Ltd. 2019
F. Sun et al. (Eds.): ICCSIP 2018, CCIS 1006, pp. 350–358, 2019.
https://doi.org/10.1007/978-981-13-7986-4_31

CO_2 source would outweigh the projected annual increase in fossil fuel emissions [9]. In order to describe the temperature sensitivity of R_s in a quantitative manner, estimates of Q_{10}, the factor by which R_s are multiplied when temperature increases by 10 degrees, have been performed at many sites around the world. But there are still considerable uncertainties associated with Q_{10}. A better understanding of Q_{10} and its environmental controls is therefore critical to reduce uncertainties in the global CO_2 budget accounting and in the predictions of the future feedbacks in the coupled carbon-climate systems [31–33].

Supposing that the responses of R_s to changes in temperature are often referred to as the temperature sensitivity, then Q_{10} can be estimated from relative changes in R_s with $10°C$ increases of temperature [6–11]. However, even R_s itself may be inadequately understood. Most publications claimed that R_s is positive, but recent studies in desert ecosystems with alkaline soils disclosed unneglectable, negative R_s values, which could not be attributed to conventional biological processes [12, 13]. R_s are useful as the measurements of CO_2 fluxes from the soils, but their values as a measure of the ecosystem processes are very limited. The R_s interpretation as biological processes (autotrophic and heterotrophic respiration) was not true for the ecosystems in alkaline land [3–5, 23]. Negative CO_2 fluxes were observed with both chambers and the open- or close-path eddy systems were still included in the nocturnal data of ecosystem respiration [28–30], so it should not be excluded from the R_s values in alkaline lands [12, 13]. Non-biological processes, such as pH-mediated CO_2 dissolution and diffusion in the soils and the surface adhesion of CO_2 onto soil minerals, have been suggested as the third dominant flux of R_s in the arid and semiarid ecosystems in alkaline land [14–17].

Non-biological processes of R_s may not be a new issue. Because of the complicated porous structure, a part of R_s were delayed, and subsequently released as a part of physical CO_2 diffusion [25]. Especially in some arid ecosystems, after precipitation, the infiltration of water reduced the stored space for CO_2 in the soil, which always aggravates the CO_2 release in R_s (this is Birch effect), which must be largely attributed to the non-biological processes [26, 27]. In order to enhance the comparability between arid regions and non-arid regions, the non-biological fluxes must be taken into account. This not only include the abiotic carbon oxidation processes, the physical CO_2 diffusion and the Birch effect that have been widely recognized [25–27], but also include some recently reported non-biological processes, such as pH-mediated CO_2 dissolution/diffusion in the soils and the surface adhesion of CO_2 onto soil minerals [14–17].

Therefore, non-biological processes significantly contributed to R_s in alkaline lands and non-biological fluxes were strongly suggested as the third dominant flux in R_s of alkaline lands [14–17]. Noting that alkaline soils characterize 5% of the total Earth's land surface [16, 17], a huge effect on the precision of carbon budget estimations is possible. It is crucial to understand how R_s in ecosystems with alkaline soils responds to abiotic factors (particularly to temperature) [16–18]. Our objectives in the present study magnitude of negative, non-biological fluxes are to interpret, calculate and model Q_{10} for alkaline soils. An assumption made in most R_s measurements and some models is that the temperature sensitivity of R_s equals the Q_{10} estimated from exponential regressions between the variations in temperature and R_s, but there is strong evidence suggesting that soil water content that simultaneously varies with temperature can exert a potential influence on the dynamics of R_s and obscure the temperature sensitivity [34, 35]. So the soil water content is also considered a determinant of Q_{10} in this study.

2   Materials and Methods

2.1   Data Sources

The analysis of Q_{10} of R_s to soil temperature at 5 cm depths (T_s) and air temperatures at 10 cm above the soil surface (T_a) at two neighboring alkaline sites (saline desert: pH = 9.1; cropped farmland: pH = 8.6) along a gradient of the soil volumetric water content at 5 cm depths (θ_s) at the Fukang Station of Desert Ecology, Chinese Academy of Sciences, which is located at the southern periphery of the Gubantonggut Desert and in the hinterland of the Eurasian continent (87°56′E, 44°17′N; elevation: 461 m). Analyses presented here are based on the R_s, θ_s, T_a and T_s values collected from some previous publications [19–21].

2.2   Analyzing the Variations of R_s with T

Day (08:00–20:00) and night (20:00–08:00) dynamics of R_s were analyzed at two neighboring alkaline sites (saline desert: pH = 9.1; cropped farmland: pH = 8.6), using the R_s, θ_s, T_a and T_s collected from the previous publications [19–21]. Variations of R_s with soil temperature at 5 cm depths (T_s) and air temperature at 10 cm above the soil surface (T_a) were disclosed in the linear regressions between R_s and T (=T_a or T_s). The regressions were compared along a gradient of soil volumetric water content at 5 cm depths (θ_s) to examine the effects of θ_s on the responses of R_s to T in alkaline lands.

2.3   Determining Q_{10} and Its Controls

The Q_{10} values used in the analysis were calculated using the following formula (for consistence, the negative values of R_s were not included in calculations of Q_{10}), using to the simple model of R_s (the derivative of the exponential chemical reaction-temperature equation originally developed by Van't Hoff) [36–38]:

$$R_{sT}/R_{sT_0} = Q_{10}^{(T-T_0)/10} \tag{1}$$

where R_{sT} and R_{sT0} are the R_s rates (μmol CO_2 m^{-2} s^{-1}) at T and T_0, respectively.

Controls of T on Q_{10} at each site were respectively analyzed in linear regressions for a between-ecosystem comparison. Results from these analyses were further compared with the analyses of the variation of Q_{10} with T. Using Q_{10} values from both sites, the effects of θ_s on the Q_{10} of R_s to T_s and the Q_{10} of R_s to T_a were analyzed in quadratic regressions. To further test the role of θ_s in determining Q_{10}, four coupling models were employed to analyze coupling effects of T and θ_s on Q_{10}.

The front two models were established under the hypothesis that the influences of θ_s and T on Q_{10} were mutually independent. The first model hypothesized that the influences of θ_s and T were linearly independent; the second model hypothesized that the influences of θ_s and T were exponentially independent. That is, these two models were respectively formulated as follows

$$Q_{10} = a\theta_s + bT + c, \ Q_{10} = ae^{b\theta_s + cT} \tag{2}$$

where a, b and c are the regression coefficients.

The latter two models were established under the hypothesis that the influences of θ_s and T on Q_{10} were not mutually independent. The third model hypothesized that the Q_{10} was dominantly determined by θ_s and T linearly interacted on the responses of the Q_{10} to θ_s; the fourth model hypothesized that Q_{10} was dominantly determined by T and θ_s linearly interacted on the responses of Q_{10} to T. These two models were respectively formulated as follows:

$$Q_{10} = ae^{(bT + c)\theta_s}, Q_{10} = ae^{(b\theta_s + c)T} \tag{3}$$

where a, b and c are the regression coefficients.

Descriptive statistics were used to calculate the R-squared values (R), root mean squared error (RMSE) and F-statistics vs. constant model and p-values of the data from each set of reduplicates. The data analysis was processed using MATLAB (Mathworks, Natick, MA, USA) and the statistical analyses were synchronously conducted, which would be reported along with the results.

3   Results and Discussions

3.1   Day and Night Variations of R_s in Alkaline Land

R_s in the saline desert (pH $\sim$ 9.1) showed an asymmetric, turbulent diurnal pattern, which dropped to a minimum in the early hours of the dawn (06:00–08:00, local time) and attained a maximum around the early afternoon (15:00–16:00; Fig. 1). The daytime range was 0–0.96 μmol CO_2 m^{-2} s^{-1}, and occasionally negative. The nighttime range was -0.87–0 μmol CO_2 m^{-2} s^{-1}, and occasionally positive. The R_s in the cropped farmland showed an almost symmetric diurnal pattern with significant differences in the daytime (0.85–3.3 μmol CO_2 m^{-2} s^{-1}) and nighttime (-0.41–1.85 μmol CO_2 m^{-2} s^{-1}) ranges. The mean value of R_s varied with θ_s: In the saline desert, when θ_s increased from 5% to 23%, the mean value of R_s increased from -0.25 to 0.14 μmol CO_2 m^{-2} s^{-1}; in the farmland, when θ_s increased from 25% to 30%, the mean value of R_s increased from 0.98 to 1.83 μmol CO_2 m^{-2} s^{-1}. However, the mean value of R_s did not monotonously increase with θ_s: When θ_s increased from 23% to 29% in the desert, the mean R_s decreased from 0.14 to -0.25 μmol CO_2 m^{-2} s^{-1}; when θ_s increased from 29% to 36% in the farmland, the mean R_s decreased from 1.83 μmol CO_2 m^{-2} s^{-1} to 1.21 μmol CO_2 m^{-2} s^{-1}. Additionally, the mean value of R_s in the desert was -0.04 μmol CO_2 m^{-2} s^{-1}, implying that alkaline soils in the desert acted as a slight C sink. With a mean R_s value of 1.34 μmol CO_2 m^{-2} s^{-1}, the alkaline soils in the farmland acted as a significant C source.

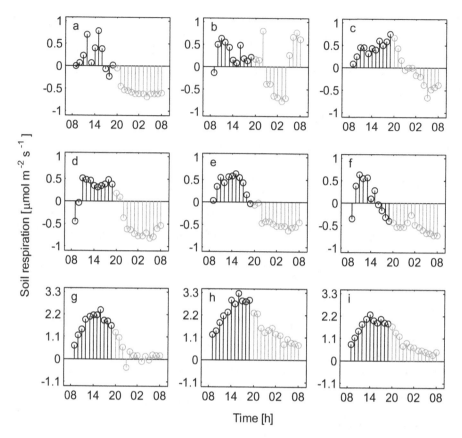

Fig. 1. The daytime (color black in line and dots) and nighttime (color green in line and dots) soil respiration at the saline desert (a: $\theta = 5\%$; b: $\theta = 16\%$; c: $\theta = 23\%$; d: $\theta = 27\%$; e: $\theta = 28\%$; f: $\theta = 29\%$) and the cropped farmland (g: $\theta = 25\%$; h: $\theta = 26\%$; i: $\theta = 36\%$). Note: θ denotes the daily mean soil volumetric water content at 5 cm depth. (Color figure online)

3.2   Relationships Between R_s and Temperature

Day and night variations of R_s with T_s in the saline desert exhibited an entirely different pattern, no matter if the soils were wet or dry (Fig. 2). In the whole diel variations, R_s monotonously increased with T_s. However, when considering the day and night variations separately, the relationships between R_s and T_s became uncertain. A negative R_s at night exerted a strong influence on the response of R_s to T_s. Response curves of R_s to T_s for night variations are below that in the day, indicating that negative fluxes occurring at night reduced the temperature sensitivity of R_s. The diel variation of R_s with the T_s in farmland was incredibly similar to that in the desert, but differences between day and night responses of R_s to T_s were obscured when no negative R_s occurred at night in the farmland. This further proved that a negative R_s occurring at night was responsible for the reduced sensitivity of R_s to T_s in these alkaline lands. Responses of R_s to another temperature index, T_a, were much different from the responses of R_s to T_s. Day and night variations of R_s with T_a in the desert exhibited a similar pattern when θ_s increased from 5% to 28% (Fig. 3). R_s universally increased with T_a and response curves of R_s to T_a in day and night variations overlapped, indicating that negative fluxes in R_s at night had no significant influence on its responses to T_a. In the extreme case in the desert (when $\theta_s = 29\%$), a significant part of daytime R_s became negative and the relationships between R_s and T_a became as uncertain as the relationships between R_s and T_s, indicating an unneglectable, negative R_s in the day and exerted a strong influence on the response of R_s to T_a.

Nevertheless, the day and night variations of R_s with T_a in the farmland exhibited a similar pattern, no matter if the soils were wet or dry (Fig. 3). It was therefore concluded that T_a values were much more determining than T_s in the diel variations of R_s in both the desert and farmland.

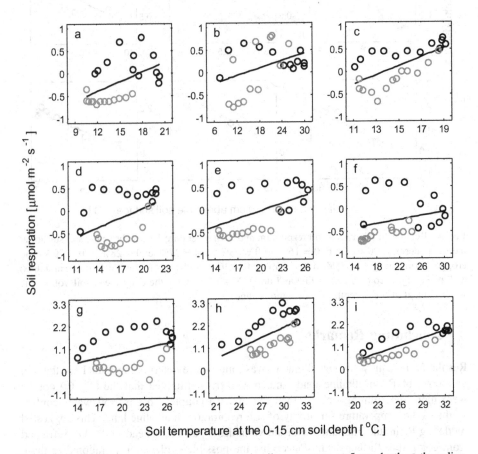

Fig. 2. Relationship between soil respiration and soil temperature at 5 cm depth at the saline desert (a: $\theta = 5\%$; b: $\theta = 16\%$; c: $\theta = 23\%$; d: $\theta = 27\%$; e: $\theta = 28\%$; f: $\theta = 29\%$) and the cropped farmland (g: $\theta = 25\%$; h: $\theta = 26\%$; i: $\theta = 36\%$) in the day (color black in line and dots) and at night (color green in line and dots). Note: θ denotes the daily mean soil volumetric water content at 5 cm depth. (Color figure online)

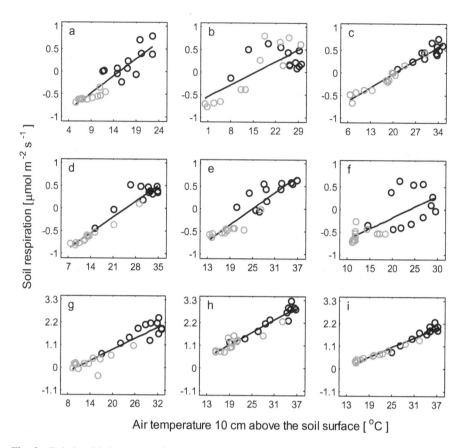

Fig. 3. Relationship between soil respiration and air temperature 10 cm above the soil surface at the saline desert (a: $\theta = 5\%$; b: $\theta = 16\%$; c: $\theta = 23\%$; d: $\theta = 27\%$; e: $\theta = 28\%$; f: $\theta = 29\%$) and cropped farmland (g: $\theta = 25\%$; h: $\theta = 26\%$; i: $\theta = 36\%$) in the day (color black in line and dots) and at the night (color green in line and dots). Note: θ denotes the daily mean soil volumetric water content at 5 cm depth. (Color figure online)

4   Concluding Remarks

Results in this study suggested that T_a was much more determining than T_s in the diel variations of R_s in alkaline land, and moreover, highlighted that the (T_a, θ_s) couple were more determining on Q_{10} than the (T_s, θ_s) couple. That is, soil water content mediates the temperature sensitivity of soil respiration in alkaline land. This suggested modeling R_s in alkaline lands with the variables T_a and θ_s instead of T_s. We refrained from going into further detail concerning the possible explanation to rationalize these results because of the currently poor understanding of Q_{10} in alkaline lands. Further explorations associated with the Q_{10} in alkaline lands and its controls are still necessary.

Acknowledgments. This research was financially supported by the National Natural Science Foundation of China (41571299) and the "Thousand Talents" plan (Y474161).

Competing Interests. None declared.

References

1. Cox, P.M., Betts, R.A., Jones, C.D., Spall, S.A., Totterdell, I.J.: Acceleration of global warming due to carbon-cycle feedbacks in a coupled climate model. Nature **408**, 184–187 (2000)
2. Schlesinger, W.H., Andrews, J.A.: Soil respiration and the global carbon cycle. Biogeochemistry **48**, 7–20 (2000)
3. Baggs, E.M.: Partitioning the components of soil respiration: a research challenge. Plant Soil **284**(1–2), 1–5 (2006)
4. Baldocchi, D.D.: Assessing the eddy covariance technique for evaluating carbon dioxide exchange rates of ecosystems: past, present and future. Glob. Change Biol. **9**(4), 479–492 (2003)
5. Valentini, R., Matteucci, G., Dolman, A.J., et al.: Respiration as the main determinant of carbon balance in European forests. Nature **404**(6780), 861–865 (2000)
6. Giardina, C., Ryan, M.: Evidence that decomposition rates of organic carbon in mineral soil do not vary with temperature. Nature **404**, 858–861 (2000)
7. Bond-Lamberty, B., Thomson, A.: A global database of soil respiration data. Biogeosciences **7**, 1915–1926 (2010)
8. Kirschbaum, M.U.F.: The temperature dependence of soil organic matter decomposition and the effect of global warming on soil organic C storage. Soil Biol. Biochem. **27**, 753–760 (1995)
9. Schimel, D.S.: Terrestrial ecosystems and the carbon-cycle. Glob. Change Biol. **1**, 77–91 (1995)
10. IPCC: Climate Change 2007: The Physical Sciences Basis: Contribution of Working Group I to the Fourth Assessment Report of the Intergovernmental Panel on Climate Change. Cambridge University Press, Cambridge (2007)
11. Wang, X.H., Piao, S.L., Ciais, P., et al.: Are ecological gradients in seasonal Q_{10} of soil respiration explained by climate or by vegetation seasonality? Soil Biol. Biochem. **42**, 1728–1734 (2010)
12. Tang, Z.X., Fan, F.L., Wan, Y.F., et al.: Abundance and diversity of RuBisCO genes responsible for CO_2 fixation in arid soils of Northwest China. Pedosphere **25**(1), 150–159 (2015)
13. Zhang, L.H., Chen, Y.N., Zhao, R.F., et al.: Significance of temperature and soil water content on soil respiration in three desert ecosystems in Northwest China. J. Arid Environ. **74**, 1200–1211 (2010)
14. Wang, X., Wang, J., Xu, M., et al.: Carbon accumulation in arid croplands of northwest China: pedogenic carbonate exceeding organic carbon. Scientific Reports (2015). https://doi.org/10.1038/srep11439
15. Stone, R.: Have desert researchers discovered a hidden loop in the carbon cycle? Science **320**(5882), 1409–1410 (2008)
16. Xie, J., Li, Y., Zhai, C.X., Li, C., et al.: CO_2 absorption by alkaline soils and its implication to the global carbon cycle. Environ. Geol. **56**(5), 953–961 (2009)

17. Yates, E.L., Detweiler, A.M., Iraci, L.T., et al.: Assessing the role of alkaline soils on the carbon cycle at a playa site. Environ. Earth Sci. **70**(3), 1047–1056 (2013)
18. Schlesinger, W.H., Belnap, J., Marion, G.: On carbon sequestration in desert ecosystems. Glob. Change Biol. **15**, 1488–1490 (2009)
19. Chen, X., Wang, W.F., Luo, G.P., et al.: Time lag between carbon dioxide influx to and efflux from bare saline-alkali soil detected by the explicit partitioning and reconciling of soil CO_2 flux. Stoch. Environ. Res. Risk Assess. **27**(3), 1–9 (2013)
20. Wang, J.P., Wang, X.J., Zhang, J., et al.: Soil organic and inorganic carbon and stable carbon isotopes in the Yanqi Basin of Northwestern China. Eur. J. Soil Sci. **66**(1), 95–103 (2015)
21. Wang, W.F., Chen, X., Luo, G.P., et al.: Modeling the contribution of abiotic exchange to CO2 flux in alkaline soils of arid areas. J. Arid Land **6**(1), 27–36 (2014)
22. Kirschbaum, M.U.F.: Will changes in soil organic carbon act as a positive or negative feedback on global warming? Biogeochemistry **48**, 21–51 (2000)
23. Decina, S.M., Hutyra, L.R., Gately, C.K., et al.: Soil respiration contributes substantially to urban carbon fluxes in the greater Boston area. Environ. Pollut. **212**, 433–439 (2016)
24. Schleser, G.H.: The responses of CO_2 evolution from soils to global temperature changes. Zeitschrift fur Natureforschung **37**(a), 287–291 (1982)
25. Fang, J.Y., Tang, Y.H., Koizumi, H., et al.: Evidence of winter time CO_2 emission from snow-covered grounds in high latitudes. Sci. China: Ser. D **42**, 378–382 (1999)
26. Wang, W., Xi, C., Zhi, P.: Negative soil respiration fluxes in unneglectable arid regions. Pol. J. Environ. Stud. **24**(2), 905–908 (2015)
27. Birch, H.F.: The effect of soil drying on humus decomposition and nitrogen availability. Plant Soil **10**, 9–31 (1958)
28. Li, Y., Wang, Y., Houghton, R.A., et al.: Hidden carbon sink beneath desert. Geophys. Res. Lett. **42**(14), 5880–5887 (2015)
29. Serrano-Ortiz, P., Were, A., Reverter, B.R., et al.: Seasonality of net carbon exchanges of Mediterranean ecosystems across an altitudinal gradient. J. Arid Environ. **115**(115), 1–9 (2015)
30. Wohlfahrt, G., Fenstermaker, L.F., Arnone, J.A.: Large annual net ecosystem CO_2 uptake of a Mojave Desert ecosystem. Glob. Change Biol. **14**, 1475–1487 (2008)
31. Huenneke, L.F., Anderson, J.P., Remmenga, M., et al.: Desertification alters patterns of aboveground net primary production in Chihuahuan ecosystems. Glob. Change Biol. **8**, 247–264 (2002)
32. Piao, S.L., et al.: Net carbon dioxide losses of northern ecosystems in response to autumn warming. Nature **451**, 49–52 (2008)
33. Daniel, D.W., Smith, L.M., Belden, J.B., et al.: Effects of land-use change and fungicide application on soil respiration in playa wetlands and adjacent uplands of the U.S. high plains. Sci. Total Environ. **514**(C), 290–297 (2015)
34. Davidson, E.A., Janssens, I.A.: Temperature sensitivity of soil carbon decomposition and feedbacks to climate change. Nature **440**, 165–173 (2006)
35. Davidson, E.A., Verchot, L.V., Cattánio, J.H., et al.: Effects of soil water content on soil respiration in forests and cattle pastures of eastern Amazonia. Biogeochemistry **48**, 53–69 (2000)
36. Nazaries, L., Tottey, W., Robinson, L., et al.: Shifts in the microbial community structure explain the response of soil respiration to land-use change but not to climate warming. Soil Biol. Biochem. **89**, 123–134 (2015)
37. Yang, K., Xiong, L., Yang, W., et al.: Effects of forest gap to soil respiration in a subalpine Picea asperata plantation of western Sichuan. J. Gymnastics **6**, 10–18 (2016)
38. Huang, J., Gao, Z.J., Chen, J., et al.: Diurnal and seasonal variations of soil respiration rate under different row-spacing in a Panicum virgatum L field on semi-arid Loess Plateau of China. J. Arid Land **8**(3), 341–349 (2016)

Mining Friendships Based on Bipartite Network Though Campus Spatiotemporal Feature

Feng Zhang[1,2], Xiaqing Xie[1,2], Jin Xu[1,2], and Xu Wu[1,2(✉)]

[1] School of Cyberspace Security, Beijing University of Posts and
Telecommunications, Beijing, China
{zhangfengshunxin, xiexiaqing, xujin, wux}@bupt.edu.cn
[2] Key Laboratory of Trustworthy Distributed Computing and Service (BUPT),
Ministry of Education, Beijing, China

Abstract. The development of the campus network results in a large number of data, which contains student behavior features with implicit spatiotemporal attributes. However, existing mining methods mostly focus on the low-dimensional. It is difficult to cover the dimension of the spatiotemporal attribute. To solve it, based on the bipartite network, this paper proposes a method for mining friendships. Aiming at the feature of the spatiotemporal dataset, a bipartite network is firstly constructed, and divided into sub-networks with the same degree of spatiotemporal nodes. In each sub-network, by using the hypothesis test, edges between co-occurrence nodes of random encounter is deleted. Finally, the friendships network of the students is a projection of the bipartite network. Experiments show that the method can effectively draw the friend relationships between students. Moreover, the friendships network helps to analyze the student behavior, which plays an important role in the decision-making of university.

Keywords: Campus spatiotemporal data · Friendships · Behavioral features · Bipartite network

1 Introduction

With the development of informatization and digitization in domestic universities, tons of data of student behavior features is generated. Great contribution can be made to multiple fields like teaching, researching, rear service and management through deep mining into these data. However, the existing mining method can only analyze the consumption data on the low dimension which makes it very hard to cover the spatiotemporal dimension. Multi-dimensional analysis of spatiotemporal data can mine the data of the feature of students' behavior and relationship which makes it an important reference to the management and decision-making of universities. Nowadays, bipartite network has become an important part in complex network theory research, it can be applied to such as the description of the transportation network and the relationship between the author and the thesis which makes it applicable to nearly all aspects of modern science in practical application. Therefore, this paper proposes a mining method for friendship construction and behavioral feature based on large amounts of

F. Sun et al. (Eds.): ICCSIP 2018, CCIS 1006, pp. 359–369, 2019.
https://doi.org/10.1007/978-981-13-7986-4_32

campus spatiotemporal data and bipartite network. This method firstly builds the bipartite network based on the spatiotemporal data of campus. Then utilizing hypothesis test to statistically analyze and test whether the co-occurrence of students comes from a random encounter and obtain the friendships network including the degree of intimacy. Finally, obtaining the information of students' behavioral features through analyzing the basic features of this network. In the second section, relative research about this field which includes the knowledge of bipartite network. In the third section, Model and design of the mining method which includes the model of bipartite network for campus spatiotemporal data and friendship. In the fourth section, display and analysis of experimental results. In the last section, the conclusion and prospection.

2 Relative Research

2.1 Relative Work

With the rapid development of campus network of domestic universities, intelligent campus [1] is already an important part of the campus construction. As the fundament of it, the campus card [2] is applied to all fields of students' life, which accumulates large amounts of information. The data mining of the information of campus card [3] is drawing more and more attention. Aiming at the behavior of study and consumption of students, Jiang et al. [4] analyzed the consumption habits of students through the optimized K-means clustering algorithm. This method uses decision tree algorithm to assess the result of clustering which helps the rear service department. Fei et al. [5] used K-means algorithm to analyze the consumption information and built the algorithm based on the results of clustering which can be used to calculate the poverty index of every student. The analysis of poor students in this method can assist the decision-making work of university funding. Qian and Shi [6] used K-means algorithm and time series algorithm to analyze and predict the behavior of students and the situation of the campus canteen. This method provides data support for the consumers and the decision makers of university. Yan et al. [7] used Apriori algorithm to analyze the data of life and study of students on campus, and mine the relevancy between the students' marks and the book borrowing information and the relevancy between attendance and the usage of Internet. It enables the supervisors on campus to guide the students in a better way based on the results of the association rule mining. The research mentioned above aids the supervision part of campus, but it still has some drawback. On one hand, the data mining is all focused on the data of study and consumption of campus card which omits the campus spatiotemporal data hidden in the campus network. On the other hand, the methods are all aimed at the financial state and marks of students which does not include the campus social network [8]. Research on spatiotemporal data [9] can identify the social relationship between two students based on the information of time and location. By learning the social relationship of students like the quantity of friend-making, we can help the university care for the mental health of students and get to know whether the students feel lonely.

2.2 Bipartite Network and Method of Analysis

Bipartite network [10] is a very important mode of presentation in complex network which can be used to depict many kinds of relationship like the relationship between commodity and consumers in sales network, the author and thesis in research network and the bus stations in transportation network of a city. Bipartite network model has become an important part of complex network research.

Usually we use a graph $G = (V, E)$ which contains vertex set V and edge set E to represent a network. The vertex number $N = |V|$ and the edge number $M = |E|$. Every edge in edge set E represents a connection of two vertices. The vertices of bipartite graph are consisted of two disjoint subsets, and the two vertices connected by one edge belong to disjoint subsets of vertices.

Definition: In figure $G = (V, E)$, if vertex set V can be divided into two disjoint nonempty subsets X and Y, and the i, j vertex of the edge (i, j) belong to two different vertex subsets, then we call figure G a bipartite graph which is marked as $G = (X, E, Y)$.

Definition: Assuming $G = (V, E)$ is a bipartite graph, $V = X \cup Y$, and any vertex of X is connected with every vertex of Y through only one edge, then the G is a complete bipartite graph.

Figure 1 is a non-complete bipartite graph containing seven vertices. The four vertices on the left and the three vertices on the right belong to set X and set Y separately.

Fig. 1. Non-complete bipartite graph

Figure 2 is a complete bipartite graph containing five vertices. The three vertices on the left and the two vertices on the right belong to set X and set Y separately.

Fig. 2. Complete bipartite graph

There are two main research methods for bipartite network model which are direct analysis and projection analysis. Direct analysis analyzes the original bipartite network model directly. This method can avoid information loss effectively and keep the original network information as much as possible. Projection analysis projects the bipartite network to get two kinds of corresponding unipartite networks and analyzes these two unipartite networks separately. The method of projection is efficient and can get the result which can not be obtained from direct analysis. The process of projection: in bipartite network, if there exist two different vertices in X which connect the same vertex in Y, the edge is built between the two vertices. This operation is applied to every two vertices in X until a unipartite network is formed. Figure 3 shows the projection of a bipartite network to two unipartite networks.

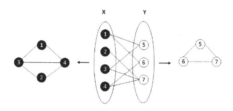

Fig. 3. From bipartite network to unipartite network

3   Design of Model and Method

3.1   Design of Bipartite Network Model for Campus Spatiotemporal Data

To establish a bipartite network model for spatiotemporal data, $G = (P, ST, E)$, the vertex set V is divided into a student set P and a spatiotemporal set ST. E is the set of edges between the student set and the spatiotemporal set. The student set P is composed of students in the school, and the spatiotemporal set ST is time-space pairs set, which composed of a time slot set and a space set. Assume that the total length of time is $[0, T)$, and Δt is the time slot, which is divided into b segments, each time segment is $[0, \Delta t), [\Delta t, 2\Delta t), ..., [T - \Delta t, T)\}$. The space set is $\{S_1, S_2, ..., S_a\}$, for a total of a elements. The number of elements in the spatiotemporal set NST = a × b. In the bipartite network, each spatiotemporal data can be represented as a connection between a node P_s in the student set and a node S_aT_b in the spatiotemporal set, meaning that a certain student appears in a certain place at a certain moment, wherein $(P_s, S_mT_r) \in E$, $s \in \{1, 2, ..., n\}, m \in \{1, 2, ..., a\}, r \in \{1, 2, ..., b\}$. Finally, a bipartite network U for campus spatiotemporal data is formed, as shown in Fig. 4.

student set: $P = \{P_1, P_2, ..., P_n\}$
spatiotemporal set: $ST = \{(S_1, T_1), ..., (S_x, T_y), ..., (S_a, T_b)\}$

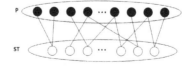

Fig. 4. Bipartite network model for campus spatiotemporal data

3.2   Method of Mining Friendships

Based on the co-occurrence of students and the degree of co-occurrence nodes, this paper mining the friendships between students, and calculate the degree of intimacy. In general, if two people appear in the same space within a similar period of time, the two people have a co-occurrence situation. Similarly, in the bipartite network for spatiotemporal data, two student vertices are connected to the same vertex in the spatiotemporal set, indicating that the two students have a co-occurrence situation, and the connected spatiotemporal vertices are called the common neighbors of the two student vertices. The number of co-occurrences of two students can be represented by the number of co-neighbors of two student vertices. To analyze the friend relationship between the student vertices, by using the projection analysis method, the spatiotemporal data binary network is projected into a unipartite network with only the student set to form a student friendships network. The projection rule: if two student vertices have at least one common neighbor, then in the student friendships network, an edge is established that connects the two vertices. In the student friendships network obtained by the above rules, the edges may not be able to truly reflect the relationship between the students, and most of the edges are originated from the random meeting. Therefore, it is necessary to use the hypothesis test method to statistically verify the students' co-occurrence situation, and delete the edges between the student vertices that have no actual relationship in the existing student friendships network, so as to obtain a more realistic network of student friend relationships.

The Method of Verify Friendships. In a bipartite network, the degree of each vertex is the number of vertices directly connected to it. In the bipartite network U for spatiotemporal data, According to the degree of the vertex in the spatiotemporal set, the original spatiotemporal set is divided into different subsets ST_d, and $ST_d \in ST$. ST_d is a set of vertices whose degree d is in set ST, and the number of vertices contained in ST_d is N_{ST}^d. The bipartite sub-networks U_d for spatiotemporal data consists of the students set P and the spatiotemporal subset ST_d. In the sub-network U_d, the degree of the student vertex i is N_j, the degree of the student vertex j is N_j, and the number of common neighbors of the two student vertices is N_{ij}^d. The process of hypothesis testing for each edge of a subnet:

The null hypothesis H_0: the edge is originated from a random encounter.
The alternative hypothesis H_1: the edge is not originated from a random encounter.

Assuming that student i and student j are randomly connected to vertices in set ST_d, the probability that student i and student j have X common neighbors in set ST_d conforms to hypergeometric distribution.

$$P\left(X|N_{ST}^d, N_i^d, N_j^d\right) = \frac{C_{N_i^d}^X C_{N_{ST}^d - N_i^d}^{N_j^d - X}}{C_{N_{ST}^d}^{N_j^d}} \tag{1}$$

For each bipartite sub-network, in fact, student i and student j have X common neighbors, and the p-value is $p(N_{ij}^d)$, in general, the significance level α is 0.05.

$$p\left(N_{ij}^d\right) = \sum\nolimits_{N_{ij}^d+1}^{\min\left(N_i^d,N_j^d\right)} P\left(X|N_{ST}^d,N_i^d,N_j^d\right) \qquad (2)$$

If $p < \alpha$, reject the null hypothesis and accept the alternative hypothesis. Edges in the sub-network are saved, otherwise, the edge is deleted. The verification process is shown in Fig. 5.

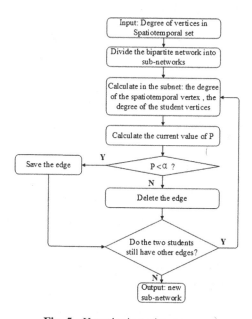

Fig. 5. Hypothesis testing process

The Method of Calculating Friendships Intimacy. In the bipartite network for campus spatiotemporal data, the student's encounter occurs in the spatiotemporal vertices of the smaller degree, the intimacy between the students is greater. Therefore, the smaller the degree of vertices, the greater the weight of the vertices' intimacy. The degree of the vertex S_xT_y is $D_{S_xT_y}$. A vertex weight W_{xy} is the ratio of the sum of the degrees of each node in all subnets to the degree of the vertex, the vertex weight value is inversely proportional to the value of the degree of the vertex. The intimacy F_{ij} between the two students is the sum of the weights of all their common neighbor vertices. Then, the intimacy is normalized so that the final student friendships intimacy F_{ij}' is within the range of [0, 1].

$$W_{xy} = \frac{\sum_{i=1}^{i=a}\sum_{j=1}^{j=b} D_{S_iT_j}}{D_{S_xT_y}} \qquad (3)$$

The intimacy F_{ij} between the two students:

$$F_{ij} = \sum W_{xy} \qquad (4)$$

The final intimacy F'_{ij} of friendships:

$$F'_{ij} = \frac{F_{ij} - \min(F)}{\max(F) - \min(F)} \qquad (5)$$

The calculation process of friendships intimacy is shown in Fig. 6.

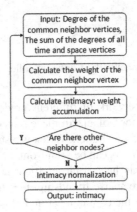

Fig. 6. The calculation process of friendships intimacy

4 Experimental Results and Analysis

4.1 Analysis of Friendships Network

The experimental dataset is the spatiotemporal data of 15,000 college students in one month, with a total of 1.2 million. Among them, the time data is provided by the student card consumption time, including date and hour, minute and second. The spatial data is provided by the information of card readers and consumption type. In all sub-networks, there are initially nearly 130 million edges. After using the hypothesis test, 46.1% of the edges are deleted. Experiments show that the method can effectively draw the friend relationships between students. Moreover, the friendships network helps to analyze the student behavior, which plays an important role in the decision-making of university. Figure 7 is a friendships network of different colleges in the same grade. The data in the figure includes the students in grade 2016 from School of electronic engineering, School of automation, and School of science, Among them, the top vertex is the student of School of Science, the number of which is 231. The right vertex is the student of School of Automation, the number of which is 562. The left vertex is the student of School of Electronic Engineering, the number of which is 359. As can be seen from the figure, students in the same grade are more closely related to each other, while the number of edges of students between different colleges is far less than those between students in the same college. It means that in undergraduate life, there is more communication between students from the same college than between students from different colleges. In addition, the results show that 67% of the connections between different colleges are boys and girls. It means that most of the students with close ties between different colleges may be lovers.

Fig. 7. A friendships network of different colleges in the same grade

Figure 8 is a friendships network of different grades in a college. It shows the student of three grades of School of electronic engineering. Among them, the left vertex is a student of grade 2015, the bottom vertex is a student of grade 2016, the right vertex is a student of grade 2017. As can be seen from the figure in the case of the same college, the same grade students have a closer friendship, while the students in the neighboring grades have a more sparse friendship, the student in the separated grades almost no contact. It shows that the communication between undergraduate students in the same grade is greater than that in different grades.

Fig. 8. A friendships network of different grades in a college

Figure 9 shows a friendships network between boys and girls in a college. In this college, the number of boys is 656, and the number of girls is 277. There are 977 edges between boys, 310 edges between girls and 30 edges between boys and girls. This figure can be used to analyze students' love situations and to understand the emotional status of college students.

Fig. 9. A friendships network between boys and girls

4.2 Analysis Clustering Coefficient of a Friendships Networks

In a network, Clustering coefficient is a coefficient that represents the degree of aggregation of vertices. Through the statistical characteristics of the network, we can judge whether a student's circle of friends circle is close or not. Clustering coefficient is the ratio of the actual number of edges between the common neighbors and the number of edges between all neighboring vertices, which each vertex connected to the others. Figure 10 is the scatter plot of the clustering coefficient of a friendships network and the number of students' friends. The abscissa is the clustering coefficient of a friendships network, and the ordinate is the number of friends. From the distribution of the students' vertices in the graph, we can see that most of the students' clustering coefficient of friendships network is between 0.1 and 0.3, and the number of friends is between 1 and 5.

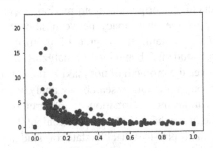

Fig. 10. The number of friends and the clustering coefficient of a friendships network

4.3 Analysis of the Lonely Man

Figure 11 is a friendships network of a class. In this network, there exist some isolated vertices whose degree are 0. The social behavior of the corresponding students is less active, which might be caused by unsociability. This kind of information provides some reference to the guidance of teachers. For the isolated vertices in friendships network, the related counselors should check in time and do well in communication work in order to avoid psychosocial disease or other accidents.

Fig. 11. A friendships network of a class

5 Summarization and Expectation

With the rapid development of campus network and the increase in need for the resource of students' information, due attention has been paid to campus data mining. For now, most of the data mining is concentrated on data of study and consumption, which cannot make the best of spatiotemporal dimension. Therefore, this paper proposes a method based on bipartite network to mining behavioral features and friendships. The bipartite network model has general applicability in practical application, which can better depict the spatiotemporal data. Firstly, building spatiotemporal data bipartite network based on campus spatiotemporal data. Secondly, statistically testifying whether students encounter originated from random encounter using hypothesis test, third calculating the degree of intimacy between students and get the students' friendships network, which contains the degree of intimacy, finally obtaining the information of features of students' behavior by analyzing the basic features of this network. This method solves the problem of not making the best of spatiotemporal data to mine campus information in previous research. By analyzing spatiotemporal data in multi-dimension, we can mine the information of the friendship and the features of students' behavior efficiently, which makes it convenient for universities to better understand both mental and physical health state of students, and it will be the important reference for the management and decision-making of the universities. In the future, we can improve the method of hypothesis test based on the fundament of this research and find a more accurate method for mining the information of friendships. We can also apply methods of spatiotemporal data mining in other scenarios to the campus scenario.

Acknowledgment. This work is supported by the National Key Research and Development Plan (Grant No. 2017YFC0820603), the Project of Chinese Society of Academic degrees and graduate education (2017Y0502) and the Open Project Fund of Key Laboratory of Trustworthy Distributed Computing and Service (BUPT), Ministry of Education. Thanks for the great help.

References

1. Tian, L.: Construction of integration and innovation of campus card. J. East China Normal Univ. (Nat. Sci. Ed.) 530–535 (2015)
2. Zhang, Y.: Overview of campus smart card system construction. Inf. Secur. Technol. 78–80 (2014)
3. Dong, X., Zhang, H.: Analysis and comparison of several clustering algorithms based on campus card consumption data. Comput. Syst. Appl. 158–161+183 (2014)
4. Jiang, N., Xu, W.: Student consumption and study behavior analysis based on the data of the campus card system. Microcomput. Appl. **31**, 35–38 (2015)
5. Fei, X., Dong, X., Zhang, H.: Analysis of impoverished college students based on campus card consumption data. Comput. Knowl. Technol. 4934–4936 (2014)
6. Qian, Y., Shi, Q.: Study on the application of data mining based on campus card platform. In: Advanced Materials Research, vols. 846–847, pp. 977–980 (2014)
7. Yan, H., Hu, H.: A study on association algorithm of smart campus mining platform based on big data. In: 2016 International Conference on Intelligent Transportation, Big Data & Smart City (ICITBS), Changsha, pp. 172–175 (2016)
8. Du, Z., Hu, L., Fu, X., Liu, Y.: Scalable and explainable friend recommendation in campus social network system. In: Li, S., Jin, Q., Jiang, X., Park, J. (eds.) Frontier and Future Development of Information Technology in Medicine and Education. LNEE, vol. 269, pp. 457–466. Springer, Dordrecht (2014). https://doi.org/10.1007/978-94-007-7618-0_45
9. Niu, J., Wang, D., Lu, J.: Mining friendships through spatial-temporal features in mobile social networks. In: 2015 IEEE 34th International Performance Computing and Communications Conference (IPCCC), Nanjing, pp. 1–8 (2015)
10. Banerjee, S., Jenamani, M., Pratihar, D.K.: Properties of a projected network of a bipartite network. In: 2017 International Conference on Communication and Signal Processing (ICCSP), Chennai, pp. 0143–0147 (2017)

Independency of Functional Connectivity States on Spatiotemporal Resolution of fMRI Data

Yuyuan Yang, Hui Shen, Zhiguo Luo, Fuquan Li, and Dewen Hu$^{(\boxtimes)}$

College of Artificial Intelligence,
National University of Defense Technology, Changsha 410073, China
dwhu@nudt.edu.cn

Abstract. Functional magnetic resonance imaging (fMRI) is widely used to explore the brain because of its high temporal and spatial resolution. Resting-state fMRI data were studied by many researchers who found the existence of dynamic functional connectivity (dFC). However, it is unclear whether estimation of functional connectivity (FC) states is dependent on temporal and spatial resolution of sampling in fMRI data. In this paper, we addressed this concern by comparing the FC states with varying spatiotemporal resolution of data where different number of regions of interest (ROIs) were randomly chosen to extract the timecourses. These timecourses were then down-sampling to different temporal resolution. Finally, a sliding-window approach was used to estimate the potential FC states in resting-state dFC. The results show that the detection of brain connectivity is insensitive to the spatial and temporal resolution of sampled data in fMRI data, which provides a dimension reduction perspective for research based on fMRI data.

Keywords: Temporal and spatial resolution · Sliding window analysis · Dynamic functional connectivity · Cluster validity index · ROI index

1 Introduction

In recent years, considering the whole brain as a sophisticated network has obtained significant attentions, which is the so-called brain connectome [1]. Resting-state fMRI data were studied by many researchers who found the existence of dFC. In previous studies, when researchers wanted to effectively extract neural signals and capture the fluctuation information of neural signals and the dynamic activities of functional networks, they often faced the problems of the selection of brain templates [2, 3] and dealing with high dimensional data. At the same time, researchers were often confused with the choice of ROIs, from less than 100 up to the quantity of voxels, when selecting brain templates without a golden standard for the selection of nodes. Researchers had assessed topological attributes of whole-brain anatomical networks over a wide range of ROIs and found that simple binary decisions about network organization were unaffected by spatial scale [4].

There were two most common topological properties, scale-freeness and small-worldness [5], tested for brain networks. The topology of both anatomical and functional

© Springer Nature Singapore Pte Ltd. 2019
F. Sun et al. (Eds.): ICCSIP 2018, CCIS 1006, pp. 370–380, 2019.
https://doi.org/10.1007/978-981-13-7986-4_33

brain networks was found to show small-world properties. These networks could be characterized highly clustered. Most researchers have used a set of brain templates chosen from the automated anatomical labeling (AAL) atlas [6] just because these brain templates have been widely used rather than the characteristic of their research object.

Which number of ROIs should the researchers employ? This problem can be considered of several practical issues. In particular, the researchers want to employ fine ROIs in order to reduce template-driven dependencies. This is a point of view to look for a better brain template. However, another possibility is that the choice of ROIs' numbers may be an intrinsic spatial property of the experiment object. Whether the estimation of resting-state FC states is influenced by the selection of ROIs, the changed spatial resolution in fMRI data. The best explanation is implicated in the intrinsic dimension of the resting-state brain states. We suppose that the intrinsic dimension of the resting-state brain states is much lower than the thousands of dimensional data. Then, when different numbers of ROIs are altered to extract the timecourses, the FC states should be similar. Different numbers of ROIs change the spatial solution of data. Furthermore, the FC states should exhibit the similar phenomenon with spatial and temporal solution changing. To verify the assumption the experiments were conducted by using different numbers of ROIs and different temporal solution timecourses to explore the effect to the brain functional connectivity under data with different temporal and spatial resolutions.

2 Datasets

2.1 HCP Dataset

Healthy subjects were selected from the public data set of the Human Connectome Project (HCP, http://www.humanconnectomeproject.org/). The data of the subjects under resting states were collected by a 3.0T nuclear magnetic resonance apparatus with the following parameters: flip angle = $52°$, time repetition = 720 ms, slice number = 72, 1200 volumes were obtained.

2.2 COBRE Dataset

The COBRE (The Center for Biomedical Research Excellence http://Functional-Connectionon_1000.projects.nitrc.org/indi/retro/cobre.html) dataset is a public data set for conducting biomedical researches.

All data were scanned with a 3.0T Siemens NMR scanner with the following parameters: time repetition = 2 s, layer thickness = 3.5 mm, slice gap = 1.05 mm, matrix size = 64×64, FOV = 240 mm, 150 volumes were obtained. The resting state fMRI data of 50 healthy subjects were randomly selected from the healthy subjects for the experiment.

3   Methods

3.1   Data Preprocessing and Spatial Sampling

The preprocessing software package was SPM8 (Wellcome Department of Imaging Neuroscience, University College London, UK, http://www.fil.ion.ucl.ac.uk/spm). (1) For each subject, the first several frames of scanned images were removed to reduce the magnetic saturation; (2) Slice timing; (3) Head motion correction; (4) Processed fMRI images for each frame based on standard templates to extract the grey-matter signals and, which was called as spatial normalization. This procedure changed the spatial solution of original data. (5) Spatial smoothing using Gaussian filtering with FWHM = 6 mm; (6) Filtering processing with frequency of 0.01 Hz–0.08 Hz (7) Regression of the whole brain's global signal (GS), head motion, white matter (WM), cerebrospinal fluid (GSF) to reduce noises.

Through the above preprocessing steps, then the ROI generated with the brain parcellation algorithm [4] could be used to extract ROI-based timecourse from 4-D fMRI data. The obtained blood oxygenation level dependent (BOLD) signal time-courses which could be used to calculate the functional connectivity were obtained [7]. When the time signal was extracted from the preprocessed data, the spatial resolution of the timecourses was changed by selecting different numbers of ROIs, and statistical methods were used to calculate the clustering validity index [8]. Exploring the relationship between the different numbers of ROIs and the number of clusters could avoid the problem of comparing FC state matrices with different dimensions. In the statistics, the evaluation criterion of FC states is the cluster validity index under different ROIs.

3.2   Data Temporal Sampling

This method was opted to use when exploring the changing temporal solution's effect on the FC states. Before carrying out the sliding window analysis, the original timecourses (TR = 0.72 s) could be down-sampled, and the timecourses with the temporal resolution of 2TR (1.44 s), 4TR (2.88 s), and 8TR (5.76 s) were obtained. Under-sampling the timecourses under resting conditions, thus changing the data temporal resolution, sliding window analysis processing is performed for the same timecourses with different temporal resolutions, and the brain connectivity state matrix is obtained by spectral clustering. The similarity of brain connectivity matrices are measured by Pearson correlation.

3.3   Sliding Window Analysis

The input data for the sliding window analysis is a set of timecourses representing the activity signals in the brain region. In the simplest case, select the window length of the time window that is parameterized with W, and using the window size (from $t = 1$ to $t = W$) [2] to calculate the connection correlation for each pair of timecourses. The Pearson correlation coefficient is used as a statistical measurement method. Then, the time window is backwards, sliding step = T, and repeating the same step with the window size $[1 + T, W + T]$ [3]. The sliding calculation process iterates through the window to the end portion containing the entire timecourses, and finally obtains the connectivity. There are N elements of different regions, and the matrix size of the data information recorded in each window is N × (N − 1)/2. At the same time, considering all the matrices together, a set of dFC is obtained [9–11].

Bivariate correlation is the most direct measure of evaluating functional connections in the sliding window approach [12]. In this experiment, the Pearson correlation coefficient commonly which used in the bivariate correlation method can be used to calculate the dynamic functional connectivity correlation of each pair brain regions [13]. The timecourses is set as a function of the time t which is an independent variable, where in the seed region is represented by s(t), t = 1, 2, ..., n. The region of interest is r(t), t = 1, 2, ..., n means, $\bar{s}$ is the mean of s(t), $\bar{r}$ is the mean of r(t). The correlation formula of the two regions is:

$$c = \frac{\sum\limits_{t=1}^{n}(s(t) - \bar{s})(r(t) - \bar{r})}{\sqrt{\sum\limits_{t=1}^{n}(s(t) - \bar{s})^2 \times \sum\limits_{t=1}^{n}(r(t) - \bar{r})^2}} \tag{1}$$

In the subsequent statistical analysis, for the convenience of statistics, the Fisher value is replaced by the Fisher value by the Fisher z-transform, and the transformation formula is as follows:

$$z = \frac{1}{2}\log(\frac{1+c}{1-c}) \tag{2}$$

This transformation causes a large change in the z value in the vicinity of c = −1 and c = 1, thereby enhancing the normal distribution characteristic of the correlation coefficient c.

In the experiment, the correlation between the timecourses of all regions is calculated, that is, all brain regions are sequentially set as seed regions.

3.4 Spectral Clustering

Spectral clustering is based on graph theory, and the essence is to transform clustering into graph segmentation problem.

Input: sample points $S = \{s_1, ..., s_n\}$, number of clusters k example
Output: label vector
Algorithm flow:
To measure the similarity of sample points, construct the adjacency matrix $A \in R^{n*n}$, where $A_{ii} = 0$;

Constructing matrix

$$D_{ii} = \sum_{j=1}^{n} A_{ij} \tag{3}$$

Laplacian matrix

$$L = D^{-\frac{1}{2}}AD^{\frac{1}{2}} \tag{4}$$

Calculate the first k largest eigenvectors $x_1, x_2, \cdots, x_k$ in L, and then rank the eigenvectors into a matrix in the order of the columns;

$$X = [x_1, x_2, \cdots, x_k] \in R^{n \times k} \tag{5}$$

Each row of the matrix X is unitized and converted into a matrix Y, where

$$Y_{ij} = X_{ij}/(\sum_j X_{ij}^2)^{1/2} \tag{6}$$

A row of Y is a sample point in the k-dimensional Euclidean space, and the k-means algorithm is used to cluster the n sample points into k-class;

Finally, the sample point s_j is assigned to the j class if and only if the i row of Y is assigned to the j class.

4 Experiments and Results

4.1 Temporal Solution Experiments

The timecourses of fMRI images were obtained with the brain template of 160, and the original timecourses were with the temporal resolution of time repetition = 0.72 s.

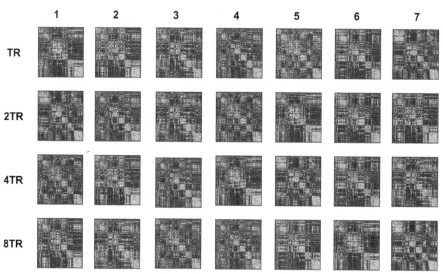

Fig. 1. The resting state fMRI data's brain connectivity under different temporal solution

The timecourses were down-sampled with the temporal resolution of 2TR, 4TR, and 8TR were obtained. When constructing the dynamic function connection matrix, the window parameters with the window size of 40 s and the sliding step length of 10 s were used to calculate and get results. During the research on resting state fMRI data conducted, a significant phenomenon appears. In the Fig. 1 (A): These cluster centroids graphs show the brain functional dynamic connectivity states. Seven clustering centers are obtained under different temporal solution when the solution of original brain timecourses' reduction varying from 1TR, 2TR, 4TR to 8TR.

Even the original data have different temporal solution. After sliding window correlation analysis and spectral clustering, their brain connectivity states do not change significantly.

For example, in the Table 1: Under 1TR's and 8 TR's temporal solution, the seven clustering centers have the most far similarity in the experiment. But we can see, the lowest central similarity is still above 93.30%. provides when the solution of original brain timecourses' reduction varying from 1TR, 2TR, 4TR to 8TR.

Table 1. The Pearson correlation between the clustering centroids under 1TR and 8TR resolution

	1	2	3	4	5	6	7
1	98.83%	70.85%	70.46%	71.65%	64.32%	71.39%	63.53%
2	71.55%	95.91%	62.67%	69.57%	63.62%	73.75%	64.51%
3	68.86%	63.51%	98.88%	70.76%	62.26%	66.11%	66.95%
4	72.55%	70.97%	70.53%	98.57%	63.92%	70.16%	71.66%
5	58.31%	66.45%	55.23%	63.71%	96.99%	64.37%	63.61%
6	67.21%	77.88%	63.95%	69.76%	67.76%	96.87%	72.70%
7	68.79%	68.83%	66.79%	67.26%	67.13%	64.29%	93.78%

4.2 Spatial Resolution Experiments

This part of the experiment used data from 50 healthy subjects of COBRE. In the process of extracting timecourses, 50, 116, 160, 257, 376, 459, 808 ROIs were used, which were randomly selected from 50–800 generated ROIs [4]. The principle of the brain template in extracting signals is actually to take the average of the signals of all voxels in a single brain region defined in the brain template, and the coordinates of the signal are defined as the central position of the region.

Due to the experiment using different numbers of ROIs, while changing the spatial resolution of data sampling, also have an impact on the dimensions of the final brain connection state matrix, in this part of the study, we couldn't measure the similarity of brain state by evaluating the similarity of the cluster centers' similarity.

The use of clustering validity index to evaluate the change of sampling spatial resolution is enough to affect the detection of the number of FC states, and to compare the relationship between clustering validity index and cluster numbers under different spatial resolutions.

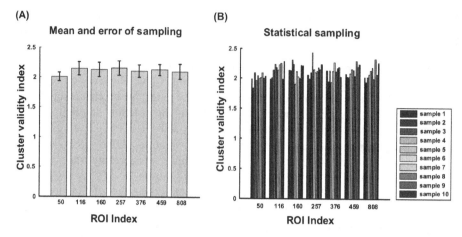

Fig. 2. The statistical analysis between the Cluster validity index and ROI index

The timecourses of 50 subjects were used to make the experimental data more general and persuasive when calculating the clustering validity index. 50 timecourses were selected each time, and 10 times were repeated to obtain ten sets of data. The ten groups of clustering validity index, the statistical analysis, are shown in the Fig. 2.

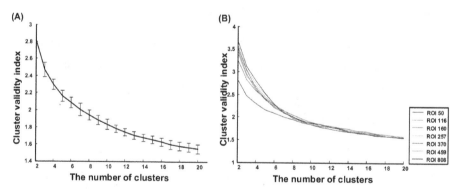

Fig. 3. The cluster validity index plotted as a function of the number of clusters. In particular, the graph (A) indicates the relation between the cluster validity index mean and standard deviation of 10 times statistical analysis and the number of clusters when ROIs are equal to 50. The graph (B) displays the relation between the cluster validity index mean and the number of clusters when ROIs are equal to 50, 116, 160, 257, 370, 459 and 808.

To get a detailed information contained in the data, we calculate the mean and standard deviation among the statistical analysis. In Fig. 4(A), the data are presented in the other style graph and cluster validity index are calculated in sampling statistics. When doing statistics, the timecourses of 50 subjects are as a sample population and 50 sets of timecourses are selected each time. Ten times were repeated to be selected to obtain ten sets of data. We obtained data on the relationship between clustering validity index and clustering numbers in 10 groups at 7 different spatial resolutions. Let us take the 10 sets of data as a Fig. 3 with the number of 50 ROIs. In the Fig. 3(A) linear graph, with the increase of the number of clusters, the trend of clustering validity index is: As the number of clusters decreases rapidly from 2 to 5, then the changes become slower and slower, and the rate of clustering index changes greatly. The number of nearby clusters is most likely the true number of brain connections we want to detect. In the Fig. 3(B), the cluster validity index all show the similar descending speed trend under different ROIs. When the number of clusters was 2 to 5, it decreased sharply with the increase of the number of clusters: when the number of clusters was 5 to 10, the change starts slowly. What's more, the cluster validity index under different number of ROIs become quickly approaching when clusters' number varying from 5 to 10.

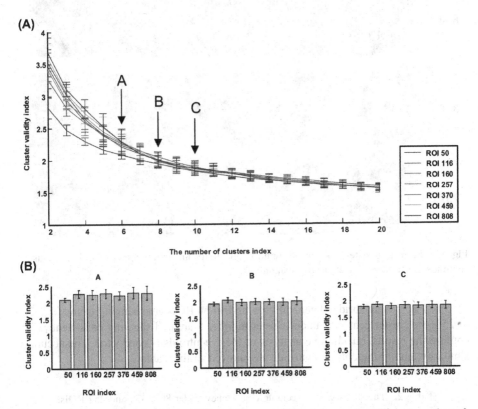

Fig. 4. The mean and standard deviation of cluster validity index under different number of clusters and different number of ROIs.

When the number of clusters is around 8, the clustering evaluation indicators are not much different. When the number of clusters is 10, the clustering index indicators calculated under different number of ROIs overlap. Mean and variance in sampling statistics under different number of ROIs are drawn. In Fig. 4(B), the slice A, B and C are obtained under different clusters' numbers from the Fig. 4(A), and for example, the slice A is obtained when cluster number equals 6. In the Fig. 4(B) A, the bar illustrates the cluster validity index are approaching closely. In the Fig. 4(B) B, when the number of clusters index equals 8, the cluster validity index is mixed under different clusters' numbers. In Fig. 4(B) C, the cluster validity index is nearly equal to each other under different clusters' numbers.

Cluster centroids under different ROIs

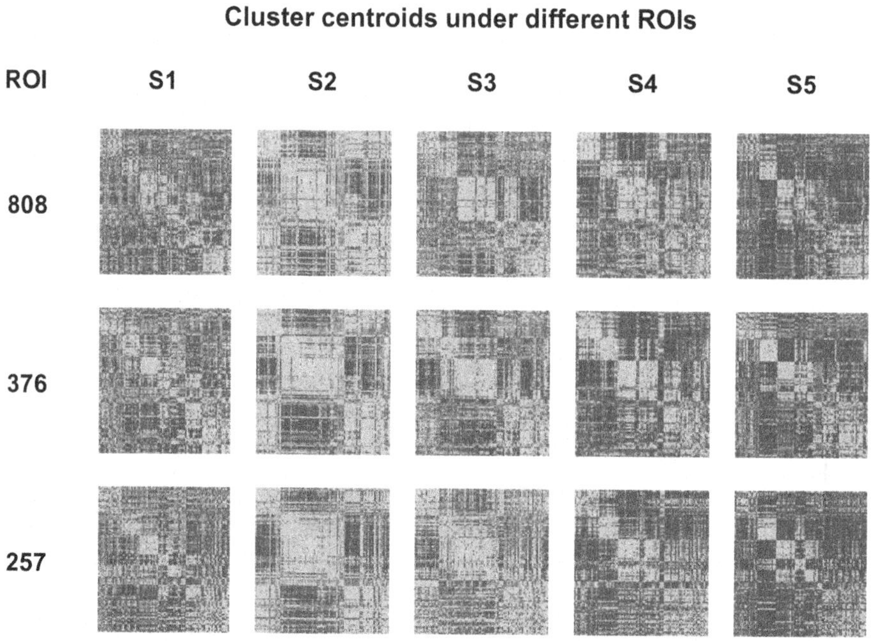

Fig. 5. The resting state fMRI data's brain connectivity under different ROIs. These cluster centroids are similar with the ROIs changing.

The Fig. 5 is an abridged general view and when ROIs are changing from 808, 376 to 257, the cluster centroids under cluster number 5 are still showing consistency. To confirm the results, quantitative analysis of these centroids is conducted. The accurate similarity among the cluster centroids are showed in the Table 2.

Table 2. The states labels' accurate consistency under 808, 376 and 257 ROIs.

	1	2	3	4	5	Ratio (%)
808	1	2	3	4	5	100
376	5	2	1	3	4	80.38
257	2	3	1	4	5	76.38

To get a more detailed information, all subjects' dynamic connectivities in correlation window are analyzed. The dynamic connectivity analysis in every subject gives a interpretation to the inconsistent of the state labels in Table 2. These inconsistency focus on the change of the subjects and the state change in every subject under cluster number 5 as shown in Fig. 6.

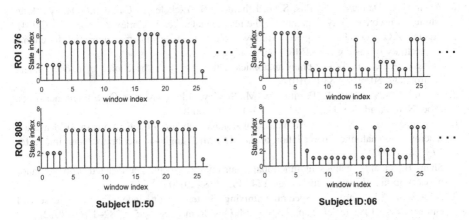

The change of corrlerational window state under different ROIs

Fig. 6. When the cluster equals 7, the dynamic connectivities are shown at every sliding window under ROI 376 and ROI 808. The inconsistency of states labels at the same sliding window mainly occurs in the boundaries of the change of subjects.

5   Discussion

In order to explore the influence of the spatiotemporal resolution of data sampling on the determination of dFC, these experiments were conducted and some interesting results were obtained. When down-sampling the timecourses, the similarity of clustering center was measured by Pearson correlation. When the time resolution was increased from 0.72 s to 5.76 s, the determination of FC states had not been greatly affected. When the spatial resolution of the timecourses was changed by selecting different ROIs, the clustering validity index calculated in statistics analysis showed a similar descending speed trend with the number of clusters changing under different ROIs.

These results confirm the estimation of FC states is independent on temporal and spatial resolution of sampling in resting-state fMRI data. At the same time, it may indicate that the brain intrinsic dimension under resting-state is lower than the number of ROIs used in this paper. The results also verify some past research findings. These researches used dimensionality reduction methods to find the brain activity patterns of global and local nerve tissue [14, 15]. The manifold decoding was used to represent the features embedded in spatiotemporal brain activity. Inspired from these studies and our findings, our future work is using dimensionality reduction coding algorithms to explore the structural of dFC states under resting-state and excavating the intrinsic information hidden in the massive fMRI data.

Acknowledgement. This research was in part supported by grants from the National Science Foundation of China (61773391, 61503397 and 61420106001).

References

1. Sporns, O., Tononi, G., Kotter, R.: The human connectome: a structural description of the human brain. PLoS Comput. Biol. **1**, e42 (2005)
2. Allen, E.A., Damaraju, E., Plis, S.M., Erhardt, E.B., Eichele, T., Calhoun, V.D.: Tracking whole-brain connectivity dynamics in the resting state. Cereb. Cortex **24**, 663–676 (2014)
3. Zhang, Z.G., et al.: Adaptive window selection in estimating dynamic functional connectivity of resting-state fMRI, pp. 1–4 (2013)
4. Zalesky, A., et al.: Whole-brain anatomical networks: does the choice of nodes matter? Neuroimage **50**, 970–983 (2010)
5. Amaral, L.A.N., Scala, A., Barthélémy, M., Stanley, H.E.: Classes of small-world networks. Proc. Natl. Acad. Sci. U.S.A. **97**, 11149–11152 (2000)
6. Tzourio-Mazoyer, N., et al.: Automated anatomical labeling of activations in SPM using a macroscopic anatomical parcellation of the MNI MRI single-subject brain. Neuroimage **15**, 273–289 (2002)
7. Shen, H., et al.: Changes in functional connectivity dynamics associated with vigilance network in taxi drivers. Neuroimage **124**, 367–378 (2016)
8. Anderson, D.T., Zare, A.: Spectral unmixing cluster validity index for multiple sets of endmembers. IEEE J. Sel. Top. Appl. Earth Obs. Remote Sens. **5**, 1282–1295 (2012)
9. Elton, A., Gao, W.: Task-related modulation of functional connectivity variability and its behavioral correlations. Hum. Brain Mapp. **36**, 3260–3272 (2015)
10. Kucyi, A., Davis, K.D.: Dynamic functional connectivity of the default mode network tracks daydreaming. Neuroimage **100**, 471–480 (2014)
11. Hutchison, R.M., Morton, J.B.: Tracking the brain's functional coupling dynamics over development. J. Neurosci. Off. J. Soc. Neurosci. **35**, 6849–6859 (2015)
12. Leonardi, N., Van De Ville, D.: On spurious and real fluctuations of dynamic functional connectivity during rest. Neuroimage **104**, 430–436 (2015)
13. Hindriks, R., et al.: Can sliding-window correlations reveal dynamic functional connectivity in resting-state fMRI? Neuroimage **127**, 242–256 (2016)
14. Kuo, P.C., Chen, Y.S., Chen, L.F.: Manifold decoding for neural representations of face viewpoint and gaze direction using magnetoencephalographic data. Hum. Brain Mapp. **39**, 2191–2209 (2018)
15. Saul, L.K., Roweis, S.T.: Think globally, fit locally: unsupervised learning of low dimensional manifolds. J. Mach. Learn. Res. **4**, 119–155 (2003)

Small Dataset Modeling and Application of Plant Medicine Extraction

Boyan Liu, Juan Chen[(⊠)], and Cuiying Dong

Beijing University of Chemical Technology, North Third Ring Road 15,
Chaoyang District, Beijing, China
jchen@mail.buct.edu.cn

Abstract. Intelligent modeling is an effective method to build prediction model of the plant medicine with ultrasonic extraction. However, there are obstacles when obtaining lots of data by the plant medicine extraction experiments, and small dataset will result in a model with low accuracy and poor generalization ability, which has a great influence on it. This paper proposes a novel virtual sample generation (VSG) approach based on Response Surface Methodology (RSM) and Extreme Learning Machine (ELM) algorithm, selecting through Cuckoo Search (CS) algorithm. The new prediction model is constructed based on ELM with the virtual sample dataset generated by this method and the original small sample dataset. The performance of the model is verified via the case of extracting the active ingredients, liquiritin, from liquorice by dual-frequency ultrasound. The experiment results show that the model established by the method proposed in this paper can significantly reduce the prediction error and improve the accuracy of the model, which provides a certain theoretical basis and reference for the industrialization of the active ingredients extraction of plant medicine.

Keywords: Small dataset modeling · Virtual sample generation ·
Plant medicine extraction

1 Introduction

The ultrasonic extraction process of plant medicine always includes numerous complex physical reactions, which brings difficulties in modeling. Data-driven modeling methods mainly focus on processing data rather than the complicated process mechanism. It is necessary to build an accurate and robust data-driven model of the optimal process parameters, which can help analyze the process of extracting the active ingredients of plant medicine [1]. However, the quantity and the quality of dataset will seriously affect the accuracy of the model. It's difficult to obtain a large size and uniformly distributed dataset gotten by measuring manually in the fields of chemical composition analysis and food detection. Therefore, the available sample dataset is limited [2, 3], resulting in the low accuracy and poor generalization performance of the established model. In the process of the ultrasonic extraction of plant medicine, the extraction rate of the active ingredients require to be measured manually by the off-line

© Springer Nature Singapore Pte Ltd. 2019
F. Sun et al. (Eds.): ICCSIP 2018, CCIS 1006, pp. 381–392, 2019.
https://doi.org/10.1007/978-981-13-7986-4_34

way. Hence, in the era of big dataset modeling, how to solve the problem of small dataset modeling is still a field worth studying.

To solve the problem of small dataset modeling, there are many academic techniques such as grey modeling, statistical learning theory, bayes network and virtual sample generation (VSG), and so on. The gray modeling is used to weaken the randomness of the original samples and improve the regularity of the sequences, so as to form a prediction model based on the gray differential equation [4, 5]. Statistical learning theory requires that the model not only achieve empirical risk minimization but also meets the condition of the confidence interval. Therefore, how to select the parameters and kernel functions is sensitive [6]. Bayes network is mainly used to infer uncertain knowledge qualitatively and quantitatively. The structure and the effect of the small dataset modeling is improved by using Expectation Maximization (EM) algorithm [7]. Based on the prior knowledge or other potential sample distribution, virtual samples were generated to fill the interval of sample information, which can improve the model performance and avoid the phenomenon of over-fitting [8].

Nowadays, Orthogonal Experimental Design (OED) and Response Surface Methodology (RSM) have been widely utilized to collect data and select the optimum parameters. These two methods can reduce workload by arranging the experiments reasonably, and the datas can be obtained efficiently. The multivariate quadratic regression equation as the prediction model of optimal parameters can be built with the sample points and their response values based on RSM, which is suitable for solving the problem of nonlinear processing [9]. The advantage of RSM is that the experimental points can be selected with a more professional design to facilitate the experiments. As a result, this method has been widely applied to the optimization of process parameters in the chemical industry [10, 11]. However, RSM also has some disadvantages. With a large number of process parameters, the model order is inevitably getting higher, which will lead to a deviation from the real situation possibility, resulting in over-fitting [12]. In addition, intelligent modeling methods such as Artificial Neural Network (ANN), Support Vector Machine (SVM) and Extreme Learning Machines (ELM) have already been widely utilized to build prediction models [13–16]. ELM algorithm is a data-driven modeling method that can realize fast learning with a single hidden layer feed-forward network. It improves the learning speed of the network and generalization ability by selecting the weight of input variables randomly. Study found that the prediction model built by ELM has better performance in accuracy, stability and uniformity [17, 18].

This paper proposes a novel virtual sample generation (VSG) approach based on Response Surface Methodology (RSM) and Extreme Learning Machine (ELM) algorithm, selecting through Cuckoo Search (CS) algorithm. The new prediction model is constructed based on ELM with the virtual sample datasets generated by this method and the original small sample datasets. The performance of the model is verified via the case of extracting the active ingredients, liquiritin, from liquorice by dual-frequency ultrasound.

2   Virtual Sample Generation

The number of samples of the small dataset modeling is less than 30 in general, which occurs in various practical applications. At present, relevant literature has proposed some methods to solve small dataset problems in image processing [19, 20] and biological system modeling [21, 22], such as grey modeling [23, 24], feature extraction [25], Virtual Sample Generation (VSG) [26, 27] and so on. VSG is an effective method to improve the accuracy of forecasting models built with small dataset. Virtual Sample was first proposed by Poggio and Vcttcr in 1992 [28]. Virtual sample refers to the auxiliary sample generated by combining the prior knowledge of the field to be studied with the known training sample, which can be defined as: for a given training dataset $D = \{(x_1, y_1), \ldots, (x_n, y_n)\}$, the virtual sample set $D' = \{(x'_1, y'_1), \ldots, (x'_n, y'_n)\}$ can be generated by some appropriate transformation T, where $x'_i = Tx_i$ and $y'_i = y_T(x_i)$. And the transformation T is obtained according to the prior knowledge of the field to be studied [29].

The relationship among the original small dataset, the virtual samples and population is shown in Fig. 1. It can be seen that the information provided by the small dataset is sparse and discrete, and the information among the sample points cannot be accurately obtained because of the interval [30, 31]. The gap among the original samples in small dataset is reduced by filling of virtual samples, which can achieve a prediction model with higher accuracy by providing more useful information [32–36]. However, the virtual samples do not all conform to the features of the population, indicating that they need to be screened by certain evaluation criteria [37].

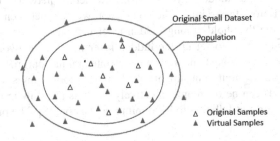

Fig. 1. Relationship among original samples, virtual samples and population

3   The Proposed Method Based on RSM-ELM

3.1   The Model Based on RSM

RSM is suitable for solving the problem of non-linear data processing. The prediction model is established by fitting the sample points and their response values into the multiple regression equation. The experiments were designed according to the Box-Behnken Design (BBD) principle and then the experimental data were obtained. The selection of experimental points is shown in Fig. 2. The obtained experimental datas were fitted with quadratic polynomial regression, which was the prediction model f_{RSM}.

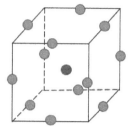

Fig. 2. Box-Behnken experimental design schematic diagram

The Root Mean Square Error (RMSE) of the testset was used to evaluate the model accuracy. The RMSE was:

$$RMSE = \sqrt{\frac{1}{n}\sum_{i=1}^{n}(y_i - y_i')^2} \tag{1}$$

Where, y_i is the actual value of the i-th test sample and y_i' is the predicted value obtained by the prediction model. The smaller the RMSE value is, the smaller the model deviation is, and the higher the model accuracy is.

3.2   The Model Based on ELM

ELM is a typical single hidden-layer feedforward neural network, the structure is shown in Fig. 3. Before the training, the connection weights between input-layer and hidden-layer and the threshold among hidden-layer neurons can be randomly generated. Hence, it only needs to set up the hidden-layer nodes of network and the activation function of hidden-layer neurons to generate unique optimal solution in the process of training without adjustment. And most shortcomings of the gradient descending methods can be overcome effectively, such as the slow training speed, the sensitive learning rate and falling into local minimum easily [38]. The prediction model

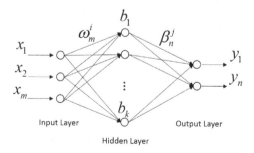

Fig. 3. Network structure of ELM

f_{ELM} is built by the experimental data designed based on BBD. The RMSE of testset in the Eq. (1), was also used to evaluate the model accuracy.

3.3 Virtual Sample Generation

The virtual sample is generated by the prediction model f_{RSM} and f_{ELM}, searched and selected by the Cuckoo Search (CS) algorithm to optimize the process of virtual sample generation. CS algorithm has comprehensive advantages in parameter setting, global search ability, universality and robustness [39]. The specific method of virtual sample generation is as follows:

First, according to the CS algorithm principle, the position of the nest is randomly generated (the vector dimension and space range of the nest are determined by the number of influencing factors and limits of related problems), which is the input of the virtual sample. And it is introduced into the above prediction model f_{RSM} and f_{ELM} based on the RSM and ELM algorithm to obtain the solution y_{RSM} and y_{ELM} respectively. The error between y_{RSM} and y_{ELM} in the Eq. (2), is used to judge the position of the nest. The smaller the error, the better the position of the nest. When the error is less than the threshold value (set as 0.05 in this paper), the position of the nest can be retained as the sample input. And the virtual sample can be constituted with it and the corresponding output y_{ELM}. The generated virtual sample can improve the accuracy of the model. The virtual samples are searched and selected reasonably by the change of the nest, and the virtual sample dataset V will be formed after several experiments.

$$\xi = |y_{ELM} - y_{RSM}| < \varepsilon \qquad\qquad (2)$$

3.4 The Operation Steps of the Proposed Method

According to the basic principles of RSM, ELM and CS algorithms, the steps of the method are summarized as follows:

Step 1: Constructing a prediction model f_{RSM} based on RSM according to the experimental datas (training dataset T) designed by BBD.

Step 2: Constructing the initial prediction model f_{ELM} based on ELM by the training dataset T.

Step 3: Generating a certain number of virtual samples according to the above process, forming the virtual dataset V;

Step 4: Constructing the new prediction model f'_{ELM} based on ELM by the virtual dataset V with the training dataset T (forming a new training dataset T-V). The accuracy of the model f'_{ELM} is evaluated by the test dataset S and compared with the original model.

Based on the above analysis, the flow chart of the proposed method is shown in Fig. 4.

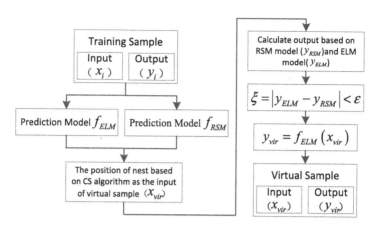

Fig. 4. Flow chart of this method

4 Case Study

Taking liquiritin, actctive ingredients of liquorice, as an example, the study was conducted on the basis of previous experiments [40].

4.1 Materials and Equipments

The main materials and equipments are shown in Table 1.

Table 1. The main materials and equipments

	Category	Manufacturer
Materials	Licorice	Beijing Tongrentang Pharmacy
	Liquiritin Standard	Shanghai Aladdin Bio-Chem Technology Co. Ltd.
Equipments	Ultrasonic Immersion Probe Device (NV-1800, 27 kHz, 900 w)	Nicle Ultrasonic Co. Ltd.
	External Groove Probe Device (42 kHz, 60 W)	Beijing Kexi Times Co. Ltd.
	UV-VIS spectrophotometer (UV-2102PC)	Dominique (Shanghai) Instrument Co. Ltd.
	Analytical Balance Sartorius (BP211-D)	Sartorius Stedim Biotech GmbH

4.2 Extraction Rate Measured Method

In this paper, the extraction rate of liquiritin require to be measured manually by the off-line way. The absorbance of the samples were measured by the ultraviolet spectrophotometer at 276 nm. The relationship between the absorbance and the concentration of the extract is determined by measuring the absorbance of the standard solution at different concentrations

$$Q = 0.0311K + 0.0332 \qquad (3)$$

Where Q is the absorbance, K is the solution concentration.

The relational expression of extraction rate is shown as

$$\eta(\%) = \frac{K(mg/L) \times V(L)}{m(g)} \times 100\% \qquad (4)$$

Where V is the total volume of the extract, m is the quality of pueraria.

4.3   Acquisition of Experimental Data

According to BBD, the extraction parameters of ultrasonic time (A), ethanol volume ratio (B) and ultrasonic duty cycle (C) were investigated for their impact on the extraction rate. The range is shown in Table 2. 17 groups of experimental datas was obtained, which form training dataset T. In addition, 7 groups of experiments were conducted to obtain datas, forming the test dataset S.

Table 2. The factors and levels

Factors and levels	Ultrasonic time (A)/min	Ethanol volume ratio (B)/%	Ultrasonic duty cycle (C)/%
−1	5	30	40
0	15	60	60
1	25	90	80

4.4   Predictive Modeling for Liquiritin Extracted by Ultrasonic

According to the datas of trainning dataset T, the prediction model of quadratic polynomial regression equation could be obtained

$$Y = -0.884 + 0.133A + 0.042B + 0.073C + 6.873 \times 10^{-4}AB - 7.195 \times 10^{-4}AC + 2.673 \times 10^{-4}BC$$
$$- 2.821 \times 10^{-3}A^2 - 6.131 \times 10^{-4}B^2 - 6.027 \times 10^{-4}C^2$$

$$(5)$$

Where A is ultrasonic time, B is ethanol volume ratio, C is ultrasonic duty cycle, Y is extraction rate.

The prediction model f_{ELM} is established by training dataset T based on ELM algorithm. According to the problems in this paper, the model is three-input $[x_i^1, x_i^2, x_i^3]$, corresponding to three factors for liquiritin extracted by ultrasonic. The model output y_i' is the extraction rate of liquiritin.

The virtual dataset V is composed of 100 virtual samples generated by the method proposed in this paper. Different prediction models are established based on ELM algorithm by combining new training dataset with the original training dataset T and different numbers of virtual samples. The comparison and evaluation of models are shown in Table 3 and Fig. 5.

Table 3. Comparison and evaluation of models

Models	Numbers of original samples	Numbers of virtual samples	RMSE	Accuracy of ascension/%
Prediction model without virtual samples	17	0	0.3480	/
Prediction model with 10 virtual samples	17	10	0.2723	21.7%
Prediction model with 30 virtual samples	17	30	0.2480	28.7%
Prediction model with 50 virtual samples	17	50	0.2346	32.6%
Prediction model with 100 virtual samples	17	100	0.2076	40.3%

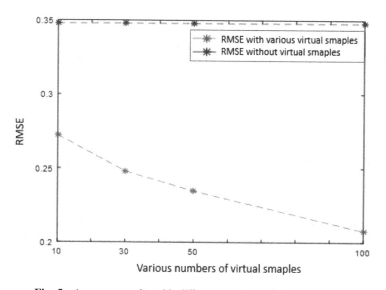

Fig. 5. Accuracy results with different numbers of virtual samples

Table 3 displays the RMSE values before and after adding different number virtual samples (including 10, 30, 50 and 100). As the results shown in Fig. 5, the prediction model with virtual samples achieves better performance compared with that without virtual samples in the term of RMSE. Also, the more virtual samples are generated, the higher accuracy and better performance the prediction model obtains. After adding 100 virtual samples, the RMSE value changed from 0.3480 to 0.2076, and the accuracy was significantly improved.

According to the above analysis, the prediction model after adding virtual samples has better generalization ability, which also improves the accuracy of the prediction model of plant medicine extracted by ultrasonic.

Figure 6(a) describes the comparison result of three values, which are the actual values from the 7 groups of test samples in the test dataset S and the predicted values obtained from the models f_{ELM} and f'_{ELM} with and without adding 100 virtual samples respectively. It can be seen from Fig. 6(a) that the predicted value obtained by the prediction model f'_{ELM} after adding the virtual sample is closer to the actual value, indicating that it has higher accuracy. Fig. 6(b) compares the errors between the predicted values and the actual values of the 7 test samples obtained from the prediction model f_{ELM} and f'_{ELM} established with and without adding 100 virtual samples. It can be seen from Fig. 6(b) that the errors of the testset after adding the virtual sample is more uniform and close to 0, which also indicates that the predicted values obtained by the prediction model f'_{ELM} after adding the virtual sample is closer to the actual value, and the model accuracy is higher. Figure 6 shows that the prediction model with virtual samples has better prediction ability and stronger generalization ability.

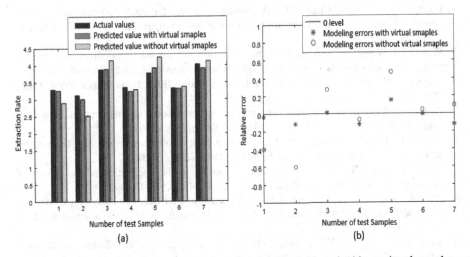

Fig. 6. Comparison of actual values and predicted values with and without virtual samples

5 Conclusions

In this paper, a new method of virtual sample generation based on the combination of RSM and ELM is proposed, and CS algorithm is used to search and select the virtual sample to improve the problem of low precision of small dataset modeling. The proposed method is applied to enhancing the prediction modeling analysis of plants medicine extracted by ultrasonic. The real case is applied in this paper to verify the effectiveness of the prediction models by comparing the errors of the models with and without adding various numbers of virtual samples. The experimental results show that the prediction model with adding virtual samples performed better than that without virtual samples in terms of the forecasting ability and accuracy. After adding 100 virtual samples, the RMSE value changed from 0.3480 to 0.2076, and the accuracy was significantly improved. In conclusion, the proposed method could be considered an effective and robust prediction tool on the small data problem.

Acknowledgment. This work is supported by the National Natural Science Foundation of China (Grant No. 21376014).

References

1. Dong, C.Y., Chen, J.: The research progress of ultrasonic extraction plant medicine effective component. Proprietary Chin. Med. **33**(7), 6:1473–6:1477 (2017)
2. Chang, C.J., Li, D.C., Huang, Y.H.: A novel gray forecasting model based on the box plot for small manufacturing data sets. Appl. Math. Comput. **265**(C) 400–408 (2015)
3. Li, D.C., Wu, C.S., Tsai, T.I.: Using mega-fuzzification and data trend estimation in small data set learning for early FMS scheduling knowledge. Comput. Oper. Res. **33**(6), 1857–1869 (2006)
4. Chang, C.J., Li, D.C., Chen, C.C.: A forecasting model for small non-equigap data sets considering data weights and occurrence possibilities. Comput. Ind. Eng. **67**(1), 139–145 (2014)
5. Wang, Y., Wang, Z., Sun, J.: Gray bootstrap method for estimating frequency-varying random vibration signals with small samples. Chin. J. Aeronaut. **27**(2), 383–389 (2014)
6. Vapnik, V.N.: An overview of statistical learning theory. IEEE Trans. Neural Netw. **10**(5), 988–999 (1999)
7. Zhu, S.F.: Research on Bayesian network classification model and its application in fault diagnosis of small samples, Harbin Institute of Technology (2009)
8. Niyogi, P., Girosi, F., Poggio, T.: Incorporating prior information in machine learning by creating virtual examples. Proc. IEEE **86**(11), 2196–2209 (1998)
9. Li, L., Zhang, H.T.: The response surface method in the application of the design of experiments and optimization. J. Lab. Res. Explor. **34**(08), 41–45 (2015)
10. Ajaz, A., Khalid, M.A., Tanveer, A.W.: Application of Box-Behnken design for ultrasonic-assistedextraction of polysaccharides from Paeonia emodi. Int. J. Biol. Macromol. **72**(5), 990–997 (2015)
11. Yang, L., Liu, Y., Zu, Y.G.: Optimize the process of ionic liquid-based ultrasonic-assisted extraction of aesculin and aseculetin from cortex fraxini by response surface methodology. Chem. Eng. J. **175**(15), 539–547 (2011)
12. Jiang, Y.J.: Complex structure model updating method based on response surface method research, Wuhan university (2011)
13. Ameer, K., Bae, S.W., Jo, Y.: Optimization of microwave-assisted extraction of total extract, stevioside and rebaudioside-A from Stevia rebaudiana, (Bertoni) leaves, using response surface methodology (RSM) and artificial neural network (ANN) modeling. Food Chem. **229**, 198 (2017)
14. Ceng, X.Y., Liang, Z.Z., Jiang, S.Y.: BP neural network to optimize the extraction process of rutin in the Sophora japonica. J. Nat. Prod. Res. Dev. **25**(3), 312–316 (2013)

15. Liang, T., Li, C.P., Zhang, J.W., Liu, H.K.: Support vector machine (SVM) of traditional Chinese medicine extract concentration soft measurement. Comput. Appl. Chem. **30**(11), 1371–1374 (2013)
16. Yu, L.M., Yan, W.G.: Model based on ELM space-time distribution of shallow embedded depth of groundwater level prediction. J. Agric. Mach. **02**(13), 215–223 (2017)
17. Huang, G.B., Zhu, Q.Y., Siew, C.K.: Extreme learning machine: a new learning scheme of feedforward neural networks. In: Proceedings IEEE International Joint Conference on Neural Networks 2004, vol. 2, pp. 985–990. IEEE (2005)
18. Huang, G.B., Zhou, H., Ding, X.: Extreme learning machine for regression and multiclass classification. IEEE Trans. Syst. Man Cybern. B Cybern. **42**(2), 513–529 (2012)
19. Li, D.C., Chang, C.J., Chen, C.C.: A grey-based fitting coefficient to build a hybrid forecasting model for small data sets. Appl. Math. Model. **36**(10), 5101–5108 (2012)
20. Chang, C.J., Li, D.C., Huang, Y.H.: A novel gray forecasting model based on the box plot for small manufacturing data sets. Appl. Math. Comput. **265**(C), 400–408 (2015)
21. Ibrahim, Z., Shapiai, M.I., Satiman, S.N.: A complete investigation of using weighted kernel regression for the case of small sample problem with noise (2015)
22. Chao, G.Y., Tsai, T.I., Lu, T.J.: A new approach to prediction of radiotherapy of bladder cancer cells in small dataset analysis. Expert Syst. Appl. **38**(7), 7963–7969 (2011)
23. Li, D.C., Lin, L.S., Peng, L.J.: Improving learning accuracy by using synthetic samples for small datasets with non-linear attribute dependency. Decis. Support Syst. **59**(1), 286–295 (2014)
24. Zheng, H., Ye, Q., Jin, Z.: A novel multiple kernel sparse representation based classification for face recognition. KSII Trans. Internet Inf. Syst. **8**(4), 1463–1480 (2014)
25. Zhu, Q., Xu, Y., Wang, J.H.: Kernel based sparse representation for face recognition. In: International Conference on Pattern Recognition, pp. 1703–1706. IEEE (2012)
26. Li, D.C., Fang, Y.H., Lai, Y.Y.: Utilization of virtual samples to facilitate cancer identification for DNA microarray data in the early stages of an investigation. Inf. Sci. **179** (16), 2740–2753 (2009)
27. Li, D.C., Hsu, H.C., Tsai, T.I.: A new method to help diagnose cancers for small sample size. Expert Syst. Appl. **33**(2), 420–424 (2007)
28. Poggio, T., Vetter, T.: Recognition and structure from one 2D model view: observations on prototypes, object classes and symmetries. Massachusetts Instof Tech **1347**, 1–25 (1992)
29. Yu, J.X., Xie, M.: Virtual sample generation technology research. J. Comput. Sci. **20**(3), 16–19 (2011)
30. Yang, J., Yu, X., Xie, Z.Q.: A novel virtual sample generation method based on Gaussian distribution. Knowl.-Based Syst. **24**, 740–748 (2011)
31. Zhu, B., Chen, Z.S., Yu, L.: Small sample overall trend of a novel diffusion technique. J. Chem. Ind. **67**(03), 820–826 (2016)
32. Yuan, T., Zhu, N., Shi, Y.: Sample data selection method for improving the prediction accuracy of the heating energy consumption. Energy Buildings **158**, 234–243 (2017)
33. Liu, P.F., Liang, H.H.: Virtual sample structure based on kernel methods. Micro Comput. Appl. **4**(3), 52–54+58 (2017)
34. Li, D.C., Wen, I.H.: A genetic algorithm-based virtual sample generation technique to improve small data set learning. Neurocomputing **143**, 222–230 (2014)
35. Jung, H.C., Jin, S.K., Heo, H.: Prediction of building energy consumption using an improved real coded genetic algorithm based least squares support vector machine approach. Energy Buildings **90**, 76–84 (2015)
36. Paudel, S., Elmitri, M., Couturier, S.: A relevant data selection method for energy consumption prediction of low energy building based on support vector machine. Energy Buildings **138**, 240–256 (2017)

37. Gong, H.F., Chen, Z.S., Zhu, Q.X.: A Monte Carlo and PSO based virtual sample generation method for enhancing the energy prediction and energy optimization on small data problem: an empirical study of petrochemical industries. Appl. Energy **197**, 405–415 (2017)
38. Huang, G.B., Zhu, Q.Y., Siew, C.K.: Extreme learning machine: theory and applications. Neurocomputing **70**(1), 489–501 (2006)
39. Layeb, A.: A novel quantum inspired cuckoo search for knapsack problems. Int. J. Bio-Inspired Comput. **3**(5), 297–305 (2011)
40. Liu, B., Chen, J., Dong, C.Y.: Optimization of ultrasonic extraction of liquiritin by response surface methodology. In: Chinese Automation Congress, pp. 5730–5734 (2017)

Adaptive Cutoff Distance Based Density Peak Pivot for Metric Space Outlier Detection

Honglong Xu[1,2] , Fuchun Sun[2(✉)] , Lijiang Tan[1] ,
and Wenjun Huang[1]

[1] Guangdong Oking Info Industry Co., Ltd., Foshan 528000, Guangdong, China
longer597@163.com, {tanlj,huangwenjun}@oking.com.cn
[2] Department of Computer Science and Technology,
Tsinghua University, Beijing 100084, China
fcsun@mail.tsinghua.edu.cn

Abstract. Outlier Detection is a key technique to discover abnormal patterns from mass data. Pivot based metric space outlier detection algorithm is designed to improve the cutoff value of outlier degree faster and terminate the detection program earlier, for saving detection time. However, due to the lack of efficient pivot selection method, the performance of existing related algorithms is not as good as it might have been. In this paper, we propose an adaptive cutoff distance based density peak pivot selection algorithm (ADP) to get a suitable pivot quickly. Moreover, we also develop an improved outlier detection algorithm based on ADP algorithm (ADPOD). Experimental results indicate that ADPOD can effectively overcome the existing relate algorithm, and achieves a 2.67 speed up over it on average and, in certain cases, up to 8.06. The distance calculation times are reduced by 53.39% on average and up to 94.84%, as well as acceptable indexing time and the universality of metric space.

Keywords: Outlier detection · Metric space · Pivot selection · Index

1 Introduction

In recent years, with the rapid development of new technologies and applications, data has increased sharply. However, as a common saying goes, "data rich but information poor". How to discover information required is becoming a difficult problem. Fortunately, with the emergence of data mining technology, this problem has got an effective way to solve. Clustering, classification, association analysis and other techniques, have made it possible for people to obtain the normal patterns beyond mass data. Nevertheless, "one person's noise may be another person's signal" [1]. The unnormal patterns may be much more valuable.

Outlier detection (also anomaly detection) is such a data mining technology used to discover unnormal patterns from mass data [2]. It is the identification of rare items, events or observations which raise suspicions by differing significantly from majority of data [3]. It is the most popular saying that, "An outlier is an observation which deviates so much from the other observations as to arouse suspicions that it was generated by a different mechanism", which was provided by Hawkins [4]. In other

© Springer Nature Singapore Pte Ltd. 2019
F. Sun et al. (Eds.): ICCSIP 2018, CCIS 1006, pp. 393–405, 2019.
https://doi.org/10.1007/978-981-13-7986-4_35

word, outliers are very few data that are significantly different from most data. Because of its unusual function, outlier detection has been widely applied in many fields, such as network intrusion detection [5], public health [6], urban traffic data [7] and so on.

In general, outlier detection algorithm can be divided into five types: statistic-based outlier detection, distance based outlier detection, density based outlier detection, depth based outlier detection and deviation based outlier detection. Metric space outlier detection, which is a typical distance based outlier detection method, consists of distance based outlier detection algorithm and distance based outlier definition, can be applied many datatypes. So that it can be used to deal with the variety challenges of big data. Further, index based metric space outlier detection has further advanced the detection speed. However, traditional algorithm randomly selects a pivot and result in instable performance. Also, the detection speed cannot be further improved because the underutilization of distance triangulation inequality.

To solve these problems, we propose an adaptive cutoff distance based density peak pivot selection algorithm to obtain pivot with high quality, and exploit an outlier detection algorithm based on it. Specifically, we make the following contributions.

(1) An adaptive cutoff distance based density peak pivot selection algorithm.
(2) A real-time stopping rule that can terminate the detection program as soon as possible with correct result.
(3) Making better use of distance triangulation inequality to remove inliers.

The rest of this paper is organized as follows. In Sect. 2, we discuss distance-based outlier detection, especially index-based metric space outlier detection. Section 3 proposes the adaptive cutoff distance based density peak pivot selection algorithm, along with our outlier detection algorithm. Experimental results and analysis are presented in Sect. 4 followed by the conclusions and future research in Sect. 5.

2 Related Work

As has been noted, distance-based outlier detection is one of the several popular outlier detection methods. Further, distance-based method can be divided into three classes, namely index-based algorithm, nested-loop algorithm and cell-based approach [8]. However, the time complexity of nested-loop is too high and cell-based method can only be applied in multidimensional data, rather than complex data type.

Unlike the above two distance-based outlier detection methods, index-based method has attracted more and more sights with its unique charm, that is significant speeding up effect. In order to detect large multidimensional data sets, Chaudhary et al. proposed a KD-tree index-based detection algorithm [9], which has got a time complexity of $O(nk)$ with the construction of KD-tree index, where n is the dataset size and k is the dimension number. However, KD-tree cannot be applied without coordinates or dimensional information. In other word, the algorithm can only be used for multidimensional data. With the help of P-tree index, Ren et al. designed a vertical distance-based outlier detection method, which processed local pruning to speed up outlier detection [10]. But as with KD-tree, P-tree has certain limitation in datatype. LSH, which is short for Locality Sensitive Hashing, is also an effective way to speed up detection. Wang et al. and Pillutla et al. took advantage of LSH and developed an outlier detection method based on different outlier definitions respectively [11, 12]. Unlike the outlier detection method stated above, LSH-based method is approximation algorithm, instead of detecting accurate result. Aiming at the outlier detection problem of distributed environment, Wang et al. exploited a data partitioning method based on space to balance the workload of different node, then pruned inliers locally based on R-tree index, in order to get the candidate outliers [13]. Though the approach obviously enhances the detection velocity, it cannot be applied in metric space. In order to solve the problem of the scalability for outlier detection, Yan et al. designed a multi-granularity pruning strategy to quickly prunes inliers, successfully reduced a huge number of k-nearest neighbor searches, but this method is developed for local outlier, which is different from this paper [14].

ORCA [15], which has been honoured as the state-of-art outlier detection algo-rithm, is closest to the algorithm this paper proposed but without index. ORCA detected dataset in random order and made use of a simple pruning rule, to be more exact, when an object's k nearest neighbors achieve an outlier degree lower than the cutoff value, it can no longer be an outlier and we can remove it directly. Experimental result showed that ORCA can give near linear time performance. The only problem is that ORCA does not benefit from index, so that its detection speed is relatively slow.

For reducing the index building time and quickly improving the cutoff value, Bhaduri et al. expanded the ORCA algorithm and developed an indexing ORCA algorithm, namely iORCA [16]. iORCA selected a pivot at random, then listed all objects in descending order by the distances between them and the pivot. iORCA detected outliers by indexing order, expecting that outliers will be processed first so that there can be a faster increase in the cutoff threshold. The algorithm achieves a considerably higher speed-up ratio, making it the most popular index-based metric space outlier detection algorithm. The main drawback to iORCA is its lack of pivot method. In detail, random pivot may result in instable performance. It also has the disadvantage of the underutilization of distance triangulation inequality, thereby the detection speed cannot be further improved.

3 ADP Based Outlier Detection Algorithm

In this section, we will discuss the adaptive cutoff distance based density peak pivot selection algorithm in detail. On the basis of pivot selection method, our outlier detection method will be proposed. At last, we will dissect their performance.

3.1 Adaptive Cutoff Distance Based Density Peak Pivot Selection Algorithm

Desity Peaks Clusering Algorithm, namely DPCA, which proposed by Alex Rodriguez and Alessandro Laio, processed a fast search for high density regions separated by low density regions, and successfully got the clustering of high quality. The algorithm's idea of density peak is just right for our pivot selection.

However, what we research is outlier detection, other than clustering. It is not necessary for us to do an immense amount of computation. In fact, it tends to just the opposite, that is, outlier detection algorithm, including pivot selection method and index construction method, should reduce time complexity as far as possible. The first problem we faced was how to set the value of cutoff distance.

As DPCA designed, cutoff distance can be set to make the average number of neighbors is around 1%–2% of the total number of objects in the data set. Obviously, it needs massive calculation and is not for outlier detection. However, even if we spend many computational resources to obtain the cutoff distance, it may still not act well, because of different distribution of datasets. Consequently, we improve it and propose an adaptive cutoff distance based density peak pivot selection algorithm (ADP).

The basic idea of ADP algorithm is consistent with iORCA that randomly selects an object will be one of the inlier objects because there are much more inliers than outliers. What the different is, we randomly select a number of candidate pivots, and design a new method to choose the one with density peak. Before detailed introduce ADP algorithm, we will describe some pruning rules at first.

As we all know, there is only distance information can be used in metric space, instead of domain-specific information. Therefore, it is very crucial for us to apply distance triangle inequality, which can evidently speed up data retrieval or outlier detection. On the basis of distance triangle inequality, three pruning rules have been derived and will be described in detail as follows.

Let D be a dataset, p be an object of D, $nn_i(p, D)$ be the ith nearest neighbor of p in D, c be the cutoff threshold, $P_c = \{p_1, p_2, p_3, \cdots, p_i\}$ be the candidate pivot set, P be the selected pivot, x be the object being detected, and $d()$ be the distance function.

Pruning Rule 1: Removing the objects that cannot be outliers.

If

$$d(x, P) + d(P, nn_k(P, D)) < c \tag{1}$$

then the detection algorithm can terminate the execution immediately with correct results.

Pruning Rule 2: Pruning the object that can never be a k-nearest neighbor.

If $\left\| d(x, P) - d(x_j, P) \right\| > d(x, nn_k(x, D))$, then x_j can never be one of the k nearest neighbors of x_t.

Proof:

From the distance triangle inequality,

$$d(x, x_j) \geq \left\| d(x, P) - dist(x_j, P) \right\|, \tag{2}$$

so that $d(x, x_j) > dist(x, nn_k(x, D))$.

That is to say, x_j is farther than the kth nearest neighbor of x, so x_j can never be one of the k nearest neighbors of x.

Pruning Rule 3: Removing k nearest neighbors that cannot be outliers.
If

$$d(x, nn_k(x, D)) < 0.5c \tag{3}$$

then x and its k nearest neighbors can be removed as inlier objects.

Proof:

It is obvious that the distance between any two objects in x and its k nearest neighbors can be smaller than c. Assume that the two objects x_a and x_b,

Then we have

$$d(x_a, x_b) \leq d(x_a, x) + d(x_b, x) \leq 0.5c + 0.5c = c \tag{4}$$

As a result, the distance of any object and its kth nearest neighbor is not larger than c, in other word, it is inlier object.

Algorithm 1: Adaptive cutoff distance based density peak pivot selection algorithm

Input: dataset D, candidate pivot number m

Output: pivot P

```
1:    P_c ← Ø, L ← Ø;
2:    P_c ← randomlySelectFromDataset(D, m);
3:    for each p in P_c
4:       Den(p) ← 0;
5:    for each o in D
6:       L(o) ← d(o, p_{c1});
7:       maxDistance ← max(d(o, p_{c1}));
8:    for each o in D {
9:        if (L(o) < 0.1* maxDistance) Den(p_{c1}) +=3;
10:       else if (L(o) < 0.2* maxDistance) Den(p_{c1}) +=2;
11:       else if (L(o) < 0.4* maxDistance) Den(p_{c1}) +=1; }
12:   for each o in D {
13:      for each p in P_c expect p_{c1}
14:      if (||L(o)-L(p)||<0.4*maxDistance) {
15:      calculate d(o, p);
16:      if (d(o, p) < 0.1* maxDistance) Den(p) +=3;
17:      else if (d(o, p) < 0.2* maxDistance) Den(p) +=2;
18:      else if (d(o, p) < 0.4* maxDistance) Den(p) +=1; }}
19:   P ← argmax(Den(p));
20:   return P;
```

Algorithm 1 shows our adaptive cutoff distance based density peak pivot selection method. After reading the dataset, it randomly selects m candidate pivots, namely P_c (line 2), then set the density value of every candidate pivot to 0 (lines 3–4), and calculates the distance between every object of the dataset and the first pivot p_{c1}, at the same time max distance will be get (lines 5–7). On the basis of max distance, we can start to calculate the density of p_{c1} now (lines 8–11). Next, this algorithm calculates the distance between each object and the remainder candidate pivots if necessary (lines 12–15) and calculate the density value of candidate pivots (lines 16–18). Finally, the candidate pivot with largest density value will be output as pivot (lines 19–20).

Significantly, it is easy to determine the value of m, which can be set as 0.1% of the dataset size but not less than 10 in a general way. On the other hand, the algorithm makes use of distance triangular inequality to reduce calculating times (lines 14–15), and constructs a multilevel weight to achieve adaptive cutoff distance (lines 9–11 and lines 16–18).

3.2   ADP Based Outlier Detection Algorithm

Algorithm 2: ADP based Outlier Detection algorithm（ADPOD）

Input: k, n, D, m

Output: D_n-outlier

```
1:      c ← 0; Dn-outlier ← Ø; B ← Ø; isStop ← false;
2:      P ← ADPPivotSelection(D, m);
3:      L ← buildIndex( D, p0);
4:      while (isStop && B ← get-next-block(L(D))) {
5:         for each b in B {
6:            if(Rule 1 holds for b) {
7:               remove b from B;
8:               ifStop ← true; }}
9:         for each b in B {
10:           if (B≠Ø){
11:           startID ← median of B ;
12:           order ← spiralOrder(L.id, startID);  }
13:           for each d in D with order{
14:              for each b in B {
15:              if(Rule 2 doesn't hold for d and b) {
16:                 dis ← d(b, d); update b.NN
17:                 if (wk(b, D) < c) {
18:                    remove b from B;
19:                    if(Rule 3 holds for b) {
20:                       for each o in b's kNN {
21:                          remove o from undetected dataset}}}}}
22:           for each b in B {
23:              Dn-outlier ← TOP(B∪Dn-outlier, n)
24:              c ← wk(Dn,k, D)   // update c;  }}}
25:     return Dn-outlier;
```

The ADPOD algorithm is shown in Algorithm 2. After initializing the cutoff value c, TOP n outliers, Dn-outlier, data block B and isStop, which is the flag of whether to stop the detecting process (line 1), ADPOD calls the pivot selection method to select pivot P from D, with parameter m (line 2). Then a simple index is built in two steps: firstly, calculate the distance of all objects and P; secondly, these distance values along with object IDs will be sorted in descending order (line 3). Then the indexing data is partition into a series of data blocks, with size of 1,000 per block in a general way. Next, in this order, detect outliers in the indexing data block (lines 4–24). For every block, at the beginning of the detection, test whether it has any inlier objects according to Pruning Rule 1. If yes, remove them directly and set the flag isStop as true, so that the program will terminate after processing this block (line 6–8). For the objects remain in data block, search the k nearest neighbors in spiral order from the middle point of the block, which is called startID (lines 11–12). For every object in the detected block, Pruning Rule 2 is used to test if it is possible for the object to be a k-nearest neighbor. If not, calculate their distance and try to update the detected object's k nearest neighbors (lines 15–16), and if its outlier degree becomes less than the cutoff value c, remove it from the block (line 16). Otherwise, ignore it and test the next one. Then outlier degree of the detected object will be calculated and if it is less than cutoff threshold, the object will be removed from the block (lines 17–18). Further, if cutoff threshold is less than 0.5c, then all its k nearest neighbors will never be outlier on the basis of Pruning Rule 3 (lines 19–21).

After detecting a block, many objects have been removed as inlier object, so there may be only a few objects left. For these remaining objects, try to insert the TOP n outliers, and update the cutoff threshold (lines 22–24). After detecting all data blocks or isStop is set as true, the detecting process is finished and TOP n outliers will be output (line 25).

3.3   Performance Analysis

For the sake of comparing and analysis, the size of dataset is set as N. With regard to ADP pivot selection algorithm, the time complexity of randomly selecting candidate pivots is O(N) at most, when m is set to a percentage of the dataset size, or indeed to be a constant level when we set m to a constant value. In fact, it is not necessary for us to set m to a value according to dataset size, suppose that the proportion of outlier is r, then outlier can never be selected as pivot unless all candidate pivots are outliers, which has a probability of r^m. By contrast, chance of selecting inlier object as pivot can be up to $1 - r^m$. Then the algorithm searches the nearest neighbors of all the candidate pivots within adaptive cutoff distance. With the help of distance triangle inequality (line 14), distance calculating times has been significantly reduced, which low to 5%. In a word, even though the time complexity of ADP algorithm may up to $O(N^2)$ in worst case, that almost certainly never happens. And moreover, we can make it lower than O(N) by control the value of m.

After selecting the density peak pivot, Algorithm 2, namely ADPOD, will build a simple index like iORCA, then process outlier detection. As a whole, they have the same time complexity. Specifically, in line 3, there are two steps for building index. Firstly, ADPOD calculate the distance between pivot to all objects of the dataset, of which time complexity is O(N). Secondly, descending sort is process and the time complexity is O(NlogN). In the procedure of outlier detection, the time complexity can be up to $O(N^2)$ in the worst case. Fortunately, this situation almost never happens, because the algorithm usually can terminate early, and the other two Pruning Rules can reduce distance calculating times in great force.

4 Experimental Results and Analysis

In this section, we describe the four datasets used in this paper, and then introduce the experimental platform and the related settings. Finally, we present the experimental results and analysis in detail.

4.1 Test Suite

All four datasets used in this section are real datasets, obtained from the UCI Machine Learning Repository [17]. We summarize them as follows.

TCP of KDD Cup 1999: KDD Cup 1999 dataset is originally from the Defense Advanced Research Projects Agency and was later processed by Professor Salvatore et al. Its 10% version consists of 190,065 TCP instances, each of which has 41 attributes.

Statlog (Shuttle): A shuttle dataset from the National Aeronautics and Space Administration (NASA), consisting of 58,000 examples, each of which has 9 attributes.

Molecular Biology: A DNA sequence dataset, which consists of 3,190 examples, all of them taken from Genbank 64.1. Each example has 60 attributes. Significantly, this dataset is suitable for applying the alignment distance metric.

Statlog (Landsat Satellite): A landsat dataset, which comes from the remote sensing data of NASA. It consists of 6,435 examples, each of which has 36 attributes.

4.2 Experimental Platform and the Related Settings

The experiments were run on a notebook with an Intel Core i7-8550U CPU @1.80 GHz, 8 GB RAM, 256 GB SSD, running Windows 10 Home. The algorithms were implemented in C++ and compiled with Visual Studio 2012 in Release Mode. Unless otherwise specified, for ease of comparison to iORCA, the parameter k in determining nearest neighbors is set to 5, the outlier detection number n is set to 30, the size of data block is set to 1,000, size of TCP dataset and Shuttle dataset is set to maximum, namely 190,065 and 58,000, and the k-distance outlier definition is applied, which takes the distance of an object to its kth nearest neighbor as outlier degree. However, APDOD is compatible with other definitions, such as the k-R outlier and the k-distance sum-based outlier. For multidimensional datasets, such as TCP, Shuttle and Landsat Satellite, we perform normalization processing before use, and apply Euclidean distance for continuous attributes, and Hamming distance for discrete attributes.

4.3   Experimental Results

In this section, we compare the ADPOD algorithm with two most popular metric space outlier detection algorithms, ORCA (without index) and iORCA (indexing). Running time and distance calculation times will be studied first, followed with the cutoff values. In order to reduce the experimental error, every experiment has been run 10 times, and the average value is used as the final result.

As a whole, we can see that ADPOD outperforms the other two algorithms on the four datasets [17], especially on the TCP and Landsat datasets, where ADPOD has got great advantages. On the other hand, it can be seen that the time complexity of ADPOD remains nearly linear, and the running time of both iORCA-index and ADPOD-index keep on so low that it is hard to distinguish them from x-axis.

However, there is an obvious exception that when the size of Shuttle dataset increases to 20,000, the running time of two indexing method are unexpectedly defeated by ORCA, which is an outlier detection method without index. To look for the reason, as Fig. 2 shows, we do a series of extra experiments, and find that the pruning rule 1 still work well on this dataset. Moreover, cutoff threshold increases much faster than ORCA. Surprisingly, on this premise, the two indexing methods' distance calculation times remain at a high level. Our analysis finds that spiral order does not speed up the searching of nearest neighbor due to the data distribution and dimensionality reduction, which processed by building index.

As we all know, distance calculation has become a very expensive procedure for data retrieval or outlier detection. In order to make a further research on the performances of the three algorithms, distance calculation times were recorded when we made the above experiments. As shown in Fig. 3, the trend of distance calculation times is very similar to running time, which has been shown in Fig. 1.

As shown in Fig. 4, benefiting from three Pruning Rules, ADPOD increase slightly in running time with increasing k. This is because with the value of k increasing, objects are easier to be removed as inliers, and more objects are found not to be k-nearest neighbors. Therefore, distance calculation time is significantly avoided.

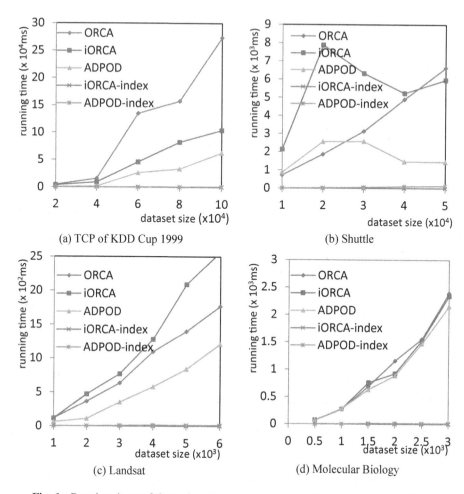

Fig. 1. Running times of three algorithms on four datasets for various dataset sizes.

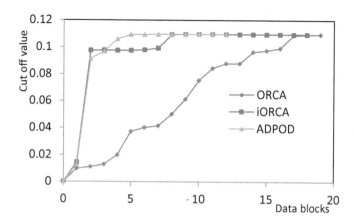

Fig. 2. Cutoff threshold of three algorithms on Shuttle dataset when size = 20,000.

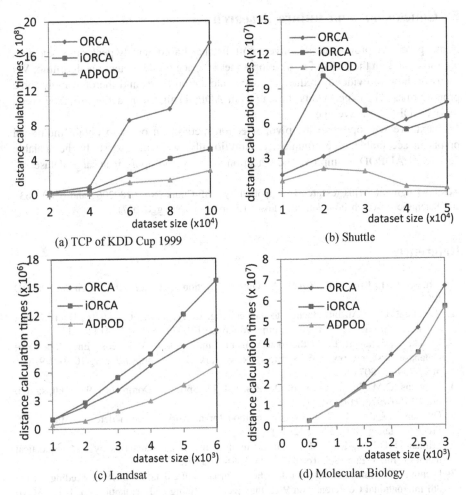

Fig. 3. Distance calculation times of three algorithms on four datasets for various dataset sizes.

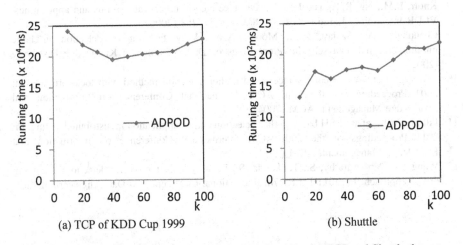

Fig. 4. Running time with various k of ADPOD algorithm for TCP and Shuttle datasets

5 Conclusions and Future Research

In this paper, we propose an adaptive cutoff distance based density peak pivot selection algorithm and on the basis of it, develop a metric space outlier detection algorithm. We focus on how to evidently reduce distance calculation times and therefor apply three pruning rules. The experiments show that our ADPOD algorithm achieves a 2.67 speed up over iORCA on average.

Next, we will optimize the pivot selection method, in order to obtain multilevel pivots in acceptable time complexity. Additionally, we will also study the scalable version of ADPOD to improve the detection velocity and apply it in large dataset.

Acknowledgment. This research is supported by NSF-China (No. 61802062 and 61802063), and Scientific Research Foundation of Foshan University (No. gg07027).

References

1. Kriegel, B.H., Kröger, P., Zimek, A.: Outlier detection techniques. In: Tutorial at PAKDD (2010)
2. Aggarwal, C.C.: An introduction to data mining. In: Aggarwal, C.C. (eds.) Data Mining, pp. 1–26. Springer, Cham (2015). https://doi.org/10.1007/978-3-319-14142-8_1
3. Zimek, A., Schubert, E.: Outlier detection. In: Liu, L., Özsu, M.T. (eds.) Encyclopedia of Database Systems, pp. 1–5. Springer, New York (2017). https://doi.org/10.1007/978-1-4899-7993-3_80719-1
4. Hawkins, D.M.: Identification of Outliers, vol. 11. Springer, Dordrecht (1980). https://doi.org/10.1007/978-94-015-3994-4
5. Othman, Z.A., et al.: Rough outlier method for network intrusion detection. Int. J. Inf. Process. Manag. **4**(7), 39–50 (2013)
6. Srimani, P.D.P.K., Koti, M.S.: Outlier mining in medical databases by using statistical methods. Int. J. Eng. Sci. Technol. **4**(1), 239–246 (2012)
7. Djenouri, Y., Zimek, A.: Outlier detection in urban traffic data. In: 2018 Proceedings of the 8th International Conference on Web Intelligence, Mining and Semantics, pp. 1–12. ACM, Novi Sad (2018)
8. Knorr, E.M., Ng, R.T., Tucakov, V.: Distance-based outliers: algorithms and applications. VLDB Int. J. Very Large Data Bases **8**(3–4), 237–253 (2000)
9. Chaudhary, A., Szalay, A.S., Moore, A.W.: Very fast outlier detection in large multidimensional data sets. In: Proceedings of Data Mining and Knowledge Discovery (2002)
10. Ren, D., et al.: A vertical distance-based outlier detection method with local pruning. In: 2004 Proceedings of the 13th ACM International Conference on Information and Knowledge Management. ACM (2004)
11. Pillutla, M.R., et al.: LSH based outlier detection and its application in distributed setting. In: 2011 Proceedings of the 20th ACM International Conference on Information and Knowledge Management. ACM (2011)
12. Wang, Y., Parthasarathy, S., Tatikonda, S.: Locality sensitive outlier detection: a ranking driven approach. In: 2011 IEEE 27th International Conference on Data Engineering. IEEE (2011)

13. Wang, X.-T., Shen, D.-R., Bai, M.: BOD: an efficient algorithm for distributed outlier detection. Chin. J. Comput. **39**(1), 36–51 (2016)
14. Yan, Y., Cao, L., Rundensteiner, E.: Scalable top-n local outlier detection. In: 2017 ACM SIGKDD International Conference on Knowledge Discovery and Data Mining, pp. 1235–1244 (2017)
15. Bay, S.D., Schwabacher, M.: Mining distance-based outliers in near linear time with randomization and a simple pruning rule. In: 2003 Proceedings of the 9th ACM SIGKDD International Conference on Knowledge Discovery and Data Mining, Washington, DC, USA (2003)
16. Bhaduri, K., Matthews, B.L., Giannella, C.R.: Algorithms for speeding up distance-based outlier detection. In: 2011 Proceedings of the 17th ACM SIGKDD International Conference on Knowledge Discovery and Data Mining, San Diego, USA (2011)
17. UCI Machine Learning Repository: Data Sets. http://archive.ics.uci.edu/ml/datasets.html. Accessed 1 Sept 2018

Robust Neural Direct Hypersonic Flight Control Under Actuator Saturation

Xia Wang[1], Bin Xu[1,2(✉)], Pengchao Zhang[3], and Yu Zhang[4]

[1] School of Automation, Northwestern Polytechnical University, Xi'an 710072, China
smileface.binxu@gmail.com
[2] Research Institute of Northwestern Polytechnical University in Shenzhen,
Shenzhen 518057, China
[3] Shaanxi Provincial Key Laboratory of Industrial Automation,
Shaanxi University of Technology, Hanzhong 723000, Shaanxi, China
[4] State Key Laboratory of Industrial Control Technology,
College of Control Science and Engineering, Zhejiang University,
Hangzhou 310027, China

Abstract. This work addresses the robust neural direct control of hypersonics flight vehicle (HFV) under dynamics uncertainty and actuator saturation. The controller is constructed with robust control and neural control. To deal with the actuator saturation, a Gaussian error function is employed to express the effect. The dynamic surface control (DSC) is studied to remove the explosion of the complexity by using a nonlinear adaptive filter. The simulation tested on the hypersonic vehicle control-oriented model (COM) shows the effectiveness of the control design.

Keywords: Hypersonic flight vehicle · Neural network (NN) ·
Actuator saturation

1 Introduction

HFVs have attained much attention due to the advantage of fast flight speed while the flight control is extremely challenging due to the special structure and the large flight envelope [1]. The dynamics uncertainty is commonly studied and intelligent control is widely used for the universal approximation ability of nonlinearity. Actuator dynamics is extensively studied since the system performance might be severely degraded if it is ignored. To be specific, the control signal is often limited due to the actuator physical constraint. In [2], the saturation model

This work was supported by Science and Technology on Space Intelligent Control Laboratory (ZDSYS-2017-05), National Natural Science Foundation of China (Grant Nos: 61622308, 61873206, 61673341), the Fundamental Research Funds of Shenzhen Science and Technology Project (JCYJ20160229172341417) and the Open Research Project of the State Key Laboratory of Industrial Control Technology, Zhejiang University, China (No. ICT1800421, ICT1900312).

F. Sun et al. (Eds.): ICCSIP 2018, CCIS 1006, pp. 406–414, 2019.
https://doi.org/10.1007/978-981-13-7986-4_36

is described by nonsmooth nonlinearity and a smooth function is introduced to facilitate the control design.

The COM of hypersonic vehicle dynamics is given in [3]. Define $\bar{\chi}_i = [\chi_1, ..., \chi_i]^T$, $i = 1, 3$ with $\chi_1 = \gamma$, $\chi_2 = \theta$, $\chi_3 = q$ and $\theta = \alpha + \gamma$. The attitude dynamics is rewritten as

$$\dot{\chi}_1 = F_1(\bar{\chi}_1) + G_1\chi_2$$
$$\dot{\chi}_2 = \chi_3$$
$$\dot{\chi}_3 = F_3(\bar{\chi}_3) + G_3u$$
$$u = \delta_e$$
$$y = \chi_1 \tag{1}$$

Since the dynamics is with the cascade structure, the adaptive back-stepping neural control is widely used. In literature, the classic back-stepping design, DSC and command filter backstepping [4] are studied. Specially, first-order filter [5] and nonlinear adaptive filter [6] are proposed. The later is superior because the asymptotic tracking of the tracking error is obtained by eliminating the effect induced by bound layer error.

It is noted that most of the NN-based control designs are conducted on the assumption that the NN estimation is always valid. Considering this problem, several attempts have been on robust adaptive design to achieve global tracking [7–9]. In [7], the unknown function approximated by NN are only based on the reference signal which is provided as a priori, so the compact domain can be determined in advance. In [10], the controller is using switching function to tune the robust design and neural design. In this way, if the states escape the approximation region, the robust design will be in effect to drive the system back to the neural working region. In the work, both indirect and direct designs are presented and the stability of the closed-loop system is discussed. For the direct design, the new function is developed and the direct controller is constructed.

Based on the previous work in [10], the convergence performance and the actuator saturation are considered in this paper. The paper is organized as follows. The control problem formulation is described in Sect. 2. Section 3 presents the controller design. Section 4 shows the simulation studies while the final conclusion is given in Sect. 5.

2   Control Problem Formulation

The control objective is to study a robust neural direct control for HFVs with unknown dynamics and actuator saturation, such that the desired tracking performance of the system is achieved.

The following assumptions are made to achieve the above-mentioned control goal.

Assumption 1. *The unknown functions $F_i(\bar{\chi}_i)$, $i = 1, 3$ satisfy $|F_i(\bar{\chi}_i)| \leq a_{im} \times F_{im}(\bar{\chi}_i)$ where a_{im} are unknown positive constants and $F_{im}(\bar{\chi}_i)$ are known functions.*

Assumption 2. *The functions G_i, $i = 1, 3$ are unknown and satisfy $G_i^L \leq |G_i| \leq G_i^U$. The signs of control gain G_i are known with $G_1 > 0$ and $G_3 < 0$.*

Remark 1. The velocity is considered as slow dynamics according to the time-scale decomposition in [10]. So the velocity is approximated as constant for the attitude dynamics control and the derivatives of G_i are considered as zero.

Definition 1. *[10] The switching functions are constructed as*

$$m_i(\bar{\chi}_i) \triangleq \prod_{k=1}^{i} B_k(\chi_k) \tag{2}$$

and

$$B_k(\chi_k)$$
$$\triangleq \begin{cases} 1 & \text{if } |\chi_k| < \lambda_{k1} \\ \frac{\lambda_{k2}^2 - \chi_k^2}{\lambda_{k2}^2 - \lambda_{k1}^2} e^{-\left(\frac{\chi_k^2 - \lambda_{k1}^2}{\tau_0\left(\lambda_{k2}^2 - \lambda_{k1}^2\right)}\right)^{2b_0}} & \text{if } \lambda_{k1} \leq |\chi_k| \leq \lambda_{k2} \\ 0 & \text{if } |\chi_k| > \lambda_{k2} \end{cases} \tag{3}$$

where the constants $\lambda_{i2} > \lambda_{i1} > 0$, $i = 1, ..., n$ are the boundaries of the compact subsets Ω_i, $b_0 > 0$ is the order of the function and $\tau_0 > 0$ is the spread of the function.

Definition 2. *For $\chi \in R$, a Gauss error function is described as*

$$\text{erf}(\chi) = \frac{2}{\sqrt{\pi}} \int_0^{\chi} e^{-t^2} dt \tag{4}$$

Remark 2. The total unknown functions are approximated by the radial basis function NN and $H_i = \omega_i^{*T}\theta_i + \varepsilon_i$, $i = 1, 3$ where ω_i^* and θ_i are the optimal weight vector and the basic function vector respectively, and ε_i is the NN construction error with $|\varepsilon_i| \leq \varepsilon_{im}$.

3   Controller Design

3.1   Actuator Saturation Model

The actuator saturation nonlinearity is described by the following smooth saturation model

$$u = u_m \times \text{erf}\left(\frac{\sqrt{\pi}}{2u_m}\bar{u}\right) \tag{5}$$

where u is the plant input and $\bar{u}$ is the control input, $u_m = (u^+ + u^-)/2 + (u^+ - u^-)/2\operatorname{sign}(\bar{u})$, u^- and u^+ are the minimum and the maximum values of the elevator deflection, and $\operatorname{sign}(*)$ is the standard sign function.

Define $\Lambda = u - b\bar{u}$ with $b > 0$ as an unknown constant. The saturation model can be represented as

$$u = b\bar{u} + \Lambda \tag{6}$$

Assumption 3. *There exist constants b_L, b_U and Λ_U such that b and Λ satisfy $b_L \le b \le b_U$ and $\Lambda \le \Lambda_U$.*

3.2 Attitude Control

For simplicity, the functions $F_i(\bar{\chi}_i)$ are denoted as F_i, define $\operatorname{sig}^{\nu_i}(e_i) = |e_i|^{\nu_i}\operatorname{sign}(e_i)$ and $b_i = \begin{cases} 0 \text{ if } e_i = 0 \\ 1 \text{ if } e_i \ne 0 \end{cases}$.

Step 1: Define $e_1 = \chi_1 - y_r$. The error dynamics of flight path angle is obtained as

$$\begin{aligned} \dot{e}_1 &= G_1\chi_2 + F_1 - \dot{y}_r \\ &= G_1\left(\chi_2 + G_1^{-1}(F_1 - \dot{y}_r)\right) \end{aligned} \tag{7}$$

Define $s_1 = [\chi_1, \dot{y}_r]^T$. On the compact set Ω_{s_1}, it is obtained as

$$\begin{aligned} H_1(s_1) &= G_1^{-1}(F_1 - \dot{y}_r) \\ &= \omega_1^{*T}\theta_1(s_1) + \varepsilon_1 \end{aligned} \tag{8}$$

The following inequality is obtained as

$$\begin{aligned} |H_1(s_1)| &\le \left(G_1^L\right)^{-1}\left(a_{1m}F_{1m}(\bar{\chi}_1) + |\dot{y}_r|\right) \\ &\le \eta_{1m}h_1(s_1) \end{aligned} \tag{9}$$

where $h_1(s_1) = F_{1m}(\bar{\chi}_1) + |\dot{y}_r|$ and $\eta_{1m} = \max\left\{(a_{1m}/G_1^L), (1/G_1^L)\right\}$.

The virtual control is designed as

$$\chi_2^c = -k_1 e_1 - b_1 l_1\operatorname{sig}^{\nu_1}(e_1) - m_1(s_1)u_1^N - (1 - m_1(s_1))u_1^r \tag{10}$$

where $k_1 > 0$, $l_1 > 0$ and $0 < \nu_1 < 1$ are the user-defined parameters, u_1^N and u_1^r are designed as

$$u_1^N = \hat{\omega}_1^T\theta_1(s_1) \tag{11}$$

$$u_1^r = \hat{\eta}_{1m}h_1(s_1)\tanh\left(\frac{\vartheta_1}{\varpi_1}\right) \tag{12}$$

where $\vartheta_1 = e_1 h_1(s_1)$, $\hat{\omega}_1$ and $\hat{\eta}_{1m}$ are the estimations of ω_1^* and η_{1m} respectively, and $\varpi_1 > 0$ is designed by users.

Using the following adaptive filter design in [6] to obtain the new state variable χ_2^d

$$\alpha_2 \dot\chi_2^d = -z_2 - \frac{\alpha_2 \hat{N}_2^2 z_2}{\sqrt{\hat{N}_2^2 z_2^2 + \mu_2^2}} - \alpha_2 e_1 \tag{13}$$

$$\dot{\hat{N}}_2 = \rho_2 \left(|z_2| - \tau_2 \hat{N}_2 \right) \tag{14}$$

where $z_2 = \chi_2^d - \chi_2^c$, α_2, μ_2, ρ_2 and τ_2 are the positive design parameters.

The update laws are designed as

$$\dot{\hat{\omega}}_1 = \gamma_1 \left[e_1 m_1(s_1) \theta_1(s_1) - \delta_1 \hat{\omega}_1 \right] \tag{15}$$

$$\dot{\hat{\eta}}_{1m} = \lambda_1 \left[(1 - m_1(s_1)) \vartheta_1 \tanh\left(\frac{\vartheta_1}{\varpi_1} \right) - \xi_1 \hat{\eta}_{1m} \right] \tag{16}$$

where $\gamma_1 > 0$, $\delta_1 > 0$, $\lambda_1 > 0$ and $\xi_1 > 0$ are the design parameters.

Step 2: Define $e_2 = \chi_2 - \chi_2^d$. The error dynamics of pitch angle is obtained as

$$\dot{e}_2 = \chi_3 - \dot\chi_2^d \tag{17}$$

The virtual control is designed as

$$\chi_3^c = -k_2 e_2 - b_2 l_2 \mathrm{sig}^{\nu_2}(e_2) - e_1 + \dot\chi_2^d \tag{18}$$

where $k_2 > 0$, $l_2 > 0$ and $0 < \nu_2 < 1$ are the user-defined parameters.

Using the following adaptive filter design in [6] to obtain the new state variable χ_3^d

$$\alpha_3 \dot\chi_3^d = -z_3 - \frac{\alpha_3 \hat{N}_3^2 z_3}{\sqrt{\hat{N}_3^2 z_3^2 + \mu_3^2}} - \alpha_3 e_2 \tag{19}$$

$$\dot{\hat{N}}_3 = \rho_3 \left(|z_3| - \tau_3 \hat{N}_3 \right) \tag{20}$$

where $z_3 = \chi_3^d - \chi_3^c$, α_3, μ_3, ρ_3 and τ_3 are the positive design parameters.

Step 3: Define $e_3 = \chi_3 - \chi_3^d$. The error dynamics of pitch rate is obtained as

$$\dot{e}_3 = F_3 + bG_3\bar{u} + G_3\Lambda - \dot\chi_3^d \tag{21}$$

$$= bG_3 \left(\frac{1}{bG_3} (F_3 - \dot\chi_3^d) + \bar{u} + \frac{\Lambda}{b} \right) \tag{22}$$

Define $s_3 = \left[\bar\chi_3^T, \dot\chi_3^d \right]^T$. On the compact set Ω_{s_3}, it is obtained as

$$H_3(s_3) = \frac{1}{bG_3} (F_3 - \dot\chi_3^d)$$

$$= \omega_3^{*T} \theta_3(s_3) + \varepsilon_3 \tag{23}$$

By Assumptions 1–3, the following inequality is obtained as

$$|H_3(s_3)| \leq \frac{1}{b_L G_3^L} \left(a_{3m} F_{3m} (\bar{\chi}_3) + |\dot{\chi}_3^d| \right)$$

$$\leq \eta_{3m} h_3(s_3) \tag{24}$$

where $h_3(s_3) = F_{3m} (\bar{\chi}_3) + |\dot{\chi}_3^d|$ and $\eta_{3m} = \max \left\{ a_{3m}/(b_L G_3^L), 1/(b_L G_3^L) \right\}$.

Define $D_3 = \Lambda/b$ with supreme $D_{3M} = \Lambda_U/b_L$. The control input is designed as

$$\bar{u} = k_3 e_3 + b_3 l_3 \mathrm{sig}^{\nu_3} (e_3) + e_2 - m_3(s_3) u_3^N + (1 - m_3(s_3)) u_3^r + u_3^U \tag{25}$$

where $k_3 > 0$, $l_3 > 0$ and $0 < \nu_3 < 1$ are the user-defined parameters, u_3^N, u_3^r and u_3^U are designed as

$$u_3^N = \hat{\omega}_3^T \theta_3(s_3) \tag{26}$$

$$u_3^r = \hat{\eta}_{3m} h_3(s_3) \tanh \left(\frac{\vartheta_3}{\varpi_3} \right) \tag{27}$$

$$u_3^U = \hat{D}_{3M} \tanh \left(\frac{e_3}{\varpi_{30}} \right) \tag{28}$$

where $\vartheta_3 = e_3 h_3(s_3)$, $\hat{\omega}_3$, $\hat{\eta}_{3m}$ and $\hat{D}_{3M}$ are the estimations of ω_3^*, η_{3m} and D_{3M} respectively, $\varpi_3 > 0$ and $\varpi_{30} > 0$ are designed by users.

The update laws are designed as

$$\dot{\hat{\omega}}_3 = -\gamma_3 \left[e_3 m_3(s_3) \theta_3(s_3) + \delta_3 \hat{\omega}_3 \right] \tag{29}$$

$$\dot{\hat{\eta}}_{3m} = \lambda_3 \left[(1 - m_3(s_3)) \vartheta_3 \tanh \left(\frac{\vartheta_3}{\varpi_3} \right) - \xi_3 \hat{\eta}_{3m} \right] \tag{30}$$

$$\dot{\hat{D}}_{3M} = \lambda_{30} \left[e_3 \tanh \left(\frac{e_3}{\varpi_{30}} \right) - \xi_{30} \hat{D}_{3M} \right] \tag{31}$$

where $\gamma_3 > 0$, $\delta_3 > 0$, $\lambda_3 > 0$, $\xi_3 > 0$, $\lambda_{30} > 0$ and $\xi_{30} > 0$ are the design parameters.

4   Simulation

The proportional-integral-derivative (PID) control for the velocity subsystem and the generated reference signals V_r, h_r and y_r are constructed as the same design in [11].

The initial conditions are $h_0 = 86000 \mathrm{ft}$, $V_0 = 7850 \mathrm{ft/s}$, $\theta_0 = 2.3°$, $\gamma_0 = 0$, $q_0 = 0$. The design parameters are chosen as $k_1 = 40$, $k_2 = 0.2$, $k_3 = 5$, $l_1 = 40$, $l_2 = 0.2$, $l_3 = 5$, $\nu_1 = 0.1$, $\nu_2 = 0.9$ and $\nu_3 = 0.9$. The parameters for adaptive laws are designed as $\gamma_i = 2$, $\delta_i = 10$, $\lambda_i = 5$, $\xi_i = 5 \times 10^{-5}$, $\varpi_i = 10^{-3}$, $\alpha_i = 0.05$, $\rho_i = 2$, $\tau_i = 0.05$, $\mu_i = 0.01$, $\lambda_{30} = 2$, $\xi_{30} = 0.05$, $\varpi_{30} = 10^{-3}$. The elevator deflection is constrained by $u^+ = 15°$ and $u^- = -15°$.

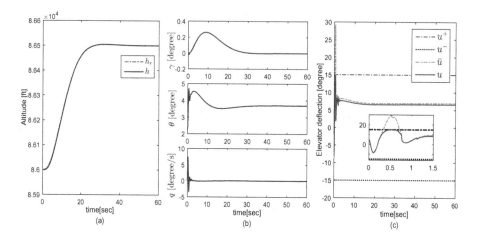

Fig. 1. System performance. (a): Altitude tracking. (b): System states. (c): Elevator deflection.

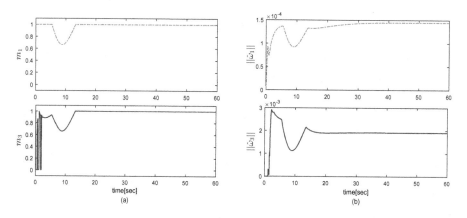

Fig. 2. Signal response. (a): Switching signals m_1 and m_3. (b): Estimate of NN weights ω_1 and ω_3.

Simulation results are given in Figs. 1, 2 and 3. From the tracking performance presented in Fig. 1, the good tracking performance is obtained in case of dynamics uncertainty. The boundedness of the elevator deflection is presented in Fig. 1(c). The response of switching signals and NN weights is shown in Fig. 2. From the parameters adaption presented in Fig. 3, it is observed that the estimations of the parameters are bounded and converge to some constants finally.

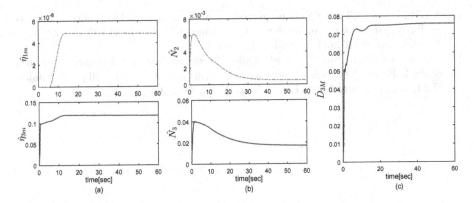

Fig. 3. Parameters adaption. (a): Estimate of η_{1m} and η_{3m}. (b): Estimate of N_2 and N_3. (c): Estimate of D_{3M}.

5   Conclusion

The robust neural direct control of HFV with unknown dynamics and actuator saturation is studied in this paper. The effectiveness of the controller design is presented by the simulation tests.

References

1. Xu, B., Shi, Z.K.: An overview on flight dynamics and control approaches for hypersonic vehicles. Sci. China Inf. Sci. **58**(7), 1–19 (2015)
2. Chen, M., Tao, G., Jiang, B.: Dynamic surface control using neural networks for a class of uncertain nonlinear systems with input saturation. IEEE Trans. Neural Netw. Learn. Syst. **26**(9), 2086–2097 (2015)
3. Parker, J.T., Serrani, A., Yurkovich, S., et al.: Control-oriented modeling of an air-breathing hypersonic vehicle. J. Guidance Control Dyn. **30**(3), 856–869 (2007)
4. Farrell, J.A., Polycarpou, M., Sharma, M., et al.: Command filtered backstepping. IEEE Trans. Autom. Control **54**(6), 1391–1395 (2009)
5. Swaroop, D., Hedrick, J.K., Yip, P.P., et al.: Dynamic surface control for a class of nonlinear systems. IEEE Trans. Autom. Control **45**(10), 1893–1899 (2000)
6. Liu, Y.H.: Dynamic surface asymptotic tracking of a class of uncertain nonlinear hysteretic systems using adaptive filters. J. Franklin Inst. **355**(1), 123–140 (2018)
7. Chen, W., Jiao, L.C., Wu, J.: Globally stable adaptive robust tracking control using RBF neural networks as feedforward compensators. Neural Comput. Appl. **21**(2), 351–363 (2012)
8. Chen, W., Ge, S.S., Wu, J., et al.: Globally stable adaptive backstepping neural network control for uncertain strict-feedback systems with tracking accuracy known a priori. IEEE Trans. Neural Netw. Learn. Syst. **26**(9), 1842–1854 (2015)
9. Huang, J.T.: Global tracking control of strict-feedback systems using neural networks. IEEE Trans. Neural Netw. Learn. Syst. **23**(11), 1714–1725 (2012)

10. Xu, B., Yang, C., Pan, Y.: Global neural dynamic surface tracking control of strict-feedback systems with application to hypersonic flight vehicle. IEEE Trans. Neural Netw. Learn. Syst. **26**(10), 2563–2575 (2015)
11. Xu, B., Yang, D., Shi, Z., et al.: Online recorded data-based composite neural control of strict-feedback systems with application to hypersonic flight dynamics. IEEE Trans. Neural Netw. Learn. Syst. **29**(8), 3839–3849 (2018)

Multiple Vehicles Merging Control via Sequence and Trajectory Optimization

Wei Tang[1,2], Ming Yang[1,2(✉)], Qiyang Qian[3], Chunxiang Wang[1,2],
and Bing Wang[1,2]

[1] Department of Automation, Shanghai Jiao Tong University,
Shanghai 200240, China
{donquixote,mingyang,wangcx,bingwang}@sjtu.edu.cn
[2] Key Laboratory of System Control and Information Processing,
Ministry of Education of China, Shanghai 200240, China
[3] School of Engineering, University of Tokyo, Tokyo 113-8654, Japan
251407133@qq.com

Abstract. In multi-lane traffic scenarios, accidents, construction, and other conditions will reduce the number of lanes, and vehicles need to decelerate, merge and pass. Therefore, vehicles merging is a hot topic in multi-vehicle cooperative driving. The existing primary methods focus on merging trajectory optimization based on the known sequence of merging and mainly consider the longitudinal model. Simulated annealing algorithm combined with Sequential Quadratic Programming is used to optimize the merging sequence and the corresponding trajectories. Numerical simulation verifies the stability and feasibility of the algorithm. Finally, the micro intelligent vehicles based simulation platform is introduced to carry out the merging experiment which proves the effectiveness of the proposed algorithm.

Keywords: Merging · Simulated annealing algorithm ·
Sequential quadratic programming

1 Introduction

In multi-lane traffic scenarios, many factors would inevitably lead to merging of vehicles from different lanes, for example, the changes of the number of lanes, regional road constructions, and the occupied sections by traffic accidents. A typical merging scene is shown in Fig. 1.

Efficient cooperative merging not only ensures the safety of vehicles during the merging process but also minimizes traffic congestion and ensures the smooth traffic flow on the roads. There have been some research results on the merging

This work was supported in part by the National Natural Science Foundation of China under Grant (U1764264/6187316), in part by Shanghai Automotive Industry Science and Technology Development Foundation (1733/1807), in part by the International Chair on Automated Driving of Ground Vehicle.

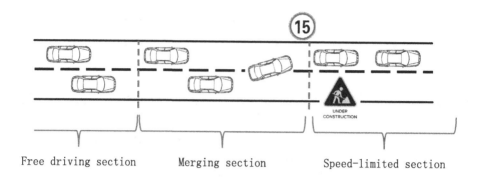

Fig. 1. A typical merging scene

problem. Using a concept of a virtual vehicle, merging control at a ramp is studied in [1,2]. In these studies, the problem is boiled down to two-car following problem or equivalent two-vehicle following problem. A HoL algorithm, which only considers the merging sequence of the two vehicles closest to the merging point, is proposed in [3]. Model predictive control is used in [4] to optimize the two-vehicle merging problem at the ramp. The lane changing trajectory planning algorithm in the multi-lane traffic scene is studied by Li et al. [5] to avoid collisions. In [5], a spanning tree in terms of vehicle safe merging sequence is used to obtain the feasible driving schedules. Cooperative merging is proposed in [6] to make vehicles on the main lane perform slight acceleration or deceleration to achieve the smooth merging. It can be found that the current research work can be divided into two categories. One of them focuses more on the optimization of merging trajectory with a known merging sequence. The other one only considers the merging schedule. There is little research on the optimization of the complete merging process. Besides, they mainly use the simplified longitudinal model and assume that the vehicle maneuvers the lateral control with a constant steering angular velocity, which is not reasonable enough.

This paper studies the whole merging process (merging sequence and correspondingly trajectory) with the full kinematic model, mainly aiming to figure out that how the vehicles on all the lanes should maneuver cooperatively to merge reasonably and effectively when the lane ahead is partially not passable. Finally, on a hardware simulation platform, the experiment is carried out to verify the effectiveness of the proposed method in this paper.

The rest of the article is organized as follows. Merging problem formation is presented in Sect. 2. In Sect. 3, the method based on simulated annealing and sequential quadratic programming is introduced. Experiments are conducted in Sect. 4 to show the effectiveness and feasibility of the proposed method. Finally, conclusion and scope of future work are presented in Sect. 5.

2   Merging Problem Formation

2.1   Problem Analysis

The merging process of vehicles is a composite problem: the first problem is the path of each vehicle in the process of merging. The second problem is the sequence of vehicles in the merging section. The different merging sequence will affect the vehicle's path. Its mathematical description is shown in Eq. (1).

$$\min_{ord \in O} J(ord) = \min_{ord \in O} \min_{s \in S_{order}} f(s) \tag{1}$$

where ord is one merging order and O is the feasible solution set to the merging order. $J(ord)$ is the objective function of ord. s is the entire states of all the vehicles for the merging trajectory. S_{order} is the feasible solution set to the s which corresponds to the merging order ord. $f(s)$ is the objective function of s.

2.2   Kinematic Vehicle Model

In [7], it has been proved that when there is little variation in tire-road friction, the kinematic model is enough to model and analyze vehicle motion. Accordingly, we use the kinematic bicycle model shown in Fig. 2. X-axis represents the parallel direction of the road.

Table 1. Notations

XOY	Global coordinate system
F	Center of front wheel
B	Center of rear wheel
CoG	Center of gravity of the vehicle
l_f	Distance from the front wheel to CoG
l_r	Distance from the rear wheel to CoG
L	Wheelbase($L = l_f + l_r$)
β	Slip angle at CoG
δ_f	Front steering angle
ψ	Yaw angle

The definitions of the parameters are given in Table 1. The angular velocity of steering wheel is α. The acceleration of the vehicle is a. Since it has been assumed that only the front wheel can be steered in this model, we can replace δ_f with δ in the following equations without any ambiguity.

The mathematical equations of the kinematic bicycle model can be written [8] as:

$$\dot{x} = v\cos(\psi + \beta) \tag{2}$$

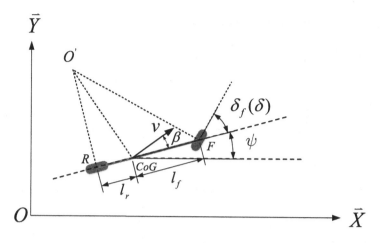

Fig. 2. Kinematic model of the vehicle

$$\dot{y} = v sin(\psi + \beta) \tag{3}$$

$$\dot{\psi} = \frac{v}{L} cos(\beta) tan(\delta) \tag{4}$$

$$\dot{\delta} = \alpha \tag{5}$$

$$\dot{v} = a \tag{6}$$

$$\beta = tan^{-1}(\frac{l_r}{L} tan(\delta)) \tag{7}$$

For the whole system, we can define:

$$S = (x_1, \ x_2, \ ..., \ x_{N_{car}})^T \tag{8}$$

$$s_i = (u_{i,0}, \ u_{i,1}, \ ..., \ u_{i,N-1}, \ t_{fi})^T \tag{9}$$

In Eqs. (8) and (9), X is the system states. x_i is the sub-state for the ith vehicle. N_{car} is the number of vehicles. $u_{i,j}$ is the control of the ith vehicle at the jth moment. N represents the number of discrete time periods. In this paper, the rate of change of acceleration of the vehicle - 'jerk' is introduced to quantify the comfort index, so $\mu_{i,k}$ is defined as the jerk of the ith vehicle at the kth moment.

$$u_{i,k} = [\alpha_{i,k}, \ \mu_{i,k}] \tag{10}$$

$$a_i(k+1) = a_i(k) + u_{i,k}(2)\delta t_i \tag{11}$$

$$\delta t_i = \frac{t_{fi} - t_{0i}}{N} \tag{12}$$

$$\begin{bmatrix} x_i(0) \\ v_i(0) \\ a_i(0) \end{bmatrix} = \begin{bmatrix} x_{0i} \\ v_{0i} \\ a_{0i} \end{bmatrix} \tag{13}$$

Equation (13) is the initial condition, in which $x_i(0)$, $v_i(0)$, $a_i(0)$ represent the position along the X-axis, velocity and acceleration of the ith vehicle at the 0 moment.

2.3   Constraint Equations

Equality Constraint. The equality constraint is the terminal condition of the problem. In the problem studied in this paper, when the vehicle approaches the end of the merging section, it must meet the limited speed. Therefore, the equality constraint is as shown in Eq. (14).

$$\begin{bmatrix} x_i(N) \\ v_i(N) \\ a_i(N) \end{bmatrix} = \begin{bmatrix} x_{fi} \\ v_{fi} \\ a_{fi} \end{bmatrix} \tag{14}$$

Inequality Constraint. The inequality constraint is the inter-vehicle distance constraint. If Vehicle j follows Vehicle i, the distance constraint between these two vehicles can be written as:

$$x_i(t) - x_j(t) \geq v_j(t)t_{hw} + l_{car} \tag{15}$$

In Eq. (15), t_{hw} is the headway. l_{car} is the length of the vehicle.

Since each δt_i can be different, Hermite interpolation [9,10] is used to calculate the inter-vehicle distance.

$$h_{j,k}(X) \triangleq H_{k_H(i,k)}(k\delta t_j) - x_j(k) - v_j(k)t_{hw} - l_{car} \tag{16}$$

$$k_H(i,k) = \frac{t_{0j} + k\delta t_j - t_{0i}}{\delta t_i} \tag{17}$$

$$k \in K_c(j) \tag{18}$$

where $K_c(j)$ is the set of k for existing constraints of Vehicle j. $H_{k_H(i,k)}$ is the Hermite interpolation function between $s_i(k_H(i,k))$ and $s_i(k_H(i,k)+1)$.

$$\begin{cases} H_k(k) = x_i(k), \ H_k(k+1) = x_i(k+1) \\ H_k'(k) = v_i(k), \ H_k'(k+1) = v_i(k+1) \\ H_k''(k) = a_i(k), \ H_k''(k+1) = a_i(k+1) \end{cases} \tag{19}$$

In this paper, we consider two optimization indicators: passing time and comfort. Therefore, the objective function is written in Eq. (20).

$$f(S) = \sum_{i=1}^{N_{car}} \sum_{k=0}^{N-1} (u_{i,k}(1)^2 + u_{i,k}(2)^2)\delta t_i + \sum_{i=1}^{N_{car}} (t_{fi} - t_{t0i}) \tag{20}$$

3   Methodology

Based on the previous analysis (see Sect. 2.1), merging optimization can be divided into the merging sequence optimization and the corresponding trajectory optimization. The merging sequence optimization belongs to the combinational optimization. Simulated annealing (SA) has a simple calculation process, good robustness, versatility, and parallelism. It can converge to the optimal global solution almost with probability 1. In the merging problem of this paper, there is a naturally existing neighborhood which can be used in the SA. Meanwhile, the primary goal of this paper is to find the optimal solution for the merging problem. So the convergence feature of SA makes it more suitable for this problem. The detailed explanation of SA can be found in [11,12].

Sequential quadratic programming is an important and efficient method to solve constrained nonlinear optimization problems. Based on the known merging sequence, the trajectory optimization is a constrained nonlinear optimization problem. Considering the speed, stability, and optimality of the algorithm, the final choice is Sequential Quadratic Programming (SQP) [13].

4   Experiments

4.1   Software Simulation

In order to choose suitable parameters of SA, numberical experiments are carried out. K_T is defined as the coefficient of the annealing schedule. T_0 is the initial temperature and is defined as $T_0 = K_{T_0} N_{car}$. K_{T_0} is the coefficient. We define L_{SA} and N_{end} as the number of inner iteration and the number of outer iteration respectively. Applying variable-controlling method to K_{T_0}, $K_{L_{SA}}$, K_T and N_{end} 1000 times, we can obtain Fig. 3. The red line represents the mean and variance of the convergence steps and the blue line represents the ratio of the experiments which converge to the optimal solution to the total number of the experiments. We can conclude that the most important factor for the correctness is N_{end}. The other three factors have little impact on the correctness. After repeated experiments, we choose: $K_{T0} = 0.05$, $L_{SA} = 2$, $K_T = 0.4$, $N_{end} = 9$.

4.2   Hardware Simulation

In this paper, we use a micro vehicle based hardware simulation platform to implement the hardware simulation. The test field which is a micro traffic environment is shown in Fig. 4. And the micro vehicle is shown in Fig. 5. Previously,

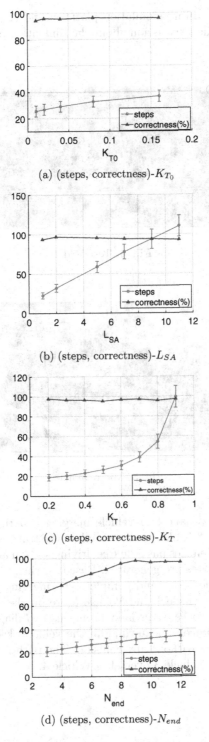

(a) (steps, correctness)-K_{T_0}

(b) (steps, correctness)-L_{SA}

(c) (steps, correctness)-K_T

(d) (steps, correctness)-N_{end}

Fig. 3. Numerical experiments of SA

we completed such hardware simulation platform and conducted many experiments on it. The detailed discussion about the simulation platform can be found in [14].

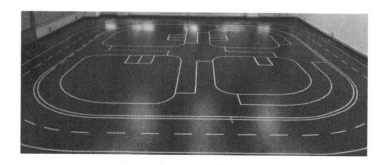

Fig. 4. Test field

Fig. 5. Micro vehicle

Figure 6 shows a two-lane four-vehicle merging experiment's segment. The two outer loops in Fig. 4 can be used to simulate the traffic scenario described in Fig. 1. When the four vehicles pass the free driving section and enter the merging section, their initial states are generated. Based on the proposed method, they get the optimized trajectories and complete the merging behavior before the speed-limited section. Vehicle 1 and Vehicle 3 are on the same lane. Vehicle 2 and Vehicle 4 are on the other same lane. From this $x-t$ diagram, we can observe the smooth merging process meanwhile all the vehicles keep the safe distance between their neighbors without any collision. The path intersection of Vehicle 3 and Vehicle 4 means Vehicle 3 overtakes Vehicle 4.

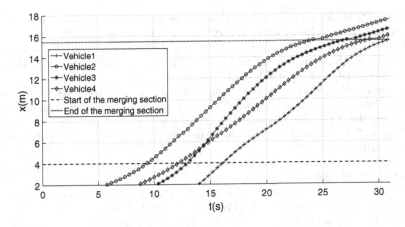

Fig. 6. Merging trajectories

5 Conclusion

In this paper, the merging problem is boiled down to an integration of a combinatorial optimization problem and a constrained nonlinear optimization problem. We use the full kinematic bicycle model rather than the simplified longitudinal model to establish the mathematical description of the merging problem. A scheme combining Simulated Annealing algorithm with Sequential Quadratic Programming algorithm is given. Software simulation proves the feasibility and effectiveness of the algorithm. At last, the hardware simulation experiment is carried out based on the micro vehicle platform, which further verifies the proposed method. Future work includes weakening assumptions, allowing repeated lane changes, and so on.

References

1. Uno, A., Sakaguchi, T., Tsugawa, S.: A merging control algorithm based on inter-vehicle communication. In: 1999 IEEE/IEEJ/JSAI International Conference on Intelligent Transportation Systems, 1999 Proceedings, pp. 783–787. IEEE (1999)
2. Milans, V., Godoy, J., Villagr, J., Prez, J.: Automated on-ramp merging system for congested traffic situations. IEEE Trans. Intell. Transp. Syst. **12**(2), 500–508 (2011)
3. Raravi, G., Shingde, V., Ramamritham, K., Bharadia, J.: Merge algorithms for intelligent vehicles. In: Ramesh, S., Sampath, P. (eds.) Next Generation Design and Verification Methodologies for Distributed Embedded Control Systems, pp. 51–65. Springer, Dordrecht (2007). https://doi.org/10.1007/978-1-4020-6254-4_5
4. Cao, W., Mukai, M., Kawabe, T., Nishira, H., Fujiki, N.: Cooperative vehicle path generation during merging using model predictive control with real-time optimization. Control Eng. Pract. **34**, 98–105 (2015)
5. Li, L., Wang, F.-Y., Zhang, Y.: Cooperative driving at lane closures. In: 2007 IEEE Conference on Intelligent Vehicles Symposium, pp. 1156–1161. IEEE (2007)

6. Hidas, P.: Modelling vehicle interactions in microscopic simulation of merging and weaving. Transp. Res. Part C: Emerg. Technol. **13**(1), 37–62 (2005)
7. Kang, C.M., Lee, S.-H., Chung, C.C.: Comparative evaluation of dynamic and kinematic vehicle models. In: 2014 IEEE 53rd Annual Conference on Decision and Control (CDC), pp. 648–653. IEEE (2014)
8. Rajamani, R.: Lateral vehicle dynamics. In: Rajamani, R. (ed.) Vehicle Dynamics and Control. Mechanical Engineering Series, pp. 15–46. Springer, Boston (2012). https://doi.org/10.1007/978-1-4614-1433-9_2
9. Burden, R.L., Faires, J.D.: Numerical Analysis, vol. 9, pp. 136–171. Cengage Learning (2010)
10. Spitzbart, A.: A generalization of Hermite's interpolation formula. Am. Math. Mon. **67**(1), 42–46 (1960)
11. De Vicente, J., Lanchares, J., Hermida, R.: Placement by thermodynamic simulated annealing. Phys. Lett. A **317**(5–6), 415–423 (2003)
12. Soares, S., Antunes, C.H., Arajo, R.: Comparison of a genetic algorithm and simulated annealing for automatic neural network ensemble development. Neurocomputing **121**, 498–511 (2013)
13. Bonnans, J.-F., Gilbert, J.C., Lemarchal, C., Sagastizbal, C.A.: Numerical Optimization: Theoretical and Practical Aspects. Springer, Heidelberg (2006). https://doi.org/10.1007/978-3-540-35447-5
14. Tang, W., et al.: MicroIV: a cooperative driving hardware simulation platform for cooperative-ITS. IEEE Trans. Vehic. Technol. **67**, 9173–9182 (2018)

Longitudinal and Lateral Coupling Model Based End-to-End Learning for Lane Keeping of Self-driving Cars

Wei Yuan[1,2], Ming Yang[1,2(✉)], Chunxiang Wang[1,2], and Bing Wang[1,2]

[1] Department of Automation, Shanghai Jiao Tong University,
Shanghai 200240, China
MingYANG@sjtu.edu.cn
[2] Key Laboratory of System Control and Information Processing,
Ministry of Education of China, Shanghai 200240, China

Abstract. Longitudinal and lateral coupling control is essential for high-precision lane keeping of self-driving cars. Recently, the end-to-end based method, which can learn high dimensional features from driving dataset, has been a new way for lane keeping of self-driving cars. However, state-of-the-art end-to-end based solutions mostly focus on the steering prediction and neglect the coupling effects of longitudinal and lateral control. This paper proposes a 3DCNN-LSTM (3D Convolutional Neural Networks-Long Short-Term Memory) model based end-to-end learning method for longitudinal and lateral coupling lane keeping of self-driving cars. A coupling controller will be designed in TORCS for lane keeping data collection. Then, the raw dataset will be augmented for better model training. Next, a 3DCNN-LSTM model with combined steering and speed loss function is proposed for model training and validation. At last, both the offline model testing and the online driving in TORCS are designed for the end-to-end model evaluation. The experiments show the proposed end-to-end coupling model achieves higher-precision lane keeping compared with the traditional end-to-end model with only lateral prediction.

Keywords: End-to-end learning · Lane keeping · Coupling model

1 Introduction

Lane keeping is an essential module for autonomous driving system, and high-precision lateral and longitudinal control can guarantee safe and comfortable autonomous lane keeping. There are two main ways to develop the autonomous lane keeping module. One is the rule-based system, which consists of several modules, such as perception, localization, decision and vehicle control. This method

This work was supported by the National Natural Science Foundation of China (U1764264/61873165).

F. Sun et al. (Eds.): ICCSIP 2018, CCIS 1006, pp. 425–436, 2019.
https://doi.org/10.1007/978-981-13-7986-4_38

requires each module to be highly robust. Otherwise, the error of the former module will impact the following modules, reducing the robustness of the whole autonomous driving system. The other one is the end-to-end learning based method, which means mapping the input from the sensors to the vehicle control command directly. The end-to-end model can learn high dimensional features from driving dataset. Currently, the end-to-end based method can be applied to the relatively simple driving scenes, such as lane keeping, lane-change decision, etc. This paper focuses on the autonomous lane keeping.

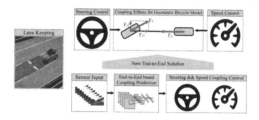

Fig. 1. High-precision end-to-end based lane keeping needs to consider the coupling effects between the steering control and speed control.

Several end-to-end models have been proposed for steering prediction in recent years, but these solutions mostly map a single image to a single steering value. All the human drivers are 'coupled system' for driving. They know it is better to slow down when turning into the curve road and it is better to speed up in the straight line, which can both guarantee the high-precision and the efficiency of the lane keeping, especially in the highway.

In fact, there are three types of coupling effects, i.e., kinetic coupling [1], tire force coupling [2], weight shift coupling [3]. For example, the lateral and longitudinal dynamics impact each other in several ways in the category of kinetic coupling, as shown in Fig. 1. On the one hand, the change of steering angle will change the direction of the lateral cornering force on the steered wheels, which will affect the longitudinal dynamics. Once the force of acceleration of the vehicle is far higher than the component in the longitudinal direction, the vehicle may lose the grip of the front wheel, which will affect lane keeping precision and even produce the car crash. On the other hand, it is easy to understand the higher longitudinal velocity will generate greater lateral centripetal force and bigger rate of lateral deviation. In the field of control, Lim has demonstrated the effectiveness of the coupled system for vehicle control and proved that longitudinal and lateral coupling control would get higher precision for path following [1].

Therefore, it is necessary to design the end-to-end learning based longitudinal and lateral coupling control for lane keeping of the future self-driving cars, which will make the lane keeping more accurate and comfortable. Moreover, the precise lane keeping requires more narrow lanes, shorter vehicle spacing and will enhance the safety of the autonomous driving in the future. This paper proposes an end-to-end learning based speed and steering coupling prediction method for autonomous lane keeping, which means an end-to-end model will learn the coupling relationship between the speed and the steering from the training datasets.

2 Related Work

The pioneering work of end-to-end learning-based autonomous driving can be traced back to 1989. Pomerleau trains a 3-layer neural network to control the car to follow the road only by the inputs from a camera and a laser range finder [4]. This milestone brings a new way to achieve autonomous driving without decomposing the whole task into different modules. LeCun et al. map the raw input image to the steering angle by CNN model for off-road mobile robots, which is the first application of CNN model in end-to-end autonomous driving [5]. Bojarski et al. propose a CNN model to map the left image, center image and right image from the front view to the steering angle [6]. Yang et al. demonstrate that the road-related features are indispensable for training a high-performance end-to-end control model [7]. Chen et al. discuss the lane keeping problem and only predict the steering of the car [8]. Yu et al. propose two independent models for steering prediction and the acceleration prediction respectively [9]. Ji et al. propose a novel 3DCNN model, which could extract features from both the spatial and the temporal dimensions by performing 3D convolutions [10]. Some LSTM related works have demonstrated the significant effect for predicting time-related problems [11–13].

The above end-to-end works only take the steering prediction as the task or decouple the steering and speed prediction, which may generate negative coupling effects. To get high-precision lane keeping efficiency in autonomous driving, a speed and steering coupling prediction model will be designed in this paper. The model will imitate as the 'Human Driver' to learn the inner coupling mechanism and output the steering angle and the expected speed simultaneously.

3 Longitudinal and Lateral Coupling Control for Data Collection

To imitate the human driver, a coupling controller similar to the human driver in TORCS is designed for lane keeping data collection. Five tracks and a car agent will be selected in TORCS [14], which is the simulation platform for certificating our approach. The coupling controller will be applied to the car agent. The speed control will be designed based on the preview control, which is based on the curvature of the track in the preview distance. The algorithm for the speed control is designed as Algorithm 1 .

The speed control will be coupled with the steering control by Stanley model, which is the high-performance path following steering controller [15,16]. As shown in Fig. 2, the vehicle will be simplified as the Geometric Bicycle Model. Stanley model is defined as:

$$\delta = \theta_e + tan^{-1}(k\frac{e}{v_x}) \tag{1}$$

Algorithm 1. Preview based Algorithm for Speed Control in Simulator

Input:
1: $gp(x)$: function for getting three preview points;
2: $gr(x_1, x_2, x_3)$: function for getting the radius of preview points;
3: $gv(x)$: function for getting expected speed based on preview radius;
4: $gc(x)$: function for getting commands for car control;
5: k_p: proportion value of preview;
Output: output t: throttle value; b: brake value; g: gear value;
6:   initial $p_c = 0$;
7: **repeat**
8:      get the current speed p_c;
9:      compute preview distance $p_d = k_p p_c$;
10:     compute preview three points $p_1, p_2, p_3 = gp(p_d)$;
11:     compute the preview radius $r = gr(p_1, p_2, p_3)$;
12:     compute the expected velocity $v = gv(r)$;
13:     compute the throttle value, brake value and gear value $t, b, g = gc(v)$;
14: **until** Stop the simulation

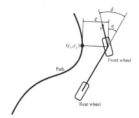

Fig. 2. The Geometric Bicycle Model.

δ is the steering value, θ_e is the difference between the tangent at the nearest point to the front wheel and the car heading, e is the distance from the front wheel to nearest point, v_x is the speed value on the X direction, which is the key parameter for coupling the lateral control and the longitudinal control.

With the coupling controller designed above, the images from the front view camera and the motion information of the car will be recorded by the data collection system in TORCS.

4   Data Collection and Augmentation

Data is one of the most important parts of the end-to-end learning. To get training and testing data as much as possible, five tracks are selected as the basic tracks to collect the dataset. The original road surface textures of the track are replaced by customized asphalt textures and asphalt darkness levels [17]. The agent car is designed to follow the center line of the lane with speed ranging from 30 km/h to 120 km/h. The training dataset is collected with the agent car by 10 frames per second (FPS), as higher FPS can only cause collecting more similar images without providing more useful information. The original screenshot will be cropped from 640*480 to 320*480 by cutting the top half of the image, because the road-related features are indispensable for training an end-to-end model [7]. The labeled images are downsampled to 200*200 for better computational efficiency. Meanwhile, the cropped images will be flipped to new images as well as flipping the steering value.

After the above two steps, the raw dataset will be defined as $\mathbf{D}_r$:

$$\mathbf{D}_r = \{(\mathbf{M}, \delta, v)_1, ..., (\mathbf{M}, \delta, v)_i, ..., (\mathbf{M}, \delta, v)_n\}(i \in [1, n], n > 15) \qquad (2)$$

As the model will operate convolution along the temporal dimension, this paper will feed the clip of video into the end-to-end model. Therefore, the single image-to-label sample will be augmented as image-sequence to label-sequence sample. Among that, the sequence of the sample which will be firstly feed into the 3DCNN structure is defined as $\mathbf{E}_j$:

$$\mathbf{E}j = \{\mathbf{M}_j, \mathbf{M}_{j+1}, \mathbf{M}_{j+2}, \mathbf{M}_{j+3}, \mathbf{M}_{j+4}\} \ (j \in [1, n - 14]) \qquad (3)$$

Secondly, the sequence of the sample which will be fitted are defined as $\mathbf{F}_j$:

$$\mathbf{F}_j = \{(\mathbf{M}, \delta, v)_{j+5}, ((\mathbf{M}, \delta, v)_{j+6}, ..., (\mathbf{M}, \delta, v)_{j+14}\} \qquad (4)$$

Therefore, one sample which will be fed into the model is defined as $\mathbf{X}_j$:

$$\mathbf{X}_j = \{\mathbf{E}_j\} \cup \{\mathbf{F}_j\} \qquad (5)$$

At last, the augmented dataset will be updated as $\mathbf{D}_a$:

$$\mathbf{D}_a = \{\mathbf{X}_1, ..., \mathbf{X}_j, ..., \mathbf{X}_{n-14}\} \qquad (6)$$

5   End-to-End Learning Method

5.1   Structure of the 3DCNN-LSTM Model

The structure of the 3DNN-LSTM model is shown in Fig. 3. The input of the model is the sequence of images. The first part of the model is a 3DCNN structure, which takes the discrete time as the first dimension. The 3DCNN structure enables the model to learn motion detectors and understand the dynamics of driving. Specifically, the 3DCNN is composed of four 3D convolutional layers and four fully-connected layers. Meanwhile, there will be a dropout for each layer. The first 3DCNN layer has a kernel size of 3*12*12. The remaining three 3DCNN layers have a kernel size of 2*5*5. All the 3DCNN layers have 64 feature maps as output. Four fully-connected layers have 1024, 512, 256, 128 outputs respectively. Here, the rectified linear unit (ReLU) is selected as the activation function. The second part of the model is LSTM cells. The predicted angle will serve as the input to the next step. For the steering and speed coupling control, the loss function is composed of three parts: the MSE (Mean-Square-Error) of the steering angle prediction in the autoregressive setting, the MSE of the speed

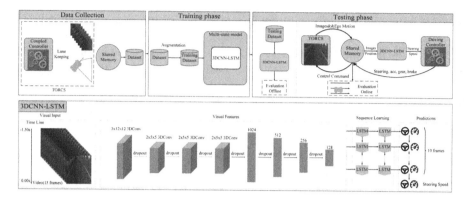

Fig. 3. The framework of the end-to-end learning based steering and speed coupling control: data collection, training and testing. The structure of the 3DCNN-LSTM model.

prediction in the autoregressive setting, and the sum of MSEs for all outputs both in autoregressive and ground truth settings.

Therefore, the final prediction of steering and speed will be defined as $[\delta_j \ v_j]$ with regarding model as mapping f:

$$[\delta_j \ v_j] = f(\mathbf{X}_j) \tag{7}$$

5.2 Evaluation Methods

Evaluation Offline. This paper will firstly evaluate the performance of the end-to-end model by testing the offline images. The first evaluation will test the root-mean-square-error (RMSE) between the prediction value and the ground truth for steering value and the speed value respectively. This evaluation method will estimate the basic performance of the end-to-end model.

$$rmse_\delta = \sqrt{\frac{\sum_{i=1}^{n} (\delta_p - \delta_g)^2}{n}} \tag{8}$$

$$rmse_v = \sqrt{\frac{\sum_{i=1}^{n} (v_p - v_g)^2}{n}} \tag{9}$$

Evaluation Online. To illustrate the coupling effects of the end-to-end model, the lane keeping error will be evaluated by online driving in TORCS. As shown in Fig. 4, the lane keeping error e_i is defined as the difference value between the ideal lane width (the width of the vehicle) and the real lane width that the whole vehicle occupies on the road (L_1).

$$L_2 = \frac{l\tan(\alpha) + w}{2\cos(\alpha)} \tag{10}$$

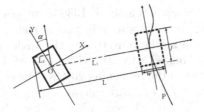

Fig. 4. The definition of lane keeping error.

$$L = L_1 + L_2 + \frac{w}{2} \tag{11}$$

$$e_i = L - w \tag{12}$$

Then, the root-mean-square-error (RMSE) will be calculated:

$$rmse_e = \sqrt{\frac{\sum_{i=1}^{n} e_i^2}{n}} \tag{13}$$

To evaluate the degree of dispersion of the error, the standard deviation (SD) of all the errors will be calculated:

$$me = \frac{\sum_{i=1}^{n} e_i}{n} \tag{14}$$

$$sd = \sqrt{\frac{\sum_{i=1}^{n} (e_i - me)^2}{n}} \tag{15}$$

6   Experiments and Analysis

6.1   Training and Validation

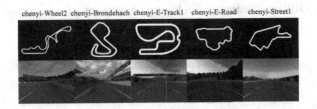

Fig. 5. Illustration of tracks selected for data collection.

The training and validation will be conducted on Ubuntu14.04 LTS with NVIDIA GTX 1080 GPU. The whole dataset comes from five tracks as shown in Fig. 5 in TORCS contains 230880 images (15392 sequence samples). The second training dataset from Udacity consists of 133935 images (8929 sequence samples). The two training datasets will train two models respectively. Here, the original steering value will not be converted to the angle value, i.e., the steering value in TORCS ranges from −1.0 to 1.0 with no unit. 80% of the dataset will be used for training model, and the remaining 20% will be used for validating. The batch size will be set to 4 for optimization step, and the epochs will be set to 1000. This paper trains the model based on TensorFlow with Adam optimization strategy [18] with a learning rate of 0.0001. After each training procedure, the validation will be conducted. During the training stage, the *dropout* will be set to 0.25 while during the validation stage the *dropout* will be set to 1.0. The loss value of both two pieces of training is stable after 1000 epochs.

6.2   Testing and Evaluation

Firstly, the **Evaluation Offline** will be conducted. The first testing dataset contains 57720 images (3848 sequence samples), which comes from the same five tracks but never been seen by the training model. The second testing dataset, which comes from Udacity, contains 33495 images (2233 sequence samples). All the samples of the testing datasets are shuffled. Meanwhile, to illustrate the high performance of our proposed model, the end-to-end CNN model proposed in Nvidia [6] and proposed in [8] are also trained and tested by the same two datasets. Figures 6 and 7 show the testing results of the two datasets. The red line denotes the ground truth of steering value and the speed from the coupling controller. The blue line shows the prediction of the 3DCNN-LSTM model. The green line shows the steering prediction of the Nvidia CNN model [6]. The magenta line shows the steering prediction of the CNN model in [8]. The 3DCNN-LSTM model performs better as the RMSE of the steering prediction is smaller than another two models in both testing datasets. As another two models do not predict the speed of the vehicle, the **Evaluation Offline** only gets the speed prediction RMSE from the proposed 3DCNN-LSTM model as shown in Table 1. The first four images in Fig. 8 are typical scenarios in Udacity dataset. The blue arrow represents the prediction value via proposed 3DCNN-LSTM model, and the red arrow represents the ground truth. More scenarios can be seen on YouTube. The **Evaluation Offline** illustrates the high performance of our proposed model.

Table 1. RMSE and SD for the prediction error

Model	Dataset			
	TORCS		Udacity	
	Steering	Speed (km/h)	Steering	Speed (km/h)
3DCNN-LSTM	0.0156	3.9923	0.0270	0.6014
Nvidia CNN Model [6]	0.0423	N/A	0.1080	N/A
CNN Model [8]	0.0511	N/A	0.1991	N/A

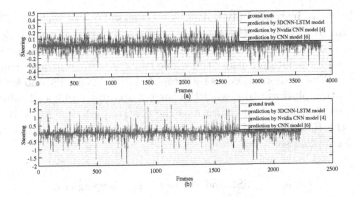

Fig. 6. Steering prediction results for two testing datasets: (a) Dataset from TORCS. (b) Dataset from Udacity. (Color figure online)

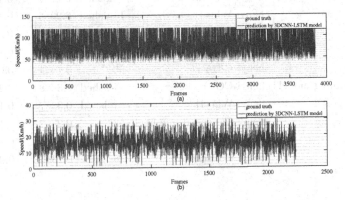

Fig. 7. Speed prediction results for two testing datasets: (a) Dataset from TORCS. (b) Dataset from Udacity. (Color figure online)

Fig. 8. Typical scenarios of lane keeping in the evaluation stage. (Color figure online)

Secondly, the **Evaluation Online** will be conducted to demonstrate the effects of the coupling prediction by another five tracks. Two experiments are designed at this stage. The first one is to control the car agent by the steering and speed coupling prediction from the proposed 3DCNN-LSTM model. The other one is to control the car agent by only steering prediction from the 3DCNN-LSTM while the speed is controlled by the traditional controller which is similar to the data collection stage, which means the steering and the speed control is decoupled entirely. The final results are shown in Table 2, 3DCNN-LSTM based end-to-end steering and speed coupling prediction finishes three tracks while the decoupled control instance only finishes two tracks. For track chenyi-CG-speed number1, the RMSE from the coupling solution is larger than the decoupled solution, the reason is that the decoupled solution only keeps in the lane for 53s while the coupled solution finishes the whole track, some significant errors might be recorded. What's more, it costs the proposed 3DCNN-LSTM model 19ms on the computation platform to predict the current steering and speed value, which is totally real time for vehicle control as the control period is 20ms. In general, almost all the RMSE and SD results demonstrate the high performance of the end-to-end coupling solution.

Table 2. RMSE and SD for the lane keeping error

Model	Track	Time/s	RMSE/m	SD/m
Coupling model	chenyi-CG-track2	Finished	0.2862	0.1820
	chenyi-Wheel1	Finished	0.2386	0.1343
	chenyi-CG-speed number1	Finished	0.4251	0.3118
	chenyi-CG-track3	9	0.1524	0.1233
	chenyi-E-track6	50	0.1321	0.0833
Decoupling model	chenyi-CG-track2	Finished	0.3588	0.2021
	chenyi-Wheel1	Finished	0.3377	0.1696
	chenyi-CG-speed number1	53	0.2392	0.1270
	chenyi-CG-track3	9	0.1544	0.1230
	chenyi-E-track6	48	0.1360	0.0942

Figure 9 shows the real steering value and the speed value of the car agent based on end-to-end coupling model along the online driving on the tack chenyi-CG-track2. The region **A** and **D** show that model behaviors lower speed with bigger steering value, while the region **B** and **C** show the deceleration process during the increasing steering value and the acceleration process during the small steering value. It is this feature of the end-to-end coupling prediction model that

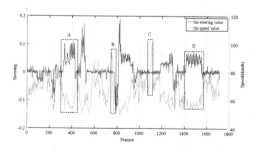

Fig. 9. The real steering and the speed value along the online driving based on coupling prediction on the track chenyi-CG-track2.

makes the lane keeping more precise. The last four images in Fig. 10 are typical scenarios during the online driving stage. The left top image is the current feeding image, the orange bar shows the current lane keeping error of the car, and the steering and speed is coupled by the end-to-end model. The demo can be seen on YouTube. In short, the end-to-end coupling prediction model performs higher-precision of lane keeping than steering only prediction end-to-end solution.

7 Conclusion

This paper focuses on the end-to-end learning based longitudinal and lateral coupling control for lane keeping of self-driving cars. The lateral control and the longitudinal control will have the kinetic effect in lane keeping, and the coupling control has been demonstrated high lane keeping precision in the previous works. Meanwhile, the human driver is a natural system for steering and speed coupling control. Therefore, a coupling controller is designed in TORCS for coupling dataset collection. A 3DCNN-LSTM model with a combined loss function is proposed for the end-to-end training. Two evaluation methods are applied for the final testing, and the experiments show our 3DCNN-LSTM model based steering and speed coupling prediction performs higher lane keeping precision. In the future, the end-to-end coupling lane keeping of self-driving in the real world will be conducted.

References

1. Lim, E.H., Hedrick, J.K.: Lateral and longitudinal vehicle control coupling for automated vehicle operation. In: 1999 Proceedings of the American Control Conference, vol. 5, pp. 3676–3680. IEEE (1999)
2. Bakker, E., Pacejka, H.B., Lidner, L.: A new tire model with an application in vehicle dynamics studies. SAE Trans. 101–113 (1989)
3. Van Zanten, A.T., Erhardt, R., Pfaff, G.: VDC, the vehicle dynamics control system of Bosch. SAE Trans. 1419–1436 (1995)
4. Pomerleau, D.A.: ALVINN, an autonomous land vehicle in a neural network. Carnegie Mellon University, Computer Science Department, Technical report (1989)
5. Abbeel, P., Ng, A.Y.: Apprenticeship learning via inverse reinforcement learning. In: Proceedings of the Twenty-First International Conference on Machine Learning, p. 1. ACM (2004)
6. Bojarski, M., et al.: End to end learning for self-driving cars. arXiv preprint arXiv:1604.07316 (2016)
7. Yang, S., Wang, W., Liu, C., Deng, K., Hedrick, J.K.: Feature analysis and selection for training an end-to-end autonomous vehicle controller using the deep learning approach. arXiv preprint arXiv:1703.09744 (2017)
8. Chen, Z., Huang, X.: End-to-end learning for lane keeping of self-driving cars. In: 2017 IEEE Intelligent Vehicles Symposium (IV), pp. 1856–1860. IEEE (2017)
9. Yu, H., Yang, S., Gu, W., Zhang, S.: Baidu driving dataset and end-to-end reactive control model. In: 2017 IEEE Intelligent Vehicles Symposium (IV), pp. 341–346. IEEE (2017)

10. Ji, S., Xu, W., Yang, M., Yu, K.: 3D convolutional neural networks for human action recognition. IEEE Trans. Pattern Anal. Mach. Intell. **35**(1), 221–231 (2013)
11. Donahue, J., et al.: Long-term recurrent convolutional networks for visual recognition and description. In: The IEEE Conference on Computer Vision and Pattern Recognition (CVPR), June 2015
12. Xingjian, S., Chen, Z., Wang, H., Yeung, D.-Y., Wong, W.-K., Woo, W.-C.: Convolutional LSTM network: a machine learning approach for precipitation nowcasting. In: Advances in Neural Information Processing Systems, pp. 802–810 (2015)
13. Hochreiter, S., Schmidhuber, J.: Long short-term memory. Neural Comput. **9**(8), 1735–1780 (1997)
14. Wymann, B., Dimitrakakis, C., Sumner, A., Espié, E., Guionneau, C., Coulom, R.: TORCS, the open racing car simulator, v1.3.5 (2013). http://www.torcs.org
15. Snider, J.M., et al.: Automatic steering methods for autonomous automobile path tracking. Robotics Institute, Pittsburgh, PA, Technical report, CMU-RITR-09-08 (2009)
16. Paden, B., Čáp, M., Yong, S.Z., Yershov, D., Frazzoli, E.: A survey of motion planning and control techniques for self-driving urban vehicles. IEEE Trans. Intell. Veh. **1**(1), 33–55 (2016)
17. Chen, C., Seff, A., Kornhauser, A., Xiao, J.: Deepdriving: learning affordance for direct perception in autonomous driving. In: Proceedings of the IEEE International Conference on Computer Vision, pp. 2722–2730 (2015)
18. Kingma, D., Ba, J.: Adam: a method for stochastic optimization. arXiv preprint arXiv:1412.6980 (2014)

Behavior Prediction and Planning for Intelligent Vehicles Based on Multi-vehicles Interaction and Game Awareness

Hongbo Gao[1,2], Guotao Xie[3(✉)], Kelong Wang[4],
Yuchao Liu[5], and Deyi Li[5]

[1] State Key Laboratory of Automotive Safety and Energy,
Tsinghua University, Beijing 100084, China
[2] Center for Intelligent Connected Vehicles and Transportation,
Tsinghua University, Beijing 100084, China
[3] Department of Automotive Engineering, Hunan University,
Changsha 410082, Hunan, China
xieguotao1990@126.com
[4] Graduate School of Chinese Academy of Social Sciences,
Beijing 102488, China
[5] Department of Computer Science and Technology,
Tsinghua University, Beijing 100084, China

Abstract. In this study, a maneuver prediction and planning framework is proposed on the basis of game theories for complex traffic scenarios. In this framework, the interaction and gaming between multiple vehicles are considered by employing the extensive form game theories, which were extensively researched for sequential gaming problems. Finally, this framework is applied and proved in different lane-change scenarios. The results show that this framework could predict other vehicles' driving maneuvers and plan maneuvers for ego vehicles by considering interaction and gaming between multiple vehicles, which helps AVs understand the environment better and make the cooperative maneuver planning in complex traffic scenarios.

Keywords: Intelligent vehicles · Behavior prediction and planning ·
Interaction and gaming awareness

1 Introduction

AVS and ADASs have received extensive research interest because they show great potential for use in more efficient, safer, and cleaner transportation systems [1]. Developments in this field will evidently increase in both quality and importance over time [2]. However, the problem is why AVs are not able to be widely used at present. Technically speaking, one of the crucial reasons is that the traffic environment is increasing complex as well as full of uncertainty [3]. To solve this problem, as human driving skills, AVs should have the ability to predict changes of the traffic environment under uncertainty, such as the trajectory of other vehicles. Also, the strategies of

© Springer Nature Singapore Pte Ltd. 2019
F. Sun et al. (Eds.): ICCSIP 2018, CCIS 1006, pp. 437–453, 2019.
https://doi.org/10.1007/978-981-13-7986-4_39

surrounding vehicles are influenced with each other. Therefore, it is crucial for AVs to have a better understanding of the traffic environment.

Situational awareness (SA) is one of the indispensable parts for AVs to understand the environment, especially in complex traffic scenarios. The work of SA is to percept the elements in the environment, comprehend their meaning and project their status in the near future, which was considered in [4]. Like driving by humans, the traffic environment prediction, which helps make right decisions, plays crucial roles in SA. In addition, other vehicles in the traffic influence the prediction and decision making of the ego vehicle and decisions of the ego vehicle also have impacts on traffic environments such as other vehicles' behaviors. And they all are aware of this, which brings out the interaction and gaming between multiple vehicles. The basic difficulty of the interaction and gaming is a circular concept: a player in the traffic makes the best decision against the conjectured strategies of the other players in the traffic but, in turn, this best decision and planning should be conjectured by the other players in the traffic and they should play the best replies as well [5]. Moreover, the elements of uncertainty are common in the traffic including observation and prediction. As a result, the uncertainty should be considered in SA. With the development of communication technology [6], vehicle-to-vehicle (V2V) communication devices could help to obtain much more information to predict and plan in the complex traffic environment. In this proposed framework for maneuver prediction and planning, multiple vehicles' interaction and gaming, and uncertainties are considered to improve SA.

The maneuver prediction and planning is to predict and plan simultaneously at a high level. The maneuver planning in this study is about High-level controller (HLC) to design the finite state machine (FSM), which was proposed and studied in [7]. Then trajectory planning and tracking models could be used to realize the automated functions [8, 9]. Since the prediction of the environment and planning of the ego vehicle influence with each other, prediction and planning should be considered at the same time. Meanwhile, surrounding vehicles also try to make the best response rationally. In other words, they interact and game with each other, which was not considered much as in [10].

There are various methods to deal with motion predictions for AVs and ADASs such as physics-based models, machine learning methods [11], and game theories [12]. Physics-based models are based on vehicle kinematic or dynamic models, which assume that some parameters stay constant. Physics-based models could only predict at a low level with a short term. Machine learning methods could learn knowledge from data by combining multiple parameters nonlinearly. However, Machine learning methods ignored the gaming of multiple vehicles in the surrounding environment. In addition, game theories have been also employed to deal with the gaming between multiple vehicles. But the uncertainty in the process of gaming and multi-act games with much longer horizon have been seldom researched. In this study, the motion prediction under uncertainty, and interaction and gaming between multiple vehicles are considered to predict and plan maneuvers at the same time based on extensive form games.

The objective of this study is to build a framework of maneuver prediction and planning for a few steps simultaneously. In this framework, the interaction and gaming between multiple vehicles in traffic are considered by employing extensive form game theories, which have been extensively researched for sequential gaming problems. And it is assumed that each player in traffic is rational and seeking for the minimized payoff cost. In the payoff function, the risk assessment model based on trajectory prediction under uncertainty, which integrates the dynamic and maneuver-based predicting models for accurate results in the long term, is employed to assess collision risks. Moreover, considering the uncertainty of traffic environments, the payoff function in this study combines risk assessments, driving efficiency and preference.

The remainder of this paper is organized as follows: Sect. 2 introduces the related work pertaining to maneuver and motion prediction. Section 3 presents the methodology used in this study, which includes the introduction of the extensive form game theory, risk assessment based on vehicle trajectory prediction as well as the payoff function for the interaction and gaming. And the application of the framework in different lane-change scenarios and the results are described and analyzed in Sect. 4. At last, Sect. 5 presents some conclusive remarks.

2 Related Work

As mentioned previously, maneuver prediction and planning are crucial for the research of AVs and ADASs. Therefore, many research efforts have been expended on motion prediction and planning for AVs and ADASs using various methods such as physics-based models, machine learning methods [13, 14], and game theories [12].

Physics-based models are the widespread techniques to predict the motions, which consider the motion prediction based on physics laws and assume that some parameters such as velocity, acceleration, and yaw rate are constant. Huang et al. [15] explored vehicle future trajectory prediction and examined the possible methodologies for trajectory prediction based on differential global positioning system. In this study, different dynamic trajectory prediction models were compared; results indicated that one of the main error causes was the changes in driver's intention. Sorstedt et al. [16] considered the driver control input parameter to obtain better predictions. Polychronopoulos, Aris et al. proposed a model-based description of the traffic environment for an accurate prediction of vehicle's path, which was situation adaptive and calculation dynamic [17]. In the study, dynamic models such as constant acceleration (CA), constant turn rate (CTR), and constant turn rate constant tangential acceleration (CTRA) models were included for the accurate path prediction. However, physics-based models can only predict with sustainable results in the short term. They could not predict at a higher level. In addition, physics-based models are not able to take the multiple vehicles' interaction and gaming into consideration.

Machine learning methods have the ability to solve the nonlinear problems in the research of motion prediction, which have been widely used to predict vehicle paths and estimate maneuvers by learning from driving data. Hou, et al. developed a model to predict driver decisions on whether to merge or not as a function of certain input variables [18], which was on the basis of Bayesian network and decision trees. In [19], a neural network-based model was developed and studied in detail to recognize the lane-change behaviors and predict the lane-change trajectory. Peng et al. [20] mentioned a back-propagation neural network model to predict lane-changing behavior. In the study, the lane-change-intent time window was designed approximately as 5 s. Machine learning methods could learn the knowledge from driving data, which are able to combine several parameters nonlinearly. However, these methods did not take the traffic sequential information into account and they failed to simulate the interaction and gaming between multiple vehicles.

By considering the sequential information, some approaches including dynamic Bayesian network, and Markov theories were employed to estimate motions and driving maneuvers. Li et al. [14] proposed a novel algorithm combining the hidden Markov model (HMM) and Bayesian filtering (BF) techniques to estimate a lane-changing maneuver. In this study, the grammar definition was inspired by speech recognition models based on Markov theories. In [21, 22], the authors built the maneuver recognition and prediction model based on data learning such as hidden Markov models (HMM). Li, et al. proposed models to infer driving intentions by considering the impact of past driving behavior on current station with add Auto-regression (AR) [23]. Gindele et al. [24] modeled the decision-making process of drivers by building a hierarchical dynamic Bayesian model that described physical relationships as well as the driver's behaviors and plans, which aimed to estimate and predict traffic situations over time. These methods estimated the motions in the maneuver level and considered the interaction between vehicles. However, gaming between vehicles was failed to consider.

Game theories have been extensively researched in a variety of areas for multi-agent interaction problems including traffic environment prediction for AVs. Talebpour et al. [25] presented a lane-changing model to understand and predict the lane-changing behavior based on a game-theoretical approach that endogenously accounted for the flow of information in a connected vehicular environment. This could improve driving awareness of surrounding traffic conditions. Liu et al. [26] modeled the vehicle inter-actions during merging process under an enhanced game-theoretic framework by adopting Nash equilibrium. And the testing results showed that this framework could achieve a relatively high accuracy of predicting vehicles' actions. In [12], the combi-nation of interaction-aware intention estimation with maneuver-based motion predic-tion based on supervised learning was proposed and the motion intention was modeled by the game theoretic idea. However, uncertainties in games were seldom researched. And the payoff function in the game had not considered the prediction of traffic environments.

3   Methodologies

In this part, extensive form game theories including different Nash equilibriums will be introduced briefly. Then, a risk assessment model based on vehicle trajectory prediction under uncertainty is proposed and studied, which lays the foundation for the interaction and gaming between multiple vehicles. In the next subsection, the payoff function for interaction and gaming is designed by considering the collision risk, driving efficiency, and maneuver preference. Finally, the framework of maneuver prediction and planning will be proposed and presented based on the single-act and multi-act games in extensive forms.

3.1   Introduction of Extensive Form Game Theories

Game theories have been researched extensively and applied in different domains such as economics, politics, sociology, and military. In addition, game theories were employed in engineering fields including automated vehicles with the aim to understand and model decision processes and SAs. In complex traffic environments, multiple agents (vehicles) make decisions in a situation where each other's payoff depends on the others' behaviors. Therefore, game theories could provide a promising framework for interaction and gaming awareness modeling [27]. The problem of maneuver predicting and planning for a few steps in the near future is a multiple time-sequential problem, which could be described as dynamic games [28]. Dynamic games can be represented by a game tree, known as the extensive form games. Based on extensive form games, the interaction and gaming between multiple vehicles in the traffic could be simulated in a sequential manner.

The basic elements of the extensive form game can be expressed by a tuple as follows:

$$S = (T, P, A, U) \tag{1}$$

T is a directed game tree with root and nodes; $P = \{P_1, P_2, \ldots, P_i, \ldots, P_N\}$ is the set of players, indexed by $i, i \in \{1, 2, \ldots, N\}$; $A_i = \{A_i^1, A_i^2, \ldots, A_i^k, \ldots, A_i^M\}$ are the actions of the player P_i; $U = \{U_1, U_2, \ldots, U_i, \ldots, U_N\}$ are the payoff functions for the players.

A game in an extensive form described by a tree includes nodes and edges. Nodes can be the player nodes or the end nodes. The end nodes are indicated by the outcomes of the sequential actions according to the payoff function. And each edge is an action of a player [29]. There are two kinds of extensive form game theories, namely perfect information, and imperfect information extensive games according to the agent's knowledge about all the prior choices including those of other agents. An imperfect-information game in extensive form is a game in which each player's choice nodes are partitioned into information sets; definitely, if two choice nodes are in the same information set then the agent cannot distinguish between them [30]. In this study, the imperfect information extensive games are employed to model the interaction and gaming between multiple vehicles because some players could not know the actions of other players definitely at the same time.

There are all kinds of Nash equilibriums to describe gaming results in extensive forms. The basic equilibrium is called pure-strategy Nash equilibrium, which selects one of the available actions in each information set of that agent [28]. But in some cases, there are no pure strategies. As a result, Nash equilibrium in mixed and behavioral strategies is proposed to describe the gaming results via probability distributions. The mixed strategies for a player is a probability distribution on the set of all the player's pure strategies. On the other hand, behavioral strategies in the extensive form games are defined as a player denoting probability distributions only on the alternatives belonging to the information set.

Based on the extensive-form game theory, the maneuver prediction and planning in the traffic could be simulated. In the following subsections, the risk assessment is firstly introduced to evaluate collision risks of the traffic environment. Then, based on the risk assessment, the pay-off function in the game theory is proposed, which considers the driving collision probability, driving efficiency, and driving preference. The final subsection is the introduction of maneuver prediction and planning with details.

3.2 Risk Assessment Based on Vehicle Trajectory Prediction Under Uncertainty

The common risk assessment models are based on defining risk functions according to dynamic features, such as time to collision (TTC), time to lane (TTL), and so on. These common risk assessment models are called dynamic feature based models. Dynamic feature based models project vehicle dynamic parameters such as the relative velocity, distance, and lateral acceleration for risk assessments. Always, machine learning methods such as support vector machine and decision trees were used extensively for projecting since they could deal with nonlinear problems with multiple features. Moreover, Inverse reinforcement learning method was employed to learn the risk assessment model from driving demonstrations. In addition, some complex mathematic models were proposed considering dynamic features such as the safety field model. These models firstly define the relationship between features and calibrate the function parameters using realistic driving data. However, these methods did not take future potential risks as well as uncertainties into consideration.

In this study, the risk assessment model proposed in this study is on the basis of vehicle trajectory prediction under uncertainty. As presented in Fig. 1, the vehicle trajectory prediction integrates the dynamic and maneuver-based approaches, which could predict accurately in the short term and look ahead to a high horizon. Based on trajectory prediction, the collision at a specific time point could be estimated under uncertainty. Then, the risk assessment for a vehicle could be obtained by considering potential risks in the near future and combining lateral and longitudinal parameters between multiple vehicles.

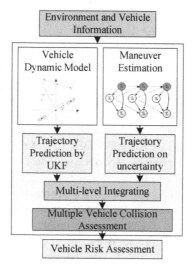

Fig. 1. Risk assessment model based on trajectory prediction under uncertainty.

Collision Assessment at a Specific Time Point: Collision assessment based on trajectory prediction of two vehicles at a specific time point can be given as follows:

$$P\left(C_{v_i,v_j}(t)\right) = \iint C\left(x_{v_i}(t), x_{v_j}(t)\right) p\left(x_{v_i}(t), x_{v_j}(t)\right) dx_{v_i} dx_{v_j} \qquad (2)$$
$$t \in \left[t_0, t_0 + T_p\right]$$

where v_i presents the vehicle i, and t is the time. And $x_{v_i}(t)$ is the predicting position of v_i at time t. $p\left(x_{v_i}(t), x_{v_j}(t)\right)$ is the position probability of the vehicle i and j. t_0 is the starting predicting point, and T_p is the predicting horizon. $C\left(x_{v_i}(t), x_{v_j}(t)\right)$ is the collision index as expressed as the following equation, which considers the shape of vehicles.

$$C\left(x_{v_i}(t), x_{v_j}(t)\right) = \begin{cases} 1, V_i(x_{v_i}(t)) \cap V_j(x_{v_j}(t)) \neq \varnothing \\ 0, \qquad\qquad\qquad else \end{cases} \qquad (3)$$

where $V_i(x_{v_i}(t))$ means the space that the vehicle i covers.

In this study, the Monte Carlo (MC) method suggested in [28] has been used to calculate the collision assessment. And an example of collision assessments based on trajectory prediction (the prediction horizon is 6 s) is shown in Fig. 2.

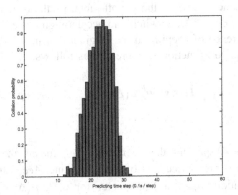

Fig. 2. Collision assessments at different time points based on integrated trajectory prediction under uncertainty (The predicting time step is 0.1 s/step and the predicting horizon is 6 s).

Risk Assessment: The risk assessment between two vehicles within the prediction horizon, $\text{Risk}\left(v_i(t_0 : t_0 + T_p), v_j(t_0 : t_0 + T_p)\right)$, can be represented as the collision prediction distribution over the future time span.

$$\mathbf{Risk}\left(v_i\left(t_0 : t_0 + T_p\right), v_j\left(t_0 : t_0 + T_p\right)\right) = \int_{t_0}^{t_0 + T_{max}} P\left(C_{v_i,v_j}(t)\right) \frac{1}{t} dt \qquad (4)$$

where T_{max} satisfies the following equation:

$$P\big(C_{v_i,v_j}(T_{max})\big) = \max_{t\in[t_0,t_0+T_p]} P\big(C_{v_i,v_j}(t)\big) \tag{5}$$

The risk assessment should be considered in multiple vehicles. The risk assessment of the vehicle v_i in a scene s_i could be expressed as follows:

$$RA(v_i,s_i) = \max_j \big(Risk\big(v_i(t_0:t_0+T_p), v_j(t_0:t_0+T_p)\big)\big) \tag{6}$$

where s_i presents the scene i, and v_i, v_j are the vehicles in the scene.

As shown above, the risk assessment model proposed in this study considers the uncertainty in the traffic environment and it is on the basis of traffic environment prediction, which considered future potential risks and could be applied in a variety of scenarios including intersection, lane changing, turning, and so on.

3.3   Payoff Function for Interaction and Gaming

The payoff function mentioned above is one of the core parts of extensive form game theories to interpret the interaction and gaming between multiple vehicles. The payoff function designed in this study is able to assess the driving risk in the near future as well as driving efficiency. Also, in the payoff function, the driving preference is considered by adding the cost of lane switch and acceleration or deceleration, which aims to describe the preference of keeping in the original driving condition.

As a result, the payoff function is expressed as follows:

$$U_i = \lambda_1 RA(v_i,s_i) + \lambda_2 \int I\big(v_i,s_i,m_t^i\big)p\big(\Delta v_{t_0+T_p},\Delta d_{t_0+T_p}\big)dp + \lambda_3 switch + \lambda_4 \frac{Acc}{\rho_v} \tag{7}$$

where $\lambda_i(i=1,2,3,4)$ present the coefficients, m_t^i means the maneuver that the vehicle takes, *switch* is preference cost of changing lane, *Acc* is the absolute value of longitudinal acceleration, ρ_v is the parameter for cost, $p\big(\Delta v_{t_0+T_p},\Delta d_{t_0+T_p}\big)$ is the probabilistic distribution of the relative parameters at the end of prediction, and $I\big(v_i,s_i,m_t^i\big)$ presents the driving efficiency for better traffic condition, which could assess the traffic beyond the prediction horizon and could be expressed as follows:

$$I\big(v_i,s_i,m_t^i\big) = \begin{cases} \frac{\Delta v_{t_0+T_p}}{\Delta d_{t_0+T_p}} & \textbf{if } \frac{\Delta v_{t_0+T_p}}{\Delta d_{t_0+T_p}} > 0; \\ 0 & \textbf{if } \frac{\Delta v_{t_0+T_p}}{\Delta d_{t_0+T_p}} \le 0; \end{cases} \tag{8}$$

where $\Delta v_{t_0+T_p}$ is the relative speed between one vehicle and the vehicle ahead at time t_0+T_p, and $\Delta d_{t_0+T_p}$ is the relative distance between the two vehicles at time t_0+T_p. If there is no vehicle ahead, then $I\big(v_i,s_i,m_t^i\big)=0$.

3.4 Maneuver Prediction and Planning Considering Interaction and Gaming

Based on the extensive form game theory with imperfect information, the maneuver prediction of other vehicles and the maneuver planning for the ego vehicle could be simulated and achieved.

In the extensive form game, define the vehicles in the traffic as players. And the ego vehicle is represented as P_0, and other vehicles in the surrounding environment are defined as $P_i(i = 1, 2, \cdots, N)$. N is the number of the vehicles except P_0.

Therefore, the players in the game can be represented as follows:

$$P = \{P_0, P_1, P_2, \ldots, P_i, \ldots, P_N\} \tag{9}$$

The actions $A_i = \{A_i^1, A_i^2, \ldots, A_i^k, \ldots, A_i^{M_i}\}$ for P_i in the game represent the maneuvers such as left lane-change, right lane-change, and lane keeping. M_i is the size of the actions for P_i.

In addition, $P_{-i} = [P_j]_{j \neq i}$ means vector of all players except P_i. In the same way, $a_{-i}^t(j) = [a_h^t(j)]_{h \neq i}, j \in M_i$ means vector of all action profiles for all players except P_i, where t means the time steps and $a_i^t(j) \in A_i$ means the jth maneuver at time t for player i. In other words, $a_0^1(j)$ is the planning maneuver for ego vehicle and $a_{-0}^1(j)$ is the predicted maneuvers of the other vehicles in the surrounding traffic at the first simulation time step.

Scenes of the environment are defined as $S = [S_1, S_2, \cdots, S_i, \cdots, S_m]$, where m is the size of the scenes. And $s_t \in S$ can be defined as follows:

$$s_t = [a_0^t(j), a_{-0}^t(\mathbf{j})] \tag{10}$$

where t is the simulation time step.

At the initial step $t = 0$, the maneuvers of surrounding vehicles are estimated based on the observable parameters using dynamic Bayesian networks. The probabilistic distribution of the maneuvers could be obtained and expressed as $p(a_i^0(j))$. Assume that the estimated maneuvers are independent as in [29]. Therefore, the probabilistic distribution of $s_0, p(s_0)$, could be obtained as follows:

$$p(s_0) = \prod_{i=0}^{n} p(a_i^0(j)) \tag{11}$$

At step t, the probabilistic distribution of maneuvers for P_i could be expressed as $p(a_i^t(j)), j \in M_i$.

The uncertainty of the maneuver estimation is considered in the payoff function of the extensive form game, as shown in (2) and (7).

3.5   Multi-step Prediction and Planning

Multi-step prediction and planning in this study are proposed to predict the environment and plan maneuvers for AVs by looking ahead in a few steps, which makes AVs react earlier to potential risks or better traffic environment in the future. Multi-step prediction and planning are based on multi-act games in extensive forms. In multi-act games, all players are allowed to act more than once in the game tree. As shown in Fig. 3, it is a 2-step prediction and planning tree, which has two players, P_0, P_1. And each player acts twice in the game.

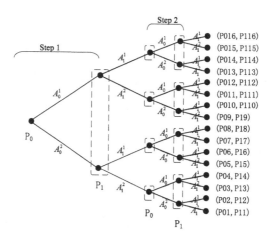

Fig. 3. Multi-step prediction and planning based on multi-act games in extensive forms with two players. P_0, P_1 are the two players in this game. A_i^j is the action of P_i. **Pij** is the payoff for Player **i**.

In the framework of multi-step prediction and planning, it is assumed that the players in the next step know exactly the actions in former steps. As shown in Fig. 3, the dashed curves of P_1 in Step-1 represents that P_1 in Step-1 do not know the action of P_0 in Step-1, which is same with the single-step prediction and planning tree. However, the players P_0, P_1 in Step-2 know exactly the actions in Step-1, which is shown by the information sets in Step-2.

The payoff costs of the multi-act games in extensive forms are defined by considering the discounted payoff of each step based on (7), which is expressed as the following equation:

$$MU_i = \sum_{k=1}^{n} \beta^{k-1} U_i^k \quad 0 < \beta \leq 1 \tag{12}$$

where MU_i means the multi-step payoff of P_i. n is number of step, for example, in Fig. 3, the number of step $n = 2$. β is the discount of the payoff at every step. And U_i^k is the payoff from (7) at Step k. The multi-step payoff function indicates that the multi-act games in extensive forms include the influences from the next several future steps.

The maneuver prediction of the other vehicles and maneuver planning for ego vehicle within several time steps can be obtained by solving the Nash equilibria in behavioral strategies. Let n denotes the number of levels of the play, then the behavioral strategies of P_i could be decomposed into n components $\hat{\gamma}_i^1, \hat{\gamma}_i^2, \cdots, \hat{\gamma}_i^n$, where $\hat{\gamma}_i^k$ is the corresponding behavioral strategy of P_i at its kth step of play. $\hat{\gamma}_i^k$ could be expressed as follows:

$$\hat{\gamma}_i^k = \{\theta_i^{k1}, \theta_i^{k2} \cdots, \theta_i^{kj}, \cdots, \theta_i^{kM_i}\} \tag{13}$$

where k means the kth step of play, M_i is the size of the maneuver vector for Player i, and θ_i^{kj} means the probability of the maneuver j at the kth step of play for Player i.

Then the set of inequalities to determine the behavioral Nash equilibrium solution can be written. For $\forall\, 0 \leq i \leq N; 0 \leq k \leq n$, (14) should be satisfied.

$$
\begin{aligned}
J_i^* &\triangleq J_i\big(\hat{\gamma}_0^{1*}, \hat{\gamma}_0^{2*}, \cdots, \hat{\gamma}_0^{k*}, \cdots, \hat{\gamma}_0^{n*}; \cdots; \hat{\gamma}_i^{1*}, \hat{\gamma}_i^{2*}, \cdots, \hat{\gamma}_i^{k*}, \cdots, \hat{\gamma}_i^{n*}; \cdots; \hat{\gamma}_N^{1*}, \hat{\gamma}_N^{2*}, \cdots, \hat{\gamma}_N^{k*}, \cdots, \hat{\gamma}_N^{n*}\big) \\
&\leq J_i\big(\hat{\gamma}_0^{1*}, \hat{\gamma}_0^{2*}, \cdots, \hat{\gamma}_0^{k*}, \cdots, \hat{\gamma}_0^{n*}; \cdots; \hat{\gamma}_i^1, \hat{\gamma}_i^2, \cdots, \hat{\gamma}_i^k, \cdots, \hat{\gamma}_i^n; \cdots; \hat{\gamma}_N^{1*}, \hat{\gamma}_N^{2*}, \cdots, \hat{\gamma}_N^{k*}, \cdots, \hat{\gamma}_N^{n*}\big)
\end{aligned}
\tag{14}
$$

where J_i is the expected payoff based on the corresponding behavioral strategies. And $\{J_0^*, J_1^*, \cdots, J_i^*, \cdots, J_{N-1}^*, J_N^*\}$ is the non-cooperative Nash equilibrium outcomes of the game in behavioral strategies.

In this study, the Nash equilibria in behavioral strategies of multi-act games with extensive forms can be obtained by solving a sequence of single-act games and by appropriate concatenation of the equilibrium strategies determined at each step of play. Therefore, we could impose further restrictions that it also satisfies (15) recursively at step k for all $\hat{\gamma}_i^k, \forall\, 0 \leq i \leq N, 0 \leq k \leq n$:

$$
\text{Step } k
\begin{cases}
\begin{aligned}
J_0^* &\triangleq J_0\big(\hat{\gamma}_0^1, \hat{\gamma}_0^2, \cdots, \hat{\gamma}_0^{k*}, \cdots, \hat{\gamma}_0^{S*}; \cdots; \hat{\gamma}_i^1, \hat{\gamma}_i^2, \cdots, \hat{\gamma}_i^{k*}, \cdots, \hat{\gamma}_i^{S*}; \cdots; \hat{\gamma}_N^1, \hat{\gamma}_N^2, \cdots, \hat{\gamma}_N^{k*}, \cdots, \hat{\gamma}_N^{S*}\big) \\
&\leq J_i\big(\hat{\gamma}_0^1, \hat{\gamma}_0^2, \cdots, \hat{\gamma}_0^k, \cdots, \hat{\gamma}_0^{S*}; \cdots; \hat{\gamma}_i^1, \hat{\gamma}_i^2, \cdots, \hat{\gamma}_i^k, \cdots, \hat{\gamma}_i^{S*}; \cdots; \hat{\gamma}_N^1, \hat{\gamma}_N^2, \cdots, \hat{\gamma}_N^k, \cdots, \hat{\gamma}_N^{S*}\big)
\end{aligned} \\
\qquad\qquad\qquad \vdots \\
\begin{aligned}
J_i^* &\triangleq J_i\big(\hat{\gamma}_0^1, \hat{\gamma}_0^2, \cdots, \hat{\gamma}_0^{k*}, \cdots, \hat{\gamma}_0^{S*}; \cdots; \hat{\gamma}_i^1, \hat{\gamma}_i^2, \cdots, \hat{\gamma}_i^{k*}, \cdots, \hat{\gamma}_i^{S*}; \cdots; \hat{\gamma}_N^1, \hat{\gamma}_N^2, \cdots, \hat{\gamma}_N^{k*}, \cdots, \hat{\gamma}_N^{S*}\big) \\
&\leq J_i\big(\hat{\gamma}_0^1, \hat{\gamma}_0^2, \cdots, \hat{\gamma}_0^k, \cdots, \hat{\gamma}_0^{S*}; \cdots; \hat{\gamma}_i^1, \hat{\gamma}_i^2, \cdots, \hat{\gamma}_i^k, \cdots, \hat{\gamma}_i^{S*}; \cdots; \hat{\gamma}_N^1, \hat{\gamma}_N^2, \cdots, \hat{\gamma}_N^k, \cdots, \hat{\gamma}_N^{S*}\big)
\end{aligned} \\
\qquad\qquad\qquad \vdots \\
\begin{aligned}
J_N^* &\triangleq J_N\big(\hat{\gamma}_0^1, \hat{\gamma}_0^2, \cdots, \hat{\gamma}_0^{k*}, \cdots, \hat{\gamma}_0^{S*}; \cdots; \hat{\gamma}_i^1, \hat{\gamma}_i^2, \cdots, \hat{\gamma}_i^{k*}, \cdots, \hat{\gamma}_i^{S*}; \cdots; \hat{\gamma}_N^1, \hat{\gamma}_N^2, \cdots, \hat{\gamma}_N^{k*}, \cdots, \hat{\gamma}_N^{S*}\big) \\
&\leq J_i\big(\hat{\gamma}_0^1, \hat{\gamma}_0^2, \cdots, \hat{\gamma}_0^{k*}, \cdots, \hat{\gamma}_0^{S*}; \cdots; \hat{\gamma}_i^1, \hat{\gamma}_i^2, \cdots, \hat{\gamma}_i^k, \cdots, \hat{\gamma}_i^{S*}; \cdots; \hat{\gamma}_N^1, \hat{\gamma}_N^2, \cdots, \hat{\gamma}_N^k, \cdots, \hat{\gamma}_N^{S*}\big)
\end{aligned}
\end{cases}
\tag{15}
$$

As a result, the maneuver planning for the ego vehicle could be achieved by finding the maximum probability behavioral strategy in the Nash equilibrium, expressed as follows:

$$A_0^{k*} = A_0^{kmx}, 0 < k \le n \tag{16}$$

where mx satisfies $\theta_0^{kmx*} = \max_{j \in M_0} \theta_0^{kj*}, 0 < k \le n$.

Moreover, the maneuver prediction for multiple steps could be obtained according to the Nash equilibrium in behavioral strategies and the former prediction results as shown in (17):

$$p\left(a_i^{k+1}(j)\right) = \frac{p\left(a_i^k(j)\right) + \theta_i^{kj*}}{\sum_{h=1}^{M_i}\left(p(a_i^k(h)) + \theta_i^{kh*}\right)} \tag{17}$$

4 Experiment and Results Analysis

4.1 Experiment Scenarios and Definition of Maneuvers

In this study, the prediction and planning framework has been applied and proved in different lane-change scenarios, where there are multiple vehicles in the surrounding environment in a three-lane road for one direction shown in Fig. 4.

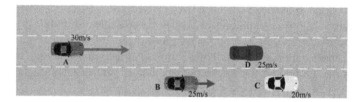

Fig. 4. Multiple vehicles in a three-lane road for one direction.

As shown in the lane-change scenarios, maneuvers used in this application including lateral and longitudinal maneuvers. The lateral maneuvers A_{lat} are defined as follows:

$$A_{lat} = \{LLC, RLC, LK\} \tag{18}$$

where LLC means left lane-change, RLC means right lane-change, and LK represents lane keeping.

Meanwhile, the longitudinal maneuvers A_{long} could be defined as follows:

$$A_{long} = \{Dec, Const, Acc\} \tag{19}$$

where Dec means deceleration, $Const$ means keeping constant velocity, and Acc means acceleration.

As a result, the maneuvers of P_i in the surrounding traffic can be obtained:

$$A_i = A_{lat} \times A_{long} \tag{20}$$

The maneuver prediction and planning in different lane-change scenarios will be analyzed in the next subsection based on the basic maneuver definition in [30].

4.2   Results Analysis

The results of the maneuver prediction and planning framework proposed in this study will be analyzed via two different lane-change scenarios. In each one, the specific lane-change scenario will be introduced first and then the results will be presented and analyzed. In each scenario, it is assumed that the ego vehicle interacts and games with the vehicle just near ahead in the three lanes.

The first lane-change scenario is shown in Fig. 5. In this scenario, there are four vehicles and it is assumed that Vehicle A is the ego vehicle. In this case, there is another more vehicle (Vehicle D) also in the middle lane with slow velocity (18 m/s). The relative longitudinal distance between Vehicle A and Vehicle B is 30 m and that between Vehicle B and Vehicle C is 20 m. And the relative longitudinal distance between Vehicle B and Vehicle D is 10 m. It is expected that Vehicle B may have the high intention or probability to make lane keeping because there is a slow vehicle in the middle lane. And Vehicle A should make the left lane-change for better traffic environment when approaching the slow vehicle D.

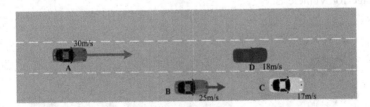

Fig. 5. The first lane-change scenario for experiment.

In this scenario, the maneuver prediction and planning results are shown in Table 1.

Table 1. Maneuver prediction and planning results for the first scenario

	Vehicle A (maneuver planning)	Vehicle B (maneuver prediction)
Observe-based model	No planning	$p(A_1^0 = LLC) = 0.05$ $p(A_1^0 = LK) = 0.95$ $p(A_1^0 = RLC) = 0$
2-step prediction and planning	$A_0^1 = \{LLC, Const\}$ $A_0^2 = \{LLC, Const\}$	$p(A_1^2 = LLC) = 0.01$ $p(A_1^2 = LK) = 0.99$ $p(A_1^2 = RLC) = 0$

As shown in Table 1, the maneuver planning for Vehicle A is $\{LLC, Const\}$ in multiple-step prediction and planning methods, which could obtain better traffic environment in the third lane because of the slow vehicle ahead in the middle lane. In this case, for the reason that there is a slow vehicle ahead in the middle lane, Vehicle B is predicted with higher probability of lane keeping than that of the observe-based model by considering the interaction and gaming aspect.

The second lane-change scenario is shown in Fig. 6. In this scenario, there are four vehicles and it is assumed that Vehicle A is the ego vehicle. In this case, there is another vehicle (Vehicle D) in the third lane compared with the first scenario. The velocity of Vehicle D is 33 m/s. The relative longitudinal distance between Vehicle A and Vehicle B is 30 m and that between Vehicle B and Vehicle C is 20 m. And the relative longitudinal distance between Vehicle A and Vehicle D is 5 m. It is expected that Vehicle B may have the high intention or probability to make lane changing for better traffic environment. Even being awareness of this, Vehicle A should keep its lane and decelerate because of the approaching of vehicle D as well as in the case of the left lane-change for Vehicle B.

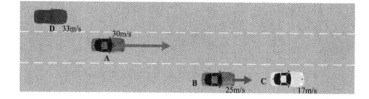

Fig. 6. The second lane-change scenario for application.

In this scenario, the maneuver prediction of Vehicle B is similar to that in the first scenario by considering the interaction and gaming with Vehicle A as shown in Table 2. However, the maneuver planning of Vehicle A is $\{LK, Dec\}$, which means Vehicle A should stay in the middle lane because Vehicle D is approaching Vehicle A with higher velocity. Also, since there is a high probability that Vehicle B would merge in, Vehicle A has to decelerate at the same time.

Table 2. Maneuver prediction and planning results for the first scenario

	Vehicle A (maneuver planning)	Vehicle B (maneuver prediction)
Observe-based model	No planning	$p(A_1^0 = LLC) = 0.05$ $p(A_1^0 = LK) = 0.95$ $p(A_1^0 = RLC) = 0$
2-step prediction and planning	$A_0^1 = \{LK, Dec\}$ $A_0^2 = \{LK, Dec\}$	$p(A_1^2 = LLC) = 0.77$ $p(A_1^2 = LK) = 0.23$ $p(A_1^2 = RLC) = 0$

5 Conclusions

In this study, a framework of maneuver prediction and planning is proposed on the basis of interaction and gaming between multiple vehicles. The payoff costs of multiple vehicles include risk assessments as well as the driving efficiency and preference. The risk assessment model proposed in this study is on the basis of trajectory prediction under uncertainty which integrates the dynamic and maneuver-based models for more accurate prediction in the long term. Based on the extensive-form game theory, the single-step and multiple-step maneuver prediction and planning frameworks are proposed. And the maneuver predicting results combine observe-based model as well as the Nash equilibrium in mixed and behavioral strategies. In addition, this framework is proved and applied in different lane-change scenarios. The results indicate that the maneuver prediction of vehicles considers the interaction and gaming between multiple vehicles. Moreover, the planning results for the ego vehicle show the cooperative decision-making strategies, which consider other vehicles strategies at the same time. Also, the multi-step prediction and planning makes the decision strategies being aware of the potential risks and respond earlier.

Acknowledgments. This work was supported by China Postdoctoral Science Foundation Special Funded Projects under Grant No. 2018T110095, Project funded by China Postdoctoral Science Foundation under Grant No. 2017M620765, National Key Research and Development Program of China under Grant No. 2017YFB0102603, and Junior Fellowships for Advanced Innovation Think-tank Program of China Association for Science and Technology under Grant No. DXB-ZKQN-2017-035.

References

1. van Arem, B.: A Strategic approach to intelligent functions in vehicles. In: Eskandarian, A. (ed.) Handbook of Intelligent Vehicles, pp. 17–29. Springer, London (2012). https://doi.org/10.1007/978-0-85729-085-4_2

2. Baines, V., Padget, J.: A situational awareness approach to intelligent vehicle agents. In: Behrisch, M., Weber, M. (eds.) Modeling Mobility with Open Data, pp. 77–103. Lecture Notes in Mobility. Springer, Cham (2015). https://doi.org/10.1007/978-3-319-15024-6_6

3. Liu, H.P., Yu, Y.L., Sun, F.C., Gu, J.: Visual-tactile fusion for object recognition. IEEE Trans. Autom. Sci. Eng. **14**(2), 996–1008 (2017)

4. Peters, H.: Game Theory: A Multi-leveled Approach, 2nd edn. Springer, New York (2015)

5. Gao, H.B., Cheng, B., Wang, J.Q., et al.: Object classification using CNN-based fusion of vision and LIDAR in autonomous vehicle environment. IEEE Trans. Ind. Inf. **PP**(99), 1 (2018)

6. Liu, H.P., Sun, F.C., Fang, B.: Robotic room-level localization using multiple sets of sonar measurements. IEEE Trans. Instrum. Meas. **66**(1), 2–13 (2017)

7. Gao, H.B., Zhang, X.Y., Liu, Y.C., et al.: Longitudinal control for Mengshi autonomous vehicle via gauss cloud model. Sustainability **9**(12), 2259–2275 (2017)

8. Liu, H.P., Sun, F.C., Guo, D., et al.: Structured output-associated dictionary learning for haptic understanding. IEEE Trans. Syst. Man Cybern.: Syst. **47**(7), 1564–1574 (2017)

9. Kim, K., Kim, B., Lee, K., Ko, B., Yi, K.: Design of integrated risk management-based dynamic driving control of automated vehicles. IEEE Intell. Transp. Syst. Mag. **9**(1), 57–73 (2017)

10. Xie, G.T., Gao, H.B., Qian, L.J., et al.: Vehicle trajectory prediction by integrating physics- and maneuver-based approaches using interactive multiple models. IEEE Trans. Ind. Electron. **56**(7), 5999–6008 (2017)

11. Bahram, M., Hubmann, C., Lawitzky, A., Aeberhard, M., Wollherr, D.: A combined model- and learning-based framework for interaction-aware maneuver prediction. IEEE Trans. Intell. Transp. Syst. **17**(6), 1538–1550 (2016)

12. Gao, H.B., Zhang, X.Y., Zhang, T.L., et al.: Research of intelligent vehicle variable granularity evaluation based on cloud model. Acta Electronica Sinica **44**(2), 365–374 (2016)

13. Li, K., Wang, X., Xu, Y., Wang, J.: Lane changing intention recognition based on speech recognition models. Transp. Res. C-Emerg. **69**, 497–514 (2016)

14. Huang, J., Tan, H.S.: Vehicle future trajectory prediction with a DGPS/INS-based positioning system. In: American Control Conference, Minneapolis, MN, USA, pp. 5831–5836, June 2006

15. Sorstedt, J., Svensson, L., Sandblom, F., Hammarstrand, L.: A new vehicle motion model for improved predictions and situation assessment. IEEE Trans. Intell. Transp. Syst. **12**(4), 1209–1219 (2011)

16. Polychronopoulos, A., Tsogas, M., Amditis, A.J., Andreone, L.: Sensor fusion for predicting vehicles' path for collision avoidance systems. IEEE Trans. Intell. Transp. Syst. **8**(3), 549–562 (2007)

17. Hou, Y., Edara, P., Sun, C.: Modeling mandatory lane changing using Bayes classifier and decision trees. IEEE Trans. Intell. Transp. Syst. **15**(2), 647–655 (2014)

18. Ding, C., Wang, W., Wang, X., Baumann, M.: A neural network model for driver's lane-changing trajectory prediction in urban traffic flow. Math. Probl. Eng. **2013**, 8 p. Article ID 967358 (2013)

19. Peng, J., Guo, Y., Fu, R., Yuan, W., Wang, C.: Multi-parameter prediction of drivers' lane-changing behaviour with neural network model. Appl. Ergon. **50**, 207–217 (2015)

20. Gadepally, V., Krishnamurthy, A., Özgüner, Ü.: A framework for estimating long term driver behavior. J. Adv. Transport. **2017**, 11 p. Article ID. 3080859 (2017)
21. Liu, P., Kurt, A.: Trajectory prediction of a lane changing vehicle based on driver behavior estimation and classification. In: 17th International IEEE Conference on Intelligent Transportation Systems, Qingdao, pp. 942–947 (2014)
22. Li, F., Wang, W., Feng, G., Guo, W.: Driving intention inference based on dynamic Bayesian networks. In: Wen, Z., Li, T. (eds.) Practical Applications of Intelligent Systems. AISC, vol. 279, pp. 1109–1119. Springer, Heidelberg (2014). https://doi.org/10.1007/978-3-642-54927-4_106
23. Gindele, T., Brechtel, S., Dillmann, R.: Learning driver behavior models from traffic observations for decision making and planning. IEEE Intell. Transp. Syst. Mag. **7**(1), 69–79 (2015)
24. Talebpour, A., Mahmassani, H.S., Hamdar, S.H.: Modeling lane-changing behavior in a connected environment: a game theory approach. Transport. Res. C-Emerg. **59**, 216–232 (2015)
25. Liu, H.X., Xin, W., Adam, Z., Ban, J.: A game theoretical approach for modelling merging and yielding behaviour at freeway on-ramp sections, pp. 197–211. Elsevier, London (2007)
26. Meng, F., Su, J., Liu, C., Chen, W.H.: Dynamic decision making in lane change: game theory with receding horizon. In: 2016 UKACC 11th International Conference on Control, Belfast, pp. 1–6 (2016)
27. Gratner, A., Annell, S.: Probabilistic collision estimation system for autonomous vehicles: evaluated in intersection scenarios using a velocity planning controller. M.S. thesis, Industrial Engineering and Management, KTH, Stockholm, Sweden (2016)
28. Bahram, M., Lawitzky, A., Friedrichs, J., Aeberhard, M., Wollherr, D.: A game-theoretic approach to replanning-aware interactive scene prediction and planning. IEEE Trans. Veh. Technol. **65**(6), 3981–3992 (2016)
29. Schreier, M., Willert, V., Adamy, J.: An integrated approach to maneuver-based trajectory prediction and criticality assessment in arbitrary road environments. IEEE Trans. Intell. Transp. Syst. **17**(10), 2751–2766 (2016)
30. Gao, H.B., Zhang, X.Y., Liu, Y.C., et al.: Cloud model approach for lateral control of intelligent vehicle systems. Sci. Program. **2016**(2), 1–12 (2016)

RMVD: Robust Monocular VSLAM for Moving Robot in Dynamic Environment

Qile Li$^{(\boxtimes)}$, Fuchun Sun, and Huaping Liu

Tsinghua University, Beijing 100084, China
lql15@mails.tsinghua.edu.cn, {fcsun,hpliu}@tsinghua.edu.cn

Abstract. For moving robot, accurate localization and mapping is important for route planning. And for mower robot, it is hard to localizing and mapping because of the dynamic working environment of mower robot, and especially hard for robot which takes use of monocular visual sensor. In this paper, we introduced our work of an intelligent monocular visual slam system which has been applied on our mower robot platform. And the system works well in our mower robots testing environment, which is outdoors and dynamic. In our work, we combines method of traditional slam algorithm and method of deep learning to deal with dynamic outdoors environment. The slam system can work in real time for robots localization. Profiting from our robust and real-time slam system, we can implement accurate route planning which takes use of localization result of the mower robots slam system.

Keywords: Monocular slam · Dynamic · Moving robot

1 Introduction

1.1 Background

SLAM is short for simultaneous localization and mapping. It is used for robots localization in its working environment and map building of its working environment.

When a robot is moving in a work space, it will capture information from its sensors, and estimate its motion as well as the structure of environment in simultaneous time.

In a slam system, various or multiple types of sensors can be utilized. As for common sensors used in slam system, there are radar, visual sensor (camera) and so on. The radar sensor can provide robot with depth information of obstacle within a limited range centered at the robot. Sensors of Visual SLAM system is also varies, such as monocular camera, RGBD camera, stereo camera. Monocular camera can only provide the robot with image information, while RGBD camera and stereo camera can provide the robot with image information as well as depth information, but the depth information provided by such camera is often limited in a range of at most several dozens of meters.

© Springer Nature Singapore Pte Ltd. 2019
F. Sun et al. (Eds.): ICCSIP 2018, CCIS 1006, pp. 454–464, 2019.
https://doi.org/10.1007/978-981-13-7986-4_40

SLAM especially Visual SLAM has attracted more and more attentions from researchers and enterprise, because of its application value in moving robot, aircraft, VR/AR and so on, and also because of the informative data captured from visual sensor.

Due to the expensive cost and outdoors limitation of RGBD and stereo visual sensor, many researchers and enterprises concentrate on the researching of monocular slam. And most of the algorithms are designed for common usage, but they are also weak in dynamic outdoors working environment. Also, in our work, we use monocular for mower robots slam system.

1.2 Related Works

Monocular SLAM has attracted more and more researchers, and there have been a lot of fine work in this field. We will simply introduce some typical work on monocular SLAM in the following.

LSD-SLAM. Large Scale Direct SLAM [7]. In tracking thread of LSD-SLAM, pose of current frame is computed by applying an optimization of minimizing intensity difference of pixels which has depth information in last frame.

In mapping thread, depth information of pixels in current frames will be used to refine those in the last key frame by eppipolar pixel match and EKF [10]. If the mapping thread determines that the current frame will become a key frame, depth information will be delivered from last key frame.

ORB-SLAM. ORB-SLAM [1] is a SLAM with multiple modes, it can work in monocular mode, stereo mode and RGBD mode. We only introduce the monocular mode here. ORB-SLAM consists of three threads: tracking thread, local mapping thread and global mapping thread. In tracking thread, ORB-SLAM is similar with PTAM, the algorithm extract ORB [12] key points and match them with last frame, solve a PNP problem to get a rough pose of current frame. Local map is also used for refining of current pose.

All the above work are designed for common use, and facing a very complex situation and works very well. But they are not designed and not suit for special case of our mower robot application, in which the robot is doing 2d motion and working in a dynamic environment. Next, we will introduce our work which is custom made for that application.

2 Algorithm

2.1 Overview

We include a recognition module in our system. Our SLAM System can be divided into 4 parts: initialization, tracking thread, mapping thread and recognition module.

The initialization part estimate relative pose of first two frames and initialize a map which consists of key points with estimated 3d coordinate and 2 key frames with estimated poses.

The tracking thread estimate pose of image frames captured from a monocular camera, and decide whether to generate a new key frame.

The mapping thread waits for new key frame generated from tracking thread. When it get a newly generated key frame from tracking thread, it will apply reconstruction, bundle adjustment local map refinement, loop closure and pose-only optimization.

The recognition thread also waits for the key frame generated from tracking thread, and will apply a convolutional neural network to deal with it. The processing result of CNN will also be used in tracking and mapping thread.

The architecture of the overall working flow after initialization can be spotted as following.

In this section, we will first introduce some important concepts in a single, and then introduce the 4 modules in independent sections (Fig. 1).

Fig. 1. The overall work flow of our slam system.

2.2   Initialization Module

The initialization module is the first step our slam systems runs. When the camera capture first 2 images, the initialization module will try to estimate the relative pose of these 2 frames and generates map points. After that a initial map contains 2 key frames with generated map points is established.

The initialization module processes in following steps. When we get first two images, we extract ORB key points [12] from those. To get plenty and correct key point matches, we apply a GMS [13] algorithm.

After we obtain the matches, we apply a RANSAC [14] algorithm to find the essential matrix of two frames, and then we can acquire the relative pose between the 2 frames by applying an SVD [15] on the matrix. Then we do a reconstruction step by taking use of eppipolar search and refine the initial map by bundle adjustment.

2.3   Tracking Thread

The Tracking thread is used for tracking cameras frame and estimating its pose. The Tracking thread consists of several step, which will be explained following.

First, we estimate a rough pose for current frame. In this step, when we capture a frame of image, we initialize the current pose with last pose plus delta pose computed by data of wheels.

Second, we apply a refinement on the pose we just estimated. After obtain a rough pose, we next take advantage of local map to refine the it.

Due to the refined matches generated from previous process of Rough pose estimation, we can get a set of map points for ORB key points on the current frame of image. A map point is an object in our slam algorithm, as mentioned above, the object consists of key point in key frame, coordinate and a score of whether belongs to a fixed object. These data can be computed in the mapping thread and recognition thread as we will explained later in the section of 2.4 and 2.5.

After estimating pose of current frame, we would check whether current frame will become a key frame. The key frame will also be sent to a recognition thread.

2.4   Mapping Thread

The mapping thread works mainly for reconstruction and refinement of the map. In the mapping thread, we wait for newly generated key frame from tracking thread. After we get key frame from tracking thread, we execute following steps to process the new key frame.

After we obtain a key frame from tracking thread, the first task to do is to estimate 3d coordinate of key points extracted on that key frame.

To estimate the coordinate of a key point on current key frame, we need to match it with key points on other key frames. It is known that the match between current key frame and other key frames follows eppipolar geometry constraint. So we can search the pixels on the eppipolar line of those old key frames. The eppipolar constraints can be spotted as Fig. 2.

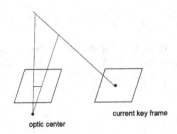

Fig. 2. The eppipolar constraints of matching on two key frames with known poses.

After the reconstruction step, we can obtain new map points. The following things to do is the optimization of pose of key frames within the local map (which of course includes current key frame) as well as key points that at least 2 key frames in the local map can observe. We apply a bandle adjustment algorithm to optimize them.

Loop Closure. The last step in the mapping thread is loop closure. In this step we apply a VLAD [3] algorithm to find similar key frames of current key frame, the difference of 2 key frame id should be larger than a threshold. After we find similar key frames. We project the map points observed by those old key frames onto current key frame and find matches. Then we solve a PNP problem to compute relative pose from current key frame to each of those key frames. If we successfully found loop closure of current key frame, we apply a 7 dof pose-only optimization of all key frames in the map. With the constraints of their relative poses computed.

2.5 Recognition Thread

The recognition thread waits for key frames fed by tracking thread. After obtaining a key frame, the recognition thread feed the image into an FCN [16] to score each pixel in the image. We recommend to use a pre-trained ResNet [17] and replace the corresponding layers as fully convolutional layers and train it in order to classify each pixel whether belongs to a fix object. The result of FCN [16] will be adopted by tracking thread and mapping thread. In tracking thread, map points with high score will be adapted to track current frame. In loop closure of mapping thread, map points with high score will be projected on to current key frame to compute pose constraint.

In our system, we design a switch to enable or disable the recognition module. In the experiment, we will compare the tracking result of these 2 different mode in different situations. Under the mode of enabling the recognition, we also test 4 different architecture of FCN in our Experiment 3. The architecture we choose from are AlexNet [18], VGG-16 [19], GoogleNet [20], and ResNet [17]. And we recommend to use ResNet [17] as the CNN architecture in the recognition thread.

3   Experiment

Our slam system is mainly designed for mower robot which works in an outdoors and 2d-emotion-major environment. And we apply a plenty of test on our slam system in the corresponding environment.

3.1   Hardware

In this subsection, we will introduce the hardware which includes sensors, processor in our test.

Sensors. The camera we use in our experiment is a 30 fps camera with resolution of 640 and 480. And we also take use of the coded discs of robot's wheels.

Processor. The processor we run our slam algorithm on is Intel Core i7-7700HQ, the ram we can use is 8 GB. Due to our Recognition module, we also use a NVIDIA GTX1060 to run the FCN [16].

3.2 Tracking Route

We first test the localization with enable the loop closure, when we drive the mower robot in outdoors dynamic environment and the following is the coordinate of the localization compare to the ground truth. As shown in Fig. 3.

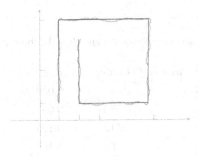

Fig. 3. In this test, we enable loop closure in the mapping thread. The green line in the graph above is the pose estimated by our slam system, the red line above is the ground truth. The smallest grid in above coordinator system is 2 m. (Color figure online)

We then test it with disabling the loop closure, we perform the same route and the result can be spotted in Fig. 4.

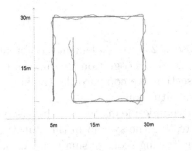

Fig. 4. In this test, we disable the loop closure in the mapping thread. The green line in the graph above is the pose estimated by our slam system, the red line above is the ground truth. The smallest grid in above coordinator system is 2 m. (Color figure online)

We can see that the error from estimate value to the ground truth during this test case is under 0.3 m.

3.3 Drift Error

We apply a plenty of testing on our slam system in dynamic environment of large scale, and calculate average drift errors of each distance. As shown in Table 1, the average drift error at different distance when we enable or disable loop closure in mapping thread. We can observe from the table that the average drift error in dynamic outdoor environment on the distance of 50 m grows around 0.4 m when we enable loop closure, and if we disable it, the drift error grows nearly 0.8 m in the end. We can conclude that if we disable the loop closure in the mapping thread, the drift error will grow more rapidly than that we enable the loop closure.

Table 1. Drift error with loop closure enabled/disabled at different distance

Distance (m)	Enable (m)	Disable (m)
5	0.041	0.043
10	0.083	0.092
15	0.119	0.129
20	0.162	0.188
25	0.203	0.253
30	0.239	0.332
35	0.280	0.429
40	0.325	0.531
45	0.371	0.652
50	0.409	0.791

3.4 Dynamic Scene

As mentioned in the Subsect. 2.5, we implement 2 different modes for recognition module, the one is enable the recognition module and another is disable the recognition. In this subsection, we compare the tracking succeed rate of these 2 different modes in several situations.

In the Table 2, the dynamic means testing the system in dynamic environment, the static means testing the system in the static environment. The small in the bracket means the testing scene is small and in our experiment, the distance is less than 10 m. The median in the bracket means the testing scene is median and in our experiment, the distance is not larger than 50 m. The big in the bracket means the testing scene is big and in our experiment, the distance is up to 100 m.

Thus we have 6 different type of test scenes. For each type of test scene, we test each mode 3 times in that type of scene and mark the succeed rate.

We can see that the mode with recognition module enabled succeed to track for all test. For test scene of big dynamic type, the working mode with recognition

Table 2. The table of tracking succeed rate under 2 recognition modes

Scene type	Enable	Disable
Dynamic (small)	3/3	3/3
Static (small)	3/3	3/3
Dynamic (median)	3/3	2/3
Static (median)	3/3	3/3
Dynamic (big)	3/3	0/3
Static (big)	3/3	3/3

disabled failed all the times. For test scene of median dynamic type, the working mode with recognition disabled failed one time. For small dynamic scenes, the 2 modes works well. From this result, we can conclude that the recognition mode is important when the robot is working in a larger dynamic scene.

Table 3. The table of tracking succeed rate with different CNN architecture

Architecture	Median	Big
AlexNet	3/3	3/3
VGG-16	3/3	3/3
GoogleNet	3/3	2/3
ResNet	3/3	3/3

In RMVD, we choose different kind of CNN architecture to use in our recognition algorithm and test the robustness of tracking in median and large scale dynamic test scene. For each type of scale, we find 3 different scenes and test all CNN choices under those 3 scenes. Thus we have 6 tests for each of the architecture. As mentioned in the Sect. 2.5, we test 4 different CNN architecture. The Table 3 shows that all the architecture pass the whole 6 tests of dynamic scene cases.

We then mark the average and minimum map point set size of each key frame for each architecture during the test. And we can view the result from the Table 4. The result shows that, for each type of CNN architecture, the average

Table 4. The table of tracking succeed rate with different CNN architecture

Architecture	Avg	Min
AlexNet	343.02	52.03
VGG-16	345.12	83.12
GoogleNet	348.05	101.54
ResNet	350.53	135.92

num map point of each key frame observes is nearly 350, and we know that the more fixed map points each key frame observes, the more robust is the slam. The average data could not show the performance of each architecture, but when we look at the minimum data, we can see the ResNet out perform others, in other word, ResNet works a lot more better than other architecture in the worst case, and that is why we prefer to use ResNet in the recognition module. To compare our work with other slam algorithms in dynamic scene, we test our work compared with ORB-SLAM [1] and LSD-SLAM [7] under 2 kinds of large scale dynamic scene, the one in which the dynamic objects move fast and the other slow. We mark the tracking succeed rate during the test, the result can be viewed in Table 5.

Table 5. The table of tracking succeed rate under 2 different dynamic type

Type	RMVD	LSD-SLAM	ORB-SLAM
Fast	3/3	3/3	3/3
Slow	3/3	2/3	2/3

We have 2 different type of dynamic test scenes. For each type of test scene, we test each slam system 3 times in that type of scene and mark the succeed rate. In this test, we enable recognition module in our algorithm. From the table we can see that when dynamic objects in the test scene move fast, all the tested slam system works well, but when the objects move slowly, only our slam system with recognition enabled tracks successfully during the whole trip in all 3 tests.

3.5   Time Cost

To test the time efficiency of each thread, we mark the mean and median time cost of processing one frame or key frame in each thread. We also test the case of enabling or disabling the loop closing in the mapping thread. parameter values era given in Table 6. The unit of time cost in the Table 6 is ms, from the table we can see that, the tracking thread can track each frame in nearly 30 fps, and then we can say that the tracking satisfy the requirement of real time.

Table 6. Time cost of each module

Time cost (ms)	Mean cost (ms)	Median cost (ms)
Tracking	34.25	33.01
Mapping	1531.75	1535.02
Mapping (no closure)	698.13	702.20
Recognition	1521.39	1519.18

As for mapping thread and recognition thread, Processing a single key frame will cost a lot more time than that in tracking thread. In the case of enabling the loop closure, the mapping thread process a key frame will cost nearly 1.5 s, and in the case of disabling the loop closure, the mapping thread will cost nearly 700 ms. The recognition module will also takes nearly 1.5 to process a key frame.

Although the time cost is much higher in mapping or recognition thread than that in tracking thread, the total system time efficiency is not influenced sharply. Because the frequency of key frame generation is much smaller than frame captured by camera, and the mapping as well as the recognition is running in individual threads which will not block the tracking thread. And from the result of experiment in the above subsections, we can see that the recognition module and

4 Conclusion

In this work, we implement a slam system which is suit for our mower robot application. Unlike other slam systems which concentrate on common problems, the slam system we proposed is custom designed for the mower robot application in which the working environment is dynamic and mainly 2d motion. We test time cost and robustness of our work and also compare with other common slam algorithm. We can see that the slam we proposed works well when facing problems of dynamic large scene.

Acknowledgement. This work was supported in part by the National Natural Science Foundation of China under Grants 61621136008/DFG TRR-169, U1613212 and the Suzhou Special program under Grand 2016SZ0219.

References

1. Mur-Artal, R., Tardos, J.D.: ORB-SLAM2: an open-source SLAM system for monocular, stereo, and RGB-D cameras. IEEE Trans. Robot. **33**, 1–8 (2017)
2. GlvezLpez, D., Tards, J.D.: Bags of binary words for fast place recognition in image sequences. IEEE Trans. Robot. **28**(5), 1188–1197 (2012)
3. Tom, W., et al.: Rare structural variants disrupt multiple genes in neurodevelopmental pathways in schizophrenia. Science **320**(5875), 539–543 (2008)
4. Trajkovic, M., Hedley, M.: Fast corner detection. Image Vis. Comput. **16**(2), 75–87 (1998)
5. Yihong, W., Zhanyi, H.: PnP problem revisited. J. Math. Imaging Vis. **24**(1), 131–141 (2006)
6. Forster, C., Pizzoli, M., Scaramuzza, D.: SVO: fast semi-direct monocular visual odometry. In: IEEE International Conference on Robotics & Automation (2014)
7. Engel, J., Schöps, T., Cremers, D.: LSD-SLAM: large-scale direct monocular SLAM (2014)
8. Leutenegger, S., Lynen, S., Bosse, M., et al.: Keyframe-based visual-inertial odometry using nonlinear optimization. Int. J. Robot. Res. **34**(3), 314–334 (2014)

9. Triggs, B., Mclauchlan, P.F., Hartley, R.I., et al.: Bundle adjustment a modern synthesis. In: Theory & Practice, International Workshop on Vision Algorithms (1999)
10. Fujii, K.: Extended Kalman filter. Reference Manual (2013)
11. Cummins, M., Newman, P.: FAB-MAP: Probabilistic Localization and Mapping in the Space of Appearance. Sage Publications, Inc., Thousand Oaks (2008)
12. Rublee, E., Rabaud, V., Konolige, K., et al.: ORB: an efficient alternative to SIFT or SURF. In: 2011 International Conference on Computer Vision. IEEE (2012)
13. Bian, J., Lin, W.Y., Matsushita, Y., et al.: GMS: grid-based motion statistics for fast, ultra-robust feature correspondence. In: 2017 IEEE Conference on Computer Vision and Pattern Recognition (CVPR). IEEE Computer Society (2017)
14. Derpanis, K.G.: Overview of the RANSAC algorithm. Image Rochester NY 4, 2–3 (2010)
15. Tsai, R.Y., Huang, T.S.: Uniqueness and estimation of three-dimensional motion parameters of rigid objects with curved surfaces. IEEE Trans. Pattern Anal. Mach. Intell. 6(1), 13 (1984)
16. Long, J., Shelhamer, E., Darrell, T.: Fully convolutional networks for semantic segmentation. IEEE Trans. Pattern Anal. Mach. Intell. (2014)
17. He, K., Zhang, X., Ren, S., et al.: Deep residual learning for image recognition (2015)
18. Krizhevsky, A., Sutskever, I., Hinton, G.: ImageNet classification with deep convolutional neural networks. In: NIPS. Curran Associates Inc. (2012)
19. Simonyan, K., Zisserman, A.: Very Deep convolutional networks for large-scale image recognition. Comput. Sci. (2014)
20. Szegedy, C., Liu, W., Jia, Y., et al.: Going deeper with convolutions (2014)

A General Monocular Visual Servoing Structure for Mobile Robots in Natural Scene Using SLAM

Chenping Li, Xuebo Zhang(✉), and Haiming Gao

Institute of Robotics and Automatic Information System (IRAIS),
Tianjin Key Laboratory of Intelligent Robotics, Nankai University,
Tianjin 300350, China
{lichenping,ghm}@mail.nankai.edu.cn, zhangxuebo@nankai.edu.cn
http://www.xuebozhang.net/

Abstract. In this paper, a general visual servoing structure for mobile robots is proposed to handle the situation that the target scene gets out of the camera view. Most existing visual servoing strategies are based on the assumption that images always share common feature points with the desired one during the servoing procedure, which actually cannot be guaranteed by the controller. To avoid such problems, simultaneous localization and mapping (SLAM) is introduced to visual servoing system, which contains the front-end for estimating the current pose and the back-end for optimizing the desired pose of the mobile robot. Meanwhile, compared with the traditional servoing system with artificial feature points, the scale of robot poses can be fixed by the map in the proposed scheme, which makes it applicable in natural scene. In addition, all position-based visual servoing controllers are implementable in the proposed servoing architecture. The servoing structure has been implemented on a nonholonomic mobile robot and experimental results are exhibited to illustrate the effectiveness and feasibility of the proposed approach.

Keywords: Visual servoing · Mobile robot · SLAM · Natural scene

1 Introduction

In recent years, mobile robots have attracted considerable interests due to their excellent performance in such tasks as search, rescue, and target tracking. Many valuable works on mobile robots, including control, planning, and visual servoing, have been reported in [1–7]. By utilizing image feedback signals, visual servoing plays an important role in environment exploration.

This work is supported in part by National Natural Science Foundation of China under Grants 61573195 and U1613210, in part by Tianjin Science and Technology Program under Grants 17KPXMSF00110.

Early research on visual servoing is mainly for industrial manipulators [8], for which both position-based [9] and image-based [10] methods are investigated. With the development of sensors, visual servoing techniques are also tested on other robots, such as mobile robots [5,6,11–13] and unmanned aerial vehicles [14–18]. Different from 6 DOF manipulators, mobile robots usually suffer from nonholonomic constraints, which means that there exist no continuous static state feedback controllers that are able to stabilize the nonholonomic mobile robot, thus making it a difficult job to regulate the robot's pose [19]. To overcome the problem introduced by the nonholonomic constraint, some novel control schemes are proposed [20,21]. Meanwhile, both position-based visual servoing [22] and image-based visual servoing [11] are studied.

As a main topic of the robotics field, monocular visual servoing usually utilizes coplanar artificial corner features due to the lack of direct observation of visual scale. Besides, it is usually based on the assumption that the target scene is always within the camera field of view during the servoing process, which cannot be guaranteed by the control algorithm in most cases, especially for nonholonomic constraints mobile robots showed in Fig. 1. In this paper, SLAM is introduced into monocular visual servoing, allowing the robot to get the position feedback even if the target scene is out of the camera field of view. Also, monocular visual servoing with SLAM is feasible in natural scene.

SLAM techniques are attracting attentions from computer vision and robotics communities in recent years. With rich information provided by cameras or laser sensors, the SLAM techniques could help to realize objectives of autonomous localization and environment perception [23–25]. To generate the metrical map, a series of pioneering methods, including both filtering based approaches and graph based ones, have been proposed. Filtering-based approaches [26,27], utilizing Bayesian Filters such as Kalman Filter and Particle Filter, transform the original problem as a system state estimation one, which require fewer computational resources due to the marginalization of past states [28]. Graph-based approaches first proposed by Lu and Milios in 1997 [29] divide the problem into two parts, front-end to construct the graph including both robot poses and landmarks in the map and back-end to optimize the graph [30]. Since the accuracy of the desired pose has an important influence on the servo results, we introduce the graph-based SLAM to avoid suboptimal results which may be caused by the early fix of linearization points in filtering-based approaches.

In this paper, a novel visual servoing structure is proposed for mobile robots. After a translation of the robot, a feature map can be created by SLAM, with which the current pose and desired pose can be estimated by front-end and back-end respectively, even on the challenging condition that the images have no feature points in common. Then the relative pose between them can be calculated as feedback for the servoing controller, by which linear and angular velocities are designed to stabilize the robot pose. The major contributions of this paper can be summarized as follows:

(1) A novel visual servoing system using SLAM is proposed to cope with situation that the target scene might get out of camera view during the servoing procedure.
(2) A general servoing framework is constructed for position-based controllers of nonholonomic mobile robots.
(3) The scale of pose estimation is fixed by feature map in SLAM rather than artificial corner features, thus making it feasible in natural scene.

The rest of the paper is organized as follows. The visual servoing problem is formulated in Sect. 2. In Sect. 3, the servoing structure using SLAM is presented. Experimental results validating our servoing structure in Sect. 4. In Sect. 5, conclusions of this paper and future works are stated.

2   Problem Formulation

As illustrated in Fig. 1, we assume that the coordinate system of the nonholonomic mobile robot coincides with that of the fixed onboard monocular camera $\mathcal{F}^c$, which can be easily achieved by installing optical centre of the camera at the midpoint of the robot wheels axis horizontally. The x^c axis of $\mathcal{F}^c$ is along the camera optical axis and the y^c axis of $\mathcal{F}^c$ is parallel to the wheel axis so that the $x^c - y^c$ plane is parallel to the motion plane of the robot. Similarly, $\mathcal{F}^0$ and $\mathcal{F}^*$ denote the robot frame in start pose and desired pose respectively. Additionally, t_x t_y and θ represent the translation and rotation angel between $\mathcal{F}^*$ and $\mathcal{F}^c$ respectively.

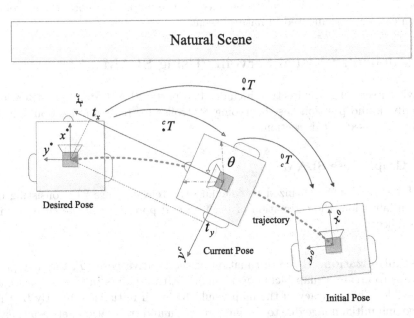

Fig. 1. Monocular visual servoing system of the mobile robot

The control objective of visual servoing is to drive the mobile robot from its start pose $\mathcal{F}^0$ to the desired one $\mathcal{F}^*$ by designing its linear velocity v and angular velocity ω calculated from the image feedback.

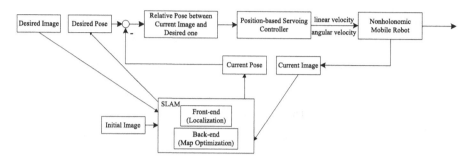

Fig. 2. System diagram

The system diagram is shown in Fig. 2. We introduce SLAM into monocular visual servoing, by which the relative pose $_*^c T$ between $\mathcal{F}^c$ and $\mathcal{F}^*$ can be calculated, so that linear and angular velocity could be designed. The SLAM process consists of two parts, front-end to locate the robot and construct a graph containing key frame poses and feature points in the environment, back-end to optimize the graph to reduce the error of desired pose, by which $_*^c T$ could be always obtained even if the desired image gets out of the camera view. Although the scale of $_*^c T$ is unknown, it can be fixed by the map. Therefore, the servoing system can be implemented in natural scene.

3   Monocular Visual Servoing Using SLAM

The visual servoing architecture includes two parts, SLAM for pose estimation as feedback and position-based servoing controller for pose stabilization, which will be discussed in this section.

3.1   Graph-Base SLAM

Graph-based SLAM is utilized to calculate the relative pose $_*^c T$, consisting of map initialization, the estimation of both desired pose $\mathcal{F}^*$ and the current one $\mathcal{F}^c$ as follows.

Map Initialization. Before estimation of the relative pose $_*^c T$, the first procedure is to create a map including as many feature points in the target scene as possible. The accuracy of the map would be low if initialized directly by the desired and initial image due to the large rotation and translation between them, which will lead to low precision of robot pose estimation. Therefore, we create

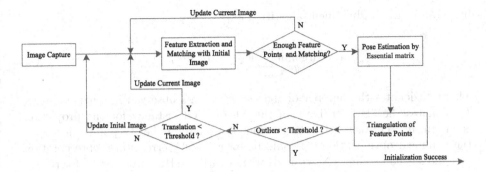

Fig. 3. Block diagram of map initialization

the map by a simple translation of the mobile robot so as to get more feature matching and avoid short-baseline in rotation motion.

Figure 3 shows the process of map initialization. A map containing enough feature points can be obtained after feature extraction and matching, pose estimation through essential-matrix-based algorithm and triangulation of the feature points. In addition, Random Sample Consensus (Ransac) is used to reject outliers in the map.

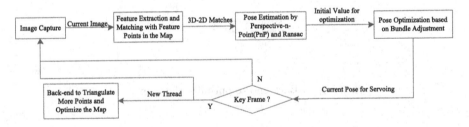

Fig. 4. Front-end to estimate the current pose of the robot

Front-End to Estimate Robot Pose. As is shown in Fig. 4, the front-end estimates the current pose of the robot by two phases. The first phase initializes the pose estimation by feature extraction and matching with points in the local map, a submap of the map used to reduce computation, consisting of 3D feature points in last frame and those who share common points with last image due to small relative motion between two adjacent images. Then Perspective-n- Point (PnP) and Ransac are used to calculate the initial value of current pose of the robot, thus making the scale unknown but constant owing to the 3D-2D matches used for estimation. In order to get the maximum likelihood estimation, the current pose $_c^0T$ is optimized by minimizing the 2-norm of the reprojection error based on Bundle Adjustment algorithm as

$$e = \arg\min_{{}^{0}_{c}T} \sum_{i=1}^{N} \|Q({}^{0}_{c}T, P_{ic}) - p_{ic}\| \tag{1}$$

where N denotes the number of the feature points observed in current image, P_{ic} denotes the 3D coordinate of the ith one, $Q(\cdot)$ stands for the projection equation, p_{ic} represents the observation coordinate of the ith point. Moreover, the nonlinear optimization (1) could be linearized by error-state representation [31] and solved by Gauss Newton algorithm with the Huber norm [32] for robust outliers rejection. The last step is to decide if the current image is a new key frame. In order to avoid short baseline degeneration and triangulate more feature points from sufficient overlap of scene, the image with enough motion and feature matching to the last key frame will be selected as a new key frame.

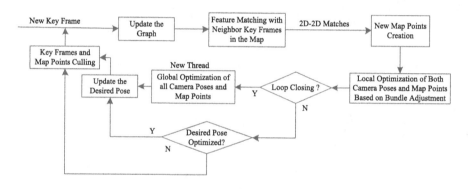

Fig. 5. Back-end to optimize the map

Back-End to Optimize the Desired Pose. Figure 5 shows the process of the back-end. Once the image is chosen as a key frame by the front-end, the new pose node and edges with other ones will be added to the map for further optimization. Besides, more map points are created by triangulating the feature matching between the new key frame and its neighbor key frames which have enough feature points with it in common. After updating the graph, local optimization of poses of the new key frame and its neighbor ones as well as map points connected with them is proceeded by minimizing the sum of reprojection error as follows

$$e = \arg\min_{{}^{0}_{j}T, P_{i}} \sum_{\mathcal{F}^{j} \in \mathcal{K}, P_{i} \in \mathcal{P}} h_{ij} \|Q({}^{0}_{j}T, P_{i}) - p_{ij}\| \tag{2}$$

where $\mathcal{K}$ denotes a set of the new key frame and its neighbor frames, $\mathcal{P}$ stands for a set of map points which are visible to frames in $\mathcal{K}$, $Q(\cdot)$ represents the projection equation, ${}^{0}_{j}T$ is the pose of the jth key frame, P_{i} denotes the 3D coordinate of the ith map point in $\mathcal{P}$, p_{ij} represents the projection coordinates of ith points in jth key frame. The value of h_{ij} is as follows.

$$h_{ij} = \begin{cases} 1 & \text{the } i\text{th point is visible to the } j\text{th key frame} \\ 0 & \text{otherwise} \end{cases} \tag{3}$$

Furthermore, if a loop is detected in the new key frame, the whole map will be optimized by a similar cost function to (2) except that $\mathcal{K}$ and $\mathcal{P}$ denote all frames and map points in the map respectively. Finally, redundancy map points and key frames will be culled to maintain the computational complexity.

Since the relative pose between the current pose and the desired one is used as the controller feedback, the precision of $_*^0T$ plays an important role in the servoing results, which, unfortunately, can only be estimated roughly at first owing to few map points in the map. However, the accuracy of $_*^0T$ can be improved continuously by the optimization in the back-end, as the robot moves to the desired position and more feature points, especially those in the desired image, are triangulated and added into the map.

3.2 Two Stage Control Scheme

As mentioned in the introduction, all position-based visual servoing control algorithms for nonholonomic mobile robots are implementable in our servoing system with SLAM. In this paper, we adopt the control scheme proposed in [33], the difference is that there is no need to take short baseline generation into consideration, because the current pose $_0^cT$ is calculated by the front-end of SLAM rather than essential-matrix.

The control objective is to design angular and linear velocity such that $\lim_{t\to\infty} t_x(t) = 0$, $\lim_{t\to\infty} t_y(t) = 0$, $\lim_{t\to\infty} \theta(t) = 0$. The two-stage controller for the nonholonomic mobile robot can be described as follows:

(1) In stage I, the linear velocity $v(t)$ and angular velocity $\omega(t)$ are designed based on the relative pose $_c^*T$ so that the translation error t_x and t_y go to zero, namely $\lim_{t\to\infty} t_x(t) = 0$, $\lim_{t\to\infty} t_y(t) = 0$.

(2) In stage II, by setting $v(t) = 0$, the angular velocity $\omega(t)$ is designed to make rotation error θ converge to zero, which is achieved by a simple proportional controller.

4 Experimental Results

In this section, experimental results are provided to verify the effectiveness of the propose visual servoing system using SLAM. As Fig. 6 shows, the experimental platform is a Pioneer3-DX mobile robot equipped with the point-grey camera BFLY-PGE-13E4C-CS at the midpoint of the robot wheels axis. The image size is 640×512 captured at 30 Hz, the same frequency as pose estimation and control, which is achieved by the Oriented FAST and Rotated BRIEF (ORB) features

Fig. 6. Experimental setup: platform (left) and environment (right)

and multithread. The experimental environment is the natural scene without any artificial features in our laboratory demonstrated as Fig. 6. All algorithms including both SLAM and servoing control is accomplished on the laptop computer communicating with the camera through the network port, with the robot through a RS232 serial port. The initial pose is $(-0.84\,\text{m}, -0.66\,\text{m}, 1.7°)$ with respect to the desired frame $\mathcal{F}^*$, where the relative pose between $\mathcal{F}^*$ and $\mathcal{F}^0$ is just like Fig. 1.

Figure 7 shows the motion path and orientation of the nonholonomic mobile robot. Figure 8 shows the linear velocity in stage I and angular velocity during the whole process, which are calculated by the controller designed in [33].

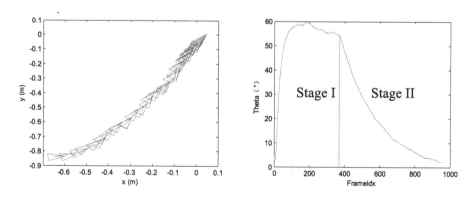

Fig. 7. The motion path (left) and rotation angle (right) of the robot

The right image of Fig. 9 is captured during the servoing process, sharing no common feature points with the desired one. Benefited from the feature map

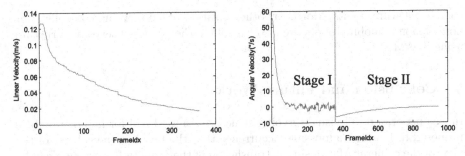

Fig. 8. The linear velocity (left) and angular velocity (right)

Fig. 9. The desired image (left) and the image in the servoing procedure (right)

Fig. 10. Features in the map (left) and the feature map (right)

created by SLAM in Fig. 10, the relative pose ${}^{c}_{*}T$ can still be estimated for controller feedback, thus making it superior over other servoing algorithms which are based on the assumption that the target scene is always in the field of view.

From the experimental results, we can see that the proposed visual servoing structure using SLAM is effective in pose stabilization for mobile robots even in the challenging situation that the desired image and the current one have no common feature points. Moreover, other position-based servoing controllers for nonholonomic mobile robots are also feasible in the proposed servoing structure using SLAM.

5   Conclusion and Future Work

In this paper, a novel visual servoing structure using SLAM for mobile robots is proposed to handle the possible occurrence that the target scene get out of the view of the camera. After a simple translation of the robot, a feature map can be established for the following estimation of the robot pose for servoing feedback in front-end of SLAM, while the back-end improves its accuracy. Specifically, the proposed scheme is feasible in natural scene without any artificial feature points, since its scale is fixed by the feature map. Experimental results showed the effectiveness of the proposed approach.

In the future, we will make effort to take advantage of additional sensors, such as encoder equipped with the mobile robot, to reduce the scale drift in the mono-SLAM and improves the precision of pose estimation. In addition, more geometric constraints in the indoor environment, including line segments, vanishing points, planes and so on, can be adopted to improve robustness and accuracy of the system.

References

1. Sun, W., Tang, S., Gao, H., Zhao, J.: Two time-scale tracking control of nonholonomic wheeled mobile robots. IEEE Trans. Control Syst. Technol. **24**(6), 2059–2069 (2016)
2. Chen, M.: Disturbance attenuation tracking control for wheeled mobile robots with skidding and slipping. IEEE Trans. Ind. Electron. **64**(4), 3359–3368 (2017)
3. Moon, C., Chung, W.: Kinodynamic planner dual-tree RRT (DT-RRT) for two-wheeled mobile robots using the rapidly exploring random tree. IEEE Trans. Ind. Electron. **62**(2), 1080–1090 (2015)
4. Montiel, O., Seplveda, R., Orozco-Rosas, U.: Optimal path planning generation for mobile robots using parallel evolutionary artificial potential field. J. Intell. Robot. Syst. **79**(2), 237–257 (2015)
5. Wang, K., Liu, Y., Li, L.: Visual servoing trajectory tracking of nonholonomic mobile robots without direct position measurement. IEEE Trans. Robot. **30**(4), 1026–1035 (2014)
6. Zhang, X., Fang, Y., Sun, N.: Visual servoing of mobile robots for posture stabilization: from theory to experiments. Int. J. Robust Nonlinear Control **25**(1), 1–15 (2015)
7. Li, B., Fang, Y., Hu, G., Zhang, X.: Model-free unified tracking and regulation visual servoing of wheeled mobile robots. IEEE Trans. Control Syst. Technol. **24**(4), 1328–1339 (2016)
8. Chaumette, F., Hutchinson, S.: Visual servo control. I. Basic approaches. IEEE Robot. Autom. Mag. **13**(4), 82–90 (2006)

9. Wilson, W.J., Hulls, C.C.W., Bell, G.S.: Relative end-effector control using carte-
   sian position based visual servoing. IEEE Trans. Robot. Autom. **12**(5), 684–696
   (1996)
10. Espiau, B., Chaumette, F., Rives, P.: A new approach to visual servoing in robotics.
    IEEE Trans. Robot. Autom. **8**(3), 313–326 (1992)
11. Mariottini, G.L., Oriolo, G., Prattichizzo, D.: Image-based visual servoing for non-
    holonomic mobile robots using epipolar geometry. IEEE Trans. Robot. **23**(1), 87–
    100 (2007)
12. Zhang, X., Fang, Y., Li, B., Wang, J.: Visual servoing of nonholonomic mobile
    robots with uncalibrated camera-to-robot parameters. IEEE Trans. Ind. Electron.
    64(1), 390–400 (2017)
13. Li, B., Zhang, X., Fang, Y., Shi, W.: Visual servoing of wheeled mobile robots
    without desired images. IEEE Trans. Cybern. (to be published). https://doi.org/
    10.1109/TCYB.2018.2828333
14. Thomas, J., Loianno, G., Daniilidis, K., Kumar, V.: Visual servoing of quadrotors
    for perching by hanging from cylindrical objects. IEEE Robot. Autom. Lett. **1**(1),
    57–64 (2016)
15. Zheng, D., Wang, H., Wang, J., Chen, S., Chen, W., Liang, X.: Image-based visual
    servoing of a quadrotor using virtual camera approach. IEEE/ASME Trans. Mecha-
    tron. **22**(2), 972–982 (2017)
16. Serra, P., Cunha, R., Hamel, T., Cabecinhas, D., Silvestre, C.: Landing of a quadro-
    tor on a moving target using dynamic image-based visual servo control. IEEE
    Trans. Robot. **32**(6), 1524–1535 (2016)
17. Guenard, N., Hamel, T., Mahony, R.: A practical visual servo control for an
    unmanned aerial vehicle. IEEE Trans. Robot. **24**(2), 331–340 (2008)
18. Cao, Z., et al.: Image dynamics-based visual servoing for quadrotors tracking a
    target with a nonlinear trajectory observer. IEEE Trans. Syst. Man Cybern.: Syst.
    (to be published). https://doi.org/10.1109/TSMC.2017.2720173
19. Do, K.D., Jiang, Z.P., Pan, J.: Simultaneous tracking and stabilization of mobile
    robots: an adaptive approach. IEEE Trans. Autom. Control **49**(7), 1147–1151
    (2004)
20. Astolfi, A.: Discontinuous control of nonholonomic systems. Syst. Control Lett.
    27(1), 37–46 (1996)
21. Yuan, H., Qu, Z.: Continuous time-varying pure feedback control for chained
    nonholonomic systems with exponential convergent rate. IFAC Proc. Vol. **41**(2),
    15203–15208 (2008)
22. Jean, J.H., Lian, F.L.: Robust visual servo control of a mobile robot for object
    tracking using shape parameters. IEEE Trans. Control Syst. Technol. **20**(6), 1461–
    1472 (2012)
23. Durrant-Whyte, H., Bailey, T.: Simultaneous localization and mapping: Part I.
    IEEE Robot. Autom. Mag. **13**(2), 99–110 (2006)
24. Bailey, T., Durrant-Whyte, H.: Simultaneous localization and mapping (SLAM):
    Part II. IEEE Robot. Autom. Mag. **13**(3), 108–117 (2006)
25. Stachniss, C., Leonard, J.J., Thrun, S.: Simultaneous localization and mapping.
    In: Siciliano, B., Khatib, O. (eds.) Springer Handbook of Robotics, pp. 1153–1176.
    Springer, Cham (2016). https://doi.org/10.1007/978-3-319-32552-1_46
26. Guivant, J.E., Nebot, E.M.: Optimization of the simultaneous localization and
    map-building algorithm for real-time implementation. IEEE Trans. Robot. Autom.
    17(3), 242–257 (2001)

27. Steux, B., El Hamzaoui, O.: tinySLAM: a SLAM algorithm in less than 200 lines of C code. In: Proceedings of the International Conference on Control, Automation, Robotics and Vision (ICARCV), pp. 1975–1979 (2010)

28. Yang, Z., Shen, S.: Monocular visual–inertial state estimation with online initialization and camera–IMU extrinsic calibration. IEEE Trans. Autom. Sci. Eng. **14**(1), 39–51 (2017)

29. Lu, F., Milios, E.: Globally consistent range scan alignment for environment mapping. Auton. Robots **4**(4), 333–349 (1997)

30. Dhiman, N.K., Deodhare, D., Khemani, D.: Where am I? Creating spatial awareness in unmanned ground robots using SLAM: a survey. Sadhana **40**(5), 1385–1433 (2015)

31. Leutenegger, S., Lynen, S., Bosse, M., et al.: Keyframe-based visual–inertial odometry using nonlinear optimization. Int. J. Robot. Res. **34**(3), 314–334 (2015)

32. Huber, P.J.: Robust estimation of a location parameter. Ann. Math. Stat. **35**(1), 73–101 (1964)

33. Li, B., Fang, Y., Zhang, X.: Essential-matrix-based visual servoing of nonholonomic mobile robots without short baseline degeneration. Int. J. Robot. Autom. (to be published). https://doi.org/10.2316/Journal.206.2015.4.206-4384

Path Planning for Active V-Slam Based on Reinforcement Learning

Borui Li[✉], Fuchun Sun, Huaping Liu, and Bin Fang

Tsinghua University, Beijing, China
lbr16@mails.tsinghua.edu.cn,
{fcsun, hpliu}@mail.tsinghua.edu.cn,
fangbin1120@163.com

Abstract. Slam (Simultaneous Localization and Mapping) is a passive system and in traditional slam algorithm robot's path is not considered when improving localization uncertainty. However, improving localization accuracy while autonomously exploring unknown environments needs to get abundant feature points and make enough loop closures. To that end we propose a reinforcement learning based active slam framework that can add path planning to existing slam algorithms. In this framework a reinforcement learning agent plans the path while slam is processing. We have tested our framework in simulation environments built in Unreal engine with unrealcv plugin and we have got excellent results.

Keywords: SLAM · Path planning · Reinforcement learning

1 Introduction

To move autonomously a robot must be able to interact with its environment, recognize, reconstruct and take appropriate action to accomplish its goal. Many techniques are suitable for solving some sub-problems of the goal above. SLAM (Simultaneous Localization and Mapping) algorithms [1, 2] can recognize the unknown environment and localize the camera. Artificial intelligence-based algorithms [3] can make navigation based on environment information. We set up a framework that can combine these two sorts of methods thus achieve robot autonomous move.

We use SLAM to continuously update the environment information and robot pose information. However, when robot experience a huge pose change, chances are the SLAM system lose track of the camera pose. We introduce reinforcement learning agent to avoid drastic robot pose change. Moreover, we use the agent to make robot explore the environment efficiently. That means we expect the robot to move shorter distance and make less pose adjustment when it finishes exploring the given space. Google [4] has made a deep learning-based SLAM module, and others has also made similar trials. Deep learning-based SLAM algorithms show poor accuracy till now, and our framework doesn't support this kind of SLAM algorithms. We only combine mainstream optimization-based SLAM algorithms. We take advantage of the SLAM output and graph-based optimization result to train the reinforcement agent.

© Springer Nature Singapore Pte Ltd. 2019
F. Sun et al. (Eds.): ICCSIP 2018, CCIS 1006, pp. 477–487, 2019.
https://doi.org/10.1007/978-981-13-7986-4_42

Section 2 presents an overview of related algorithms. Section 2.1 presents the design and implement of a direct-based SLAM algorithm used in experiment. Section 3 presents the design of our framework. Section 4 presents our experiments. Section 5 presents the conclusion and future work.

2   Algorithms

2.1   SLAM

Simultaneous Localization and Mapping (SLAM) problem is widely researched in recent decades. V-SLAM is especially centered in recent years. In general slam process consists of tracking and mapping. Tracking part is to estimate the 6-dof camera pose (3-dof rotation and 3-dof translation), which is also called front-end. Mapping part is the corresponding back-end and uses triangulation to estimate the depth of feature points in environment. Optimization can be applied to improve the accuracy of the two parts' estimation. Filter-based slam is the former trend. FastSLAM and EKF-SLAM are representatives. They all lack control of the localization drift in motion, and nowadays they are replaced by keyframe-based slam methods. Keyframe-based slam algorithms share a common execution routine. First it gets frame input and select key frames for analysis. Some (or all) of the points selected from neighboring keyframes to figure out the correct match. According to the rules of point selection, optimization-based SLAM can be classified to be direct-based and feature-based. Direct-based means select points according to the grayscale gradient, and LSD-SLAM [2] is a representative. Feature-based means select points according to given rule, such as ORB. ORB-SLAM [1] is the leading representative. Same point can be observed in several keyframes and in several different matches, so the SLAM system make optimization to minimize the conflicts in different matches. According to the matches, we can calculate the geometry coordinates of the selected point while figuring out the robot motion. In our work we utilize the calculated geometry coordinates and the optimization result to feed information to reinforcement agent. Our framework supports both feature-based algorithm and direct-based algorithm. In experiment we use ORB-SLAM and a direct-based semi-dense SLAM algorithm implemented by us.

2.2   Reinforcement Learning

We should first introduce the basic set up of A Reinforcement leaning agent. A Reinforcement leaning agent interacts with an environment over time. At each time step t, the agent receives a state s_t in a state space S and selects an action at from an action space A, following a policy $\pi(a_t|s_t)$, which is the agent's behavior, i.e., a mapping from state s_t to actions at, receives a scalar reward rt, and transitions to the next state s_t, according to the environment dynamics, or model, for reward function R(s, a) and state transition probability $P(s_{t+1}|s_t, a_t)$ respectively. In an episodic problem, this process continues until the agent reaches a terminal state and then it restarts. The return $R_t = \sum_{k=0}^{+\infty} \gamma_k r_{t+k}$ is the discounted, accumulated reward with the discount factor $\gamma \in (0, 1]$. The agent aims to maximize the expectation of such long-term return from each state.

The problem is set up in discrete state and action spaces. In the traditional set up, state space and action space must be represented in low dimensions to avoid "dimension disaster". However nowadays it is not hard to extend it to continuous spaces. We can utilize deep network to fit the policy $\pi(a_t|s_t)$, value function Q(s, a) or reward function R(s, a). This is deep reinforcement learning. In our framework both policy-based (fit the policy $\pi(a_t|s_t)$) agent and value-based (fit the value function Q(s, a)) agent are supported. Value-based agent is first proposed in DQN [5]. DQN makes a large replay buffer to store state transform history (s_t, a_t, s_{t+1}, r_t), and use DNN to fit Q(s, a).DNN is trained by random selection of replay buffer. Pure policy-based agent (i.e. REIN-FORCE) performs bad because it only updates parameters after a whole episode and only get sparse reward. We can use actor-critic method to overcome it. Actor-critic based agent for continues state space and action space is first proposed in DDPG [6]. Now A3C [7] and ACKTR [8] are more up-to-date choices. ACKTR (Actor Critic using Kronecker-factored Trust Region) is a combination of actor-critic, TRPO (Trust Region Policy Optimization), and Kronecker factorization. Actor-critic is oriented from policy gradient. It consists of actor network and critic network. Actor network output the continues action while critic network judges the performance of actor network. To accelerate the training process, natural policy gradient [6] is used to follow the steepest descent direction that uses the Fisher metric as the underlying metric. Trust-region policy optimization (TRPO) can avoids explicitly storing and inverting the Fisher matrix by using Fisher-vector products. TRPO utilize advantage function A(s, a) = Q(s, a) − V(s) to estimate the actions. Kronecker-factored approximated curvature is an estimation of natural gradient and used to boost the calculation. TRPO and K-FAC are combined by applying trust region formulation of K-FAC. In our experiment we use DQN and ACKTR to represent value-based methods and policy-based methods.

2.3 Path Planning for SLAM

Path planning for active slam is a new branch of slam research. Many previous work [9–11] are centered on Radar SLAM. References [9, 10] make the path planning by moving to the point with most information gain. Reference [9] uses sensitive analysis to sample from the discrete points in robot's moving range per unit time and utilizes support vector regression to predict the information gain. Reference [10] categorize the information gain in 2 classes: loop closure gain and exploratory gain. The former one denotes uncertainty loss and the latter denotes new discovery area increase. Reference [11] state the problem in a reinforcement learning form, and it utilize a naïve state representation to output the moving direction. In the environment manual labels are given to indicate the traversality of certain directions. We transform some concept in above 3 papers into V-SLAM situation. Loop closure gain and exploratory gain both represent the optimization uncertainty loss of estimated environment model. In optimization-based V-SLAM, global optimization is to reduce the uncertainty of the coordinates of robot and environment points. That is also the optimization of environment uncertainty loss. We can easily derive the identity of the two expressions.

One of the main goals of our path planning is to optimize the global optimization loss. Moreover, as is known to all, loop closure plays an important role of the drift optimization. In exploration process of unknown environment, we encourage large loop closure. Large loop closure can make more stable observation of given space than combination of small loop closures. In our path planning we add some policy restriction so that the robot can avoid small loop closures.

Obstacle avoidance is also considered, this is auto implemented by our path planning network.

3   Framework

We set up the framework to combine keyframe-based SLAM and reinforcement learning, it is shown in Fig. 1.

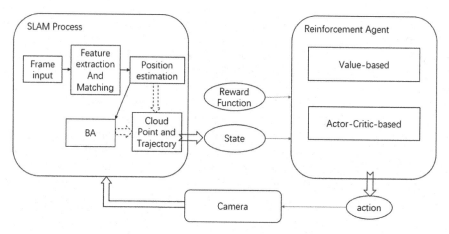

Fig. 1. Framework of combining keyframe-based SLAM and reinforcement learning.

SLAM process is running parallel to Reinforcement Agent while they are dependent on each other. SLAM process continuously receiving frames and estimate the camera pose change and feature points' coordinates. Besides utilizing the information from neighboring frames, SLAM process makes bundle adjustment to optimize the global estimation. They can generate point cloud and camera trajectory. We transform these outputs into the input state of reinforcement agent and feed them to the agent along with the manual designed reward function. The agent output actions to make the camera change its 6-dof pose, thus changing the input frames of SLAM process.

We can see the definition of state, action and reward is of vital importance. We will illustrate them below.

3.1   Action

Action Space can be defined below:

$$A^{sparse} = \left\{ (dir, pace) | dir \in \frac{\pi}{D_0} \{ (-D_0 + 1)/2, \ldots, 1, 2, \ldots, D_0/2 \}, pace = D_1, D_0, D_1 \in N^* \right\}$$

$$A^{continues} = \{ (dir, pace) | dir \in (-\pi/2, \pi/2], pace \in (0, 2D_1) \}$$

Dir means the radius change of camera orientation (clockwise change is above zero). Pace means the l2-norm of camera translation. D_0, D_1 are also hyper-parameters.

Note that we 've done experiments in virtual environment, which is a discrete environment. So, when receiving any action, the camera will move to the discrete point nearest to the destination point of the action.

3.2   Reward

Reward function is designed below:

$$R(s_t, a_t) = \begin{cases} -1e4 & a_t \text{ is unsafe} \\ -\Delta L & a_t \text{ is safe and SLAM keep in track} \\ -1e4 & a_t \text{ is safe and SLAM loses track} \end{cases}$$

Action a_t is safe means after the camera perform a_t there is no collision. Our basic demand is to make sure that the camera can avoid obstacles and SLAM system can work normally, so we add huge penalty on the deviation situations. L is the loss of global bundle adjustment, and ΔL is the L in s_{t+1} minus the L in s_t. As is mentioned in Sect. 2.3, L also means the environment uncertainty. In SLAM process, L is on the increase except for when loop closure is detected. Our reward can lead the agent towards less moving steps (negative reward in most situation) and more loop closure.

3.3   State

Our State is composed by global map information, local map information, and uncertainty information. We can get the point cloud representing the estimated environment from SLAM process. As to simplify the representation, we clear the points whose x-coordinates are smaller than hyper-parameter H, and project the remaining point cloud to the Z-O-Y plain (X axis is vertical) and down sample it to be an $N * N$ normalized grid G. Each cell C_{ij} contains a number g_{ij} denoting the density of projected points in that cell.

$$g_{ij} = \frac{\text{point quantity in } C_{i,j}}{\text{Point quantity in } G}$$

N is a hyper-parameter. Small N brings poor granularity thus making the training useless. Big N brings large space occupation of state and can cause storage exception or slow training speed. N also directly determines the input layer parameters of reinforcement agent. N should be set according to environments assessment beforehand.

Global Map Information. Global map information contains G^{global}, and camera trajectory information T. G^{global} is the generated by the projection of all feature points recorded in temporary SLAM process. T is a vector representing recent actions. Length of T is set to be 10.

Local Map Information. Local map information contains G^{global} and camera trajectory information T. G^{global} is the generated by the projection of all feature points recorded in a $2D_1 * 2D_1$ square area S^a. Current camera position is in the center of S^a. T is shared with global map information.

Uncertainty Information. Uncertainty information is mainly composed by global bundle adjustment loss L. We have mentioned the tight relationship between L and environment uncertainty information.

4 Experiments

We have done experiments in the virtual environment established by unreal4 engine. Unreal Engine 4 is a complete suite of development tools made for anyone working with real-time technology. Achieve Hollywood-quality visuals out of the box. Unreal Engine's physically-based rendering, advanced dynamic shadow options, screen space reflections and lighting channels provide the flexibility and efficiency to create awe-inspiring content (Fig. 2).

Fig. 2. Common elements in unreal4 engine

To get the vision information and ground truth (i.e. obstacle boundary, camera 6-dof pose, camera intrinsics), we use a plugin named unrealcv [12] (Fig. 3).

| Image | Object Mask | Depth | Surface Normal |

Fig. 3. Unrealcv interface examples [9]

We have bought a scene named "the medieval village" from unreal engine shop and after some edit it is used as our experiment environment. The bounding box size of building area is 300*240*60. There exists a loop closure that can traverse the whole map (Fig. 4).

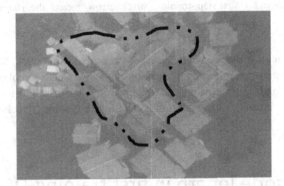

Fig. 4. Virtual environment of experiments with a large loop

When it comes to training, some details should be explained here. In this situation, $N = 20$, $D_0 = 36$, $D_1 = 2$, H is the height of the camera. Camera obeys the pin-hole model with the $FOV = 90°$.

For a certain kind of reinforcement agent, we made two split sub-agents to receive global state and local state separately. Sub-agent No. 1 receives global state, and we only care about the $a_1[dir]$ part of output, which lead to the global exploration direction. Sub-agent No. 2 receives local state, and we care about all the output: the $a_2[dir]$ part and $a_2[pace]$ part, which denote the point we can arrive at this time stamp. Final output should be performed in two steps:

Camera turn $a_2[dir]$ radius and move $a_2[pace]$ long

Camera move backward $a_2[pace]/5$ long, then turn $\pi/D_0 * sign(a_1[dir]-a_2[dir])$ radius.

We design this action execution mode to give the agents a smooth moving mode, which can accelerate our training; In fact without this measure the agents cannot achieve convergence.

We train value-based and actor-critic-based agents in three steps shown below:

First, we want to train an agent that can "drive" the camera smoothly and avoid obstacles. In this step we only explore a limited range in the map. Each episode the camera starts from the same position with the same orientation sketched in Fig. 5. The episode ends when collision occurs or moving steps reaches 200.

Fig. 5. Limited range for first-step training, black arrow means the starting position and orientation

We arrange our code to receive image input via unrealcv interface. We only process one grid G per time step. In the realization of DQN, we make a replay buffer with 1 million in length and apply epsilon-greedy. Epsilon falls from 0.6 to 0.1 in 100000 episodes. Leaning rate is 0.02, momentum is 0.9. Figure 6 shows the change of episode length.

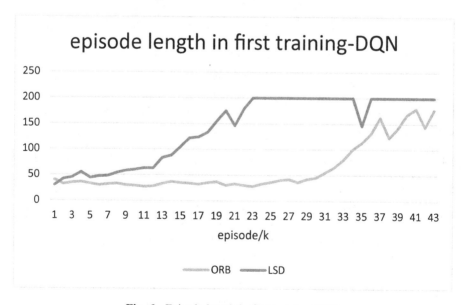

Fig. 6. Episode length in first training-DQN

In the realization of ACKTR, we also apply epsilon-greedy. Epsilon falls from 0.4 to 0.15 in 1 million episodes. Leaning rate is 0.01, momentum is 0.9. Figure 7 shows the change of episode length.

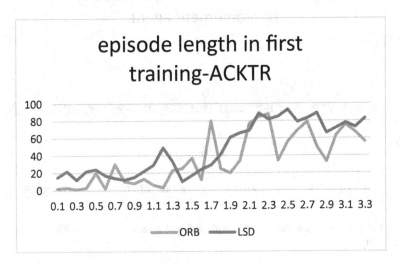

Fig. 7. Extended range for second-step training, black arrow means the starting position and orientation

In Figs. 7 and 6, we can see not all the agents converge well, but the trend is clear that all combinations are performing smoother camera control and more conscious of avoiding obstacles. ACKTR acts poorer than DQN, and that is because continuous-control agent is hard to train and converge, we need more time and more training episodes for ACKTR to converge properly.

We finetune the model trained in step 1, continue the step 2 training. As is shown in Fig. 8, we extended the area and change the initial camera pose. We still want to improve the agents' performance on smooth path planning and obstacle avoidance. Hyper-parameters are the same with above. Almost every episode ends up with 200 steps. Figure 9 shows the change of optimization loss CL_i with different combination of SLAM algorithm and reinforcement agent. Here $CL_i = \underline{L}_{i + 10000} - \underline{L}_i$. $\underline{L}_i$ represent the average of L at the end of surrounding 200 episodes ($i - i + 200$).

Fig. 8. Extended range for second-step training, black arrow means the starting position and orientation

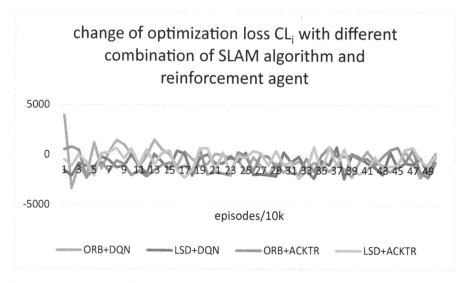

Fig. 9. Change of optimization loss CL_i with different combination of SLAM algorithm and reinforcement agent

We can see more than half of the sampled CL_i numbers are beneath zero, which means while reinforcement agent is converging, optimization loss of slam is reducing, and localization accuracy is improving.

5   Conclusion

We have proposed a reinforcement learning based active slam framework that can add path planning to existing slam algorithms. In this framework a reinforcement learning agent plans the path while slam is processing. We have tested our framework in simulation environments built in Unreal engine with unrealcv plugin and we have got some excellent results. However, there are also some problems to solve in further research. We split the agent into global planning agent and local planning agent. When using epsilon-greedy method to train them, we just give them a random safe action, but this cannot help them show the divergency. Also, the training now costs very long time, especially the training of ACKTR. I should consider using distributed cluster to accelerate.

Acknowledgement. This work is supported by National Key R&D Program of China under with Grant No. 2017YFB1302302.

References

1. Mur-Artal, R., Montiel, J.M.M., Tardós, J.D.: ORB-SLAM: a versatile and accurate monocular SLAM system. IEEE Trans. Robot. **31**(5), 1147–1163 (2017)
2. Engel, J., Schöps, T., Cremers, D.: LSD-SLAM: large-scale direct monocular SLAM. In: Fleet, D., Pajdla, T., Schiele, B., Tuytelaars, T. (eds.) ECCV 2014. LNCS, vol. 8690, pp. 834–849. Springer, Cham (2014). https://doi.org/10.1007/978-3-319-10605-2_54
3. Smart, W.D., Kaelbling, L.P.: Effective reinforcement learning for mobile robots. In: Proceedings of the IEEE/RSJ International Conference on Intelligent Robots and Systems, pp. 3404–3410 (2008)
4. Gupta, S., Davidson, J., Levine, S., Sukthankar, R., Malik, J.: Cognitive Mapping and Planning for Visual Navigation (2017)
5. Mnih, V., Kavukcuoglu, K., Silver, D., et al.: Playing atari with deep reinforcement learning. Comput. Sci. (2013)
6. Lillicrap, T.P., Hunt, J.J., Pritzel, A., et al.: Continuous control with deep reinforcement learning. Comput. Sci. **8**(6), A187 (2015)
7. Mnih, V., Badia, A.P., Mirza, M., et al.: Asynchronous methods for deep reinforcement learning (2016)
8. Wu, Y., Mansimov, E., Liao, S., et al.: Scalable trust-region method for deep reinforcement learning using Kronecker-factored approximation (2017)
9. Valencia, R., Miro, J.V., Dissanayake, G., Andrade-Cetto, J.: Active pose SLAM. In: 2012 IEEE/RSJ International Conference on Intelligent Robots and Systems (IROS), pp. 1885–1891 (2012)
10. Lauri, M., Ritala, R.: Planning for robotic exploration based on forward simulation. Robot. Auton. Syst. **83**(C), 15–31 (2016)
11. Qiu, W., et al.: UnrealCV: virtual worlds for computer vision, pp. 1221–1224. ACM (2017)
12. Bai, S., Wang, J., Doherty, K., Englot, B.: Inference-enabled information-theoretic exploration of continuous action spaces. In: Bicchi, A., Burgard, W. (eds.) Robotics Research. Springer Proceedings in Advanced Robotics, vol. 3, pp. 419–433. Springer, Cham (2018). https://doi.org/10.1007/978-3-319-60916-4_24

HDAA: High-Speed Data Acquisition Algorithm of IoT

Zhijin Qiu[1(✉)], Suiping Qi[1], Zhengyu Zhou[2], Tong Hu[1], Jing Zou[1],
and Dongming Wang[1]

[1] Institute of Oceanographic Instrumentation,
Qilu University of Technology (Shandong Academy of Sciences),
Qingdao 266000, China
qzjouc@163.com
[2] Shandong University of Technology, Zibo 255012, China

Abstract. As the 'Industry 4.0' has been proposed, the Internet of Things (IoT) has been widely used in more and more fields, and the higher demand for data acquisition efficiency. Unfortunately, the format, type, and access methods of data sources in different areas are diverse, making low efficiency of data acquisition. To address this issue, based on the data acquisition middleware of IoT (DAQ-Middleware), a novel **H**igh-speed **D**ata **A**cquisition **A**lgorithm of IoT (HDAA) is proposed. The algorithm includes parallel data acquisition algorithm and acquisition efficiency optimization heuristic method. According to the characteristics of different data sources and data interfaces, the mapping relationship is established between data sources and data interfaces, which improves the data acquisition efficiency of IoT. In the practical application and simulation environment, the data acquisition efficiency of HDAA is analyzed and compared with other algorithms. The results show that HDAA greatly improves the efficiency of data acquisition. In particular, the advantage of the algorithm is more obvious in the case of more data sources and less data interfaces.

Keywords: Internet of Things · Data acquisition · Middleware · Parallel acquisition · Heuristic

1 Introduction

With the development of pervasive computing, RFID, and sensor networks, the application and development of IoT technologies have been promoted. In different fields, the IoT realizes the acquisition, storage, analysis and display of global sensor data by connecting intelligent instruments, completes the analyzsis of big data, and guides enterprises to make strategic decisions and upgrades [1].

In order to realize data integration for existing IoT systems, the access data source also includes existing databases and data files, so the data source of the IoT is mainly divided into two parts: (a) sensing instruments including smart

F. Sun et al. (Eds.): ICCSIP 2018, CCIS 1006, pp. 488–499, 2019.
https://doi.org/10.1007/978-981-13-7986-4_43

sensors, RFID tags, computers and mobile devices; (b) databases and data files. At present, no matter which kind of data source, there are different kinds of data types, communication protocols and access methods, which make the development of the IoT system extremely complicated. Obviously, it is incredible to have a uniform communication protocol and data format for different instrument manufacturers.

In terms of IoT system design, many related studies have been conducted. Most of them mainly focus on the overall architecture design [2–5] and data display method [6–9] in IoT systems. There is no much study about the diversity of the data sources' format. In the research area of distributed systems, the relevant scholars have designed different architectures or algorithms for data acquisition system. Kovac [10] propose the use of virtual instrument technology and GPIB interface to achieve the acquisition of sensor data, which increases the convenience of access to the sensing instruments to a certain extent. Qiu et al. [11] propose a high performance data acquisition algorithm based on the analysis of dynamic delay characteristics of data acquisition. But this algorithm is only suitable for specific sensing instruments, and does not apply to multiple data sources. At the same time, the algorithm still using a serial data acquisition method for sequentially acquiring data from multiple data sources. Until recently, in [12] propose the concept of Complex Virtual Instrument System to handle multiple data sources. However, their architectures and application areas are still restricted. The Open GIS Consortium (OGC) [13] proposes to use Programmable Underwater Connector with Knowledge (PUCK) protocol to integrate the physical instruments automatically. Although, this has solved lots of problems in system integration and development, it must modify the ocean observing instruments and add PUCK model. Doing so increases the cost of instrument manufactures as well. In summary, none of the solutions above can settle comprehensively all the mentioned problems in data acquisition of IoT systems.

In this paper, according to the experiences of participation in the development of IEEE 1851, IEEE 2402 international standard and GB/T 33137-2016 national standard, we propose a data acquisition middleware based on IoT: DAQ-Middleware. DAQ-Middleware can provides sensing data for IoT system of the different areas through the standardized data interface.

In summary, the major contributions of this paper can be summarized as follows: (a) A scalable IoT data acquisition middleware is proposed, which not only supports access to the sensing instruments with interfaces of serial, network, GPIB and USB, but also supports access to various types of databases and files with interfaces of FTP, Web Service and MQ. (b) HDAA is proposed, which include a parallel data acquisition algorithm and an acquisition efficiency optimization heuristic method. (c) In the application scenario and simulation environment, the data acquisition efficiency of HDAA is compared with other algorithms. The purpose of this work is reduce the development cost and improve the data acquisition efficiency.

The rest of this article is organized as follows: Sect. 2 presents the architecture model of data acquisition system. Section 3 is an overview of DAQ-Middleware, and the HDAA is proposed in Sect. 4. Section 5 analyzes and compares the performance of HDAA. Concluding remarks are presented in Sect. 6.

2   Architecture Model

2.1   Hierarchy Model of IoT

Recently, many scholars put forward the object hierarchy model of IoT according to the different requirements, in order to facilitate the development and maintenance of IoT systems. According to [7], as shown in Fig. 1, the object hierarchy model is divided into four layers (sensing layer, acquisition layer, management layer, and application layer). Each layer is independent of each other, and only through the data interfaces to interact between the adjacent layers. The output of a layer is the input of next level. In some cases, management and application layers are collectively called application system.

2.2   Structure Model of DAQ-Middleware

As shown in Fig. 2, DAQ-Middleware is located in the acquisition layer of the IoT hierarchical model. Its functions include receiving control commands from the application system, periodically obtaining the data of data sources, and transmitting the obtained data to the application system through the standardized data interfaces. DAQ-Middleware uses Socket to communicate with application system. In different circumstances, DAQ-Middleware connects to the sensing instruments via interfaces, such as RS232, RS485, Ethernet and USB, and connects to the existing databases and data files through other interfaces, such as Web Service, MQ and FTP.

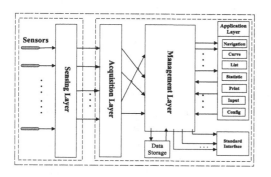
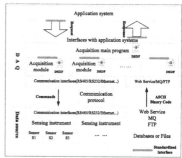

Fig. 1. Hierarchy model of IoT.   **Fig. 2.** Architecture of DAQ.

3   Overview of DAQ-Middleware

This section describes the data source description model, defines the interface between the application system and the middleware, and defines the interaction between the main program and the acquisition module. It can not only provide unified monitoring data for IoT applications in different fields, but also realize the addition, deletion and modification of data sources by modifying the data source description information.

3.1   Data Source Description File

The data source description file (DSDF) describes all the information of the data sources that are accessed. DAQ-Middleware can obtain various information, such as attributes, interfaces and sensor parameters of the data sources by analyzing DSDF. In order to facilitate the DSDF analysis, the format of DSDF is defined.

DSDF is described in XML format. DSDF contains multiple data sources, and each data source includes information of attributes, interfaces and parameters. The node of attributes holds information such as serial number (GlbID), the name of data sources (Name), the name of acquisition module (Model), acquisition module's storage path (Path), the number of sensor parameters (ParameterNum), and data sources' provider (Manufacturer).

DSDF describes the ways of access, and the interface parameter's information of each data source, so that we can achieve the connection from DAQ-Middleware to the data sources. Different data sources are connected uses different interfaces, and the parameters of different data interfaces are not the same. The description of the interface information includes the RS-485, RS-232, Ethernet, GPIB, USB, Web Service, FTP and MQ. Different types of interfaces need to describe the parameters are different. For example, RS-232 needs to describe the information of serial number, baud rate, data bits, stop bits, and checksum, but RS-485 also includes the information of sensing device's address.

3.2   Interface Standardization

DAQ-Middleware is an independent system, so if you want to achieve no matter which the field of IoT can access to DAQ-Middleware, we need to standardize the interfaces between DAQ-Middleware and the application system. The communication parameter description file is used to describe the interface information, which includes four parameters: IPAddress, FilePort, ControlPort and DataPort. All these interfaces adopting Socket. For details of the interface, refer to the GB/T 33137-2016 national standard (China).

3.3   Acquisition Module

Figure 2 shows that DAQ-Middleware includes the acquisition main program and the acquisition module. DAQ-Middleware uses communication interfaces to acquire the data from the data sources based on specific protocol. We have developed a unique acquisition module for each data source based on different communication protocols.

The functions of acquisition main program: It accepts control commands and data request commands from the application system, and returns DSDF and the processing results. It is responsible for obtaining DSDF, and synthesizing-analyzing the information to implement the loading of the acquisition module. It instantiates the communication interface, interacts with the acquisition module, organizes the obtained sensor data in a standard format, and returns the sensor data to the application system.

The functions of acquisition module: It obtains sensor data from data sources via communication protocol, and the information of communication interfaces, which have been instantiated by the acquisition main program. It interacts with the acquisition main program through the standard interface, obtains the sensor list, and returns the sensor data to the acquisition main program.

The standardization of interface between the acquisition main program and the acquisition module enables the dynamic modification and deletion of the data source by modifying DSDF.

4   High-Speed Data Acquisition Algorithm for IoT

4.1   Parallel Data Acquisition

As Fig. 2 shown, the main program receives data request commands from application system, which contain the sensor list of multiple sensing parameters for multiple data sources. In general (Serial Data Acquisition), the data acquisition middleware analyzes the sensor list, obtains the data sources to be acquired, and then performs the data acquisition *in turn*. However, as shown in Fig. 3a, with the increasing number of data sources, this method leads to long acquisition cycle and low efficiency. Since the characteristics of data acquisition module are independently designed in the DAQ-Middleware, we propose a novel parallel data acquisition algorithm, aiming to improve the efficiency of data acquisition.

According to the principle of computer interfaces, there is a situation in which the same interface can access multiple data sources. For example, an RS-485 interface can access multiple sensing instruments (with different addresses). But in order to accurately analyze the returned sensor data, every time the data acquisition middleware can only communicate with a single device on the same interface. As Fig. 3b shown, since data acquisition between different data sources is independent of each other, we can perform them in parallel.

Let I_i denote interface information, where i is the index of interface and $i = 1, 2, \cdots m$. The data source information is defined as R_j and j is the index of data source for each interface connection. The number of data sources connected to the I_i interface is n_i', i.e., $j = 1, 2, \cdots n_i'$. As shown in Fig. 3b, we define a matrix D_{m*n}, which represents the data source information of each accessed interface, obviously, $n = max(n_i')$, $i = 1, 2, \cdots m$. Because different data interfaces are independent of each other, we divide the data acquisition into n rounds, and

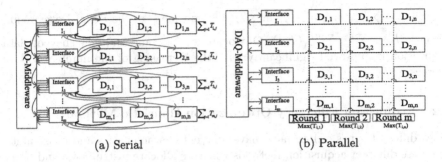

Fig. 3. Serial/Parallel data acquisition algorithm.

each round we acquire data from a data source on m interfaces. Note that, there is a possible situation where no data source corresponding to the elements of matrix $D_{i,j}$, so we set that value 0. Otherwise, the data source's ID. The parallel data acquisition algorithm is described in detail as Algorithm 1.

Algorithm 1. Parallel Data Acquisition Algorithm

Input: Matrix D_{m*n} obtained from DSDF
Output: Acquired sensor data and acquisition time T_{m*n}
1   **for** *round* $j = 1$ *to* n **do**
2   **for** *interface* $i = 1$ *to* m **do**
3   **if** $D_{i,j} \neq 0$ **then**
4   Acquisition main program **sends** the sensor list to the acquisition module corresponding to data source $D_{i,j}$;
5   **end**
6   **end**
7   **for** *interface* $i = 1$ *to* m **do**
8   **if** $D_{i,j} \neq 0$ **then**
9   Acquisition modules **collect data** according to the communication protocol and **record the time** $T_{i,j}$ required for data acquisition;
10   **end**
11   **if** $D_{i,j} = 0$ **then**
12        $T_{i,j} = 0$;
13   **end**
14   **end**
15 **end**

Algorithm 1 can in certain degree improve the efficiency of data acquisition. According to the obtained acquisition time T_{m*n}, we can calculate the time required to complete one round of data acquisition. The time required for each round of data acquisition is the maximum value of each column of matrix T_{m*n}, namely $t_j = \max_i T_{i,j}$. The time t required to complete a complete data acqui-

sition is $t = \sum_{j=1}^{n}(t_j) = \sum_{j=1}^{n}(\max_i T_{i,j})$. The time t' of the Serial Data Acqui-
sition is $t' = \sum_{i=1}^{m}\sum_{j=1}^{n}(T_{i,j})$. Obviously, $t \leq t'$, and the efficiency of data acquisition is improved significantly with the increasing of the number of data sources.

4.2   Acquisition Efficiency Optimization Heuristic Method

Since different types of interfaces have different characteristics and constraints, there are different acquisition methods when we allocate instruments and interfaces. In order to improve the efficiency of data acquisition, we can adjust the matrix D_{m*n} to reduce the total acquisition time t, while satisfying the constraints of interface attribute. This optimization problem can be described as follows.

$$\min \; t = \sum_{j=1}^{n}(t_j) = \sum_{j=1}^{n}(\max_i(T_{i,j}))$$

$s.t. \; I_i \; is \; satisfied.$

$Each \; data \; source \; only \; belongs \; to \; one \; interface.$

We can find the optimal distribution using brute-force method. There are m^n allocations. Thus, brute-force method has an exponential time complexity. Instead, we now propose a heuristic method, which can obtain a reasonable data resource and interface matching efficiently. Each round of data acquisition time is decided by $t_j = \max_i(T_{i,j})$.

The basic idea of heuristic is to put the data sources of different interfaces with similar data acquisition time in the same round to save data acquisition time. The detailed algorithm is given in Algorithm 2. Firstly, there are often circumstances that the interfaces with different IDs belong to the same interface type, so we consolidate data sources of the same type of interface in T_{m*n} to obtain G'_{p*q}. p is the number of interface types and q is the number of data sources owned by that type interfaces. Obviously, $p \leq m$ and $q \geq n$. The data source communication time for each interface type is then sorted in descending order to obtain G_{p*q}. Next, keep the columns of $D_{i,j}$ unchanged, and the rows gradually increasing. According to the interface I_i and matrix G_{p*q}, we assign data sources to the interface in turn, and then move to the next column. Repeat this until all the data sources are completed. Lastly, the relationship matrix $D_{i,j}$ is obtained between the data sources and the interfaces.

5   Performance Comparison and Analysis

In the practical application and simulation experiment scene, the performance of HDAA is analyzed and verified.

Algorithm 2. Acq-Efficiency Optimization Heuristic

Input: I_i, T_{m*n}
Output: $D_{i,j}$
1 Consolidate data sources of the same type interface and get G'_{p*q};
2 **for** *each number of interface types* **do**
3 | Sort data source communication time in descending order in G'_{p*q} to get G_{p*q};
4 **end**
5 **for** *each round j* **do**
6 | **for** *each interface i* **do**
7 | | **if** *data source with interface type i of G_{p*q} has not been allocated* **then**
8 | | | $D_{i,j}$=ID of the data source;
9 | | **else**
10 | | | $D_{i,j} = 0$;
11 | | **end**
12 | **end**
13 **end**

5.1 Practical Application

Experimental Environment. The field of household appliances testing has a wide range of needs for IoT application systems. Table 1 summarizes the 9 data sources, which consist of sensing instruments, databases and data files (40 instruments and 410 parameters). Each data source corresponds to a data acquisition module, so we have developed a total of 9 acquisition modules, and configured each DSDF.

Result Analysis. DAQ-Middleware adopts Algorithms 1 and 2. The result show that the acquisition efficiency of HDAA is five times that of serial data acquisition algorithms.

We consider an IoT system where 40 sensing instruments (Table 1) are connected to the proposed middleware via 14 interfaces. The serial data acquisition algorithm sequentially obtains the data from 40 sensing instruments, while Algorithm 1 can obtain data in parallel and use Algorithm 2 to schedule the acquisition.

Particularly, we sort the acquisition time of different data sources to obtain matrix G_{7*10}. According to matrix G_{7*10}, and adopting the acquisition efficiency optimization heuristic, D_{14*5} is obtained. Then perform the parallel data acquisition algorithm based on D_{14*5}, T_{14*5} also is obtained. The time required t for HDAA to complete a data acquisition is only $t = \sum_{j=1}^{n}(t_j) = \sum_{j=1}^{n}(\max_i(T_{i,j})) = 387\,\text{ms}$, while the time required for the serial acquisition t' is $t' = \sum_{i=1}^{m}\sum_{j=1}^{n}(T_{i,j}) = 1,979\,\text{ms}$. It is obviously that t is only about 1/5 of t'. So the proposed HDAA (parallel data acquisition algorithm and acquisition efficiency optimization heuristic) can improve the efficiency of data acquisition.

Table 1. Information of data sources.

Name	Function	Parameters	Instruments	Total of parameters
Data sources: Sensor Devices *(Interface types: RS-232, RS-485, USB, Ethernet)*				
MX100	Acquisition temperature	60	5	300
SR93	Temperature controller	2	4	8
8775A	Power meter	5	4	20
UT35A	Indicating controller	4	4	16
Anemometer	Measuring winds	2	5	10
Data sources: Database and Data File *(Interface types: Web Service, FTP, MQ)*				
Flowmeter	Measure flow rate	2	2	4
Manometer	Measure liquid pressure	2	2	4
Counter	Record switching doors	2	4	8
Vibrator	Measure vibration	4	10	40

In addition, when the number of access instruments and interfaces increases, such enhancement is more obvious.

At the same time, under the condition of satisfying the interface attribute constraints, we compare the proposed Algorithm 2 with random allocation method in the acquisition of data sources. As shown in Fig. 4, the random acquisition method is based on Algorithm 1, but use random scheduling. Its data acquisition time is lower than the serial data acquisition algorithm, but higher than HDAA.

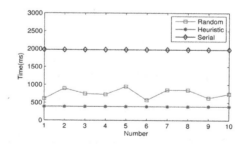

Fig. 4. Acquisition efficiency in practical application.

5.2   Simulation

Simulation Environment. In order to further verify the acquisition efficiency of the algorithm in large-scale data sets, we simulated the data acquisition delay time and then compared it with different data acquisition algorithms. The article [14] analysis shows that the data acquisition delay time obeys the Gaussian distribution of $N(10,4)$. Ten delay time data sets are randomly generated based on the distribution. For different algorithm, the average of the acquisition efficiency on the data set was compared and analyzed.

Comparison Algorithm. Compare the acquisition efficiency of different algorithms.

- Serial data acquisition algorithm (Serial): Acquire all sensing instruments one by one.
- Randomly assigned parallel data acquisition algorithm (Parallel-random): Based on Algorithm 1, the acquisition order of sensing instruments on each interface is randomly assigned.
- HDAA (Parallel-heuristic): Combining Algorithms 1 and 2, based on the parallel data acquisition algorithm, using the acquisition efficiency optimization heuristic method, the acquisition order of the sensing instruments on each interface is allocated.

Result Analysis. The data acquisition efficiency of the three algorithms was compared and analyzed under different numbers of sensing instruments and different numbers of interfaces.

When the number of interfaces is 10, 50 and 100, the relationship between accessing different numbers $(50-500)$ of sensing instruments and the acquisition efficiency, and the ratio of data acquisition efficiency of different algorithms are analyzed and compared. The result as shown in Fig. 5a, b and c, since Serial requires a long time, we use a log non-uniform interval for the ordinate.

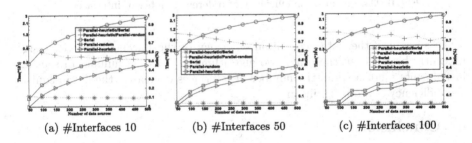

(a) #Interfaces 10   (b) #Interfaces 50   (c) #Interfaces 100

Fig. 5. Data acquisition efficiency of different number of data sources.

In Fig. 5a, b and c, it can be concluded that with the same number of interfaces, as the number of sensing instruments increases, the data acquisition time increases. The time of Serial is significantly higher than the Parallel-heuristic. When the number of interfaces is 100 and the number of sensing instruments is 50 and 100, the data acquisition time is the same. Because the number of interfaces is greater than or equal to the number of sensing instruments, only one sensing instrument is connected to each interface, and the data acquisition time is the same and the efficiency is the highest. As the number of sensing instruments increases, the acquisition efficiency ratio becomes smaller between the Parallel-heuristic and the other two algorithms.

When the number of sensing instruments is 50, 250 and 500, the relationship between different numbers (10 − 100) of interfaces and data acquisition time, and the ratio of data acquisition efficiency of different algorithms are analyzed and compared.

In Fig. 6a, b and c, under the same number of sensing instruments, as the number of interfaces increases, the acquisition efficiency is gradually increased. Since the number of sensing instruments is constant for each experiment, the data acquisition time of Serial does not change as the number of interfaces increases. When the number of sensing instruments is 50, the number of interfaces is greater than 50, and the data acquisition time is no longer reduced. At the same time, with the increase of the number of interfaces, the ratio between Parallel-heuristic and Parallel-random is reduced, and the ratio is increased between Parallel-heuristic and Serial.

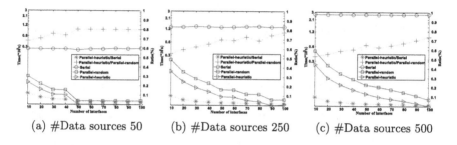

(a) #Data sources 50   (b) #Data sources 250   (c) #Data sources 500

Fig. 6. Data acquisition efficiency of different number of interfaces.

In summary, the data acquisition efficiency of the Parallel-heuristic is significantly higher than the other two algorithms, and as the number of sensing instruments increases and the number of interfaces decreases, the data acquisition efficiency is more significant.

6   Conclusion

Based on the DAQ-Middleware, this paper analyzes the characteristics between data source and interface, establishes the mapping relationship between data source and interface, and proposes a HDAA. In the practical application and simulation, the data acquisition efficiency of Serial, Parallel-random and HDAA are analyzed and compared. The results show that HDAA greatly improves the data acquisition efficiency. What's more, with the number of sensing instruments and the data interface decreases, the data acquisition efficiency is more significant.

Considering that the IoT application system is very widely used, future work in more IoT applications will verify, compare and analyze the performance of middleware and algorithm performance.

Acknowledgment. The study is supported by the National Natural Science Foundation of China (Nos. 41606112 and 41705046) and Key Research and Development Program of Shandong Province (No. 2016JMRH0538).

References

1. Gubbi, J., Buyya, R., Marusic, S., Palaniswami, M.: Internet of Things (IoT): a vision, architectural elements, and future directions. Futur. Gener. Comput. Syst. **29**(7), 1645–1660 (2013)
2. Peng, M., Li, Y., Zhao, Z., Wang, C.: System architecture and key technologies for 5G heterogeneous cloud radio access networks. IEEE Netw. **29**(2), 6–14 (2015)
3. Riedel, T., Fantana, N., Genaid, A., Yordanov, D., Schmidtke, H.R., Beigl, M.: Using web service gateways and code generation for sustainable IoT system development. In: 2010 Internet of Things (IOT), Tokyo, pp. 1–8. IEEE (2010)
4. Ning, H., Wang, Z.: Future internet of things architecture: like mankind neural system or social organization framework? IEEE Commun. Lett. **15**(4), 461–463 (2011)
5. Qiu, Z., Hu, T., Qi, S., Liu, S., Wang, X., Guo, Z.: Automatic matching method for ocean observation elements based on edge computing. In: International Conference on Big Data Computing and Communications, pp. 174–180, Chicago. IEEE (2018). https://doi.org/10.1109/BIGCOM.2018.00035
6. Gigli, M., Koo, S.G.: Internet of Things: services and applications categorization. Internet Things **1**(2), 27–31 (2011)
7. Qiu, Z., et al.: IoTI: internet of things instruments reconstruction model design. In: Instrumentation and Measurement Technology Conference Proceedings (I2MTC), Taiwan, pp. 1–6. IEEE (2016). https://doi.org/10.1109/I2MTC.2016.7520533
8. Kelly, S.D.T., Suryadevara, N.K., Mukhopadhyay, S.C.: Towards the implementation of IoT for environmental condition monitoring in homes. IEEE Sens. J. **13**(10), 3846–3853 (2013)
9. Qiu, Z., Hu, N., Guo, Z., Qiu, L., Guo, S., Wang, X.: IoT sensing parameters adaptive matching algorithm. In: Wang, Y., Yu, G., Zhang, Y., Han, Z., Wang, G. (eds.) BigCom 2016. LNCS, vol. 9784, pp. 198–211. Springer, Cham (2016). https://doi.org/10.1007/978-3-319-42553-5_17
10. Kovac, V.S.K.: Virtual instrumentation and distributed measurement systems. J. Electr. Eng **55**(1–2), 50–56 (2004)
11. Qiu, Z., Guo, Z., Liu, C.: Adaptive high-speed data acquisition algorithm in sensor network nodes. J. Southeast Univ. Nat. Sci. Ed. **42**(A02), 238–244 (2012)
12. Qiu, Z., Guo, Z., Wang, Y., Hu, T., Liu, C., Li, T.: Reconstruction model of ocean observing complex virtual instrument. J. Ocean. Univ. China **17**(5), 1159–1170 (2018). https://doi.org/10.1007/s11802-018-3445-6
13. Toma, D.M., et al.: Smart sensors for interoperable smart ocean environment. In: OCEANS 2011 IEEE, Spain, pp. 1–4. IEEE (2011)
14. Chen, Z., Huang, Y., Tang, C., Qu, L.: Estimation of transmission delay of time synchronization information for Internet of things of coal mine underground. Ind. Mine Autom. **40**(12), 37–41 (2014)

Mixed Iterative Adaptive Dynamic Programming Based Sensor Scheduling for Target Tracking in Energy Harvesting Wireless Sensor Networks

Fen Liu[1,2(✉)], Shuai Chen[1,2], Chengpeng Jiang[1,2], and Wendong Xiao[1,2(✉)]

[1] University of Science and Technology Beijing, Beijing 100083, China
liufenustb@163.com, wdxiao@ustb.edu.cn
[2] Beijing Engineering Research Center of Industrial Spectrum Imaging, Beijing 100083, China

Abstract. Target tracking is a typical application of wireless sensor networks (WSNs), in which improving the tracking accuracy with the limited network resources is remaining as a challenging problem. Hence target tracking often relies on sensor scheduling approaches to optimize the resource utilization. With the development of energy acquisition technologies, the building of WSNs based on energy harvesting has become possible to help weaken the limitation of battery energy in WSNs, where theoretically the lifetime of the network could be extended to infinite. Hence, the development of energy harvesting technologies provides a new challenge of infinite-horizon sensor scheduling with the finite energy harvesting capability for high performance target tracking. This paper proposes an adaptive multi-step sensor scheduling approach based on the mixed iterative adaptive dynamic programming (MIADP) to minimize the global performance composed of tracking performance and energy consumption. MIADP consists of two iterations: P-iteration to update the iterative value function and V-iteration to obtain the iterative control law sequence. The simulation results demonstrate that the proposed scheme has advantages in the global trade-off between tracking performance and energy consumption compared with adaptive dynamic programming (ADP) based single-step sensor scheduling.

Keywords: Adaptive dynamic programming · Target tracking · Sensor scheduling · Wireless sensor networks · Energy harvesting

1 Introduction

Usually, a wireless sensor network (WSN) is composed of some static or moving sensors in the self-organized and multi-hop way. They can collaborate for perceiving, collecting, processing and transmitting the information of the monitored phenomena in the geographic area covered by the network. WSNs are widely used in many fields, such as environmental monitoring, medical care, pension service, intelligent transportation [1] and so on. In the numerous practical applications of WSNs, the development of target tracking technologies has received more and more attention.

© Springer Nature Singapore Pte Ltd. 2019
F. Sun et al. (Eds.): ICCSIP 2018, CCIS 1006, pp. 500–511, 2019.
https://doi.org/10.1007/978-981-13-7986-4_44

Since WSNs consist of low cost, self-organizing small-sized sensors with good concealment that lead to rapid deployment, WSNs are widely used for moving target tracking, but there also exist some challenges. For example, the battery energy carried by sensor node is finite and the sensing, computing and communication resources of sensor nodes are limited. Hence, new requirements are needed for the study of target tracking in WSNs by considering these challenges.

To address these problems, the available sensor scheduling algorithms are demanded to task the appropriate sensor for target tracking in order to get accurate estimates and effective resource utilization in WSNs. For example, an adaptive sensor scheduling was introduced in [2] by scheduling next tasking sensor for the next time step according to the predicted tracking accuracy which is derived from the trace of the covariance matrix of the state estimation. In the adaptive sampling interval approach for single target tracking [3], the sensors are scheduled in alternative tracking mode which realized the energy-efficient tracking according to the predicted tracking accuracy based on extended Kalman filter (EKF).

However, this above work is single-step sensor scheduling scheme. To improve the speed of target tracking, multi-step sensor scheduling can be adopted in WSNs. For example, to minimize the estimation error over multiple time steps in a computationally tractable fashion, an information-based pruning algorithm for multi-step sensor scheduling was proposed by using the information matrices of the sensors and the monotonicity of the Riccati equation [4]. However, it is based on the local performance (the performance for the current time steps) optimization to dispatch the sensors, and there are few scheduling methods based on the global performance (particularly, with regarding to the performance for all the time steps from the current to the end or infinite) optimization, especially the adaptive multi-step sensor scheduling.

Theoretically, in the energy harvesting WSNs, the lifetime of the network is infinite, subsequently the key problem for sensor scheduling to address is no longer to maximize the network's lifetime, but to optimize the network's performance under the given energy harvesting capability. Hence, the development of energy harvesting technologies has provided a new challenge of infinite-horizon sensor scheduling with the finite energy harvesting capability for high performance target tracking. In this paper, we will apply adaptive dynamic programming (ADP) to obtain the infinite-horizon optimal sensor scheduling for target tracking in energy harvesting WSNs.

The typical structure of ADP is constructed by three modules: model, critic and action. Characterized by strong abilities of self-learning and adaption, ADP has demonstrated strong capability to find the optimal control policy and solve the dynamic programming problem of discrete system [5], including adaptive critic designs, reinforcement learning and so on, which obtains the index function of approximate optimal performance and the approximate optimal control to satisfy the Bellman optimal principle through the approximate structure of function. ADP is used to media access control protocol [6] and optimal scheduling for target tracking [7] in the energy harvesting WSNs, which can get the approximate optimal control based on global tradeoff between tracking accuracy and energy consumption. But it is a single-step sensor scheduling scheme. This paper will propose an adaptive multi-step sensor scheduling approach for target tracking in energy harvesting WSNs based on the approximate optimization of global performance.

In this paper, we will study the optimal sensor scheduling for target tracking in a WSN with solar energy harvesting. First, the energy harvesting model and EKF based prediction and estimation for the target state are given. Second, the energy consumption for each sensor is analyzed and the optimal sensor scheduling problem is abstracted to mathematical model. Then, the mixed iterative ADP (MIADP)-based multi-step sensor scheduling is proposed. Finally, the simulation results show that the proposed scheme has advantages in the global trade-off between tracking performance and energy consumption compared with ADP based single-step sensor scheduling.

2 Problem Description

The aim of this article is to obtain the optimal sensor scheduling for target tracking in a solar energy harvesting WSN. In this paper we assume the WSN is composed of a sink node and M sensor nodes, and the knowledge with the location of every sensor is known. Each sensor node with enough energy can sense the target and pass the perceived information to the sink node. The sink node fuses the received measurement, predicts the target state and schedules the next tasking sensor nodes by minimizing the trade-off between the tracking error and energy consumption.

2.1 Modeling for Solar Energy Harvesting

In this paper the nodes can harvest energy when the solar energy is available. If the capacity for sensor's energy storage is infinite, the harvested energy is [8]

$$E_h(t_0, \Delta T) = \int_{t_0}^{t_0 + \Delta T} \eta_e f_e(t) dt = \eta_e \int_{t_0}^{t_0 + \Delta T} f_e(t) dt \qquad (1)$$

where t_0 is the beginning of the energy harvesting time, ΔT is the time duration, $f_e(t)$ is the statistical distribution of the solar energy, and η_e is the conversion efficiency of the solar panel. However, the unlimited storage capacity is impractical. Suppose that the maximal capacity for energy storage of sensor i is $H_i^{\max}(0 < H_i^{\max} < \infty)$. Then, the harvested energy of sensor i with the residual energy E_{left} is $\min\left(E_{left} + E_h(t_0, \Delta T), H_i^{\max}\right)$.

2.2 EKF-Based Prediction and Estimation for Target State

We will apply EKF to the target tracking problem. The basic idea of EFK is: using minimum mean square error as the best estimation criterion, updating the current estimated state with the previous estimation and the current measurement. We assume a linear target motion model and a non-linear measurement model, both with Gaussian noise distributions. The state of the target at the t-th time step that happens at τ_t is

$X(t) = [\, x(t) \quad v_x(t) \quad y(t) \quad v_y(t) \,]^T$, where $(x(t), y(t))$ are the location coordinate at τ_t, and $(v_x(t), v_y(t))$ are the velocity of the target along the X axis and the Y axis. The target motion is described by the following constant velocity model:

$$X(t+1) = AX(t) + Gw(t). \tag{2}$$

Let Q be the covariance matrix of the process noise $w(t)$. The expression of A, G and Q can be obtained from [3]. If sensor i is used to obtain the t-th measurement $Z_i(t)$ of the target at τ_t, the measurement model is

$$Z_i(t) = h_i(X(t)) + v_i(t), \tag{3}$$

where $v_i(t)$ is the measurement noise from sensor i with the covariance matrix $R_i(t)$. Both w and v_i are independent and assumed to be with zero-mean, white, Gaussian probability distributions. h_i is a (generally non-linear) measurement function depending on $X(t)$, the measurement characteristic and the parameters (e.g., the location) of sensor i.

The time update is operated as

$$\hat{X}(t+1|t) = A\hat{X}(t|t),$$
$$P(t+1|t) = AP(t|t)A^T + GQG^T. \tag{4}$$

The state update is operated as

$$K_i(t+1) = P(t+1|t)H_i^T(t+1)\left[H_i(t+1)P(t+1|t)H_i^T(t+1) + R_i(t+1)\right]^{-1},$$
$$\hat{X}_i(t+1|t+1) = \hat{X}(t+1|t) + K_i(t+1)\left(Z_i(t+1) - h_i(\hat{X}(t+1|t))\right), \tag{5}$$
$$P_i(t+1|t+1) = (I - K_i(t+1)H_i(t+1))P(t+1|t),$$

where $H_i(t+1)$ is Jacobian matrix of the measurement function h_i at τ_{t+1} with respect to the predicted state $\hat{X}(t+1|t)$. In the simulation of this paper, h_i and $H_i(t+1)$ are the same with [3].

In the above equations, $\hat{X}(t+1|t)$ means the $(t+1)$-th priori estimation of the state under the condition of t-th state has been known. $\hat{X}_i(t+1|t+1)$ is the $(t+1)$-th posterior estimation of the state from sensor i under the condition of the measurement $Z_i(t+1)$ has been known. $P(t+1|t)$ represents the error covariance matrix of the priori estimation which is a real symmetric matrix and $P_i(t+1|t+1)$ is the error covariance matrix of the posterior estimation from sensor i. I is a unit matrix. $K_i(t+1)$ is the Kalman gain of sensor i to minimize the variance of $P_i(t+1|t+1)$. If just given $X(1)$ and $P(1)$, the $(t+1)$-th estimation $\hat{X}_i(t+1|t+1)$ $(t=1,2,\cdots)$ can be estimated iteratively after the $t+1$ measurements.

2.3   Tracking Performance

At τ_t, the sink schedules the sensor to minimize the global performance. However, the measurement is unobtainable in advance, so it is infeasible to calculate the error with state estimation. Nevertheless, the error covariance is obtainable before measuring, which describes the degree of difference between the estimation and the expectation. Hence $T(t) = Trace(P(t|t))$ can be used to evaluate the tracking performance.

3   The Optimal Sensor Scheduling Problem

3.1   Target Tracking Mechanism

In this paper, we assume that the sink node has strong computing ability and enough energy. The general tracking system in the energy harvesting WSN works as follows:

(1) Initialization. The energy harvesting sensor with enough energy, that detecting the target for the first time when the target enters the sensor field becomes the first tasking sensor. It sends the observation to the sink node.
(2) State prediction. When the sink gets a new measurement, it predicts the state and error covariance by EKF.
(3) Sensor scheduling. After the prediction, based on the solar energy harvesting model, the sink selects adaptively the tasking sensors for each time step by MIADP according to the trace of the updated error covariance and the predicted energy consumption.
(4) Mode switch and information transmission. The sink wakes up the scheduled tasking sensors for the corresponding time step via the low-power paging channel. The other nodes switch to sleeping mode.
(5) Sensing, data processing and state estimation. The scheduled sensors sense the distance between themselves and the target and send them to the sink.

3.2   Energy Consumption

We assume the communication between the sensor node and the sink node is a single-hop link. At the t-th time step, the detection model of sensor i is described as follows

$$D_i(t) = \begin{cases} 0, & E_i(t) < E^h \\ 1, & E_i(t) \geq E^h \end{cases} \tag{6}$$

E^h is a threshold value, $E_i(t)$ represents the received signal level, and $E_i(t) = E_i^0 e^{-\beta d_{(x,i)}}$ in which E_i^0 and β are constant, and $d_{(x,i)}$ is the Euclidean distance between the target and sensor i. The set of tasking sensors to track the target $\Omega_T(t)$ is a subset of

$\Omega_D(t) = \{i \in \Omega_D(t), D_i(t) = 1\}$ which denotes the set of all candidate nodes that possibly detect the target. At τ_t, the energy consumption of sensor i is

$$E_{con}(i) = \begin{cases} E_r + E_t(i) + E_p, & u_i(t) = 1 \\ E_s, & u_i(t) = 0 \end{cases} \tag{7}$$

If $u_i(t) = 1$, the sensor i is scheduled, otherwise the sensor i is sleeping. $E_r = e_r b_r$ represents the energy consumed in receiving b_r bits' data. $E_t(i) = (e_t + e_d d_{(s,i)}^2)b_t$ represents the energy consumption due to transmitting b_t bits' data to the sink node s. $E_p = e_p b_p$ represents the energy consumption due to sensing and data processing of b_p bits, and E_s represents the energy required for sleeping. e_r, e_t, e_d and e_p are decided by the specifications of the sensor.

At τ_t, before being scheduled, the residual energy of sensor i is

$$\begin{aligned} E_i^{bf}(t) &= \min\left(E_i^{af}(t-1, u_i(t-1)) + E_h(\tau_t, \Delta t), \ H^{max}\right) \\ &= f(E_i^{af}(t-1, u_i(t-1))), \end{aligned} \tag{8}$$

where $E_i^{af}(t-1, u_i(t-1))$ is the residual energy of sensor i after being scheduled at the $(t-1)$-th time step. If being scheduled, the sensor i must satisfy the restriction $E_i^{bf}(t) \geq E_r + E_t(i) + E_p$. Let $\Omega_u(t)$ be the sensors meeting the condition in $\Omega_D(t)$. While scheduling at each time step t, the control must be a subset of $\Omega_u(t)$.

At the t-th time step, after being scheduled the consumed energy of sensor i is

$$E_i^c(t, u_i(t)) = \left(E_r + E_t(i) + E_p\right)u_i(t) + E_s(1 - u_i(t)) \tag{9}$$

and the residual energy of sensor i is $E_i^{af}(t, u_i(t)) = E_i^{bf}(t) - E_i^c(t, u_i(t))$.

3.3 The Optimal Sensor Scheduling Problem

Set the system control of the t-th time step is $u(t) = (u_1(t), u_2(t), \cdots u_M(t))$ where M is the number of the sensors. To balance the tracking performance and the energy consumption, we define the utility function as $\Gamma(t, u(t)) = \beta T(t) + \sum_{i=1}^{M} E_i^c(t, u(t))$ in which $\beta > 0$ is a coefficient to adjust the weight of tracking error. Define the performance index as

$$J(t, u(t)) = \sum_{j=t}^{\infty} \gamma^{j-t} \Gamma(j, u(j)), \tag{10}$$

where $0 < \gamma \leq 1$ is a discount factor. Then, we can derive that

$$J(t, u(t)) = \Gamma(t, u(t)) + \gamma J(t+1, u(t+1)). \tag{11}$$

Hence, the objective function of the optimal sensor scheduling problem is

$$\min_{u(k)} J(t, u(t)).$$

$$s.t. \begin{cases} D^i(t) = 1 & \forall i \in \{i | u_i(t) = 1\} \\ E_{af}(t) \geq \mathbf{0} \end{cases} \tag{12}$$

Let $J^*(t, u(t)) = \min_{u(t)} J(t, u(t))$. Then we can get the following Hamilton-Jacobi-Bellman (HJB) equation

$$J^*(t, u(t)) = \min_{u(t)} \{\Gamma(t, u(t)) + \gamma J^*(t+1, u(t+1))\}, \tag{13}$$

and the optimal control sequence $u^*(t)$

$$u^*(t) = \arg\min_{u(t)} \{\Gamma(t, u(t)) + \gamma J^*(t+1, u(t+1))\}. \tag{14}$$

Generally, the optimal performance function $J^*(t, u(t))$ is nonlinear and it is hard to obtain the optimal control by solving (13) directly. To solve this problem, MIADP based multi-step sensor scheduling for target tracking in energy harvesting WSNs will be put forward.

4 MIADP-Based Optimal Sensor Scheduling

Let the sink node schedule the sensors for n ($n \in \mathbb{N}, n > 1$) time steps every time. For any $t = 0, 1, \cdots$, there exists $m_1 = 0, 1, \cdots$ and $m_2 = 0, 1, \cdots, n-1$ that satisfy $t = m_1 n + m_2$. Let $k = m_1 n$ and $\omega(k)$ be the control law sequence from k-th time step to $(k+n-1)$-th time step. Then $\forall k \in \{0, n, 2n, \cdots\}$, we can define a new utility function as

$$U(k, \omega(k)) = \sum_{j=0}^{n-1} \gamma^j \Gamma(t+j, u(t+j)). \tag{15}$$

Let $\Lambda^*(k) = J^*(k, \omega(k))$ and $\eta = \gamma^n$, the HJB equation can be derived as

$$\Lambda^*(k) = \min_{\omega(k)} \{U(k, \omega(k)) + \eta \Lambda^*(k+n)\}. \tag{16}$$

The optimal control law sequence can be obtained by

$$\omega^*(k) = \arg\min_{\omega(k)} \{U(k, \omega(k)) + \eta \Lambda^*(k+n)\}. \tag{17}$$

Let $\mu(k)$ be the control law at time step k and $\varpi(k) = (\mu(k), \mu(k+1), \cdots, \mu(k+n-1))$ such that the following performance index function is finite.

$$\Psi(k) = \sum_{q=0}^{\infty} \eta^q U(k+nq, \mu(k+nq)). \tag{18}$$

Let $W(k)$ be defined as $W(k) = \{\varpi(k) : \Psi(k) < \infty\}$. For the MIADP, there are two iterations in the algorithm, which are P-iteration and V-iteration. Let $i = 0, 1, \cdots$ be the index of P-iteration. For $i = 0$, let $V_0(k) = 0, \forall k = 0, \ n, 2n, \cdots$ and $U_0(k) = (u_0(k), u_0(k+1), \cdots, u_0(k+n-1))$ be an arbitrary control law sequence and $U_0(k) \in W(k)$. For $i = 1, 2, \cdots$, let $V_i(k)$ be the iterative value function constructed by the control law sequence $U_{i-1}(k)$ that satisfies the following HJB equation

$$V_i(k) = U(k, U_{i-1}(k)) + \eta V_{i-1}(k+n). \tag{19}$$

Then, the iterative control law sequence $U_i(k)$ can be obtained by

$$U_i(k) = \arg\min_{\omega(k)} \{U(k, \omega(k)) + \eta V_{i-1}(k+n)\}. \tag{20}$$

The above iteration can be called as P-iteration. For any $i = 1, 2, \cdots$, the iterative value function $V_i(k)$ is constructed by the control law sequence $U_{i-1}(k)$. But $U_i(k)$ cannot be obtained by solving (20) directly and the V-iteration is used to obtained $U_i(k)$ by iteration. Let j be the index of V-iteration. For any $j = 0, 1, \cdots n-1$, the iterative control law is

$$\mu_i(k+j) = \arg\min_{u(k+j)} \{\Gamma(k+j, u(k+j)) + \gamma V_i(k+j+1)\}, \tag{21}$$

and the iterative value function is

$$\begin{aligned} V_i(k+j) &= \min_{u(k+j)} \{\Gamma(k+j, u(k+j)) + \gamma V_i(k+j+1)\} \\ &= \Gamma(k+j, \mu_i(k+j)) + \gamma V_i(k+j+1). \end{aligned} \tag{22}$$

For any $i = 1, 2, \cdots$, let the final value function be

$$V_i(k+n) = V_{i-1}(k+n). \tag{23}$$

Then, the iterative control law sequence $U_i(k)$ is

$$U_i(k) = \{\mu_i(k), \mu_i(k+1), \cdots, \mu_i(k+n-1)\}. \tag{24}$$

5 Simulation Results

In the simulation, the tracking region is a 10 m × 10 m square and sensor nodes are deployed in it with the number changes from 4 to 24. The target speed changes from 1 m/s to 10 m/s. The energy consumption parameters are borrowed from [3]. Assume that every communication delivers 10 bits' data and the time required for communication is ignored.

We assume the solar panel' area is 5 cm × 5 cm. The harvested energy rate is 0.1 W/cm², and energy conversion efficiency is 15%. We consider the randomness of energy harvesting and assume that the probability of energy arrival is 50% [8]. The max capacity of each battery is 2 J with the initial energy being 0.1 J, and it has infinite recharge cycles.

While the target moving, the sink adaptively schedules two-step tasking sensors to detect the target according to the tracking performance and energy consumption by EKF estimation and MIADP. The tasking sensors detect the target, and send them to the sink. As an example, a MIADP based two-step sensor scheduling is shown in Fig. 1, while the single-step sensor scheduling based on ADP is shown in Fig. 2. Comparatively speaking, the sensors are scheduled evenly and reasonable based on MIADP.

The tracking performance is analyzed through the number of network's nodes and the target speed, as shown in Figs. 3 and 4. We can find that the tracking error tends to increase with the rising of sparsity of sensor density and target speed. It is obvious that the tracking performance of MIADP based target tracking is better than the tracking performance of ADP based target tracking. In conclusion, the proposed MIADP based

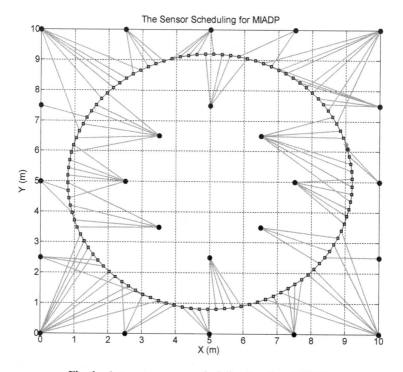

Fig. 1. A two-step sensor scheduling based on MIADP.

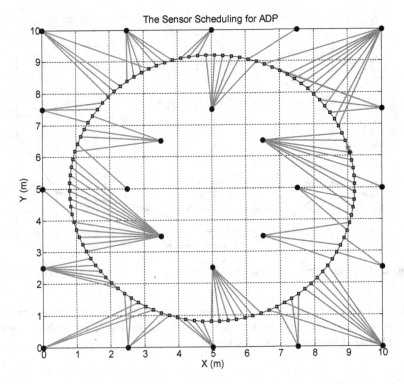

Fig. 2. A single-step sensor scheduling based on ADP.

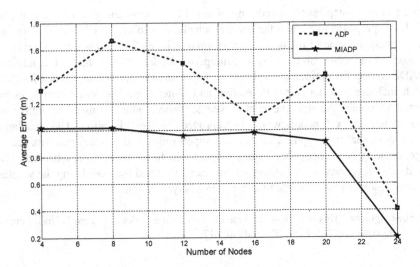

Fig. 3. The average tracking error while the number of nodes in the WSN changes from 4 to 24.

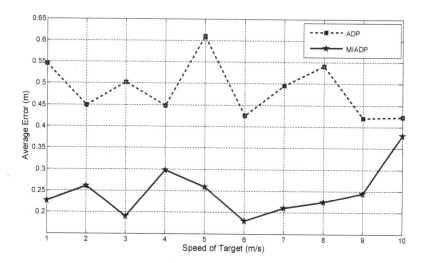

Fig. 4. The average tracking error while the target speed changes from 1 m/s to 10 m/s.

multi-step sensor scheduling has advantages in infinite horizon while considering the global performance for target tracking in the energy harvesting based WSNs compared with ADP based single-step sensor scheduling.

6 Conclusion

Aiming at multi-step sensor scheduling of target tracking in energy harvesting WSNs, MIADP is proposed to address the optimal scheduling problem. EKF is used to predict and estimate the state of the target. A performance index function is established based on tracking accuracy and energy consumption. Under some constraint conditions, MIADP can get the optimal control law by optimizing the performance index function, which includes two iterations: P-iteration and V-iteration. The V-iteration is implemented to obtain the iterative control law sequence, which aims to minimize the performance index function which is improved by the P-iteration. The simulation results show that the proposed method has superiorities in the global performance for target tracking in an energy harvesting WSN. As the future work, more advanced ADP based cross-layer sensor scheduling scheme can be studied by considering the wireless network resources such as bandwidth via cross-layer design.

Acknowledgment. This work was supported in part by the National Natural Science Foundation of China (Grants No. 61673055 and No. 61773056).

References

1. Odat, E., Shamma, J.S., Claudel, C.: Vehicle classification and speed estimation using combined passive infrared/ultrasonic sensors. IEEE Trans. Intell. Transp. Syst. **19**(5), 1593–1606 (2018)
2. Xiao, W.D., Wu, J.K., Xie, L.H., Dong, L.: Sensor scheduling for target tracking in networks of active sensors. Acta Automatica Sinica **32**(6), 922–928 (2006)
3. Xiao, W.D., Zhang, S., Lin, J.Y., Tham, C.K.: Energy-efficient adaptive sensor scheduling for target tracking in wireless sensor networks. J. Control Theor. Appl. **8**(1), 86–92 (2010)
4. Huber, M.F.: Optimal pruning for multi-step sensor scheduling. IEEE Trans. Autom. Control **57**(5), 1338–1343 (2012)
5. Wei, Q.L., Liu, D.R., Lin, H.Q.: Value iteration adaptive dynamic programming for optimal control of discrete-time nonlinear systems. IEEE Trans. Cybern. **46**(3), 840–853 (2016)
6. Xiao, W.D., Liu, F., Zhang, J.J.: Adaptive dynamic programming for multi-point scheduling in energy harvesting wireless sensor networks. In: 2015 IEEE 12th International Conference on Ubiquitous Intelligence and Computing and 2015 IEEE 12th International Conference on Autonomic and Trusted Computing and 2015 IEEE 15th International Conference on Scalable Computing and Communications and Its Associated Workshops (UIC-ATC-ScalCom), pp. 1498–1502. IEEE, Beijing (2015)
7. Liu, F., Jiang, C.P., Chen, S., Xiao, W.D.: Multi-sensor scheduling for target tracking based on constrained ADP in energy harvesting WSN. In: 13th IEEE Conference on Industrial Electronics and Applications (ICIEA), pp. 1579–1584. IEEE, Wuhan (2018)
8. Chen, H.B., Zeng, Q., Zhao, F.: Efficient sleep scheduling algorithm for target tracking in double-storage energy harvesting sensor networks. Int. J. Distrib. Sens. Netw. **2016**(2), 1–8 (2016)

Simulation and Modeling of Modbus Protocol Based on Petri Net

Lei Guo, Xiaochuan Yang$^{(\boxtimes)}$, and Yuan Song

School of Automation, Beijing University of Posts and Telecommunications,
Beijing 100876, China
guolei@bupt.edu.cn, 1914143411@qq.com

Abstract. Petri net is a widely applied tool, and is very efficient in the area of network protocol modeling. A method for modeling and simulating Modbus protocol is proposed in the paper based on Petri net. According to the Modbus protocol data frame state machine, the corresponding Petri net structure model is presented. The Petri model is described with Petri net graphics and formal language. Meanwhile, and the Petri net reachability graph analysis method is applied to analyze the Petri net model of Modbus protocol, the properties of Modbus protocol model is verified. This modeling method has both good intuitiveness and reliability analysis for Modbus protocol.

Keywords: Petri · Modbus · Reachability graph

1 Introduction

In the modeling method of network model, various tools are widely adopted. Petri net is a formal modeling tool which can describe the dynamic behavior of the system. And it has good practical value in the process of real-time analysis of the network. The modeling method based on UML can only be used as a static modeling method, which cannot directly reflect the dynamic characteristics of the system. It turns out that Petri nets are suitable for simulation models with dynamic, concurrent and real-time characteristics. Boundedness analysis, reachability analysis and deadlock analysis of Petri nets can be applied to analyze and describe the properties of communication protocols.

Petri net is widely adopted in the analysis of communication protocols. In [1], Zhang and Zhang et al. proposed a method to model and describe the Kerberos protocol by Petri net base on CPNTools. They adopted the graphical method to visualized the characteristics of the Kerberos protocol. And the method is intuitive. Aiming at the vulnerability of time synchronization protocol in railway time synchronization network, Li and Zhang combined stochastic Petri net (SPN) with Markov chain, and they analyzed the vulnerability of Protocol in [2]. This method is of great significance to the vulnerability analysis of protocols. Zhou, Li and others introduced a method to analyze the performance of token networks based on Petri nets in [3]. The method combines stochastic Petri nets

© Springer Nature Singapore Pte Ltd. 2019
F. Sun et al. (Eds.): ICCSIP 2018, CCIS 1006, pp. 512–522, 2019.
https://doi.org/10.1007/978-981-13-7986-4_45

with queuing theory, and this method can describe and analyze a wide range of token networks, such as the nodes with buffer capacity constraints. A method of modeling CAN bus protocol with deterministic stochastic Petri net (DSPN) was introduced by Lu in [4], the performance indexes such as bus throughput, average message delay and transmission success probability are analyzed in detail with the DSPN model of CAN bus. Petri nets are also well used in modeling and performance analysis of computer networks. As introduced in [5], Li and Li et al. put forward a method of modeling computer networks based on generalized Petri nets, at the same time, several main performance indexes of computer networks are effectively analyzed with the properties of Petri nets.

Modbus protocol has found an increasingly wide utilization in power system, monitoring system, petroleum industry and PLC system in [6]. Controllers of different manufacturers can communicate with other types of equipment based on Modbus protocol in [7]. Modbus protocol specifies that the nodes participating in communication are 'master station' and 'slave station'. When the master station sends a request to the slave station, and the slave station will send a response to the master station. Each slave station has its own unique address number ID. The number of slave stations can reach up to 247 in [8]. The Modbus protocol is divided into three forms: RTU, ASCLL and TCP. The RTU form of Modbus is studied in this paper. Generally, serial kinds of communication (such as RS485, RS232) are adopted in RTU. And the communication mode is half duplex. Modbus specifies specific protocol frame formats and instructions that allow the data exchange between the master and slave stations, a unique protocol frame format and instructions enable data exchange between the master and slave (the minimum memory unit is a register or a coil). When the data frame including a read instruction sent by the master station is received by the slave station, the slave station will send the data with the specified address to the master station. Then the slave station transmits data of the specified address to the master station. At the same time, the master station can also send the instructions of writing data to the slave station. When the slave station receives the data frame, it will write the data to the corresponding address according to the request form master station. Then the read and write functions of the Modbus protocol can be realized.

In this paper, Modbus protocol communication state machine model is established. At the same time, the Petri net is applied to model the Modbus protocol, and the modeling tool is CPNTools. Combining Petri net formal definition with reachability graph to analyze the properties of the network. The changing state of the data frame in the communication process is represented based on a kind of colored Petri net. The modeling method in this paper well guiding significance for information security and reliable transmission communication of Modbus protocol.

2   Communication State Machine of Modbus Protocol

The finite state machine model is widely used in the formal description of communication protocols in [9], The state machine of communication on protocol defines the communication message sequence and the interaction behavior between the protocol entities, which is indispensable in protocol specification. The state machine mainly consists of a limited number of states and transitions between each other. The state machine model established in this paper is proposed to represent the state change in the process of Modbus protocol communication. According to the state machine principle, the legality of the judgment data frame is taken as the transition condition, as shown in Fig. 1:

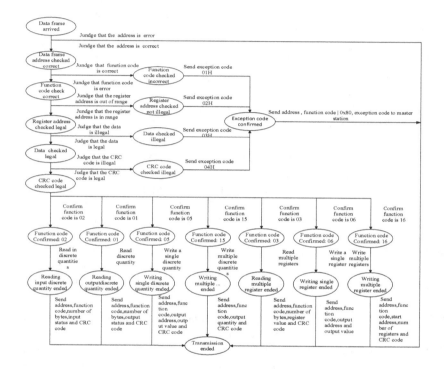

Fig. 1. Modbus protocol state machine model

During the communication between the Modbus slave station and the master station, when the master station sends a frame of data to the bus, the slave station need to check whether the data frame is legal according to the format of the Modbus protocol. Firstly, the slave judges whether it is a data frame sent to itself according to the address ID. Then the rationality of the function code, the register address range, the data, and the CRC code are required to be checked. If the data frame does not compatible to the protocol, the slave will return the corresponding exception code to the master. The slave station performs the corresponding read/write action according to its function code from the legal data frame. After the read/write operation is completed, the slave will return the corresponding response code to the master station which represent the ending of one communication process between the master and slave stations.

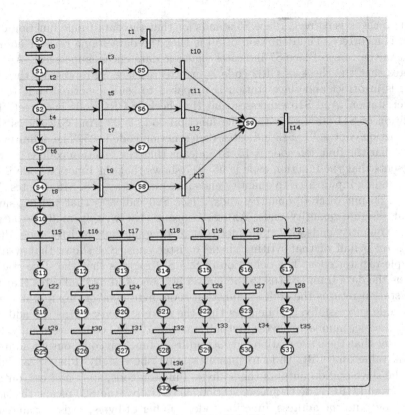

Fig. 2. Petri net model of Modbus protocol

3 Petri Net Model of Modbus Protocol Communication

The state machine can describe the state of system very well. However, it can't show the dynamics intuitively. Compared with most other tools, Petri net provides a clearer description of the state and action of the system. The Petri net model is intuitive. And it provides great convenience for protocol verification in [10]. Therefore, according to the state of the Modbus protocol communication and the data frame change described with the state machine, the Petri net can be applied to model and simulate the Modbus protocol dynamically based on CPNTools. The model structure is shown in Fig. 2.

In the Petri net model, the working status of the network is described with places. The time-consuming actions and events are described with transitions. We use arcs to describe the relationship between location and transition, the arcs mean the connections and changes between states and events. As shown in Fig. 2, S donates the place and t stands for the transition. The definition of S0 means that the data frame arrived. S1 indicates that the data frame address check is correct. Place S2 denotes that the data frame function code check is correct. That the data frame register address is in the range is expressed by S3. S4 shows that the data check is correct. Place S5 stands for that the data frame function code check is incorrect. The definition of S6 is that the data frame register address is not in the range. Place S7 indicates that the data check is incorrect. And S8 denotes that the check of CRC code is incorrect. Place S9 represents that the check is incorrect and slave station is prepared to send abnormal code to the master station. And S10 expresses that the check of CRC code is correct. The definition of S11 stands for that the function code is 02. And S12 shows that the function code is 01. S13 indicates that function code is 05. The definition of S14 is that the function code is 15. S15 means that the function code is 03. S16 represents that the function code is 06. S17 shows that the function code is 16. That reading input discrete quantity ends is expressed by S18. S19 denotes that reading output discrete quantity ends. Place S20 indicates that writing single output discrete quantity ends. And S21 means that writing multiple output discrete quantity ends. S22 stands for that reading multiple register ends. Place S23 is on behalf of that writing single register ends. S24 shows that writing multiple register ends. The definition of S25 S31 express that the slave station returns the data frame status to the master station. And S25 indicates that the slave station returns the address, function code, byte number, input status and CRC code successfully. S26 denotes that the slave station returns the address, function code, number of bytes, output status and CRC code successfully. S27 stands for that the slave station outputs address, function code, output address, output value and CRC code to master station successfully. Place S28 shows that the slave station outputs the address, function code, start address, output quantity and CRC code to master station successfully. And S29 means the slave station outputs the address, function code, number of bytes, register value and CRC code to the master station successfully. S30 indicates that the slave station returns the address, function code, output address, output value and CRC code to master station successfully. The definition of S31 expresses that the slave station returns the address, function code, start address, number of registers and CRC code to master station successfully. The definition of S32 is that the message transmission ends. Transition t0 indicates that the address is correct. t1 verifies that the address is error. And t2 shows that the function code is correct. The definition of t3 is on behalf of that the function code is error. And t4 determines the register address is in range. Transition t5 means that the register address is out of range. And t6 judges that the data is legal. t7 confirm that the data is illegal. The definition of t8 shows that the CRC code is legal. t9 expresses that the CRC code is illegal. And t10 sends exception code 01H. t11 sends exception code 02H. t12 sends exception code 03H. t13 sends exception code 04H. t14 sends address, function code and exception code to the master station. And t15 t21 detect the function code (order is $02, 01, 05, 15, 03, 06, 16$). Transition t22 is on behalf of the operation of reading in discrete quantities. And t23 indicates the operation of reading discrete quantity. The definition of t24 stands for the operation of writing a single discrete quantity. And t25 means the operation of writing multiple discrete quantities. Transition t26 shows the operation of reading multiple registers. The definition of t27 is the operation of writing a single register, t28 denotes the operation of writing multiple registers. t29 sends address, function code, number of bytes, input status and CRC code to the master station. t30 sends address, function code, number of bytes, output status and CRC code to the master station, t31 sends address, function code, output address, output value and CRC code. And t32 sends address, function code, output quantity and CRC code to the master station. t33 sends address, function code, number of bytes, register value and CRC code to the master station. t34 sends address, function code, output address and output value to the master station. t35 sends address, function code, start address, number of registers and CRC code to the master station. t36 indicates the operation of ending the process of data frame transmission and reception.

4   Formal Definition and Analysis of Petri Net

Petri net consists of three elements $N = (P, T, F)$, among that $P = \{p_1 p_2 \ldots p_m\}$ is on behalf of a collection of place; $T = \{t_1 t_2 \ldots t_n\}$ means a set of transitions; $F = (P \times T) \cup (T \times P)$ is the set of input functions and output functions, known as stream relations; three tuple $N = (P, T, F)$ constitutes a necessary and sufficient condition for a Petri net: $P \cap T = \phi$, it provide that the place and the transition are two different types of elements; $P \cup T \neq \phi$, indicates that there is at least one element in the network; $F = (P \times T) \cup (T \times P)$, established a one-way relationship from the place to the transition, from the transition to the place, and the same elements cannot be directly connected. Defining the emission of a transition t can cause the emission mark M to be transformed into a new mark M', the transformation rules of M to M' are as follows:

$$
M'(P_i) = \begin{cases}
M'(P_i) & \forall P_i \notin \cdot t U t \cdot \\
M'(P_i) - \alpha(P_i, t) & \forall P_i \in \cdot t - (\cdot t \cap t \cdot) \\
M'(P_i) + \beta(P_i, t) & \forall P_i \in \cdot t - (\cdot t \cap t \cdot) \\
M'(P_i) + \beta(P_i, t) - \alpha(P_i, t) & \forall P_i \in \cdot t \cap t \cdot
\end{cases}
$$

Supposed that δ is a finite transition sequence $t_1, t_2, \cdots, t_k$, δ is a legal transition sequence starting with M_1, if and only if $\exists M_2, \cdots, \exists M_{k+1} : M_1 M_2 \cdots M_{k+1}$, $M_1 [\delta > M_{k+1}, M_1 M_2 \cdots M_{k+1}$ is called Marker sequence in [11], the reachable mark set $[M_0]$ of Petri nets is a set of marks consisting of all the legal transition sequences starting from the initial mark M_0.

For bounded Petri nets, the reachable mark set is a finite set, a directed graph is constructed from the set of reachable relations between marks, the directed graph is called a reachability graph, all possible global states can be given through reachability graph. Some application problems concern the possible global state in system, the reachability graph can meet the requirements of such problems. In this paper, M_0 is the initial mark of the network, and $R(M_0)$ is used as the vertex set. According to the Petri net model in Fig. 2, the reachability graph of the Modbus protocol communication state is constructed as shown in Fig. 3:

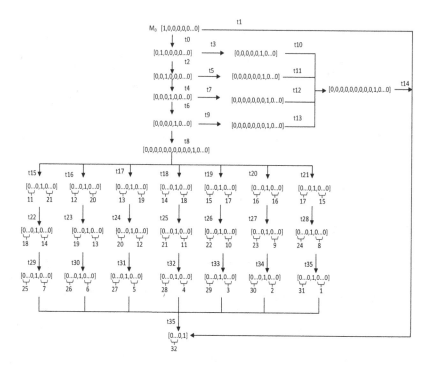

Fig. 3. Petri net model of Modbus protocol

The properties of bounded Petri net $R(M_0)$ can be analyzed by means of $RG(\Sigma)$. We can clearly find out the state transition process and events in the network by reachability graph.

Boundedness: The maximum number of tokens that the place can accommodate is its bounds. If the bounds of the place are finite, the place becomes bounded. If each place in the network is bounded, then this network is a bounded Petri net. Supposed that $\Sigma = (S, T, F, M_0)$ is a Petri net, if each $s \in S$ has bounded, then it is called a bounded Petri net, $B(\Sigma) = max\{B(s) | s \in S\}$ is the boundary of Σ, when it is equal to 1, it is safe, and the model is in a safe state. It reflects that the maximum number of tokens that can be obtained during each operation is 1, it means that no unlimited resources are needed during Modbus communication.

Activity: For Petri net $\Sigma = (S, T, F, M_0)$, if $t \in T, \forall M \in [M_0$ then $M[t >$, it is shown that t is alive. Related to the right to generate under all reachable mark, starting from any mark of M_0 in the reachability graph, t can be triggered by executing a certain transition sequence. Then t is alive under the mark M_0, and there is no deadlock. It can be seen from the reachability graph that all transitions of the system can be triggered, which proves that the system is alive, it indicates that the Modbus protocol will not deadlock during the transmission and reception of each frame of data.

Reversibility: It means the recoverability from any reachable mark to initial mark. We can find out from the reachability graph that the Modbus protocol frame cannot be restored to the initial state in the communication process. From the reachability graph, we can see that the model is irreversible, indicating that the Modbus protocol frame cannot be restored to its original state during the communication process. The data frame transmitted between the master station and the slave station is transmitted only once, and there is no data frame retransmission mechanism.

5   Colored Petri Net Model and Security Analysis

In order to intuitively display the state of data frames in the Modbus protocol communication process, colored Petri net is applied to model the process of Modbus data frame status, each place has a color set to determine what type of the data is included in [12]. The colored Petri net model of the data frame state in Modbus protocol is shown in Fig. 4.

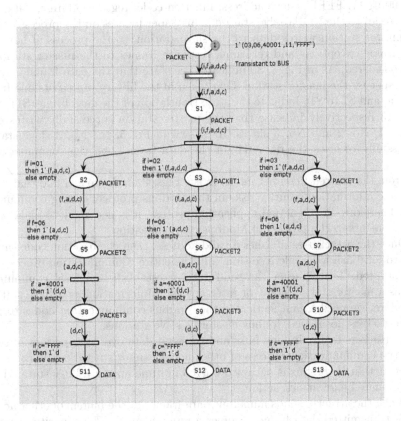

Fig. 4. Colored Petri net of Modbus protocol data frames (Color figure online)

The colored set of this model contains the following definitions, the slave address: $colset\ ID = int\ with\ 1..10$, the function code: $colset\ FUN = int$, the register address: $colset\ ADR = int\ with\ 40000..49999$, define the data: $DATA = int$, CRC code: $CRC = string$. In addition, the four libraries in the model that stand for the state of the data frame are defined as following: $colset\ PACKET = product\ ID * FUN * ADR * DATA * CRC$, $colset\ PACKET1 = product\ FUN * ADR * DATA * CRC$, $colset\ PACKET2 = product\ ADR * DATA * CRC$, $colset\ PACKET3 = product\ DATA * CRC$, $colset\ DATA = int$. And the circulating variable in the directed arc are defined as follows: $val\ i : ID$, $val\ f : FUN$, $val\ a : ADR$, $val\ d : DATA$, $val\ c : CRC$. The state in the Petri net is represented by the place (usually an elliptical or circular place). The simulation includes 14 place in S0–S13. The tokens in the library represents the number of data frames, and the translation represents the behavior or action occurring in the process of the communication. The colored Petri net has a specific initial mark, indicating the initial state of the system.

In this modeling process, one master station and three slave stations are adopted in the simulation process. The master station sends the data frame 03, 06, 40001, 11, FFFF' (slave address, function code, register address, data, and CRC code) to the NO. 3 salve station. This paper focuses on the process of how the master station writes data to the slave station, so the process of handling data frame exceptions and returning response frames to the master station is not considered. As in Fig. 4, S0 indicates the state that the data frame is ready to be sent by the master station. One token in the library represents one frame of data, and S1 to S10 indicate the state translation of the data frame. S11, S12, and S13 respectively indicate that the master station successfully writes data to No. 1, No. 2 and No. 3 slaves. As shown in Fig. 5, the No. 3 slave station successfully receives the data '11' in the data frame, and the communication ends.

From the colored Petri net model in the Figs. 4 and 5, we can find that there are some information security risks in the Modbus protocol during communication. Therefore, in the actual application process, it is necessary to make some improvements in the process of Modbus communication.

Once the attacker establishes a valid address, then the function code can be used to establish a complete session, and the entire communication process will be disrupted. The attacker can send data or establish broadcast communication as a master station node, or intercept valid information as a slave station. Therefore, we need to authenticated the Modbus communication nodes to prevent attackers posing as Modbus master or slave stations.

If attackers maintain long links and transmit data over long periods of time, then the communication process of other nodes cannot start. So it is necessary to detect that if the bus is occupied for a long time and in a busy state all the time, it may be an attack action.

When the attacker sends numerous data frames to the buffers of other nodes, or the transmitted data frame occupies a large memory. The capacity of buffer will reach the upper limit, leading to the communication process to fail. Hence,

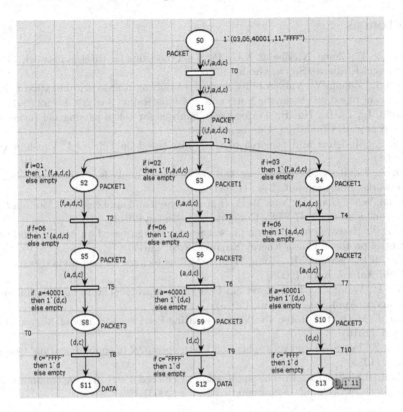

Fig. 5. No. 3 slave station successfully received data (Color figure online)

it is necessary to judge that when the throughput of the buffer is too large in a short time, there may be an attack behavior.

6   Conclusion

Modeling and simulation of the network protocols has always been an important issue in the fieldbus technology research. Focus on the state of the Modbus protocol communication process and the changes of the data frame, the states in the Modbus protocol communication process are displayed through the Petri net model intuitively. This method provides convenience to study the reliability and security of Modbus protocol. And it has positive driving effect and certain use value on the model research of other fieldbus protocols.

References

1. Zhang, T., Zhang, X., Zhang, X.G.: Petri net modeling for wireless network security protocol Kerberos. Softw. Guide (2017)
2. Lan, L., Zhang, Y.: Vulnerability analysis of railway time synchronization network protocol based on stochastic Petri net. J. China Railw. Soc. **39**, 85–92 (2017)
3. Zhou, L., Li, R., Hu, B.: Performance analysis for token-passing networks using Petri nets. J. China Inst. Commun. (1990)
4. Lu, J.: Modeling and research of CAN bus based on DSPN. J. Yanshan Univ. (2008)
5. Li, Z., Li, R.: GSPN modeling and performance analysis methods of computer networks. Microcomput. Dev. (1995)
6. Yuan, W.B., Hong, B., You, W.F., et al.: Research and application of Modbus/TCP communication on S7-PLC. Comput. Eng. Design (2014)
7. Niu, B.: Research on vulnerability excavation design based on Modbus industrial control protocol. China Energy Environ. Prot. (2017)
8. Yan, H.H., Wang, X.H., Tong, W.M.: Modbus technology and node development. Tech. Autom. Appl. (2006)
9. Wu, L., Wang, C., Hong, Z., et al.: Overview on protocol state machine inference: a survey. Appl. Res. Comput. (2015)
10. Cai, J.: Method of protocol validation by using Petri network model. Microcomput. Appl. (2016)
11. Hua, Z.: Petri-Net and its application for the protocol of communication. Comput. Eng. (1985)
12. Zhou, B.S., Hong, L.I.: The application of colored Petri nets in communication protocol. Acta Simulata Systematica Sinica (2003)

Research on Time-Triggered Ethernet Security of Integrated Electronic System

Rui Liu[1,2(✉)]

[1] North Automatic Control Technology Institute,
NORINCO GROUP, Taiyuan 030006, China
`liurui0822@sina.com`
[2] Automatic Department, Tsinghua University, Beijing 100084, China

Abstract. Based on the information flow model with time-triggered Ethernet architecture of integrated electronic system and the requirements of system encryption and authorization, information flow configuration, APP configuration and key data encryption are designed, and dynamic system encryption and authentication process is established. Combining with the operational requirements of integrated electronic system, authorization design of command system, file authentication and authorization management and information flow configuration are carried out. Encryption authorization design such as APP management.

Keywords: Time-triggered Ethernet · Integrated electronic system · Information flow model · Encryption authorization

1 Introduction

Integrated electronic System is an integrated processing system integrating the information and control of the weaponry and equipment [1]. It takes overall consideration of the collection, transmission, processing, application and display of platform including fire control information, vehicle information, platform command information and sensing information, and contains the unification management, configuration and sharing of information resources; Integrated electronic System completes the target searching, tracking and identification, fire control, ammunition loading and launching control, vehicle monitoring and control, integrated protection, network communication command and control functions; mainly consists of the processing and control of computers, network bus devices, display control equipment, command communications equipment, sensors and other components. A typical integrated electronic system shown in Fig. 1, including interactive devices, computer integrated platform, command and communication equipment, search and tracking equipment, positioning and navigation equipment, servo control equipment and fire control equipment, power sensors and actuators, sensors and actuators of the turret.

The integrated electronic system is the core of the information system of the vehicle system, and the network is the basis of information transmission. Josephe Sifakesi (Josephe Sifakis, awarded the 2007 Turing Award of ACM) pointed out that the existing information technology can be divided into communication network and control network in two categories. because of communication network's open general

F. Sun et al. (Eds.): ICCSIP 2018, CCIS 1006, pp. 523–530, 2019.
https://doi.org/10.1007/978-981-13-7986-4_46

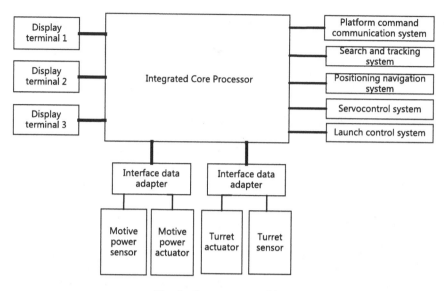

Fig. 1. System composition

protocol, high bandwidth and large data transmission capacity, it is usually used in communication business with low level of deterministic and real-time requirements. It usually includes commercial standard Ethernet and industrial Ethernet. Because it is based on Best effort (priority and queue alignment), and met the max of satisfaction instead of performance. The network are always "too busy". On the contrary, because of control network's transmission real time, information integrity and special internal protocol, the control network is applied to the control services. Because system degradation may cause failure, the control network is used in critical-key system, can make sure information integrity and time certainty without risk in any time. It usually includes AFDX, FC, 1553B, Flex-ray and so on. The characteristics of the two type of network are shown in Table 1.

Table 1. Analysis of the characteristics of communication network and control network

Content	General communication network	Vehicle communication network	Traditional vehicle control network
Certainty	Low Allow messages to be retried, timeout, and discarded	Low Allow messages to be retried, timeout, and discarded	High Time characteristics must meet the requirements of system transmission
Integrity	Failure and non detection probability for 1E-5pfh	Failure and non detection probability for 1E-5pfh	Failure and non detection probability for 1E-6pfh

(*continued*)

Table 1. (*continued*)

Content	General communication network	Vehicle communication network	Traditional vehicle control network
Security	Low After failure, keep ability by maintain and replace	Low After failure, keep ability by maintain and replace	High Once the failure, the impact the task completion and traffic safety
Ways of communication	Best Effort	Best Effort	Rate-Constraint, Best Effort
Type data	Audio and video service, data service	Audio and video service, data service	Control service, data service
Traffic flow	Free flow	Free flow	Planning flow
Fault tolerant	Timeout retransmission, breakpoint resume, state recovery	Timeout retransmission, breakpoint resume, state recovery	State monitoring, self detection, redundancy management
Resource scheduling	Competition, best effort to transmit	Competition, best effort to transmit	Traffic control of transmit, determination of the transmission

2 Time-Triggered Architecture

Time-triggered network for control networks are gaining more prominence for hard real-time communications. Time-triggered network support the AFDX and FC network. In time-triggered networks, all message communication is synchronized to a common time base [2]. Clock synchronization algorithms ensure that a notion of global time is maintained in each network node [3]. For information on distributed clock synchronization algorithms. The global time forms the basis of all message communications in a time-triggered network. Message schedules are defined offline and all messages are communicated at time intervals synchronized to global time.

TTE has three Ways of communication: Time-Trigger (TT), Rate-Constraint (RC), Best Effort (BE) [4]. What's more, TTE supports: hardware real-time, Rate-Constraint, Rate-no- constraint, tolerant topology, state monitoring, protocol fault tolerance, self-detection, reconstruction or degrading, voting and redundancy management. If synchronous TT packets are not sent, the bandwidth is immediately released and free for other asynchronous Ethernet traffic.

3 Network Security Design Based on Time-Triggered

3.1 Information Flow Process

The data is sent from the A application to the B application process:
Send node local APP: application data processing, send to network operation process;

Send node local operating system: operating system process scheduling, queuing waiting;

Send node OSI environment: 7th layer receive user process data;

Send node OSI environment: 7th layer to 1st layer;

Network communication line: cable transmission data;

The receiving node OSI: 1st layer to the 7th layer;

Receiving node OSI environment: 7th layer of data are sent to the user process;

Local operating system of receiving node: operating system process scheduling, queuing waiting;

The local APP of the receiving node: the user process completes the final data operation.

3.2   Aim of Build Information Flow Model

Based on the information flow model of integrated electronic system, combined with the requirements of system encryption and authorization, we realize the information flow configuration, APP configuration, key data and other encryption requirements, and establish a dynamic system encryption and authentication process.

Based on the specific scene (power up initialization and dynamic encryption authentication), the process of information flow propagation is simulated. In the add or reduce the system encryption and authentication process design changes the configuration of the information flow in the APP scenario, and other integrated electronic systems are simulated with APP redundancy encryption and authentication process; design, information flow encryption and authorization design under the agreement based on the time triggered.

3.3   Information Flow Model of Integrated Electronic System

The information flow model takes the actual process of the integrated electronic system business process as the prototype, abstracts the information flow model. For function decoupling and improving system scalability, function decoupling is decomposed into functional modules with moderate particle size, and information flow abstraction is described on this basis [5, 6]. The flow of information flows through the node, the type of interactive information, the size of the information flow and the temporal relationship of information interaction, including the communication flow and the control flow.

In Fig. 2, the proposed information flow model shows that the communication network and the control network exist at the same time in the integrated electronic system. Among them, communication network is responsible for transmitting task class data, with high delay and large bandwidth. It generally belongs to event triggered information. It usually includes formatting password, target information, location and navigation information, environmental information and all kinds of management information. The control network is responsible for transmitting and controlling data. The delay is low, and the bandwidth is usually small. Generally, it includes trigger class information and periodic information. It usually includes vehicle posture information, self-detection target information and all kinds of state information of controlled objects.

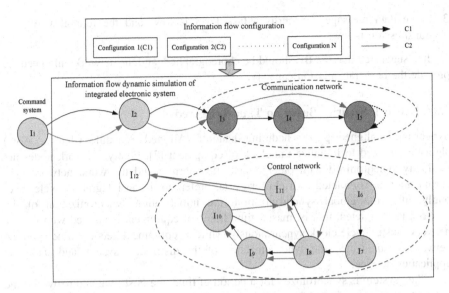

Fig. 2. Information flow dynamic simulation of integrated electronic system

3.4   Interface Control Document (ICD) Design

After analysis information flow by the proposed model, message can be divided in three types in the integrated electronic system: emergency, event, cycle, large data. And message properties contain: security level, task level, delay, cable receiving/sending time, Check-in time, Check-out time. The details of the three types are as follows:

1. Strong periodic message - high security level, low response delay (US) and determined, message generation time is determined and periodic.

It is proposed to be arranged according to TT. The network needs to provide a time delay upper bound according to the time required by the control system and a high priority.

The time period of the message occurs, it can be planned in advance, and the utilization of resources is high.

Send window: (sending time–Check-in, sending time), the latest application should send a message before "sending time–Check-in".

Receiving window: (reception time-Checkout, reception time), the application should wait until "reception time-Checkout" to wait for the message to receive.

2. Weak periodic message - Security, low task level, response delay but the determined time is determined and periodically generates a message.

It is proposed to be choreographed by RC, and the network needs to provide a delay upper bound, a low priority.

The message occurrence time cycle can be preprogrammed, but it is not recommended to use TT to increase the complexity of scheduling and scheduling. After failure, it affects the TT message scheduling with high security level.

3. Large data message - Security - task level is low, and the reliability of data transmission is low.

It is suggested that the BE should be choreographed, and the network only needs to provide the best transmission capacity.

3.5   Network Security Based on Time-Triggered

Synchronous aligned post scheduling handoff (Aligned Schedule Change, ASC) algorithm is used to initialize the clock of equipment [7]. Firstly, network nodes are gradually synchronized with other nodes after startup, and the worst network synchronization is completed in a cluster cycle, preferably in an integration cycle. Secondly, after the global synchronization, the initialization synchronization of the network is completed, that is, master time frame of equipment is aligned with the TT network cluster cycle clock synchronously. Thirdly, equipment gets the time from the network, ensures the time synchronization of the distributed system and starts the application service.

When system is synchronized for a period of time, the host time and network time will drift, continuous Resynchronization (CR) algorithm can be used to synchronize the clock [8]. Firstly, begins with the equipment execution, periodically calculating the offset of the TT network cluster cycle clock relative to the equipment clock. And then, lengthen or shorten the partitioned MTF according to the deviation, and the deviation correction needs to set the threshold to avoid excessive correction. At last, align cycle synchronization (Figs. 3, 4 and 5).

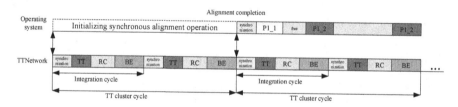

Fig. 3. Power up initialization

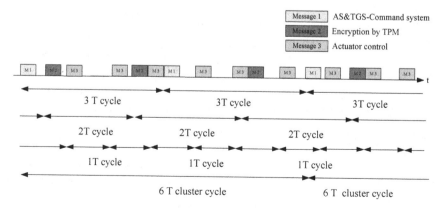

Fig. 4. Network security design based on Time-Triggered

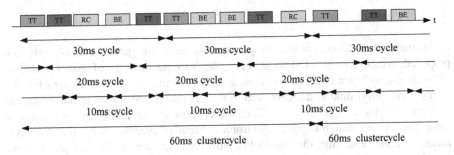

Fig. 5. Major time frame

3.6   Network Security Workflow Design

See Fig. 6.

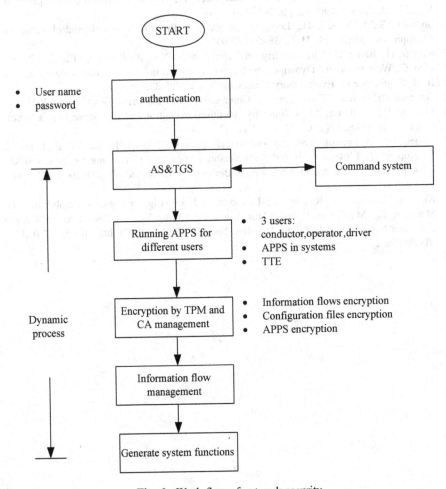

Fig. 6. Work flow of network security

4 Conclusion

In this paper, the information flow propagation model of integrated electronic system is proposed, which can be used to simulate the information state of nodes including network and software function modules, and the information types and characteristics of integrated electronic system are analyzed, ICD design, power up initialization and network security design based on TTE, the encryption and authorization process of command system and integrated electronic system is established by the AT&TGS method. At the same time, the information flow configuration, application program and key data encryption design are carried out. Finally, based on the above results.

References

1. Liu, R.: The development trend of integrated electronic system for ground combat platform. In: ICICTA 2018, Changsha, pp. 246–250 (2018)
2. Shaheen, S., Heffernan, D., Leen, G.: A gateway for time-triggered control networks. Microprocess. Microsyst. **31**(1), 38–50 (2007)
3. Kopetz, H., Bauer, G.: The time triggered architecture. Proc. IEEE **91**(1), 112–126 (2003)
4. Pico, C., Wainwright, R.: Dynamic scheduling of computer tasks using genetic algorithms. In: IEEE Conference on Evolutionary Computation, pp. 829–833 (1994)
5. Obermaisser, R. (ed.): Time-Triggered Communication. CRC Press, Boca Raton (2011)
6. Fleming, P., Purshouse, R.: Evolutionary algorithms in control systems engineering: a survey. Control Eng. Pract. **10**(11), 1223–1241 (2002)
7. Kopetz, H.: The time-triggered approach to real-time system design. In: Randell, B., Laprie, J. C., Kopetz, H., Littlewood, B. (eds.) Predictably Dependable Computing Systems. ESPRIT Basic Research Series, pp. 53–66. Springer, Berlin (1995). https://doi.org/10.1007/978-3-642-79789-7_4
8. Katz, S., Lincoln, P., Rushby, J.: Low-overhead time-triggered group membership. In: Mavronicolas, M., Tsigas, P. (eds.) Distributed Algorithms. WDAG 1997. Lecture Notes in Computer Science, vol. 1320, pp. 155–169. Springer, Berlin (1997). https://doi.org/10.1007/BFb0030682

Author Index

Printed in the United States
By Bookmasters